Herbert Junghanns

Clinical Implications of
Normal Biomechanical Stresses on Spinal Function

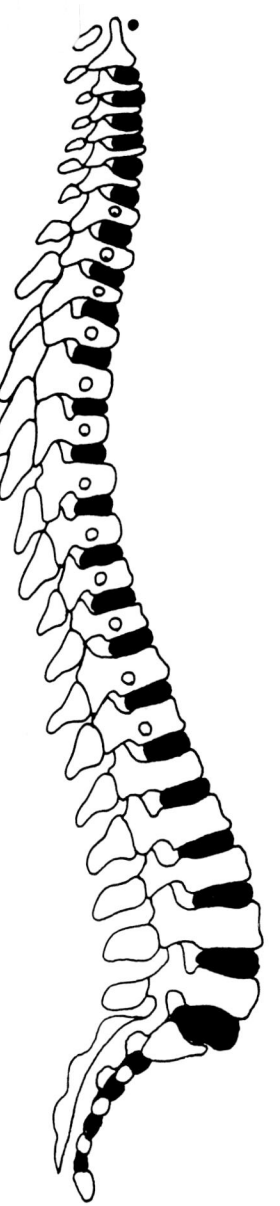

English Language Edition
Edited by
Hans J. Hager, DC
Northwestern College of Chiropractic
Bloomington, Minnesota

AN ASPEN PUBLICATION®
Aspen Publishers, Inc.
Rockville, Maryland
1990

Library of Congress Cataloging-in-Publication Data

Junghanns, Herbert, 1902-1986
[Wirbelsaul unter den Einflussen des taglichen Lebens, der Freizeit, des Sportes, English]
Clinical implications of normal biomechanical stresses on spinal function / Herbert Junghanns & Hans J. Hager, U.S. editor.
p. cm.

Translation of: Die wirbelsaule unter den einflussen des taglichen Lebens, der Freizeit, des Sportes.
"An Aspen publication."
Includes bibliographical references.
ISBN: 0-8342-0109-7
1. Human mechanics. 2. Spine--Physiology. 3. Stress (Physiology). I. Hager, Hans J. II. Title.
[DNLM: 1. Biomechanics. 2. Spine--physiology. 3. Stress, Mechanical. WE 725 J95wb]
QP303.J8613   1990
612.7'6--dc20
DNLM/DLC
for Library of Congress
89-18547
CIP

English language edition, copyright © 1990 by Aspen Publishers, Inc.
All rights reserved.

Aspen Publishers, Inc., grants permission for photocopying for limited personal or internal use. This consent does not extend to other kinds of copying, such as copying for general distribution, for advertising or promotional purposes, for creating new collective works for resale. For information, address Aspen Publishers, Inc., Permissions Department, 1600 Research Boulevard, Rockville, Maryland 20850.

Originally published Die Wirbelsaulei unter den Einflussen des taglichen Lebens, der Freizeit, des Sportes © 1986
Hippokrates Verlag

Editorial Services: Ruth Bloom

Library of Congress Catalog Card Number: 89-18547
ISBN: 0-8342-0109-7

Printed in the United States of America

1 2 3 4 5

Table of Contents

Publisher's Note ix

Preface to the German Edition xi

Preface to the English Language Edition xiii

1. **Introduction: Problems of the Stressed Spinal Column** 1
   1.1 Stress, Sports Injury, and Sports Damage 1
   1.2 Adaptation 3
       1.2.1 Muscular System 4
       1.2.2 Bones 4
       1.2.3 Tendons and Cartilage 5
       1.2.4 Hyaline Cartilage 5
       1.2.5 Articulations 6
       1.2.6 Intervertebral Disc 6

2. **Basic Compendium of Development, Morphology, and Biochemistry** 9
   2.1 Normal Development 9
       2.1.1 Development until Birth 9
       2.2.2 Development until Conclusion of Growth 12
   2.2 Morphological Characteristics 15
       2.2.1 Vertebral Bones and the Sacrum 17
       2.2.2 Intervertebral Disc 18
       2.2.3 Ligaments and Muscles 20
       2.2.4 Nerves and Blood Vessels 21
       2.2.5 Articulations 26
       2.2.6 Vertebral Body—Intervertebral Disc Junction 31
       2.2.7 The Motor Unit 32
       2.2.8 Curvatures and Angles 32

2.3	Biochemistry	36
	2.3.1 Bones	36
	2.3.2 Intervertebral Disc	37
	2.3.3 Mechanical-Biochemical Interaction	46

3. The Intervertebral Motor Unit or Segment — 49

3.1	The New Concept of the Spine	49
3.2	Anatomy and Functions	49
	3.2.1 General Overview	49
	3.2.2 Intervertebral Disc	50
	3.2.3 Bony Elements and Articulations	62
	3.2.4 The Vertebral Body-Intervertebral Disc Boundary	62
	3.2.5 Ligament System and Muscle Corset	64
	3.2.6 Blood Vessels	65
	3.2.7 Nerve Supply in and at the Intervertebral Motor Segment	65
3.3	Important External Influences	68
	3.3.1 Introduction	68
	3.3.2 Sinus Vibrations	68
	3.3.3 Stochastic and Impacting Vibrations	68
	3.3.4 Lack of Motion	69
3.4	The Performance-Impaired Intervertebral Motor Segment	69
	3.4.1 Intervertebral Insufficiency	69
	3.4.2 Intervertebral Instability	70
	3.4.3 Intervertebral Immobility	72
	3.4.4 Vertebral Blockade	72
	3.4.5 Load-Bearing Capacity in Intervertebral Insufficiency	74
	3.4.6 Spondylogenic Symptoms and Syndromes: Clinical Perspective	75

4. Factors Interfering with Functional Capacity — 77

4.1	Introduction	77
4.2	Variations and Abnormalities	77
	4.2.1 Variations	77
	4.2.2 Abnormalities in the Vertebral Body-Intervertebral Disc Series	79
	4.2.3 Malformations in the Vertebral Arch Series	80
	4.2.4 Compounded Spinal Abnormalities	81
	4.2.5 Narrowness of the Vertebral Canal and Intervertebral Canals	82
	4.2.6 Significance of the Transitional Regions	82
	4.2.7 Impairments of Functional Capacity through Variations and Malformations	83
4.3	Malformations of the Spine	83
	4.3.1 Kyphosis	83
	4.3.2 Juvenile Kyphosis/Scheuermann's Disease	84
	4.3.3 Senile Kyphosis	89
	4.3.4 Scolioses	90
	4.3.5 Lordosis: S..aightening and Extension	94
	4.3.6 Stress Resistance of Faulty Curvatures	95
4.4	Vertebral Slippage and Vertebral Displacement	98
	4.4.1 Vertebral Slippage	98
	4.4.2 Causes of Spondylolysis	100
	4.4.3 Stress Resistance of Spondylolysis/Spondylolisthesis	101

		4.4.4	Vertebral Displacements	102
		4.4.5	Stress Resistance of Vertebral Displacements	104
	4.5	Additional Changes		104
		4.5.1	Introduction	104
		4.5.2	Impairment Factors Determined Mostly by the Intervertebral Disc	105
		4.5.3	Ligaments and Muscles	115
		4.5.4	Skeleton and Muscle Corset	119
		4.5.5	Arthrosis at the Articulations of the Spine	125
	4.6	Decreased Performance Capacity through Additional Influences		131
		4.6.1	Consequences of Infections (Spondylitis/Spondylodiscitis)	131
		4.6.2	Rheumatism	133
		4.6.3	Ankylosing Spondylitis (Bechterew's Disease)	135
		4.6.4	Metabolic Abnormalities	136
		4.6.5	Chemical Substances and Ionizing Rays	137
		4.6.6	Tumors	138
		4.6.7	Space Flight	138
		4.6.8	Injuries	139
		4.6.9	Surgery of the Spine	139
	4.7	Prognosis of Spinal Disorders		139
		4.7.1	Self-Protection/Adaptation	140
5.	**Strain Caused by External Influences**			**141**
	5.1	Introduction		141
		5.1.1	Functions of the Spinal Column	141
		5.1.2	Four Groups of External Influences	141
	5.2	General Biomechanical Functional Requirements		142
		5.2.1	Shape and Posture	143
		5.2.2	Mobility/Movement	148
		5.2.3	Involvement of Muscles, Nerves, and Blood Vessels	154
		5.2.4	Skeleton	160
		5.2.5	Intervertebral Disc	164
		5.2.6	Ligament System	165
	5.3	Special Mechanical Influences		165
		5.3.1	Lack of Exercise	165
		5.3.2	Total Body Vibrations	166
		5.3.3	Partial Body Vibrations	171
	5.4	Biomechanical Behavior of the Entire Spinal Column		172
6.	**Examination of the Spinal Column**			**175**
	6.1	Examination Principles		175
		6.1.1	Normal Mobility	175
		6.1.2	Shape and Postural Impairments	175
		6.1.3	Mobility Impairments	178
	6.2	Medical Examination		178
		6.2.1	Case History	179
		6.2.2	Physical Examination	180
		6.2.3	Imaging Procedures for Diagnostics	187
	6.3	Preventive, Fitness, and Follow-Up Examinations		191
		6.3.1	School Examinations	191
		6.3.2	West German Experience	191
		6.3.3	Mandatory Radiodiagnostics	192

7. Effects of Daily Life on the Spinal Column **193**
- 7.1 Introduction 193
  - 7.1.1 Daily Life, Susceptible Periods, and Disorders Caused by Lack of Exercise *194*
- 7.2 Spinal Column in Childhood and Adolescence 195
  - 7.2.1 Introduction *195*
  - 7.2.2 Preschool Age—Time of Mobility *196*
  - 7.2.3 School Age and Adolescence—Beginning of the Sedentary Period *196*
  - 7.2.4 Transition to Adulthood *208*
- 7.3 Spinal Column of the Adult 209
  - 7.3.1 Standing *209*
  - 7.3.2 Walking *210*
  - 7.3.3 Sitting *212*
  - 7.3.4 Correct Lifting and Carrying *213*
  - 7.3.5 Spinal Column Stress Affecting Women *213*
  - 7.3.6 The Adult at Home *216*
  - 7.3.7 Total Body Vibrations *216*
  - 7.3.8 Partial Body Vibrations *223*
  - 7.3.9 Lack of Exercise *223*
  - 7.3.10 Additional Exogenous Influences *224*
  - 7.3.11 The Spinal Column in Old Age *225*
  - 7.3.12 Prophylactic Measures *226*
- 7.4 Treatment and Rehabilitation 229
  - 7.4.1 Conservative Treatment *229*
  - 7.4.2 Surgical Procedures *239*
  - 7.4.3 Rehabilitation *249*

8. Stresses on the Spine in Sports, Gymnastics, and Leisure **251**
- 8.1 Introduction 251
- 8.2 Leisure Sports and Fitness Programs 251
  - 8.2.1 Leisure Sports *251*
  - 8.2.2 Fitness Programs *253*
- 8.3 General Information on Sports-Related Spinal Disorders 257
  - 8.3.1 Limits of Biomechanical Stress Resistance *257*
  - 8.3.2 Statistics *259*
- 8.4 Stress and Damage Potential in Various Types of Sports 260
  - 8.4.1 Introduction *260*
  - 8.4.2 Driving Sports *263*
  - 8.4.3 Track and Field Sports *264*
  - 8.4.4 Golf and Racket Sports *273*
  - 8.4.5 Contact Sports *276*
  - 8.4.6 Weight Training *283*
  - 8.4.7 Air Sports *286*
  - 8.4.8 Equestrian Sports *287*
  - 8.4.9. Gymnastics *290*
  - 8.4.10 Aquatic Sports *298*
  - 8.4.11 Winter Sports *306*
  - 8.4.12 Throwing Sports and Shooting Sports *310*
  - 8.4.13 Teachers and Trainers *315*

8.5	Ballet and Dance		316
	8.5.1	Classical Ballet	316
	8.5.2	Other Dances	317
8.6	Acrobatics		317
	8.6.1	Contortionists	317
	8.6.2	Trampoline Acrobatics	319
	8.6.3	Ski Acrobatics	320
8.7	Detrimental Stress on the Vertebral Arches through Sports and Gymnastics		320
	8.7.1	Spondylolysis and Spondylolisthesis	320
	8.7.2	Separations (Avulsion Fractures) of Vertebral Arch Processes and the Odontoid Process	321
	8.7.3	Tendopathy, Tendinosis, and Baastrup's Disease	322
	8.7.4	Articulations	322
8.8	Sports Fitness in the Case of a Previously Damaged Spine		322
	8.8.1	Juvenile Kyphosis	323
	8.8.2	Scoliosis	327
	8.8.3	Bone Damage (General)	327
	8.8.4	Spondylolysis, Spondylolisthesis, and Vertebral Dislocations	327
	8.8.5	Damage Caused Mostly by Intervertebral Discs or Articulations	327
	8.8.6	Surgery	327
8.9	The Juvenile Spine and Performance Sports		328
8.10	Prophylactic Examinations in Sports Medicine		329
	8.10.1	Examinations for Sports Fitness	329
	8.10.2	Medical Observation of Young Athletes	329
	8.10.3	Follow-Up Examinations and After Care	329
8.11	Prophylaxis, Rehabilitation, and Reintegration		330
	8.11.1	Prophylaxis	330
	8.11.2	Rehabilitation and Reintegration of Adolescents and Persons with Disabilities	330
	8.11.3	Sports for Older Persons	330
	8.11.4	Sports As Therapy	332

Bibliography	333
Index	381
About the Author	395

Publisher's Note

Aspen Publishers, Inc. is proud to be publishing the English language edition of this classic work about the spine written by renowned German doctor, Herbert Junghanns, and published in Germany by Hippokrates-Verlag Publishers. This book represents Dr. Junghanns' life-long examination of the biomechanics of the human frame, especially the spine, and his convictions that early diagnosis of environmental stresses paired with conservative care are the key ingredients to proper back care. With the trends in many disciplines of health care turning toward conservative care, ergonomics, early intervention, and preventative techniques, this book will certainly be a valuable addition to the libraries of practicing orthopaedic, back care, and sports medicine professionals in medicine, chiropractic, osteopathy, and physical therapy.

We would like to point out that the extensive references were taken directly from the original German text and are a mixture of English language and foreign language. During the course of translation, language editing, and content editing, we found that there were several instances where in-text references did not appear in the bibliography in the original German edition. Our editors have attempted to eliminate these omissions but in some cases the in-text references were kept, for content purposes, without a full reference at the end of the book. We hope that this will not cause the reader any inconvenience.

We would like to express our sincere appreciation to all who helped to bring this book to fruition: Dr. Marianne Gengenbach and Dr. Bernard Busch, original reviewers of the German edition, for their thoughtful and encouraging evaluations; Annette Schiller, for smoothing out a most difficult translation; and Dr. Hans J. Hager, for persevering through a very long and arduous editing process.

The German language edition of this book has already proved to be a highly respected bestseller in the European health care community; we hope that the English language edition will serve its readers equally well.

Preface to the German Edition

It is the author's goal in this book to discuss the many nontraumatic influences on the spine that often provide the crux of his medical practice. These nontraumatic influences furtively originate at the spinal column, which is the constantly stressed central organ of the support and motor system, and lead to serious chronic pathological conditions—less of the bony portions, but rather at the more than 100 various joints and especially at the intervertebral discs. It is the important objective of this book to pathomorphologically, pathophysiologically, and clinically differentiate these various forms of damage in order to enable a suitably targeted treatment.

Introductory chapters—advanced as a compendium—convey the fundamental knowledge of the basic concepts. Without this knowledge, prophylaxis, differential diagnosis and therapy are often unsuccessful.

Those spinal column problems which are encountered repeatedly by everyone in their daily lives are given the most emphasis in the book. We all will suffer from back problems, to some extent, during the course of our lives.

The time spent sitting at school, the behavior during leisure time, overexertion during sports and gymnastics, youthful addiction to motorcycles, the far-spread use of automobiles with their spine-damaging vibrations, and finally, the often premature-aging of the bony element and of the soft tissue components of the spinal column are all unfortunately frequent causes that turn the spine into a center of suffering for many people. But it is possible to help the sufferer of back problems and it is the central concern of this book to portray the possibilities for such help. It follows the triad of medical help: prevention, therapy, follow-up care.

It is fortunate that many people regard various sports and physical workouts after work and in leisure time as relaxation from everyday life and as a way of preventing a decline of physical strength. Therefore they will be considered in detail, but there must also be a warning for instances where the sport or activity greatly overexerts the constitution of the spinal column or when training and competition in highly competitive sports turn into the enemies of physical health.

It is important to depict all the requirements and possibilities for keeping the spinal column healthy, using the principles of medical research as well as practical experience. It is hoped that the interested health care professional will be encouraged in this manner and it is also hoped that the person afflicted with a spinal column disorder will gain insight and finally success for the maintenance and—as far as necessary—improvement of the performance of the spine, as well as its ability to resist stresses.

The concepts of this author are based on thought processes which reach back more than fifty years to the time when Georg Schmorl in Dresden began to focus on the spine as the center of his scientific interest. This author was privileged to participate in these scientific studies by participating in the examination of 10,000 spines from 1927 to 1931. The resulting basic pathomorphological knowledge was expanded by new scientific findings and experiences gained in clinical practice and consultation. Surgeries allowed a look into many aspects of diseases, that broadened the field of vision and also contributed to an increase in the long-standing desire to write a book concerning this topic.

This book is intended to come to the aid of health care professionals who look for more than just hastily compiled treatment recommendations for their general practice or specialty. Therefore, it contains principles that encourage systematic differential diagnosis and preventive measures based on it.

In spite of all research findings concerning the spine, there are still many unanswered questions. For this reason, this book attempts to uncover and explain such problems in order to encourage scientists of the various medical subspecialties as well as nonmedical specialties to join in interdisciplinary joint studies with the objective of more thoroughly penetrating the manifold problems. The amount of our ignorance in the area of spinal research is still significant.

It is impossible to conclude this preface without thanking my numerous medical coworkers in practice and research. In addition, I thank my long-time secretarial coworkers, Mrs. Herta Birner and Mrs. Annaliese Reinhard, and to the librarian of the Emergency Hospital of the Professional Cooperative Association in Frankfurt/Main, Mrs. Helga Walter. They performed the tedious preparation and facilitated the completion of the manuscript.

Last but not least, my appreciation goes to the long-time director of the Hippokrates Publishing House Mr Ehrenfried Klotz, who retired recently, to his successor Mr Albrecht Hauff, and to the proofreading department and all participating employees of the publishing house for their valuable publication suggestions and the good design of the book.

Herbert Junghanns
Bad Nauheim
December 1985

Preface to the English Language Edition

In the text at hand, Dr. Herbert Junghanns culminated more than 50 years of special interest in the human spine that started through his association with Dr. Georg Schmorl. Dr. Junghanns has organized his accumulated knowledge in a form that makes this book especially useful to all physicians that are involved in the care of the spine.

It is the emphasis on normal everyday stresses in conjunction with leisure time activities including sports that make this book so informative and special. The section on specific sports and their particular influence on the normal or susceptible spine will be of invaluable help to the physician dealing with prevention, therapy, and supportive care of sports injuries.

Contrary to available texts, *Clinical Implications of Biomechanical Stresses on Spinal Function* offers detailed descriptions of anatomical characteristics of the approximately 100 articulations of the spine as well as the intervertebral structures.

At this point, I would like to acknowledge the support of my wife Marianne as well as my daughters Rika and Katrina in editing this extremely difficult text. Furthermore, the assistance of Martha Sasser and Ruth Bloom of Aspen Publishers, Inc. was very much appreciated.

Hans J. Hager, D.C.

1

Introduction: Problems of the Stressed Spinal Column

1.1 STRESS, SPORTS INJURY, AND SPORTS DAMAGE

The subject of stresses exerted on the spinal column by such different realities as daily life (including leisure activities), sports, and exercise requires an introductory explanation. Many textbooks discuss the fact that sudden, unexpected, and forceful influences (ie, accidents as defined by insurance companies) may cause injury to a healthy spinal column and, to an even larger degree, to a previously abnormal one if the impact force exceeds the load tolerance. On the other hand, the way in which the spinal column is affected by work-related stresses caused by hard physical labor repeated over a long period of time, poor body posture, lack of movement during long hours of work at a desk, or exposure to vibrations is a topic of debate in occupational medicine, biomechanics, and biochemistry as well as in other specialty disciplines. This book is justified by the fact that the problematic nature of these scientific inquiries and reflections on their consequences also affect every day life.

Many questions concerning the possibility of spinal column damage caused not by one-time traumatic influences but rather by long-term, abiding, and repeated stresses that occur especially in sports and exercise remain unanswered. The resulting pathomorphology, predisposing factors for damage to occur in certain locations, and the progressive development of damage once it begins also require further study. In addition, the concurrence of endogenous individual influences in conjunction with personal circumstances of exogenous origin opens up new questions which must be answered.

Scientific studies have attempted to elucidate the mechanism of damage and the types of damage that occur in chronically stressed tissue. Discussions have involved both compact bony tissue and soft tissue. For the spinal column, studies have focused on the intervertebral discs with their hyaline cartilaginous, fibrous, and gelatinous parts, certain ligaments and their attachments to bone, and the cartilaginous coverings of bony articular surfaces.

Gaining an overview of stress injuries is further hindered by the multitude of articulated and mixed articulated movements that are possible in the spine. Those movements are described in section 2.2.5.1. Often, finding the required answers was already hampered during the attempt to find clear descriptive terminology. Some of the terminology was determined by the genesis of the injury or the final disease state: wear and tear damage, loading shock, tissue derangement, overexertional damage, or physiological stress.

To differentiate the damage of chronic stress from a single sudden impact force, the damage of force, terms that are intended to act as modifiers of trauma, fracture, or fissure were added: frequently repeated microtrauma, specific microtrauma, accumulation of repeated trivial injury, subclinical chronic trauma, slowly progressive fracture, chronic stress fracture (in contrast to a force fracture), fatigue fracture, microfissures occurring in outbursts, and quite a few other terms. Many terms contain clues to the origin of the injury, as in the following examples: destructive alteration of function, overstressing of mechanical function, "influence of the mechanical drumroll," nutritional deficiency, stress syndrome as an endogenous injury, tissue fatigue due to mechanical stress, disproportionate balance between stress and stress tolerance, dysfunction as a result of simple overuse, weakening of mechanical resistance, and damage (eg, sports damage) in contrast to sports accident.

There is always a grain of truth in these various descriptors, but there often remain doubts where the evaluation of damaging chronic influences on the organs of support and movement is concerned. The central axial organ, the spinal column, is particularly often involved in such doubts. Therefore it is necessary to discuss at various places in this book *which* mechanical chronic stresses, such as the rapid and repetitive movements and impacts of some types of athletic training and competition, may be damaging to the spine's elements. The same is true for the skeleton, the hyaline cartilage layer of the many joints, and the soft tissues, especially the intervertebral discs.

Every attempt to clarify injury possibilities caused by chronic mechanical influences leads to an important question: If the influence of pressure, of a short vibration phase or of a strain (eg, overextension) is not sufficient to cause an injury, is the sum of such influences then ascribed a role of pathogenic significance? It is impossible, however, to answer this question generically. It is necessary to consider special circumstances, including personal habits or inevitable exogenous influences caused by daily life, recreational activities, sports, and exercise.

This results in several separate questions, some of which are roughly sketched out below:

- Do individual, fast, and consecutive subliminal mechanical influences or long-term, rarely interrupted, forced postures prevent the intermediate recovery of the affected tissue to such an extent that a wear and tear damage results?
- Does this also take place if the individual exogenous forces are far below the mechanical stability limits of the affected tissues?
- Which *combinations* of various forces—eg, pressure, torsion, vibrations—[carry with them] as a result of running up a special susceptibility to injury through summation?

So far, satisfactory answers are not available because of the lack of sufficient results of experimental studies. Even the numerous attempts at clarification from epidemiological studies have thus far not yielded clear results. This is true both for the bones of the spinal column and the structural elements of the involved motor units and for corresponding intervertebral discs that have their own special problems.

[The many tasks that the spinal column must fulfill in static and kinetic respects and for which it is prepared, extend over the entire span of human life.] The maintenance of these functions throughout life, however, is dependent on "normal" stress: a natural interchange of walking, standing, and lying preferably reinforced with muscle-strengthening exercise therapies. The excessive physical influence on the spine on the one side and a lack of exercise on the other are damaging factors to which every person may be exposed during daily life (injuries through sudden single impact such as the effects of accidents are not appropriate to this topic and are mentioned only occasionally for comparison).

It is difficult to draw clear lines between a lack of exercise and overexertion where normal daily demands are concerned. Another factor to be considered is how far personal stress tolerance fluctuates. Malformations of the anatomic structure (both congenital or caused in childhood), pathological influences on the muscles (eg, paralyses, even though they may be residual), and other factors may result in a greatly restricted stress-bearing ability of the spinal column. In such cases even the stresses of "normal" daily life may already result in unfavorable consequences. They may worsen over the decades because of an age-related reduction of muscle strength and bone substance and because of wear in the soft tissues, mostly in the intervertebral discs and the layers of articular cartilage.

A look at the varied suggestions for terminology in regard to a distinction between sports injury (sports accidents) and sports damage also uncovers quite a few difficulties. Most people working in this area agree on the principles, but the terminology is still confusing. For physicians to understand each other better, the discussion should be continued with scientifically proven results of long-term studies involving different sports. In addition, the results must be numerically sufficient and must be based on practical sports-medical diagnoses.

Until new findings have been agreed on in this manner, only three terms should be used (expanded below): sports injury, secondary damage after sports injury, and synonyms for the causes of sports damage. The long list for the last contains a selection of terms often discussed in the literature that are predominantly used for injuries of the spinal column. It is necessary to simplify and combine this list as known information increases.

1. Sports injury results from a single, sudden, and unexpected event (corresponding to the commonly defined work accident).
2. Secondary damage after sports injury includes especially the post-traumatic arthroses that continue to worsen after joint fractures, chondral fracturing, and meniscal tearing. Secondary damage may be found in the spinal column after impact forces (eg, after avulsion of joint components at single vertebral arches or uncovertebral articulations, vertebral body fractures, vertebral luxations with intervertebral disc damage, and the like).
3. Synonyms for the causes of sports damage refer to tissue damage caused by sports-specific motion or force vectors that are frequently or constantly within the borderline are of tissue tolerance; tissues mostly affected are bradytrophic tissues such as articular cartilage, interior articular discs, and intervertebral discs. Effects of induced dysfunction on such bradytrophic tissues are as follows:

- an imbalance between individual biochemical stress tolerance and required athletic performance
- wear damage caused by a small force that is long term and constantly repeated
- latent, chronic sports damage with tissue wear
- chronic trauma caused by training and athletic performance
- distortions that are frequent and subliminal
- physiological stress
- fatigue fracture
- subliminal, frequent trauma
- microfissures occurring in clusters
- microtrauma (as the initial trauma)
- accumulation of repeated trivial injuries
- disabling articular damage in athletes

In all areas of life (e.g., in sports, exercise, leisure activity, etc.), stresses affect a healthy or previously damaged spinal column either as an entity or peripherally. This book does not systematically deal with stresses caused in the work place but rather touches only on pertinent topics.

1.2 ADAPTATION

Stresses that must be borne by the spinal column often reach or even exceed stress tolerance. The stress influences are countered in many respects by the spine's compensatory ability, but this ability is not always able to ameliorate all effects of the stress. It is especially the presence of such a variety of very distinctly reacting tissue types which cause some of the many difficulties in assessing the spinal column's compensation for stress.

Hesse (1980) explicitly addresses the adaptation processes of posture and the motor system and their limitations: "Adaptation processes to stresses are basic characteristics of life per se and without them [human] existence in the biological area is unthinkable." Hesse explains this important fact with the example of muscle tissue and bradytrophic tissues such as ligaments and cartilage. Hesse derives his findings mostly from his own extensive experiences in sports. In his examples of the adaptation of muscle tissue, ligaments, and cartilage, however, he fails to mention the spinal column, even though it plays an important role as the central axial organ in the area of adaptation in practically all types of athletic activity. The fact that the adaptational possibility is particularly bleak for the intervertebral disc is discussed at the end of this chapter.

Three principles that are confirmed again and again in the following discussions are mentioned here:

1. One basic purpose of sports training consists of incrementally increasing the adaptational ability of the various tissue types.
2. The adaptational possibility reaches its limit when the stress tolerances of the tissue are exceeded.
3. Continuously repeated overstressing in training by forces that exceed normal physiological function decreases performance potential (eg, diminishes stress tolerance) because of developing pain.

1.2.1 Muscular System

Sports physiology and internal medicine have determined through extensive studies the ways in which cardiac as well as skeletal muscles respond to training: increase in mass, performance, and resistance. Details are contained in the extensive studies of Tittel (1973).

The excellent adaptability of muscles disciplined by specific training to athletic requirements is well known. It results in an increase in fiber diameter and cross-sectional capacity and in the capillary network of the muscle fibers. Even more dramatic results can be observed in a more effective muscle metabolism. This is essential to many organs and tissues, including indirectly the cartilaginous layers of the spinal articulations and the bradytrophic tissues of the intervertebral discs.

More extensive, newer series of tests reported by Howald (1984) showed the possibility of conversion of several muscle structures depending on whether the athletic training required continuous performance or short sprint distances. Hereditary predispositions also play a role in this process. Nevertheless, these findings are additional proof of sports-specific muscle adaptation. It is also known, however, that these adaptations undergo a fast reversal when the specialized athletic training is interrupted.

Muscles of the trunk that are strengthened through training, together with the "assisting" muscles of the spine (at the thorax, in the abdominal wall, at the transition from pelvis to legs, and at the shoulder girdle), adapt to each athletic performance (see section 2.2.4). Ideally, in this way the static dynamic musculoligamentous units form a "hyperphysiological corset" during activity. For details and examples see sections 3.2.5, 4.7, and 5.2.3.1.

Adaptation processes of the individual structural elements of the spine are diverse. The following discussion merely attempts to explain how different stresses of exercise or sports activity affect the tissue components of the spine. The literature has increased considerably within the last two decades. Nevertheless, there are still some gaping holes, not least because of the difficulties of experimental examination of the spinal column. Therefore, the information in the following sections is only partial.

An important part of athletic training is the necessity of fulfilling increasingly higher requirements through such adaptation. This process is limited by pre-existing physiological stress tolerances. This is a fact that sports physicians, trainers, and athletes themselves must constantly consider.

1.2.2 Bones

Questions concerning adaptation to athletic influences take up a steadily increasing space in the literature. The bones of the spinal column are discussed in this regard in section 5.2.4.1, and the stress-dependent structural changes of trabecular bone is especially emphasized. Such change appears after the healing of fractures but also during growth when abnormally distributed stresses take effect (eg, coxa valga or vara).

Because of the distinct metabolism of bone, which enables fast anabolism and catabolism, adaptation processes in the form of mass increase, broadened diaphyses, and strengthened trabeculae may be created in the bone through exercise and training. In heavy axial loading of the spinal column, as occurs in weight lifting (see Chapter 8), the adaptation consists of the creation of increased density in the vertebral bodies.

Increased trabeculation may also be present asymmetrically in the vertebral bodies if the spinal column is overloaded unilaterally (eg, on the throwing side of javelin throwers; see Chapter 8). Animal studies confirm such unilateral effects of stress on bones (Schoenholzer 1962).

Bone growth in the form of an obtuse projection of the anterior vertebral body edge in the thoracic vertebral region was observed by Muenchow and Albert (1969) in roentgenograms of weight lifters (see Chapter 8). These adaptation processes to special stress influences on the anterior portions of the spinal column increased with training. The question of whether a relationship existed between juvenile kyphoses and such adaptations and what damage was incurred in the anterior portions of the adjacent intervertebral discs remained unanswered.

In the case of a spondylolysis, spontaneous repair occasionally takes place in adolescents: the transitional zone in the interarticular portion does not develop into an open furrow but ossifies. An elongated, bony, compact pars interarticularis remains (see figures in section 4.5.1). Such an adaptation prevents further slippage and simultaneously reinforces the load-bearing capacity of the vertebral arch. A special adaptation process often takes place in the spondylolisthesis of L5–S1: any further slipping is prevented by a slowly developing bony buttress at the sacral base (see figures in section 4.5.1).

1.2.3 Tendons and Cartilage

In animal experiments, Tilscher and Oblak (1973) found evidence of training effects on Achilles tendons: hypertrophy with increased tensile strength and a small decrease in elasticity. Even though a large number of shorter ligaments and tendons are greatly stressed in many sports disciplines, no findings concerning the effect of training on tendons and ligaments exist for the spinal column area because such experiments would be difficult to perform. These ligaments and tendons include the ligamentum flavum, anterior and posterior longitudinal ligaments of the spinal column, interspinous and supraspinous ligaments, tendon attachments of the long back muscles, articular ligaments of the approximately 50 vertebral arch articulations, and tendons of the atlanto-occipital articulations.

All spinal tendons and ligaments are undoubtedly increasingly stressed through traction and torsion during the slowly intensifying training of the trunk muscles. It is not possible to undertake close studies because the tolerance limits of the individual ligament systems of the spinal column are unknown. Because the above mentioned animal experiments have basically proven the trainability of tendons, trainability and therefore an increase in the tolerance limit of ligaments and tendons in the spinal column area may be assumed. It will probably be a by-product of general muscle training.

A constant exceeding of the stress tolerance of ligaments and tendons may lead to acro-osteopathy. In such cases any further training or excessive physical and massage therapy worsens the sports damage and increases the pain. Only an appropriate rest period may re-establish the original adaptation.

1.2.4 Hyaline Cartilage

In contrast to the articulations of the extremities, no large continuous areas of hyaline cartilage exist in the spinal column. Nevertheless, the total mass of hyaline cartilage is significant. It is distributed over the vertebral arch and the atlanto-occipital articulations (ie, over more than 100 small articular surfaces; see section 2.2.5.1). Several mixed articulations are also included: costovertebral articulations, sacroiliac articulations, and the pubic symphysis. The approximately 25 mixed articulations at the intervertebral disc (see section 2.2.3) each include two hyaline cartilage plates together with a pulpaceous and lamellar fibrous cartilage. Their adaptability is discussed subsequently.

1.2.5 Articulations

The question of adaptability of the hyaline cartilaginous articular surfaces in the numerous smaller articulations distributed along the entire length of the spinal column was discussed in the preceding section.

The bony articular surfaces below the cartilaginous layer possess, together with the articular processes, a rather good adaptability if, for example, a scoliosis forms during the growth period. The articulations with their cartilaginous layers follow the increasing curves. During this process, and because of the abnormal development associated with scoliosis, the cartilaginous and bony articular surfaces may significantly change in size and axial orientation within the spinal column.

In the case of unstable vertebral fractures, the vertebral arch articulations of the fractured and adjacent areas often assist in achieving stabilization through ossification. Such stabilization is a necessary adaptation to these traumatic conditions. This ossifying process also takes place during the healing of destructive infection centers and after stabilizing surgical procedures.

Animal studies on the adaptability of the articular cartilage demonstrated that, after a running program (ie, a uniform, repetitive movement), several articulations of the extremities showed a slight thickening of the cartilaginous layers. These results, which were reported in 1973 by Tittel, are not entirely applicable to the human spinal column. Because of the complex movements of the spinal column in high-performance athletics, the mechanical influences are distributed over a multitude of small articular surfaces that are intermittently exposed to pressure with rotational, shearing, sliding, and torsional forces. There are some sports, however, in which the spinal column is specifically affected. It is therefore next to impossible to show that the cartilage in certain articulations thickens (adapts). Therefore the questions remain as to whether the hyaline cartilage tissues of the spinal column adapt to the increased requirements of athletic activity and whether their layers become thickened, better able to glide, more impact and wear resistant, and more elastic.

1.2.6 Intervertebral Disc

Different fundamentals exist concerning the problems of adaptation of the intervertebral disc. This is because it possesses a complicated structure consisting of various types of tissue and fulfills special functions compared with all other types of spinal column tissue. It is also not enough to regard the intervertebral disc only as a structure made of fibrous cartilage and to study only the adaptability and stress tolerance of that fibrous component. The fibrous cartilage in the lamellar rings plays an important role. For comprehensive function of the susceptible intervertebral disc, however, the pulposus as a grid-gel system and the two hyaline cartilage plates also fulfill certain roles and together form the integrated tissue system (see Chapter 2).

Up to now direct adaptability of the intervertebral disc to athletic training could not be proven. If in many sports an increased performance of the spinal column is achieved, then this must be attributed to the trunk muscles (see sections in Chapters 3 and 4) that have been strengthened through the training. These muscles are tied together with the ligaments into a static as well as a dynamically acting musculoligamentous corset that regulates the adaptation of the entire spinal column to the activity's requirements. Back pain may indicate that the pressure on the intervertebral discs—possibly connected with a unilateral load or torsion—has reached the stress tolerance level or has even exceeded it. In the case of light or short painful episodes, the training may be initially carefully continued. If the complaints intensify, a rest from training is urgently needed to ensure a proper fluid exchange for nutritional supply and removal of wastes in the bradytrophic tissues of the intervertebral discs; this is recovery through alteration between mechanical stresses and rest.

The thickening of articular cartilage mentioned in the preceding section as an adaptational process occurring after long-term stress has not been confirmed by all investigators. This may be a result of different experimental methods, however. PG Schneider (1972), for example, concluded from his animal experiments and model studies that an overstressing of articulations results in an escape of synovial fluid and therefore is the origin of cartilage damage because pressure resistance is lowered and damaging friction results. This can be considered parallel to the behavior of the intervertebral discs under pressure: stagnation or a back-and-forth gliding motion with ultimate expulsion of the fluid. High-intensity training, often enhanced by accompanying workouts with weight, may involve load influences in accordance with this conclusion.

Frequently in daily activity, requirements beyond normal physiology are demanded of the spinal column and therefore of the intervertebral disc, which is the most important biomechanical and biochemical part of the motor unit but also the most damage prone (see sections in Chapter 7). Sports and exercise training tax the intervertebral discs to an even greater extent, especially in the case of a high load pressure in combination with faulty load distribution through rotation and shearing influences. This exceeds simultaneously the load tolerance and adaptation capacity that are inherent in a well-trained musculoligamentous corset. The results are damages in the intervertebral discs. The discs are unable to adapt further, and even recovery through alteration (see sections 2.3.3.1 and 8.3.1) is no longer effective anymore. The well-being of the intervertebral disc is especially threatened by fast, continuously repeated pressure impacts (the "drumroll" of training; see sections in Chapters 3 and 8) if it impairs the required nutritional supply and waste removal from the tissue because fluid exchange is dormant or ineffective. More information about this is given in section 3.2.4. It is questionable in such cases whether a return of the normal fluid exchange may even be obtained after a pause (often too short) in training and whether it will bring back an adaptation to the normal nutritional conditions of the bradytrophic disc tissue. If restoration is unsuccessful, or if an excessive impacting axial pressure has already damaged parts of the disc tissue with tears and fissures, a slow death of the disc commences and progresses from simple disc wear (chondrosis disci); to disc attrition (intervertebral osteochondrosis) (see Chapter 4). These conditions allow no adaptation, that is, no return to former performance levels. Athletes who still successfully participate in high-level competition at this point are rare because it requires a positive inner attitude and great energy to overcome the pain (this process might be called the "psychoenergetic adaptation" and can be seen in many professional acrobats, contortionists, and the like; see Chapter 8).

The following is a summary of the adaptability of the damage-prone intervertebral disc to requirements of sports and exercise. Important is "external" adaptation, which fights off overexertion through a strengthened musculoligamentous corset developed through training. This may be called a secondary adaptation. It includes well-considered and trained movements that dissipate in a controlled manner the stresses associated with various specific sports (eg, the technique of weight lifting; see Chapter 8). An "inner" adaptation caused by the efforts of the intervertebral disc itself seems to be nonexistent. In any case, it is not proven that the fibrous cartilage layers of the lamellar rings are thickened through training, that the pulposus receives an increasing load-bearing tension, or that the hyaline cartilage plate of the intervertebral disc becomes more resistant.

2

Basic Compendium of Development, Morphology, and Biochemistry

2.1 NORMAL DEVELOPMENT

Prenatal development, maturation until growth is concluded, and the final development of shape and posture of the spinal column are processes that result in a "normally" structured spinal column (or, more exactly, *should* result in it). Anyone possessing knowledge of the topic is aware, however, that most people do not possess a flawless bony or soft tissue construction of their spinal column. Many formative stages are necessary to let the numerous basic elements mature individually according to a predetermined time table and to fuse them. During this long developmental process, which is genetically predetermined in its details, it is possible for neurological, vascular, or other impulses to induce unexpected shifts in the time table or other changes that result in more or less obvious developmental flaws. In addition, the long developmental process, which only comes to a complete standstill at the end of the second decade (occasionally even somewhat later), is subject to individually diverse although not absolutely abnormal environmental influences that may cause malformations. Section 4.3 discusses the final results of variations and malformations thus created. The beginnings of such developmental phases are described in the following chapters on normal development.

In the following sections the normal development of the spinal column is broadly depicted. It is discussed only to the extent to which it may form a foundation for the understanding of spinal column stress (especially in the case of preexisting damage) in the context of the main theme of this book.

The biomechanical principles that dominate the genesis of many spinal problems are discussed in Chapter 3, with special emphasis on the motor unit itself. References to other biomechanical issues also appear in several other locations where appropriate, especially in Chapters 4 and 5.

This preliminary commentary must also contain a look back, to the evolution of *Homo sapiens*. Over millions of years, the curved spinal column attained its new specific function as the central support organ and, by extension, the central motor system. The evolving posture, which became increasingly more upright and finally biped, as well as biped ambulation (Fig. 2-1, A to C) completely changed the biomechanics of the spinal column. The most difficult changes affected the cervical spine and the lumbosacral-lumbopelvic regions. Even today both these areas provide the crux medicorum: the "upper" and the "lower" back.

2.1.1 Development until Birth

From the precartilaginous state on, the notochord and mesoderm control the differentia-

10 CLINICAL IMPLICATIONS OF NORMAL BIOMECHANICAL STRESSES ON SPINAL FUNCTION

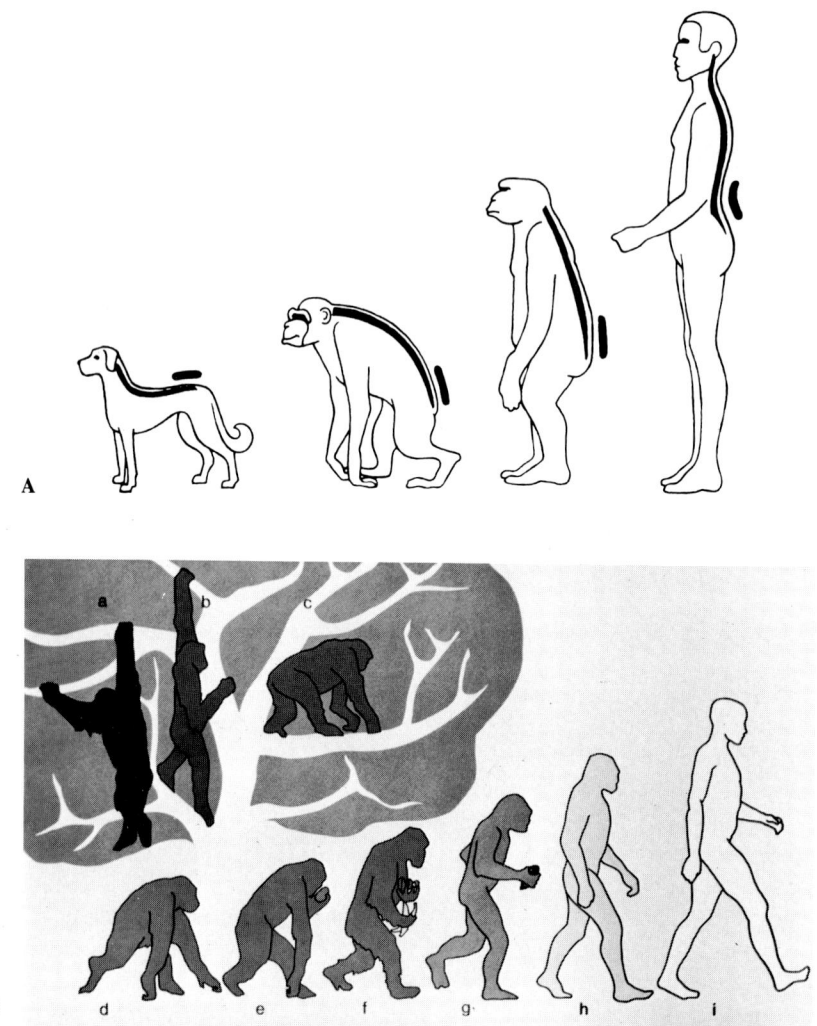

Fig. 2-1 The evolving spinal column. (**A**) From quadruped to upright human posture: the thoracic lordosis changes to kyphosis, and the lumbar kyphosis changes to a lumbar lordosis, because of the progressively extending posture. (**B**) From quadruped to two legs, from trees to savannahs: The evolution of *Homo erectus* [according to Reinhardt (1983)].

---

tion of primitive vertebral structures, bone formations, and the intervertebral discs, which run crosswise to the vertical axis [a detailed description with many illustrations and references may be found in Schmorl and Junghanns (1968) and in Toendury (1958)].

Figure 2-2 shows the important retrogressive metamorphosis of the dorsal notochord, which runs vertically through the vertebral bodies and their discs from head to buttocks. These phases are schematically depicted in Fig. 2-2 from top to bottom. In each of these phases of retrogressive metamorphosis of the notochord lies a possibility for failure. Occasionally, a short notochordal canal remains in a vertebral body (Fig. 2-3). In the case of more extensive imperfections during the metamorphosis of the notochord, the vertebral bodies are affected to an extent that may result in future serious problems in the vertebral bodies: hemivertebra, butterfly vertebra, and many others (the chart in Fig. 4-3 contains a detailed overview).

In 20% to 30% of all spinal columns, more or less distinct cavities remain during the final

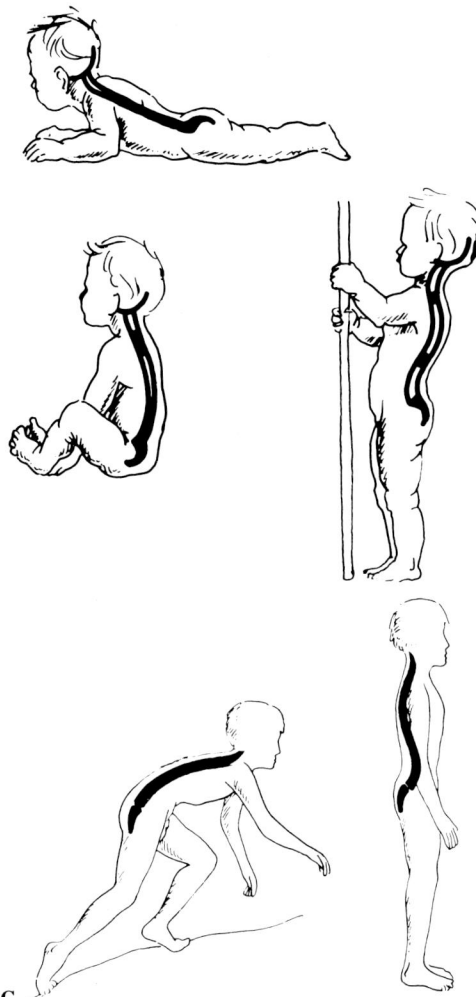

(C) Ontogenic development of typical spinal column shape in infant (top) [according to Tittel (1976)], and the evolution from quadruped to two legs (bottom) [according to Kapandji (1972)].

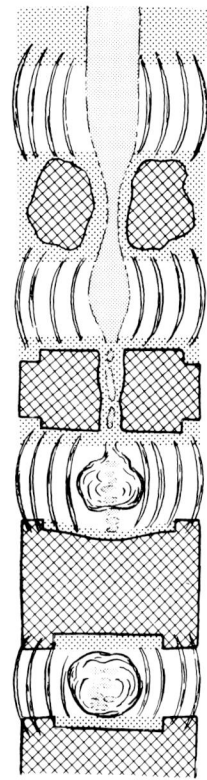

Fig. 2-2 The regressive metamorphosis of the notochord. In the upper part of the illustration the notochord traverses the cartilaginous vertebral body structure (dotted area) and the intervertebral disc structures in the cephalocaudal direction as an intact round wand. Concomitant with formation of the ossification center (hatched area), the notochord is constricted in the vertebral body and is distended at each intervertebral disc level to the intervertebral chordal enlargement. Inside the vertebral body it finally disappears altogether, but remainders of chordal cells may again be found in the pulposus of the intervertebral disc. If the penetration point of the notochord in the cartilaginous end plate is not completely closed, an indentation with a thinned cartilage plate remains (see Fig. 2-5).

phase of the regression of the notochord. These Schmorl's nodes may be easily recognized on roentgenograms (see Fig. 4-8). At the concavities the thickness of the cartilage plate layers is decreased and therefore must be regarded as biomechanically susceptible. The photomicrograph in Fig. 4-7 illustrates how such spots look in later years. For more related information about juvenile kyphosis see section 4.4.2.

In connection with the horizontal segmentation of the vertebral bodies and their discs, neural processes grow from the vertebral body on both sides and form the vertebral arch with its processes, which enclose the spinal chord. They contribute to the formation of the spinal canal as well as to the formation of the intervertebral foramina. The numerous joints in the vertebral arch series alter both form and axial orientation from their embryonic arrangement (see sections 2.2.5 and 3.2.3).

The ossification processes in the vertebral body series and the vertebral arch series do not

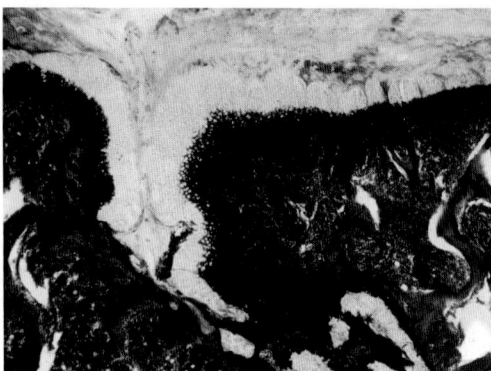

Fig. 2-3 Photomicrograph of a persisting short notochordal canal segment at the T-10 level in a 16-year-old patient (slide and picture by G. Schmorl, 1928).

take place simultaneously in each segment. Ossification centers form first in the vertebral bodies, and the vertebral arches ossify later. Those processes are not concluded during the embryonic period, however, only partly at the time of growth completion.

The intervertebral disc already distinguishes itself as a separate segment from the vertebral system during early embryonic development. These and other developments are depicted in the schematic illustration in Fig. 2-4. The intersegmental notochordal enlargement, which is the future pulposus, is also visible in this developmental stage. The annular fibrous tissue is located around the notochordal enlargement and is peripheral to it. It gradually forms the taut lamellar rings. The fibers are deeply anchored in the initially cartilaginous and later ossified vertebral body epiphysis and in the hyaline cartilage layer of the intervertebral disc. This is a predisposing factor for future functional problems (see section 3.2.2).

2.1.2 Development until Conclusion of Growth

When the fetus is born, the spinal column must still compensate for a significant underdevelopment. It is only after about 20 years (late in comparison with other organ systems) that the cartilage layer at the vertebral body–intervertebral disc border finally stops growing. Until this point is reached (at puberty or later), active

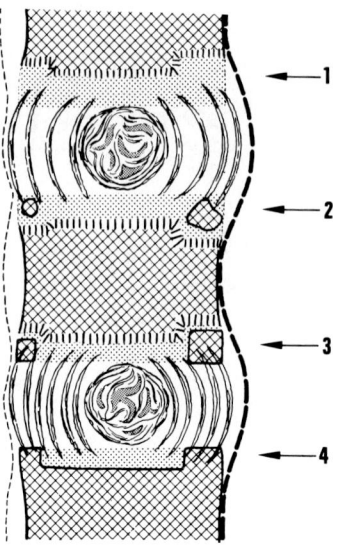

Fig. 2-4 Drawing of the development of vertebral body edges (epiphyses) according to Junghanns. After formation of the vertebral body ossification center (top) a closed cartilage plate exists in the growth zone (hatched region). The raised borders of the cartilage plate are still set in the ossification center, or the cartilaginous epiphysis (1). Here various ossification centers (2) develop, which fuse first into the ring-shaped bony epiphysis (3) and then fuse firmly with the vertebral body ossification center. In this way the raised bony epiphysis (4) is created. It encircles the cartilaginous plate (near 4). Fibers of the lamellar rings (fiber rings) are firmly anchored in the bony epiphysis and in the bony end plate. The anterior longitudinal ligament (right) runs along the anterior and lateral vertebral body wall and is firmly attached. It detaches at the point where the cartilaginous epiphysis was located in the ring of the vertebral body ossification center (1) and traverses the intervertebral space to attach at the adjacent vertebral body, again somewhat distant from its bony epiphysis (4). The posterior longitudinal ligament is connected with the rear side of the intervertebral disc and passes over the rear of the vertebral body.

growth zones exist at the vertebral body end plates and the adjacent hyaline cartilage plates of the intervertebral discs. Even the vertebral body epiphysis, which encircles the vertebral body edge and is supported by it, shows growth cartilage long after birth (Figs. 2-4 and 2-5). This is clearly exemplified by roentgenograms of adolescents (Fig. 2-6). In these growth zones along the vertebral body–intervertebral disc border, uniform growth does not always occur. Therefore, possibilities for damage exist during puberty, those especially sensitive active growth periods (eg, during puberty growth spurts), as is

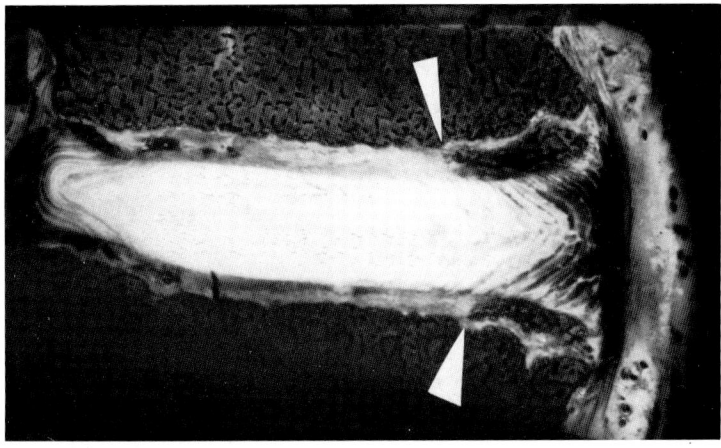

Fig. 2-5 Sagittal section of the intervertebral disc of an adolescent. Both arrows point to the rear border of the front section of the ring-shaped vertebral body epiphysis. It is not yet fused with the vertebral body edge. This is shown by a fine, light-colored streak.

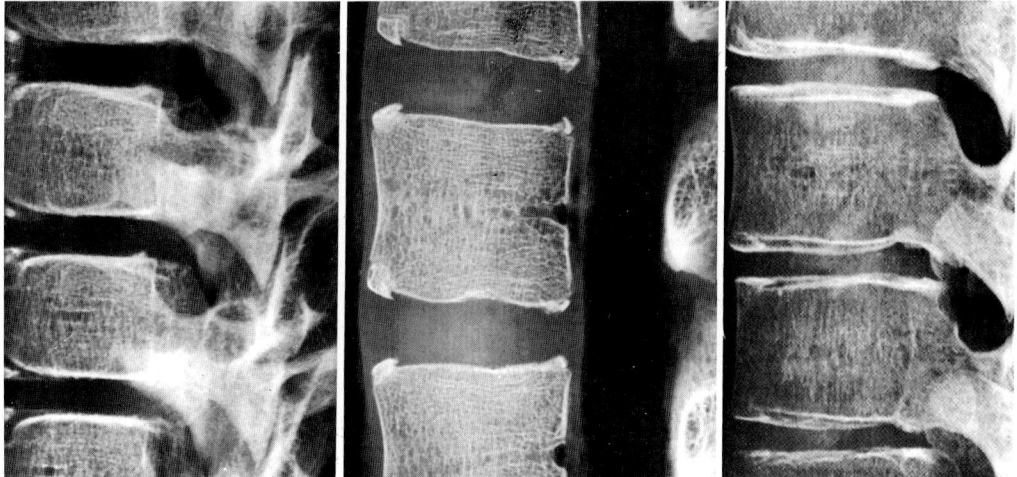

Fig. 2-6 Roentgenograms of sagittal sections of the spinal column of a 12-year-old (left) and of a 15-year-old (middle); roentgenogram of the spinal column of a 17-year-old. These figures show a progressive development of vertebral body epiphyses not yet connected with the vertebral bodies (left; see Fig. 2-4, numbers 2 and 3), increasing bony transition to the vertebral body edge (middle), and complete fusion with the vertebral body (right; see Fig. 2-4, number 4).

often seen in juvenile kyphosis (Scheuermann's disease). External influences often interfere dangerously with regular development. Those influences include sports, especially highly competitive or elite sports during adolescence, which cause a susceptibility to damage that is often overlooked. The consequences of these influences are often not recognized until later, and at times too late. For more details see Chapter 8.

The size and form of the vertebral bodies are determined in spinal column sections at different times. Extensive data about this topic may be found in standard texts and handbooks.

The biomechanical necessities may be clearly recognized in the structures of the vertebral bodies. For example, the superior and inferior end plates of the vertebral body must fulfill various tasks, as may be seen in Fig. 2-7. The interior structure of the vertebral bodies provides

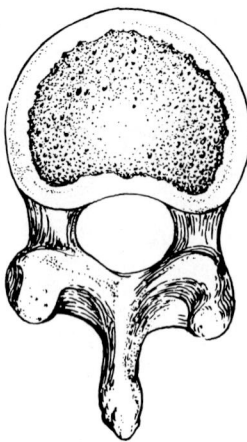

Fig. 2-7 Drawing of a macerated lumbar vertebra. The vertebral body end plate is perforated like a sieve. In the middle section the holes are sparse. This pressure receptacle corresponds to the pulposus of the intervertebral disc. The bony ring of the vertebral body epiphysis surrounds the area of the hyaline cartilage plate, which has been removed through maceration.

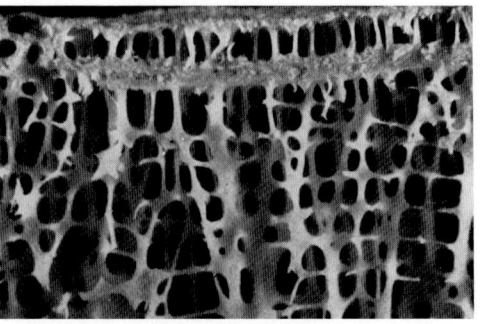

Fig. 2-8 Sagittal section of a macerated lumbar vertebral body portion (slight magnification). The spongiosa consists of criss-crossing, perforated lamellae. Beneath the vertebral body end plate there is a parallel reinforcement tract.

both lightness and the required support through the criss-crossing, perforated spongiosa plates of spongy bone (Figs. 2-8 and 2-9). This is true for both thoracic and lumbar vertebrae. Because of their specialized function and required stress tolerance, the cervical vertebral bodies possess a different trajectory structure.

In the vertebral arches the sutures gradually disappear during the postnatal years. The most important of these are depicted in Fig. 2-10. If ossification is delayed in one or more sutures or is absent altogether, the consequences are severe and will limit stress-bearing capability (see section 4.3). Recent studies repeatedly address the question of whether stresses during the adoles-

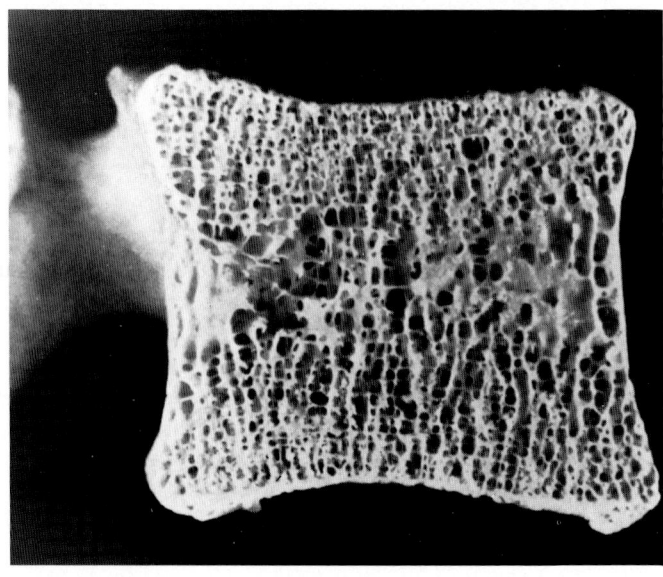

Fig. 2-9 Sagittal section through the vertebral body of L-3. The arrangement of the trabeculae shows economical construction of a support system designed to withstand pressure applied over a wide area. In the center and toward the exterior surfaces, which carry less load, the density of the bone structure decreases.

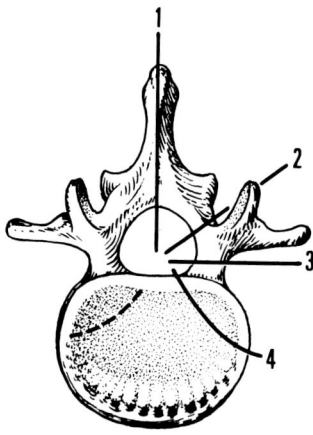

Fig. 2-10 Neural arch sutures. 1, spinous process suture; 2, superior articular process suture; 3, pedicle; 4, vertebral arch epiphysis.

Fig. 2-11 Horizontal superficial section through a fibrous ring with depiction of lamellar rings (Photo by G Schmorl, 1928).

cent growth period will result in gaps in already properly ossified interarticular sections (suture 2 in Fig. 2-10). The final answer has yet to be found. It is not unusual to find that the sequential ossification processes in the vertebral bodies and the vertebral arches result in malformations (see Chapter 4). During horizontal segmentation, irregularities in regard to the number of vertebrae for individual segments may occur. This results in transitional vertebrae, which are most often characterized by variations in vertebral arch structure (see section 4.3.1).

The transformations begun during the embryonic stage continue postnatally in the intervertebral disc. The fibers, which become more compact, join to form lamellae, which proceed in spirals from one vertebral body to another. The adjacent layers proceed at an angle of 120° in opposite directions to each other. They are anchored in the bony vertebral body margins with their fibers (see Figs. 2-2 and 2-4). A superficial section through a fully formed intervertebral disc shows the layers of the fibrous lamellae (Fig. 2-11). The closely woven fiber tissue was described by Toendury (1958) (Fig. 2-12). The significance of this bioarchitectural structure is discussed in section 4.2.2. The blood vessels that enter the edge zones of the annular fibers from the outside during the embryonic period (see Fig. 2-27) regress by the age of 4.

The extent of lifelong neurological supply to the intervertebral disc is not yet fully understood. Branches of the ramus recurrens (see Fig. 2-22) can be found at the exterior surfaces of the disc. Further details are presented in section 2.2.5. The sagittal curves change between the embryonic growth period and the time of complete maturity. The lumbar lordosis clearly protrudes in front of the functionally significant head-to-coccyx line. The thoracic kyphosis moves behind this line.

2.2 MORPHOLOGICAL CHARACTERISTICS

Of all the parts of the support and motor system, only the spinal column has a developmental path that is pieced together from so many elements. This has been discussed in a simplified manner in the preceding sections. The spinal column is constructed of the initially independent vertebral body–intervertebral disc series and the neural arch series, which is also initially independently developed. These sequentially independently developing elements form the final segmental structure, which is subdivided into individual bony vertebrae with interposed intervertebral discs.

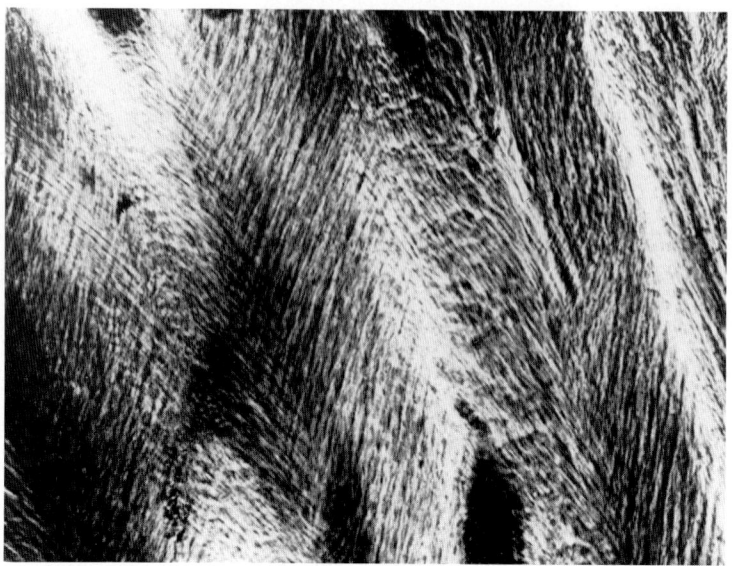

Fig. 2-12 Section through the fibrous ring of a vertebral disc [from Toendury (1958)]. Interwoven cross-fibers between fiber lamellae proceeding in opposite directions are clearly seen.

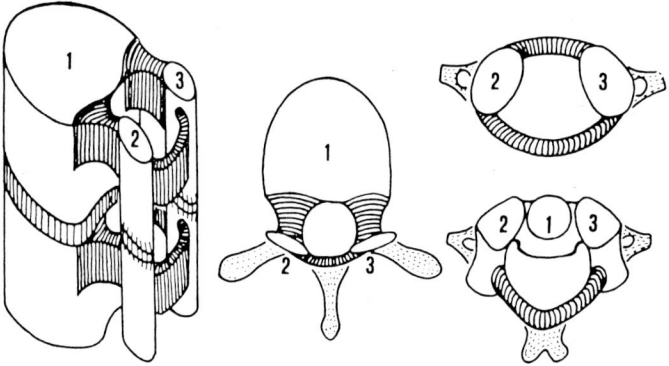

Fig. 2-13 Spinal column structure according to Louis (1978). The three vertical loading lines and horizontal stabilizing bridges are shown.

The support of vertical loads (and also of all motion) is provided anteriorly by the vertebral body–intervertebral disc units. Posteriorly the responsibility for stability lies with the taut neural arch articulations. These mutually cooperate with the articular processes as partners of the anterior support column, as shown in Fig. 2-13. The stability of the individual bony segment is created through three bridges (hatched areas in Fig. 2-13). Only the two superior cervical vertebrae deviate from this structure.

The normal anatomical structure of the spinal column, together with tendons and muscles, leads to the biomechanical masterpiece of a segmented mobile column with central tasks in the support and motor system. It also encloses and protects important structures such as the spinal cord, nerve roots, blood vessels in the spinal canal, and the numerous intervertebral foramina.

The spinal column is only able to fulfill its required tasks because it has an impressive extent of possible motion as a result of its segmentation with numerous mixed articulations and articular elements (see the discussion of motor units in Chapter 3). This also creates the capability to withstand static and dynamic loading. The most important characteristics of anatomical structure are discussed in the following sections because these characteristics contribute to a basic understanding of damage-induced failure. Failure may be primarily mechanical, but biochemically controlled processes may also lead to mechanical consequences and therefore may have a negative effect on the function of the spine.

2.2.1 Vertebral Bones and the Sacrum

The vertebral body consists of the already mentioned structures (see Figs. 2-8 and 2-9). The cortex is relatively thin. This is consistent with average load conditions. Superior and inferior vertebral body end plates are finely perforated (cribriform) except for a slightly denser point (the pressure receptacle plate) opposite the pulposus of the intervertebral disc (see Fig. 2-7).

The joint-forming bony processes include a caplike bony epiphysis that originates at an ossification center and is kept separate from the corresponding bone by a growth zone. No closed bony epiphysal disc develops on the human vertebral body, however; instead, an initially cartilaginous and later ossified ring-shaped margin forms (see Figs. 2-4 to 2-6).

Fibers from the annular rings of the intervertebral disc are deeply anchored in the bony vertebral body margins. This, together with the fibers anchored in the hyaline cartilage plate, results in a biomechanically important, firm clasp between vertebral body and intervertebral disc. More information about this may be found in section 3.2.4.

Special characteristics of the vertebral bodies of the cervical spine column include the uncinate processes, which extend from the left and right sides of the vertebral arch. Those two processes ossify and fuse with the vertebral body and subsequently top it laterally as scooplike (half moon–shaped) tubercles. On each side they form the caudal part of the lateral vertebral body articulation (Luschka or uncovertebral joint). The uncovertebral articulation thus created is described in section 2.2.5.5. Simultaneously a groove forms in the intervertebral disc.

The vertebral arch is anchored together with its root (radix arcus vertebrae) in the vertebral body on both sides. During fetal development the arch epiphysis, which is an intervertebral cartilage, exists at this location (see Fig. 2-10, number 4). It is closed by 6 years of age. Special characteristics of the vertebral arch are the sutures (grooves) (see Fig. 2-10). In spondylolysis, a notch in the interarticular portion between the superior and inferior articular processes (Fig. 2-10, number 2) holds the most interest. It may be the precursor of spondylolisthesis and may have a different shape from normal (see Fig. 4-30). Disagreements concerning its origin have existed for decades (see section 4.5).

The vertebral arch surrounds more than two-thirds of the foramenal wall. The remainder is formed by the back of the vertebral body. The intervertebral foramen, which is better termed the intervertebral canal, varies in radiographic appearance in the individual sections of the spine: in the cervical region it has the shape of a shoe sole, in the thoracic region it is rounded, and in the sacral region it looks like an auricle. Because the orifice levels sit at various angles to the sagittal plane, an appropriately oriented central ray must be chosen for roentgenography. The orientation of the intervertebral canals relative to the intervertebral discs varies in the different parts of the spine. In the cervical region, close connections with the lateral vertebral body articulations exist (uncovertebral joints). In the sacral region, the posterolateral circumference of the disc forms a portion of the intervertebral canal. In the thoracic region, the intervertebral canals open to the exterior into the intercostal spaces. In all regions of the spine the intervertebral canals have great practical significance because they protectively enclose their neurological and vascular contents. Pathological changes and abnormal mobility between the vertebrae result in a predisposition to malfunction that is too often underestimated.

There are three anatomical processes of the vertebral arch that provide important mechanical properties to the spine. They are the articular pillars, the spinous processes, and the transverse processes. The superior and inferior articular processes have differently oriented axes in the different spinal regions, which affects the vertebral articulations that they form. It is only during growth in early childhood that they attain the permanent orientation of the articular surfaces. For more details see section 2.2.5.2.

The spinous process is formed during the first year of life by fusion of the two vertebral arch halves. It has no independent ossification center. In the atlas and sacrum the fusion of the vertebral arch is often delayed until the age of 6. The length, width, and orientation are different in the various sections of the spine. In early childhood small ossification centers (apophyses) attach to the tip of the spinous processes as well as to the ends of the transverse processes. Their bony fusion with the main bones is often delayed and sometimes is nonexistent, which may hinder the diagnosis of actual fractures.

The fusion of a large number of osteochondral structures (vertebral bodies, vertebral arches with their anatomical processes, costal rudiments, and apophyses) into the compact sacrum is conspicuous and must be noted as a peculiarity in terms of developmental history and morphology. The lateral masses of the sacrum do not become fully ossified until between the ages of 15 and 25 years and include incorporation of dorsal accessory processes as the sacral tubercles. The tips of the fusing spinous processes remain visible as the median sacral crest. The spinal column is joined with the pelvic girdle by means of the two sacroiliac articulations (see section 2.2.5.3).

2.2.2 Intervertebral Disc

The intervertebral disc, which was termed a mixed articulation by Luschka in 1858, represents a morphological peculiarity with regard to both its own structure and its connections with the two adjacent vertebral bodies (see section 2.2.7). More details about the gradual reorganization of the intervertebral disc structure during the fetal period may be found in section 2.1.2. The structure of the intervertebral disc permits dynamic coordination because of the close interconnection of the pulposus and the fiber ring lamellae. Dependent on this microstructure and in functional synchrony with the pulposus, the fiber ring forms a shock-absorbing and pressure distributing system. The fiber ring attains important functional mechanical significance through its firm bonding with the bony margin and hyaline cartilage end plate of the vertebral body. This is illustrated in Figs. 2-2 and 2-4. The fibers are firmly anchored in deep insertion canals (Sharpey's fibers). Such biomechanically important attachments are also found at tendinous, ligamentous, and fascial attachments (eg, at the tips of the spinous and transverse processes; see Chapter 4).

The nature of the tissue of the intervertebral disc and its connection with the adjacent vertebral bodies is important for the proper function of the segmentally organized spinal column. This is described in section 3.2.4. The microstructure of the tissues of the intervertebral disc was mostly elucidated through the use of electron microscopy and histochemical studies. The biconvex fiber cells of a given lamellar ring are embedded between collagen fibers in parallel fiber bundles. Mucopolysaccharides play a significant role in their connection. The nucleus pulposus cells lie in a three-dimensional network (grid-gel system). A summarized explanation may be found in Junghanns (1979). In the metabolism of the intervertebral disc, the transition zone between the pulposus and the annular fibers attains special significance. Improvements in understanding of histomorphology will provide further insight into these structural relationships.

In newborns the nucleus pulposus consists mostly of notochordal cells, which disappear during subsequent development (see Fig. 2-2). Occasionally notochordal cells are also found in adults. Stability in the pulposus is attained through the already mentioned grid-gel system. Gradually the adjacent interior lamellar layers fuse and bond with the pulposus. The result is a fibromucoid system with bifid spaces (Fig. 2-14). These appear on roentgenograms after injection of radiopaque fluids. (The first photographs of discs were taken in 1931 by Junghanns with the help of microscopic sectioning techniques; see Fig. 2-15). During the course of life the fluid in the initially tautly filled pulposus decreases, and therefore the intrinsic elasticity of the pulposus also diminishes. This elasticity is of great importance for the biomechanical behavior of the entire disc (see sections in Chapters 3 and 5) and may also be changed by biochemical influences (section 2.3.2.3).

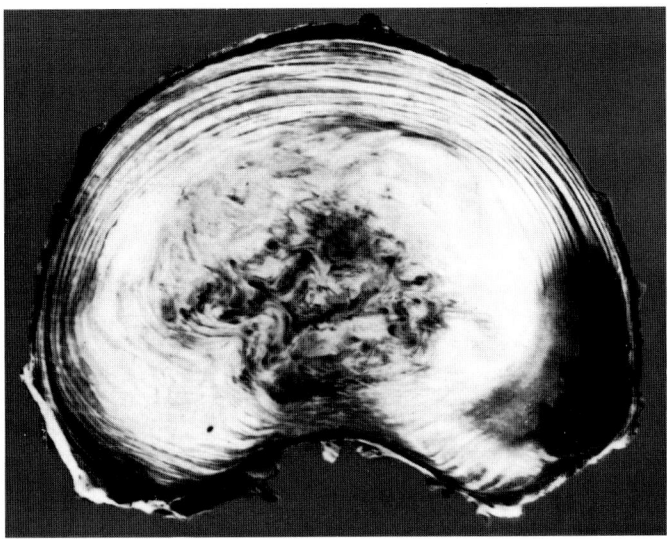

Fig. 2-14 Superficial section of a lumbar intervertebral disc. The lamellar rings and pulposus region are clearly distinguishable. An early chondrosis of the disc already exists, however (see section 4.6.2.3). The normally mucoid pulposus has already lost fluid, which is why its fibers appear to be dry and wrinkled. The interior fiber layers of the lamellar rings are no longer compact and taut but are slightly wavy (left) and torn (top). The black spot to the right is a sectioning artifact.

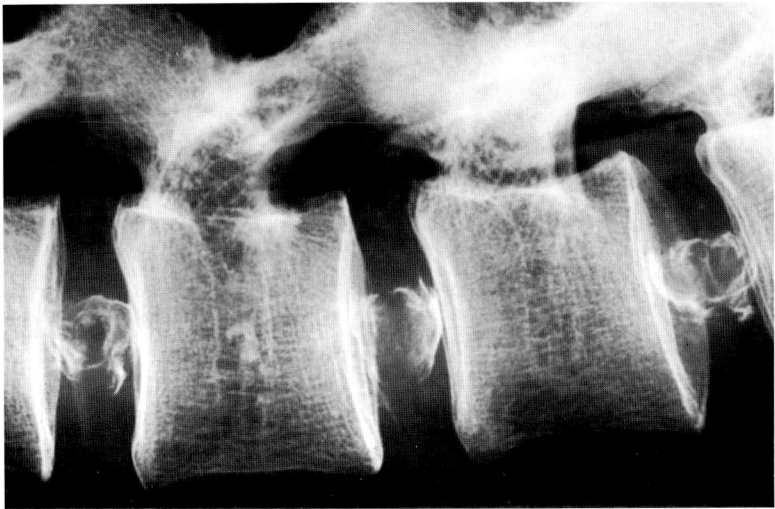

Fig. 2-15 Lateral view of the lumbar spine of a 47-year-old man. The bifid spaces of the pulposi have been injected with radiopaque fluid. Normal expansion of the narrow, notch-shaped spaces of the pulposi cause them to overlap in onion skin manner.

The fibrous lamellae, which are such important components in the intervertebral disc, were initially studied by Schmorl and his students (1928 to 1931). Interest in these studies prompted Toendury to continue working on it at a later time (see Figs. 2-11 and 2-12). Because of their functional significance to the disc space and therefore to the motor unit, the anatomical

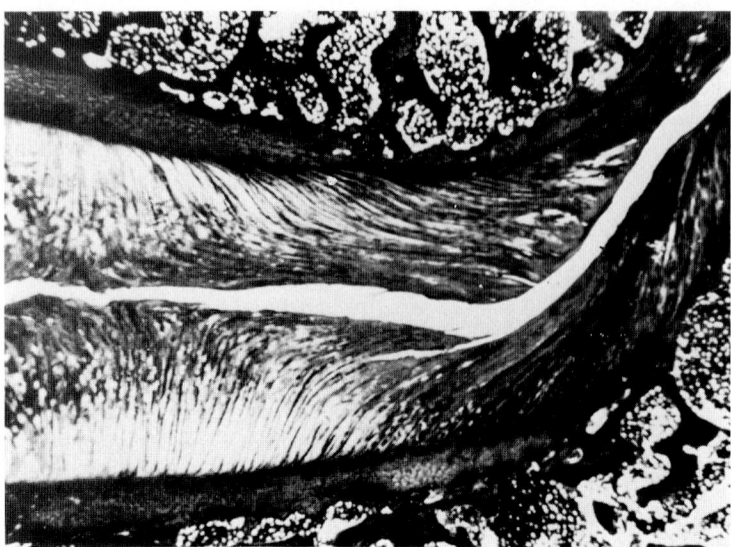

Fig. 2-16 Transverse groove in an intervertebral disc of the cervical spine, which originates slowly, expands, and leads to the formation of the uncovertebral articulation (right).

details of the annular fibers with their division into an interior zone and an exterior area of lamellar rings are discussed in section 3.2.

Special uncovertebral grooves exist at the intervertebral discs of the cervical spine (C2–3 to C-7). They originate at the end of the first decade of life in the previously properly established annulus fibrosus bilaterally in the region of the uncovertebral processes. This takes place while the uncovertebral processes are developing in a cephalad direction. Later the lateral notches in the center of the intervertebral disc unite to form a continuous transverse notch (Fig. 2-16). Toendury explicitly described this process in 1958 and 1981. He stated that occasionally fat folds (articular villi and menisci) push into the notches from the side. Finally the uncovertebral joint is transformed into an articulation that can be called mixed articulation. The term uncovertebral articulation (Luschka joint) of the cervical spine has been generally accepted, however.

2.2.3 Ligaments and Muscles

2.2.3.1 Ligaments

The two longest ligaments of the spinal column, the anterior and posterior longitudinal ligaments, are peculiar because of their contrasting modes of attachment. The posterior longitudinal ligament attaches at the back of the intervertebral discs in a fan shape and crosses the posterior of the vertebral body as a narrow band (Fig. 2-17). In contrast, the anterior longitudinal ligament is firmly attached to the front and sides of the vertebral body and connects with the periosteum. An important peculiarity of the anterior spinal ligament is that it detaches from the exterior surface of the body at the point where during growth the osteochondral margin and later the bony margin existed, passes over the intervertebral disc with which it is connected only by loose fiber bundles, and attaches again at the adjacent vertebral body at the proper point (see Fig. 2-14). This morphological characteristic becomes significant in spondylosis deformans (see section in Chapter 4).

The ligamentum flavum also forms a rather strong support system (see Fig. 3-1). It is located at the back of the vertebral canal at the ventral vertebral arch surface and proceeds from arch to arch while passing over the vertebral arch articulations themselves. It functions as an important stabilizer for articular movements and prevents, to a large degree, slipping of the vertebral arch articular surfaces.

A multitude of other ligaments form a unidirectionally functioning support system on and

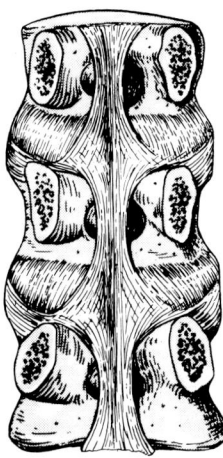

Fig. 2-17 Posterior longitudinal ligament showing fan-shaped expansion and interweaving with the back of the intervertebral disc. The rear surfaces of the vertebral bodies are passed over.

---

between the spinous processes (even though they are individually small). The many small ligaments between the transverse processes also function as a uniformly functioning unit because they run from the occiput to the pelvis. The interspinous ligament and the supraspinous ligament also form continuous systems. Prestar (1982) described the interrelationship of ligaments and their relationship with the surrounding fascia. For additional information about ligament systems see sections in Chapters 3 and 5.

2.2.3.2 Muscles

As with ligaments, there are many short, mutually complementary muscles, especially along the vertebral arches, that either move from vertebral segment to segment or pass over segments to perform over a broad functional spectrum. This broad functional spectrum results in the capability for balanced movement. Muscles must be frequently exercised to remain healthy, however, or their insufficiency augments other damages such as those of normal aging or excessive wear on the discs.

An integral function of the back muscles is their integrative connection of the head, neck, thorax, and lumbopelvic regions as well as their indirect connection with the appendicular portions of the skeleton. If this is considered, the complexity of tasks in both directly and indirectly involved muscles as well as their significant role in the dynamics of the entire support and motion system (eg, walking, standing, and sitting) may easily be recognized. Additional muscle groups that aid in the movement and stabilization of the spine include the pectoral muscles, the intercostal muscles, the diaphragm, and the entire abdominal musculature (see Chapter 5).

If only those muscles belonging directly to the spinal column are considered, there are 4 pairs of short and 8 pairs of long cervical muscles and 11 pairs of short and 15 pairs of long and wide back muscles in the main trunk (including 8 pairs of muscles that have both their attachments on the spinal column). Approximately 25 ligaments and fascial membranes support the function of these muscles. These structures form an entire physiological corset, which is a principal element in form and posture of the spine. Because of the connections of this corset to the head and appendicular skeleton, it functions as a single muscular and ligamentous unit in the structure and function of the central support and motor system of the body. This process also involves gravity.

Details of the distinct functions of the gluteal muscles may be found in well-known textbooks. The objective here is to discuss only a few functional muscle groups with their static and dynamic functions. Information is also provided in Figs. 2-18 to 2-21.

2.2.4 Nerves and Blood Vessels

The spinal cord and its segmentally arranged nerve roots are already linked at the time of the development of the spinal column. Together with the notochord they provide a decisive influence on the formation of the spinal column. The topography resulting from this is well known from textbooks [see also Jackson et al (1966)]. Drawing the nerve roots and their branches aids in the understanding of many pathological changes that are primarily linked with motor unit function; these are discussed below. (Fig. 2-22). It is also important to consider the position of the

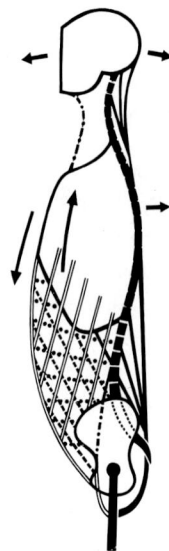

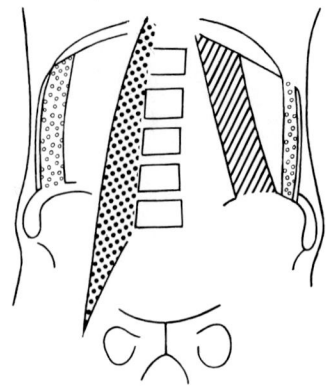

Fig. 2-19 Lateral muscle control of the lateral curvature of the spinal column. The oval shape of the intervertebral disc in the upper region of the lumbar spine provides a certain countersupport against rotation [according to Farfan (1975)].

Fig. 2-18 Muscular contraction of the spinal and gluteal regions in a person standing upright [resketched and appended according to Kummer (1961)]. The reversed arch-tendon principle with dorsal contraction through the ligaments and the erector spinae muscles in the cervical and lumbar region is seen. The abdominal muscles function as a ventral traction girdle and may also support the erector spinae muscles by increasing intra-abdominal pressure [according to Schenk (1964)].

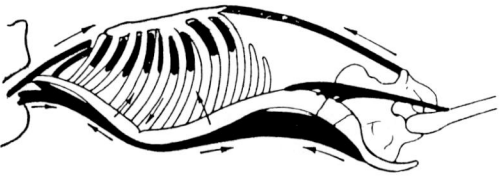

Fig. 2-21 Schematic depiction [according to Guentz (1965)] of muscular forces affecting the spinal column during a spasm leading to thoracic compression fracture. The great ventral muscle tract between the feet and head along with the intercostal muscles in spasm tries to bend the entire spinal column forward. The strong erector spinae muscles antagonistically fixate the cervical and lumbar section in a lordosis. The flexing force can only be released through the thoracic spinal column, and there the collapse of the thoracic vertebral bodies takes place.

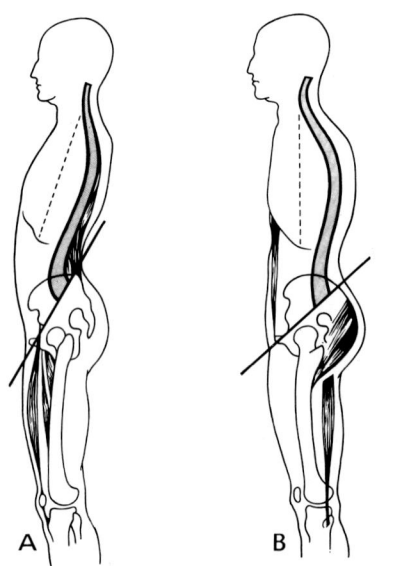

Fig. 2-20 Relationship between spinal column shape, pelvic position and posture-controlling muscles. (**A**) Normal posture. (**B**) Tilting of the pelvis with an increase in lumbar lordosis, as is seen with juvenile kyphosis.

autonomic nervous system in relation to the spinal column, in particular the sympathetic trunk and its ganglia. The nerves of the intervertebral disc and of the vertebral arch articulations are described in section 3.2.7.

The spinal cord, which is protected by the vertebral canal, does not need a special description at this point. There are approximately 25 pairs of spinal roots, which enter the intervertebral foramina from the protective vertebral canal and are protected by them. Because of the relatively narrow passages of the intervertebral foramina, however, the roots are often susceptible to damages. The fact that the connective

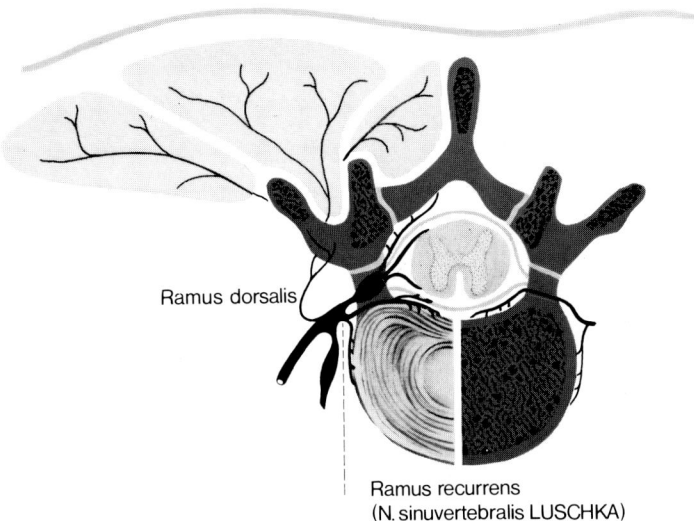

Fig. 2-22 Schematic cross-section through the spinal column at the intervertebral canal depicting the division of the spinal nerve.

fibers to the sympathetic nerves also leave the spinal canal through the intervertebral foramina has received less attention. Luschka depicted these fibers in 1850 and pointed out their significance, but it was not until the present century that they were studied to any extent. These fine fibers are often involved in pathological conditions caused by a malfunctioning motor unit (see section 3.4). Even more significant is the sinuvertebral nerve, which was also described by Luschka (1850) (Fig. 2-22). This nerve supplies the periosteum, the blood vessels, and the tissues within the vertebral canal. Information about all other nerves in the motor unit and its periphery may be found in section 3.2.7.

The different orientations of the nerve roots in the intervertebral foramina (Fig. 2-23) are adapted to anatomic conditions and also correspond to the possibilities for motion at each segment. If they are interrupted by pathological conditions, however, serious consequences result from pressure, obstruction of motion, or similar occurrences. These consequences may affect the peripheral as well as visceral organs to a large extent. Therefore, the intricate relationships among individual nerve tracts, which run in bundles through the spinal nerve, must be considered during diagnosis.

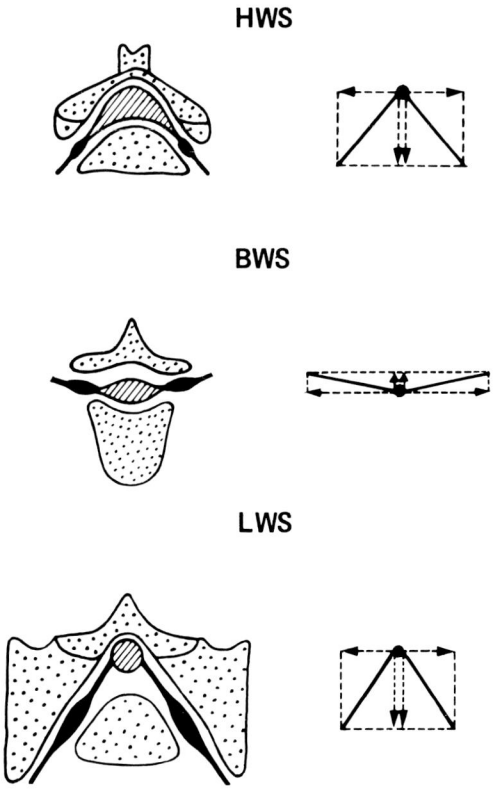

Fig. 2-23 The various orientations of the spinal cord roots at the cervical spine, thoracic spine, and lumbar spine (according to Felten 1958).

The spinal column contains an expansive vascular system that is connected with the surrounding area and especially with the vertebral canal and spinal cord. Arteries penetrate the vertebral body from the posterior, anterior, and anterolateral aspects. The vertebral arches are also generously supplied. The arterial flow is somewhat segmentally controlled by the intercostal arteries, which send prelaminar branches from their radicular trunk through the intervertebral foramina. In this way they supply not only the vertebral body, which they penetrate from the exterior surfaces, but also the spinal cord and the dura mater. Finally, other branches run to the inferior back muscles and further on to the skin. From the spinal cord, capillaries and blood pools reach the hyaline cartilage plate (Fig. 2-24; see also sections 2.2.7 and 3.2.6). Those capillaries and blood pools also have some neurological supply. This was described by Jackson et al. in 1966 (see also section 3.2.7). A small branch artery (that has been much discussed in spite of its small caliber) penetrates the interarticular space. Its possible connection with spondylolysis is discussed in sections 4.4 and 5.2.3.

The vertebral artery, which comes from the subclavicular arch, has close connections with the cervical spinal column. Its roentgenographic portrayal has become increasingly more important (see illustrations in section 4.6.5.5). Abnormalities of this artery are frequent (Fig. 2-25). The vertebral artery runs from the transverse process of the C-6 into the foramen transversarium and is close to the lateral vertebral articulations (uncovertebral joints) and to the lateral exits of the intervertebral foramina. After it traverses the transverse process of the atlas, it lies in the osseus arterial sulcus vertebralis and penetrates with its loop, at the point above the posterior arch of the atlas, the posterior atlantooccipital membrane to run through the occipital foramen into the cranial cavity (possible damages are described in section 5.2.3). Before the two vertebral arteries unite to form the basilar artery, each gives off two posterior spinal arteries and a wider anterior spinal artery.

The variability of blood flow through the vertebral artery must be considered for anatomical and pathophysiological reasons. The flow is already significantly decreased by frequent

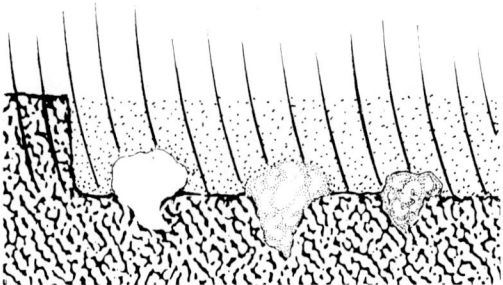

Fig. 2-24 Special capillary loops and blood pools that provide nourishment by diffusion through the intervertebral disc exist in the marginal layer between the vertebral body end plate and the hyaline cartilage plate of the intervertebral disc. The long striations suggest the bonding fibers, which run from the lamellar rings into the cartilage plate.

movements of the head (Fig. 2-26). This may lead to decreased brain circulation. This leads to questions about therapy and diagnosis, as Gutmann et al. described in 1985. The anterior and posterior spinal arteries combine from the right and left in a longitudinal tract that runs alongside the spinal cord; this tract is connected there in a ladderlike structure with the recurrent spinal artery and the intervertebral arteries.

The location of the aorta at the ventral side of the spinal column also has biomechanical significance according to Schanz (1930) (see Chapter 5). The venous flow from the vertebral body drains at the back through large pores and proceeds into the vertebral longitudinal sinus. The significance of the venous plexuses for clinical practice is described in detail in Chapter 5.

The close interrelationship between the blood supply of the spinal column and that of the spinal cord is often addressed in the literature (Felten 1958). Important findings concerning these relationships are obtained by injecting contrast medium into the bone marrow of the spinal processes in a living person (Clemens 1966).

The blood supply of the intervertebral disc plays a special role during the developmental stage. Fine capillaries develop between the exterior layers of the annular fiber rings (Fig. 2-27). Numerous vascular loops run from the vertebral ossification center into the marginal portions of the cartilaginous end plate and into the ossification centers forming there. It is still debated whether an axial vessel that approximately fol-

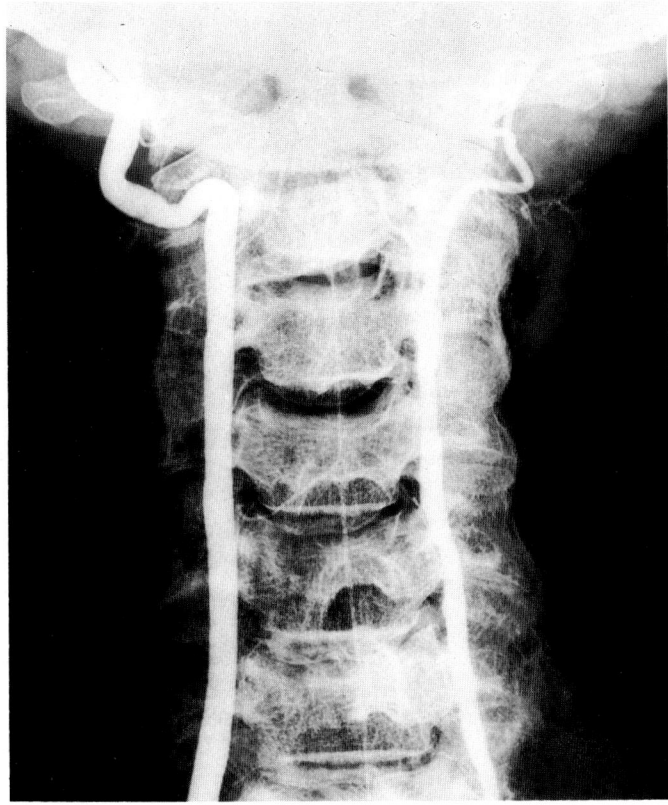

Fig. 2-25 Roentgenogram of the cervical spinal column while the vertebral artery is filled. On the right the proper course of the artery with its loop may be seen. The left shows a significant change of the arterial lumen, especially in its loop.

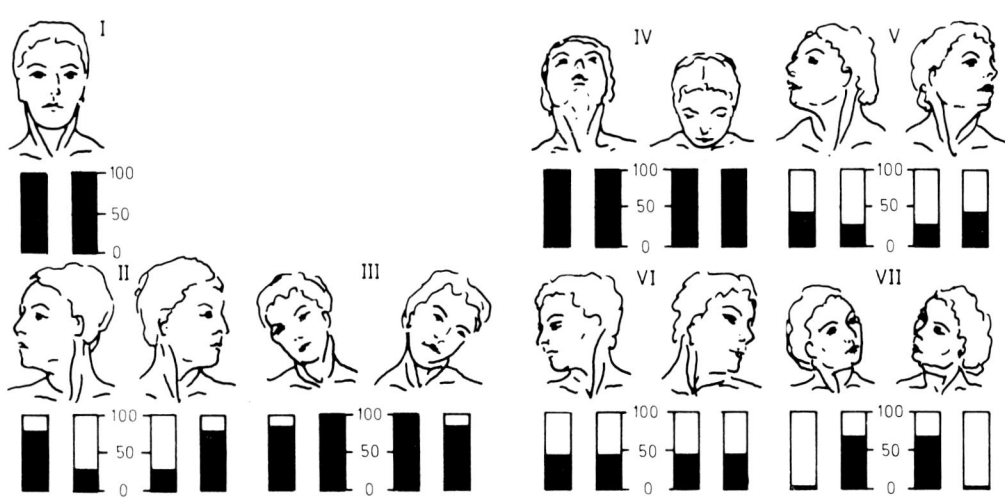

Fig. 2-26 Influence of head position on cerebral circulation: schematic depiction of obstruction of the vertebral artery during various head movements. (I) neutral position, (II) head rotation, (III) lateral flexion, (IV) extension and flexion, (V) extension and rotation, (VI) rotation and lateral flexion to the same side, and (VII) rotation and lateral flexion to the opposite side. Circulation is given in percentages [from Gutmann et al. (1985)].

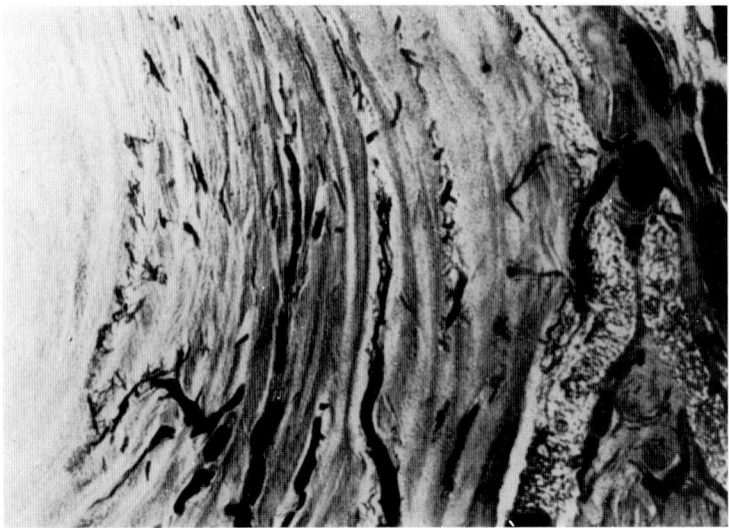

Fig. 2-27 Cross-section through the marginal areas of the presacral intervertebral disc of a premature infant. The blood vessels penetrating from the side form fine nets between the lamellae in the exterior zone of the fiber ring (according to Toendury 1958).

lows the path of the notochordal canal from the vertebral body runs only to the center of the hyaline cartilage plate or whether it sends out fine capillaries into the disc tissue. During its retrogressive metamorphosis it leaves a small "scar" behind in the cartilage plate that, together with the notochordal penetration point, constitutes a point of low stress resistance. After growth is completed, no blood vessels remain in the intervertebral disc. Capillary loops and blood pools penetrate the hyaline cartilaginous plate of the vertebral disc from the osseous vertebral body (see Fig. 2-24). This ensures the metabolism (nutrient supply and waste removal) of the rather sluggishly nourished intervertebral disc material.

2.2.5 Articulations

2.2.5.1 "The 100 Articulations of the Spinal Column"

The importance of the spinal column as a static (load-carrying) and dynamic (movable) central organ of support and motor function is found to a large extent in the well-graduated biomechanical connection of many motor units. Variations occur in large numbers and with great frequency, so that they are not identical for all spinal columns. The spinal column is composed of the previously discussed mixed-articular intervertebral disc, which number varies from 23 to 25 according to variations, and two more mixed articulations, the sacroiliac joints. The symphysis pubis, which is the mixed articulated anterior pelvic junction, must also be included among these structures. Its functions are closely related to the movements and loads of the spinal column; this interrelationship often receives too little consideration.

In addition to the large number of mixed articulations (about 25 to 28), the spinal column also includes 63 to 65 true articulations: 50 vertebral arch articulations, 10 uncovertebral articulations, and 5 occipital articulations. These 24 vertebrocostal articulations, which consist of 2 partial articulations each, (see section 2.2.5.6) are also significant since they may cause an often overlooked painful arthrosis. Together, these more than 100 mixed articulations and articulations result in an obvious significance of the spinal column that is not even approximated in any other part of the body's support and motor system.

2.2.5.2 Vertebral Arch Articulations

The approximately 50 vertebral arch articulations, whose development is described in section 2.2.1, resemble other true articulations in their anatomical structure. They may be classified as gliding mortise joints. Their load capacity is dependent on various corresponding anatomical articular surfaces, a smooth cartilaginous surface, articular fluid that is distributed according to exertional forces, and a limiting ligamentous capsule. In addition, the spinal muscles assert exogenous forces for control and stabilization of posture and for motion in unison with the corresponding external ligamentous systems either by initiation or checking of motion.

The vertebral arch articulations constitute a self-contained functional unit for the central skeletal system and are functionally connected with the intervertebral discs. Each segmental pair of articulations as well as each individual articulation has special tasks that frequently correspond to their anatomical structure. This structure is related in form and function to the biomechanical requirements of the various spinal column sections (Figs. 2-28 and 2-29). In addition there are divergences in form and axis orientation of the vertebral arch articulations at the transitional areas between spinal column sections, with occasional differences between right and left (Fig. 2-30). Such changes often predispose individuals for arthroses.

The vertebral arch articulations are well supplied with nerves (see section 3.2.7 illustrations). Nerves are evident in the fibrous capsules of the articulations and in the cartilage coverings of the articular surfaces.

The presence of menisci is an unusual feature of the vertebral arch articulations. They are infrequently seen as a continuous meniscal disc between the articular surfaces (Fig. 2-31). Often one finds cuspidal articular villi that project together with the articular capsule into the articular cavity (Fig. 2-32). The main task of these villi, however, is not primarily an adjustment of the articular shape or of the articular cavities. Instead, they function as an elastic pressure cushion and thus as shock absorbers. Although these structures have been the focus of many studies, it is not certain whether they are sec-

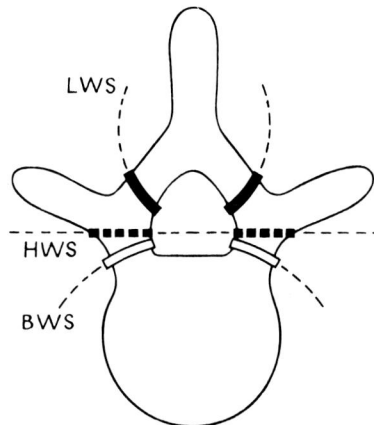

Fig. 2-28 Orientation of the vertebral arch articulations in the cervical, thoracic, and lumbar spinal column [according to Sullivan and Farfan (1975)].

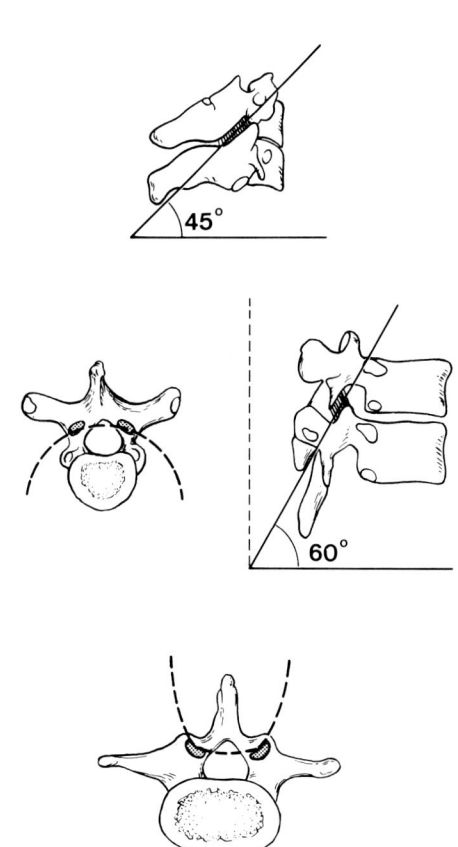

Fig. 2-29 Schematic depiction of orientation variations of vertebral arch articular surfaces in the sagittal plane in three areas of the spinal column (top, cervical; middle, thoracic; bottom, lumbar spinal column) (according to Schenk 1964).

28 CLINICAL IMPLICATIONS OF NORMAL BIOMECHANICAL STRESSES ON SPINAL FUNCTION

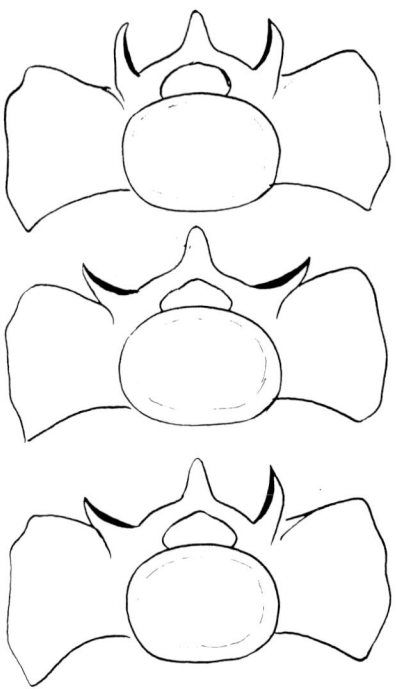

Fig. 2-30 Schematic drawing of the sacral base as seen from above. Different orientational possibilities of the articulations at S-1 correspond to similar articular positions at the L-5. (Top) half-moon shaped (12%), (middle) shallow (57%), (bottom) half-moon shaped and shallow (31%).

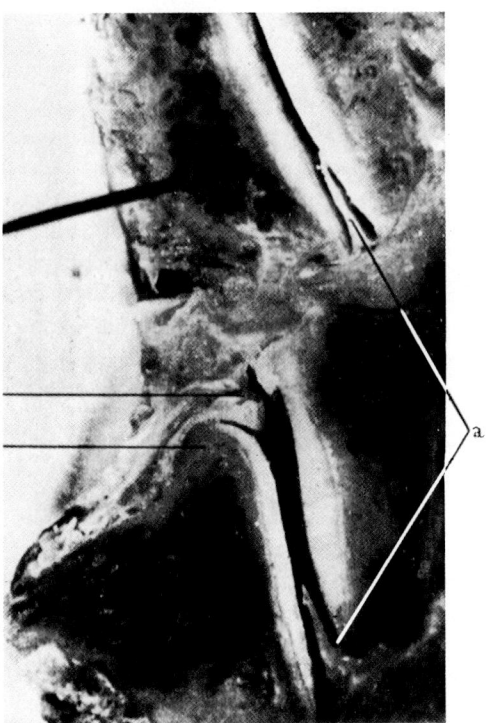

Fig. 2-32 Cuspidal articular villi in the articular arch articulations.

Fig. 2-31 Disc-shaped meniscus in the vertebral arch articulation.

ondarily created articular folds or whether they have their origins in the mesenchyme of the articular surfaces. Nevertheless, their presence causes a susceptibility of the vertebral arch articulations for painful obstruction of the motor unit (see Chapter 3). The eleventh conference (1979) of the Society for Spinal Column Research dealt exclusively with vertebral arch articulations; see "The Spinal Column in Research and Practice," vol 87 (1982). See also Gerner (1978), Med (1975, 1979), Ritsema (1980), Toendury (1968), and Wigh (1980).

2.2.5.3 Sacroiliac Articulations and the Symphysis Pubis

Both sacroiliac articulations consist in their superior (posterior) part of a rigid syndesmosis but are true articulations in their inferior (anterior) section, complete with articular cartilage and a narrow articular cavity (Fig. 2-33). The opposing articular surfaces are curved so that they can stabilize the joint and prevent slipping. This combined morphological structure allows only small movements; these may be measured by means of radiographic stereometry (Schmid 1980). The pelvic girdle, however, supports the large forces that arise between the spinal column and the pelvis when the spinal column or the legs are strained.

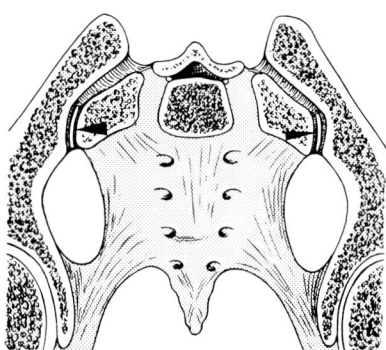

Fig. 2-33 The sacroiliac articulation, which consists superiorly of a rigid syndesmosis. The inferior section (arrows) is articular and has a cartilage covering. When the syndesmosis is relaxed, an arthrosis with osteophytosis can occur.

The pubic symphysis is also involved in cushioning and carrying the loads that the pelvic girdle supports. Its morphological structure has been compared (Luschka 1858) with that of the intervertebral disc because there are many similarities between these two mixed articulations (Schlenzka, 1980). Arthroses of the sacroiliac articulations and of the symphysis pubis are discussed in Chapter 4, the articular obstruction in Chapter 6 and the obstruction in section 3.4.4.

2.2.5.4 Occipital Articulations

In their developmental history the five occipital articulations are derived in part from the vertebral bodies and in part from the vertebral arches. The occipitoatlantoaxial articulation group is the most complex articulation of the human body in both anatomical and kinetic respects (White and Panjabi 1978). A description of its anatomy and movement possibilities is given in Woersdoerfer and Magerl (1980) and Dul et al. (1982). Its special place in articular mechanics, physiology, and clinical practice was described in 1983 by Wolff, who explained the nerve interferences that may originate at these articulations as well as chiropractic therapeutics for such problems. In 1983, Kamieth described in detail radiological evidence of normal motion at the occipital articulations. He elucidated diagnostic pitfalls and their prevention through special photographic methods and discussed improper and proper chiropractic manipulations.

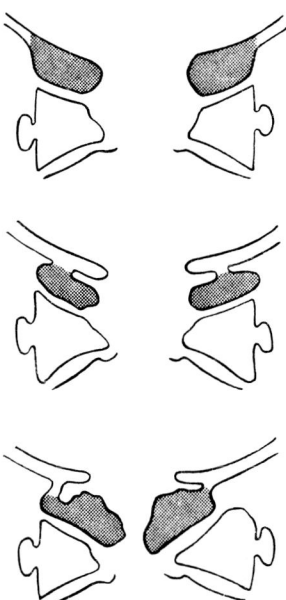

Fig. 2-34 Occipital vertebra.

In the horizontal plane one finds the paired articulations of occiput with atlas and atlas with axis. These are true articulations with menisci. In addition, there is the trochoid articulation between the back of the anterior arch of the atlas and the anterior surface of the dens. It is a morphological peculiarity that the paired articulations between atlas and axis do not rest congruently on each other because both the cranial and the caudal articular surface have a slightly convex shape. More detailed descriptions are contained in "Pathology and Clinical Practice of the Occipital-Cervical Region" from the 9th conference of the Society for Spinal Column Research (1975) (published by Hippokrates, Stuttgart, 1978). More information about arthroses of the occipital articulations is found in Chapter 4.

The manifestation of an occipital vertebra at the cervico-occipital junction is a rare phenomenon. Most often this anomaly exists only partially as cone-shaped appendices (Fig. 2-34). Another rare occurrence is atlas assimilation (occipitalization). Basilar impression is an often unnoticed abnormality in the cervico-occipital transition area. Other pathological problems, however, may result in secondary basilar impression and a distinct clinical picture; these

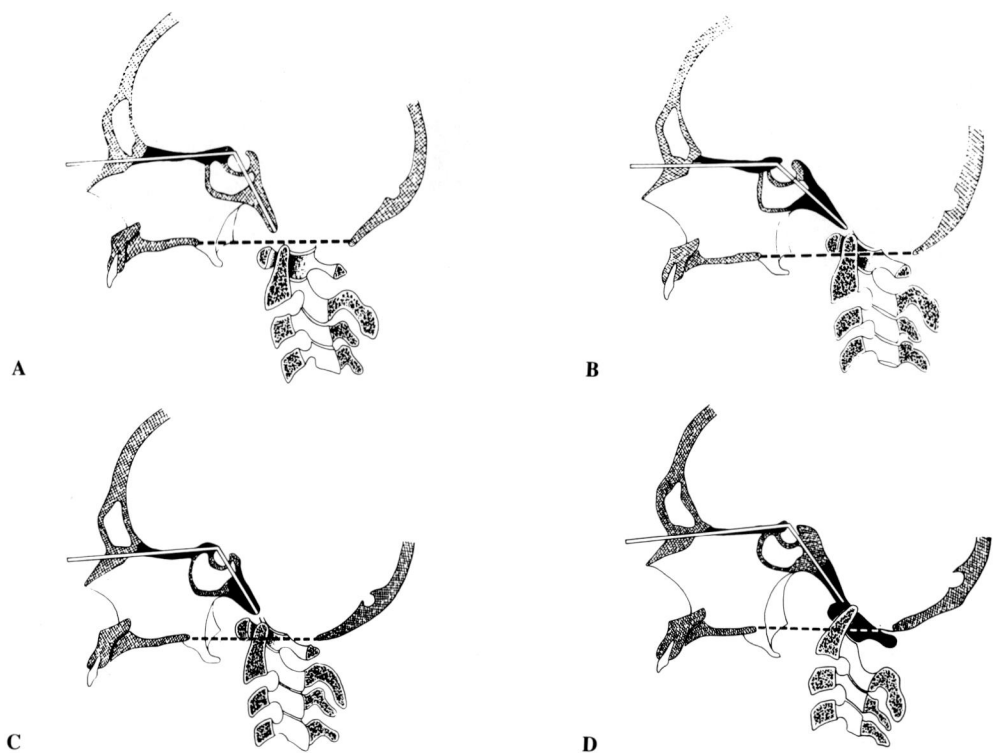

Fig. 2-35 Schematic depiction of various forms of occipital dysplasia compared to normal [from Erdmann (1963)]. (**A**) Normal; (**B**) decreased angle of the clivus, leading to basilar impression; (**C**) hypoplasia of the clivus, leading to basilar impression; (**D**) osseous occipitalization and elevation of the dens axis.

---

include osteoporosis, tuberculosis, and rheumatic spondylitis, among others. In the past, basilar impression was only of anatomical interest. A better knowledge of symptoms aided by new imaging procedures has attracted more attention to this abnormality. Some of the most common malformations at the cervico-occipital transition (the occipital dysplasias) have been described by Erdmann (Figs. 2-35 and 2-36).

2.2.5.5 Uncovertebral Articulations

The development of the lateral vertebral body articulations in the cervical spinal column was described in section 2.2.3 (see Fig. 2-16). This late transformation of previously clearly established morphological structures is a conspicuous peculiarity. It has also been studied comparatively in various other vertebrates. Such studies found progressive adaptation to the requirements of motion. In 1980, Stahl and Huth described in detail the synovial gaps of the uncovertebral articulations, their genesis, and their significance from a morphological and functional standpoint.

An often overlooked peculiarity of the uncovertebral articulations is found at the cervicothoracic transition. The normal shape of the lateral vertebral body articulations is slightly raised toward the exterior. This raised curve levels off at the transition point either on one or both sides and thus adapts to the conditions of the thoracic spine. If this process takes place only unilaterally (Fig. 2-37, arrow), it may lead to disrupted mobility and therefore to early uncovertebral arthrosis.

2.2.5.6 Vertebrocostal Articulations and the Rib Cage

Vertebrocostal articulations form in the area of the rib-supporting vertebrae during the precartilaginous stage. After the conclusion of development, a characteristic double articulation

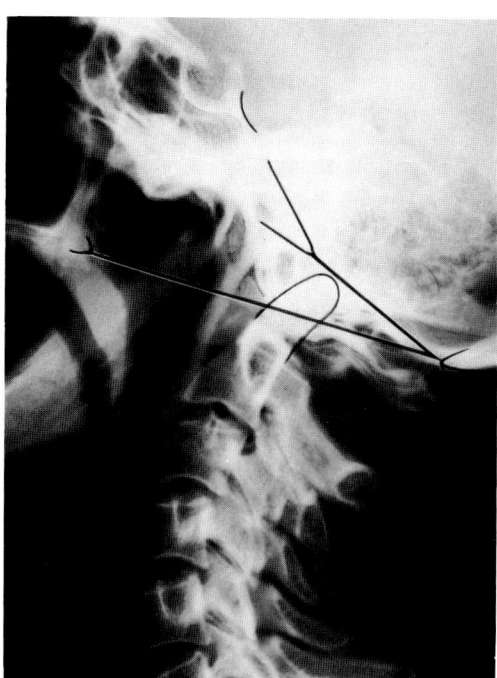

Fig. 2-36 Basilar impression. The dental process far surpasses Chamberlain's line in its height, and its tip reaches McRay's line [from Erdmann (1965)].

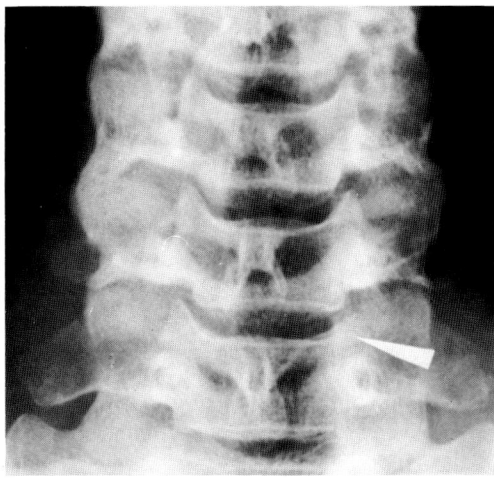

Fig. 2-37 Uncovertebral articulation at C-7 (arrow). C-7 is characterized as a transitional vertebra because of the shallow position of its uncovertebral articulation.

forms with the spinal column: an articular connection between rib and transverse process (costotransverse articulation). A second one forms between the head of the rib and the intervertebral disc (costovertebral articulation). Because of the presence of an intra-articular ligament, the vertebrocostal articulation has a rigid syndesmosis between the rib and the posterolateral portion of the intervertebral disc, which is the main contact area of the rib head. The vertebral edges that border it both superiorly and inferiorly form a small (sometimes absent) socket. The costotransverse articulation is an amphiarthrosis between the tip of the vertebral transverse process (socket) and the rib head. Intra-articular discs (menisci) have been found on those articulations (Emminger 1955). Section 4.6 reports on the frequent arthroses of these articulations and obstructions of their motion.

Together with the sternum, the ribs and their described articulations form the rib cage, which provides additional spinal stability in all directions of motion. The rib cage is also a large part of the auxiliary support system for the viscera according to Schanz (1931) (see Chapter 5). In addition, the rib cage is purported to increase the resistance of the spinal column to axial compression by a factor of 4 (Woersdoerfer and Magerl 1980).

The lumbar spinal column lacks articulations that correspond to the vertebrocostal articulations. The ossification centers for the ribs and transverse processes, which separate during development, fuse into the large lumbar mamillary processes, however.

2.2.6 Vertebral Body–Intervertebral Disc Junction

The connection of the vertebral body to the intervertebral disc is, in its development and final structure, probably the most important anatomical structure in the support and motor system of the human body; for descriptions see sections 2.2.2, 2.2.3, 3.2.2.1, and 3.2.4. A similar structure exists only in primates. In other mammals and all other animal species a closed osseous epiphyseal plate separates the vertebral body from the content of the intervertebral (disc) space.

The principles of nourishment of the intervertebral disc are explained on the basis of the anatomical characteristics of the vertebral body–intervertebral disc junction (extensively studied by Schmorl and his students from 1927 to 1931) in other chapters. The structures enable the spine to manage the static and dynamic loads required at the junction between a mobile part and a rigid part (the vertebral body). Consideration of the boundary between the disc and the vertebral body (which also contains the growth zones) becomes especially important when one considers this construction occurs approximately 50 times on the approximately 25 motor units of the spine (see section 2.2.5.1).

The capillaries that stretch from the vertebral body marrow through the pores of the cribriform plate to the hyaline cartilage plate, and the blood pools formed there, were shown in microscopic studies in the Schmorl Institute during Schmorl's lifetime (see Fig. 2-24). These studies demonstrated the blood diffusion path, which is crucial to the life and well-being of the slowly nourished intervertebral disc (although it must be said that 50 years ago the full impact of these anatomical structures remained unrecognized). Because they carry a high disease potential, it has become obvious just how important these structures at the vertebral body–intervertebral disk transition are. Many consequences derive from this potential, as will be seen in the following chapters. Horst (1982) has also examined the mechanical tensions in the vertebral body end plates and has gained new findings concerning the question of ruptures in the annular fibers as well as in the transition zones between intervertebral disc and vertebral body.

2.2.7 The Motor Unit

A peculiarity that is restricted to the spinal column is the motor unit, which is interposed approximately [23 to 25 times] between each two adjacent vertebrae (see Fig. 3-1). The term motor unit was introduced in 1950 (see Chapter 3 for definition). This unit is dominated by the intervertebral disc, which is a taut, mixed articulation and therefore also an elastic buffer. It absorbs loads and distributes pressure over the bony end plates of each two adjacent vertebral bodies.

The second important element in the functional space between vertebrae is the paired vertebral arch articulations (see section 2.2.5.2). They participate in all movements and support the functions of the intervertebral disc. The ligaments, muscles, blood vessels, and nerves in this area all have close connections with the motor unit.

From the point of view of functional anatomy, the 23 to 25 motor units in their entirety represent an organ system because movements of the spinal column regularly require the involvement of several segments. Thus even if only one segment is diseased, the adjacent segments are affected as well (see, for example, section 3.2.1).

2.2.8 Curvatures and Angles

The normal curvatures of the spinal column lie in the plane of the sagittal suture. The profile of the spinal column (total kyphosis during the early embryonic period) develops during childhood into the curved final shape (Fig. 2-38): two kyphoses (thoracic spinal column and sacrum) and two lordoses (cervical and lumbar spinal column). This double S curvature absorbs vertical forces in a springlike fashion and thus has shock-absorbing qualities.

During the formation of the final kyphosis, it becomes more and more clear that this curvature is determined by the shape of the vertebral bodies themselves. The lumbar lordosis, on the other hand, seems to develop its curvature because of the influence of the intervertebral disc shape, which is slightly raised in the front. In this respect the last presacral intervertebral disc often plays an important role. From the many more or less important curvature arches, the ideal shape was elucidated by Killus (1973, 1976) with the help of computer analysis. Killus superimposed 150 measurement results (Fig. 2-39). With the help of further conversions, Killus found the "ideal" spinal column (Fig. 2-40).

An occasional slight right convex curvature of the thoracic spinal column is attributed to pronounced right-handedness. Scoliotic curvatures exceeding this rather common minor finding are classified as pathological abnormalities (see Chapter 4). The most important and most frequently measured angle is located at the lumbosacral transition. It shows significant differences determined by individual and heredi-

Basic Compendium of Development, Morphology, and Biochemistry 33

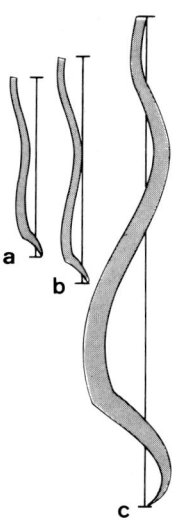

Fig. 2-38 The development of the human spinal curvature during the growth period. (**A**) 3-month-old infant, (**B**) 10-month-old infant, (**C**) 18-year-old [according to Platzer (1975)].

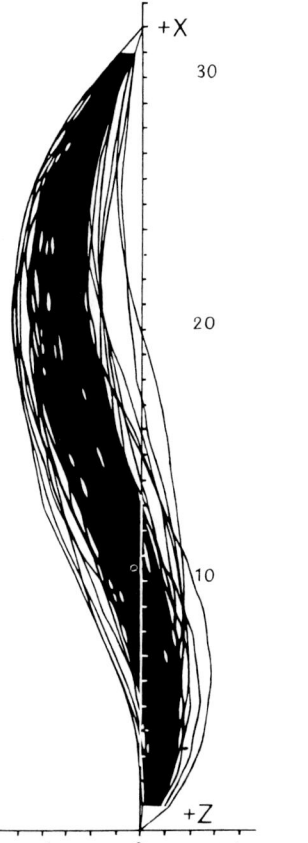

Fig. 2-39 Superimposed diagrams of thoracic and lumbar spinal column path from 150 full-spine roentgenograms [according to Killus (1973, 1976)].

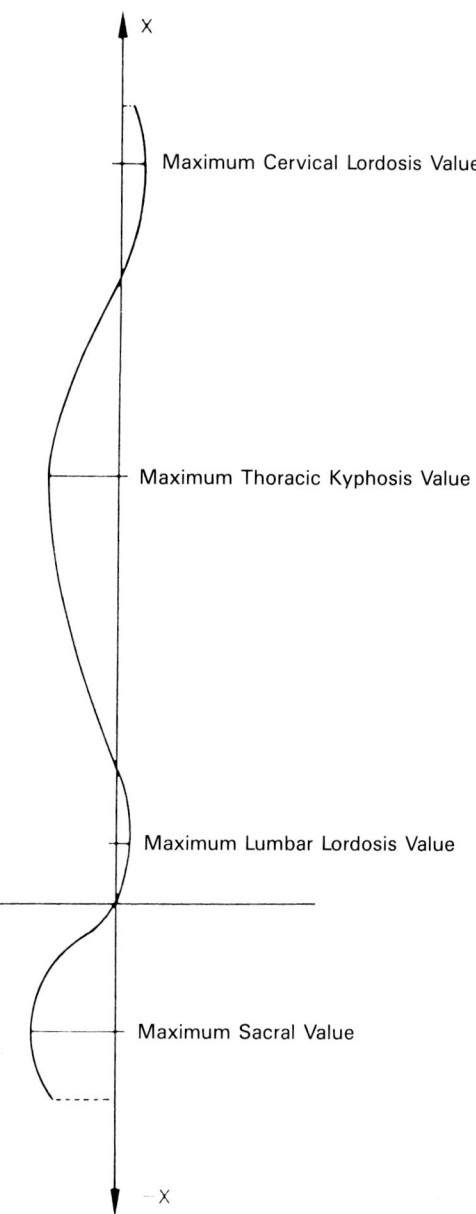

Fig. 2-40 The "ideal" spine from the computations of Killus (see Fig. 2-39).

tary tendencies. The lumbosacral curve is the principal factor in establishing the position of the entire spine because it rests on the sacral base. Its inclination toward the horizontal and the wedge shape of the presacral intervertebral disc provide the decisive factors for the curvature formation of the spinal column in the sagittal plane (ie, for the described lordoses and kyphosis up to the

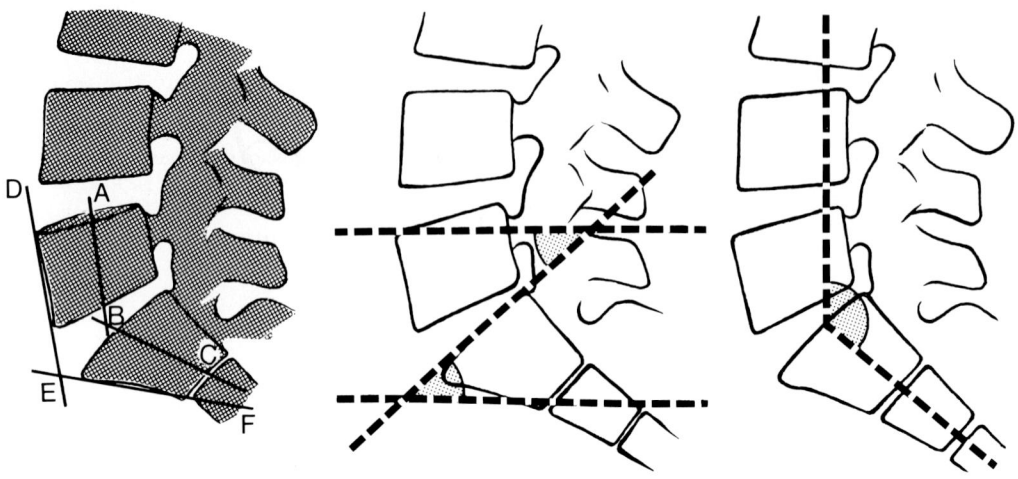

Fig. 2-41 Various methods of angle determination at the lumbosacral transition.

cervico-occipital transition). For this reason the angle conditions at the lumbosacral transition have always been of interest.

Measuring the angles is not easy at this location. Therefore, persons concerned with this problem use various points and lines of reference. Junghanns reported on the lumbosacral and promontory angles in detail in 1929 and 1977a,b; further details are given in Schmorl and Junghanns (1968). For measurements in the lumbosacral, see, for example, Erdmann (1956, 1965a,b) and Swiderski and Swiderski (1977). The various measuring methods are based in part on reference points connected with the skeleton. Some investigators, however, also consider the intervertebral space (ie, the shape and condition of the intervertebral disc) or use a horizontal or vertical axis as reference lines. According to some measuring systems, the lumbosacral angle is determined by the obtuse angle of the middle axes of the L-5 and S-1, which is open to the back (line ABC in Fig. 2-41, left). For men it is on average 142° (123° to 157°), and for women it is 144° (124° to 164°). Other investigators define the lumbosacral angle as that between a horizontal line and the superior surface of the sacrum, which is open to the front (Fig. 2-41, middle). Lackum (1924) used the median bisecting lines of S-1 and S-2 together with a vertical line for the lumbosacral angle (Fig. 2-41, right).

The promontory angle is determined by the lines at the anterior surfaces of the L-5 and S-1 (line DEF in Fig. 2-41, left). The average values are 129° for men (112° to 151°) and 130° to 156° for women. Erdmann (1956) points out that the last presacral vertebral body often has a variable shape at this transition, which influences the promontory angle decisively (Fig. 2-42). If the last presacral vertebra is more or less integrated into the sacrum as a transitional vertebra (sacralization), a double promontory may result (Fig. 2-42, B and C). Several investigators suggest vertical or horizontal reference lines. Because these depend on the positioning of the spinal column during radiography or on the direction of the central roentgen beam, however, there is uncertainty in the comparison of measurements (see Fig. 2-41, middle and left).

The lumbosacral transitional area, with its individually distinct angles, is closely interrelated with pelvic leveling and the plane of orientation of the pelvic cavity. More information about the pelvic inlet may be found in textbooks on gynecology and orthopedics.

The interior architecture of each vertebra is based on angular and arch structures that mostly affect the relationship between vertebral body and vertebral arch. The body-isthmus angle (Fig. 2-43, left), the isthmus (arcuate) angle (Fig. 2-43, lower right), and the articular angle (Fig. 2-43, upper right) are important factors in

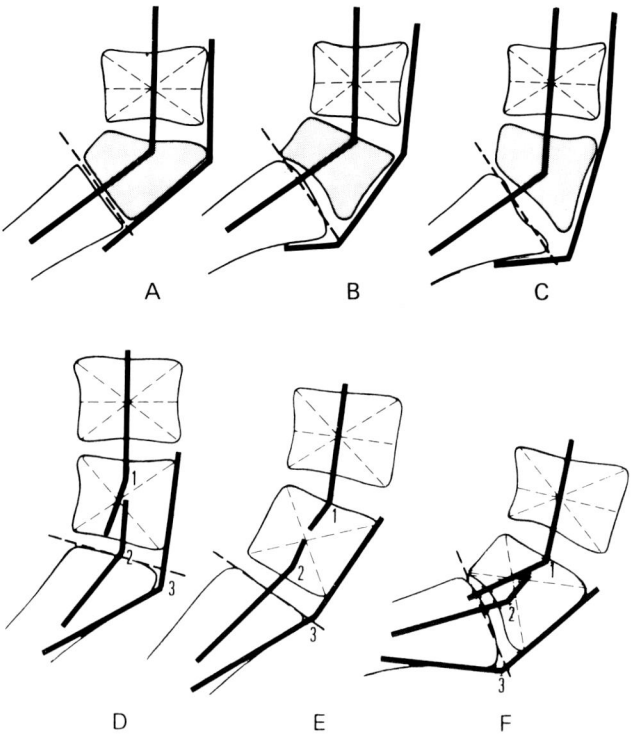

Fig. 2-42 The promontory angle. Different shapes of the last presacral vertebra significantly change the promontory angle. In the case of a transitional vertebra a double promontory results (**B** and **C**). Different measurements are used for different inclination angles of the sacral base and shape abnormalities of the last presacral vertebral body (**D** to **F**).

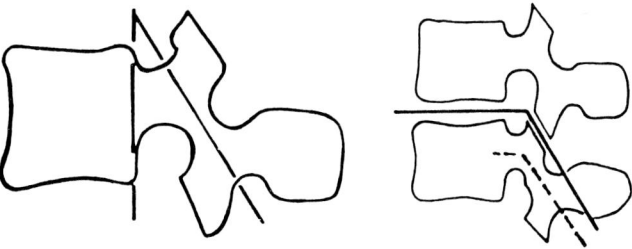

Fig. 2-43 (Left) Body-isthmus angle, (upper right) articular angle, (lower right) isthmus angle.

the stable construction of the vertebral arch and for the transmission and distribution of loads, especially in cases of bending or rotating forces. If those angles deviate from the normal value during or even after the growth period, a gradual transformation of trajectory orientation takes place (see Chapter 5). This can create or increase spondylolysis or spondylolisthesis or pseudospondylolisthesis.

The crooked development of the juvenile spine, such as in juvenile kyphosis (Scheuermann's disease), may be found in more than 50% of all adolescents to varying degrees. A detailed description along with many illustrations is given in Chapters 4 and 8. Juvenile scolioses are not quite as common. Their causes are manifold. Their curvatures of different degrees—often connected with torsions and rotational slipping—have for centuries occupied physicians more than have the kyphoses. Details and many illustrations are given in Chapters 4 and 8.

2.3 BIOCHEMISTRY

As is true for the entire body, the supply and removal of metabolic fluids and substances in the spine depends on more than neurological control and unobstructed circulation (including lymphatic circulation). Nutrition, rest, exercise, and muscular movement must play their proper parts to secure a physiologically balanced metabolism. This dependence of metabolism on the musculature affects the entire body. Decreased muscular movement (lack of exercise; see sections 3.3.4 and 5.3) as well as overexertion of the muscular corset of the spine are significant in several aspects. The muscles that closely border the spine in extensive sections and attach in part to the osseus structural elements participate in the metabolic environment, which spreads through the loose connective tissue layers and also through the attached ligament tracts. In addition, other important components of the spinal column (the intervertebral discs) depend on diffusion of nutrition controlled by spinal movements (see section 2.2.3). For this reason, muscles have additional importance with respect to spinal motion.

2.3.1 Bones

It is not proper to regard the bony tissue of the human body as a mere frame for shape, posture, and movement. In addition to those functions, bone serves, through steady anabolism and catabolism, as an important metabolic organ. Besides its storage function, bone also represents a constantly mobile mineral depot. Its controlling influence on the calcium and phosphorus metabolism may be compared to the importance of the liver in the carbohydrate metabolism.

Although the red marrow in the long bones is replaced gradually with yellow marrow during childhood, the bone marrow in the pelvis, ribs,

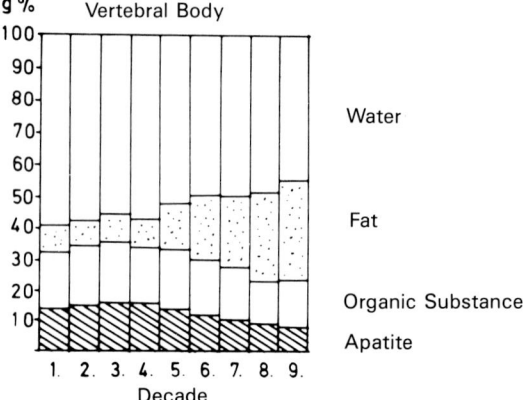

Fig. 2-44 Results of analysis of the quantitative composition of bony substance in the vertebral body during several stages of life [according to Heuck (1976)].

and vertebrae, which are included in the list of bones with the highest restructuring potential, is preserved into later decades. A positive influence on this maintenance is an ample blood supply. Therefore, as a rule the osseous parts of the spinal column, especially the vertebral bodies, possess a balanced metabolism with all necessary conditions for the maintenance of normally structured bone.

Because of high levels of anabolism and catabolism in these bones, metabolic disturbances such as increased osteoblastic activity or increased osteoclastic activity have their largest effect in the vertebral skeleton. Even the symptoms of such changes are often manifested first or even solely in the vertebrae (Schmorl and Junghanns 1968). As a consequence, many pathophysiological conditions can be considered a targeted influence of bone metabolism at the spinal column. The ample blood circulation of the spongiosa-rich vertebral bodies as well as the hematogenously active bone marrow make possible this fast and extensive ability to react to any change in metabolic balance.

Biological aging also taxes bony tissue extensively in the form of age-dependent behavior of soluble and insoluble collagen fractions. Figure 2-44 depicts just how much the mass of individual elements of the vertebral body spongiosa is shifted during life. The decrease in the water content, fatty infiltration, and mineral content is conspicuous.

In addition to aging processes, other causes of change in the bony tissue may occur when, because of biochemical influences (such as hormonal imbalances or nutritional deficiencies), an incorrect composition of the necessary metabolic supply occurs and interferes with the physiological anabolism and catabolism of bone. Several principles that touch on both biochemistry and biomechanics are discussed in Chapter 5. These include concepts of bone mineralization.

The formation and transformation processes in the vertebral bones use biochemical and mechanical principles that apply to all other parts of the skeleton. Most of these processes take place in the same manner in the entire bony tissue. Especially in the case of biomechanically and biochemically coupled functions, however (see section 2.3.4.1), there are a few peculiarities because mechanical loads are different for the vertebrae than for the remaining skeleton. This is because of their segmental structure and the close physiological dependence between bones and intervertebral disc cartilage. Therefore, the vertebral bones have additional tasks compared with the bones of the extremities. This is discussed in further detail in other chapters.

Discussion of biochemical processes must not neglect the transition between the vertebral body and the intervertebral disc. Only if this zone is correctly structured in relation to the bone will it be able to perform its proper function as an important point of fluid supply and removal for intervertebral disc metabolism (see section 3.2.4).

2.3.2 Intervertebral Disc

2.3.2.1 Preliminary Comment

The biochemical processes in the intervertebral disc that science has given only slight consideration in the past have become increasingly important during recent decades. Research should supply important answers to questions concerning aging and chronic tissue wear of the intervertebral disc. Although in the past the unanswered questions concerned only the fluid content in general, analytical results have shown increasingly detailed differentiation of individual chemical components. The microstructure has also been further clarified. In this regard interdisciplinary cooperation, including the involvement of several research techniques, is indispensible: radiological crystallography, infrared spectroscopy, biochemical studies, immunological studies, and so forth. The newer findings concerning the biochemistry of the intervertebral disc justify the conclusion of Maroudas et al. (1975), which has become a guiding principle: nutritional conditions are significantly more important for the intervertebral disc than for the articular cartilage. Between 1975 and 1977, Adams' research team analyzed the chemical processes in the intervertebral discs of different age groups in many respects. The researchers demonstrated a close connection between mechanical function and chemical composition of the individual tissue types in the disc (see section 2.3.4.2). In their opinion, local variations in chemical composition may lead to mechanical failure. Lipson and Muir (1980) induced anterior prolapses of the nucleus pulposus in mice. Biochemical changes and gradually ossifying cartilaginous bulges appeared on the edges of such prolapses. The following works provide details about the problems and practical issues of intervertebral disc biochemistry: Naylor (1958; 1975); Nachemson et al. (1968; 1970); Hamerman and Rosenberg (1970); Kaiser (1972; 1975); Kraemer (*Biochemie*, 1976); Silberberg and Gerritsen (1976); Silberberg, Aufdermaur, and Adler (1979); Junghanns ("Die Wirbelsaeule," 1979); Urban and Maroudas (1980); Ogata (1981).

2.3.2.2 Metabolic Pathways in the Intervertebral Disc

The pathways for the supply and removal of nutritional materials for the intervertebral disc hold primary importance in the entire metabolism of the disc and therefore in its biochemical behavior in general. The fluid exchange between the intervertebral disc tissue and its surrounding area takes place in part directly through the blood vessels on top of the exterior lamellar rings. Another aspect of metabolism crosses the boundary between vertebral body and disc: the

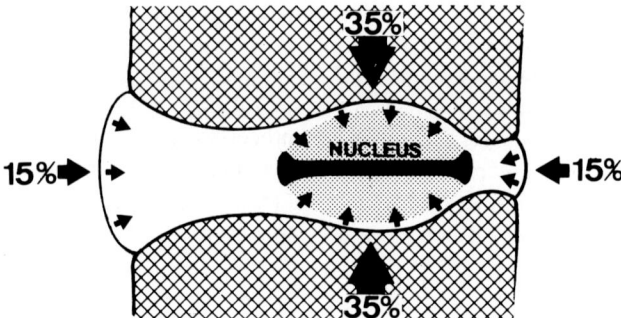

Fig. 2-45 Diffusion path for glucose and oxygen. Note that the pathway favors the boundary layer of the vertebral body–intervertebral disc (70%); the fiber ring layers are less favored (30%). The cross-hatched areas represent the pulposus, which is susceptible to nutritional deficiency [Nachemson (1976)].

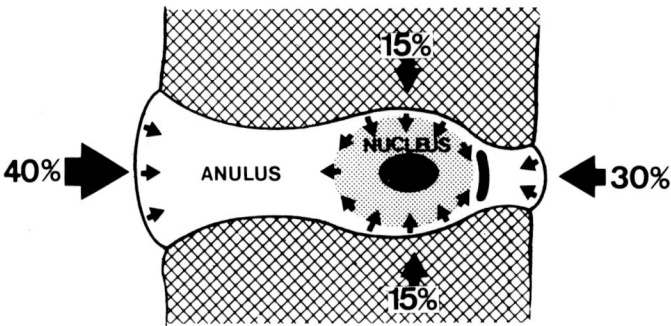

Fig. 2-46 Diffusion path for sulfates. Note that the pathway favors the anterior and posterior layers of the fiber ring (40% and 30%); the boundary layer of the vertebral body–intervertebral disc is less favored (30%). The cross-hatched areas represent areas with physiological susceptibility to nutritional deficiency [Nachemson (1976)].

osseous and hyaline cartilaginous end plates (see section 3.2.4). These two pathways each provide different nutrients. With increasing age, but also as a consequence of exogenous forces, damage originates that may hinder or even completely obstruct the free access of one of the pathways, most often the vertebral body–intervertebral disc boundary. The result is changed composition of the fluid in the disc. The consequences of such changes are discussed in section 3.2.

Maroudas et al. (1975a,b) and Nachemson (1970 to 1976) both investigated the aforementioned pathways for nutrients into the disc. According to their findings, 70% of the supplied glucose and oxygen derives from the vertebral body vessels; that is, they come through the osseous and hyaline cartilage plates and cross the body-disc border. Only 30% comes from the exterior lamellar fiber rings (Fig. 2-45). Of all supplied sulfates, 30% comes across the body-disc border, 30% comes from the posterior across the fiber ring, and 40% comes antero-laterally across the fiber ring (Fig. 2-46). These findings stem from animal studies as well as from experiments with human spinal column sections, so that comparisons should be made with caution. Further biological experiments must be undertaken to achieve final clarification of conditions in vivo.

Supply and removal of the intervertebral disc fluid are directly dependent on a regularly alternating pressure within the disc. The intervertebral disc takes on fluid and low–molecular weight substances when the intradisc pressure is low. Pressure greater than 80 kPa prevents this intake. In the case of a unilateral pressure increase, fluid and other substances only reach the low-pressure areas. See section 2.3.4.2 for further details.

In 1977, Urban et al. reported the results of extensive studies on the nutrition of the intervertebral disc in live dogs and in spinal slide sections. They described the three known pathways of influx (fiber ring and two vertebral body–intervertebral disc boundary layers), diffusion times across them, and the involved fluids and substances (including sulfates, glucose, and Ringer's solution). Calcification of the disc's hyaline cartilage plates or variantly ossified end plates (see section 2.2.2) or both may be the cause of decreased diffusion. Because of the different structures of the boundary between the vertebral body and intervertebral disc in animals, these findings cannot be directly transferred to humans. They do, however, supplement the findings of past studies [see also Inoue (1981)].

At this point, the indispensible pump mechanism induced by spinal column motion must be mentioned. It represents the major functional component for maintenance of sufficient diffusion in the disc (see section 3.2.4). Sections in Chapters 2 and 5 discuss these interrelationships and their significance.

Not all questions concerning the nourishment of the disc by diffusion pathways have been clarified yet. Nevertheless, the decisive function of the boundary between the vertebral body and the intervertebral disc is undisputed, and therefore the summary statement at the end of section 3.2.4 is justified: The fate of the intervertebral disc is decided at the vertebral body–intervertebral disc boundary.

In addition to a general retardation of metabolism in aging, damages of these 50 boundary layers cause a local metabolic fatigue and result in loss of diffusion. The resulting metabolic insufficiency carries serious dangers to the health of the intervertebral disc.

Prophylaxis in maintenance of a functional intervertebral disc is characterized by another principle: The basic biological law of recovery through alteration holds true for the intervertebral disc. This principle is absolutely essential for understanding athletic training, for example. This principle also holds for the muscles of the spinal column (see section 5.2.3.1). Muscular fatigue or spasm as a result of lack of exercise, vibrational influences, or chronic tension contributes to the already decreased metabolism of the intervertebral disc. This results in a vicious cycle in which the very viability of the intervertebral disc is impaired. To understand these processes, one should keep in mind the following statement: Nutritional conditions are much more important for the intervertebral disc than for the articular cartilage.

2.3.2.3 Fluid Content

The fluid content of the disc tissue is the primary determinant of its turgor and elasticity, particularly in the fluid-rich nucleus pulposus. In addition, a decrease in fluid content with resulting pressure differences results in decreased metabolism in the same manner as a change in the fluid composition. Serious consequences for the disc can be expected in such cases. This affects especially the aging disc (see section 2.3.2.10) with its greatly decreased fluid content: 88% for a newborn, 83% for a juvenile, and 70% for a septagenarian.

An important role in aging processes is played by the hydrophilic properties of the disc tissue, which also decrease with age. The hydrophilic capacity for hyperosmotic solutions is twice as high in the nucleus pulposus as in the fiber ring. The function of this fluid as a means of nutrient transport and waste removal from the disc must not be underestimated.

The content of interstitial fluid is not uniform across the tissue of the intervertebral disc. During adolescence the fluid amount in the nucleus pulposus far exceeds that of the fiber ring. In old age these fluid values approximate each other to a large extent. Although the adolescent nucleus pulposus appears to be gelatinous because of its high fluid content, the aging pulposus with its low fluid content increasingly approaches a fibrous state.

Long-term pressure loads, especially when applied to the intervertebral discs (eg, during long sitting), decrease the fluid content. The decrease in height of many discs that results from prolonged pressure can be measured. During the night (relaxation), normal body height returns. This difference in body height between day and night decreases with age (Kraemer and Gritz 1980). This may be explained by the age-related

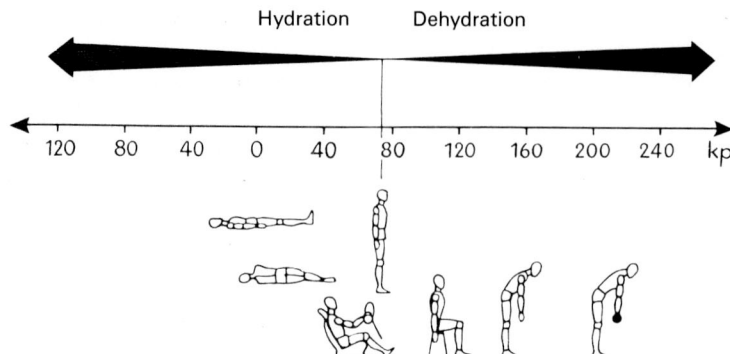

Fig. 2-47 Theoretical depiction of fluid intake and output combined with intradiscal pressure measurements in L3–4 in a living person [from Nachemson (1975)].

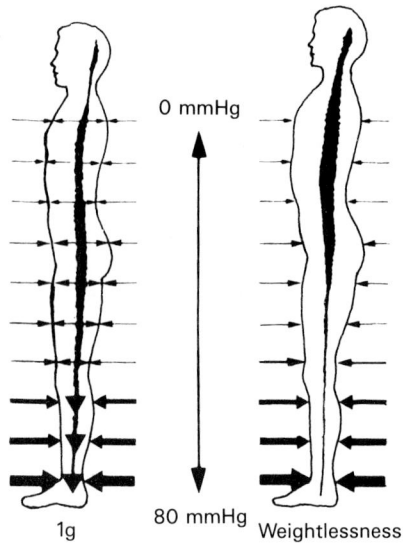

Fig. 2-48 Fluid pressure and volume displacement during a state of weightlessness.

decrease of the osmolarity level in the intervertebral disc. Simultaneously, a decreased hydrophilic tendency and decreased water-binding capacity appear.

In 1975, Nachemson produced a scale that depicted the relationship between the mechanical influences of different body postures and pressure-mediated fluid exchange in the intervertebral discs (Fig. 2-47). These findings again supported the extent of mechanical influence on biochemical processes (see section 2.3.3).

An extensive literature exists in regard to the water content of the human body, but only a small portion of it deals with the chemical composition of the intervertebral disc fluid (Bush et al. 1956; Kraemer 1977; Krzywicki et al. 1971; Oest 1962; Pueschel 1930).

Space flight creates peculiarities in the behavior of fluid in the intervertebral disc (Junghanns, ''Die Wirbelsaeule,'' 1979). Weightlessness reduces the total fluid in the lower half of the body, especially in the legs (Fig. 2-48). Vascular congestion results in the upper trunk, cervical spine, and head. Unavoidably, fluid congestion also results in the intervertebral discs. As a consequence, the height of the intervertebral disc spaces increases, and body height increases measurably as well. The pump mechanism (see section 3.2.4) required for metabolism is missing, and a change in the chemical composition of the intervertebral disc fluid results. The question of whether this results in secondary damages to the disc remains unanswered, and certainty concerning this question cannot be gained until long-term studies have been performed on persons in space for several months.

The height increases measured in astronauts by Burchard (1975) and Gierke (1971) showed noteworthy peculiarities. At the end of space travel the height increase of the spinal column quickly receded, temporarily even to a point less than the original height (Figs. 2-49 and 2-50). This was probably related to diuresis, which was aided by drugs, and partially to a lack of tone of the still weakened spinal column muscles. Normal height was not reestablished until 5 to 17 days after landing. Differences in the circumferences of the rib cage (excursion during respi-

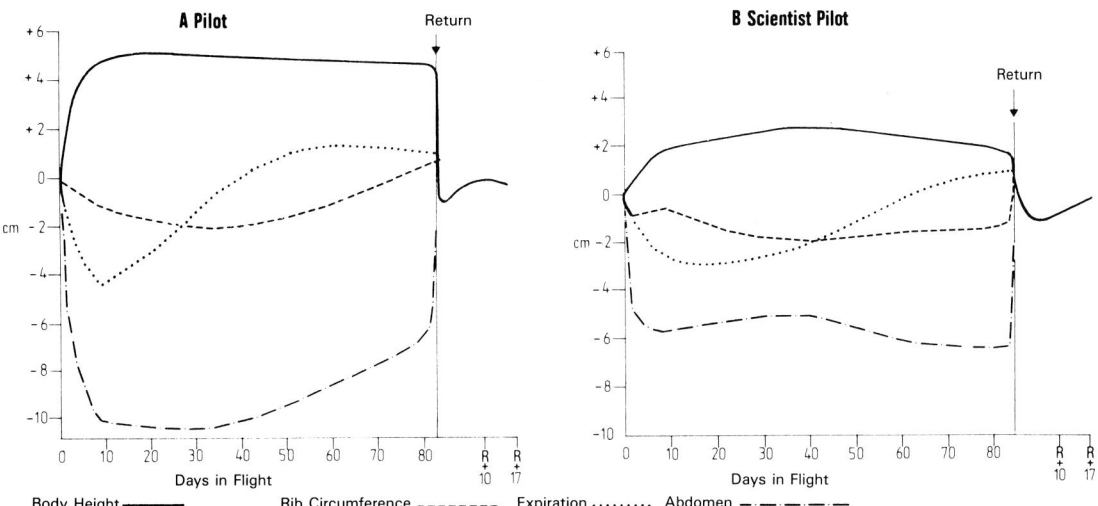

Fig. 2-49 Changes in body height and trunk circumference in astronauts of Skylab 4 during and after a flight time of 80 days (according to Thornton et al.). Legend: body height (solid line), rib cage circumference during inspiration (dashed line) and expiration (dotted line), circumference of abdomen (dotted and dashed line).

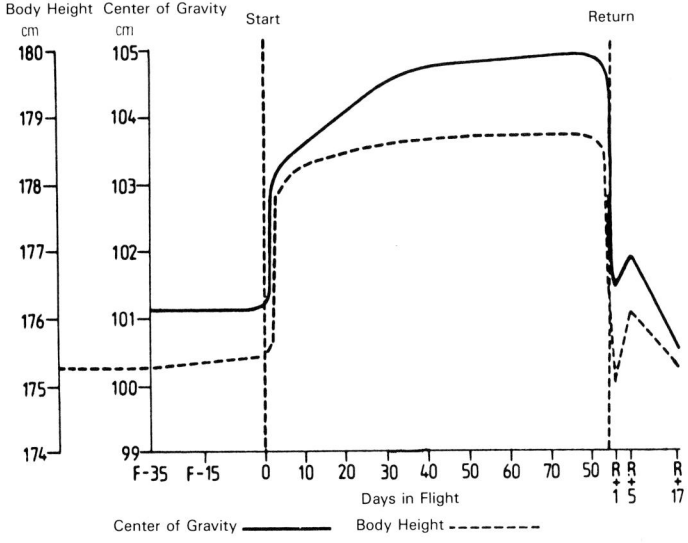

Fig. 2-50 Height increase (dashed line) and displacement of the center of gravity (solid line) of an astronaut during and after the flight of Skylab 4. The height increase is less than the original value on landing, increases again until day 5 after landing (R + 5), and returns to its original value on the day 17 after landing (R + 17) (graphs according to Thornton et al.)

ration) and the abdomen were also considerable (Fig. 2-49).

2.3.2.4 Minerals

Much information has been gained over the last decade concerning the mineral content of the intervertebral disc. The calcium content doubles during life. The bonding of calcium ions with acidic mucopolysaccharides leads to a calcium receptivity. This probably represents an explanation for the frequent calcium deposits in the fluid-rich nucleus pulposus observed after infections and trauma, especially in children. The behavior of the other minerals varies a great deal. Potassium and sulfur concentrations decrease with age. Stoefen (1975) reported on the correlations between the sulphur content of the intervertebral disc and the resulting possibilities for damage. Magnesium content decreases during the first and second decade of life but increases again later. Like calcium content, nitrogen content increases steadily with age. This may lead to formation of apatitic calcium phosphate crystals. The inorganic ions are in part bonded to the organic matrix and in part are present in the extracellular fluid in solution.

2.3.2.5 Organic Matrix

Basic substance and fibers form the organic matrix of the intervertebral disc, with a protein content of between 50% and 90% in the dry mass. The important components of the ground substance are glycoproteins and high–molecular weight polysaccharides. Hydrophilic properties and viscosity are determined mostly by the types of proteins and carbohydrates of the glycoproteins. In addition to the less common hyaluronic acid and heparin, the most frequent mucopolysaccharides in the intervertebral disc are chondroitin sulfate and keratan sulfate, which are formed intracellularly. Chondroitin-4-sulfate and chondroitin-6-sulfate play important roles in the aging process of the intervertebral disc tissue.

The important components of the basic substance are glucoproteins and high molecular polysaccharides. Water solubility and viscosity are necessarily determined by proteins and the carbohydrates of the glucoproteins. Aside from the less apparent hyaluronic acids and heparin, there are chondroitonic and ceratanic sulfates, which are intracellularly formed, and are the main part of the mucopolysaccharide in small children (90%). Chondroitin-4-sulfates and chondroitin-6-sulfates play an important role because of the age of the disc tissue.

Through inbred metabolic disruptions (gene mutations) of the acidic mucopolysaccharides, there are a number of serious types of illness known as the mucopolysaccharidoses. They are recognized through altered developments of cartilage and bone tissue—multiplex dystosis. This affects most of the developmental zones of the spinal body tissue borders and leads to spinal malformations through simultaneous lack of composition of the basic substance of the intervertebral tissues (Spranger 1974). The disc tissue is less capable of resistance against mechanical strains. Therefore, the mucopolysaccharidoses depict problems for resistance capability, often in their especially abortive and more meaningful forms. There is, therefore, an apparent connection with adolescent kyphosis (4.4.3).

Elasticity and viscosity of the basic substance, which are also very important mechanical qualities of the intervertebral tissue, depend upon the hydration power of the mucopolysaccharides and link a greater part of their liquidity through the macromolecules (with a molecular weight of more than a million). Water absorption ability is important for the mucopolysaccharides with sulfate groups that appear in the vessel-free parts of the intervertebral tissue. In contrast, those mucopolysaccharides in areas of the intervertebral tissue where vessels exist possess no sulfate groups. They are, therefore, less water soluble, and less definite in the embryonic tissue.

Whether or not the synthesis of the mucopolysaccharide-macromolecule takes place intracellularly or extracellularly, the main part of the metabolic process lies in the cartilage cells. The limited lifespan of the macromolecular groups necessitate an everlasting new formation in order to maintain an equilibrium between the synthesis and depolymerization. Thus, a well-balanced metabolism in intervertebral disc tissue is necessary, which again depends on regulated liquid exchange for the neighborhood. Badly maintained tissue cells produce macromolecular groups of minimal quality and quantity. The difficulties in the nourishment of diffusion, which increase with age (2.3.3.10), diminish the total mucopolysaccharide in the tissue. Oncotic pressure is reduced and, therefore, the water content and the water absorption ability are narrowed. In addition, the increase of the hyaluronidesis favors the breaking apart of the macromolecule. Further enzymatic breakdown restricts the size of the fission product. They flow through the semipermeable spinal body/intervertebral tissue in the bloodstream. Finally, because of aging or other processes, damaged intervertebral tissue is expanded in a vicious circle from which the tissues cannot be separated.

2.3.2.6 Collagenous and Elastic Fibers

Collagenous fibers, which are an additional important structural component of the intervertebral disc, form bundled mature fibrils in the fiber ring and are organized in tracts. They fulfill their mechanical tasks by means of their concentric, onion skin–like arrangement into lamellae (see Figs. 2-11 and 2-12). In contrast to the fibril density in the fiber ring, a loose network of fibrils with extensive intervals between them exists in the nucleus pulposus. The collagen content in the matrix is about 44% to 51% of the dry substance (elastin accounts for only about 0.2%). Temperature and pH are known to affect the macromolecular condition of the collagen.

The structure and distribution of polysaccharides in the fiber ring are changed significantly in the aging disc (see section 2.3.2.10). The parallel fiber arrangement is gradually lost, and the cells concentrate collagen. The collagen content of the nucleus pulposus increases as well. A striking increase in granulation of some components of the intracellular substance can be demonstrated on para-aminosalicylic acid (PAS) staining.

The collagen fibers are initially formed intracellularly as the soluble precursor tropocollagen, which is eventually transformed through extracellular polymerization into insoluble collagen. This synthesis and breakdown of collagen balance each other in early life. This is also true for the already described mucopolysaccharides. The collagen in the fibrils (with a biological half-life of 30 to 60 days) is broken down by collagenases. This collagen turnover slows with aging. Because of age-dependent diffusion loss, exterior influences, and other biochemical processes in the intervertebral disc, the collagen turnover finally comes to an almost complete halt, which supports the insurmountable vicious cycle of intervertebral disc degeneration. Eckert and Decker (1947) found hyalinization of the fiber ring lamellae that increases with age and is connected with the thickening of individual lamellae. These changes and the initial ring-shaped fissures in the fiber ring, whose early appearance was emphasized by Farfan (1973), are followed by the collagenization of the nucleus pulposus (Naylor, Shentall, and Micklethwaite 1977).

Intervertebral discs on the convex side of scolioses have a different chemical composition than those on the concave side. This was first described by Bushell (1979) and Ghosh et al (1980).

Elastic fibers were not mentioned in early works concerning intervertebral disc structure. Buckwalter, Cooper, and Maynard (1976) described electron microscopic studies that found an amorphous elastic fiber structure with sparse peripheral microfibrils in the nucleus pulposus. In accordance with their difference in function, the elastic portions of the fiber ring possess a more fibrous character. Knese (1978) also reported results of electron microscopic studies showing a central homogeneous portion and an exterior fibrillary portion of the disc. Elastic and nonelastic lamellae seemed to alternate. Some investigators consider the intervertebral disc a viscoelastic system (Barbieri and de Franceschi 1975).

2.3.2.7 Enzymes, Immunoglobulins, and Lysozymes

The enzymes contained in the intervertebral disc fulfill decomposing as well as synthesizing tasks in accordance with their surroundings. These enzymes are formed in lysosomes of the intervertebral disc cells. As biocatalyzers, they have an accelerating effect on metabolism (ochronosis; see section 2.3.2.9). The following are found in the intervertebral disc: acid phosphatases, cathepsin, β-galactosidase, β-glucouronidase, and β-acetylglucosaminidase. A strong nucleotidase activity is found in the nuclei of all sections of the intervertebral disc in adolescents but is completely absent in middle-aged individuals. After 55 years of age, nucleotidase activities are again found. The enzyme collagenase (nucleolysin) and its toxic effects were described by Bromley et al. in 1980.

According to Gertzbein et al. (1977), an inflammatory component, probably autoimmune, is part of intervertebral disc degeneration. Numerous investigators also emphasize the importance of lymphocytes in the intervertebral disc. Immune reactions in the intervertebral disc are created only when ruptures have reached the spinal canal and a connection with the immune system has been established, however. It remains to be established whether such ruptures may be a result of simple vibratory forces. This question is important in the understanding of disc degeneration and its consequences (see Chapter 4).

Intensive experiments are still needed to establish the role of immunoglobulins formed by lymphocytes in various diseases (eg, rheumatoid arthritis) or in degeneration or spondylo-discitis (see Chapter 4). From 1953 to 1976, Naylor provided the ground work for the understanding of the immunology and enzymology of the disc.

2.3.2.8 Microstructure

The chemical composition of the organic matrix of the intervertebral disc is closely tied to its microstructure. Many recent electron microscopic studies have shown that the cells of the nucleus pulposus lie in a three-dimensional grid-gel system. The cells of the fiber ring are deposited in biconvex form between the fibrils. Before their expulsion, the newly formed collagen fibrils are located mostly at the cell ends.

In the layered fiber ring, the fibers lie in parallel bundles. Mucopolysaccharides are essential for the cohesiveness of these bundles. Their molecules form a macromolecular superstructure that is fortified by the three-dimensional network of collagen fibers. Longitudinal sections and cross-sections of the fibrils have been studied extensively by electron microscopy. The cross-section of the anulus fibrosus seems to decrease after the age of 20 years, whereas that of the nucleus pulposus increases. Degeneration (see section 4.5) is manifested by a progressive decline in organization of the ultrastructure.

Even more exact differentiation of the microstructure will be gained as research technology improves (Auquier et al. 1974). Such studies are urgently needed to further clarify the interrelationships among the lamellae, which cross each other in opposite directions (see Figs. 2-11 and 2-12). So far the traction and shearing forces that can be tolerated by the connective fibers are unquantified. It is possible that during spinal rotation, even that caused by horizontal vibrations, strong tensions and mechanical overexertion may be created. It is possible that this leads to a loosening between adjacent lamellae and even to tears in connective fibers. It has yet to be determined which initiating or exacerbating effect is caused by faulty metabolism.

2.3.2.9 Effects of Hormones, Nutrition, and Drugs

It seems obvious that a structure as complex as the intervertebral disc is, because of its relatively slow nutritional influx, especially susceptible to external influences. This is true for the decreased flow of normally composed diffusion fluid as well as for the influx of damaging substances and difficulties in the removal of metabolic waste products. It is probable, as Ruth Silberberg (1971) described in regard to growth and aging of the epiphyseal and articular cartilage, that some metabolic aspects of the tissue of the intervertebral disc are genetically predisposed. Silberberg further reported that hormone metabolism and certain nutritional influences may significantly change the cartilaginous tissue. Silberberg's conclusion was that the increased disposition to an arthrosis in endocrine diseases (such as acromegaly and diabetes) clearly indicates that human articular cartilage may react to general hormonal factors in a manner similar to that of laboratory animals. Therefore, human articular cartilage may be assumed to react not only to chronic endocrine diseases but also to smaller metabolic disturbances that are common during life. If these reactions accumulate, the changes may become irreversible and may influence the aging process, therefore leading to the development of osteoarthritis.

These conclusions suggest that similar assumptions may be made for the chronic wear of intervertebral disc tissue, that is, for the fibrous as well as for the hyaline cartilaginous portions. In this process, influences must be considered that, according to the results of Silberberg, affect osteoarthritis in either an accelerating or a retarding manner (Table 2-1). Silberberg (1974) has also reported on hormonal damages, with special regard for the cartilaginous portions of the spinal column.

In addition to nutrition, which Klavehn (1976) regards as important for the development of wear in the articular system, a changed hormonal metabolism, exogenous hormones, and other metabolic abnormalities may result in damage to

Table 2-1 Influences on Osteoarthritic Changes

Accelerating	Retarding
Biochemical	
Somatotropin	Hypopituitarism
Testosterone	Castration (estrogens)
Nortestosterone	
Progesterone	Glucocorticoids of the adrenal cortex
Nutrition	
High caloric intake	Low caloric intake
High-fat diet	

the disc. An obvious example is ankylosing hyperostosis (see section 4.5.2.2), which correlates closely with gout and diabetes and in addition to causing damage to the intervertebral disc (like spondylosis deformans) is also characterized by conspicuous, flowing ossification at the anterolateral surfaces of the vertebrae, especially in the thoracic area.

M. Heide (1968, 1983) reported that sulfur from sulfur baths penetrates the skin and reaches the intervertebral discs and articular cartilage and may help maintain proper metabolic balance. Ochronosis (alkaptonuria) is a hereditary metabolic abnormality that results from the lack of a specific enzyme. A peculiarity is the black color of the intervertebral disc tissue and spinal ligaments, which is conspicuous on the slide. On the roentgenogram, spinal osteochondrosis is apparent. In the late stages it is joined by marginal peaks on the vertebral body that tend to bridge the intervertebral spaces (Schmorl and Junghanns 1968; Deeb and Frayha 1976). Because of the rarity of this condition it has thus far not been possible to determine whether flowing ossification occurs, as it does in diabetes. Such questions must be asked to clarify the susceptibility of intervertebral disc tissue to metabolism (Aufdermaur et al. 1980; Hirsch et al. 1952; Van den Hooff 1964; Mladenovic and Mihajlovic 1977; Silberberg, Aufdermaur, and Adler 1979).

2.3.2.10 Aging of the Intervertebral Disc

The metabolic exchange continuously taking place in the tissues of the intervertebral disc slows down with age, so that the tissue simultaneously changes in biochemical quality and fluid content. This leads to metabolic deficiency of the intervertebral disc. In this respect the individual is less decisively affected by chronological age than by biological age, which often deviates from generally accepted assumptions about aging. Even certain specific organs and organ systems may differ widely from the general aging scheme by longer preservation or premature degeneration. The decline in performance of the spinal column actually begins in the early decades of life. Only seldom does it begin in the bony elements; much more frequently, damage begins early in the intervertebral disc tissue. This leads to an intervertebral insufficiency with the consequences described in section 3.4.2, which limits physical stress tolerance at an early point, even beyond the area of the spinal column itself.

The chemical processes affecting the tissue and interstitial fluid of the disc, which become gradually retarded, are determined in part genetically and in part by nutritional diffusion, which is susceptible to malfunction. Additional influences play roles that vary in frequency and intensity. Thus the aging of the intervertebral disc is a complex as well as an individually variant process. Statistically, the intervertebral disc belongs among the body tissues that age early and to a great degree. This is evident by statistical frequency analysis of pathomorphological slides and roentgenograms (see Chapter 4). In addition, it is confirmed by a conspicuous amount of lost time from work, applications for early disability, and a high incidence of necessary occupational assistance measures due to back injuries (Junghanns 1976; 1979). The main reason for this is the aforementioned metabolic deficiency, which increases with age. This leads to a biochemical and therefore biomechanical crisis of the intervertebral disc (Peerebom and Copius 1971).

Silberberg, Aufdermaur, and Adler (1979) reported on animal experiments that demonstrated deleterious effects of domestication and other "unnatural" environmental influences and described the spontaneous degeneration of the aging intervertebral disc tissue from protrusion to prolapse. The damages in laboratory rats strongly parallel those seen in aging processes in humans: intervertebral chondrosis with tissue necrosis and spondylosis deformans with marginal osteophytes. In the area of the thoracic spine, osteophytes were found at the posterior edges of the vertebral bodies pressing against the spinal cord. Erosions of the vertebral body end plates were also discovered. In conjunction with such damages, arthroses were found at the vertebral arch articulations. These can be secondary signs of both spondylosis deformans and a herniated intervertebral disc.

In summary, the influences on the life span, wear, and aging of the intervertebral disc require further experimental investigation until a complete understanding is reached.

2.3.2.11 Chemical Changes as the Cause of Pain

The extent to which chemical changes may result in the development of pain in the area of the intervertebral motor unit (see section 2.2.7 and Fig. 3-1) has not been fully determined. According to present knowledge, however, it is clear that in spite of the manifold changes in the biochemistry of the intervertebral disc no pain seems to develop within the intervertebral disc tissue itself. In 1950, Lindblom assumed that pain receptors were present in the interior of the intervertebral disc on the basis of his contrast-injection studies. This assumption was contradicted by Stilwell (1965) and Coventry (1968), however.

Pain may develop in other portions of the motor unit because the capsules and ligaments of the vertebral arch articulations and other immediately adjacent soft tissues and ligaments are amply supplied with nerves. At these points, pain probably develops not only from immediate mechanical pressure on nerve endings but also from chemical influences on the pain receptors. The possibility of chemically caused pain may only be clarified after additional clinical observations and laboratory tests. The so-called discogenic pain, which is created during discographies or during the injection of hypertonic saline solutions, may possibly be created when the injection preparation, which directly affects the nerves, leaves the intercorporal space (eg, through tissue fissures). Another aspect that requires investigation is the question of whether the pain that appears during chronic exertion of greatly changed intervertebral discs (as in osteochondrosis) is caused solely by mechanical influences or whether the changed biochemical environment spreads out from the intervertebral disc and causes nerve pain.

Diamant et al. (1968) have reported some observations in this context. As in ischemia of other organs, a deficient nutritional state causes the concentration of certain substances to increase in the intervertebral disc, which changes the tonus and pH value of the basic substance. On the basis of these and similar findings, Kramer (1975) assumed that dissolved acid metabolites leave the intervertebral disc during a period of sustained increased hydrostatic pressure and cause inflammatory reactions of adjacent nerve fibers. Nachemson described the sheathing of nerve roots with thickened reactive scar tissue in the area of herniated intervertebral disc portions when strongly decreased pH values (6.1) were present. When, during prolapses, the pH values of the intervertebral disc were more than 7.0, such reactions near the nerve roots were nonexistent.

2.3.3 Mechanical-Biochemical Interaction

2.3.3.1 Bones

The bony vertebrae as stable elements are segmentally arranged in the spinal column. The direction of their mechanical load changes frequently during the manifold requirements of motion. This is determined by the more than 100 possible articulations discussed above (23 to 25 intervertebral disc articulations, 46 to 50 vertebral arch articulations, 12 to 14 uncovertebral articulations, several head articulations, and 2 sacroiliac articulations). Several articulations always participate in static and dynamic tasks, and in most cases many of them do. The varieties of motion require adaptive bone tissue, which again requires continuous metabolic turnover.

Vibrations are among the negative influences on the sequence of biochemical processes. A lack of exercise caused by lengthy confinement and immobility during illness or psychological and other influences also belong in the same category. Changes in atmospheric pressure, time spent at high altitudes, and repeated sudden accelerations (mostly during space flight) have also recently come to play important roles in the scientific research covering bone chemistry, although such changes so far affect only a small number of people in daily life.

Questions also arise concerning the transformation of notches in the intra-articular portion of the vertebral arch in formation of spondylolysis or spondylolisthesis. These processes are closely related to a biomechanically mediated structural transformation (Mau 1977).

The age-dependent biochemical processes in the vertebral bones are especially sensitive to mechanical stresses. In the course of the degeneration of osteoporotic vertebral bodies, the metabolism of the bone tissue continuously changes in accordance with the current state of deformation.

2.3.3.2 Intervertebral Disc

The main purpose of the vertebral bones is maintenance of stability. Especially in early and middle life, the vertebral bones undergo only a few basic chemical transformations that lead to threatening damages of the spine. In contrast, in early life the intervertebral discs are affected by chemical influences that seriously interfere with their biochemical function because of their nutritional diffusion, which is susceptible to malfunction. The fact that the intervertebral disc thrives from motion indicates the interrelationship of mechanical influences and the chemical processes of metabolism. They are of decisive importance for a healthy intervertebral disc. The essential diffusion flow must continuously penetrate the hyaline cartilage plate of the intervertebral disc and can only be maintained through the motion-induced pump mechanism. The turgor of the fluid-rich nucleus pulposus guarantees the tension of the fibers, which enables them to exercise their mechanical function. This includes the chemically correct fluid composition and its proper distribution in the cells and interstices, which for their part depend on the hydrophilicity of the structures (that is, on the chemical quality of the fiber ground substance). The experiments of Wassilev (1970) with bipedal mice revealed a significantly altered chemical composition in the fiber ring as a result of the changed axial load and the consequently changed pressure direction.

Fluid loss of aging tissue and lack of exercise in later life with additional diffusion fatigue (metabolic inactivity) inevitably change the chemical quality of the fluid in cells and fibers. These conditions result in a vicious cycle that determines the further decline of biochemical processes and possibilities in terms of mechanical function. Only additional clinical observation and scientific experiments will answer the question which body internal and external influences have similar destructive consequences in early life. Damages caused by overexertion or lack of exercise (ie, decreased pump mechanism) can be traced back to the activities of sports and daily life.

Osteoporosis (see section 4.6.4.2) is not only related to the declining stability of the bony tissue but is also determined by the biochemical attitude of the intervertebral disc. If, on the basis of diagnosed vertebral osteoporosis, the adjacent intervertebral discs still show high interior pressure as a result of high fluid content, dents in the vertebral body end plates will occur, and "codfish vertebrae" are formed. There is still a lack of studies on the biochemical situation in the high intervertebral discs that lie between the "codfish vertebrae" (see section 4.6.4.2). Their volume has increased, but how do fibers, cells, and interstitial fluid act? Finding an answer requires that many biochemical questions be explored first.

The biochemical influences on adjacent nerve roots have not been sufficiently scrutinized to determine whether a mechanical disturbance (instability of the intervertebral motor unit; see section 3.4.2) caused by the intervertebral disc has the ability to discharge faulty products of a malfunctioning disc metabolism through fissures and gaps, thus causing pain through diffusion to segmental nerve roots (section 2.3.2.11). Furthermore, the question still remains if pain, caused by lack of motion in conjunction with added pressure (eg, during prolonged sitting) can be explained this way. In such cases prophylactic physiotherapy on a regular basis is necessary to regulate a malfunctioning diffusional flow.

Standing and sitting in an erect position create pressure on the spinal column, which leads, in spite of motion inherent in the usual course of the day, to a reduced vertical dimension of the intervertebral space. During the night, however, an adjustment can be observed. During a prolonged confinement to bed due to illness, the interplay of motion as well as the day-night adjustment is nonexistent. Nevertheless, such occasional mechanical influences on biochemical processes will not result in a chronic condition. The collection of fluid in the intervertebral discs during space flight is to be judged differently. In this case the condition is caused by low pressure and manifests itself in an increase in body height (see Figs. 2-48 to 2-50). This condition has consequences for the metabolic value of the fluid. So far it has not been determined whether secondary damages to the intervertebral discs of astronauts occur.

The significance of an initially small damage is described in sections in Chapters 3 and 8. The damage results in more or less extensive fluid loss or adjustments in the diffusion process (or both). This alters the metabolic conditions and creates a disposition for progressive discopathy.

Vibrational influences on the spinal column are on the rise because of present lifestyles. Especially from long-term vibrational influences, there is a high probability of changes in the influx and efflux of fluid in the intervertebral spaces. No general statements can be made so far, however. The interplay of long-term pressure, such as that experienced during long sitting in a motor vehicle, and simultaneous vibrations as well as spontaneous shocks and shaking requires further studies in regard to changed biochemistry of the intervertebral disc tissue and interstitial fluid. Special consideration should be given to the possibility of vibrational damages that may result from neurovascular influences at the capillaries.

3

The Intervertebral Motor Unit or Segment

3.1 THE NEW CONCEPT OF THE SPINE

During the 19th century and the beginning of the 20th century, investigators in biomechanics and clinical practice directed their attention almost exclusively to the bony elements of the vertebral column. In 1927, Schmorl and his students began to focus on research of the normal and pathomorphological anatomy of the spine. From a clinical and biomechanical point of view, it became necessary to analyze the function of the motion potential that is present between each two vertebrae (Fig. 3-1). The term *intervertebral motor segment* was suggested in 1950, and research, medical practice, prophylaxis, and rehabilitation began to focus on this important area of the spine.

Thirty years after the initial description of the intervertebral motor segment, an overview of the conclusions reached so far is needed. The knowledge of the importance of the motor segment opens up a new dimension in the study of the biomechanics of the spine and facilitates clarification of biochemical relationships by which damage of the intervertebral disc finally results in an intervertebral insufficiency (see section 3.4.2).

3.2 ANATOMY AND FUNCTIONS

3.2.1 General Overview

The intervertebral motor segment (Fig. 3-1) is the functionally significant structure between each two vertebrae and consists of different anatomical base elements. The development and morphological characteristics of the final anatomical structure are described in Chapter 2. The arrangement of the base elements in the segment is described briefly in section 2.2.7.

The largest volume (by mass) in each intervertebral space is taken up by the mixed-articulation intervertebral disc (Fig. 3-1). The disc works together with the anterior and posterior longitudinal ligament, paired vertebral arch articulations, corresponding vertebrocostal articulations in the thorax, and yellow ligament. Therefore, the segment harbors many potential biomechanical problems. The biochemical principles involved are discussed in section 2.3.2.

The functional space of the intervertebral motor segment also includes the portions of the vertebral canal in the same motion plane as well as the right and left intervertebral canal, spaces between the superposed vertebral arches with the spaces between the spinous processes, and

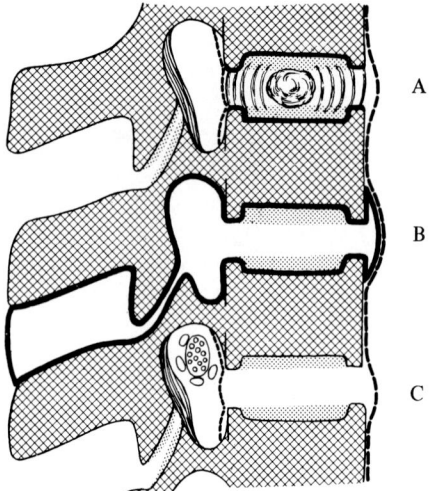

Fig. 3-1 Schematic drawing of the intervertebral motor segment [from Junghanns (1951)]. (**A**) Mixed-articulation intervertebral disc (note fiber penetrations into the bony vertebral body epiphyses and hyaline cartilage plates); (**B**) Intervertebral motor segment; (**C**) content of the intervertebral canal.

spaces between the paired transverse processes. It also includes the portions of the anterior longitudinal ligament that pass the intervertebral space in the front, portions of the posterior longitudinal ligament that are attached at the back of the intervertebral disc, venous plexus of the spinal canal, nerves and blood vessels in the two intervertebral canals, and muscle attachments and ligaments in the area of the spinous and transverse processes. The structural elements of the intervertebral motor segment are anatomically and functionally coordinated but nevertheless interdependent. This is true, for example, if the vertebral arch articulations have been affected because of changes in the intervertebral disc or vice versa.

Every study of the biomechanical issues in connection with the intervertebral motor segment requires a basic knowledge of the anatomical structure of the adult segment and additional knowledge about changes at the boundary between the vertebral body and intervertebral disc in the juvenile growth period. These gradual transformations of the entire surface of the vertebral disc–intervertebral disc boundary, including the vertebral body edge, are important because of their sensitivity to pressure, traction, and shearing. Figures 2-3 and 2-4 show the development of the vertebral body–intervertebral disc series during growth.

Details about functionally important morphological characteristics and the biochemistry and biomechanics of the intervertebral disc (consisting of the nucleus pulposus, fiber ring, and hyaline cartilage plates) are explained in sections 2.2.2, 3.2.2, and 5.2.5 (biomechanics) and in section 2.3.2 (biochemistry). The important transition comprised by the vertebral body and intervertebral disc is described in sections 2.2.6, 2.3.2, and 3.2.4. Sections 2.2.3, 3.4, and 5.2.6 provide details concerning the ligaments responsible for the stability of the intervertebral motor segment. The structure and function of the paired vertebral arch articulations of each intervertebral motor segment are described in sections 2.2.5.2 and 4.5.5.2, and the structure and function of the vertebrocostal articulations are described in sections 2.2.5.6 and 4.5.5.7.

The intervertebral motor segment requires sufficiently strong muscles for kinetic as well as static functions. Weak muscles may worsen a slackening condition of the intervertebral motor segment (intervertebral instability, section 3.4.3), and may, in the case of serious muscle weakness, contribute to its formation.

An isolated look at the intervertebral motor segment is not opportune. The entirety of the segments forms the organ system of the intervertebral motor segment, which enables the modulation-rich mobility necessary for the central position of the spine. Because every individual part of the segment is susceptible to malfunction, serious difficulties with regard to the performance of parts of the back or the entire spine may result. External performance requirements often reinforce the disorders originating in the segment (see sections 3.3 and 3.4).

3.2.2 Intervertebral Disc

3.2.2.1 Functional Anatomy

The structure of the various tissue types that are architecturally oriented toward the fulfillment of many biomechanical and biochemical functions and the fluid content of the various tissues guarantee the necessary resiliency resistance of the intervertebral disc. The intervertebral disc ensures the functional ability of the spine.

The nucleus pulposus, as the functional center of the intercorporal space of the intervertebral disc, has a high degree of turgor because of its high fluid content and acts as a shock-absorbing water cushion that absorbs impacting forces and distributes them according to their initial impact direction. Because of these tasks, the nucleus pulposus is a functional power source.

During its development the fiber ring undergoes the transformations described in section 2.1. Its internal zone is not clearly distinguished from the nucleus pulposus. Fibers penetrate into the hyaline cartilage plate from the internal zone of the fiber ring and from several lamellae. The wider external zone (lamellae are organized in layers) is subject to the distension pressure of the nucleus pulposus. This stretches the lamellae fibers, which are firmly and tautly bonded on all sides to the bony epiphysis (Fig. 3-2). This pressure-tension system binds the adjacent vertebral bodies together, prevents excessive tilting, and retards rotations caused by lamellae rings, which run in opposite directions.

In addition to the nucleus pulposus and fiber ring, the hyaline cartilage plates adjacent to the vertebral body form the third tissue element of the intervertebral disc. They connect with the bony vertebral body epiphysis (Figs. 2-4 and 2-5) but do not completely cover the surface of the finely perforated bony vertebral body end plate (Fig. 2-7). They are demarcated on all sides by the internal raised edge of the bony vertebral body epiphysis. Histologically, this is shown in the sagittal section (Fig. 2-5). The close retention of the hyaline cartilage plate and the intervertebral disc caused by penetrating fibers of the lamellae ring, as well as their significance for the metabolism of the intervertebral disc (see section 3.2.4), justifies the association of the cartilage plates with the intervertebral disc. A developmental comparison would show them to be cartilaginous "articular" cover layers of the adjacent vertebral bodies. Only the close functional relationship with the intervertebral disc reveals the "mixed" articulation first described by Luschka in 1858. The intervertebral disc is the central element in the intervertebral motor segment.

More detailed information concerning the biochemical bonding of the intervertebral disc to the vertebral body is shown in Figs. 2-2 and 2-4. The fibers of the external lamellae rings run into the bony epiphysis where they are securely bonded, which is also the case for the entire bony epiphyseal ring. This epiphyseal ring is widest in the front and narrows laterally and backward (Fig. 2-7). This linking of intervertebral disc with vertebral bone comprises fastening of the disc tissue with the adjacent vertebral bodies and forming a resistant wrapper around the softer internal parts of the fiber ring by the rough external fiber ring layers. Their purpose is to enclose tightly the fluid-rich nucleus pulposus and support the tensional function of the fibers of the external lamellae rings (which are deeply bonded in the bony epiphyses through penetration of their fibers into the cranial and caudal hyaline cartilage plates, Fig. 2-4, #3 and 4).

The anatomical structure of the intervertebral disc corresponds to the biomechanical and biochemical functions the mixed articulation must control and supports their functioning through the stress and motion-determined pump mechanism, which aids in diffusional nutrition (see section 2.3.3.2).

The close interplay between the nucleus pulposus and fiber ring and their alternating functional mechanism, together with the involvement of the adjacent cartilage plates, create the function of the "mixed articulation intervertebral disc" within the segment. Although certain comparisons between this mixed articulation and a proper joint can be drawn, the tasks of this mixed articulation are significantly more complex than those of a proper articulation. In addition to the usual articular function, which includes mobility and the restraining of excessive motion, the tissue structure of the intervertebral disc with its load-determined interplay between the pressure force of the nucleus pulposus and the traction force of the fiber ring creates the elastic system. Therefore, the intervertebral discs are the most important elastic elements of the motor systems, which protects the bone system from fractures and alleviates impacts that are too forceful for many internal organs (eg, brain and spinal cord). With respect to normal requirements, the elastic system maintains the static and dynamic balance of the spine. Erect walking and vibrations in vehicles, which mostly affect the longitudinal axis of the spine, put a severe strain on the dynamic balance. Because of the constant mechanical demands of daily life, the normal functional demands and performance capacity of the intervertebral disc tissue are unbalanced, which negatively affects the stability of the intervertebral disc tissue. It inevitably has tragic consequences.

3.2.2.2 The Significance of Internal Pressure

The nucleus pulposus (Fig. 2-6) is the stress-absorbing and load-distributing center of the intervertebral disc and, therefore, the source of its functional power. Because of its inherent turgor, which is determined by its fluid content, the nucleus pulposus exerts pressure in all directions, even in its load-free state. This internal pressure maintains the interval between the adjacent vertebral bodies. Simultaneously, this pressure affects the surrounding fiber ring and tightens the lamellae of the epiphyseal fiber ring that run from vertebra to vertebra. This guarantees a tight embracement of the adjacent vertebral bodies (Fig. 3-2). In the relaxed position, the nucleus pulposus is spherical. Any change in the spherical shape is created by pressure or tensional forces.

In simplified schematic illustrations of the intervertebral motor segment and its function, the nucleus pulposus is shown in the approximate center of the intervertebral space (Fig. 2-4). In reality, corresponding to its biomechanical function, the nucleus pulposus is located at the transition of the middle third to the posterior third, approximately halfway between the anterior boundary of the intervertebral disc and the connecting line between the two vertebral arch articulations. Depending on the kyphotic or lordotic sagittal curve of a section of the spine, this location may change. It is always closely interrelated with biomechanical factors. But in any location, the nucleus pulposus, due to its internal pressure, always plays the central role in the dynamic interplay with the lamellae ring.

Fig. 3-2 The internal turgor of the fluid-filled nucleus pulposus tightens the fibers of the fiber ring, which enter a state of traction because of their bond with the bony epiphyses.

Depending on the biochemical environment of the nucleus pulposus, which is determined by the metabolism, the fluid absorption capacity fluctuates. The turgor in the nucleus pulposus may increase to a swelling pressure. This increases the elasticity, ie, the force of mechanical resistance. The "water cushion" nucleus pulposus distributes the axial pressure on the intervertebral disc in such a manner that only half of the pressure force affects the fiber ring. Tangential pressure, which is created by certain positions and motions, exerts a force on the posterior fiber ring that is 3 to 5 times higher than the pressure force exerted on the entire intervertebral disc.

Figure 3-3A shows the pressure increase on the transitional intervertebral disc L5/S1 while a

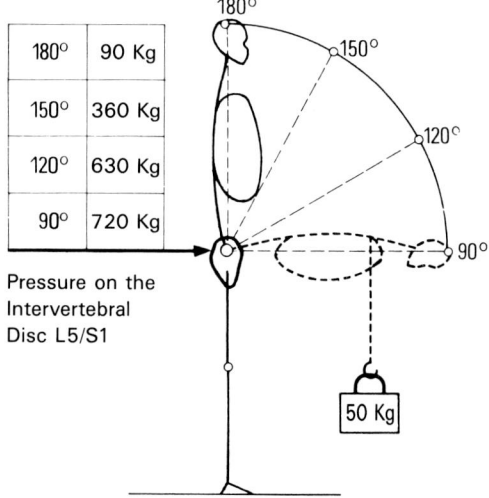

180°	90 Kg
150°	360 Kg
120°	630 Kg
90°	720 Kg

Pressure on the Intervertebral Disc L5/S1

Fig. 3-3A Pressure on the transitional intervertebral disc L5/S1 during the carrying of a 50-kg weight (Matthiass 1979).

person carries a 50-kg weight and bends the upper torso forward: the pressure increases from 90 kg (upright position) to 720 kg (forward bend of 90°). Diagrams by Muenchinger show how load pressure is better distributed by lifting with the back in the upright position (Figs. 3-3B and 3-4). The ability of the fluid inside and outside the nucleus pulposus to quickly shift significantly contributes to this fact. If the external pressure subsides (space flight, confinement to bed, day-night difference, etc.), the intervertebral disc absorbs more fluid, the spine stretches, and body height increases measurably.

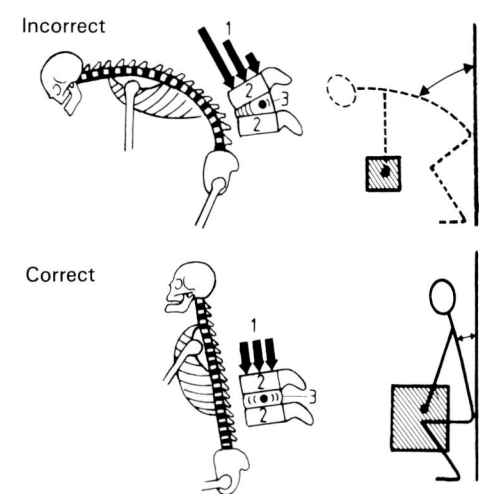

Fig. 3-4 Pressure distribution of the lifted load over the intervertebral discs of the lumbar spine with correct and incorrect lifting technique.

3.2.2.3 In Vivo Pressure Measurement

Impressive studies were designed to measure the static and dynamic intervertebral disc pressure in vivo. The development of the intervertebral disc puncture and discography (in vivo discometry) allowed these studies. Pricking with thin hollow needles enables pressure measurements (preferably performed at the accessible intervertebral disc L3/4 in different postures and positions and with different loads on the spine) (Figs. 3-5, 3-6A, and 3-6B).

The pressure-absorbing internal tension of the intervertebral disc tissue changes in slightly damaged intervertebral discs, for example, the normal pressure in the dorsal part of an intervertebral disc measured 60 kg/cm^2 and 30 kg/cm^2 when the tissue structure was abnormal. Nachemson and Elfstroem (1970) provided details of these studies with data of the pressure under different loads.

Important findings for medical practice were obtained by comparing the pressure measured in the intervertebral disc L3/4 with simultaneously obtained EMG findings at the lumbar muscles (Andersson et al. 1974, 1977). The tests were taken in various locations (experimental chair, common office chair, wheelchair, and car seat). Figure 3-7 shows the EMG results, intraabdominal pressure, and intradiscal pressure during various lifting techniques. The studies

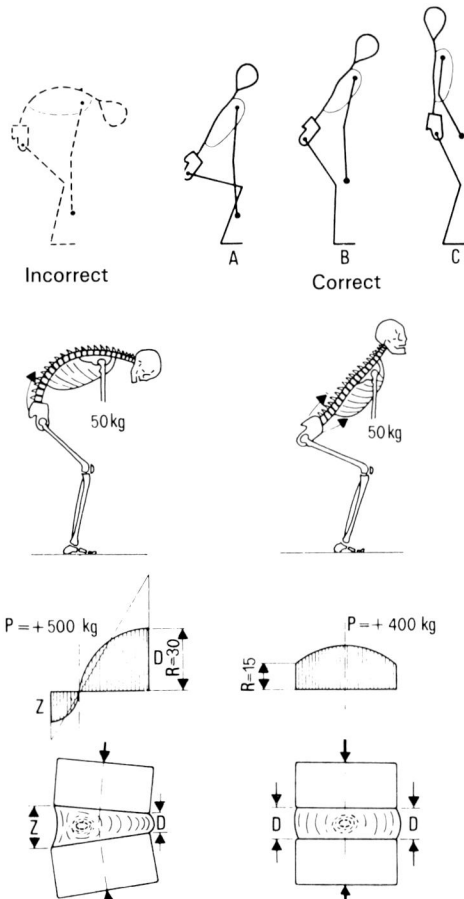

Fig. 3-3B Lifting from a bending position (Muenchinger 1960). **1st and 2nd row:** lifting technique; **3rd row:** intervertebral disc load diagrams during the lifting of a 50-kg weight with bended back and a trunk inclination of 45°; **4th row left:** incorrect lifting with strong anterior pressure on the intervertebral disc and posterior traction; **4th row right:** correct lifting: no traction and little pressure with even distribution over the entire intervertebral disc.

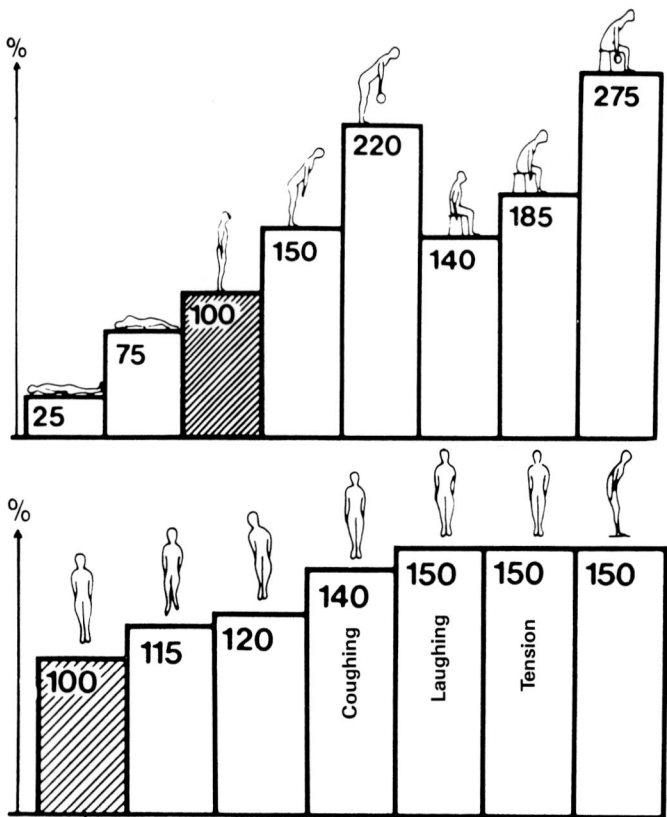

Fig. 3-5 Relative pressure changes in the intervertebral disc L3/L4 in vivo. **Upper row:** different body positions without and with load; **lower row:** different postures while standing with different tension of the muscles [from Nachemson (1976)].

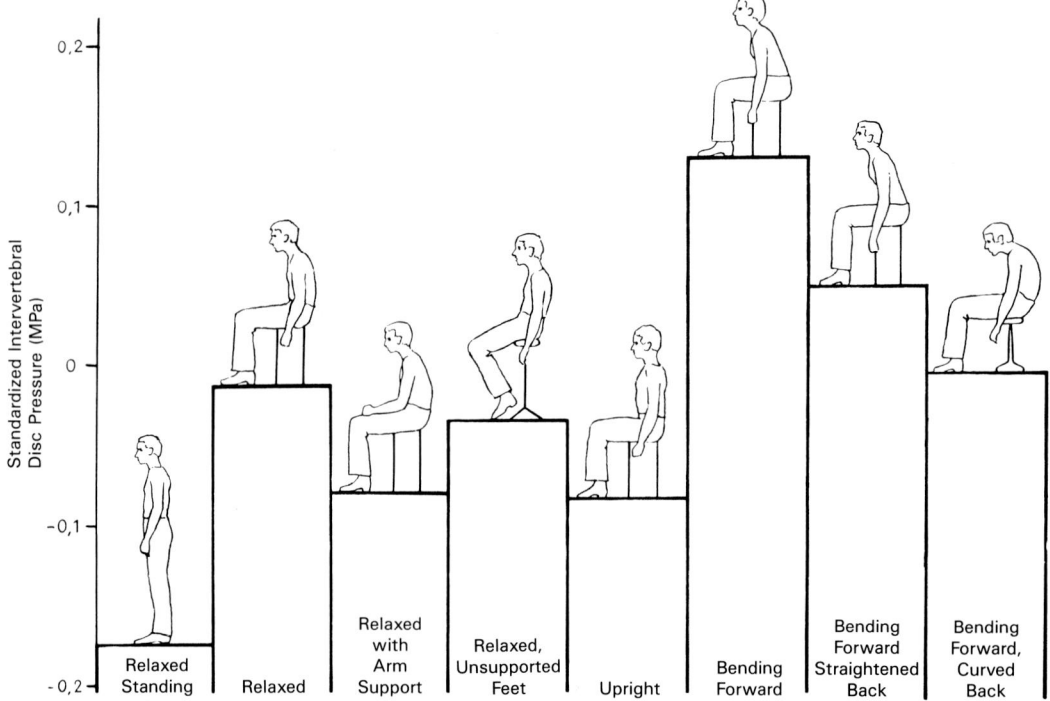

Fig. 3-6A Average values of standardized intervertebral disc pressure during standing and sitting without back support. The nonstandardized intervertebral disc pressure in the reference position is 0.51 MPa (Andersson et al. 1975).

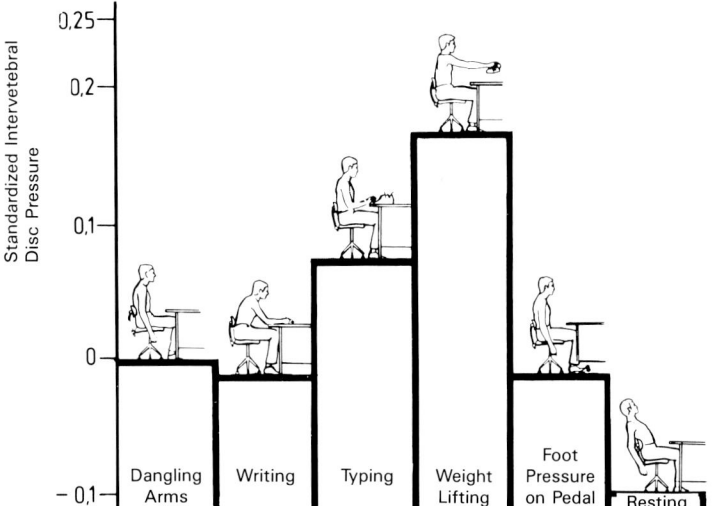

Fig. 3-6B Average values of standardized intervertebral disc pressure during sitting in an office chair with usual back postures and with back support at L4/5. The nonstandardized intervertebral disc pressure measured 0.47 MPa in the reference position (Andersson et al. 1975).

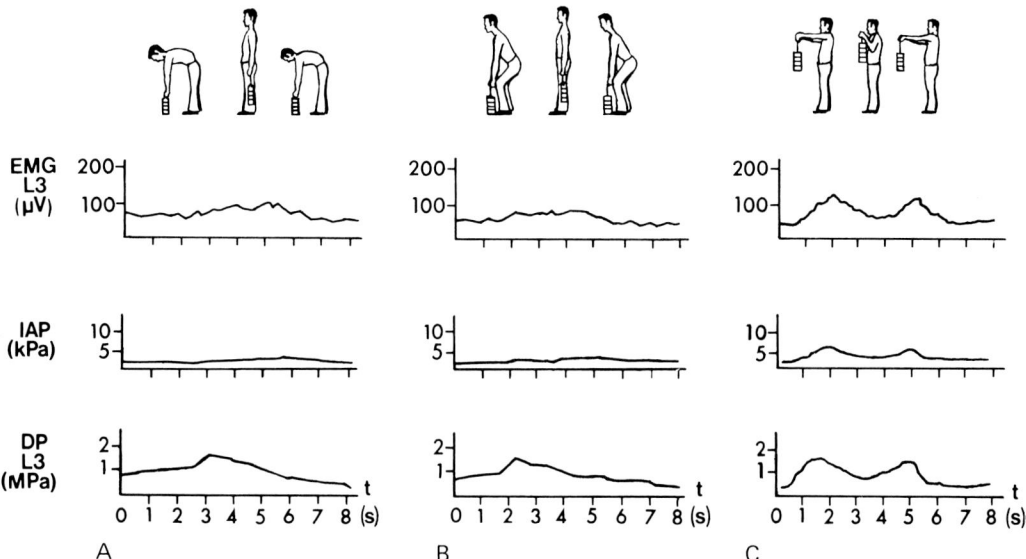

Fig. 3-7 Comparison between the curves of the EMG (at L3), the internal pressure (IAP), and the intradiscal pressure (DPL3) in various positions with loads.

were expanded to daily activities, such as operating a shift stick in a motor vehicle, bending the body over a desk, typing, etc. Increased pressure on the intervertebral disc always occurs. Figure 3-8 portrays the pressure load created in the intervertebral disc by the different lifting techniques.

In 1981, Hattori et al. reported on the internal pressure of intervertebral discs of the cervical spine. The highest values in normal spines were found during the bending backward of the back: 9.3 kg/cm^2. Forward bending resulted in a value of 6 kg/cm^2. Rotation with a lateral bending resulted in a pressure between 4 and 5.4 kg/cm^2. Longitudinal stretching significantly decreased the pressure. The authors found differing results in the case of intervertebral chondrosis.

The pressure measurements performed on volunteers (mostly physicians) form the ergometric foundations for the exertion of the spinal

56 CLINICAL IMPLICATIONS OF NORMAL BIOMECHANICAL STRESSES ON SPINAL FUNCTION

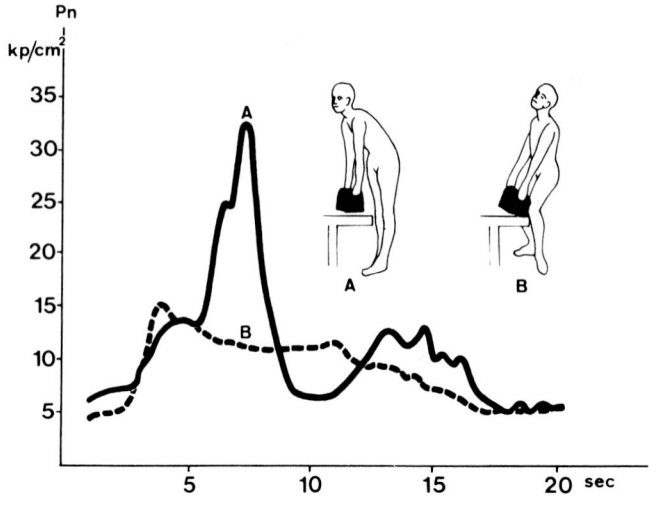

Fig. 3-8 Pressure measurement in the intervertebral disc L3/4 of a 25-year-old man during the lifting of 20 kg with bended back, straight knees (**A**), with straight back, bended knee and hip joints (**B**): 1 kg/cm^2 = 1 kgf/cm^2 (Nachemson 1975).

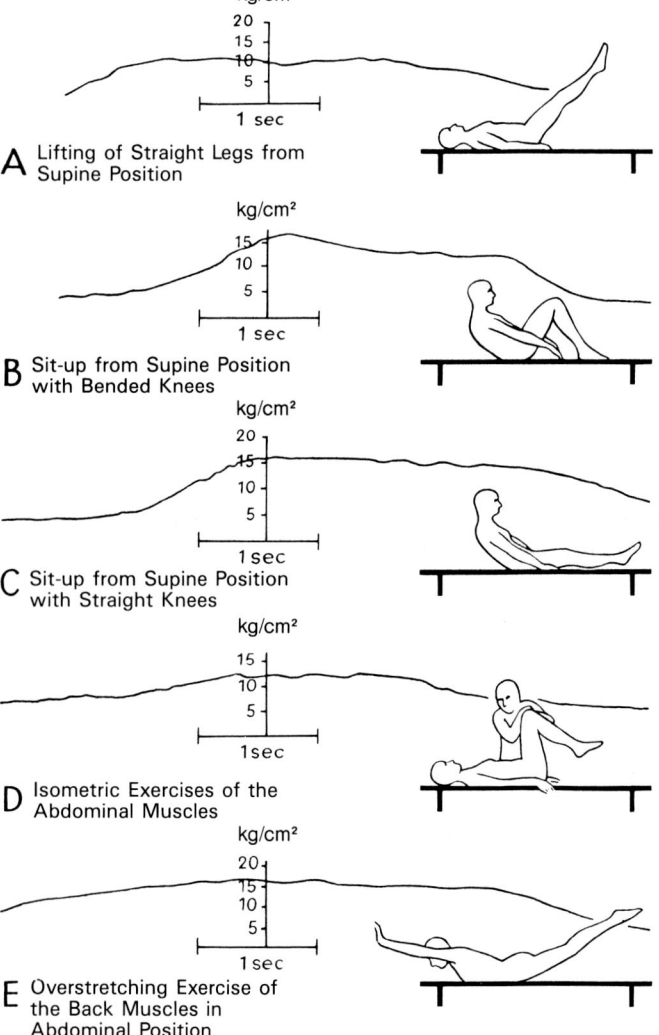

Fig. 3-9 Intervertebral disc pressure during various body exercises (Nachemson and Elfstroem 1970). (See Table 3-1.) (**A**) lifting of straight legs from supine position; (**B**) sit-up from supine position with bended knees; (**C**) sit-up from supine position with straight knees; (**D**) isometric exercises of abdominal muscles; (**E**) overstretching exercise of back muscles in abdominal position.

column and help in the formulation of rules for lifting and carrying as well as the design of chairs for school, home, and leisure. In addition, the findings of intradiscal measurements are important for therapy techniques (Fig. 3-9) that affect the influx and outflow of nutrients in the intervertebral disc because the intervertebral disc thrives on motion (Junghanns 1973).

The findings of intradiscal measurements are especially important for sports, eg, for weight lifters; their loads reach the extreme capacity ceilings. The lifting technique is important and must ensure a vertical axial load on the lumbar intervertebral discs. A slanted or rotary force exceeds the load capacity and may cause serious tissue damage.

3.2.2.4 Pressure, Traction, Rotation, and Shifting Stability

Many investigators have focused their attention on the stability of the intervertebral disc tissue. The findings demonstrate again the central role of the intervertebral disc within the intervertebral motor segment. Table 3-1 shows a compilation of stress tolerances found in comparisons of intervertebral discs with vertebral bodies in pressure, traction, and rotation studies. They are summarized from series of tests performed by Sonoda (1962). According to those results, the intervertebral discs are able to withstand a higher axial pressure load than the vertebral bodies, but they show less resistance to axial traction. With regard to torsion, the intervertebral discs are more resistant than the vertebral bones. Because they can be compressed, intervertebral discs decrease in height before they burst. This decrease is 5 to 7 times higher than the decrease in the vertebral body (Table 3-2).

Table 3-1 Approximate Loading of the Intervertebral Disc L3/4 of a Test Person Weighing 70 Kg under Various Conditions

Load Type	Load Pressure (kg)*
Supine position	30
Standing	70
Sitting upright, unsupported	100
Walking	85
Rotating	90
Bending sideways	95
Coughing	110
Skipping	110
Straight trunk position	120
Laughing	120
Forward bending, 20°	120
Lifting 20 kg with straight back, bended knees	210
Lifting 20 kg with curved back, straight knees	340
Forward bending, 20°, with 10 kg in each hand	185
Lying with longitudinal traction of 30 kg	10
Lifting straight legs from supine position	120
Sit-up from supine position with bended knees	180
Sit-up from supine position with straight knees	175
Isometric exercises of abdominal muscles	110
Overstretching exercise of back muscles in abdominal position	150

*Nachemson (1975). See Figure 3-9.

If the intervertebral disc is exposed to pressure for only a few seconds, elasticity returns. Such short compressions may be repeated without resulting in damage if they do not exceed the tolerance of the load. Several experiments showed a high adaptability of the tissue to mechanical pressures. However, in vivo studies

Table 3-2 Height Loss Caused by Axial Pressure Up to the Rupture Limit Compared with Pressure-Free Normal Height for Intervertebral Discs and Vertebral Bodies*

	Cervical Spine (%)	Lower Thoracic Spine (%)	Lumbar Spine (%)
Intervertebral disc in 4th/5th decade of life	35.2	31.4	35.5
Vertebral body in 2nd/3rd decade of life	8.1	5.6	5.6

*Sonoda (1962).

have not determined how much fluid is being expelled from the intervertebral disc under particular pressures, how much fluid will reenter before the next pressure impact, and whether this fluid has the necessary metabolic composition.

The gradual increase of axial pressure results in ruptures in the cartilage plate with subsequent microfissures at the bony end plate of the vertebral body. During this pressure exertion, the fiber ring is still unaffected, ie, its resistance tolerance has not yet been exceeded. Therefore, the cartilage plates are the most sensitive elements of the intervertebral disc, and the bony end plates are the most elastic parts of the vertebral body. The manner in which vibrations may contribute to damage of the cartilage plates and the bony end plates is discussed in chapter 5.

If slides of intervertebral discs are exposed to continuously alternating forward and backward bends, an internal destruction of the tissue results, but the external ring layers remain unaffected. With the help of a durometer, Ritchie and Fahrni (1970) studied the stability at various locations on lumbar intervertebral discs: anterior, lateral anterior, lateral, and lateral posterior. By the age of 30, the stability has declined, especially at the lateral posterior (Fig. 3-10). At these locations, radial tears may also be found in the ring fibers and are precursors of the imminent prolapse of the intervertebral disc tissue (Figs. 3-11 and 3-12). In addition, these illustrations show the protrusions of ring fibers in the direction of the nucleus pulposus, which are also a symptom of a beginning inter-

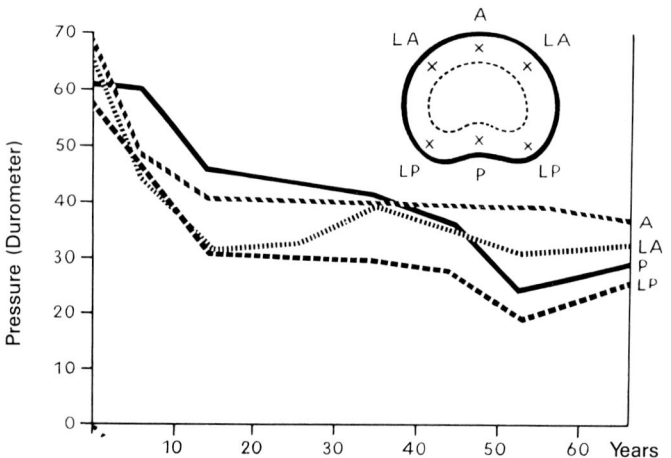

Fig. 3-10 Differences of intervertebral disc pressure measured with a durometer at different sections of the intervertebral disc circumference. The low values point to a relative softness of the tissue (Ritchie and Fahrni 1970).

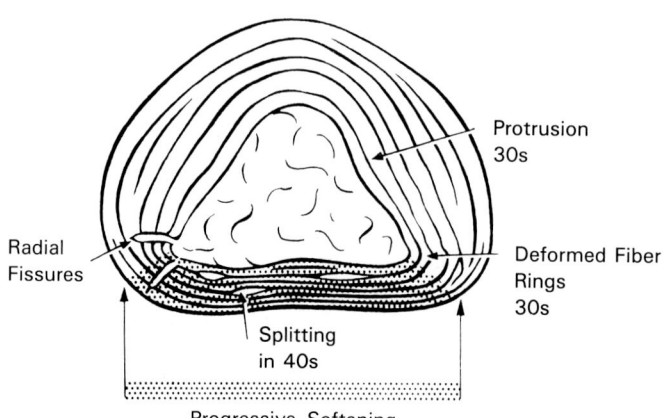

Fig. 3-11 Changes in the tissue structure of the intervertebral disc according to age, mostly in the posterior part with longitudinal and transverse fissures (Ritchie and Fahrni 1970).

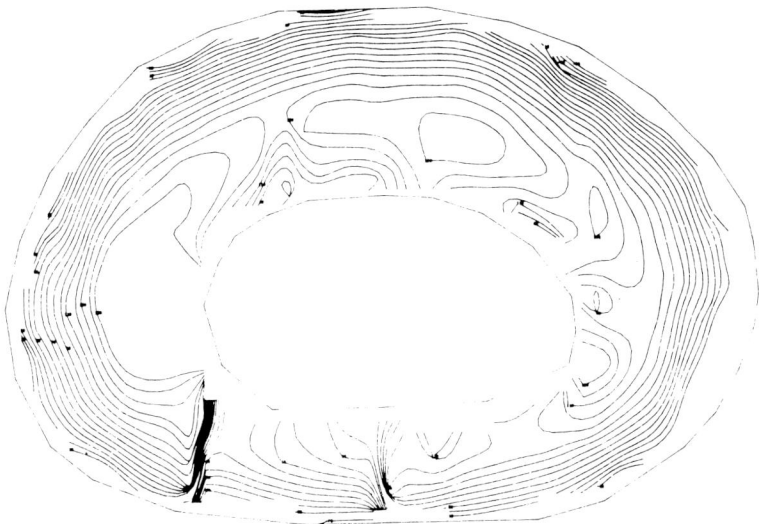

Fig. 3-12 Model of a tension chart of a lumbar intervertebral disc (Farfan 1970). The measured tension lines concentrate in the posterior portion where most ruptures also originate during rotation studies.

vertebral chondrosis. Along with its progression, the height of the intervertebral disc decreases and the segment slackens. Physical exertion and vibrations may directly affect the progression of such damage.

The intervertebral disc that is already under a pressure load may become damaged as the result of subliminal, but sudden, additional pressure. Such an unexpected pressure impact plays a role as an "additional impulse" (Schmorl and Junghanns 1968), and in clinical practice should be taken into account by searching for damage caused by carried loads in daily life. In conjunction with already existing loads, additional impulses frequently have damaging effects on the intervertebral disc.

The elastic nature of the intervertebral disc was experimentally tested by Plaue et al. (1974). In 1981, Koeller et al. reported on extensive studies on the deformation behavior of lumbar intervertebral discs exposed to a prolonged axial dynamic pressure force. According to their results, the material characteristics of the fibrous anulus determine to a great extent biomechanical behavior during pressure as well as recovery. Higher exertion necessitates a longer recovery; ie, the highest possible relaxation of back muscles is necessary. The intervertebral disc fluid that has been expelled by a prolonged pressure load may be reintroduced into the metabolism (supply and removal) only through a slowly returning pump mechanism if the load is decreased.

Axial longitudinal traction plays only a small role in the usual course of daily life. Athletic training often includes a longitudinal traction of the spine, eg, gymnastics at the horizontal bar and on the trapeze, and is often paired with forward or backward bending, including rotation.

During the course of traction studies (Sonoda 1962), sprain fractures of the vertebral body or the rupture of the intervertebral disc resulted from forces that varied tremendously in their strength (Table 3-3). They fluctuated for the intervertebral disc from 105 kg (cervical spine) to 394 kg (lumbar spine). The rupture of vertebral bodies after exceeding the traction load tolerance resulted in a transverse fissure in the thoracic spine and in slanted or multidimensional fissures in the lumbar spine. However, fissures in the intervertebral discs appeared along the cartilage plate (often accompanied by fragments in the posterior part and overflowing of nucleus pulposus tissue into the fissure).

Rotational stability is considered particularly important for the intervertebral disc since many essential motions of the spine include rotation,

Table 3-3 Overview of Values for Maximum Load Tolerances*

	CS		Upper TS		Lower TS		LS	
	IVD	VB	IVD	VB	IVD	VB	IVD	VB
Axial pressure (kg)	320	289	450	336	1,150	502	1,500	569
Axial traction (kg)	105		142	173	291	336	394	464
Rotation								
(kg/cm)	56		87	60	273	165	463	255
(kg/mm^2)	.52		.46	.37	.48	0.34	.51	.32

*CS = cervical spine; TS = thoracic spine; LS = lumbar spine; IVD = intervertebral disc; VB = vertebral body.

often with simultaneous bending or tilting. This led to experiments on rotation potentials and limits of rotational stability using specimens of the human spine (Table 3-4). According to these experiments, the rotational load tolerance up to the rupturing point ranges from 56 kg/cm in the cervical intervertebral disc to 463 kg/cm in the lumbar intervertebral disc. Exceeding the rotational load tolerances resulted in ruptured fissures in the external layer of the fiber ring, near the cartilage plate. Many investigators have agreed on the essential points; the exact figures, however, differed.

The position of the rotation axis (Figs. 3-13 and 3-14) and the shapes of the vertebral arch articulations determine the extent as well as the restriction of the rotation potential, which is different during walking, standing, and sitting with simultaneous lateral, forward, and backward bending.

The question arises whether prolonged lateral rotation caused by unfavorable body posture leads to tissue fatigue to the extent that a susceptibility to damage is being created.

According to Farfan (1979), 90 percent of all rotational forces are absorbed by the intervertebral discs in connection with the vertebral arch articulations. The experimental exceeding of the rotational stability limit leads to ruptures at locations that pathoanatomical mass examinations (Schmorl 1930) also frequently revealed damage of the intervertebral disc. Such tears may be the precursors of a dorsolateral prolapse of the intervertebral disc.

Table 3-4 Rupture Tolerance Levels during Rotation Studies and Axial Longitudinal Traction at Intervertebral Discs and Vertebral Bodies*

	Cervical Spinal Column	Upper Thoracic Spinal Column	Lower Thoracic Spinal Column	Lumbar Spinal Column
Intervertebral discs	56 kg/cm 0.52 kg/mm^2	87 kg/cm 0.46 kg/mm^2	273 kg/cm 0.48 kg/mm^2	463 kg/cm 0.51 kg/mm^2
Vertebral bodies	— —	60 kg/cm 0.37 kg/mm^2	165 kg/cm 0.34 kg/mm^2	255 kg/cm 0.32 kg/mm^2

	Cervical Spinal Column	Upper Thoracic Spinal Column	Lower Thoracic Spinal Column	Lumbar Spinal Column
Intervertebral discs	105 kg 0.33 kg/mm^2	142 kg 0.24 kg/mm^2	291 kg 0.26 kg/mm^2	394 kg 0.30 kg/mm^2
Vertebral bodies	— —	173 kg 0.37 kg/mm^2	336 kg 0.38 kg/mm^2	464 kg 0.40 kg/mm^2

*Sonoda (1962).

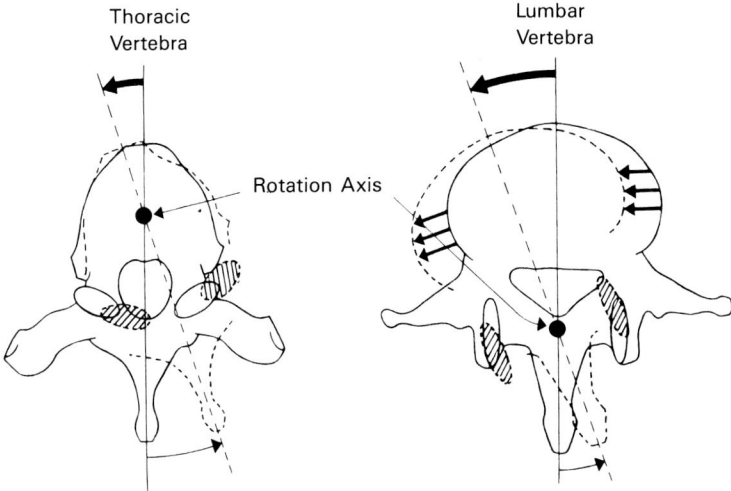

Fig. 3-13 Rotational motion of the vertebral arch articulations. **Left:** thoracic vertebra with axis in the vertebral arch center; **right:** lumbar vertebra with rotation axis in the anterior part of the arch. *Source:* Gregersen and Lucas 1967.

In the course of experiments (Tuetsch and Ulrich 1973), intervertebral disc rupture has been induced by exertion of 4.5 mkg during a 20° rotation. The intervertebral disc ruptured at the transition point to the vertebral body. This point, with the lowest rotational resistance, is particularly exerted in gymnastics through forcefully performed spins with hard landings, and damage must be anticipated (see Chapter 8).

Reaching the rotation angles without causing damage depends on the direction of motion, various load combinations, muscle strength, and condition of the intervertebral disc (Pope et al. 1977). Rotations are hindered if abnormalities exist in the vertebral arch articulations at the borders of spinal columns, ie, different inclination angles of articular surfaces on the left and right sides and different orientations of the motion axis. Such variations, which were created during the growth period, explain the special susceptibility for premature wear of intervertebral discs in transition areas.

The described values for rotation load tolerances of the human spine suffice for the necessary practical conclusions. Load tolerances of the vertebral bodies are significantly lower (see Chapter 5) and must be considered. Computer simulations will allow new insights.

The stability with regard to shifting (shearing) is ensured for loads required in daily life as far as unchanged intervertebral discs are concerned. Without the addition of any special conditions, the tautness of the lamellae rings with their firm bondings in the bony epiphysis and hyaline cartilage plate and the ligamental system of the paired vertebral arch articulations form a biomechanical unit (intervertebral motor segment) and will prevent the damaging parallel shifting between two vertebrae.

The lateral sliding in the vertex of scolioses (section 4.4.4) is known as rotational sliding. This rotation-determined lateral shifting is pre-

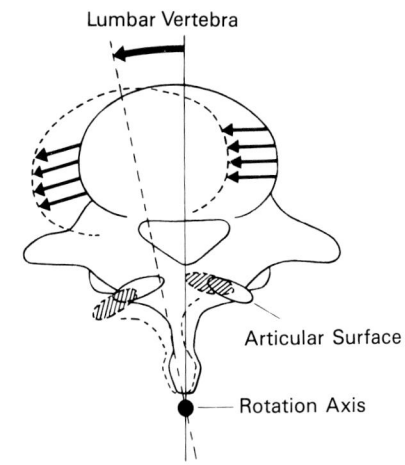

Fig. 3-14 Rotational motion of the presacral vertebra around the axis lying at the tip of the spinous process with shifting in the vertebral arch articulations in the direction of the rotation (Gregersen and Lucas 1967).

ceded by transformation processes in the vertebral arch articulations and a progressive wear of the intervertebral disc tissue. (See sections in Chapters 4 and 8 for pathomorphological damage and transformation forces that are active in spondylolysis/spondylolisthesis and pseudospondylolisthesis during the parallel shifting in the affected intervertebral motor segment.)

3.2.3 Bony Elements and Articulations

With regard to the two vertebral bodies that cranially and caudally limit the intervertebral motor segment in its ventral half, the bony epiphysis of the vertebral bodies and the perforated end plate are of intrinsic importance for the biomechanical ability of the anterior segment portion (see section 2.2.2, Fig. 2-7). However, with regard to axial pressure, the bony end plates are the most elastic parts of the vertebral bodies. The extent of their functional significance for the biochemically regulated viability of the adjacent intervertebral disc is discussed in section 3.2.4.

In the posterior part, the segment space is bordered by the cortical surfaces of the two vertebral arches. The cartilage layers of the left and right vertebral arch articulation are also border surfaces of the segment space. Both vertebral arch articulations of a segment are functional partners of the ventral segment section, ie, the intervertebral disc. Because of their shape, the articular surface position, and their rotation axis, they regulate the intervertebral motion process. Their limited mobility prevents excessive rotational exertions of the intervertebral disc. Difficulties arise (eg, at the transitional regions between spinal column sections) if there is one caudal and one cranial articulation of the segment (see Niethard 1981). The accordingly altered functional relations within the articular pairs and with regard to the ventral part of the segment lower the performance in this level and promote intervertebral disc damage.

3.2.4 The Vertebral Body–Intervertebral Disc Boundary

The participating bone sections and hyaline cartilage plates of the intervertebral disc continuously exercise mechanical and biochemical functions in this transitional area which exists in two places in each intervertebral motor segment (approximately 50 places in the spine) and includes the sensitive growth layers. This transitional area serves as an important intermediate station for fluids for nutrition of the intervertebral disc. The key for recognizing the causes of damage in the intervertebral disc tissue is often found here. (See Chapter 2 for information concerning the development of the biomechanical structure and biochemical problems.)

The intervertebral disc has no blood vessels, and this is the cause of the susceptibility to damage. As a child grows, the intervertebral disc sheds the embryonic blood vessels, and the intervertebral discs form one of the largest avascular tissues of the human body that is dependent on nutritional diffusion.

Schmorl and his students (1927 to 1932) performed the basic macroscopic and microscopic studies on the important relations at the vertebral body–intervertebral disc boundary. They described the positions of the hyaline cartilage plate in reference to the vertebral body and its bony epiphysis as well as the bondings of the lamellae fibers in the epiphysis and cartilage plate (section 2.1). The perforations in the end plate of the vertebral body were discovered and received the name *cribrum*. The middle section with fewer perforations and therefore higher stability has since been called the pressure absorption plate (Fig. 2-7). This plate is located opposite the pressurized nucleus pulposus, and its entire surface makes contact with the hyaline cartilage plate, which is considered part of the intervertebral disc.

The end plate of the vertebral body (cribrum) and the hyaline cartilage plate are border layers, which the nourishing and removing diffusional flow for the rather sluggishly nourished intervertebral disc has to cross. The capillaries that penetrate from the vertebral body marrow into the perforations of the cribrum support this process. Their loops (buds) reach the hyaline cartilage plate. In addition, parts of the capillaries flow into blood pools, which probably serve as regulating reservoirs for the pressure compensation of the diffusional flow (Fig. 2-4). The fine wall layers of the capillary buds and blood pools are semipermeable contact membranes for the diffusional flow.

Virgin (1958) showed the close contact of the capillaries with the cartilage plates. In 1971, Donisch and Trapp described the penetration of the blood vessels into the cartilage plate, where they end with no outlet. However, they examined only children up to the age of 11 years.

Whether the normal blood pressure in the capillaries is sufficient to maintain the necessary diffusion of fluid and substances while the body is in a resting position remains questionable. It is certain that pressure and suction significantly support the diffusion in both directions. This occurs by body movements in daily life and is augmented by athletic activity, therapeutic measures, or vibrations. Such external influences activate a pump mechanism regarded by many investigators as indispensible for the viability of the intervertebral disc.

The dependency of fluid diffusion on pressure has been discussed in several studies. Brown et al. (1957), Cloward and Buzard (1952), and Farfan (1973) obtained proof that injected fluids quickly penetrate from the intervertebral disc into the adjacent vertebral body. Detailed studies concerning these questions have been undertaken by Kraemer (1973). There is no doubt that diseases of the capillary network in the end plates of the vertebral bodies or compressed bone tissue inevitably obstruct the fluid exchange by constricting the blood vessels. Ogata and Whiteside confirmed this with new experiments in 1981. If the cartilage plate is compressed or even destroyed through calcium deposits or other structural damages, the exchange process also changes.

In 1969 Bechtold performed histological studies of the layers of the vertebral body–intervertebral disc boundary and discovered numerous changes:

- *in the area of the cartilage plate and bony epiphysis:* foci of degeneration in the cartilage plate, lacerated and detached anular fibers, and irregularities in or nonexistence of the calcification line
- *in the area of the bony cribrum of the vertebral body:* fragmented zones with necroses and cysts and numerous metaplastical changes; in the vertebral body marrow adjacent to the cribrum: transformation of the hematopoietic marrow into yellow marrow, fibrosis with increased number of blood vessels, and transformation of sclerotically thickened trabeculae
- *at the lateral vertebral body wall:* transformation of the thickened vertebral body corticalis to osteophytes and to a supporting sclerosis of the epiphysis, which differs from the serrae of spondylosis and arthrosis both in histology and function

Bechtold called this damage consequences of overexertion in conjunction with existing degeneration of the intervertebral disc. This interpretation may be correct in some cases. However, the cause of the histological findings may also be found at the side of the vertebral body if capillary damage exists. Often, both will be present. A vicious cycle worsens the pathological conditions through mutual aggravation. The second pathway through the external part of the intervertebral disc may also be obstructed. This creates additional damaging factors, which reinforce the vicious cycle and make it more difficult to research details.

Even though some questions remain unanswered, distinct relationships do exist between the lowered or terminated permeability of the transitional layer between the vertebral body and the intervertebral disc and chronic damage of the intervertebral disc. Many investigators are convinced that damaged boundaries are at least one (probably the most important) of several possible causes of chronic damage of the disc. In some cases, however, it cannot be clearly determined whether the impermeability of the cartilage plate–bone plate boundary is the cause or the consequence of intervertebral chondrosis and other damage of the disc.

Many additional factors may be involved in the damage and may obstruct the normal supply and waste removal in the transitional layers: microfissures, fragmental zones, calluses on the bony cribrum and the hyaline cartilage layer, tears, calcified spots, lamellae fibers breaking loose, and—at bone and cartilage—healing processes of the damage. (These and similar impairments are also discussed in Chapters 3 and 5.)

It is not yet known how aging affects the tissues of the intervertebral disc. Is increasing dryness for the most part due to the loss of substances that cross the bone-cartilage boundary, ie, glucose and oxygen (Fig. 2-45) or to the generally age-determined fatigue of metabolism?

It remains to be shown whether by loss or decrease of fluid flow particular formations or locations of wear-and-tear damage of the disc occurs in the anterior-lateral or cranial-caudal access path. The studies of Hartung and Anna (1976) need to be continued in order to find the necessary answers. Their studies determined the irreversibility of load and deformation conditions of biological tissue. According to their report, this also holds true for precapillary sphincters and cartilage tissue. Since these particular anatomical structures are closely connected with the diffusional pathway of the intervertebral disc, additional studies might clarify whether mechanical load changes due to vibrations (sections 3.3.2; 5.3) may cause irreversible tissue damage at the bone plate and cartilage plate of the vertebral body–intervertebral disc boundary and therefore induce necrosis in the various tissues of the disc.

Unanswered questions remain with regard to the issue of vibrational influences on the spine and particularly at the boundary and vertebral body–intervertebral disc. These questions must be diligently researched because low input vibrations hift fluid and substances back and forth in the transitional layer between vertebral disc due to a swift succession of trough and crest.

Consequently, there is no complete exchange of fluid and substances as is required for maintaining the viability of the intervertebral disc. So far, there are no experimental studies of whether such a vibration-caused "fluid stagnation" results in additional nutritional difficulties for the susceptible bradytrophic tissue that, after a prolonged and frequent repetition of this disturbing mechanism, would create damage or worsen existing damage. A damaging shifting of the intervertebral disc fluid—as in the case of vibrations—may also occur as a result of athletic training (Chapter 8). Further discussions on the influence of vibrations on the soft parts of the spine are in Chapter 5. Lack of exercise also belongs in the category of external influences that might damage the intervertebral disc tissue (see Chapter 5).

A review of the discussion in this chapter justifies the summary statement: "The fate of the intervertebral disc is decided at the vertebral body–intervertebral disc boundary (Junghanns 1973).

3.2.5 Ligament System and Muscle Corset

The ligament system of the spine serves the purpose of static stabilization of the spine (see description of ligaments in section 2.2.3). It allows motions but also limits them depending on the respective task of the individual ligament. The system ensures normal posture and is responsible for stabilization in the final position of various movements insofar as it supports the active muscle functions. In addition, the entire system, as each individual ligament, is also able to absorb traumatic influences up to the load tolerance limit. Each of the intervertebral motor segments is tied into the extensive ligament system. The footholds of the longitudinal ligament are particularly important for changes in the segment (eg, spondylosis deformans).

The muscles have a dynamic function for posture and movement and are considered the active stabilizers of the spine, in contrast to the passively stabilizing ligament system. Together they form a static-dynamic musculoligamentous corset. In this way, they act as a physiological corset on each intervertebral motor segment in connection with the corresponding section of the musculoligamentous chain reaching from the head to the pelvis (see Chapter 5). If a segment has slackened, for whatever reason, the two static-dynamic stabilizers will sooner or later no longer be able to fulfill their common task for this or several intervertebral motor segments. The consequences are described in section 3.4.3: The latent performance insufficiency becomes a perceptible disease. The EMG may determine the extent of insufficiency of individual muscles or corset groups.

The influence of vibrations not only affects the intervertebral motor segment (mostly its intervertebral disc) but also impairs the muscles of the back.

3.2.6 Blood Vessels

In the intervertebral motor segment, blood vessels play an essential role in the influx of arterial blood and the venous return because the nutritional diffusion of the rather sluggishly nourished intervertebral disc depends on them. The supplying arteries run across the lateral and anterior outside walls of the vertebral bodies and finally separate into capillaries, which end in the perforations of the bony cribrum (see Chapter 2). Another supply path consists of arteries, which proceed in the paradiscal tissue on the external ring layers of the intervertebral discs in the front, on the side, and in the back (see Chapter 2). The extensive networks of avalvular veins that run in the spinal cord canal provide the return. The embryonical blood vessels in the intervertebral disc that recede during the first months of life are portrayed in Figure 2-27.

The blood supply of the vertebrae has an important function at the vertebral body–intervertebral disc boundary. It is responsible for nutritional supply and waste removal in the intervertebral disc and is also significant for the interarticular portion. A further discussion of the blood supply is found in Chapter 2.

3.2.7 Nerve Supply In and At the Intervertebral Motor Segment

In 1850, Luschka described a nerve in the lumbar spine that originates from the spinal nerve and runs back along the external surface of the intervertebral disc and vertebral body: the meningeal branch of spinal nerve (ramus recurrens) (Fig. 2-22). It was named the sinuvertebral nerve. Since it disposes fibers to the dura, it is also called the dural nerve (Clara 1959).

Studies are contradictory. Jung and Brunschwieg (1932) were not able to find either nerve fibers or peripheroceptors. Tsukuda (1939), in contrast, described the existence of nerve fibers in the interior of the intervertebral disc and the nucleus pulposus. According to studies by Roofe (1940) fine, marrowless nerve fibers exist in the anular fibers of the 4th and 5th lumbar vertebral disc, but he was not able to establish their origin. Jackson et al. (1966) reported on the nerves of the lumbar spine and corresponding soft tissue. With the cholinesterase technique, they studied numerous human spines of all ages. In embryos and newborns, they found Vater-Pacini corpuscles at the lateral-anterior surface of the fiber ring and concentrated around the vertebral arch articular capsules. They also found free nerve fibers and neural nets in the external layers of the fiber ring and in the anterior and posterior longitudinal ligament. No nerves were found in the deeper layers of the fiber ring or in the nucleus pulposus. In the cartilage plates of embryos and newborns, nerves existed in connection with capillary loops and capillary sinuses (Fig. 3-15; cf. Fig. 2-24). In the spine of adults, they found fine, free nerve endings in the periost of the lumbar vertebrae as well as in the capsules of the vertebral arch articulations. In contrast, no nerves could be found in the nucleus pulposus. The external zones of the fiber ring contained a nerve supply even in older persons (Fig. 3-16). Intervertebral discs with wear-and-tear drainage (intervertebral chondrosis and intervertebral osteochondrosis, called degeneration by Jackson [1966]) show no nerves. So far, no nerves have been found in connection with the rather frequent growth of fiber tissue into a destroyed intervertebral disc, which results in a fibrous stiffening of the intervertebral motor segment, even though blood vessels have been found regularly. In summary, no agreement about the issue of nerves existing in the interior of the adult intervertebral disc has been recorded.

Whether future studies will be able to prove the existence of the neural control mechanism that Farfan assumed in the intervertebral discs of the lumbar spine and that Garkovetsky described in 1975 remains an open question. In the author's opinion, this mechanism supposedly activates signals for spinal functions. However, according to Wyke and Molina (1972), the nerves in the fiber capsules of the neural arch articulations play an important role in the reflex series of motions of the cervical spine. They de-

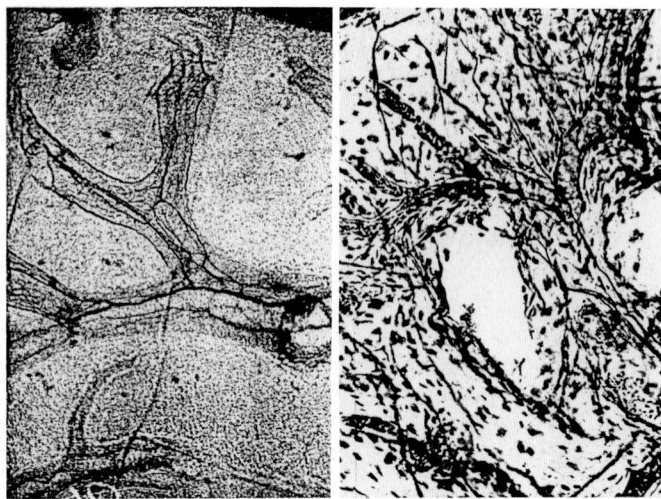

Fig. 3-15 Left: Nerve endings in vascular canals of the hyaline cartilage plate of a 1-month-old girl (cholinesterase technique); **Right:** very fine reticular net at the vascular sinusoids in the hyaline cartilage plate of a 2-month-old girl (Bielschowski-dyeing) [from Jackson et al. (1966)].

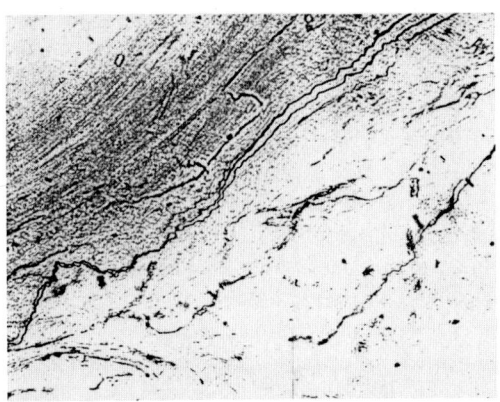

Fig. 3-16 Nerve fibers in the external layers of the fiber ring of a 76-year-old man (cholinesterase technique) [from Jackson et al. (1966)].

scribed two types of corpuscular nerve endings that act as fast and slow adaptational receptors. In their opinion, their functions may be interrupted by damage resulting from infection or degeneration.

Jackson et al. (1966) extensively studied the neural supply in the area of lumbar vertebral arch articulations (see Fig. 3-17).

Impressed by the studies of Wyke (1975), Dvorak and Dvorak (1982) furthered the study of the neurology of vertebral arch articulations and their plurisegmental innervation, which can be of importance in connection with peripheral changes of soft tissue due to interference with the segments (such as spondylogenic reflex syndrome, spondylogenic nocireaction). Chiro-

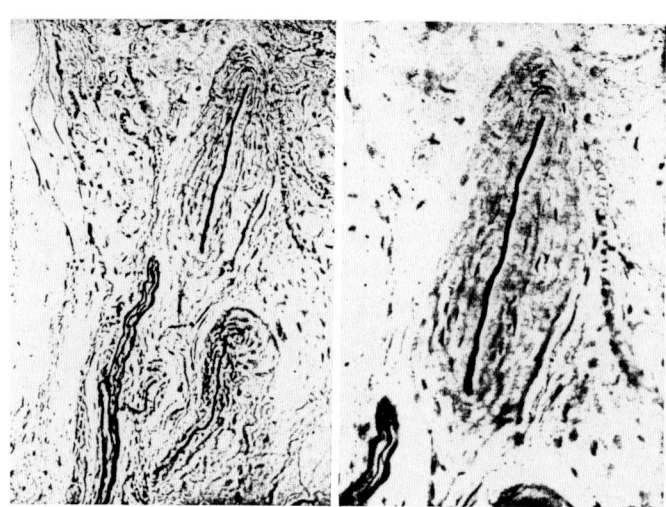

Fig. 3-17 Vater-Pacini nerve endings in the synovia of vertebral arch articulations of a 2-month-old infant. *Enlargement:* left 250x, right 360x (Jackson et al 1966).

practic manipulations via influences on the articular receptors may help in the case of segmental dysfunction (obstruction). Figure 3-18 portrays the neural relations in the area of the vertebral arch articulations.

In order to understand the origin and nature of spondylogenic pain, it is important to know that in the adult body, nerves exist in the periost of the vertebral body, the capsules of the vertebral arch and vertebrocostal articulations, the spinal ligaments, the peridural area, and plexiform around the vertebral artery. In addition, connective fibers run to the sympathetic nervous system. This extensive neural net that has developed in and at the intervertebral motor segment and is connected with other parts of the body through the spinal roots is shown in Figs. 2-22 and 3-18. It is easy to see the impairment potential of a damaged intervertebral motor segment. Impairment factors determined by the intervertebral disc, arthroses of the corresponding articulations and similar damage dominate the functionally impaired segment with all the consequences of an intervertebral insufficiency. They are transferred on predetermined neural pathways and often amplified by vibrations or by a lack of exercise. Additional mechanical impulses activate neurological symptoms in the respective nerve area even far from the spine. Pain radiations that are controlled by damaged intervertebral motor segments are often called soft tissue, or muscle, rheumatism (see Chapter 4).

In the past, little attention has been brought to the vertebrocostal articulations, which are biomechanically integrated into the intervertebral motor segment and possess a densely meshed neural net (Wyke 1975). As a consequence of arthrotic disorders (which are often coupled with arthroses of the vertebral arch articulations) they may radiate pain into the intercostal spaces in the case of intervertebral instability. These are projected pains, mostly of the pseudoradical type. Occasionally, they are noticed as pseudoanginal heart pain (Floeel 1980; Steinruecken 1980).

Therefore, the characteristics of source pain and disease symptoms depend significantly on the type of nerve fibers damaged by diseases or afflicted by mechanical pressure due to incorrect motions of an unhealthy intervertebral motor segment. In the case of spondylogenic pain, the described biomechanical facts must be considered and diagnostically clarified. An examination must terminate in a specific treatment method—but not polypragmasy.

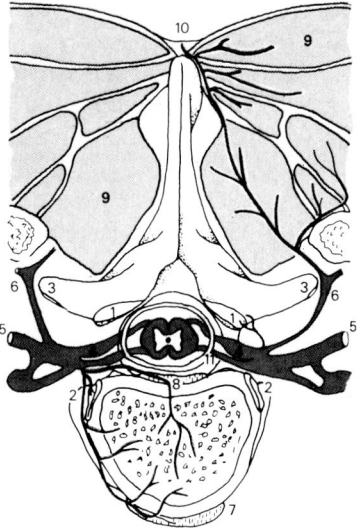
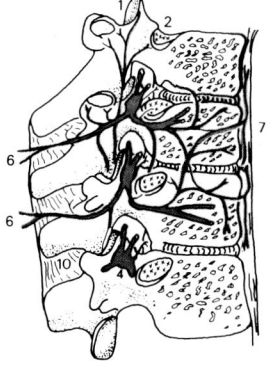

Fig. 3-18 Schematic portrayal of articular, muscular, ligamentous, and periost innervation in the area of the thoracic spine (Wyke 1976): (**1**) apophyseal articulation; (**2**) vertebrocostal articulation; (**3**) costotransversal articulation; (**4**) spinal ganglion; (**5**) ramus ventralis of the spinal nerve; (**6**) ramus dorsalis of the spinal nerve; (**7**) anterior longitudinal ligament; (**8**) posterior longitudinal ligament; (**9**) paravertebral muscles; (**10**) interspinal ligament (Dvorak and Dvorak 1982).

Other investigators who studied the neural supply in the area of the intervertebral motor segment include Edgar and Ghadially (1976); d'Eshougues and Waghemacker (1975); Hirsch et al. (1963); Jackson et al. (1966); Jelinek and Malinsky (1956); Wiberg (1949), and many others.

3.3 IMPORTANT EXTERNAL INFLUENCES

3.3.1 Introduction

The approximately 25 intervertebral motor segments that are integrated in the spine between each two vertebrae form an organ unit according to their biomechanical and biochemical functions. Each part of the unit is affected by more or less significant external influences. These include, for example, all motions caused by muscles and created outside the spine, possibly under the influence of gravity. The following discussions deal only with a few important external influences that are occasionally underestimated by physicians even though almost everyone is subject to these influences daily and often for hours: they may result in damage of the spine. These include total-body and partial-body vibrations in a sinus rhythm—often interspersed with irregular (stochastic) vibrations (see 3.3.3). They affect us at the work place, in leisure and sports, and when traveling.

Each intervertebral motor segment is affected by these influences. Because of its elastic nature, the intervertebral disc is most often affected since it must resist excessive tilting and rotation in its function as buffer and load distributor; but also—often in connection with the vertebral arch articulation pair belonging to the segment—it must act as a brake. Frequently the external loads exceed the performance capacity of the intervertebral disc, especially in the case of prolonged vibrations. Serious damage may result as described in detail in Chapter 5.

The described conditions not only affect the intervertebral disc but also its important partner: the vertebral arch articulation pair of the segment (see vertebral arch articulation arthrosis in Chapter 4). On the other hand, arthroses of the vertebral arch articulations may induce damage of the intervertebral disc when they disturb the centralized function of the segment.

3.3.2 Sinus Vibrations

Many vibrations affect the body to an extent that may damage many organs. The term *vibrational disease* exists justifiably. Chapter 5 explains that vibrations are considered the secret interference of metabolism of the intervertebral disc, which eventually leads to destruction of the intervertebral disc structure. Lack of exercise often contributes to the damaging effect. The spine is most often affected by total-body vibrations, whose transmission path and characteristics are portrayed in Chapter 5.

Serious continuous influences caused by total-body vibrations may induce damage in the vertebral body–intervertebral disc boundary or may worsen existing damage. Vibration-caused stagnation of fluid is an imminent danger to the nutrition of intervertebral disc tissue and may be the cause or concomitant cause of intervertebral disc wear.

Partial-body vibrations are mostly caused by occupational activities (see Chapter 5). Their transmission path runs across the hand, arm, and shoulder joint to the cervical and upper thoracic spine. They are evaluated differently with regard to their damage potential in the intervertebral motor segment. Partial-body vibrations may, however, have a worsening effect in connection with total-body vibrations. This may be especially true for the cervical spine since it is more frequently exposed to rotations and three-dimensional rolling motions than other sections of the spine.

3.3.3 Stochastic and Impacting Vibrations

Persons in motor vehicles (who are mostly in a sitting position) are essentially affected by sinus-shaped total-body and partial-body vibrations as well as by their irregular (stochastic) mixed forms. Those vibrations are absorbed by the spine and its muscle corset. Often, unexpected and irregular shaking, pounding, tilting, and rotational tremors (impacting vibrations) contribute to seriously disturbing the intervertebral motor segments in question. The stochastic and impacting influences have particularly unfavorable consequences. Without doubt, they worsen damage in the discs and the transitional zones to the adjacent vertebral bodies (section 3.2.4).

3.3.4 Lack of Motion

One external influence is certainly lack of motion, which leads to a slower pump mechanism or even to a complete halt of the pump mechanism. Because of the insufficient interplay in the diffusional flow, nutrients and substances that need to be removed accumulate in the intervertebral disc tissues that are insufficiently supplied. Therefore a lack or insufficient motion may damage the segmental element with the largest mass, ie, the intervertebral disc (see Chapter 5).

Lack of motion also results from a long confinement to bed due to illnesses and from space flights. The spine suffers from a relative lack of motion during a prolonged sitting position, particularly if connected with an unfavorable forced posture. All of these varieties of insufficient bodily motions lead to irregularity of the fluid and substance exchange. Prolonged lack of motion also leads to calcium decomposition in the entire bony tissue. Vertebrae are particularly affected by this inactive osteoporosis. Decomposition of the vertebral bodies leads to microfissures in the bony cribrum. In addition, the diffusional flow for supply and waste removal in the disc is slowed.

3.4 THE PERFORMANCE-IMPAIRED INTERVERTEBRAL MOTOR SEGMENT

3.4.1 Intervertebral Insufficiency

Each interference of the normal structure of the intervertebral motor segment lowers the performance capacity of the entire segmental unit, even if it is only partially affected in an "obvious" manner. This is because the functions of the individual parts are very closely interrelated, eg, the frequent damage of the intervertebral disc (intervertebral chondrosis, intervertebral osteochondrosis) affect the second essential functional unit, ie, the two vertebral arch articulations of the segment and their corresponding ligaments, articular capsules, and menisci (see Chapter 2). Damage of the vertebral arch articulation may not only affect the second, parallel articulation, but also directly the function of the intervertebral disc and even its anatomical structures—and therefore its functional ability. This affects the intervertebral interplay of motion, and quite often spondylogenic symptoms and syndromes appear.

In order to emphasize the homogeneous function of this intervertebral mobility, it was labeled the intervertebral motor segment (1951) (see section 3.1). It unifies freedom of motion as well as certain impediments for excessive motion, which are regulated by the fiber system in the intervertebral disc tissue, ligaments, and mobility limits of the vertebral arch articulations and vertebrocostal articulations.

Damage of essential structural elements of the segment (intervertebral disc, vertebral arch articulations) directly threaten the adjacent structures: the spinal cord and its membranes, segmental nerve roots, and adjacent autonomous nerves and blood vessels. Such damage is initially only brief and subliminal. The more frequent and the longer friction, pressure, and traction are, the more permanent damage is, eg, radiculopathy, myelopathy.

It is not appropriate to consider the individual, segmentally arranged intervertebral motor segments alone. However, individual segments are subject to significant impairment. No matter what damage appears in the individual elements, in each case a performance deficiency or degeneration occurs in the entire unit. Therefore, functional interferences in the segment are summarized as *intervertebral insufficiency*, a term that should not be confused with *vertebral insufficiency*, which was created by Schanz (1931). He thought of vertebral insufficiency as a misproportion of the load and load-bearing capacity of the vertebral bones. However, this applies to intervertebral insufficiency, which is due to damage of the segment and the functional condition of muscles and ligaments.

In order to understand *intervertebral insufficiency* as a comprehensive term and as the main interest for specific diagnosis and causative therapies, a clear nomenclature is necessary. So far there are still disagreements concerning the medical nomenclature. Further research, practice, and diagnoses require clear, technical terms based on anatomy and consistent with pathomorphological and pathophysiological findings (Junghanns 1977). Therefore, the intervertebral motor segment as a decisive factor for static, kinetic, and external impairment potentials requires clearly classified terminology. In this context attention should be paid to

- internal interrelations among the individual structures: intervertebral disc, vertebral arch, vertebrocostal articulations, etc.
- effects of damage of the segment on the surrounding bones, muscles, ligaments, spinal nerves, spinal cord, and blood vessels
- external influences on the segment: structural changes and changes in the resistance capacity of the adjacent bony tissue, flawed static caused by axial deviations, etc.

Damage in the interior of the segment or external influences affect the performance capacity of the intervertebral motor segment. Potentials of decreasing performance span the gap between excessive mobility, hampered mobility, or even complete immobility. Intervertebral insufficiency leads to impaired mobility as well as an impaired stress capacity of the spine. A physician, however, might focus on intervertebral insufficiency only if a patient reports severe problems and back pain although the impairment was triggered long before.

Intervertebral insufficiency may manifest itself in increasing mobility, ie, a slackening in the intervertebral motor segment: intervertebral instability. Some pathological changes lead to intervertebral immobility via stiffness, ie, rigor or ankylosis. In addition, there is the possibility of intervertebral incarceration, the so-called blockage of the intervertebral motor segment.

For the physician who considers impairments caused by the spinal column as intervertebral insufficiency, the "new concept of the spinal column" (see section 3.1) will determine his or her diagnostic considerations, therapeutic activity (conservative or surgical), evaluation fitness for sports, interest in occupational medicine, and all further questions.

3.4.2 Intervertebral Instability

Excessive mobility in the segmental unit, the slackened intervertebral motor segment (intervertebral instability), may have its origin in any part of the segment: intervertebral disc or vertebral arch articulation pair. Figure 4-38 portrays the susceptible areas 1 to 6 in the intercorporal space, ie, at the intervertebral disc and at the transition to the vertebral body. At these points, damage originates that almost always results in an intervertebral instability. This may happen rather quickly if damage of several susceptible areas of the intervertebral disc space exists or if damage exists in adjacent segments. Chapter 4 describes details, especially the resulting illnesses and impairment factors.

Slackening of a segment may also originate in the vertebral arch articulations, the essential partners of the intervertebral disc. Arthroses in these articulations lead gradually via cartilage-bone abrasions to deformed articulations and instability, which consecutively destroys the intervertebral disc, eg, in a pseudospondylolisthesis. Surgery may become necessary (see Chapter 7). The most frequent slackening occurs in the intervertebral motor segments of the cervical and lumbar spine.

The beginning instability is not painful as long as muscles and ligaments are still strong enough to absorb the shifting and torsion. Initially a latent instability exists: the latent performance insufficiency. The insufficiency develops into a noticeable disease when damage to the intervertebral motor segment worsens by involvement of several segments or when external circumstances participate, eg, when an additional impulse is involved. This influence, which "causes" the disease, is often a mechanical impulse: coughing, sneezing, pressing, rhythmic or stochastic impacts of a motor vehicle or motor bike, sudden body rotation, forward bending or straightening of the body, sitting in an unfavorable body position for a long period of time, etc. The additional impulse may also be thermal, climatic, allergic, toxic, endocrine, or even psychological. In psychologically unstable patients an additional impulse such as a curved posture or anxiety may often be sufficient to shift an unstable intervertebral motor segment (eg, at the cervical spine) because of muscle contractions and induce a serious neck-shoulder-arm neuralgia.

Continuous unfavorable loads and additional impulses in connection with a slackened intervertebral segment may induce various complaints: three types of instability.

The consequences of the first type appear to the patient as lumbago: back or neck pain. For many patients, these complaints are the only symptoms, with several pain-free intervals over many years. The intervertebral instability causes pain when several slackened segments allow stair-like shifts.

The second type of instability includes spondylogenic symptoms and syndromes. They result from a transfer of complaints via neural or vascular pathways to the head or periphery of the body: eg, neck-head pain, neck-shoulder-arm pain, lumboischialgia. The most frequently used pathway is the neural one; the vascular pathway is rarely used. The irritations of the segmental nerve roots are initially small (subliminal). Gradually repeated irritation causes pathoanatomical damage at and in the spinal nerve (radiculopathy) and consequently an almost uninterrupted disturbance: continuous radiations to the internal organs.

Spondylogenic diseases may occur when effects of the instability have exerted prolonged pressure on the spinal cord, spinal nerve roots and their ganglia, or blood vessels and autonomic nerves. Often, they are found far from their point of origin and become so self-contained that a spontaneous process of healing has become impossible. These conditions characterize the third type of instability. Examples are:

- prolapse of the intervertebral disc with pareses
- pressure against the cervical cord with chronic myelopathy as a result of constriction of the vertebral canal (tweezer mechanism) (see Fig. 3-19)

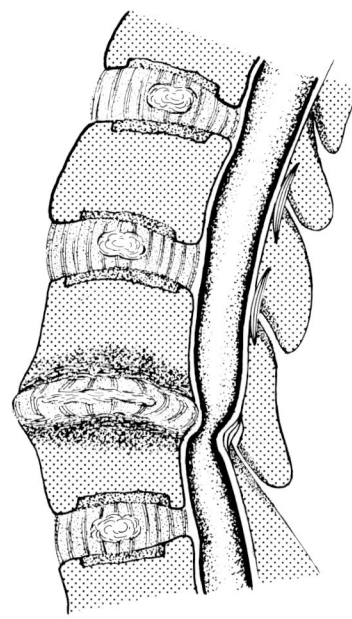

Fig. 3-19 Tweezer mechanism: slight backward shifting of a vertebra with bony tori at the rear vertebral body edge. Intervertebra with bony spurs at the rear vertebral body edge. Interticulation, results in a tweezer-like strangulation of the spinal cord (cf. Fig. 3-20).

- pressure on spinal roots due to backward shifting with additional intervertebral osteochondrosis in the cervical and lumbar area (Fig. 3-20)
- irritation of autonomic nerves with serious consequences, such as heart disorders or circulatory insufficiency and other chronic diseases whose origin was formerly not presumed to be the spine

The described effects of instability appear not only in the case of severe hypermobility. Even small shifts, which are only seldom portrayed in roentgenograms, may cause the described complaints. During a longer course of the disease, processes coexist (or alternate), which include increasing mobility (intervertebral disc wear, intervertebral disc decomposition), decreasing mobility, or complete loss of mobility: scarred ligament sections, stiffening bony clasps. So far it has not been possible to determine to what extent internal strangulation or progressive ligamentous fibrosis results in excessive mobility. It is also unknown how often instability results in

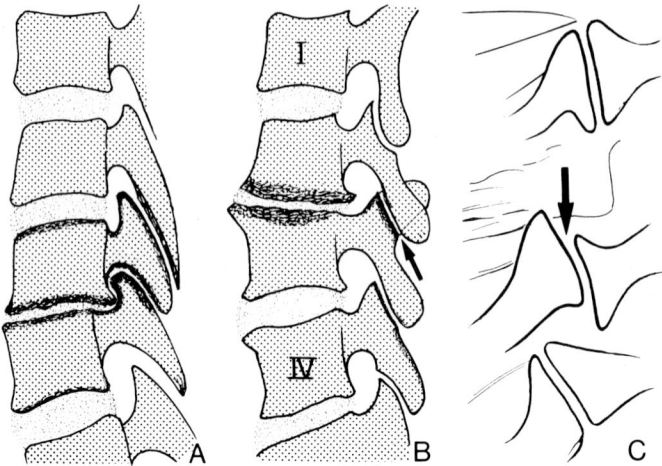

Fig. 3-20 Schematic of a retrolisthesis drawing in the intervertebral motor segment of the cervical spine (**A**) and the lumbar spine (**B**), drawn according to roentgenograms. Intervertebral osteochondrosis at the cervical and lumbar spine. Constriction of the intervertebral canal at the cervical spine as a result of retrolisthesis and arthrosis in the vertebral arch articulation (cf. tweezer mechanism in Fig. 3-19). Telescopic shift in the vertebral arch articulation at the lumbar spine (**arrow**). This position can be seen especially clearly with a slant tomogram (**C**).

immobility due to growth of fibrous tissue or bones into the intervertebral space, eg, in the healing process of bone fractures.

The distinct as well as the hidden syndromes of intervertebral insufficiency require a treatment adapted to the state of the illness. Often, manual therapeutic manipulations, physical therapy, and massages will be emphasized (see Chapter 7). Many treatment procedures may become necessary, including surgery.

3.4.3 Intervertebral Immobility

Intervertebral insufficiency may also appear as intervertebral immobility:

- by growth of blood vessels in connection with tissue growth into the intervertebral disc, intervertebral fibrosis results (after trauma, infection)
- if intervertebral ossification forms (after infection, trauma, congenital block vertebrae)
- if the intervertebral motor segment stiffens due to ligamentous ossification, as in the case of spondylarthritis ancylopoetica or spondylosis hyperortotica
- if a bridging ossification of the intervertebral disc space by spondylosis deformous occurs (after trauma or infection)

These changes result in a permanent mobility impairment of one or several intervertebral motor segments. If the segments stiffen, the normal position of vertebrae in relation to each other may be maintained. In most cases, the height of the intervertebral disc space decreases. Occasionally, the immobility appears in a more or less distinctly shifted, tilted, or rotated position.

3.4.4 Vertebral Blockade

The term *vertebral blockage* or *vertebral blockade* (obstruction of an intervertebral motor segment as a functional pathomechanism) means a temporary mobility obstruction. This blockage, which can disappear either suddenly or slowly by itself or by manipulations, may have its origin in the intervertebral disc space or in the vertebral arch articulation. The first occurs mostly in connection with intervertebral osteochondrosis by impingement of a partially or completely loosened part of the intervertebral

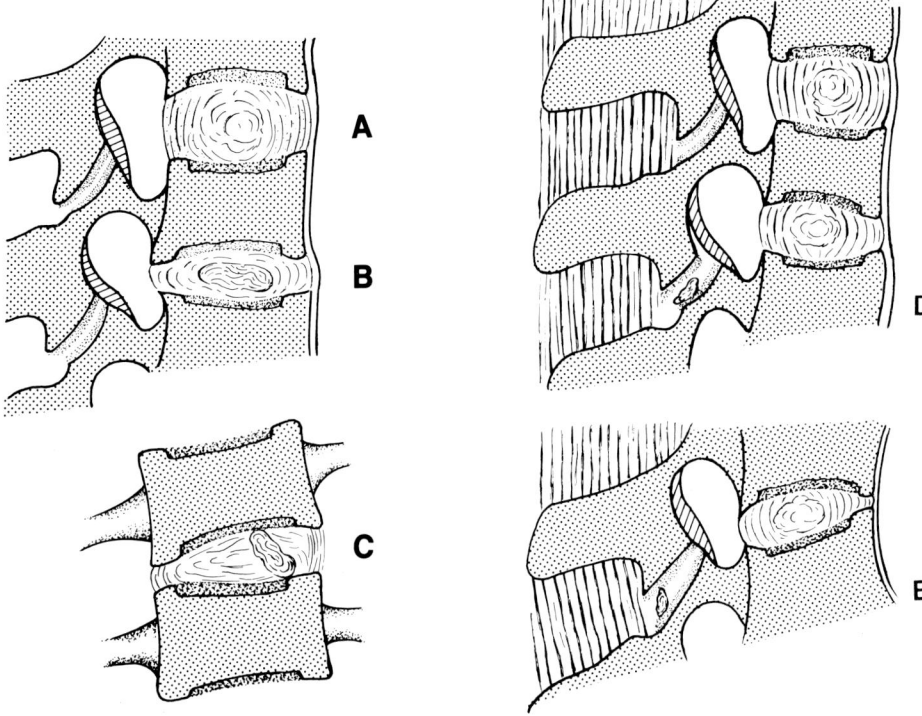

Fig. 3-21 (**A**) Sagittal section of a normal intervertebral disc; (**B**) intervertebral chondrosis with central sequester of intervertebral disc, lowered intervertebral space; (**C**) laterally positioned, tilted, and pinched sequester in the frontal plane (incarceratio intradiscalis); (**D**) corpus librum in gap of vertebral arch articulation; (**E**) tilted, free body in the vertebral arch articulation.

disc (see Figs. 4-47 and 3-21). The second (Fig. 3-21) may be caused by an impingement of a sequestered portion; there is a similarity with the pinched meniscus of the knee joint.

The mobility obstruction suddenly occurring as a result of a blockage is rather painful. By predisposition, it may occur any time in daily life, particularly as a sport-specific pain attack. In recent years, sports medicine has increasingly described blockades in the sacroiliac articulations (incarceratio iliosacralis). This is seen in connection with more demanding training and competition. The painful blockade appears mostly in the lumbar area by torsion of the lumbar-pelvis-hip region (occasionally also in connection with blockades of vertebral arch articulations).

Often, the term *subluxation* is used for intervertebral and interarticular incarceration. However, this process is not a subluxation but the obstruction during an articular motion that does not or only insignificantly exceeds the anatomically limited extent of mobility. Physicians would not call a blockade in the meniscus of a knee joint a "subluxation." This term is also unsuitable for blockade of the intervertebral segment or sacroiliac articulation.

It is still difficult to clarify the cause of incarceration for each case with physical and radiological examinations. Specific manipulations may be able to loosen the blockage, which eliminates pain and brings back mobility. Relapses are frequent as long as the exact cause has not been found and treated.

The load-bearing capacity of the spinal column is greatly or completely impaired by partial stiffness or pain during the period of acute blockade. After the blockade is remedied, the previous condition returns. It is, as described, mostly an intervertebral chondrosis/intervertebral osteochondrosis or an arthrosis of the vertebral arch articulation, with complaints corresponding to the intervertebral insufficiency.

The vertebrocostal articulations can be regarded as part of the unit of the intervertebral motor segment because of their close biomechanical relationship. Therefore, blockades may also be observed in those articulations. Floeel (1980) described muscle spasms as a result of neural misregulation, which may lead to blockade. Projected pain in the intracostal space and pseudoanginal symptoms indicate articular blockage. To remedy this condition, chirotherapy is recommended (Moehrle 1981; Steinruecken 1980).

3.4.5 Load-Bearing Capacity in Intervertebral Insufficiency

Even the smallest initial damage in the case of an intervertebral chondrosis involves a decrease in the performance capacity of the affected intervertebral motor segment. However, initially, a latent performance insufficiency exists, which by slowly increasing the damage in the intervertebral disc, gradually evolves into a perceptible performance insufficiency. An "inconvenience" may finally lead to serious illness and may result in slight handicaps on the job, in sports, or in daily life or a long confinement to bed, even in the case of intervertebral osteochondrosis of a single intervertebral motor segment. The three types of intervertebral insufficiency (described in section 3.4.2) are of decisive significance. They cause the radiating pain, spondylogenic diseases, etc. whose characteristics affect the load-bearing capacity of the spine in different ways (which must be clarified for each individual case by a medical examination). The importance of this syndrome with its significant complaints lies in the performance insufficiency: the slackening of the intervertebral segment.

In most cases of intervertebral disc wear, more than one segment is affected. Because the illness is based on general physical causes, it spreads into numerous intervertebral discs. However, this takes place with a varying extent of changes and different distribution to smaller or larger spinal sections. The most serious form of intervertebral chondrosis, intervertebral osteochondrosis, however, appears mostly only at one or a few intervertebral spaces.

The chondrosis/osteochondrosis poses an individually different pathological risk, which often manifests itself through initial pain and the first performance insufficiency during the important periods of puberty and the transitional period between school and a job. The "age-determined" intervertebral disc wear affects the individual to a smaller or larger extent, usually unexpectedly in the late 40s. Since singular prophylactic checkups are unable to provide certain indications concerning the fate of the intervertebral discs, monitoring examinations are recommended immediately at the occurrence of complaints and in older persons. Their results may lead to a timely introduction of necessary therapy, which may divert or alleviate damage so that daily activities can be pursued as usual. Prophylactic measures, therapy, rehabilitation procedures, and in some cases, surgery, can stabilize a performance insufficiency (see Chapter 7). Chapters 3 and 7 discuss the manner in which vibrations, heavy physical exertions, or prolonged forced postures may cause intervertebral chondrosis and influence its further development.

Isolated intervertebral disc damage, which may deteriorate to intervertebral osteochondrosis because of various circumstances, is accompanied by significantly lowered load-bearing capacity of the spine if the tissue of the intervertebral disc has sufficiently slackened (see Chapter 4).

Insufficiency in the most important section of the intervertebral motor segment (ie, the intervertebral disc, but also in the two vertebral arch articulations), may have a negative effect on work, daily life, leisure, and sports if the permanent load capacity limit has been reached, must be endured over a prolonged period, or is exceeded (see Chapter 8). Studies exist on average load-bearing capacities. More information in this regard may be found in *The Spinal Column in Research and Practice* (volume 78, Hippokrates Publishing House, Stuttgart, 1979).

3.4.6 Spondylogenic Symptoms and Syndromes: Clinical Perspective

The performance-deficient intervertebral motor segment was formerly held responsible for essentially purely segmental complaints and diseases, which were discussed and divided into three types as effects of intervertebral instability in section 3.4.2. As research results and practical medical experiences were combined, it became clear that segmental spondylogenic syndromes spread further in neural (as well as vascular) respects than seemed possible from a singular segmental spondylogenic focus. Organs outside the central organ of the support and motor system (eg, lung, stomach, heart) showed neurally determined interrelationships with the spine and pseudoradical pain, which may be explained only through intersegmentally neural cross-linking (Bergsmann and Eder 1982; Eder and Tilscher 1982).

The extensive consideration of these issues poses many new tasks for the diagnostician and therapist and requires a change in patterns of thinking. In this book, it is impossible to discuss sufficiently the surfacing questions so that practical therapeutic conclusions may be drawn. This may be seen from the large number of new syndromes (see Table 3-5). The diagnostics of these causes of pain include, in addition to exact history, the specific physical examination and a series of roentgenograms according to the plan presented in Chapter 6. The person interested in therapy will soon realize that each syndrome requires its own treatment plan but that specific manipulational therapy is an essential part of success if it is used properly. The problem of the cause of origin of spondylogenic symptoms and syndromes also includes the question of how they are activated. Additional impulses in daily life play a role (see Chapter 8) since they convert a predisposition as a result of previous damage into a spondylogenic syndrome.

In spite of the findings of the last decades, therapy still poses several problems because the medical approach cannot be immediately determined in many cases. Often, it is found only because of experience. Procedures that do not affect the intervertebral motor segment but rather attempt to influence the autonomic nervous system from the point of radiation (ie, retrograde) often lack powerful theoretical foundations and efficacy. These procedures include subcutaneous and intracutaneous injec-

Table 3-5 Relationships of Ischemic Heart Disorders and Cardiovertebral Syndromes*

	Cardiovertebral Syndromes with Ischemic Heart Disorder	Cardiovertebral Syndromes without Ischemic Heart Disorder
Location of pain	Retrosternal, shoulder, left arm	Intermittently precordial
Pain activation	Stress-determined	Not stress-determined
Vegetative concomitant symptoms	Rare	Frequent
ECG	Signs of ischemia	No signs of ischemia (periodic rhythm disorder)
Blockage pattern	Multisegmental thoracal, cervicothoracal Difficult to resolve	Changing localization involvement of head articulations therapeutically beneficial
Diagnosis of connective tissue	Relapse tendency	Uncharacteristic
Organ therapy	Clear organ zones	No effect
Nitro drugs	Primarily	No effect
Analgetica antirheumatica	Immediately effective	Temporarily effective
Chirotherapy	No effect As concomitant therapy for segmental irritation	Principally

*Bergsmann and Eder (1982).

tions in the head zones. (For acupuncture, see section in Chapter 7.) In each case, careful consideration must be given to the question of whether new therapies should be preferred to proven, successful procedures.

Newer findings, obtained by Bergsmann and Eder (1982), may be a guideline for treatment. Geiger (1979), Heide (1972, 1979), and Kunert (1981) report on the issue the spine and the heart. Eder and Tilscher (1982) discuss in detail the viscerovertebral relationships. Valuable books on diagnostics and therapy for the cervical syndrome and shoulder-arm pain have been written by Jenkner (1982) and Mumenthaler et al. (1980). In the case of spondylogenic symptoms, a psychological factor is often present: (Buran and Novak 1984). Fusion impairment of the eye has also been described (Mohr and Schimek 1984). In 1984, Sagebiel reported on a postoperative vertebrocostal syndrome.

4

Factors Interfering with Functional Capacity

4.1 INTRODUCTION

Depending on the seriousness of the condition and on whether several irregularities coexist, changes in morphological structure and physiological behavior interfere with static and physiological functional capacity. In addition to changes in the spine, skeleton, intervertebral discs, and ligaments, effects that originate in muscles, nerves, and the blood supply must also be considered insofar as they have many links with the spine. For example, even when only moderate damage exists in the intervertebral discs, an overtrained muscle corset may exert increased bending or rotational pressure and create additional damage.

Vibrations can directly damage the soft tissue of the spine—particularly the intervertebral discs—and occasionally bones. However, more frequently, directly damaged nerves and/or blood vessels affect the spine indirectly. Such neural and vascular damage potentials are discussed in Chapters 3, 5, and 7. The physician is encouraged to consider all such potentials in diagnosis and therapy.

A large group of impairment factors is often termed *endogenous*. However, the term is too limited. The following chapters discuss those factors that impair function and result from a disposition, are congenital, or occur during the course of life. These also include the consequences of exogenous influences, such as infectious diseases that result in permanent changes in the bones and soft tissue of the spine. They may finally become serious impairment factors that lower the static and dynamic function of the spine.

Damage of the spine can often be related to the prolapse of tissue portions of the intervertebral disk into the surrounding area:

- Prolapse toward the head or sacrum into the vertebral body results in the nodulus intraspongiosus (Schmorl's node, section 4.5.2.5).
- Prolapse to the posterior or lateral posterior is called prolapsus posteromedialis/posterolateralis.
- Prolapse to anterior and lateral anterior portions is rare and often appears initially in the form of a protrusio anterior/anterolateral protrusion.

4.2 VARIATIONS AND ABNORMALITIES

4.2.1 Variations

The variations of the spine, ie, the genetic irregularities in the usual number of vertebrae and malformations of vertebral bodies and arches in boundaries between the spinal sections, are relatively insignificant if they affect only short intervals. In addition to the bones, the intervertebral discs are also varied. Additional influences (eg, aging or exogenous noxae, such as prolonged sitting, result in additional problems.

Because of limited movement, the variations and malformations at the head–cervical spine boundary (basilar impression, occipitalization of the atlas, atlas assimilation, manifestation of an occipital vertebra, etc.) lead to premature wear of adjacent intervertebral discs and to arthrosis of the head articulations, especially if they appear unsymmetrically and result in a slanted posture of the head. Depending on their intensity, impairing symptoms result (eg, after prolonged sitting with the head tilted). These varied, often congenital, abnormalities at the head–cervical spine boundary, which are sometimes also the result of disease, have been discussed by many investigators [see Erdmann (1963), H. Dieckmann (1966), and Kamieth (1983)].

Unilateral and bilateral cervical ribs with a bony connection to the first thoracic rib, or compact connective tissue tracts that run from the tips of short cervical ribs to the next genuine rib, are often accompanied by changes in the course of scalenus muscles and abnormalities of nerves and blood vessels. In the case of unilateral strain, this may result in increasing problems: cervical rib or scalenus syndrome.

The variations at the thorax-loin boundary, the lumbar ribs, do not play an important role but appear in many forms. In differentiating between lumbar rib and transverse process breakoff, they become more significant.

Frequent variations at the loin-sacrum boundary are unilateral or bilateral transitional vertebrae (lumbalization or sacralization) (Figs. 4-1 and 4-2). Pseudoarthroses (Fig. 4-2), which develop in such cases between the widened transverse processes and the lateral ala on the sacrum, become arthrotic during the course of life. The accompanying arthroses of the vertebral arch articulations are also involved in algogenesis.

An unsymmetrical transitional vertebra is often connected with sacroscoliosis (Fig. 4-1). The connection among lumbosacral transitional

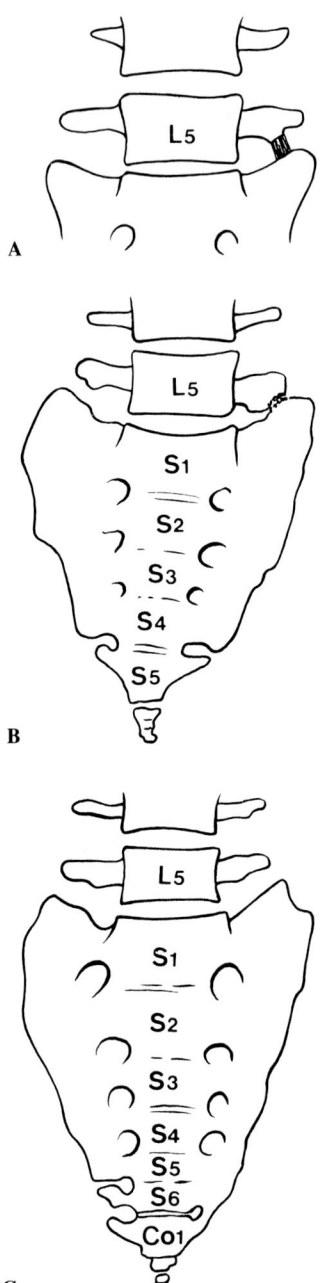

Fig. 4-1 Various forms of transitional vertebrae L5/S1. (**A**) compact ligament link, left; (**B**) jointlike link, right; (**C**) increased lateral mass of S1.

vertebrae, intervertebral osteochondrosis, as well as lumbosacral transitional vertebrae, and lumboscolioses should not be overlooked. Section 4.2.6 further discusses the influence of variations on the four transitional regions of the spine.

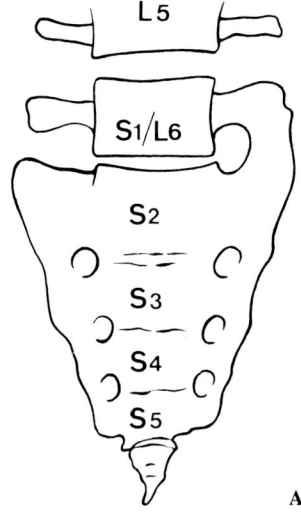

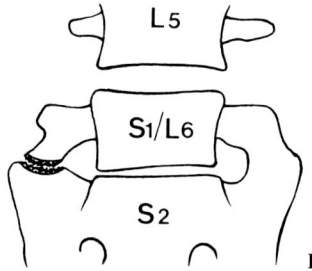

Fig. 4-2 Transitional vertebra S1/L6. (**A**) compact left bone link; (**B**) left bony articular (to the right) link, which often undergoes arthrotic change.

4.2.2 Abnormalities in the Vertebral Body–Intervertebral Disc Series

Growth irregularities in the cord or its impaired retromorphosis results in defects of the segmental structure of the vertebral body–intervertebral disc series. In this context, malfunctions in the segmental blood vessel course or external influences during the embryonic period, such as hypoxemia, X-rays, lead consumption, and various drugs, play a role in addition to primary genetic effects. In 1958, Degenhardt reported results of animal experiments concerning such problems.

A schematic overview of the maturation of vertebral bodies and vertebral arches is shown in Fig. 4-3. The upper row shows the proper development. The cord canal disappears, as do the gaps (sutures) in the vertebral arch (I–III). Ossification centers form at several locations (IV and V). For some time, however, the arch root remains unconnected with the vertebral body. Through the vascular buds, several ossification centers develop in the vertebral body (I: A and B and with delay I: C and D). A transverse cartilage band can remain during the anterior and posterior formation of ossification centers (see frontal vertebral body gap at V [lower row]). During the long developmental process, a sagittal vertebral body gap with the remaining cord canal (I: C) may form. Another possible result is a lateral semivertebra (I: D).

Figure 2-2 is a drawing of a normal retromorphosis of the embryonic cord. Often, indentations remain in the area of its penetration points at the cover or base plates of one or several vertebral bodies (juvenile kyphosis). Such indentations are to some degree found in 20% to 30% of all spines. They are always accompanied by a decreased thickness and resistance of the cartilaginous and bony end plates. Therefore, a Schmorl's nodule frequently forms at this location (see section 4.5). In addition, the indentations may be concomitant causes of juvenile kyphosis (see section 4.3).

The cord only occasionally remains in a vertebral body and is called persistent notocord (Fig. 2-3). This results in a soft tissue tract running in the head-sacrum direction and often accompanies a slightly wedge-shaped vertebra. At the same time, the tissue of the adjacent intervertebral discs is affected and has little resistance. The height of the intervertebral spaces above and beneath the vertebra is decreased.

The congenital block vertebrae are frequent defects in the segmentation: The fusing between two or more vertebrae consists mostly of a bony connection of the vertebral bodies. The intervertebral space may later be recognized in a roentgenogram by more or less distinct transverse spongiosa tracts (Fig. 2-6). The block vertebra may have the height of the fused vertebral bodies including the interposed intervertebral spaces. If the block vertebra is shorter than this total height, slight kyphosis occurs. The vertebral bodies are either partially or completely enclosed in this block. This is an important differential diagnostic symptom in contrast to block

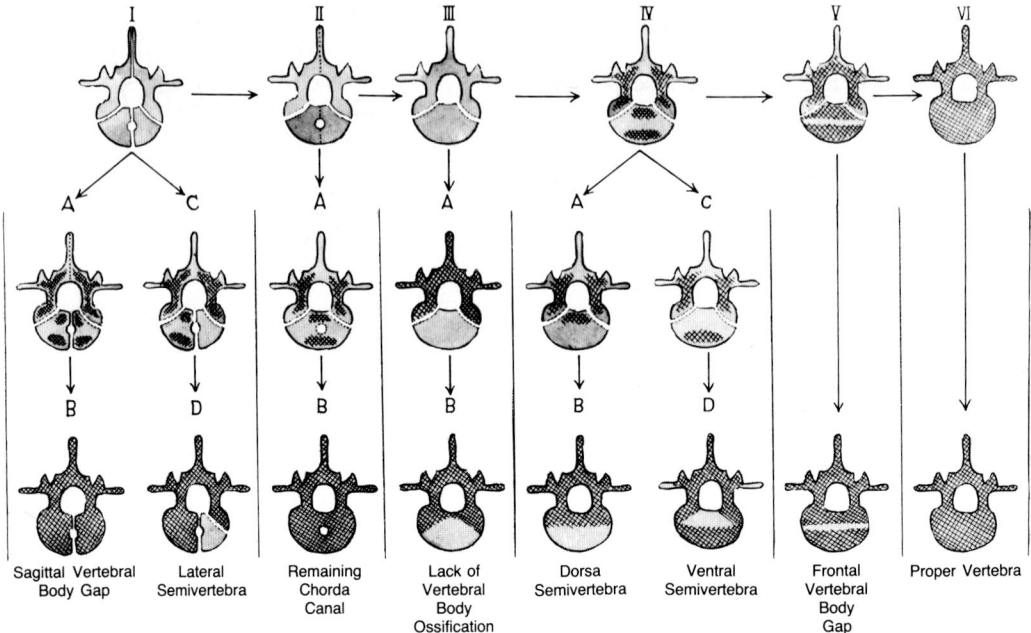

Fig. 4-3 Model of proper vertebral body development (**upper row**) and various vertebral body malformations (**middle and lower row**) that may be associated with developmental stages I–V. Bone tissue striated (Junghanns). (For further description, see the text.)

vertebrae, which appear after a receded pyesis. The intervertebral canals nevertheless remain open for the passage of the segmental nerves and blood vessels. With progressive age, the intervertebral discs adjacent to a vertebral block are threatened by a premature intervertebral chondrosis or intervertebral osteochondrosis.

In connection with developmental defects of the cord, the rare vertebral body cleft occurs in the sagittal suture plane with the formation of a butterfly vertebra: vertebra alata, which lowers the stress resistance of the spine.

Substantial flexionlike scolioses form as the result of lateral congenital semivertebrae. A semivertebra that has developed in the back (hemispondylus dorsalis) is accompanied by an acute-angled kyphosis with intervertebral disc impairment and represents a significant point of weakness in the load-bearing capacity.

4.2.3 Malformations in the Vertebral Arch Series

Gaps (sutures) are the most frequently occurring developmental defects in the vertebral arch series. They are mostly determined by growth irregularities of the neural canal. The median gap in the spinous process, the spina bifida, is the best known. Depending on their occurrence on one or more adjacent spinous processes and the involvement of the spinal cord and its membranes, these gaps show different degrees of neural damage, which result in corresponding stress problems. Most of them occur in the sacrum: 20% to 25%, mostly men are affected. The lower lumbovertebral spinous processes are involved in 1.5% to 3% of all cases, mostly as spina occulta. The width of the gaps determines the stress resistance. Singular gaps with only a small cleft are of neither clinical nor biomechanical importance. Gaps 3 and 4 shown in Figure 2-10 cause problems in diagnostics [see Schmorl and Junghanns (1968) and Toendury (1958)].

The apophyses at the tips of the vertebral arch processes sometimes lead to differential diagnostic considerations. They are supposed to ossify with the processes by the time growth is completed, but they sometimes remain as persistent apophyses. This may create problems in radiodiagnostics with regard to sudden fractures or "break-offs" resulting from bone fatigue (see Chapter 8).

Bone bridges between transverse processes (also with interposed nearthrosis) in the lumbar spine are found only occasionally. They must be individually evaluated with regard to stress resistance, especially if they are connected with scolioses.

The lateral disruption of the vertebral arch, the interarticular gap (interarticularis spondylolysis) (Fig. 2-10) may have different shapes and may be located at different heights (see Fig. 4-29). It is the precondition for spondylolisthesis and appears irregularly. The detailed discussion of its many problems is in section 4.4.

4.2.4 Compounded Spinal Abnormalities

Compounded spinal abnormalities result from varied combinations of malformations. At times, they are complex and result in kyphoses, scolioses, and kyphoscolioses, often in connection with fusions of vertebrae and vertebral body and arch gaps. Many affect the dynamics of the axial skeleton so significantly that their individual stress resistance must be determined on a case-by-case basis. Regular follow-up examinations are required. The best known syndrome is Klippel-Feil syndrome in which the head

Fig. 4-4 Diagram of displacement of semisegments with scoliosis (hemimetameric segment displacement).

appears to be resting directly on the shoulders. Often, it is accompanied by neural syndromes.

Some congenital scolioses are caused by lateral or multiply alternating semivertebrae as they exist in the hemimetameric segment displacement (Fig. 4-4). Often, they are accompanied by vertebral arch gaps. Schlegel (1979) described the diagnostic characteristics of congenital malformations.

Bony fusions of vertebral bodies are mostly linked with the fusion of vertebral arch portions (vertebral block) (Fig. 4-5).

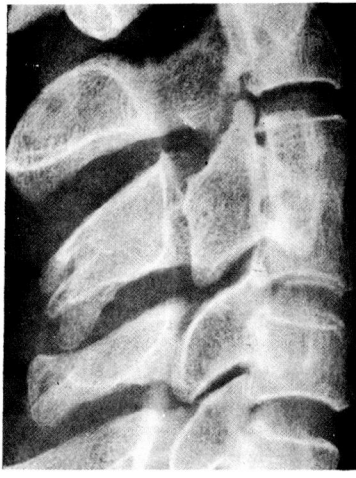 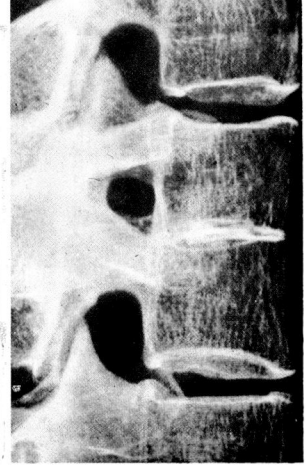

Fig. 4-5 Block vertebrae. **Left:** bony fusion of 3rd and 4th cervical vertebral body and fusion of their articular and spinous processes in a 45-year-old man; **right:** congenital block vertebrae block in a 56-year-old woman. Substantial narrowing of the intervertebral canal.

4.2.5 Narrowness of the Vertebral Canal and Intervertebral Canals

The shape and width of the vertebral canal and the recessus lateralis in the area of the lower lumbar vertebrae are genetically determined. Monoradicular sciatic symptoms may appear in the case of congenital narrowness of the recessus if the height of the intervertebral space decreases, often in conjunction with a slight retroposition of a vertebra (Krayenbuehl and Benini 1979). This results in a latent performance insufficiency, which causes perceptible symptoms of insufficiency, eg, during rotation. Occasionally, surgery becomes necessary (see Chapter 7).

During the past few years, there have been increased studies of these and other potentials of vertebral canal narrowness: for the cervical spine, see Caille (1970), Chahal et al. (1982), Grobovschek and Fischbach (1979), Harris (1977/1978), and Yamamoto et al. (1979) (ossification of posterior longitudinal ligament); for the lumbar spine, see Echeverria and Lockwood (1979), Rousseaux et al. (1979), Schroeder and Lackner (1980), and Varughese and Quartey (1979). Narrowness of the lumbar vertebral canal can be clearly portrayed with radiculography (Hawkes and Roberts 1980). Special radiculography and computer tomography (CT) may be helpful in diagnostics [Klumair and Fochem (1980), Lancourt et al. (1979), and Schubiger (1984)].

In addition to narrowness of the vertebral canal, narrowness of the intervertebral canals (intervertebral foramina) is important in many syndromes. Each intervertebral osteochondrosis, whether accompanied by displacement in the segment or not, results in a narrowed passage width of the paired intervertebral canals. There is pressure on nerves and blood vessels, which results in remote effects.

4.2.6 Significance of the Transitional Regions

The four transitional regions of the spine (head–cervical spine, cervical–thoracic spine, thoracic–lumbar spine, lumbar spine–sacrum) must fulfill important functions with regard to the dynamics of the central axial organ. These are most important at the two extremities of the spine.

Maigne (1984) provides an overview of impairment potentials (Table 4-1) and discusses developing dysfunctions and their consequences. Certain habitual postures activate problems in certain transitional regions. Maigne describes examination and chiropractic therapy procedures only briefly, but clearly.

The intervertebral motor segments in transitional sections suffer mostly from premature

Table 4-1 Syndromes of Transitional Regions

Cervico-Occipital Transition

Headaches[4]
  supraorbital
  occipital (distribution area of ramus auriculus nervi vagi)
  occipitomaxillar (these forms may also appear together)
Vertigo[1]
Hearing impairments[1]
Unconsciousness[1]
Depression tendency etc.[1]

Cervicothoracic Transition

Cervicalgia[3]
Cervicobrachial neuralgias[2]
Interscapulovertebral dorsalgias[4]
Tendinalgias of the shoulder[3]
Epicondylalgias[3]
Epitrochlealgias[1]
Acroparesthesia etc.[1]

Thoracolumbar Transition

Low lumbalgias with high point of origin[4]
Pseudovisceral pain[2]
Hemipubalgias[2]
Adductor pain[2]
Pseudoperiarthritis of the hip[2]

Lumbosacral Transition

Lumbalgias
  discal[4]
  originating from posterior articulations[3]
  ligamental[1]
Ischialgia[4]

Note: 1–4 indicate increasing frequency.

Data from Maigne

wear in the intervertebral discs and arthrosis of the corresponding articulations. Therefore, the frequency of arthrosis is high in transitional regions, and arthrosis occurs even in youth. Resulting mobility problems may lead to ankylosis, and localized and radiating pain frequently affect several intervertebral motor segments above or beneath the transitional region. The syndromes are varied, and segmental diagnostics are required. Often, reinforcing surgery is required.

Thus, substantial impairment factors may originate at the transitional sections and lead to decreased functional capacity. The head articulations and the lumbar spine–sacrum boundary are the most difficult transitional regions with regard to diagnostics and therapy. In the area of the five head articulations, arthroses often remain undiagnosed as the cause of symptoms. An exact diagnosis of this condition is possible only with radiological procedures.

The lumbar spine–sacrum boundary must bear substantial loads. This region simultaneously forms the boundary between the spine and pelvis and therefore has close links with the pelvic girdle: sacroiliac articulations, pubic symphysis (see sections 2.2 and 4.5).

Additional difficulties are caused by high load conditions of the lumbar spine–sacrum boundary. They occur when there is simultaneous spondylolysis/spondylolisthesis and pseudospondylolisthesis. Frequent wear of the presacral intervertebral disc with bony edge spikes and arthrosis of the vertebral arch articulations in this area augment the occurrence of difficulties for the aging patient. The axes for carrying the torso load and external loads increase the problems. In addition, frequent change in the position of the pelvic entrance level occurs. If additional arthrosis of the pelvic articulations exists, the load problems originating there also have unfavorable effects. The entire lumbar-pelvic-hip region (LPH) requires a diligent diagnostic analysis and coordinated therapy. A pelvic girdle relaxation caused by such conditions in the LPH section may also occur and is often overlooked, even though it may be an essential concomitant cause of difficulties. Chirodiagnostics and chirotherapy should be considered (see section 7.4).

4.2.7 Impairments of Functional Capacity through Variations and Malformations

Slight variations and malformations rarely cause perceptible impairments in youth but may in later years or when they are subject to special external strain. In youth, even substantial changes of the spine caused by variations or malformations are compensated for by strongly developed muscles and youthful, taut, ligament systems. Therefore, static as well as dynamic strains do not cause pain.

Special problems occur for the impaired spine by the frequent presence of intervertebral disc wear and/or arthroses in the vertebral arch articulations. In later life, arthrosis almost regularly forms also in the adjacent regions, above and beneath the changed sections of the spine. Similar reactions of adjacent regions often appear after surgical reinforcement, ie, anterior or posterior spondylodesis. In 1981, Goymann and Konermann reported on these problems.

4.3 MALFORMATIONS OF THE SPINE

4.3.1 Kyphosis

During the stage of the sitting position and at the time an infant starts to walk, the large curvature kyphosis of the spine of a newborn develops into the important kyphosis of the thoracic spine and the biomechanically less important kyphosis of the sacrum (Fig. 4-1B). The frequent, intensified thoracic kyphosis, which is caused by a decline in muscle strength and ligament relaxation, is called posture instability, or posture degeneration: "student kyphosis" of the growth period (section 7.2). However, such diagnoses should not be allowed to cover up a potentially serious disease: juvenile kyphosis. Each increase in the natural curvature of the thoracic spine requires clarification with regard to its stress resistance by the use of all diagnostic possibilities.

The causes of congenital kyphosis were discussed in section 4.2. Additional and often obvious kyphosis also forms following certain systemic diseases of the bones. These include hereditary constitutional diseases as well as age or nutrition-determined osteoporosis, osteomalacia, or osteodystrophy. If systemic diseases of the skeleton are found, the spine must always be considered in diagnostics. In the case of progressive—mostly painful—kyphosis, it is advisable to search for such diseases since stresses in daily life may worsen the condition.

Kyphosis after vertebral fractures and after osteomyelitis (eg, gibbus caused by tuberculosis) leads to the known problems of treatment, medical after-care, and future stress resistance.

4.3.2 Juvenile Kyphosis/Scheuermann's Disease

Juvenile kyphosis with its various intensities is without doubt the most frequent spinal disorder in adolescents and carries with it consequences that last until old age. There is radiological evidence of Scheuermann's disease in at least half of all adolescents, and 50 percent of those experience difficulties. Juvenile kyphosis ranges from slight damage of the vertebral body end plates to substantial malformations of the vertebral bodies, which mostly increase during growth and in many cases lead to the characteristic hunchback. The development is shown in Figure 4-6. Cover plates and rims of the vertebral bodies may be involved to different degrees. The cause of damage lies in the growth zones of the vertebral body–intervertebral disc boundary (Figs. 4-7, 4-8, and 4-9). In addition, these transition zones are not reinforced during the sometimes spurtlike, sometimes slower growth period, ie, until the 14th to 16th year of life, and are therefore unstable and susceptible to damage if they are subject to strain.

Another finding is remarkable: If growing vertebrae are affected by kyphosis, the distractional forces in the arch section are increased. This leads to a height increase of the arches and elongation of the articular processes. Thus, kyphosis is fixated, and the erection capacity is hindered (Heine 1981).

Christ and Dupuis (1968) diagnosed 51 percent of cases of serious juvenile kyphosis during the examinations of young farmers. With this frequency in mind, it is understandable that Gschwend (1965, 1972) determined a connec-

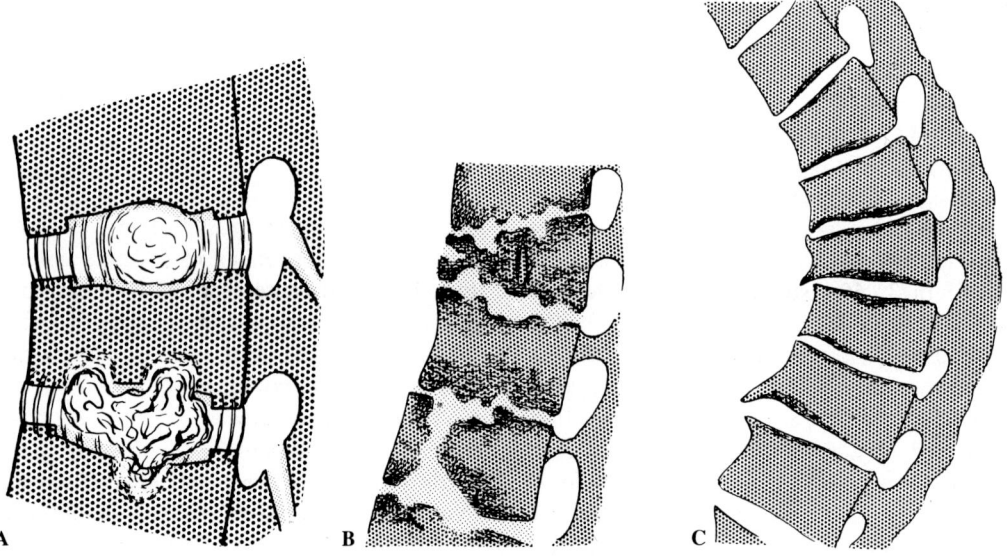

Fig. 4-6 Schematic drawing of the development of juvenile kyphosis. (**A**) initial damage at the vertebral body–intervertebral disc boundary; (**B**) drawing of a tomograph of a serious juvenile kyphosis; (**C**) drawing of a roentgenogram of Scheuermann's disease that has healed with complete stiffness.

Fig. 4-7 Section in the sagittal level of a thoracic vertebra portion (14-year-old) with distinct juvenile kyphosis. In the anterior intervertebral disc section, the vertebral body rims are still cartilaginous. Adjacent hyaline cartilage plates are unchanged up to the **arrows**. The cartilage plate sections further back are destroyed. The nucleus pulposus is greatly changed, with fissures distending upward and downward into the vertebral body end plates. Lamellae rings are impaired in their direction in the front.

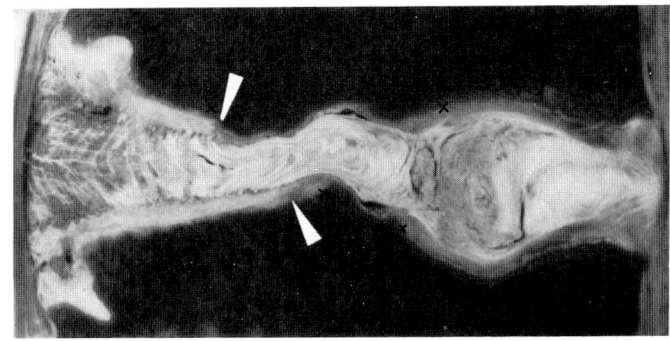

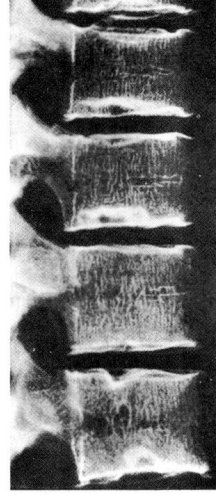

Fig. 4-8 Distention of the intervertebral discs in the area of the former cord penetration point: Schmorl's nodule in serial arrangement.

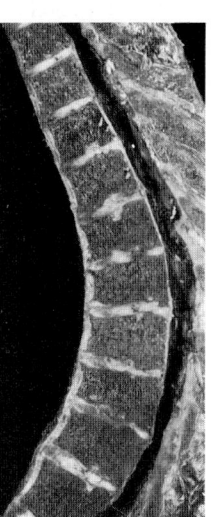

Fig. 4-9 Sagittal section through the thoracic spine of an 18-year-old with characteristic juvenile kyphosis. Intervertebral spaces have decreased height and there are irregular borders with adjacent vertebral bodies. There are several protrusions of intervertebral disc tissue into the vertebral bodies: Schmorl's nodules.

tion with juvenile kyphosis in 70% to 80% of all cases of chondrosis and osteochondrosis in older patients.

Ross (1962) conducted radiological studies of the spines of 5,000 healthy, complaint-free youths from age 15 to 22. Only 31.6% were normal. In 33.6%, slight damage existed; in 27.6%, intermediate damage; and in 7.2%, serious damage. In spite of the high number of test persons, the statistical validity is limited (the persons studied had already been selected as "complaint-free, healthy youths" who reported voluntarily for the medical fitness physical to join the police force). However, the findings of Ross do provide points of reference for the distribution pattern of frequent spinal damage. Several of the drawings in Figure 4-10 show the various conditions of juvenile kyphosis.

As already mentioned, about 50% of all juvenile spines show signs of juvenile kyphosis. In about half of these cases, distinct kyphosis is evident in the lower thoracic spine. Frequently, the characteristic symptoms also predominantly exist in the upper section of the lumbar spine (Fig. 4-11) and cause especially serious complaints. If the therapy is insufficient, kyphosis may worsen and result in load-bearing problems in later life.

Vertebral bodies that are indented at the cover or base plates, which may appear consecutively in adjacent vertebral bodies, form Schmorl's nodules (Figs. 4-8 and 4-9). They play a role in the development of juvenile kyphosis and are accompanied by developmental defects that belong in the group of enchondral dysostoses. A connection with the abortive forms of muco-

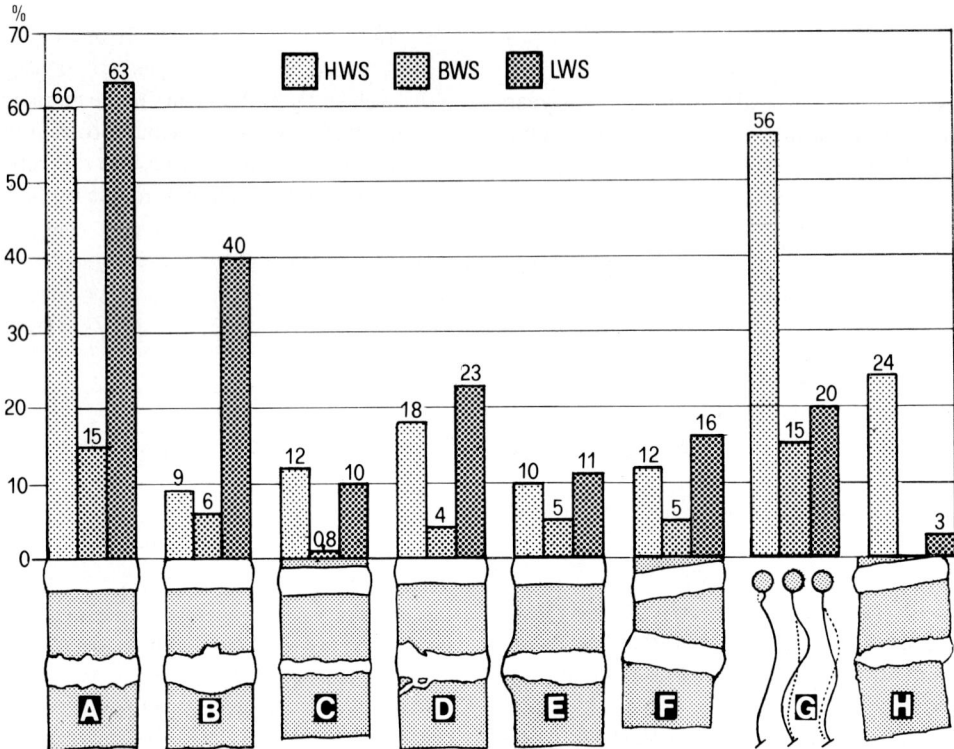

Fig. 4-10 Frequency of spinal roentgenogram findings of adolescents (Ross 1962). (**A**) irregular vertebral body end plates; (**B**) single Schmorl's nodule (**top**), indentation of the vertebral body end plates; (**C**) height decrease of the intervertebral disk; (**D**) irregularities of anterior vertebral body rims; (**E**) bony edge lips; (**F**) wedge-shaped vertebra; (**G**) kyphosis of the cervical spine, thoracic kyphosis with compensating lordosis, flat back; (**H**) vertebral displacement.

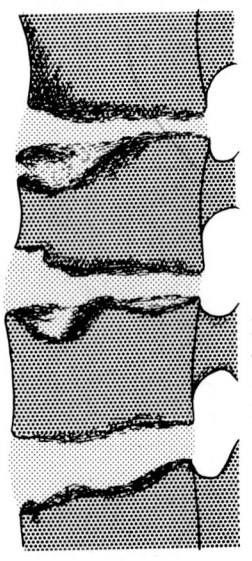

Fig. 4-11 Schematic drawing of spinal roentgenogram findings. If the juvenile kyphosis progresses into the lumbar spine, the damage is often serious. Protruding intervertebral tissue may result in a sequestering of the vertebral body rim.

polysaccharidoses is probable. Mau (1958, 1972) discussed damage of cartilage ossification in the vertebral body end plates with the involvement of intervertebral discs.

The damage described by Scheuermann appears on the cover and base plates of the growing vertebral body. They form primarily during the growth spurt in puberty (Aufdermaur 1976; Schmorl and Junghanns 1968). The pressure that is exerted on the anterior portions of the thoracic spine in all instances of load, particularly during curved sitting, additionally obstructs the impaired growth at the vertebral body–intervertebral disc boundary. Kyphosis of the thoracic spine is also increased through the shortening of the major pectoral muscle because the shoulder joint and shoulder blade are pulled forward. In this way, wedge-shaped vertebrae that are tapered at the front are established. The wedge-shaped vertebrae and the cover and base plates of the vertebral bodies, which maintain their irregular wavy shape after growth ceases, are the life-long signs of the disease. Medical experience justifies the assumption that endogenous influences are essentially responsible for the development of the associated hunchback. Nevertheless, exogenous strain is not negligible, especially with regard to urgently required prophylactic measures and therapy. According to Mitzkat (1980), physical exertion in later years reintroduces back problems if residues of juvenile kyphosis are present.

Since juvenile kyphosis may be of different intensities, the three to five stages of classification are usual; gradual transitions exist. The classification describes characteristic roentgenogram findings as follows:

- *stage 1:* isolated and slight irregularities at the vertebral body end plates
- *stage 2:* stronger irregularities (growth unrest) at the vertebral body end plates as are generally present at the beginning of Scheuermann's disease
- *stage 3:* classic picture of juvenile kyphosis with numerous Schmorl's nodules, decreased height of the intervertebral spaces, and wedge-shaped vertebrae in the affected area
- *stage 4:* final state of Scheuermann's disease with wavy but smooth vertebral body end plates, decreased height of the intervertebral spaces, and wedge-shaped vertebrae
- *stage 5:* most severe final state with round-curved kyphosis of the thoracic spine or low kyphosis at the boundary of the thoracic and lumbar spine and serious protrusions of intervertebral disc tissue into the vertebral bodies in the front and middle portions

The beginning of kyphosis may already be recognized in stages 1 and 2 by inspecting the back profile and becomes more and more obvious as it enters later stages (Fig. 4-12). Radiodiagnostics should be used even in the initial stages because they allow the observation of details that are important for the evaluation and progress of the disease and therefore also for therapy. The classification of border cases always creates a discretionary margin that creates problems, even for the expert. The Moire topography may be helpful for the long-term observation of kyphosis progression (Horst and Drerup 1980) (Fig. 4-13).

The often controversial pathological value of Scheuermann's disease was discussed by Richter et al. (1982). They showed that the ^{99m}TC scanning did not aid in the evaluation of Scheuermann's disease.

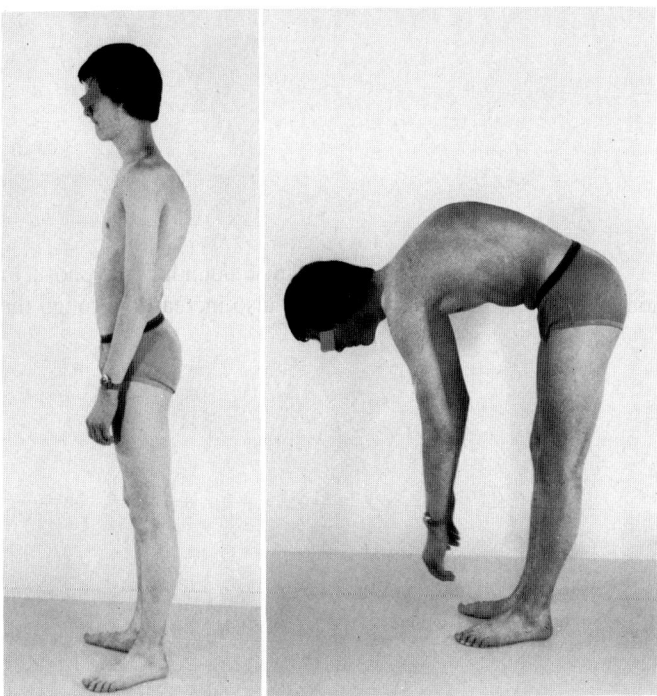

Fig. 4-12 Clinical finding of a 19-year-old patient with a serious thoracic Scheuermann's kyphosis. Note the increased kyphosis of the middle and lower thoracic spine and the extended position of the lumbar spine in the forward trunk bend [from Goetze et al. 1980]

88 CLINICAL IMPLICATIONS OF NORMAL BIOMECHANICAL STRESSES ON SPINAL FUNCTION

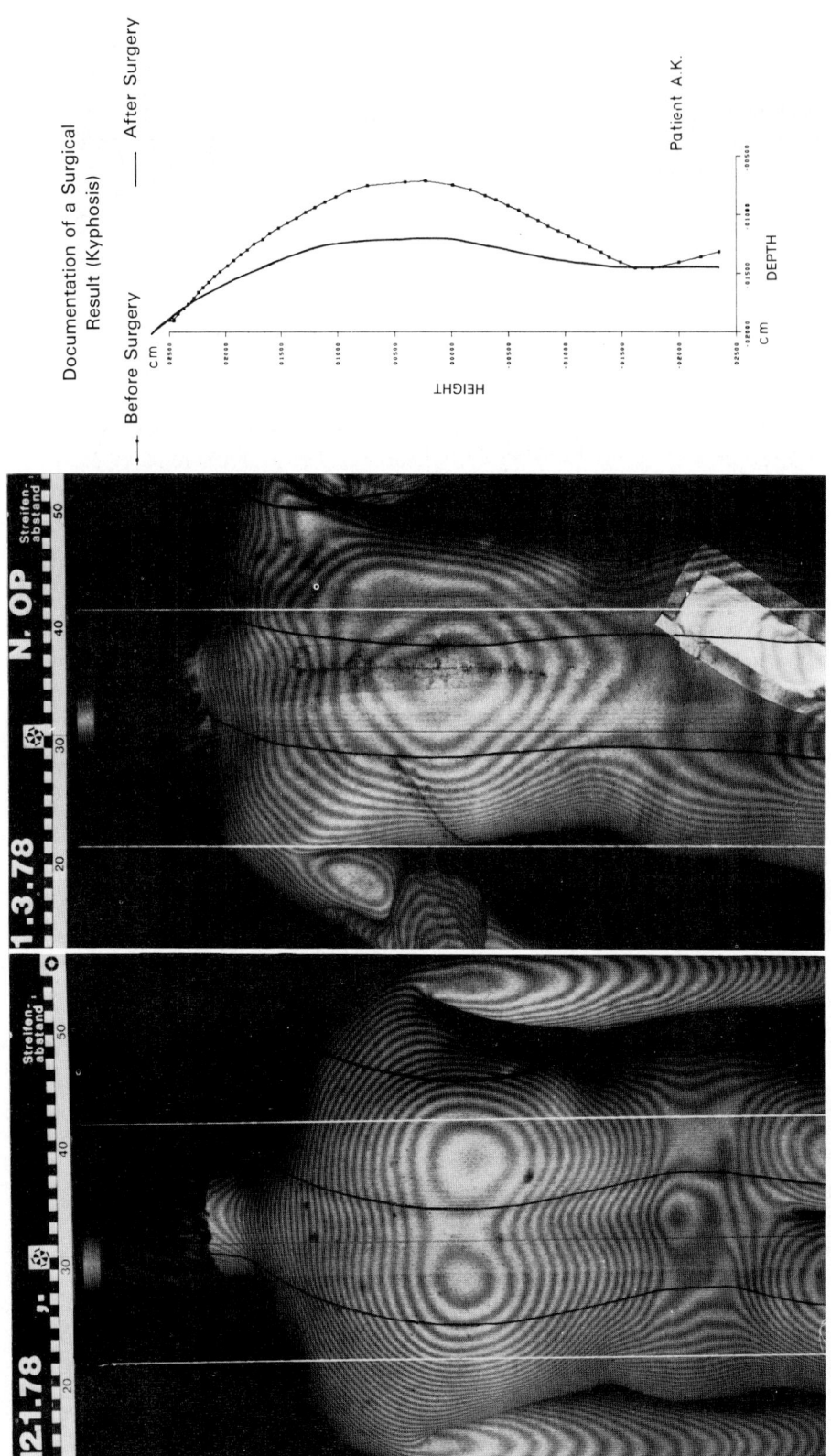

Fig. 4-13 Documentation of erection surgery for juvenile kyphosis. **Left:** Moire topogram before surgery and after surgery; **right:** comparison of sagittal middle profile [from Drerup 1980].

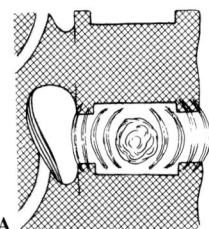 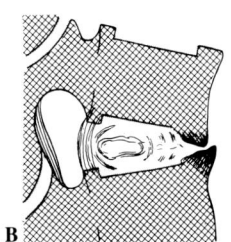 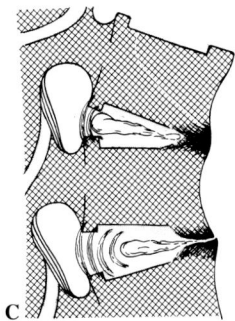

Fig. 4-14 Schematic drawing of the gradual development of senile kyphosis. After degeneration of the anterior portions of the epiphyseal fiber ring, the height of the anterior portions of the intervertebral space decreases; then, there is pressure and friction on the anterior edges of the adjacent vertebral bodies, including sclerosing (**A**, **B**) and finally ossification (**C**).

Many texts discuss the topic of treatment, for example, Matthiass (1980) and Rathke (1980). Edelmann, Groeneveld, Henssge, Weiss, Zapfe, et al. report on conservative therapy in *The Spinal Column in Research and Practice* (1980). Heine et al. (1981) acquired statistical documentation on the prognosis of Scheuermann's disease. Additional literature includes Krahl et al. (1980); Niethard and Gaertner (1980); Puhl et al. (1980) (radiology); Rathke (1980); and Steinbrueck et al. (1980) (fitness for sports).

4.3.3 Senile Kyphosis

A specific change of the intervertebral disc in the spine of aging persons was first differentiated by Junghanns in 1932 from other forms of kyphosis. This change of the intervertebral disc results in a senile kyphosis: kyphosis senilis. Its gradual development is shown in Figure 4-14. In contrast to juvenile kyphosis where the curvature vertex sits in the lower portion of the thoracic spine and often even at the lumbar spine, the center of the hump in senile kyphosis is in the upper to middle portion of the thoracic spine. Because of the declining erection power of the muscles, permanent pressure rests on the anterior portions of the intervertebral discs. This, in connection with simultaneous age-determined nutrition impairment, causes tissue necroses. The intervertebral space loses height in the front. The direct pressure on the anterior por-

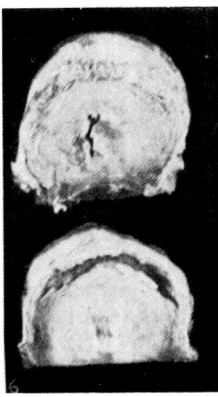

Fig. 4-15 Photographs of horizontally sectioned intervertebral discs showing precursors of senile kyphosis in two older persons. **Top:** the development of fissures in the nucleus pulposus and brittle necrosis of the anterior portion of the fiber ring; **bottom:** a somewhat irregularly limited, gaping, sickle-shaped fissure in the anterior of the fiber ring, along the posterior edge of the rim. The bony end plate of the adjacent vertebral body is visible in the depth of the fissure.

tions of the vertebral bodies results in a consolidation of bones. Finally, a compact, bony link forms in the anterior section. The process advances from top to bottom. Details concerning the progression are shown in Figures 4-15 through 4-19.

The result of the decade-long painful development is arched, often substantial kyphosis (Fig. 4-20). During the initial phase, pain appears but recedes again during the ossification. Nevertheless, the great curvature of senile kyphosis is perceived as very unpleasant, since

90 CLINICAL IMPLICATIONS OF NORMAL BIOMECHANICAL STRESSES ON SPINAL FUNCTION

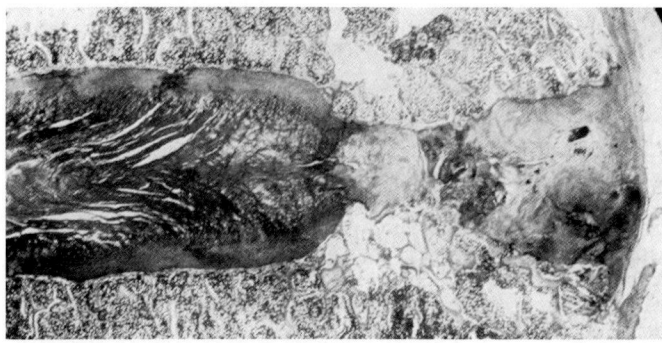

Fig. 4-16 Photomicrograph of a sagittal section through an intervertebral disc. Anterior half shows beginning senile kyphosis. Note the ingrowth of blood vessels, fibrous tissue, and spongy bone into the intervertebral disc at the posterior edge of the bony rim.

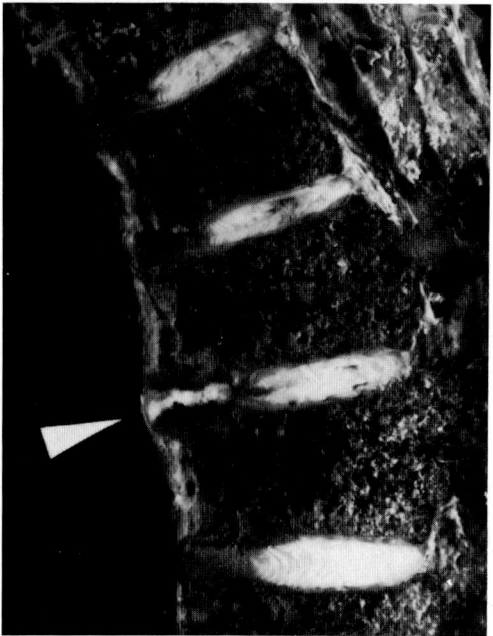

Fig. 4-17 Photograph of a sagittal section of the thoracic spine of an 85-year-old woman. Moderate senile kyphosis. Intervertebral discs are decreased in height; the anterior sections are ossified. One intervertebral disc (**arrow**) has undergone fibrous transformation in the front.

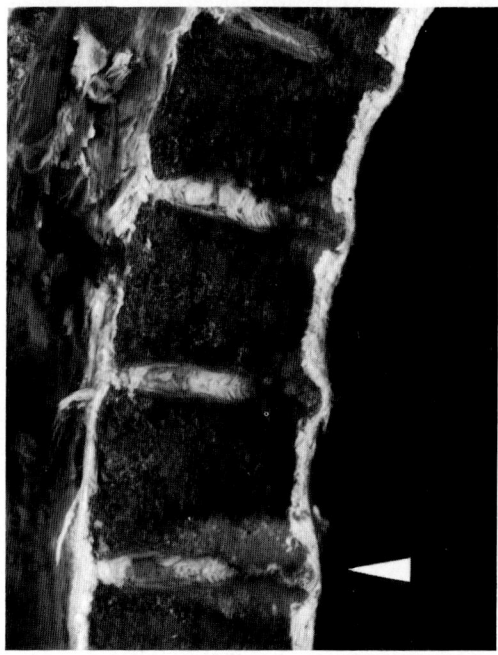

Fig. 4-18 Sagittal section of the thoracic spine of a 74-year-old man. Senile kyphosis with typical characteristics: low intervertebral discs that have already ossified (**upper part of picture**). At the **arrow**, active destruction of the anterior intervertebral disc section with a wide, surrounding ossification area upward and downward.

the eyes are forced to look on the ground. Often, senile kyphosis appears in combination with osteoporosis and sintered osteoporotic vertebral bodies (Fig. 4-21). This results in a further increase of the curvature. Even though treatment cannot restore mobility, warming and massage of the long back muscles; the lumbar, rump and leg muscles; and the neck-shoulder-arm muscles can slow the progression of the stooped posture to a certain extent.

4.3.4 Scolioses

Scolioses are abnormalities of the spine that originate mostly during the growth period. Noeh and Behnecke (1975) found scolioses in one third of students examined ranging in age from 10 to 12 years.

Frequent causes of lumbar scolioses are a scoliotic pelvis (18.8%), abnormalities at the lumbosacral boundary (33%), and asymmetries

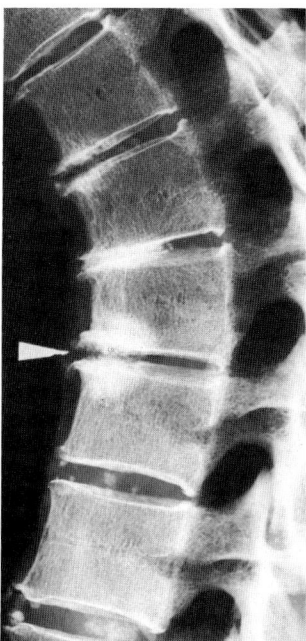

Fig. 4-19 Lateral roentgenogram of the thoracic spine sectioned in half in the sagittal plane of a 63-year-old woman. Senile kyphosis developing. Low, anterior intervertebral disc sections with sclerosis of the adjacent spongiosa. Ingrowth of bone tissue. Small spurs on the edge. At the **arrow**, especially wide ossification phases. These will soon disappear after the ossification from vertebra to vertebra is complete.

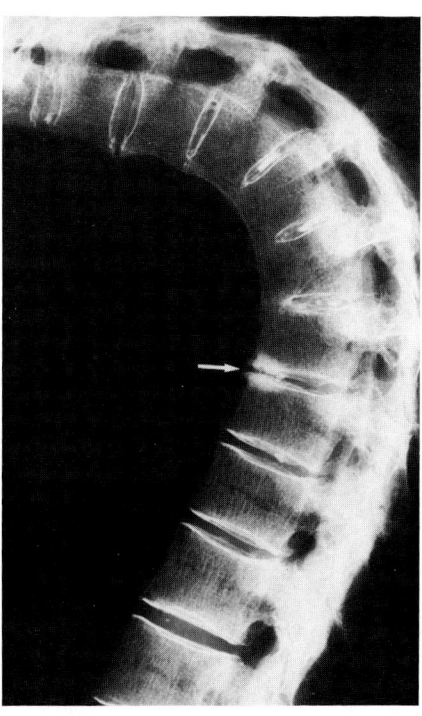

Fig. 4-20 Lateral roentgenogram of the thoracic spine of a 67-year-old woman, sectioned in the sagittal plane. Ankylosed, severe senile kyphosis. Four intervertebral discs are spongy on the anterior sections; the preserved middle and posterior sections contain several small calcium deposits. The next lower intervertebral disc is low in the front with ingrown bone tissue and compression of the adjacent spongiosa (**arrow**). Small edge spurs on the adjacent vertebral bodies; spurs have already disintegrated at the higher (ossified and stiffened) intervertebral discs.

in L-5/S-1 (18.8%). In all scolioses, countercurvatures are required in order to maintain statis. The well-known *S*-shape of scoliosis occurs. Depending on the degree of the main curvature and the additional countercurvatures, scolioses result in difficulties in motion and stress resistance. With progressive age, "supporting" bone spurs of various sizes form at the interior side of the curvature (Figs. 4-22 and 4-24). They stabilize, relieve pain, and thus improve the stress resistance of the central axial organ. In the main curvature of severe rotation scolioses, an especially distinct torsion vertebra appears (Fig. 4-23). This may result in a lateral slippage (rotational sliding) (Fig. 4-24). The connection of kyphoses and kyphoscolioses with consequences affecting the cardiovascular system and respiration are determined by the stress resistance of the individual person.

In order to facilitate evaluation, classifications have been introduced that distinguish the degrees of severity. The classification by Jentschura (1977) follows:

- *first degree:* low grade, but fixated, curvature with slight torsion; partial active and passive correction possible
- *second degree:* distinct *S*-shaped or *C*-shaped scoliosis; individual curvatures are developed from light to intermediate and compensate each other; clear signs of torsion
- *third degree:* serious curvature affecting the entire spine; serious rib hump and lumbar bulging; unilateral projection, considerable deformation of the rib cage
- *fourth degree:* extreme scoliosis; obvious diminution of trunk; thorax rests on pelvis; ribs project into pelvis

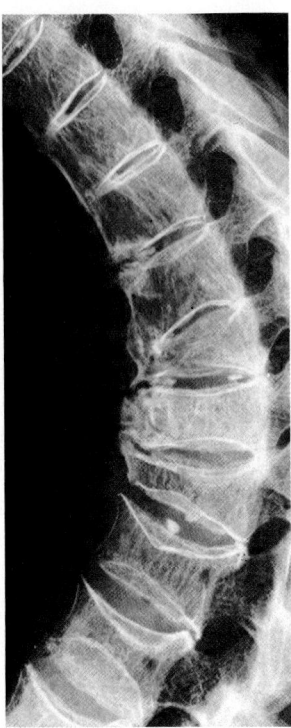

Fig. 4-21 Lateral roentgenogram of the thoracic spine of an 83-year-old woman, sectioned in the sagittal plane. Combination of senile and osteoporotic kyphosis. Typical senile kyphosis in the top with ossification of intervertebral discs in the front. Wedge-shaped vertebral collapses and beginning fish vertebrae due to osteoporosis at the bottom.

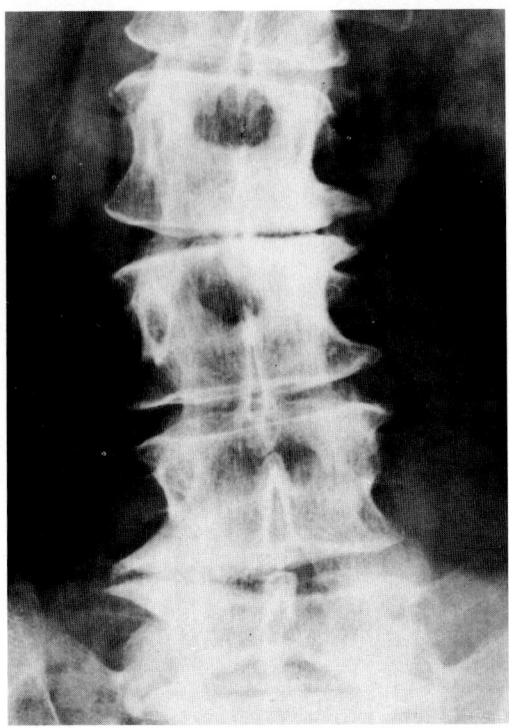

Fig. 4-22 Lumbar scoliosis, 66-year-old woman. Various-sized edge spurs, always at the inner side of the curvature. Special load centers are the interiors of the curvatures at L2-3 and L4-5.

Mau (1982) presented details of the various causes of scoliotic curvature. The synoptic chart contains seven groups of symptomatic scolioses with a total of 40 individual forms and an additional 5 variants of idiopathic scolioses. The differences in classifications by various investigators illustrate the difficulty of classifying scolioses.

In addition to growth-determined "idiopathic" scolioses, scolioses that cause increasing pain with progressive age and that appear because of variants or malformations mostly at the lumbosacral boundary and in combination with intervertebral osteochondrosis play an important role. Posture scolioses must be distinguished from structural scolioses. Persons so affected require expert prophylactic therapy, eg, frequently repeated muscle-strengthening exercises. By successful therapy, behavioral changes in terms of protecting the spine are unnecessary. This is also true for occupational retraining. However, athletic activities of a person with scoliosis should be regularly supervised by a physician (see section 8.8).

Figure 4-25 is a characteristic photograph of views of scoliosis in different body postures. Many anatomic and clinical museums exhibit scoliotic trunk skeletons (see Fig. 4-26).

The measuring of scoliotic curvatures has been described in the literature, taught in text books, and conducted in many ways. The procedure described by Cobb (1948) is preferred, especially for presurgical measuring and postsurgical success controls (Fig. 4-27).

In 1975, Scheier introduced an overview of the etiological aspects provided by Cobb (1948) for the classification of scolioses: osteochondropathic, neuropathic, myopathic, fibropathic, and idiopathic. Scheier considered the

Factors Interfering with Functional Capacity 93

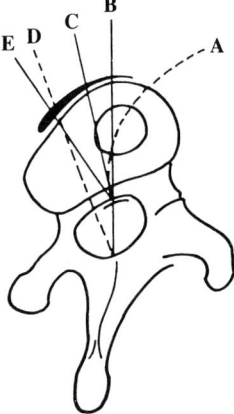

Fig. 4-23 Torsion vertebra in scoliosis with location of original sagittal plane according to different investigators. (**A**) Riedinger; (**B**) Engel (1981); (**C**) Albert (1899); (**D**) Nicoladoni; (**E**) Albert (1890).

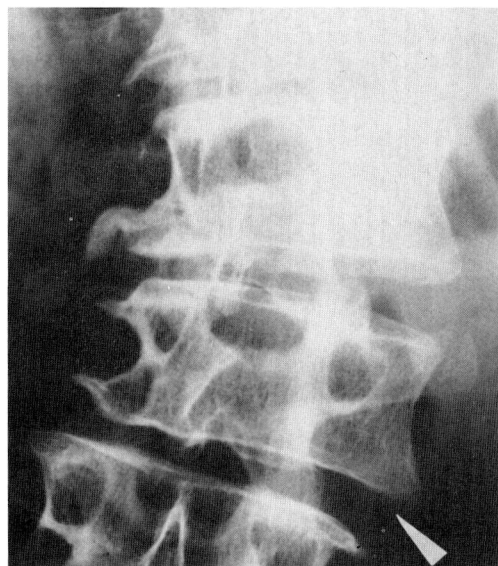

Fig. 4-24 Lumbar scoliosis with vertebral body spurs at the interior of the curvature. Additional torsion displacement at L3-4 (**arrow**).

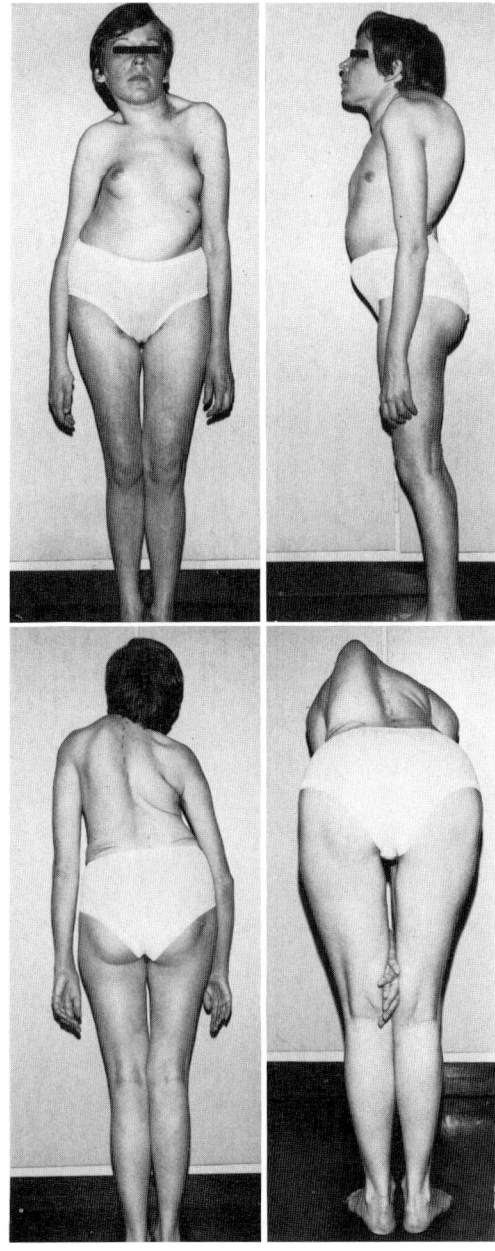

Fig. 4-25 Severe thoracic and lumbar idiopathic scoliosis in a 31-year-old woman from the front, side, standing from the back and bending over [from Schulze (1981)].

category of idiopathic scoliosis to be questionable. Harrington (1977) also held several factors in addition to genetic disposition responsible for the development of idiopathic scoliosis: nutrition and hormonal and mechanical influences.

Moire topography (Fig. 4-28) has been used to portray and document scoliosis [Drerup et al. (1983) and Willner (1979); see also Chapter 6].

Additional discussions are by Banzer et al. (1980) (measuring of rotation angle in computer tomogram); Dick (1980) (surgical treatment); Gueth and Abbink (1980) (electromyography); Mau (1982) (etiopathogenesis); and Zielke (1982) (surgery of scoliosis).

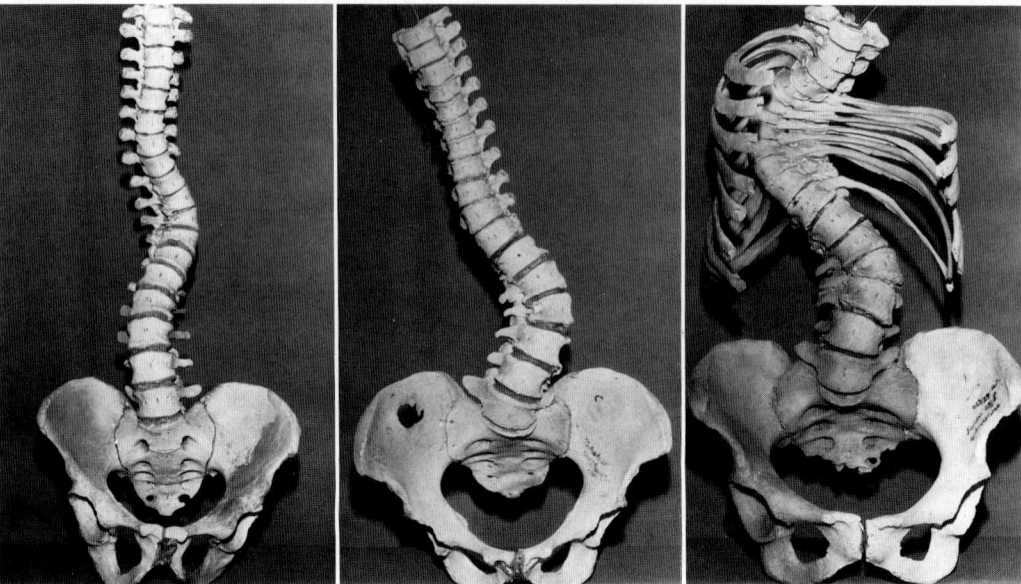

Fig. 4-26 Scolioses of the spine (collection of Schmorl in Dresden). These various scoliotic forms all have the distinct wedge-shaped vertebral body in the center of the inner curvature side. The far right picture shows a seriously deformed rib cage.

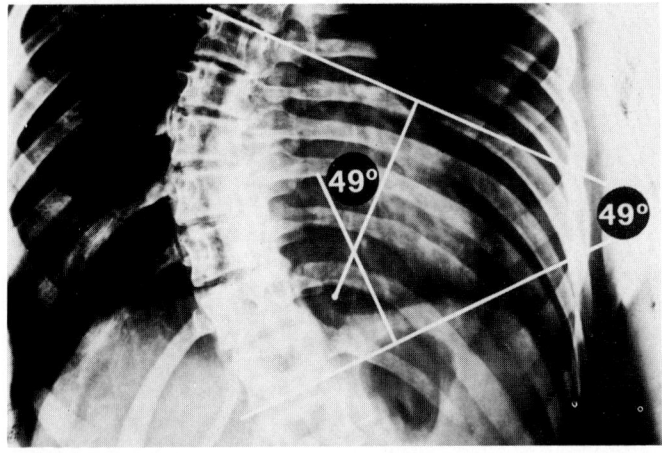

Fig. 4-27 Measuring of the scoliosis angle (Cobb 1948).

4.3.5 Lordosis: Straightening and Extension

Except for the usual lordoses in the cervical and lumbar region that serve, in connection with thoracic kyphosis, to maintain the static compensation of the *S* shape of the central axial organ, lordoses caused by pathomorphological changes of the skeleton or intervertebral discs are found only rarely. It does appear in the context of some malformations. The lordosis most often caused by pathological changes is the compensational lordosis (Fig. 6-2), which exists in combination with increased thoracic kyphosis in the large-curvature juvenile kyphosis or after vertebral body fractures heal in wedge shapes. The compensational lordosis helps reestablish the perpendicular axis or upright head position with a horizontal view.

In the case of flexed kyphosis, strong compensational lordosis often occurs, as seen in tuberculosis of the spine. If lordosis forms during the growth period, compensating height increases in

Factors Interfering with Functional Capacity 95

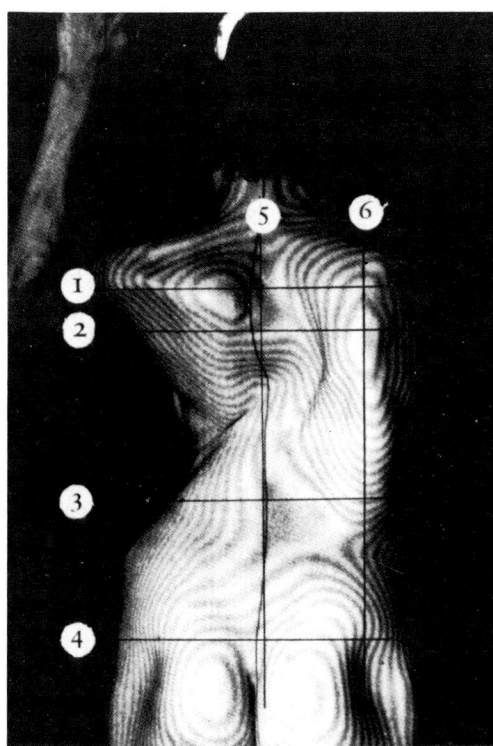

Fig. 4-28 Moire photograph of scoliosis (see Chapter 6).

the lumbar vertebral bodies occur: vertebrae elongatae. Bilateral hip luxations, pendant abdomen, and hip stiffness almost regularly cause compensational lordoses. The often obvious posture lordosis that results from wearing very high heels is well known. Pain may occur.

An accompanying symptom of substantially curved lordosis is the contact of the spinous processes in the vertex with the formation of nearthroses that show spurs and scleroses. This is frequently observed at the lumbar spine but rarely at the cervical spine (Baastrup's syndrome; see Fig. 4-60).

The usual spinal curvatures in the sagittal plane may not only curve further but may also straighten. This may affect one isolated portion of the spine, but in most cases the straightening of one section results in compensating adjacent countercurvatures. Many of these straightenings are fixated (extension stiffness), may be discovered during the physical examination, and can be portrayed radiologically. However,

sometimes they simply reflect incorrect postures (straight posture) that may be compensated for.

A permanently fixated extension of normal kyphosis in the thoracic area may be observed when two vertebral fractures far from each other or two foci of infection are present. Lumbar and cervical lordoses also extend between two vertebral foci or vertebral fractures.

Very frequently, an extension over a larger area exists in the lordotic as well as kyphotic spinal sections above an unstable intervertebral motor segment. An extension of the superior spinal column sections also exists when a vertebral body displacement toward the posterior occurs (retrolisthesis). During forward vertebral sliding (spondylolisthesis), a tilted pelvis combines with a displacement stage between the spinous processes and a flattening of the lumbar lordosis above.

The frequent lumbar extension stiffness (often combined with hip stiffness) also belongs in this group. It is found in the presence of caudal tumors, inflammations, and arthrosis of the vertebral arch articulations but may also be caused by other reasons. An extension posture almost always appears after laminectomy and is controlled by the muscles. At the cervical spine, vertebral blocks, but more frequently intervertebral disc damage and/or uncovertebral arthrosis, are the causes of a steep extension that may transform into kyphosis.

Especially at the lumbar spine, the flattened lordosis is an important clue in searching for the cause, and serious damage is often found. Extension stiffness of normal spinal curvatures are accompanied by pain and hinder stress resistance.

The angles at the lumbosacral boundary may be substantially changed by lumbar stiffness but may also influence lumbar lordosis through damage in the region (eg, osteochondroses).

4.3.6 Stress Resistance of Faulty Curvatures

The stress resistance of kyphoses depends on the cause (healing of a primary disease, eg, tuberculosis) and on the clarification of the present developmental tendency (progression or final). Documentation of the progress, including measurements of the curvature (section 6.3) must be recorded. Radiodiagnostics should be repeated intermittently. As long as the curvature progresses, any overexertion should be avoided, physical therapy should be performed, forward bending during sitting in school and leisure should be avoided, if possible, and an inclined writing surface should always be used.

In the final stages of kyphoses, the bone does not play a significant role. The same is true for pain as long as there is no occurrence of infection. The causes of a sudden or repeated occurrence of pain after exertion must be investigated. The stress resistance of a curved spine may be impaired by pain if damage at the intervertebral motor segment appears or if existing damage becomes perceptible. The pain may be connected with intervertebral disc damage (intervertebral chondrosis, intervertebral osteochondrosis) or may originate from arthrosis deformans developing in the overexerted vertebral arch articulations. Specific physical and radiographic examinations are helpful in clarifying these symptoms. A multitude of symptoms are activated by muscles stressed unphysiologically. Therapy must focus on this.

In spite of lowered mobility, it may be possible to load serious kyphoses and flexions (gibbus) extensively if they originated in youth—even if they resulted from trauma or infection—for several decades. Because of the decreasing force of compensating muscles, their stress resistance, however, decreases in later years. Therefore a job with little physical exertion and alternating walking, standing, and sitting is recommended. Long sitting should be avoided on a daily basis and in leisure.

Juvenile kyphosis (Scheuermann's disease) is particularly interesting with regard to stress resistance. In serious cases, the requirement for medical supervision and therapy may stretch over decades. Questions of stress resistance will repeatedly appear. Since the progress is uncertain when the first symptoms appear, the physician should observe the condition regularly. During this time, stresses, including vibrations, may constitute worsening factors.

Slight indications of the disease, such as small irregularities of individual vertebral bodies and singular Schmorl's nodules, always require the attention of a physician. Temporary abstinence from sports is recommended to prevent aggravation. Simultaneously, specific physiotherapy and muscle training are required, during the course of which all exercises with forward bending must be avoided. Upright sitting at the school desk must be constantly supervised (see Chapter 7). If a youth with distinct signs of juvenile kyphosis wants to become seriously involved in sports, the condition of the spine must be examined with regard to stress resistance.

Ross (1962) published a sequence of instances of minimal to serious damage that was found in roentgenograms of young applicants for police training (Fig. 4-10). Some of the findings, which he classified into eight categories (usually only five are mentioned), are only "suggestions" of the syndrome. Minimal damage to a spine (often in spinal sections that are far apart) may result in an increased pathological risk. Whether this constitutes unfitness for certain types of stress (sitting, prolonged posture, etc.) needs to be determined by collecting the verified results of long-term studies, including comparisons between roentgenograms and physical findings.

Juvenile kyphosis plays an important role in certain jobs or sports because of its frequency and the deterioration potential posed by stress. [Details may be found in *The Spinal Column in Occupational Medicine* by Junghanns (1979).]

Results of functional treatment of juvenile kyphosis lead Henssge (1976) to the conclusion that a functional examination should also be considered with regard to occupational activity. Even though abstinence from continued hard labor is necessary, light and intermediate work may be performed while standing or sitting as long as it is not connected with prolonged forced postures of the spine. According to Henssge, the restrictions required in normal occupational activity in the case of juvenile kyphosis are small. He considers individual findings at the vertebral body rims (eg, Schmorl's nodule) to be insignificant. The evaluation of the performance potential is determined by the extent of the contracture and its effects on the adjacent spinal sections. These conclusions may also be extended to daily life as well as to sports and leisure.

In any case, Scheuermann's disease may be greatly aggravated by stressful vibrations. Prior to participation in exercise and sports, the person with Scheuermann's disease must be tested with regard to stress resistance (see Chapter 8). Investigators dealing with the prognosis of juvenile kyphosis arrive justifiably at the following warnings and suggestions: Activities that involve heavy lifting and carrying, prolonged bent posture, or permanent lack of motion should be avoided. In order to avoid progressive damage, suitable, medically supervised physiotherapy should be implemented that has the objective of counteracting detrimental influences from a job and personal life style with the help of compensating motions and strengthening of the spine–muscle corset. Additional information may be found in Reinhold and Tillmann (1968), Rompe (1965), Scheier and Saner (1970), and Schmitt (1975).

Exertion with senile kyphosis depends on the momentary condition and therefore requires medical counsel. The typical damage in the anterior portions of the intervertebral discs (Figs. 4-14 through 4-20) such as the increasing curvature in the vertex of thoracic kyphosis, also progresses slowly. The cause of the present pain is often recognized only after the curvature has become obvious. However, the condition may have started in the fifth decade of life and therefore before retirement age. The progress of the disease and especially the pain—which stems partially from an accompanying senile osteoporosis—require abstinence from stresses that may cause pain. This may possibly lead to premature retirement. A therapy for strengthening the back and neck muscles and the avoidance of forward bending during treatment and while sitting are recommended.

Even though the stress resistance for intermediate physical exertion exists without substantial complaints until the middle or end of the fourth decade of life, even for more serious scoliosis developed during adolescence, complaints may occur in later decades. Therefore, the most advantageous situation on the job or in daily life is alternating walking, standing, and sitting. In addition, ongoing physiotherapy is suggested in order to avoid damage caused by overexertion in the intervertebral motor segments, in the muscles, and of the cardiovascular system. Also of decisive significance is the choice of the work place. Goetze and Rompe (1977) gave recommendations for expert evaluation of persons with scoliosis.

Special attention must be paid to rotational scoliosis with torsion displacement in the vertex of the lateral curvature. The accompanying insufficiency of the stabilizing functions of the intervertebral disc tissue relaxes the intervertebral motor segment and thus substantially impairs the stress resistance until a fixation occurs by way of ossification in the intervertebral space or by bridging spurs.

The simultaneous presence of transitional vertebrae at the lumbosacral boundary constitutes an additional stress limit for scoliosis since osteochondrotic damage in the upper/lower adjacent intervertebral spaces results almost regularly in later years. Pain susceptibility results in the event of pseudoarthrotic additional articulations (nearthroses), which are frequently interposed between the ala of the sacrum and the widened transverse process of the transitional vertebra (Figs. 4-1 and 4-2). They are joined by accompanying arthroses in the strongly stressed vertebral arch articulations. These pain-activating conditions prohibit hard physical exertion or prolonged forced posture of the spine. Postural scolioses (4.4.4) require systematic therapy aimed at strengthening muscles. As far as permanent exertions of the spine are necessary in daily life and/or on the job, regular checkups are necessary. Even more important is treatment during the school years (Heipertz and Turnen 1976). At this age, a surgical erection should be considered for suitable cases in order to achieve better stress resistance in the future (see Chapter 7).

Persons with the less frequent traumatic scolioses or those resulting from infections may in spite of their motion impairment be able to resist stress for several decades if the scolioses originated in youth. Because of the decreasing strength of the compensating muscles, however, their stress resistance decreases in later years.

So far, it has not been shown that a healthy spine can develop scoliosis because of permanent mechanical influences. In contrast, an increase in the curvature frequently occurs during the adolescent growth period in scolioses caused by endogenous factors (if mechanically stressful exogenous factors coexist). To avoid the possibility of such aggravations, regular school physicals are suggested. Therapy introduced in time may relieve symptoms and in many cases circumvent aggravation if the patient stays with the therapy over a sufficiently long period.

The differentiation between endogenous, previously existing damage and exogenous influences (from a job or life style) is difficult and must be based on a verified diagnosis and in consideration of a diligently analyzed stress requirement in daily life or on the job. The suggestions for the diagnosis of scolioses by Goetze and Rompe (1977) are helpful in this context.

The stress resistance of lordoses, extension postures, and extensions depends less on the changed shape of the spine and more on the specific cause. Varied causes for erections and extensions are described in section 4.3. If the cause can be eliminated, mobility and stress resistance may be reestablished. Preparatory auxiliary measures in this context consist of systematic muscle training.

The extension posture above an osteochondrosis that is especially painful when subjected to stress may improve if the instability of the intervertebral motor segment gradually turns into fibrous/bony ankylosis or after an intercorporal spondylodesis. However, the extent of mobility and the stress potential increase only after training and strengthening of the muscles.

The establishment of an improved or complete stress resistance depends very much on the therapy and individualized after-care by the physician and the willpower of the patient.

4.4 VERTEBRAL SLIPPAGE AND VERTEBRAL DISPLACEMENT

4.4.1 Vertebral Slippage

The paired interarticular portions are the important locations of stability for the vertebral arch. Spondylolysis, a gap in the interarticular portion of the vertebral arch, is the precursor of the most frequent form of vertebral slippage (spondylolisthesis). Its location is shown in Figure 2-10. Some of the varied forms of gaps are shown in Figure 4-29. Additional forms are shown in the roentgenograms in Figure 4-30.

The frequency of spondylolysis/spondylolisthesis varies between 2% and 27% according to population group, race, and probably various sitting and squatting habits. For whites, the average is 5% to 7%; for Bantus, 9%; for Japanese, 10%, and for Eskimos, 27%. Eisenstein (1978) reported on approximately 485 skeletons of adolescents, both from whites and blacks from South Africa. Both groups had an average incidence of gaps in the pars interarticularis of 3.5%. The average incidence of simultaneous spina bifida was 1.9%, but 11.8% for skeletons with spondylolyses. Similar numbers were reported earlier (Junghanns 1929, 1930, 1931).

Several investigators calculated the incidence according to gender at 50:50. Others reported the

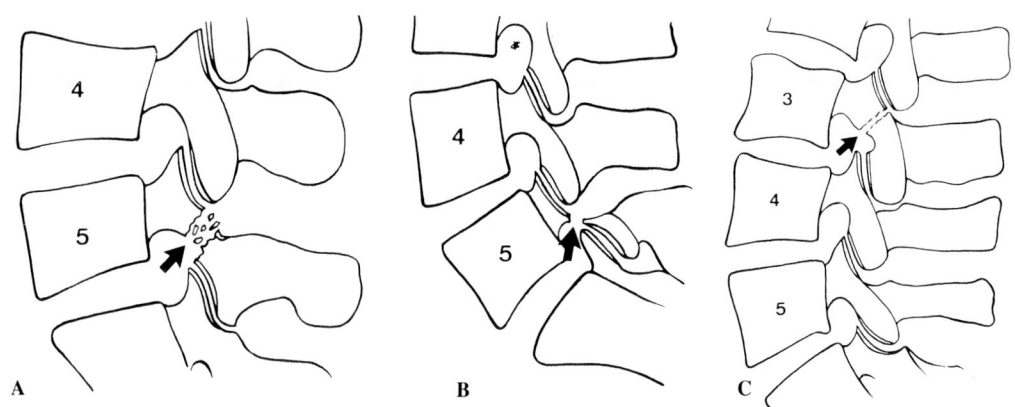

Fig. 4-29 Different types of gaps in the interarticular portion (spondylolysis) in the 5th (**A, B**) and 3rd (**C**) lumbar vertebral arch.

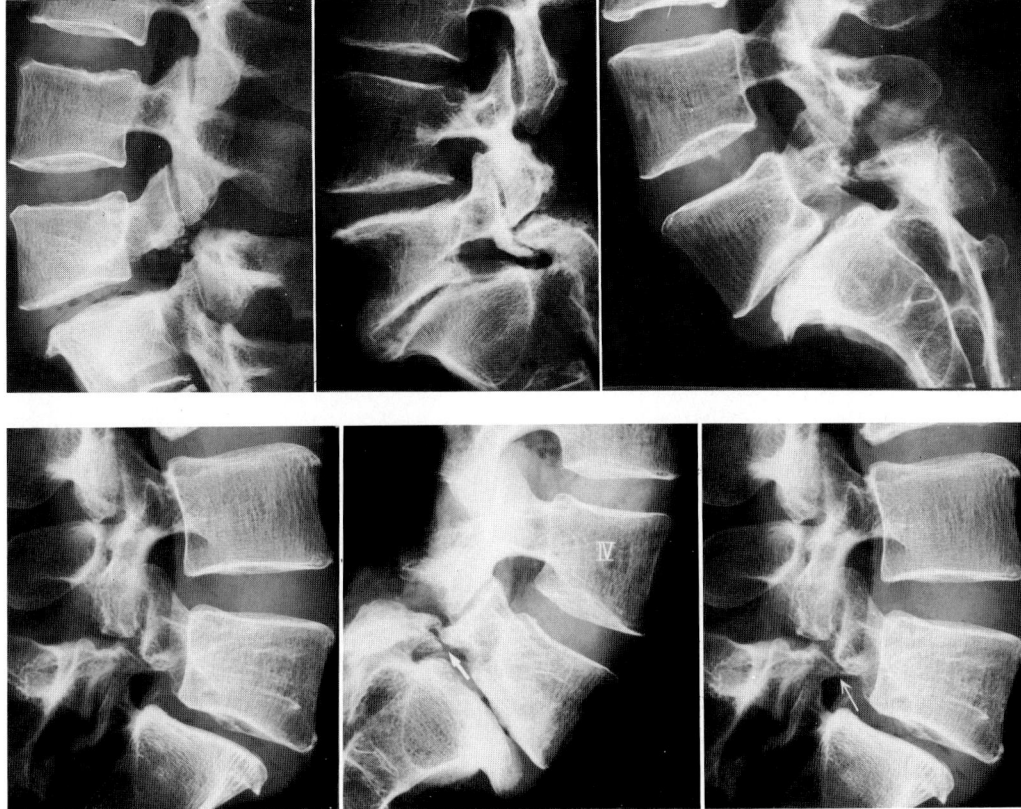

Fig. 4-30 Roentgenograms of unmacerated vertebral column halves of deceased men and women (56 to 84 years old), gained by sagittal section (Pathological Institute, Dresden, 1928–1930). Spondylolysis in L-5 of different forms as well as vertebral slippage with large or small consolelike bone projections at the anterior edge of the left sacral vertebra.

---

ratio as one third for women and two thirds for men. This was attributed to higher physical stresses for men. One half to two thirds of the gaps are combined with olisthesis.

If a vertebral slippage is induced by bilateral gaps in the interarticular portion or by "dysplastic" reduction of bone stability or fragmental zones, then the posterior portion of the arch, including both inferior articular processes, the vertebral arch plates, and the spinous process, remains at the original location. The slipping vertebra slides forward together with both arch roots, the superior articular processes, and both transverse processes and with the entire spine lying above. The intervertebral disc of the slipping level degenerates gradually and loses height. Bone spurs may form in the front. Often a stress-absorbing, consolelike projection appears at the sacrum. Unilateral lyses result in a forward slippage with moderate rotation. Spondylolistheses may also result in vascular disorders (Wegener et al. 1980).

The preferred location of spondylolysis is the last presacral vertebra: in two thirds or more of observed cases. The next most frequent is the 4th lumbar vertebra, with 15% to 30%. Combinations of several slipped vertebrae occur in the lumbar spine, as does complete slippage into the pelvis (spondyloptosis).

Numerous investigators have reported on the presence of slipped vertebrae in different sections of the spine, eg, Junghanns (1930, 1931), Schmorl and Junghanns (1968), and Zippel (1976). Vertebral slippage at the cervical spine is rare and was first described by Rauber (1907).

The cause of gaps in the interarticular portion is assumed to be congenital. The following investigators reported on this topic: Azouz et al. (1974), Bellamy et al. (1974), Boehler (1968), Charlton et al. (1978), Cotta (1980), Dawley

(1971), Gehweiler et al. (1977), Kosnik et al. (1979), Moseley (1976), Prioleau and Wilson (1975), Robson et al. (1980), Sheikholeslamzadeh et al. (1977), and Zippel (1976).

The extent of the slipping process plays an important role in determining reasonable stresses in the lumbar as well as the cervical spine. Many investigators have formulated suggestions for comparable measuring in order to provide a model of stress resistance. The slipping distance is best measured at the posterior vertebral body edges since the anterior edges frequently show spur formation.

Penning and Blickman (1980) studied the mobility of spondylolisthesis in roentgenograms showing forward and backward bending as well as forward or backward displacement. In the case of spondylolysis in the 5th lumbar vertebral arch, no slippage occurred between L-5 and S-1. However, this motion led to a change in the height of the intervertebral space L4-5: anterior height loss during forward bending and during backward displacement and a height increase during backward bending and during forward displacement. These findings confirm that after the forward slippage comes to a stop in an intervertebral motor segment of the lumbar spine, the next higher segment (or several of the higher segments) are able to take over "replacement functions" if allowed by the condition of the intervertebral discs. Such replacement functions are also indicated above and below a section stiffened by spondylodesis. If the replacement function is overexerted, a chondrosis/osteochondrosis with intermittent pain may result.

There are detailed indications on the further progress of spondylolytic gaps for spondylolysis/spondylolisthesis that is still in a state of slippage. Possibilities are the progression of dysplastic processes or ossification (Fig. 4-31), which terminates any further forward slippage (Zippel and Pfeil 1980).

4.4.2 Causes of Spondylolysis

The causes of spondylolysis, the precursor of the characteristic vertebral slippage, has repeatedly been studied. For a long time, ontogenic,

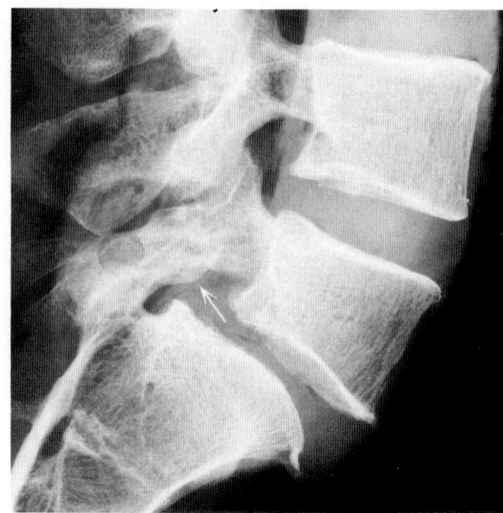

Fig. 4-31 Roentgenogram of a spinal column sectioned in half in sagittal direction. The interarticular portion of the vertebral arch is elongated and thickened: osseous healed spondylolytic gap. Negligible forward slippage (spondylolisthesis) of L-5.

traumatic, trophostatic, and dysplastic theories were offered in connection with gaps in the interarticular portion: Meyer-Burgdorff (1931), Schmorl and Junghanns (1968), and Taillard (1959 to 1963). Based on histological studies of fetal (22) and infantile (32 between 0 and 6 years) spines, Runge and Zippel (1976) reported in detail on the growth at the interarticular portion of the vertebral arch. They concluded that nonfusion of two enchondral ossification centers in the isthmus was not a formational-genetic factor for the development of a lateral vertebral arch gap. However, they allowed the possibility of a congenital gap developing before the ossification phase [see Kestler (1979), Taillard (1980), and Zippel and Pfeil (1980)].

According to the findings of other investigators, the interarticular portion may have already been separated into an anterior and posterior portion (possibly because of congenital or hereditary causes) in the early growth period (Shariaree et al. 1979). In addition, the development of dysplasias or hypoplasias with relaxation and elongation of the stressed interarticular portion is also possible in the growth period. The angulus isthmocorporalis may also play a role.

For the development of gaps in the interarticular portion (important for the stability of the vertebral arch), additional genetically determined conditions at the vertebral arch must also be considered, eg, variations and malformations. In 1980, Arct pointed to assimilations, such as contact of enlarged transverse processes, which he postulated to be 30% of assimilations in the lumbosacral region. He considered anatomical-functional incongruence to be a concomitant cause of the development of spondylolysis.

There remains the question of a congenital reduction of arterial blood flow in the interarticular portion of the vertebral arch from which a central artery ensures the main supply of the isthmus (see section 5.2). Jamiokowska (1980) demonstrated an insufficient blood supply and an additional lack of arterial anastomoses in 50% of his specimens. This may be an additional factor for the development of gaps with a poor healing tendency [see also Suezawa and Jacob (1981)].

Recently, the trophostatic theory for the development of lysis in the isthmus has been used extensively, ie, transformational zones or latent fractures caused by pressure-determined biochemical disorders in the bone: the tweezer effect of the articular process tips that contact the isthmus. Several investigators studied whether rhythmic-mechanical permanent influences on the lumbar spine create gaps in the interarticular portion. The question remains whether forward or backward bending is responsible for damage in the interarticular portion (see Chapter 5). Groher (1980) considered 5% to 6% of endogenous causes to preexist in the general population and suggested that in many cases, spondylolysis or spondylolisthesis is caused by exogenous influences.

There is a frequent connection between spondylolisthesis and scoliosis. According to McPhee and O'Brien (1980), this occurs more frequently at L4-5 than at L-5/S-1. Mau (1980) extensively studied this topic. Recently, reports have been published on extensive experiments concerning aggravation of spondylolysis: Henssge (1980), Niethard (1981), Schultz and Niethard (1980), Suezawa (1980), Suezawa and Jacob (1980, 1981). These works also discussed the influence of sports on the lumbosacral region (see Chapter 8).

4.4.3 Stress Resistance of Spondylolysis/Spondylolisthesis

In each case of spondylolysis or spondylolisthesis, the case history (beginning and progress of symptoms at the back, radiation, and pain by movement) combined with an expert medical examination (including roentgenograms for several levels) is indispensible for the physician in establishing the potentials of future stress resistance. Because the beginning of a slippage (spondylolisthesis) cannot be recognized in adolescents affected by spondylolysis and because its progress cannot be predicted, caution in exertion is recommended. Stresses on the lumbar spine-sacrum boundary must be especially avoided since the aggravation risk is significant. Baumgartner and Taillard (1971) studied persons suffering from such damage who finished their military service without problems. Ten years later (when they were 30), 62% of those studied were unfit for service because of complaints.

Spondylolysis without slippage or with only slight slippage noticed in roentgenograms near the end of the growth period (between 18 and 25 years of age) will not necessarily continue to slip. Often, patients are able to withstand intermediate to heavy physical stresses without complaint. However, many develop complaints after the age of 45. In addition, additional slippage occurs in many cases. Therefore, caution in exertion must be exercised.

Newly developed or aggravated complaints should be considered cautiously. They are signs of further instability of the intervertebral disc under the slipped vertebra and also indicate myogelosis of overexerted muscles. Noncompetitive swimming without dives is recommended as therapy. Many investigators consider damage of the intervertebral disc to be the essential cause of slippage. Others regard the damage as a consequence of mechanical weak points in both interarticular portions. There is also a widespread opinion that a stabilized intervertebral disc prevents forward slippage. Increasing pain and evidently increased slippage are reasons to consider surgery (see Chapter 7). Zippel and Pfeil (1980) report in detail on the athletic stress resistance of spondylolysis/spondylolisthesis (see also Chapter 8).

4.4.4 Vertebral Displacements

Pseudospondylolisthesis (Junghanns 1930), ie, forward vertebral displacement, develops without any connection with damage in the interarticular portion (Figs. 4-32 through 4-34). It always appears in connection with a height loss in the corresponding intervertebral space, which soon develops into distinct intervertebral osteochondrosis. In comparison with the adjacent upper articulation, the articular surfaces of the vertebral arch are inclined forward. The vertebral arch/articular process angle is clearly more obtuse than is normal. Both vertebral arch articulations of the segment are arthrotically changed, and the width of the articular space is decreased. Their arthrotic spurs constrict the intervertebral canal (Junghanns 1930). In 1977, Taillard and Lagier called this condition erosive

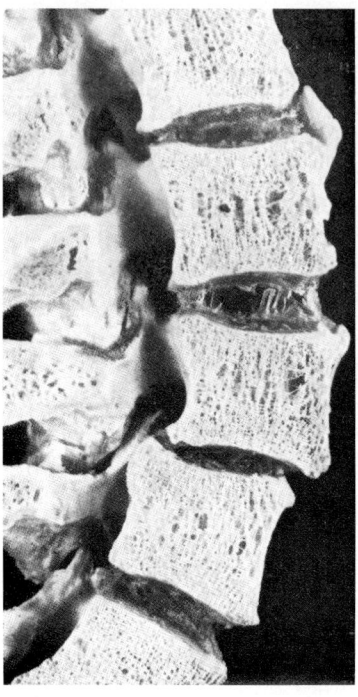

Fig. 4-33 Surface of a sagittal section of the lumbosacral region of a 72-year-old woman. Pseudospondylolisthesis of the 4th lumbar vertebra. Note the spur of the articular process projecting into the intervertebral canal.

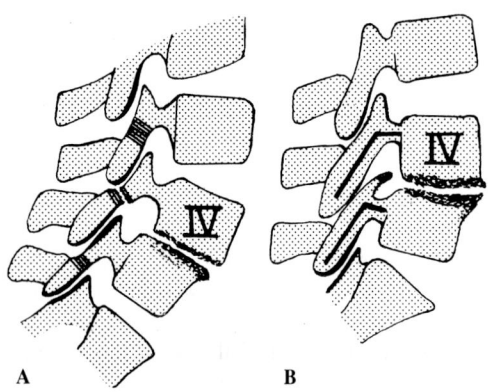

Fig. 4-32 Schematic tracings of lateral roentgenograms of the lumbosacral area. (**A**) pseudospondylolisthesis of the 4th lumbar vertebra with a gap in the interarticular portion; (**B**) pseudospondylolisthesis of the 4th lumbar vertebra. Its inferior articular process is positioned somewhat more level than the rest. Level position of the gap in the vertebral arch articulation between L4-5. Angle enlargement between arch root and inferior articular process as seen by the sketched axes. A small spur projects into the 4th lumbar intervertebral canal from the superior articular process of the 5th lumbar vertebra, and the angle between this one and the corresponding arch root is decreased.

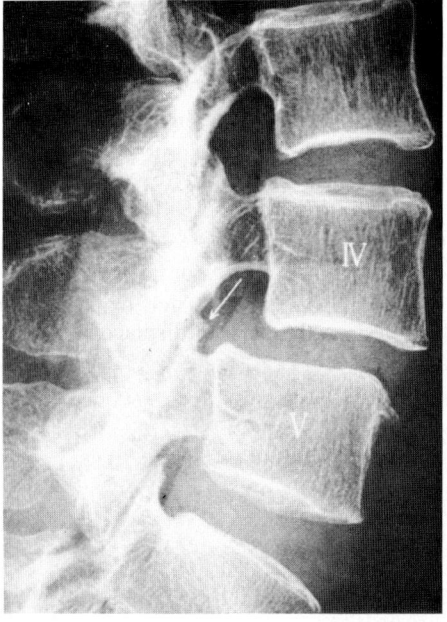

Fig. 4-34 Lateral roentgenogram of half of the lumbosacral area of a 58-year-old woman (sectioned in the sagittal level). Pseudospondylolisthesis of the 4th lumbar vertebra.

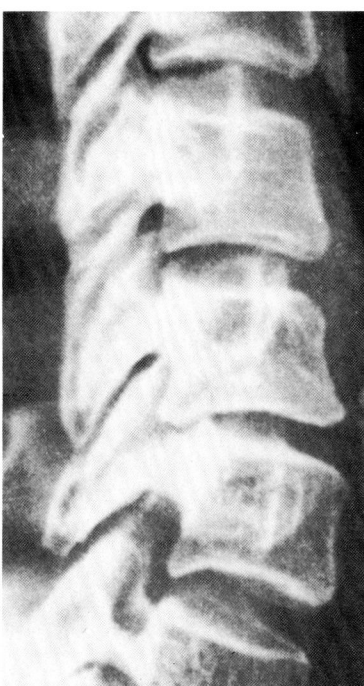

Fig. 4-35 Backward displacement of the 5th cervical vertebra (retrolisthesis) with height loss of the intervertebral space (58-year-old man).

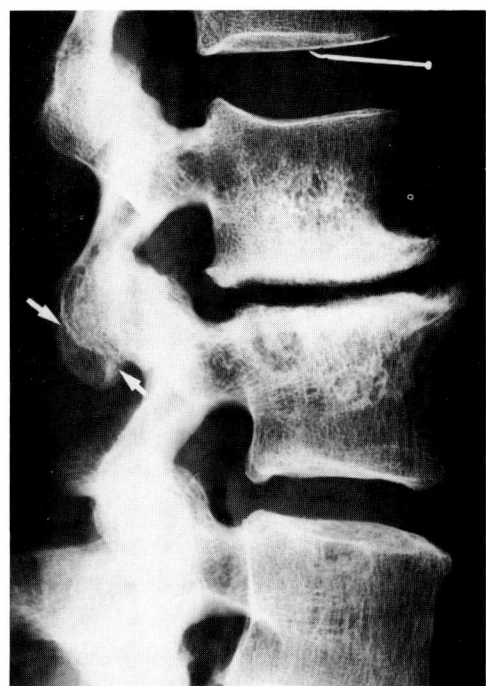

Fig. 4-36 Lateral roentgenogram of half of the lumbar spine of a 67-year-old man, sectioned in the sagittal level. Severe height loss of the 2nd lumbar intervertebral disc with sclerosis of adjacent vertebral body spongiosa. Displacement of 2nd lumbar vertebra backward, with telescopic displacement of its inferior articular process to the lower back, so that it projects over the articular surface of the superior articular process of the 3rd lumbar vertebra (**arrows**). Constriction of the intervertebral canal.

osteoarthrosis. In 1980, Zippel and Pfeil named it degenerative-involutive spondylolisthesis. In 1980, Farfan described it as spondylolisthesis degenerativa, which occurs in connection with rotation.

No symptoms can be detected during adolescence. In most cases, symptoms are not observed until after the age of 40. It is mostly the 4th lumbar vertebra that is displaced, and the displacement occurs more often in women than in men. A noteworthy aspect of pseudospondylolisthesis is the parallel displacement on the lower vertebra. There is no tilting of the vertebra, and therefore the intervertebral space does not have a wedge shape. Walker et al. (1980) rejected osteoporosis as a concomitant cause of the displacement.

The relaxed intervertebral segment that is linked to the displacement, intervertebral osteochondrosis, and vertebral arch articular arthrosis may be portrayed in functional roentgenograms. Complaints correspond with those of intervertebral instability. Treatment should be the same as for spondylolisthesis. Surgical treatment is described in section 7.4.

According to statistics in the literature, the backward vertebral displacement (retrolisthesis) (Figs. 3-20, 4-35, and 4-36) is found at the cervical spine (3.2%) and at the lumbar spine (4.7%). The intervertebral disc in the slippage level is conspicuously degenerated (intervertebral osteochondrosis), and the intervertebral motor segment is relaxed to the point of intervertebral instability. The displacement level is easily recognized in the lateral roentgenogram at the vertebral body edges running to the vertebral canal; the locations are not obstructed by edge ridges. In the affected intervertebral motor segment, the entire upper spine is slightly displaced backward compared with the lower spine. Frequently, there is a steep inclination above the displacement: Guentz's sign. Planoparallel narrowing of the affected intervertebral space is possible only if the vertebral arch articular processes belonging to the intervertebral motor segment slip past each other (telescopic displacement) (Fig. 3-20). Because of the articulations that are tilted downward and backward, the vertebra is forced backward. The complaints correspond to those of intervertebral instability and are especially severe if several adjacent lumbar vertebrae slip backward in a step-ladder–like manner. Retrolisthesis may lead to the tweezer mechanism at the cervical spine if arthroses of the vertebral arch articulations with spurs are also present (Fig. 3-19). Because of the developing constriction of the vertebral canal, both from the anterior and posterior, serious spinal cord injuries may result, and surgery may be urgently needed (see section 7.4).

Lateral displacement (rotation displacement) (Figs. 4-24 and 4-37) is found almost exclusively at the lumbar spine in combination with scoliosis and is a symptom of intervertebral instability. In such cases, attention must also be paid to the interarticular portions of the vertebral arches at the level of the torsion vertex since various spondylolisthetic scolioses and scoliotic spondylolyses exist (Mau 1977, 1980).

In children and adolescents, slight forward or backward displacements of a vertebra(e) in the cervical spine can often be detected by lateral roentgenogram performed during backward and forward bending (see section 6.3). Displacements may be within normal limits. However, in the case of chronic complaints, roentgenograms should be taken every six to nine months. These displacements may lead to the often misdiagnosed "school headache" in adolescents. A slanted desk is helpful (see section 7.3).

4.4.5 Stress Resistance of Vertebral Displacements

All forms of vertebral displacement have one aspect in common: the displaced segment shows a combination of intervertebral osteochondrosis and arthrosis of the two vertebral arch articulations. The severity of this combination determines the complaints and therefore the stress resistance of the spine. The displacements

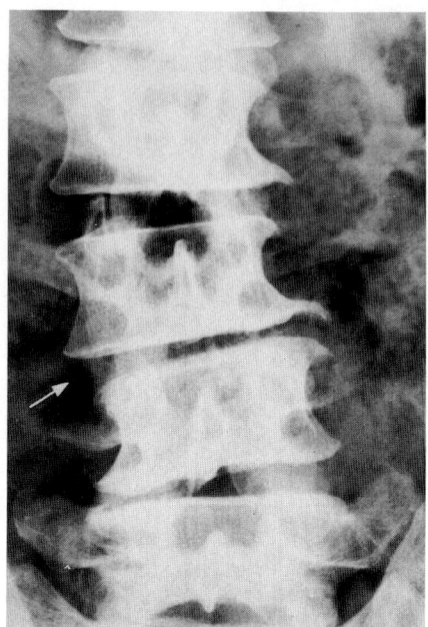

Fig. 4-37 Roentgenogram of the lumbar spine of a 44-year-old man. Rotation slippage in scoliosis (**arrow**).

described in section 4.4.4 often affect only one segment. However, often severe pain and problems do not occur until later life when intervertebral instability surfaces. Lack of exercise, especially in conjunction with vibrations, increases the pain. The progressive weakness of the back muscles that have been damaged by sitting is responsible.

In the case of rotation displacement, which is always combined with scoliosis, the early appearance of pain necessitates the testing of stress resistance by a physician. The beginning functional insufficiency (latent insufficiency, section 3.4) must be recognized in time. Derotation surgery may bring relief in some cases (see section 7.4).

Stress resistance must be determined for each recurring episode of pain so that progressive therapy may result in new stability. Medical counsel should be considered for leisure and sport activities.

4.5 ADDITIONAL CHANGES

4.5.1 Introduction

Some damages affect only the skeleton of the axial organ, and other damages affect the bones

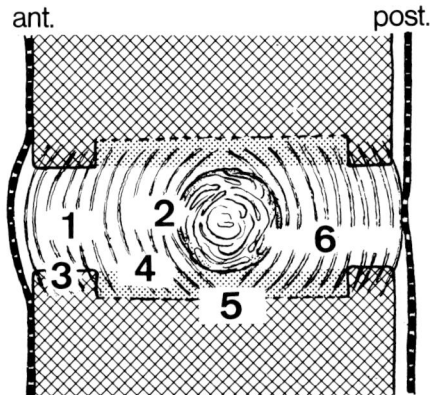

Fig. 4-38 Schematic drawing of a sagittal section of an intervertebral disc with the vertebral body–intervertebral disk boundary. Numbers designate areas susceptible to influence by permanent mechanical factors (including vibrations). (**1**) Figures 2-11 and 2-12 portray the connective fiber penetrations. They run between the fiber ring lamellae and are subject to alternating tension during torsion movements, especially quick torsion waves. This may encourage the formation of concentric cracks. (**2**) Transitional zone between nucleus pulposus and internal fiber ring layers. (**3**) Penetration zone of lamellae ring fibers into the bony vertebral ring epiphysis. (**4**) Transitional area of penetrating fibers into the hyaline cartilage. (**5**) Vertebral body–intervertebral disc boundary with vertebral body end plate (porous cribrum) and adjacent hyaline cartilage plate. (**6**) Posterior area of the intervertebral disc where radial tears from the nucleus pulposus to the external ring layers appear most frequently and prepare the way for the protrusion or prolapse in posterior or posterolateral direction.

---

only secondarily. Damages in the tissue of the intervertebral disc are often the cause of stress resistance problems. Figure 4-38 shows six areas of susceptibility. Each may be the point of origin for damage that impairs the biomechanical equilibrium in the affected section. In this context, potentials for remote effects arise.

Pain relationships between alternations in the spine and visceral disorders based on viscerovertebral reflex paths are often difficult to diagnose. Because of such neural plexi, "lumbar syndromes" that point to a spondylogenic origin may prove to be organ-specific pain radiations: liver, kidneys, and abdominal organs. On the other hand, there is the possibility of simulation of an organ disorder by spondylogenic pain radiation (see section 3.4). These complex organ interrelationships carry different names: vegetative pain, pseudoradicular pain, projection pain, etc. Extensive literature on this topic includes Eder and Tilscher (1982), Kunert (1975), Lewit (1973), Novotny and Dvorak (1973), Tilscher et al. (1977), and Tilscher (1983).

4.5.2 Impairment Factors Determined Mostly by the Intervertebral Disc

4.5.2.1 Spondylosis Deformans

Spondylosis deformans, the bone spur disease, is rightly considered one of the most frequent disorders of the spine. At the same time, it is the most frequently occurring damage caused by the intervertebral disc. A graphic portrayal of its frequency in the thoracic and lumbar spine was calculated by Junghanns (1931) after a pathomorphological study of more than 4,000 spines. The fast increase in changes (Fig. 4-39) to age 35 is remarkable, 40% in both genders; until the age of 49, 80% of men and 60% of women; until the age of 59, 90% of men and 80% of women.

Many investigators have reported similar results, mostly documented with roentgenograms: Suesse (1957), Tepe (1956), and many others. In 1962, Nathan studied the connection of spondylosis deformans with age, gender, and race. Several investigators reported that spondylosis deformans is caused by exogenous stresses (job) and in such cases is located at the lower thoracic spine: Kersten (1967), Liebeskind (1970), Louyot et al. (1954), Schroeter (1961), and Schulze and Polster (1979).

The precondition of the initially cartilaginous-bulging and gradually ossifying spurs is the detachment of the annular fibers from the bony vertebral ring epiphysis (Figs. 4-40 and 4-38). The detachment of the fibers from their bondings destroys the firm bond between the vertebral body and intervertebral disc. Functional-mechanical parallels exist with regard to tendon bonding (Junghanns 1979). If the nucleus pulposus has not changed substantially and is still filled with fluid (ie, its turgor is essentially maintained), an incorrect displacement potential to the front and sides develops for the relaxed intervertebral disc tissue. As a consequence, the

106 CLINICAL IMPLICATIONS OF NORMAL BIOMECHANICAL STRESSES ON SPINAL FUNCTION

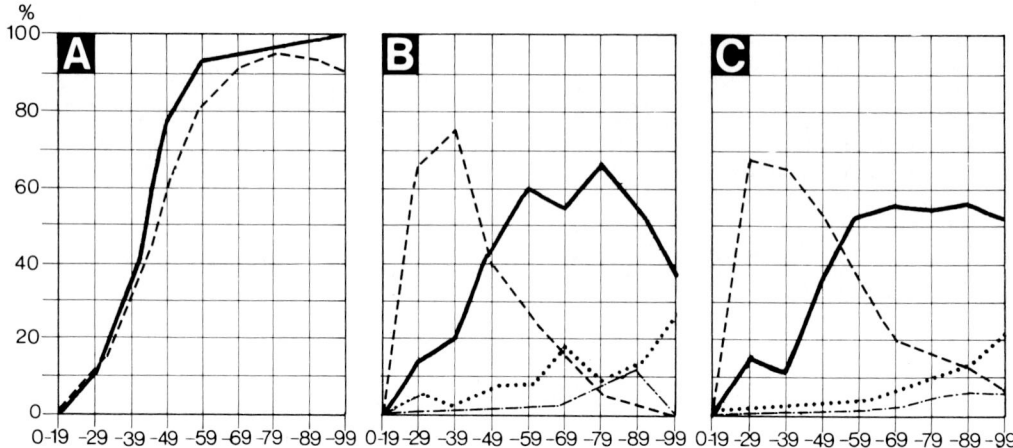

Fig. 4-39 Frequency of spondylosis deformans. (**A**) increase in men and women; (**B**) distribution over lumbar and thoracic spine in men; (**C**) in women. Equally minor findings in lumbar and thoracic spine, findings in thoracic spine without involvement of lumbar spine, substantial findings in lumbar spine, minor involvement of thoracic spine, lumbar and thoracic spine with equal substantial findings.

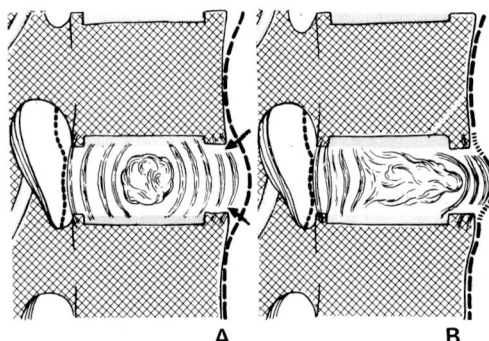

Fig. 4-40 Detachment of fiber ring layers from the bony epiphysis (cf. Fig. 4-38). Because of the developing relaxation (**A**), the fiber ring pushes forward. (**B**) Gradually, the typical, bony epiphysis of spondylosis deformans develops (Figs. 4-41 and 4-42).

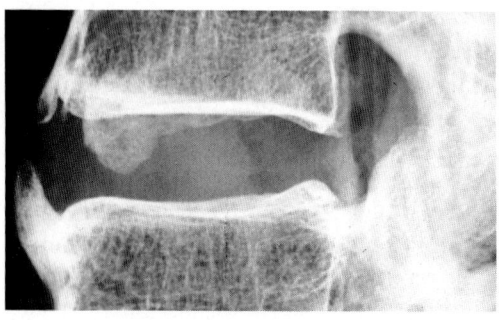

Fig. 4-41 Bone spurs of spondylosis deformans develop at the attachment points of the anterior longitudinal ligament. Note the unchanged height of the intervertebral space.

intervertebral disc tissue that is relaxed at the annular epiphysis presses by motion and stress against the anterior longitudinal ligament. This repeated forward pushing of the intervertebral disc and the additional incorrect motions result in a constant tug at the attachments of the longitudinal ligament. In a reaction to this irritation, bone spurs develop (Fig. 4-41), but no significant narrowing of the intervertebral space occurs. There is an increasingly popular opinion that "bone spur disease" is less of a disease than a defense (attempt of stabilization) against intervertebral instability. What remains is the bony memorial of a prolonged malfunction. Biochemical processes play a role, as shown in studies by Lipsen and Muir (1980).

Spondylosis deformans appears only rarely in a single intervertebral motor segment. Almost regularly, several adjacent intervertebral motor segments are affected. Occasionally, it affects different regions of the spine and may exist in all three sections of the axial organ either at the same intensity or at different intensities. The spurs form along the attachment points of the lateral longitudinal ligament (Fig. 4-41). In contrast, often only one intervertebral motor segment is affected by intervertebral osteochondrosis.

Incorrect displacement potential (relaxation in the intervertebral motor segment; see section 3.4) is rare in spondylosis deformans and, if it

Fig. 4-42 Drawing of the development of spondylosis deformans of the lumbar spine according to a series of roentgenograms over a period of 15 years (first picture at age 58). **Top:** "intercalary bone" in the longitudinal ligament between two spondylotic spurs with gradual enlargement of the intercalary bone and bone spurs developing toward it; **bottom:** bone spurs steadily enlarge from **A** to **C** and lead to ossification (**left**) and nearthrosis (**right**).

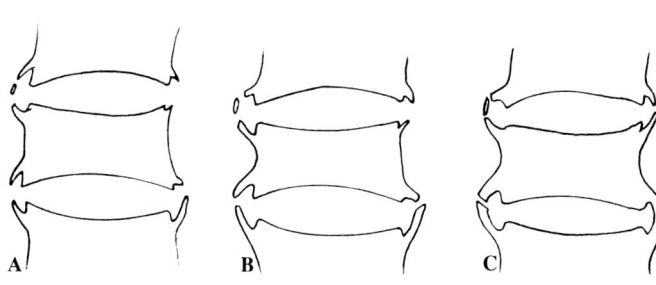

exists, is negligible. However, it is one syndrome of intervertebral osteochondrosis.

The bulges and spurs of spondylosis deformans differ in size and expansion. They may develop quickly or slowly and may be of grotesque shapes that occasionally bridge the intervertebral space by growing toward each other in a beaklike manner (Fig. 4-42). They form bony connections and thereby cause immobility of the intervertebral motor segment. Because of the many symptoms of spondylosis deformans, the large differences in the complaints of patients, and the stiffness that finally develops, an individual evaluation of stress resistance is necessary.

The diagnosis of spondylosis deformans can be confirmed only with the roentgenograms. The bone spurs (Figs. 4-41 and 4-42) that develop at typical locations on the vertebral body differentiate this disease from other disorders. Spondylosis deformans must be differentiated from intervertebral chondrosis (intervertebral disc wear) and also from intervertebral osteochondrosis, the degeneration of the intervertebral disc. Intervertebral chondrosis is characterized by narrowing of the intervertebral space and spurs of the vertebral ring epiphysis, which are small in spite of the relaxed intervertebral motor segment and may so be distinguished from spondylosis. For various reasons, spondylosis deformans, intervertebral chondrosis, and intervertebral osteochondrosis may occur in the same spine. More details concerning the differentiation between these syndromes, which all are caused by intervertebral disc damage but are otherwise caused by very different pathomorphological causes, are found in Table 4-1. These essential differences determine the stress resistance risk. The damage caused by the intervertebral disc is quite different in origin and therefore in its consequences. Mistakes in diagnostics and possibly wrong conclusions about the significance of exogenous factors can be avoided only if damage is clearly differentiated.

The characteristic bone spurs can be seen early in roentgenograms. Since the pathological process starts with the detachment of the fibers of the fiber ring from their bonding point in the bony vertebral ring epiphysis (Fig. 4-38), parallels with acro-osteopathy can be observed (see Chapter 3). Microscopic studies have shown that detachment of tendons from their bonding points occurs in this painful disorder.

There are indications of a possible causal connection with vibrations for spondylosis deformans. The combination of vibrations with rotational stress is an additional exogenous factor for the aggravation of spondylosis deformans.

Since spondylosis deformans begins in middle age and is almost always aggravated in later years, the patient's occupation is often seen as its cause. Details concerning this problem may be found in *The Spinal Column in Occupational Medicine* (1979).

Mobility and stress resistance depend on the particular clinical picture presented. The bone spurs offer no indication of the degree of pain or stress risk. Even bone beaks extending over large sections of the spine or with grotesque shapes do not necessarily result in severe disability. However, they lead to limited mobility, which is without major influence on daily life. Animated leisure activities, exercises, or sports may be impeded. Some affected persons occasionally suffer from pain attacks with limited stress resistance potential when they reach middle age. However, with progressive age, pain converts to pain-free, localized, or complete stiffness of the spine.

With painful disability, another cause of pain must always be considered. The cause may be simultaneous intervertebral osteochondrosis in one or several intervertebral motor segments. The frequency of this combination has not been established. This should be done in a large number of cases with physical and radiological examinations in order to create a basis for evaluation. It is not known to which extent an isolated spondylosis deformans without accompanying intervertebral osteochondrosis or other pain-activating spinal disorders represents the cause for the high percentage of patients with premature disability. Spondylosis deformans cannot generally be classified as either a painful and stress-diminishing disorder or a pain-free and nondisabling disorder. Medical examinations and counseling are required in each case.

4.5.2.2 Spondylosis Hyperostotica

It is not possible to differentiate all cases of spondylosis hyperostotica from spondylosis deformans. However, there is hardly a chance of mistaking spondylosis hyperostotica with its distinct forms since the compact, smooth bone appositions that "flow" along the vertebral bodies and have wide bridges across the intervertebral spaces are distinct characteristics (Fig. 4-43). The close connection with gout and diabetes points to relations with metabolism, which are unknown in spondylosis deformans.

Physical condition plays a role in spondylosis hyperostotica (pyknic), and an increased excretion of growth hormones is being discussed. Biomechanically interesting is the increased right-sided "icing" deposit on the thoracic spine that often occurs in this disorder. The lack of this deposit on the left side is explained by aortic pulsation. [See Boss and Rehr (1969), Caplan et al. (1966), Chaiton et al. (1979), Ott et al. (1978), and Schilling et al. (1965).]

It is difficult to evaluate spondylosis hyperostotica with regard to its effects on stress resistance because its relationships with constitutional and metabolic changes have not been demonstrated sufficiently, and verified series of tests are lacking. According to past findings, afflicted persons become pain-free after the

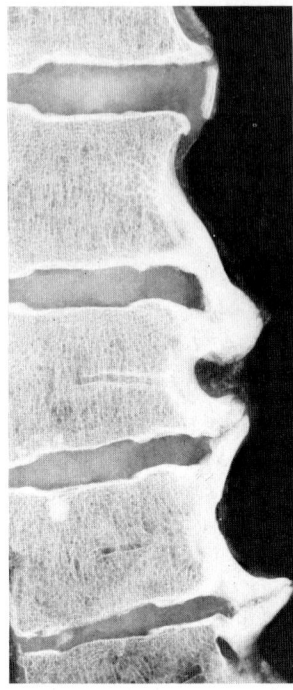

Fig. 4-43 Roentgenogram of a section taken sagittally from a spine. Spondylosis hyperostotica with very distinct "icinglike" appositions that bridge the intervertebral spaces.

wide-banded ossification (mostly at the thoracic spine) with an ankylosed bridging of several intervertebral spaces is concluded. This determines the stress resistance in the daily life of an individual. The bridging, "flowing" bone tracts give a new, stressable stability to the thoracic spine if trajectory arches with radial supports have formed and are adapted to the pressure conditions (Fig. 4-44).

4.5.2.3 Intervertebral Chondrosis (Intervertebral Disc Wear)

The tissue of the intervertebral disc suffers premature and extensive damage more than any other organ or organ system in the human body. Biochemical changes in the nucleus pulposus and fiber ring are connected with intervertebral disc wear. The majority of such biochemical changes are attributable to aging processes, ie, an endogenously determined transformation of the intervertebral disc tissue, which is also found in laboratory animals. The question of whether or to what extent genetic causes play a decisive role for humans in this context has not been

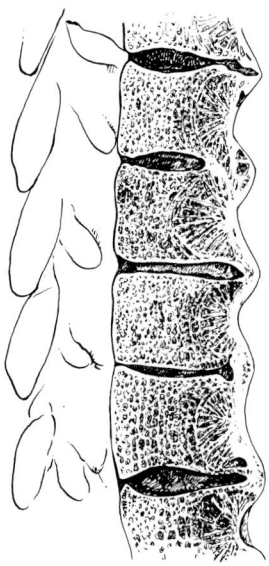

Fig. 4-44 Adaptation in the trajectory course of the vertebral body spongiosa caused by pressure and stress changes of progressive ankylosis: spondylosis hyperostotica (drawn after an anatomic specimen).

completely answered. In 1961, Berry described genetic causes in mice. DeSèse observed differences in mice according to species in the frequency of degenerative arthritis of the spine. This term included chronic intervertebral disc disorders such as intervertebral chondrosis and intervertebral osteochondrosis. The question of whether autoimmune processes play an essential or accompanying role in intervertebral disc wear requires extensive study [see Gertzbein (1977); see also section 2.3].

A changed chemical environment (section 2.3), the progressive drying, the loss of internal turgor, and the appearance of tears and cracks characterize intervertebral chondrosis, the wear of the intervertebral disc (ie, the first stage of age-related damage). Early stages of intervertebral chondrosis may be recognized in superficial sections of intervertebral discs (see Fig. 2-14) before narrowing has occurred.

Narrowing occurs at a later time because of further drying. Concentric cracks and horizontal tears are decisively involved in this process. They may be demonstrated in pathoanatomical specimens (Fig. 2-15) and in vivo by injecting a radio-opaque medium. After the injection of dye, they show up in axial or horizontal sections. Some of the many forms of cracks are shown in Figures 4-45 and 4-46. The cracks are small in intervertebral chondrosis. Schmorl's nodules and other forms of intervertebral disc displacement are almost regularly preceded by intervertebral chondrosis. The changed intervertebral disc tissue allows incorrect motions and affects the entire intervertebral motor segment because of its functional insufficiency.

In the initial stages, the radiographic diagnosis of intervertebral chondrosis is difficult. However, diligent comparisons of the intervertebral spaces confirm the diagnosis through the gradually more obvious narrowing and the first development of the small edge spurs of the beginning spondylosis. A larger decrease in the intercorporal space indicates the beginning of intervertebral osteochondrosis. Roentgenograms with radio-opaque medium, which should be performed only if they are urgently needed for diagnosis, may be helpful. If no other causes for progressive stress and mobility complaints can be found, it is appropriate to suspect beginning wear in the intervertebral disc tissue.

With regard to the development of intervertebral disc wear, section 2.3 discusses biochemical influences and the influence of metabolism, which is possible only by diffusion in the rather sluggishly nourished tissue of the intervertebral disc. Section 3.2 discusses possible problems in the diffusional pathways, especially at the bony cribrum–hyaline cartilage plate boundary. The thus impaired nutritional supply and waste removal system is an essential precondition for the development of intervertebral chondrosis, which may progress to intervertebral osteochondrosis (intervertebral disc degeneration).

In the past, when biochemical conditions had not been sufficiently clarified, fatigue damage was seen as the primary origin of intervertebral chondrosis. There is no doubt that such fatigue accompanies chemically determined tissue damage. However, in all diagnoses of intervertebral disc damage and secondary disorders, a distinction between previously existing damage and stress consequences must be made.

Trauma to the anatomic structure and therefore the biochemistry of the intervertebral disc tissue may result in serious consequences. The initial impact creates tears and separations in the area of the fiber rings. There may also be detach-

110 CLINICAL IMPLICATIONS OF NORMAL BIOMECHANICAL STRESSES ON SPINAL FUNCTION

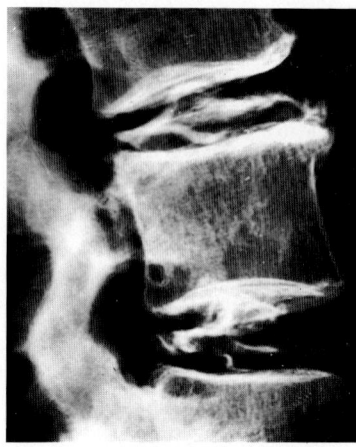

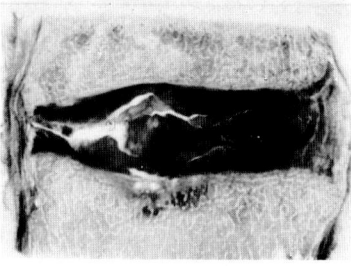

Fig. 4-45 Intervertebral chondrosis with cracks in the intervertebral disc tissue (filled with radio-opaque medium) that affect the area of the nucleus pulposus as well as the fiber ring. **Top:** Roentgenogram of the spine of a corpse; **bottom:** sagittal section through the lower intervertebral disc shown in the roentgenogram (75-year-old man).

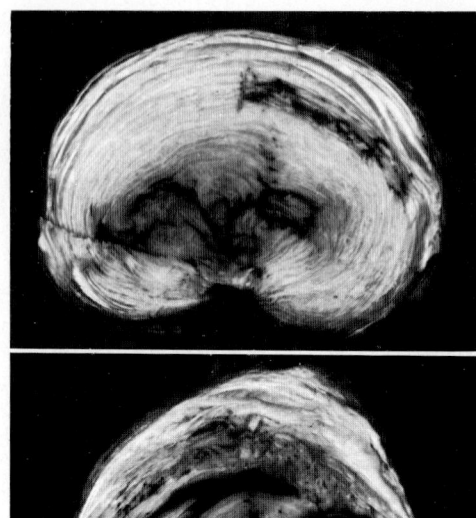

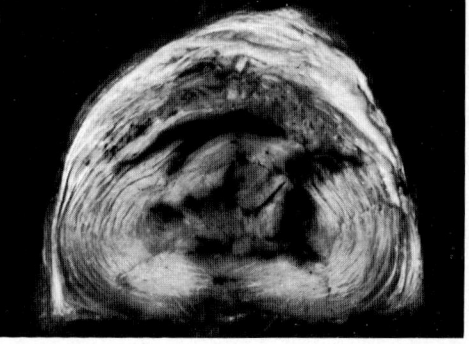

Fig. 4-46 Horizontal sections through intervertebral discs that were injected with dye before sectioning. The cracks are not limited to the nucleus. Cracks in the fiber ring are filled with the injection medium and show a concentric orientation, following the layers of the fiber ring. In addition, there is a tear, running from the nucleus pulposus toward the back and cutting through all fiber ring layers.

ment of penetrating fibers at the bony epyphysis of the vertebral body or at the hyaline cartilage plate. Most frequently, such consequences of an initial impact result from axial pressure or an extension in the axial direction with simultaneous torsion in the intervertebral space, with a shearing momentum and forceful countertraction at the fiber ring layers. Such situations often occur in daily life, in certain occupations, and in many sports and exercises. Damage may progress from intervertebral chondrosis to intervertebral osteochondrosis and all of its secondary consequences (see section 3.4).

4.5.2.4 Intervertebral Osteochondrosis (Intervertebral Disc Degeneration)

The most severe chronic intervertebral disc damage (a continuation and final stage of intervertebral chondrosis) is intervertebral osteochondrosis–intervertebral disc degeneration. In the pathomorphological picture, it is recognized by a progressive destruction of intervertebral disc tissue. The cracks in the dried tissue have many shapes, and intervertebral disc sequestra may appear (Figs. 4-47 and 3-21 A, B, and C). Injected radio-opaque medium leaves the intervertebral space if tears have destroyed the outer fiber ring layers.

The narrowing of the intervertebral space results in pressure and friction on the bony cover and base plates of the adjacent vertebral bodies. This may happen in the entire area of the vertebral body–intervertebral disc boundary, including the ring epiphysis. Roentgenograms show sclerosis of the vertebral body end plates with a rugged surface or small bone spurs, which originate in the rim of the vertebral body (Fig. 4-48). In contrast, the bony projections of spondylosis originate somewhat far from the vertebral body rim at the point of attachment of

Factors Interfering with Functional Capacity 111

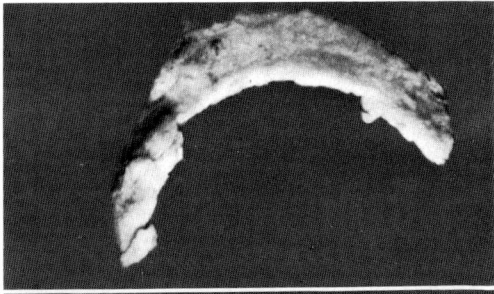

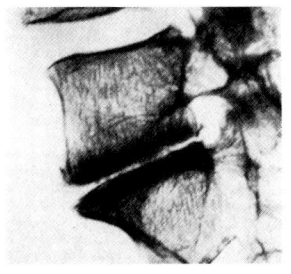

Fig. 4-48 Severe intervertebral osteochondrosis of L-5/S-1. Intervertebral disc tissue completely destroyed. Spurs on rim, front, and back. Sclerosis of adjacent vertebral body spongiosa.

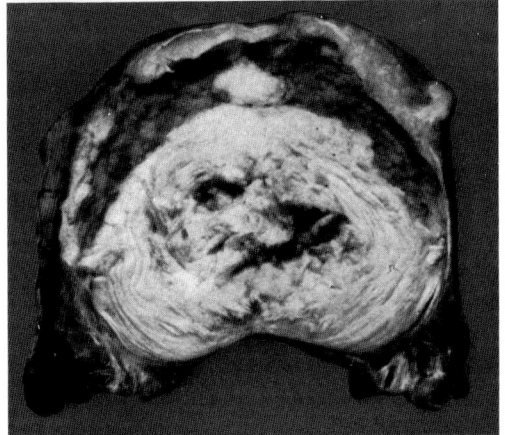

Fig. 4-47 Photograph of a superficial section through a lumbar intervertebral disc. Intervertebral chondrosis in transition to intervertebral osteochondrosis with complete detachment of a sickle-shaped portion (large intervertebral disc sequestrum, free articular body. The sequestrum may result in a blockade (see section 3.4).

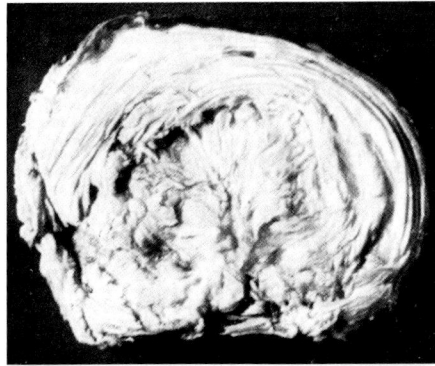

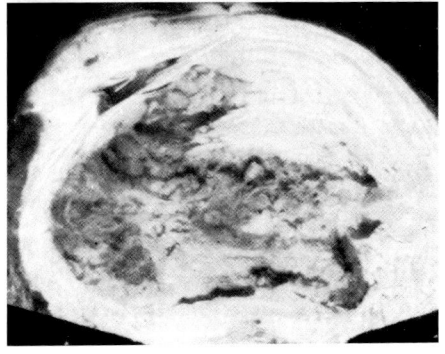

Fig. 4-49 Superficial sections of lumbar spines showing intervertebral osteochondrosis. Degeneration of the dried nucleus pulposus area, spreading to the extensively torn fiber ring.

the anterior longitudinal ligament (Figs. 4-41 and 4-42).

Intervertebral osteochondrosis is a regular companion of spondylolysis or spondylolisthesis and also of backward and lateral displacements (see Figs. 3-19, 3-20, 4-30, 4-32, 4-36, and 4-48). Often, arthroses of the uncovertebral articulations are combined with osteochondroses of the corresponding intervertebral spaces. This leads to clinical pictures in which pain radiates to the head and/or into the neck-shoulder-arm areas. Figure 4-49 shows the dryness and structural degeneration of intervertebral discs during the final stages of intervertebral osteochondrosis. The anterior spurs on the rim in intervertebral osteochondrosis may occasionally constrict the esophagus (Fig. 4-50). As described in section 7.4, large spurs on the vertebral body rim may in rare cases necessitate surgical intervention.

Basic research still leaves open the question whether intervertebral osteochondrosis always plays an important role in the sclerotic processes affecting the vertebral body end plates or whether the prior sclerosis of the bone (which in certain cases may be the healing process of microfrequent fractures) prevents metabolism

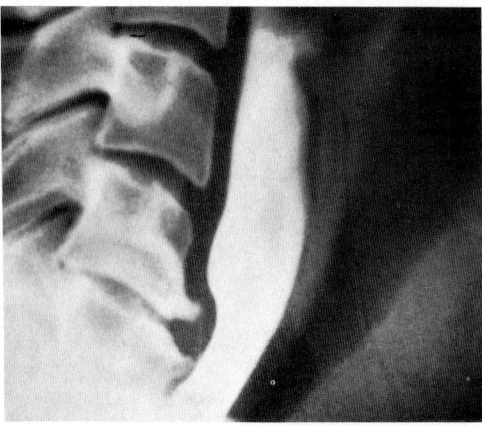

Fig. 4-50 Lateral roentgenogram of the cervical spine of a 42-year-old woman showing intervertebral osteochondrosis. Radio-opaque filling of the esophagus. The bony edge spurs of intervertebral osteochondrosis at the 5th and 6th cervical vertebral body constrict the esophagus. Significant complaints during swallowing.

for the intervertebral disc and thus causes damage. A detailed discussion of this issue is found in section 5.2.

Intervertebral osteochondrosis rarely appears simultaneously at several intervertebral discs. It often occurs in conjunction with vertebral displacements. Section 3.4 discusses the serious and permanent influence on stress and motion of the spine (intervertebral insufficiency). The frequent occurrence of intervertebral osteochondrosis next to lumbosacral transition vertebrae was observed by Erdmann (1953). He regards the variations as endogenous factors for intervertebral disc damage, whereas stresses caused by special life styles or behaviors were only additional factors.

Intervertebral osteochondrosis is the main symptom or accompanying symptom of many systemic diseases such as chondrocalcinosis, ochronoses, neuropathy, tabes, syringomyelia, etc. If back pain appears in any of these diseases, a roentgenogram of the spine (preferably the lumbar spine) will support the diagnosis. The role of autoimmunization in intervertebral disc tissue and activated lymphocytes is described in section 2.3.

In a small number of cases (there are no precise data), the relaxation and displacement tendency connected with intervertebral disc degeneration may be stabilized by the ingrowth of taut connective tissue or bones into the intervertebral space (or also by bridging bone braces). Surgical stabilization is indicated for cases with significant pain (section 7.3).

The radiological diagnosis of intervertebral osteochondrosis is determined by height loss of the intervertebral space and excessive displacement. Roentgenograms performed during forward or backward bending and occasionally a physical examination can confirm the diagnosis. Effects of intervertebral disc degeneration with regard to the stress resistance of the spine are described in section 3.4 [see Lagier and MacGee (1979) and Jumashev et al (1976)].

4.5.2.5 Protrusion and Prolapse of the Intervertebral Disc

The protrusion of intervertebral disc tissue out of the intervertebral space may occur in all directions (Fig. 4-51). Each direction is connected with a distinct clinical picture. The most common prolapse of intervertebral disc tissue presses

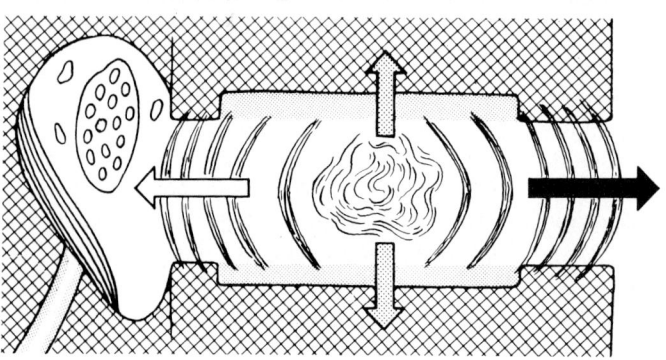

Fig. 4-51 Model of various types of intervertebral disc prolapse. **Dotted arrows** indicate prolapse toward the head or sacrum, resulting in a Schmorl's nodule. **White arrow** indicates the path of posterior prolapse. **Black arrow** indicates directions of intervertebral disc displacement in spondylosis.

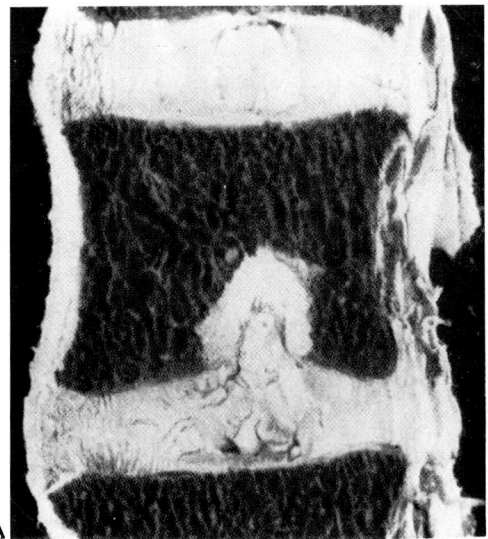 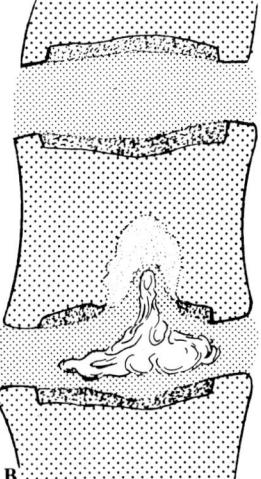

Fig. 4-52 Characteristic Schmorl's nodule. **(A)** Sagittal section of spine. Prolapse of intervertebral disc tissue into vertebral body after penetration of bone and cartilage plate. Basketlike cartilage cover of the prolapsed intervertebral disc tissue. **(B)** Schematic illustration.

against and into the adjacent vertebral body: the characteristic Schmorl's nodule (Fig. 4-52). It occurs occasionally after trauma, eg, as a residue of a vertebral body fracture with a collapse of the cover plate (Fig. 4-53). More frequently, the intervertebral disc tissue penetrates the vertebral body spongiosa at the former penetration point of the chorda dorsalis (Fig. 2-2) slowly, and often via the described indentations of the intervertebral disc (Fig. 4-54). A single Schmorl's nodule does not cause pain or impairment. If they appear in numerous, adjacent vertebral bodies, they may be precursors of juvenile kyphosis (Fig. 4-8). There are connections to the clinical picture of endochondral dystopia.

A severe prolapse of the intervertebral disc may be associated with biomechanical risks, especially if it is located in the anterior part of lumbar vertebral bodies. This frequently occurs in juvenile kyphosis (Fig. 4-11). Every other larger isolated prolapse of the intervertebral disc in a vertebral body also changes the biomechanical conditions of the intervertebral disc where the prolapse originated and, to a certain extent, of the respective intervertebral motor segment. Occasionally, complaints that appear or are aggravated during special motions or axial stresses seem conceivable in such cases. The connection of an isolated Schmorl's nodule with athletic influences is discussed in section 8.8.

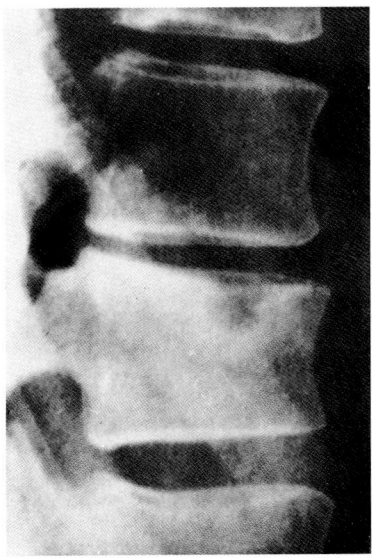

Fig. 4-53 Development of a characteristic "traumatic" Schmorl's nodule three years after a depression fracture of a thoracic vertebral body. The basketlike callus prevents further prolapse of intervertebral disc tissue.

There are further biomechanical problems linked with the penetration of intervertebral disc tissue into the vertebral body, ie, with the development of a Schmorl's nodule. The development of a Schmorl's nodule as a result of prolonged stress, lack of exercise, or forced posture of the spine has not been confirmed for cases where the intervertebral disc–vertebral body boundary was

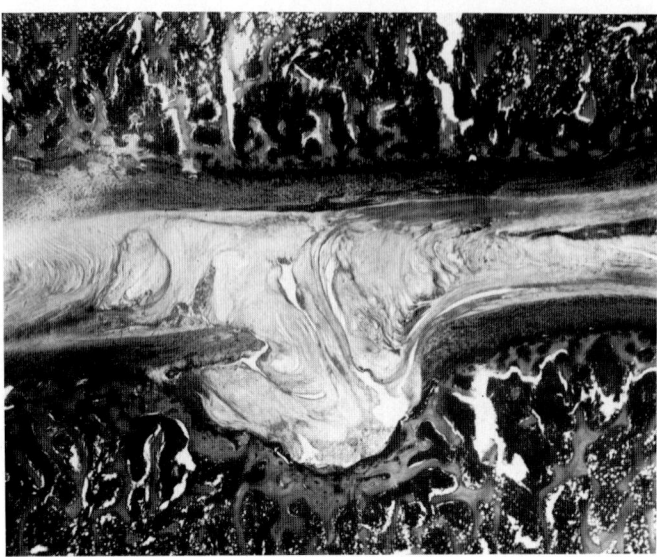

Fig. 4-54 Schmorl's nodule. Prolapse of intervertebral disc tissue through a wide-open gap in the intervertebral disc–vertebral body boundary. Tears in intervertebral disc tissue in both sides. Enclosure of prolapse with bone tissue. Prolapsed nucleus pulposus tissue has moved under the bony vertebral body cover plate to the left.

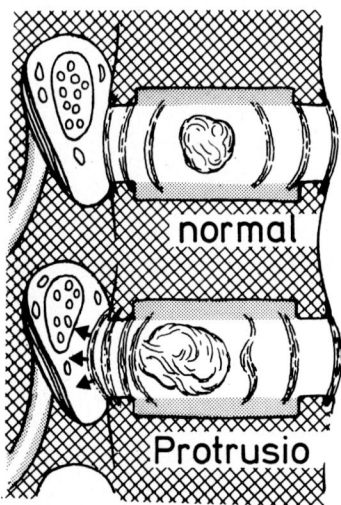

Fig. 4-55 Protrusion of the back wall of an intervertebral disc which may be a precursor of prolapse.

anatomically correct. Recently, there has been discussion about whether prolonged vibrations can cause microfractures and fragmental zones in the area either as direct fatigue damage or through decreased blood circulation. If, after prolonged vibration, tissue damage should actually appear at the hyaline cartilage layer of the intervertebral disc and/or in the bony vertebral body end plate, then the developed "weak point" may represent an opportunity for a slow prolapse of intervertebral disc tissue into the vertebral body, ie, a vibration-determined development of a Schmorl's nodule.

Protrusion of the intervertebral disc may develop as a mutual protrusion of the posterior, lateral, and anterior layers of the fiber ring by intervertebral chondrosis if a loss of elasticity results in a height loss of the intervertebral space. If there are simultaneous posteromedial or posterolateral radial tears into which portions of the fiber ring or nucleus pulposus penetrate, a distinct protrusion of the back wall of the intervertebral disc develops (Fig. 4-55). It presses against nerve roots and causes varying complaints, depending on the pressure exerted on the intervertebral disc (lifting from a bending position, coughing, sneezing, etc.). After the last fiber rings have broken, the various forms of prolapse may occur (Fig. 4-56). Depending on the form, the prolapse produces the known complaints. The prolapse of the intervertebral disc belongs pathomorphologically to the syndrome of intervertebral chondrosis and develops less often with existing intervertebral osteochondrosis.

Posteromedial and posterolateral prolapse are the main painful forms of intervertebral disc prolapse (Fig. 4-57). Such a prolapse may occur suddenly, accompanied by great pain and almost without perceptible warnings. It may also gradually produce an incapacity in daily life because

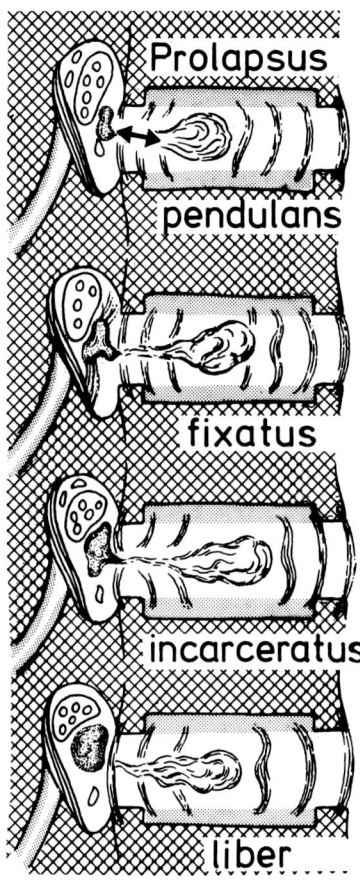

Fig. 4-56 Schematic drawing of various types of intervertebral disc prolapse: pendulous, fixated, incarcerated, free.

of its frequent recurrences and may finally require surgery (section 7.4).

Doubts about the functional capacity after surgical correction of an intervertebral disc prolapse keep surfacing. There is no generally applicable solution, and medical counsel is required. This is especially true for the increasing number of young people who undergo surgery. In such cases, complete stress resistance and mobility of the spine may be re-established with timely surgery. The resumption of former athletic activity is documented (Fischer 1976). In no case should intervertebral disc surgery be the reason for significant limitations in personal life or even for premature disability without further consideration. However, some cases will require a specially selected work place adapted to the condition of the spine. Additional information concerning prolapse in adolescents may be found in Børgesen and Vang (1974), Grobler et al. (1979), and Kurihara and Kataoka (1980).

4.5.2.6 Detachment of a Portion of the Vertebral Body Rim

The displacement potential of intervertebral disc tissue (Fig. 4-51) points essentially to the cause of the bone spurs of spondylosis appearing at the anterior and lateral vertebral body. Another type of prolapse to the front (more exactly to the lateral front) is the detachment of a portion of the vertebral margin in connection with the penetration of intervertebral disc tissue from the internal margin of the vertebral ring epiphysis laterally to the front (Figs. 4-58 and 4-59). This type of prolapse dissects an anterior (only rarely lateral) bone portion that is shaped like an orange section. The prolapsing intervertebral disc tissue almost regularly shows a crack. Pseudoarthrosis may develop if no bridging, ossified brace in the vertebral body periosteum exists that fixates the dissected bone portion. The differential diagnosis with regard to the dissection of the vertebral margin is often difficult. The dissection of the vertebral margin is mostly combined with the collapse of a shallow vertebral body cover plate and forms a firm bony connection with the vertebral body during the healing process of the fracture. The gradual margin detachment appears at one or simultaneously at several vertebral bodies but occurs almost exclusively at the upper margin of the vertebral body. Often, this margin detachment occurs in connection with juvenile kyphosis.

Some investigators have hypothesized a traumatic origin for all separations of the vertebral margin. Others have labeled them persistent vertebral body epiphyses [see Junghanns (1930)]. The extensive literature with regard to the development of the orange section–shaped vertebral margin portion is reviewed in Schmorl and Junghanns (1968).

4.5.3 Ligaments and Muscles

4.5.3.1 Baastrup's Disease

Baastrup (1933, 1936) was the first to describe the chronic damage between the spinous proc-

116   CLINICAL IMPLICATIONS OF NORMAL BIOMECHANICAL STRESSES ON SPINAL FUNCTION

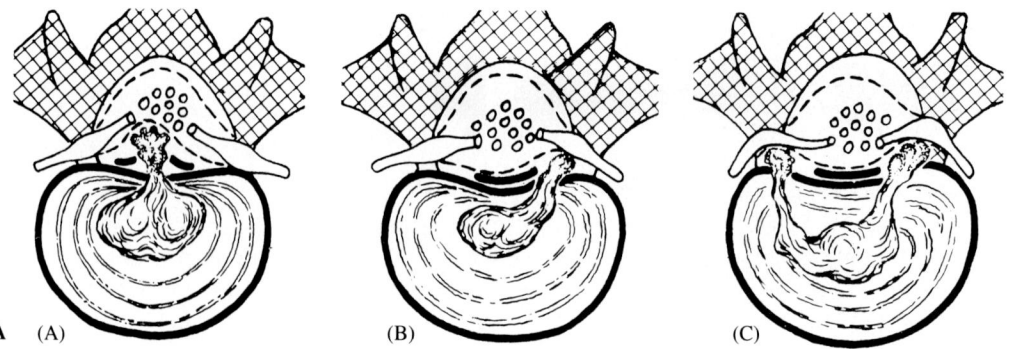

Fig. 4-57 A. The various types of backward intervertebral disc prolapse. **(A)** posteromedial with fibrillation (tear) of the posterior longitudinal ligament; **(B)** unilateral posterolateral; **(C)** bilateral;

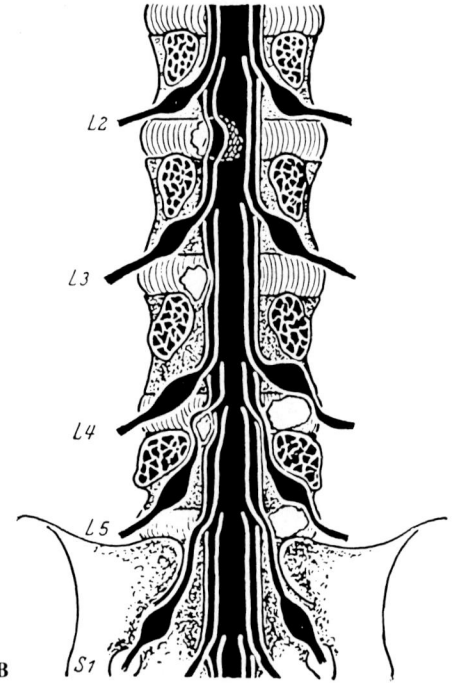

Fig. 4-57 B Relationships of prolapsed nodules of the intervertebral discs with spinal roots. Medial prolapse (L-2) displays few characteristic symptoms and may affect several roots of the cauda equina. Unilateral prolapse (L-3 left) presses root L-4 from the outside. It may also prolapse between the dura side and the root exits so that it simultaneously affects two roots (L-4 left). Larger, lateral prolapses can exert simultaneous or alternating pressure against two roots (L-4 and L-5 right).

esses of the lumbar spine, which may also rarely be found at the cervical spine. It is caused by the wear of interspinal ligaments. Severe lordosis, excessive spinous processes, and height loss of the intervertebral space (eg, through intervertebral osteochondrosis) are related to the development of this painful disorder. According to Eger (1966), its origin must be traced to mechanical influences (eg, shearing and extension forces) on the ligaments. Additional causes are possible. Rissanen (1960) assumes a rheumatic component. Baastrup's disease may also result from sport-specific causes (see section 8.7).

Damage in the interspinal ligaments does not originate in the bonding canals or at the bone attachment but in the ligament itself. Initially, cavities and cracks develop, which may be revealed by injection of radio-opaque medium. Finally, pseudoarthrosis forms between the spinous processes together with progressive sclerosis of contact surfaces: "kissing spines." The roentgenogram is impressive (Fig. 4-60). The disorder substantially limits the static stress resistance and mobility of the spine because of the gradually developing chronic pain. Injection therapy is indicated (occasionally also surgery if the pain becomes unbearable). For extensive literature reviews, see Schmorl and Junghanns (1968) and Knoch (1962).

4.5.3.2 Spinal Acro-ostealgia

Spinal acro-ostealgia, an extremely painful disorder appearing at bone projections, is known to develop at several locations of the support and motor system. Laarmann (1977) addressed these disorders as bonding disorders or muscle tract periostoses. They start in the long bonding canals, which are lined with cartilage and in

Factors Interfering with Functional Capacity 117

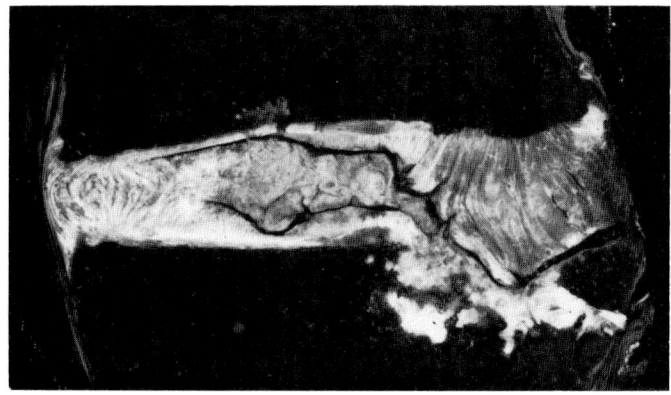

Fig. 4-58 Slightly enlarged picture of a sagittal section of an intervertebral disc. Intervertebral disc tissue has protruded into a tear between the cartilage plate and ring epiphysis and has further moved to the lower front and thus has detached a wedge-shaped portion of spongiosa. Numerous cartilaginous growths in the tear area. Fiber ring dissected from the ring epiphysis.

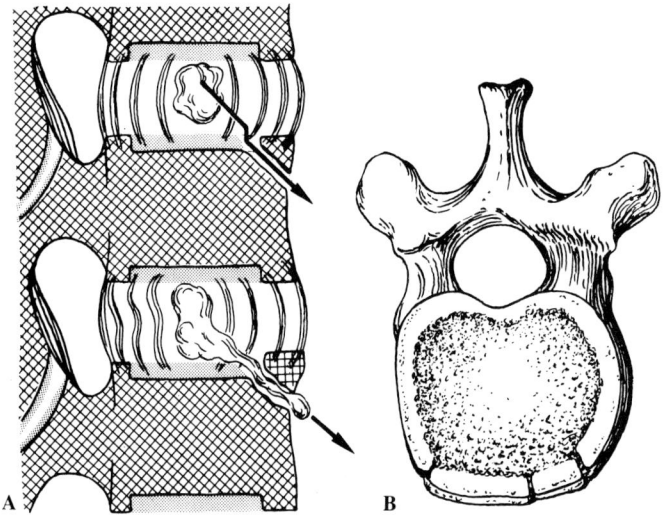

Fig. 4-59 Schematic drawing of a developing separation of a vertebral margin. The intervertebral disc tissue penetrates obliquely from the boundary between the cartilage plate and posterior vertebral ring epiphysis into the vertebral body and squeezes off a portion of the margin (**A**). View of margin dissection at the macerated bone (**B**).

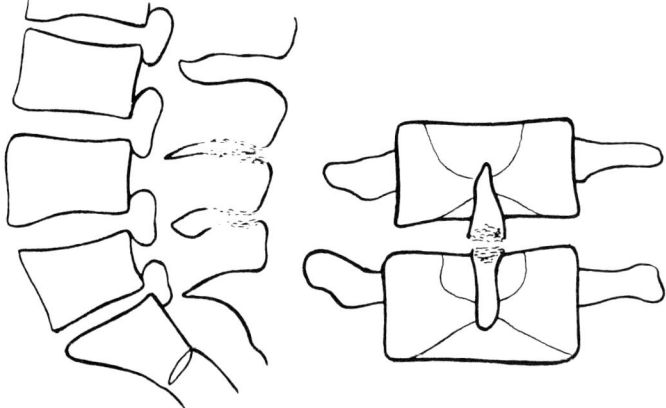

Fig. 4-60 Drawings of Baastrup's disease according to roentgenograms.

which the fibers of tendons, ligaments, and occasionally muscle fascias are bonded in such a way as to form a functional tissue symbiosis with the bone (Drasche 1975; Rettig 1975). At the penetration points, wear of the hyaline cartilaginous contact point (tissue deterioration, tissue fatigue) develops.

Thurner and Bodner (1963) discussed a colloidal collapse of interfibrillar and intercellular substance. Therefore, the tendons lack the elastic cushion of their bonding. They are affected by the deterioration process and tear off. Simultaneously, rugged surfaces and deposits develop and may lead to bone spurs at the painful attachment points: the clinical picture may be radiographically portrayed. A drawing of a periosteum-free tendon attachment is shown in Figure 4-61. Franke (1977) critically discussed this in connection with athletic overstraining of tendon attachment points that are susceptible to frequent tendinoses.

Often, there is a chronic development that strongly resists therapy. Since such damage is explicitly determined by posture and stress, these syndromes are aggravated if the exogenous influences (which are often sport-specific) continue. The usual physiotherapy may aggravate these disorders (Gutmann 1980a).

4.5.3.3 Instability/Hypermobility

The impairments most frequently resulting in instability of the spine originate in the intervertebral motor segment. The decreased functional capacity remains unnoticed for a long time. Only when tissue damage results in a relaxed segment does a pathological, perceptible functional insufficiency result. Three groups of instability were discussed in section 3.4.

Hypermobility may be constitutional (Rompe and Steinbrueck 1981/1982) but may also appear as the cause of back pain as a consequence of decreased muscle strength and ligament insufficiency in connection with a relaxed segment or sometimes independently. A weakness of the musculoligamentous corset (eg, by polio or transverse lesion syndromes) is a severe impairment factor and may lead to painful relaxations in a segment fully exposed to stress (eg, curvature vertex) or in larger sections of the spine. Ligament insufficiency can be compensated for only by muscle tension for a short period. An overstressed back muscle tract slackens or results in a painful extension stiffness. Therefore, overexertion of muscles and ligaments in spondylolisthesis, retrolisthesis, and torsional slippage also finally leads to chronic damage. Even though radiographical functional pictures show a displaced segment in the case of acute pain, they do not provide information regarding its total displacement potential since the pain stimulus results in a defensive stiffness and, therefore, immobility.

During pregnancy, the generally relaxed ligament systems in the pelvic area and at the lumbosacral transition result in a physiological

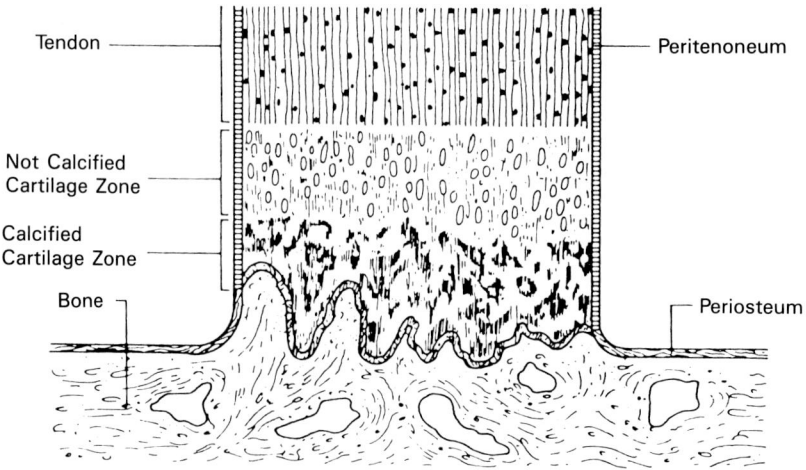

Fig. 4-61 Model of a periosteum-free tendon attachment (Schneider 1954).

hypermobility. In 1980, Gutmann recommended timely, prophylactic measures.

4.5.3.4 Ligament Ossifications

All ligaments of the spine may ossify for various reasons. Depending on the extent of the ossification, mobility and stress resistance are lowered. The most extensive ossifications occur with Bechterew's disease. Extensive, ossified ligaments are found in spondylosis hyperostotica. The wide bone surfaces develop especially at the anterior longitudinal ligament of the thoracic spine (see Figs. 4-43 and 4-44). With spondylosis deformans, bone spurs develop in the anterior longitudinal ligament.

A ligament ossification impairing the spinal cord and spinal roots (which is often difficult to diagnose) develops at the posterior longitudinal ligament that attaches at the back walls of the intervertebral disc. The bone protuberances develop in isolation at one or more locations and also in larger connected bone rims over several segments. They may cause severe neural damage. Often, the bones that project into the spinal cord canal are discovered only by computerized tomography.

The ligamenta flava bridge the vertebral arch articulations at the back wall of the vertebral canal in each segment, but they are a part of the stabilizing ligament system of the vertebral arch series (which is not detailed here). The ligamenta flava are involved in the ossification process of ankylosing spondylitis.

All larger bone protuberances into the ligaments or articular capsules result in impairment potentials: bridging of intervertebral spaces or vertebral arch articulations. Arthrosis at the head articulations, uncovertebral articulations, and sacroiliac articulations also result in impairment and fusing, bridgelike bone spurs. Articular and vertebral fractures may result in similar consequences.

4.5.4 Skeleton and Muscle Corset

4.5.4.1 Introduction

The vertebral skeleton is the essential load-bearing component of the trunk. Therefore, static stress resistance depends to a large extent on unchanged bone tissue and proper structure of the vertebral body and arch shape, including its processes. The load-bearing capacity of the spine must be ensured for the various dynamic and kinetic stresses that are required of the spine by upright posture or changing body postures. Thus, each changed skeleton must be scrutinized with regard to stress resistance insufficiency and/or possibilities of inducing pain.

The bones of the spine are especially and prematurely subject to aging. For example, the vertebral body (next to the head of the femur) shows the deossification of the organ bone in Figure 4-62. Damage in the spinal skeleton can cause severe diseases, including the most widely spread bone disease: osteoporosis. The diffuse back discomfort that accompanies this disease is initially unsubstantial and becomes more obvious with the decline in calcium content (which may be traced radiographically). If osteoporosis is accompanied by a gradual contour distortion of the vertebral bodies, the stress discomfort sometimes increases up to the point where bed rest is required.

The structure of the skeleton is severely impaired or affected in all changes that are congenital or determined by growth. In addition, the consequences of many other influences affect the skeleton unfavorably.

In all cases of bone damage or disease, the bone is usually not the primary cause of pain after it has attained its final internal structure and external shape after accretion, disintegration, and transformation. If pain remains after these processes, different causes should be considered. They may be found in simultaneous damage of soft tissue (ie, at intervertebral discs, ligaments, and the muscle corset), involvement of nerves and blood vessels, and consequences of static changes. The most frequent cause of "back pain" is damage in the intervertebral motor segment.

Painful phases of the disorders (eg, in osteoporosis, bone infections or bone fractures) necessitate appropriate restraint in daily life (eg, no prolonged sitting or riding in automobiles), leisure, and sports. Universal guidelines are not available. The physician must counsel the patient about gradual reintegration and rehabilitation.

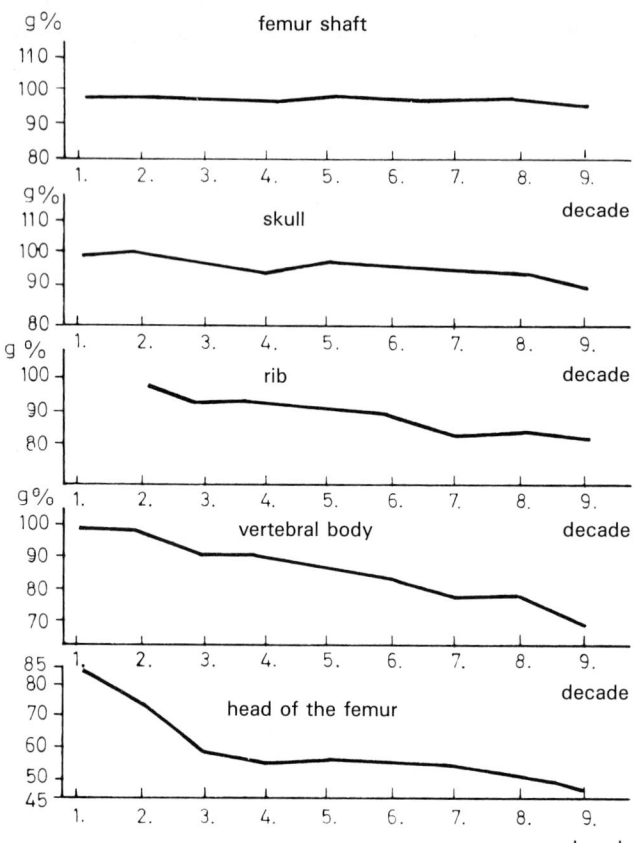

Fig. 4-62 Changes of the bone tissue volume in the total bone during aging. Results of chemical analyses of five bone regions clearly show the "deossification" of the organ bone (Heuck 1976).

4.5.4.2 Osteoporosis

Osteoporoses are the most frequent disorder of bone tissue and are almost exclusively systemic diseases of the skeleton of internal origin, coupled with metabolic disorders. They develop more frequently in women than in men (Jesserer 1981). The best known and most frequent form, senile osteoporosis, results from an increase in physiological bone disintegration. This causes the bone mass to decline, starting at the age of 30. In men, it declines by 3% per decade; in women, by 8%. This finally results in a total bone mass loss of 10% to 40%. Because of a decline in the thickness of the trabeculae, the spongiosa is involved in this process at an earlier time and to a larger degree than the corticalis, which follows only later in the process. The bone disintegration starts in the center of the vertebral bodies and gradually progresses toward all sides.

During this process, the vertical, load-bearing bone lamellae remain initially unaffected (Fig. 4-63). Osteoporosis may be portrayed in roentgenograms when the mineralized bone tissue has been diminished by approximately 3%. The load-bearing capacity of such bones declines progressively since flexibility, compactness, and elasticity decrease with age (Vinz 1975).

Osteoporoses that are localized or restricted to one bone occur only rarely. They are caused, for example, by tumors, inflammations in the bone interior or its surrounding area, and exposure to radiation. Dennert and Muenzenberg (1975) discussed radiographical diagnostics.

Osteoporoses resulting from endogenous causes, which are mostly endocrine impairments of metabolism, are almost always more distinct in the bones of the spine than in other bones. This is a consequence of the good blood circula-

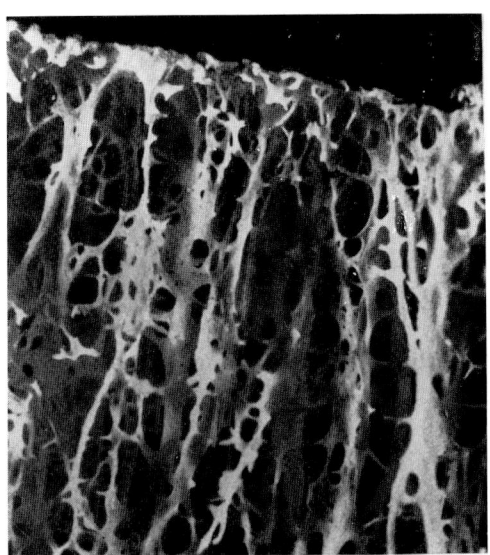

Fig. 4-63 Macerated vertebral body portion of an aged woman. Slightly enlarged. View of the strongly porotic spongiosa structure. Compared to proper spongiosa, the spongiosa plates are decreased in number and thickness and contain more holes (see Figs. 2-8 and 2-9).

tion of the red bone marrow, which is plentiful even in old age. The age-determined decline of calcium in the vertebral bones is more distinct in women than in men.

Krokowski and his associates (1974–1977) attributed osteoporosis to diminished blood circulation in the bones. According to their theory, osteoclastic activity is encouraged if the blood flow in the sinusoidal venous plexus of the bone interior is impaired, be it through stasis following a decreased arterial flow, venous congestion, or reduced extravascular fluid pressure. This theory must be confirmed by additional studies. Krokowski and Peter (1977) emphasized the influence of muscular insufficiency, with additional studies being done by Heuck (1970).

According to Jesserer (1981a,b; 1982), osteoporosis is an individual clinical syndrome but is not a disease that fits into any classification. Therefore, a specific therapy must be used, which he describes. Sodium fluoride is presently the most common drug used. It requires a careful dosage and is successful only after prolonged application [see also Ziegler (1984)]. Osteoporosis is always caused by an endogenous impairment factor for the stress resistance of the bony portion of the spine.

The combination of biochemical changes and continuous biomechanical influence (2.3.5.1) in substantial vertebral osteoporoses results in isolated or multiple vertebral body contour changes, even without an additional accidental event during daily or athletic stresses and leisure activities (Figs. 4-64 and 4-65). These transformations of vertebral bodies may develop in isolation but are in most cases found repeatedly in a spine. Often, there are various transformations of shapes in one spine. In the lumbar region, fish vertebrae dominate with their characteristic biconcave shape and are clearly visible in a roentgenogram. Such obvious vertebral contour changes encouraged the development of measuring methods with a comparative index. Heuck (1976) explained the biconcave index (central index) of Barnett and Nordin. In his opinion, these morphometric procedures in connection with radiodiagnostic measurements support the early diagnosis of vertebral osteoporosis.

Senile osteoporosis and postmenopausal osteoporosis, which appears somewhat earlier in women, are well-known examples of the low resistance capacity of osteoporotic vertebral bones. According to data provided by Havelka (1975), there are approximately 1.6 million women in the United States who suffer from senile osteoporoses and vertebral body contour changes. Problems concerning daily stress requirements and pain are frequent.

Osteoporosis of astronauts was extensively studied during the past few decades. It is remarkable that in spite of daily food rations enriched with calcium, the astronauts suffered the following per diem losses: 635 mg Ca, 296 mg K, and 6.4 mg Fe. Hormonal changes caused by weightlessness and forced inactivity are the essential causes for the development of astronautical osteoporosis.

Examples of osteoporosis of other origins is barotactic osteoporosis of astronauts and fish vertebra disease of adolescents. Osteoporosis can also be caused by drugs, estrogenic and androgenic deficiency, and inactivity.

Osteoporoses of the spine also result in large-curvature, or occasionally bent, kyphoses, rarely in scolioses. Existing scolioses, like existing kyphoses, are aggravated by an additional osteoporosis when subject to daily pressures. Often, osteoporotic kyphosis is associated with

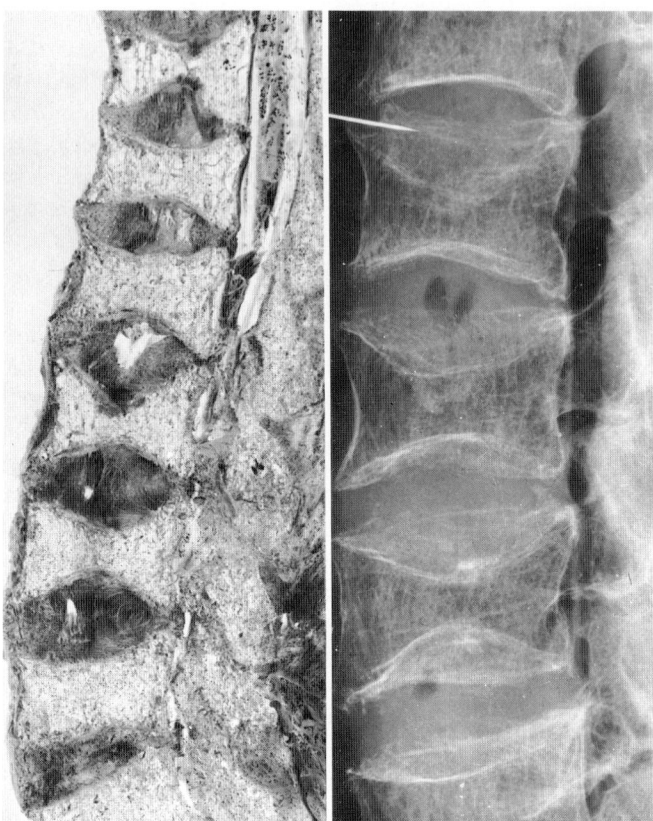

Fig. 4-64 Sagittal section of a severely osteoporotic lumbar spine (77-year-old woman). Centrally indented vertebral bodies: fish vertebrae. In several of the swollen intervertebral discs, there are "hollow spaces" (fluid-filled cysts). In the roentgenogram, some appear to be translucent.

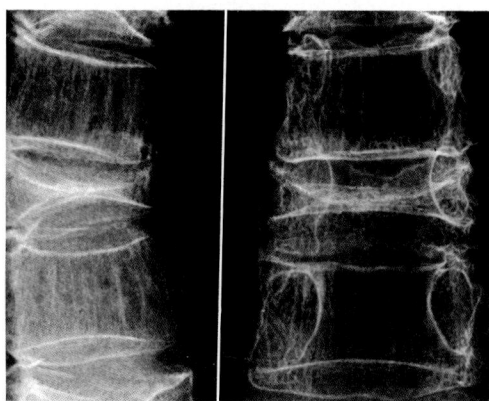

Fig. 4-65 Osteoporosis. **Left:** Lateral roentgenogram of the middle thoracic spine of a 76-year-old woman. Substantial osteoporosis with compression of several vertebral bodies; in the middle, a flat vertebra. **Right:** Roentgenogram of the same thoracic spine, frontal view. Note the "frog head" shape of the collapsed vertebral body.

senile kyphosis, which according to Junghanns (1931) has its origin in damage from strain in the anterior part of the intervertebral disc (see Figs. 4-14 through 4-20).

Questions concerning the development or aggravation of osteoporoses through continuous mechanical influences (increased load or lack of exercise) are discussed in sections 5.3 and 7.3. Conservative treatment methods and diet are discussed in section 7.4.

4.5.4.3 Generalized (Malacic) and Localized Osteopathies

Malacic osteopathies include rachitis caused by a lack of vitamin D, osteomalacia (D-hypovitaminosis of adults), hunger osteopathy (spondylomalacia), and bone damage in sprue and scurvy. Similar bone damage is found in hyper-

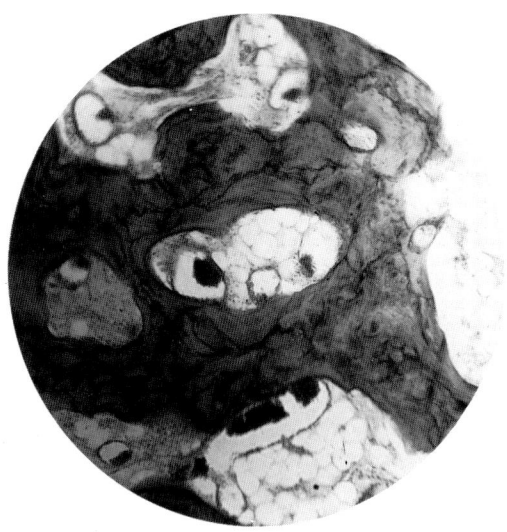

Fig. 4-66 Paget's disease. Photomicrograph of a section through the vertebral body. Widened trabeculae with mosaic structures [photo by Schmorl (1932)].

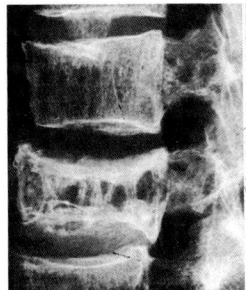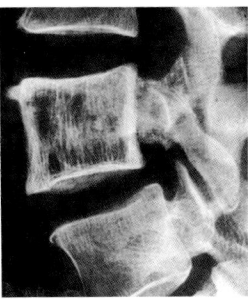

Fig. 4-67 Paget's disease. Lateral partial roentgenograms of the spinal column halves of two men over the age of 60. **Left:** flat vertebra with pagetic structures, thickened vertebral arches, and constricted intervertebral canals; **right:** framework of a diseased vertebral body, thickened vertebral arch.

parathyroid and renal osteopathies and in infantile diabetes and other rare diseases.

The characteristic bone structure in malacic osteopathies results from an accumulation of wide osteoid seams on the trabeculae. However, there is no calcification of the osteoids while the bone degeneration caused by osteoclasts continues uninterrupted. Radiographically, this results in a mellowed vertebral body structure, whereas osteoporosis leaves a clear mark on the trabeculae, whose thickness is decreased. Osteomalacias result in a significantly lowered stress resistance, similar to osteoporosis. Contour changes of vertebral bodies and the resulting kyphosis, or less frequently scoliosis, is common. For more information, see Jesserer (1980, 1981a,b), Kruse (1977), Ritz et al. (1977), and Thurner and Amato (1977).

The cause of the Paget's disease, which Jenner (1980) called a localized osteopathy, is still disputed. It is characterized histologically by mosaic structures (Fig. 4-66) and is probably caused by a virus. It originates in the bone marrow and appears in 3% to 4% of all persons over the age of 40. The spine may be affected monoostotically or polyostotically. In 6.5% of all cases, Paget's disease spreads to all skeletal elements of the spine see Hallermann (1929), Jesserer (1981), and Schmorl (1932).

The bone tissue is soft, can be cut with a knife, and consists of rough streaks or honeycombs with widened bone lamellae. Often "ivory bones" develop. The diseased bone often causes a malformation of the vertebral shape (ie, the vertebral body and vertebral arch increase in their mass). This may induce pressure on the spinal cord or root pain caused by constriction of the intervertebral canal (Fig. 4-67).

4.5.4.4 Osteopetrosis (Osteosclerosis)

The bones in osteopetrosis (ivory vertebrae, marble vertebrae) are characterized by compressed spongiosa. The compression may appear in a roentgenogram as an only moderate widening of the still clearly distinguishable trabeculae or, after a prolonged existence of the cause, it may result in such a complete density of structure that the differentiation of a single trabecula is no longer possible. In some types of carcinoma, up to 33% of metastases are found in the spine. They appear frequently osteoblastically with localized compressions or result in ivory vertebrae. For more information, see Jesserer (1977a, 1982), Junghanns (1979a), Schmidt (1976), and Schmorl and Junghanns (1968).

4.5.4.5 Hereditary Systemic Diseases

Several hereditary systemic diseases that involve the spine cannot be diagnosed in childhood or during the usual physical examinations of the adult. They often do not result in damage with a decline of stress resistance until the later decades of life. In addition, they are difficult to diagnose since they are not always present in a distinct form. In the case of a misjudgment of stress tolerance, this may have severe consequences. In such cases, the examination of the entire skeletal system, the family, and respective laboratory results cannot be avoided.

Chondrodystrophy fetalis, whose prototype is the (chondrodystrophic) dachshund breed with this hereditary disease, seldom appears in humans in a distinct form. The spine is regularly involved. Hunchbacks in the thoracolumbar transition resulting from wedge vertebrae with anterior edges are found in the adult with this disease. In contrast, the substantial vertebral body changes in the infant (irregular flat discs) are present in later life only by way of suggestion.

In the past, a certain demarcation between chondrodystrophy fetalis and the group of endochondral dysostoses was established. The spine is involved in the latter. The vertebral bodies are characterized in youth by round-shaped edges and are decreased in height. The ossification centers in the cartilaginous vertebral ring epiphysis appear less frequently, and the end plates of the vertebral bodies are irregular. These characteristics are similar to those of juvenile kyphosis. However, it is still unclear whether juvenile kyphosis always develops according to this process, to what extent Schmorl's nodules are involved in this process, and which additional influences (eg, mechanical) participate in the development of the final changes of the spine.

Additional diseases belonging to the group of hereditary systemic diseases are congenital fragility of the bones, cleidocranial dysostosis, Albers-Schönberg disease, neurofibromatosis, osteopoikilosis, Down's syndrome, and ochronosis. Details in this context can be found in Hellner (1961) and Schmorl and Junghanns (1968).

These diseases represent decreased resistance against dynamic and static load stresses. In part, this results from bone tissue but is often reinforced by the accompanying variations of the shape of the spine. The physician must consider these stress risks for physical activity.

4.5.4.6 Additional Impairment Factors of Bone Stability

Benign tumors (eg, angiomas) as well as malignant tumors and the rather frequent bone metastases are especially dangerous impairment factors for the functional capacity of the spinal skeleton. Depending on the location and extent of the tumors, the stress resistance of the affected spinal section varies. If a tumor or metastasis spreads from the vertebral body toward the two vertebral arch roots, the collapse at this location occasionally occurs earlier than in the center of the vertebral body. Even small tumors in the interarticular portion cause a collapse because of the tweezerlike pressure of the vertebral arch articulations and therefore may induce spondylolysis or spondylolisthesis (Taillard 1980). Tumor metastases in the vertebral bodies cause wide-ranging destruction: from bone destruction to sudden vertebral body collapse, with pain. In such cases, the patient is unable to name the cause of the collapse (fall, especially forceful forward bend, etc). The collapse of a tumor vertebral body may occur very slowly and leads in most cases to a wedge vertebra, which is tapered toward the front. If the destroyed bone tissue is located laterally, there is also the possibility of scoliosis.

Vertebral body metastases do not always result in bone-destructing processes with collapse since not all metastases show destructive characteristics with decreased bone stability. As already described, some tumors may result in increased bone accretion (up to 33% osteoblastic metastases). The thus developing ivory vertebrae are, in general, as stress resistant as a vertebral body with a normal structure. Nevertheless, it does not seem advisable to expose an individual with an osteosclerotic vertebra to especially high stresses.

4.5.4.7 Muscle Corset

The spine is enclosed by an extensive, strong, and diversely structured muscle corset from which a large number of connecting muscles run to the head, shoulders, and arms; rib cage; pelvis; and legs. In addition, there is a ligament system with many bondings. It is therefore justified to speak of a static-dynamic musculoligamentous corset. Each decline in function in the various sections of the musculoligamentous corset or the failure of larger portions has a harassing effect on the functional capacity of the spine. Fortunately, the spine can adapt to a certain extent (see sections 4.7 and 8.2).

4.5.5 Arthrosis at the Articulations of the Spine

4.5.5.1 Introduction

In addition to the intervertebral discs, which are called semiarticulations, there are a number of semiarticulations and genuine articulations within the intercorporal space at the spine (more than 100) (see section 2.2).

Articulations and semiarticulations are important for the function of the spine, even from a numerical point of view. Unfortunately, they do not always receive the required attention, and because of difficult diagnostics, the search for the true causes of symptoms that appear in the spine and are caused by arthroses of the articulations, semiarticulations, and nearthroses is left undone. Those disorders belong in the group of spinal disorders that are all too often encompassed by the undefined term "rheumatism of the back." Articular arthrosis, especially in the initial stages, can be confirmed only through specific roentgenographic examinations (see Chapter 6).

Since there is usually a connection between articular arthroses and intervertebral chondrosis or intervertebral osteochondrosis (eg, Fig. 3-20), this two-fold damage in the intervertebral motor segment represents a high risk for the stress resistance of the affected spinal sections. An initially latent functional insufficiency is followed by the syndrome of intervertebral insufficiency (see section 3.4).

4.5.5.2 Vertebral Arch Articulations

Anatomical descriptions of vertebral arch articulations may be found in Chapters 2 and 3.

Since the 25 pairs of vertebral arch articulations, which are connected in a complete biomechanical functional chain, are practically exerted together in each movement of the spine, arthroses (which are often diagnosed late) are significant. In addition, there is segmental coupling of arthrotic articulation pairs in connection with damage in the structure of the intervertebral disc, eg, chondrosis and osteochondrosis (Figs. 3-20 and 4-32). The relationship between arthrosis of the vertebral arch articulation and spondylotic spurs on the vertebral bodies is typically determined by whether the articular damage is unilateral or bilateral.

It is often forgotten that during the frequent abuse of the spine (lack of exercise, vibrations, high-performance sports, etc), the intervertebral disc as well as the respective pair of vertebral arch articulations within the intervertebral motor segment are subject to axial pressure. During motion, stress-absorbing and load-distributing tasks are assigned not only to the intervertebral disc but also to the vertebral arch articulations. The development and aggravation of articular arthroses of the spine are significantly influenced by vibrations.

Arthrosis of the vertebral arch articulations causes early and progressive pain. It remains to be determined to what extent the arthrotically changed cartilaginous layer of the articular facet or the nerve endings alone absorb pain in the affected articular capsule and transmit pain (see section 2.2). Expert radiography of the vertebral arch articulations (ie, oblique tomography) (Fig. 4-68) was described by Erdmann (1979). New imaging procedures (section 6.3) will lead to even better diagnostic methods.

Arthrosis of vertebral arch articulations is often quite distinct in the cervical spine (Fig. 4-69). Its significance for discomfort in the neck and for neck-shoulder-arm syndromes increases if it coincides with arthroses of the uncovertebral articulations.

The frequent arthroses of the vertebral arch articulations have long fascinated science. Lange (1934) and Guentz (1933) established a 50% incidence of arthroses in 60-year-old persons in 1934. The frequency in individual intervertebral motor segments was calculated by Guentz to be 70% at T4-5 and 50% to 60% each at L3-4, L4-5, and L5-S1 [see also Schmorl and Junghanns (1968)]. Endogenous and exogenous influences play different roles, with the main influence being of endogenous origin. Often, the diagnosis of accompanying arthrosis of the vertebral arch articulations follows that of intervertebral chondrosis. A unilateral arthrosis of the

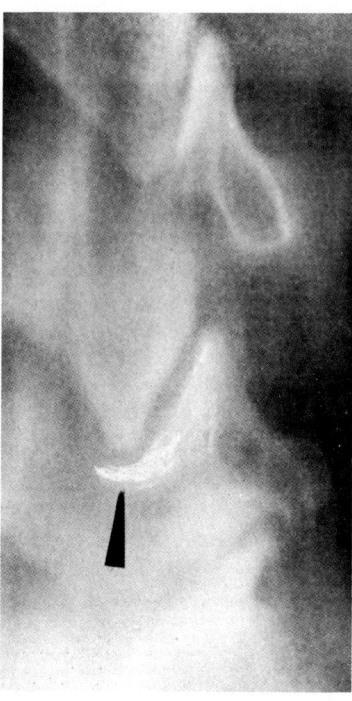

Fig. 4-68 Partial view of an oblique tomograph of the inferior lumbar vertebral arch series of a 40-year-old man. Arthrosis of the vertebral arch articulations, partially with large arthrotic spurs (**arrow**) (from Erdmann 1979).

vertebral arch articulations develops in scoliosis [described by Heine (1981) in juveniles with an average age between 15 and 16 years] and is also found after injury of the vertebral arch articulation, after detachment of the articular tip, etc. The connection between pseudospondylolisthesis and other vertebral displacements was discussed in section 4.4.

Vertebral arch articulations are subject to regressive changes with pain by motion and stiffness in ankylosing spondylitis and chronic polyarthritis (Aufdermaur 1981).

Arthrosis of the vertebral arch articulations has been studied rarely in spite of its great practical significance. In 1977, Vernon-Roberts and Pirie reported on the formerly unknown penetration of cartilage tissue into the adjacent spongiosa. They demonstrated a rounded cartilage center in the subchondral bone surrounded by a compact capsule. Schmorl (1930) observed similar penetration in the bones at the vertebral body–intervertebral disc boundary in intervertebral osteochondrosis. In contrast to the typical Schmorl's nodules, he called those pearl-like structures arthrotic cartilage nodules. Newer histological studies of arthrosis of vertebral arch articulations were conducted in 1979 by Heine and Rodegerdts.

Because of the frequency and significance of the painful arthrosis of vertebral arch articulation, this disorder is classified in the group of spinal damage with an inherent risk for motion and stress. For additional information, see Groher (1979) and Niethard and Gaertner (1980). Computerized tomography allows more detailed insights into arthrotic damage of the vertebral arch articulations.

The arthrotic vertebral arch articulation, via its swollen capsule tissue and/or pressure of the

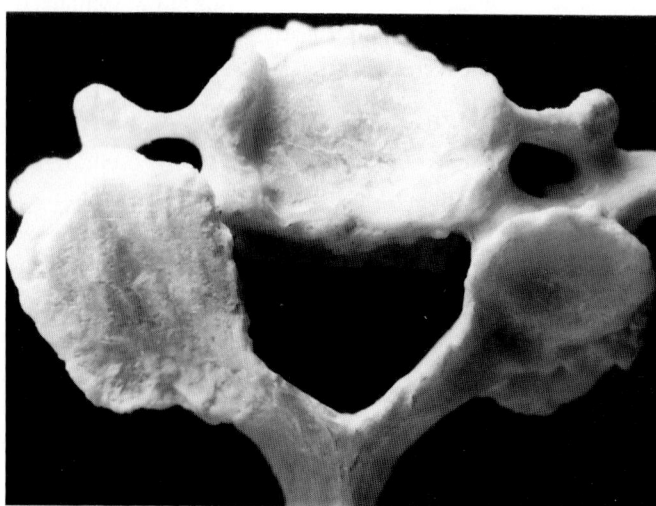

Fig. 4-69 Photograph of a macerated cervical vertebral body. The severe left-sided arthrosis in the vertebral arch articulations with beveled grooves, widening of the entire articular surface, and severe arthrotic edge spurs greatly constrict the foramen costotransversarium. Less severe arthrosis on the right side (from Hinz 1970).

rims, may cause distant effects that simulate, accent, or significantly contribute to organ damage because of its autonomic neural connections (Kunert 1981). Because of their partly common nerve supply, damage in the intervertebral discs and vertebrocostal articulations must also be considered in addition to vertebral arch articulations (Kunert 1981).

The rare tumors of the vertebral arch articulations (Willert and Enderle 1981) result in arthroses if they are located close to the articular surface or if they destroy the articular facet. Motion, stress, and vibrations cause great pain.

The necessity of considering the painful arthroses of the vertebral arch articulations in diagnostics is discussed in Chapter 7, insofar as conservative treatments are preferred. In the past few years, the number of successful surgical treatments has increased (see Chapter 7).

4.5.5.3 Sacroiliac Articulations and the Symphysis Pubis

Both of the sacroiliac articulations (section 2.2), like the vertebral arch articulations, must be regarded as an articular pair in the segmental structure. They must withstand static and dynamic stresses (and often also sinoid or stochastic vibrations) and must distribute them between the pelvic girdle and sacrum, and finally from the spine-sacrum boundary to the pelvic girdle. Their internal structure, consisting of a genuine articulation in the front and a taut fibrous joint in the back, is well adapted to these tasks (Fig. 2-33).

Stresses that are mostly asymmetrical and abnormal (hip joint disorders, limping walk) result in arthrosis in the sacroiliac articulations and a painful blockade or instability of one or both articulations. The inevitable compensation (balancing) stress of the swaying walk finally leads to muscle fatigue, back pain, and similar symptoms of insufficiency and to sacroiliac overstress damage (Dihlmann 1975). In 1979, Dihlmann recommended sacroiliac computed tomography in order to refine diagnostics.

Subacute, chronic, latent arthritides in the sacroiliac articulations, as are present in ankylosing spondylitis and in the vinylchloride disease, pose a great impediment in terms of load-bearing because of the accompanying pain.

The suspicion of arthritis or arthrosis in the sacroiliac articulations is confirmed by pain induced in the course of a physical examination. On the roentgenogram, there are edge spurs in the frontal view at the lower portion of the sacroiliac joint as well as band-shaped compressed spongiosa with relaxed transitional layers along the joint. In Bechterew's disease and other inflammatory diseases, the sacroiliac articulations may ossify and fuse unilaterally or bilaterally.

Incorrect sitting habits in daily life (in part combined with influences of occupational sitting), motor biking, riding in automobiles, and probably many sports activities connected with pelvic rotation encourage the development of sacroiliac arthroses. Pelvic articulations relaxed by difficult deliveries (including symphysis) may also be responsible for arthroses. The acute, juvenile sacroiliac articular syndrome and its differential diagnosis were described by DuPan and Widmer in 1979. For additional information, see Elhabali et al. (1979), Helbing (1978), and Schlenzka (1980).

The symphysis pubis (section 2.2), according to Luschka (1858), a semiarticulation, must absorb stresses in connection with the sacroiliac articulations, which reach the pelvis either from the spine or from the legs as a prolonged or rhythmical (vibration) pressure. A scoliotic pelvis (caused, for example, by different leg lengths, walking disorders caused by hip joint problems, and similar influences) results, especially through the swaying stress during walking, in painful arthroses at the symphysis. As in the sacroiliac articulations, ossification can develop.

4.5.5.4 Head Articulations

Anatomical descriptions are provided in section 2.2.

Pain by motion and vertebral blockades are indications of arthroses of the head articulations (Fig. 4-70). Long-term studies of the connection between arthroses of the head articulations and influences in competitive sports have not been performed. Buetti-Baeuml (1954), and others, found serious damage in the central and lower cervical spine (spondylitis deformans, osteochondrosis, uncovertebral arthroses) of 30- to

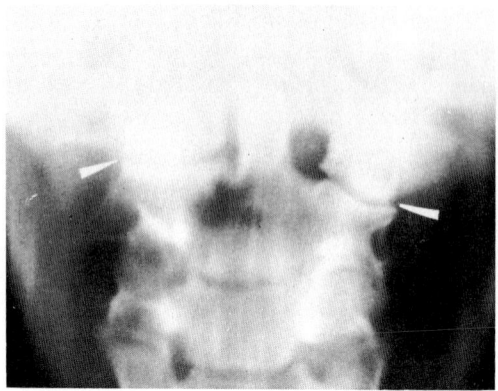

Fig. 4-70 Arthrosis deformans in the atlantoaxial articulation as a result of constitutional slanting of the articular surfaces (computed tomograph).

40-year-old individuals who had been free-style wrestlers since the age of 14 to 15. In studies of athletes, attention must be paid to the many variations and abnormal shapes in the head-neck boundary that are especially susceptible to forceful impacts. They cause prolonged headaches, especially in connection with simultaneous arthrosis. The damaging influence of the motorcycle helmet, which must be expected because of the constant forward tilting of the head (especially during cross-country rides with more difficult conditions), has not been the topic of sufficient, systematic studies. In addition, vibrations and stochastic impacts affect the spine via the motorcycle seat.

4.5.5.5 Uncovertebral Articulations

The hook articulations (half-moon articulations, uncovertebral articulations) at the left and right side of the cervical spine develop only gradually after birth through the growth of half-moon–shaped bone processes proceeding upward (Fig. 4-71) and through the connected development of gaps in the intervertebral disc tissue (Fig. 2-16). Arthrosis develops early in these uncovertebral articulations (Fig. 4-71) and is almost always coupled with a height loss of the intervertebral space (Fig. 4-72) caused by intervertebral disc wear (up to degeneration). The arthrotic bone ridges projecting into the intervertebral canal especially constrict the penetration area of the spinal roots (Fig. 4-72). This coupled damage finally results in intervertebral insufficiency with the usual painful consequences (section 3.4). These changes are visible in the frontal roentgenogram taken centrally and in the oblique tomograph. Computed tomography portrays details even better.

In addition to the intervertebral canal, the bony ridges of uncovertebral arthrosis also threaten the vertebral artery (Figs. 4-73 through 4-75). The impairment of the vertebral artery, which leads to an obstructed blood flow in some head positions, may negatively affect the inner ear and may cause or aggravate kinetosis.

Uncovertebral arthroses are troublesome in daily life, in some jobs, and in leisure because the symptoms appear suddenly. Therefore,

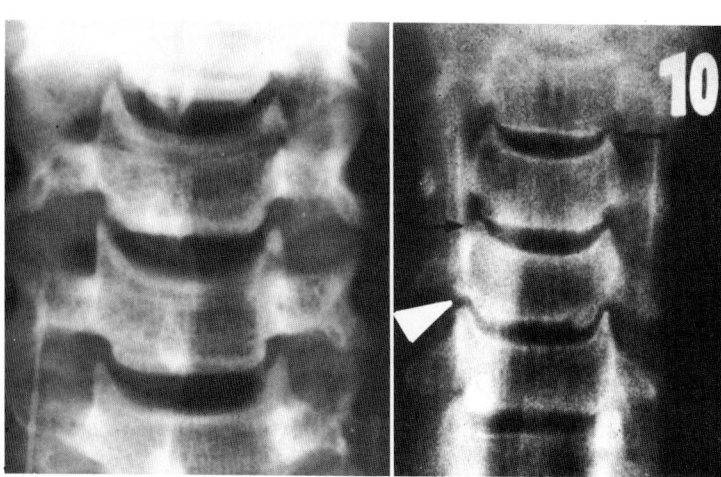

Fig. 4-71 Tomograph of uncovertebral articulations. **Left**, normal; **right**, beginning arthrosis (**arrow**).

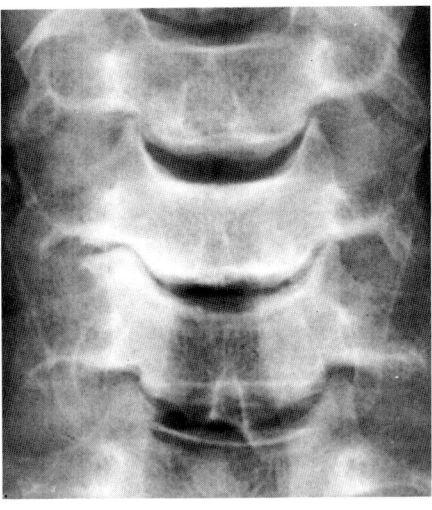
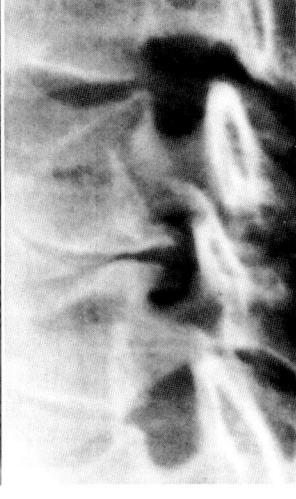

Fig. 4-72 Arthrosis of the uncovertebral articulations. **Left:** unilateral severe arthrosis of the uncovertebral articulation (in the initial stage on the other side). Simultaneous height decrease of the intervertebral space (beginning intervertebral osteochondrosis) (oblique X-ray). **Right:** bony edge ridges of the arthrotic uncovertebral articulation severely constricting the intervertebral canal.

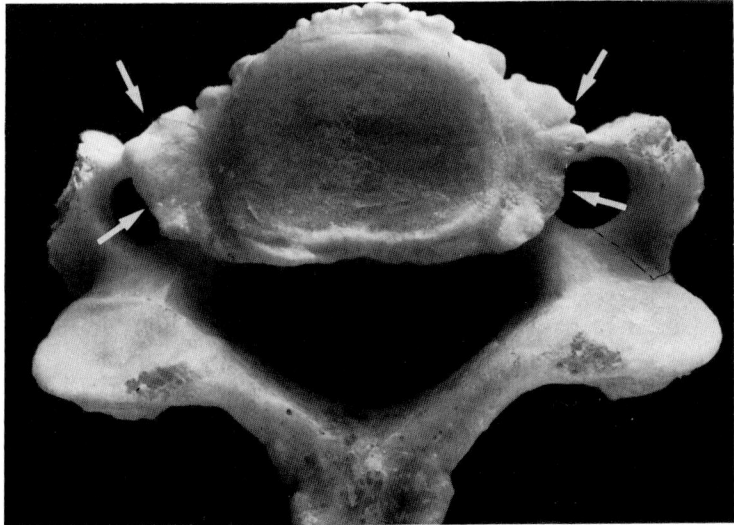

Fig. 4-73 Macerated cervical vertebral body. Large, bony bilateral edge ridges in uncovertebral arthrosis (**arrows**). They constrict the foramen costotransversarium (more on the left than the right) and therefore the penetration canal of the vertebral artery (picture from Hinz 1970).

arthroses are also serious impairments in exercise and sports. Often, surgical treatment is required (section 7.4).

4.5.5.6 Pseudoarticulations

Transition vertebrae at the lumbosacral boundary are characterized by unilateral or bilateral widening of the transverse processes (Figs. 4-1 and 4-2). Frequently, jointlike connections (pseudoarticulations) form and undergo arthrotic changes during the course of life. Often, there is a simultaneous intervertebral osteochondrosis. Pain is always present during static and dynamic stress: painful transitional vertebrae (Fig. 4-76).

The endogenously predetermined progression of arthrosis in pseudoarticulations and of chondrosis in the "inferior" structure of the intervertebral disc is often aggravated by exogenous stresses, which, however, are only secondary causes. The painful transitional vertebrae interfere with heavy physical labor and many activities in daily life. They also impair athletic performance.

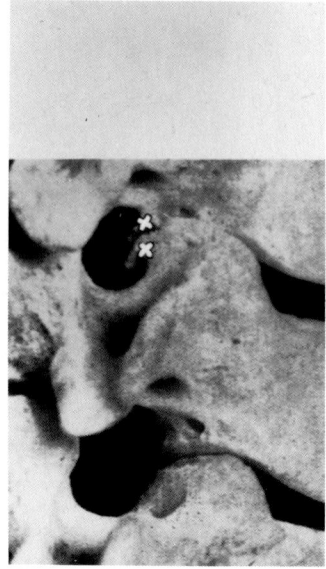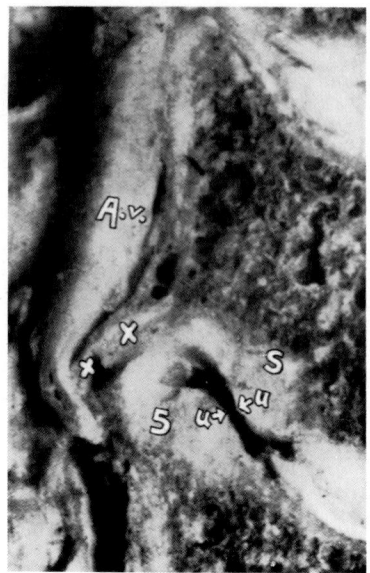

Fig. 4-74 Uncovertebral articulation in the cervical spine. **Left:** in a macerated specimen, normal conditions in the lower part with a wide intervertebral canal; on top, arthrotic edge ridges (**XX**), with constriction of the intervertebral canal. **Right:** frontal section through the right half of the cervical spine with severe arthrosis of an uncovertebral articulation; severe edge spurs (**XX**) that displace and constrict the vertebral artery (Krogdahl and Torgensen).

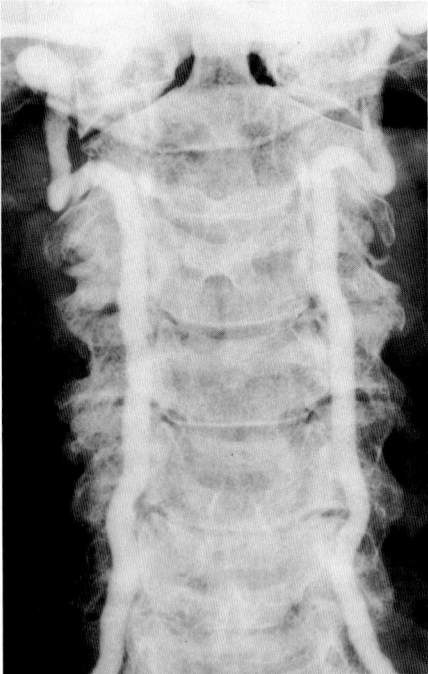

Fig. 4-75 Angiogram of both vertebral arteries showing uncovertebral arthrosis in a 67-year-old man. Archlike evasion of both arteries at C5-6 caused by uncovertebral arthroses (normal condition of arteriography at neck is shown in Figure 2-25).

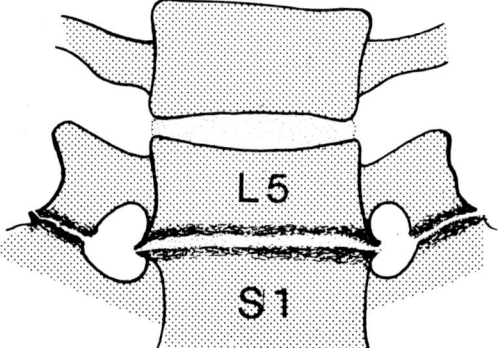

Fig. 4-76 Transitional vertebrae L-5/S-1 with pseudoarticulations between widened transverse processes and ala of the sacrum. Arthrosis in pseudoarticulations and intervertebral osteochondrosis (drawn according to roentgenogram).

4.5.5.7 Vertebrocostal Articulations

The development and final condition of the vertebrocostal articulations were discussed in section 2.2. The anatomical conditions often result in vertebrocostal arthrosis combined with intervertebral osteochondrosis. The corresponding progression of arthrosis is felt as a strong, lancinating lumbago in the rib area (intercostal neuralgia) when a respiratory motion of the rib cage coincides with an unfavorable posture, movement, or stress of the trunk (Maigne 1970) resulting from a blockade in the vertebrocostal articulation, which is caused by neural misregulation attributable to muscle spasms. The vertebrocostal arthrosis may be demonstrated radiographically with a radiological technique described by Hohmann (1968). For additional

Table 4-2 Frequency of Changes in the Spine

Authors: No. Cases	Runge 4654	Lindemann 4291	De Sèze 1000	Le Go 4161	Fargeot 100	Foehr 684	Cremona 5580
Changes	(%)	(%)	(%)	(%)	(%)	(%)	(%)
Abnormalities	32.00	43.00	5.50	25.40	36.00		
Spina bifida	3.09	11.00				24.00	0.74
Symptoms at lumbosacral boundary	6.16	7.70		15.71	11.00	11.00	8.76
Spondylolysis/spondylolisthesis	2.08	1.40	3.80		5.00	4.00	10.36
Discopathy	2.53		0.4			11.00	
Arthrosis	19.20	17.50				39.00	28.76
Static symptoms	2.32		0.90	5.85	0.90	65.00	18.41
Juvenile kyphosis	0.81	0.40	0.50		0.50	82.00	2.78

Data from Cremona (1972).

---

information, see Andrian-Werburg (1979), Arct (1978), Bergsmann and Eder (1982), Floeel (1980), Geiger (1983), and Steinruecken (1980b).

4.6 DECREASED PERFORMANCE CAPACITY THROUGH ADDITIONAL INFLUENCES

4.6.1 Consequences of Infections (Spondylitis/Spondylodiscitis)

Infections frequently cause perceptible chronic damage of the spine. It would exceed the scope of this book to describe all infectious agents with consequences for the spine. Only a few frequent types are discussed (see Table 4-3).

Tuberculosis is the most frequent cause of bone infection; spondylitis tuberculosa results most frequently in severe consequences [see Kastert (1974) for statistics]. Spinal tuberculosis characteristically begins in one vertebral body and then penetrates the adjacent intervertebral disc and destroys it rapidly [see Brocher (1973), Caroit et al. (1975), Kastert (1974), and Schmorl and Junghanns (1968). Radical treatment possibilities were described by Chahal and Jyoti (1980).

Only in the past few decades has vertebral infection through brucellosis (Bang's disease, Maltese fever) been reported. The course of the disease is often subacute: the real cause remains undetected for a long period. Especially in the case of a subliminal, uncharacteristic progress, a bacterial invasion of organs, bones, and articulations occurs. The spine becomes involved one to four months after the infection. Infections may develop either in the vertebral arch articulations or the vertebral bones in the form of spondylitis brucellosa with intervertebral disc liquefaction (an early symptom).

Special attention should be paid to the brucella infection of the sacroiliac articulations described by Mergold (1963). It accompanies the acute disease but may also develop further when the brucella bacilli have been successfully eliminated from the organism. In the same way brucellosis induces arthritis in many articulations of the body, it may induce an infection of the vertebral arch articulations (spondylarthritis brucellosa) with symptoms that are often incorrectly diagnosed. For additional information, see Diethelm and Kastert (1974), Fenollosa (1975), Hall (1974), Henderson et al. (1975), Kaben et al. (1976), Lederer (1972), Mohr (1969), di Rienzo (1950), Schmorl and Junghanns (1968), and Schnurrenberger et al. (1975).

Salmonella infections play an increasingly important role. The more than 100 types are pathogenic in part for humans (eg, typhus abdominalis and paratyphus), in part for animals, and often for both. Salmonella infections transmitted from animal to human cause acute intestinal disorders. Endemic transmission to humans may in part be attributed to "unphysiological" animal husbandry in stock farms

Table 4-3 Causative Agents of Inflammatory and Parasite-Induced Diseases of the Spine

Specific Vertebral Diseases

Mycobacteria, especially
  M. tuberculosis and M. Bovis
questionable or rare
  m. avium
  m. Calmette-Guerin
  m. leprae
and a-typical mycobacteria treponemas, especially
  t. pallida
  congenital and acquired syphillis
  tabes dorsalis
questionable or rare:
  t. recurrens (recurrence fever)
  t. pertenue (frambesia)

Unspecific Spinal Diseases

bacterial infections
staphylococci
streptococci
pneumococci
salmonella
rickettsiae
brucellae
coli bacteria
klebsiella
enterococci
gonococci
pseudomonades

Mykoses
  blastomycines
  histoplasma
  cryptococci
  coccidia
  sporotricha
actinomycomas
nocardia
viruses

Parasite-induced Spinal Diseases

echinococci
cysticercus

Data from Schulze (1979).

[see Diethelm and Kastert (1974), Hall (1974), and Schmorl and Junghanns (1968)]. According to statistics reported by Kempf et al. (1972), spondylodiscitis specific to the causative agent develops in 0.2% to 0.3% of salmonellosis, most often at the lumbar spine. As in tuberculosis and abdominal typhus, the intervertebral disc is affected at one vertebral body, with a rapid transition to the adjacent vertebral body.

The clinical picture in general proceeds more rapidly than with tuberculosis.

Unspecific pyogenic agents, mostly staphylococci but also streptococci and others, may directly penetrate the spine and result in vertebral osteomyelitis. More often, this disorder develops as a consequence of metastases (ie, directly) during a septic systemic disease. According to several surveys, this disorder accounts for approximately 2% of all cases of osteomyelitis. Often, the bacteria accumulate at several locations in the spine. The vertebral bodies and their processes, including the vertebral arch articulations, are affected much more frequently than in case of the specific infections (eg, tuberculosis, brucelloses, and salmonelloses). During the chronic course of an unspecified vertebral infection, there are, in addition to vertebral body foci with liquefaction of adjacent intervertebral discs, occasional bone compactions that look like ivory bones (Deplante et al. 1974) [see also Schmorl and Junghanns (1968)]. Schulze (1979) provided a list of infectious agents causing vertebral osteomyelitis compiled on the basis of the work of Diethelm and Kastert (1974) (see Table 4-3). Schmorl and Junghanns (1968) also provided a compilation.

Spondylodiscitis, the destruction of an intervertebral disc by infection, is mostly caused by the transition from an adjacent vertebral body. The term *spondylodiscitis* refers to the consequences of a direct penetration of infectious agents or chemical substances into the intervertebral disc tissue, as far as the specific changes of rheumatic spondylodiscitis are not present.

Only rarely is a direct stab or the penetration of a projectile the cause of spondylodiscitis. Just as rare are iatrogenic "liquefactions" of the intervertebral disc tissue. They may be present after surgery at or near the spine and after punctures (discography, vertebral body puncture, lumbar puncture, lumbar sympathetic trunk blockade, aortography, etc.) (Fig. 4-77) [see also Hoppenfeld (1980), Stoehr (1980), and section 7.4].

Spondylodiscitis after punctures is regarded by some not as an infection but rather as a chemical reaction to the injected fluid (eg, after discography), which results in a rapid dissolution and resorption of the cartilage ground sub-

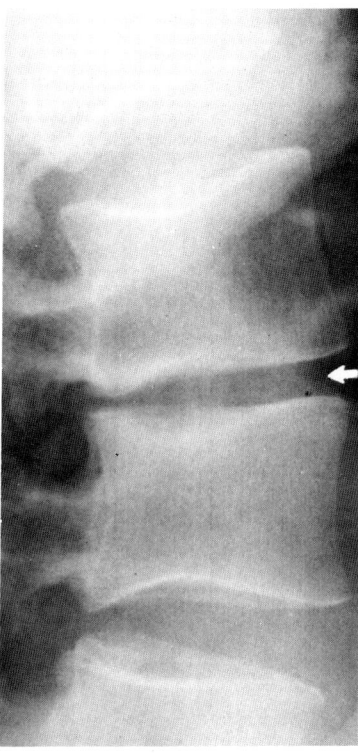

Fig. 4-77 Spondylodiscitis at L3-4 (**arrow**). Partial view of a lateral roentgenogram. Significant height decrease in the intervertebral space and relaxation of the bony vertebral body end plates, especially in the central and dorsal section, with sclerosis.

stance in the fibrous-cartilaginous annulus as well as in the hyaline-cartilaginous end plates (Farfan 1979). If a direct infection develops after the puncture of an intervertebral disc (artificial spondylodiscitis), it is often limited to the tissue of the intervertebral disc and the immediate area. The final result is usually a height loss of the intervertebral space with a fibrous or bony stiffness.

Spondylodiscitis is very painful in its acute stage and often requires a long healing time with immobilization. Surgical removal with localized antibiotic treatment and bone chip filling may be helpful and may shorten the healing process (section 7.4). After complete ossification, an unimpaired stress resistance is reestablished.

Details concerning the therapeutically desired spondylodiscitis (nucleolysis) resulting from injection of the proteolytic enzyme chymopapain or through collagenosis (including possible damage) may be found in section 7.4.

For more information, see Busse et al. (1976); (postoperative discitis); Ford (1976); Hoelzl and Riedler (1976) (lumbar sympathetic trunk blockade with infection); Kerdiles et al. (1975) (aortography with infection); Manani et al. (1980) (discogenic vertebral sclerosis after surgery).

4.6.2 Rheumatism

The connections between "rheumatism" and the spine are various and for many reasons very complex. The largest obstacle to organizing these relations in terms of pathophysiology and pathomorphology is the nonuniform, often controversial nomenclature and the persistent attempts of many rheumatologists to expand the term *rheumatism* to include all articular pain and skeletal muscle disorders. According to Anderson (1971) and others, this would also include pain after a trauma if it lasts longer than six weeks. The term includes osteoarthroses and chronic (degenerative) intervertebral disc damage of the spine (ie, intervertebral chondrosis as well as intervertebral osteochondrosis) and also the symptoms of a prolapse of the intervertebral disc. "Unexplainable rheumatic symptoms" are also included, as is ankylosing spondylitis and spondylosis deformans. According to Bros (1965), the term also includes damage of the skeleton caused by chemical toxins in fluorosis, bone necrosis resulting from embolisms in decompression illness with their consecutive symptoms at the articulations, and other exogenous bone and spinal damage. In contrast to this unsystematic expansion, Wright (1979) advocated a clear definition of *seronegative spondylarthropathies*.

Even though the pathophysiological foundations for the delimitation of the various forms of inflammatory rheumatism have not been established in a satisfactory manner and basic research has in no way been concluded, the unlimited expansion of the term *rheumatism* nevertheless remains inexplicable. This is especially true for the increasingly used term *rheumatic group*, which comprises many diagnosable and pathoanatomically delimited symptoms of age-induced and trauma-induced articular wear together with less well defined or undefined painful symptoms. The path toward clear differential diagnostics is further obstructed by the introduction of the term *degenerative rheumatism* for the group of chronic, painful spinal disorders (de Blecourt 1963). Tilscher (1983) recommended that the diagnosis ''degenerative rheumatism'' be applied only with the utmost reservation. Hopefully, the introduction of the subspecialty ''rheumatology'' will have a clarifying effect on many controversial questions concerning the terms *rheumatism* and *rheumatic disorders*. This subspecialty is intended for internal medicine and orthopedics and comprises only ''inflammatory rheumatism.''

With regard to the spine, the ''inflammatory rheumatic disorders,'' which are often called ''genuine'' rheumatism are of interest: rheumatic fever (acute polyarthritis), chronic polyarthritis (primary chronic polyarthritis, rheumatic polyarthritis), and ankylosing spondylitis or ankylopoietica (Bechterew's disease). The relationships of these three forms of disease with the spine vary. To a large extent, this can be attributed to the multitude of inflammatory rheumatic diseases and their many symptoms. The decisive factor is the interaction of genetic predispositional factors, ie, endogenous factors. In addition, viral influences, streptococcal infections, autoantigens, dysfunction of lysosomal ferments, etc., play a role.

The stress resistance of the spine declines during the painful, acute periods of rheumatic symptoms to such a degree that substantial impairments for personal life and athletic activity exist. Medical counsel is essential during the chronic conditions of progressive stiffness, but motion and stress of the spine should not be prohibited. For additional information, see J.A.D. Anderson (1971), Behrend and Behrend (1971), Fassbender (1978), Fritze et al. (1971), Jung (1977), Junghanns (1975), Lederer (1972), Miehlke (1975), von Arnim and Hoecherl (1976), and Zaitseva, 1970.

Rheumatism as a systemic disease of the derivatives of the mesoblast (Fassbender 1973, 1975) affects mostly the cartilage tissue. At the spine, this means a susceptibility of the intervertebral discs. In severe cases, it results in spondylodiscitis, ie, the destruction of the intervertebral disc with encroachment of the adjacent vertebral bodies (Fig. 4-77).

Spondylodiscitis may be a concomitant symptom of primary chronic polyarthritis and also of Bechterew's disease (Fig. 4-78) and other influences. One or several intervertebral discs are affected. The serious destruction induces instability of the relaxed intervertebral motor segment accompanied by severe pain.

Spondylodiscitis develops especially frequently in adolescents and affects mostly the cervical spine. It destroys ligaments and causes relaxations, which may result in spinal cord compression. The difficult radiological diagnostics were discussed by Wackenheim (1974). For additional information, see Eulderink and Meijers (1976), Frank and Gleeson (1975), Gschwend et al. (1981), Martel (1977), and Roques et al. (1977).

An important finding (Caplan 1953) was the frequency of silicoarthritis: Caplan's syndrome. It appears in miners as a progressive polyarthritis and increases with exposure and age. The way and manner in which a combination of a severe quartz dust silicosis and primary chronic rheumatism is formed have not been determined [see Behrend and Behrend (1971), Dechoux (1972), Fritze (1974), and Rosmanith (1971)]. Since spinal damage has been increasingly observed in connection with primary chronic rheumatism, especially at the head-neck boundary, attention should also be paid to the spine in all cases of silicoarthritis.

It has not yet been sufficiently established whether juvenile rheumatic cervical spondylosis, which Reinhardt (1974) described as severe ossification following rheumatic polyarthritis, is the consequence of spondylodiscitis developed and healed primarily at the cervical spine or whether it needs to be classified into the usual pattern of spondylarthritis ankylopoetica. Schilling (1963, 1984) explicitly discussed the questions associated with rheumatic cervical arthritis [see also Caplan et al. (1962), Mattson (1971), Petry (1954), and Rettig (1975)].

Prolonged pain in projecting bone points (eg, at the spinous and transverse processes of the spine), acro-osteoalgia, is occasionally seen as a concomitant symptom of infectious rheumatism.

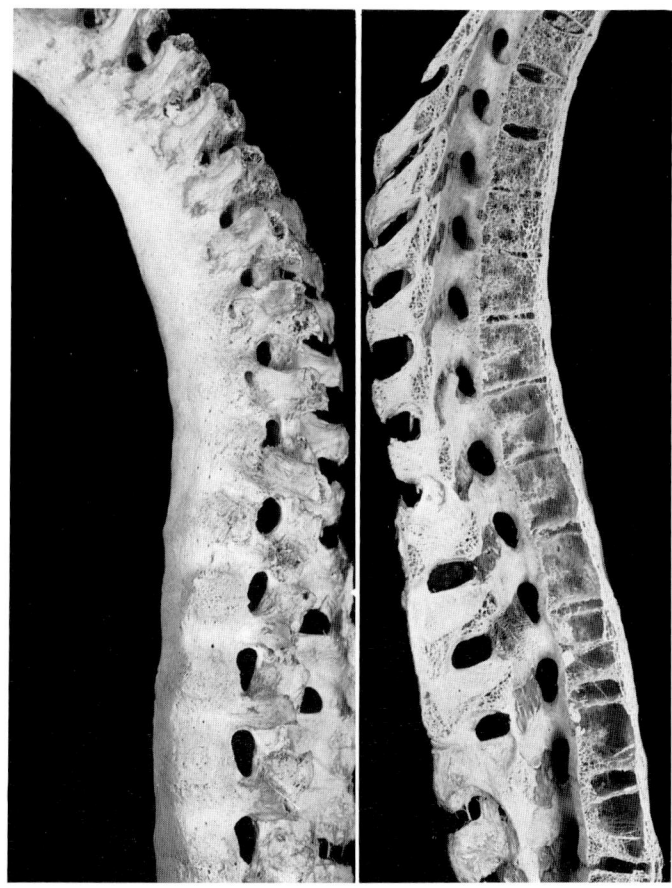

Fig. 4-78 Ankylosing spondylitis. (**A**) macerated spine (60-year-old man). Complete ossification of the external surface of the vertebral body–intervertebral disc series. Ossification of the ligaments in the vertebral arch area. In the sagittal section, ossification and thickening of the anterior longitudinal ligament, intervertebral discs in their external parts, ligamenta flava, vertebral arch articulations, and interspinal ligaments at the spinous processes; severe loss of vertebral body spongiosa. (**B**) bone scintigram. Inflammatory symptoms in both sacroiliac articulations (Grebe 1972).

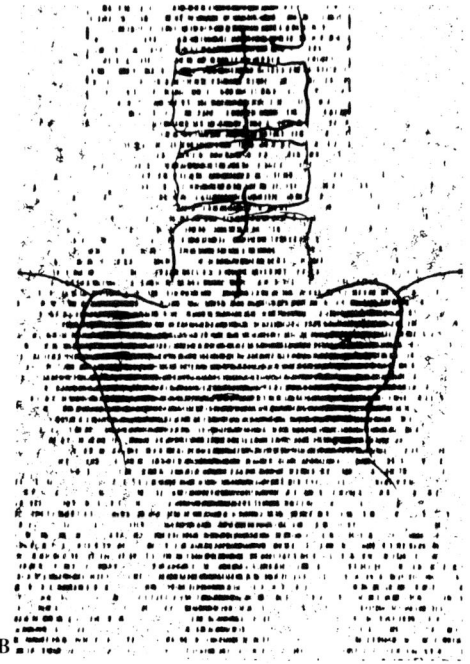

4.6.3 Ankylosing Spondylitis (Bechterew's Disease)

Even though there are several differential diagnostic relationships between some forms of rheumatism (eg, benign seronegative chronic polyarthritis) and the distinct clinical picture of ankylosing spondylitis (Fig. 4-78), the etiology of the disease remains undetermined [see Ott and Wurm (1957) and Schmorl and Junghanns (1968)].

The pathogenetic progress in the vertebral arch articulations is still disputed [see Aufdermaur (1981), Guentz (1933), and Ott and Wurm (1957)]. This also applies to the vertebrocostal articulations. The early involvement of the sacroiliac articulations is manifested by progressive pain. The diagnosis of articular involvement may be determined through scintigraphy (section 6.3) (Fig. 4-78).

A variety of influences has been suggested as causes of Bechterew's disease. These include primarily coldness and wetness, physical exertion, and toxic damage resulting from lead (Werthemann and Rinetlen 1932). The primarily unanimous opinion of investigators dealing with the question of exogenous influences is that a person's job has apparently no influence on the development of ankylosing spondylitis, that its origins can be traced in most cases to adolescence, and that a distinct genetic component exists. However, prolonged unfavorable influences such as heavy physical exertion and shock to the spine, as well as coldness and wetness, may at least temporarily aggravate the progression of the disease (Behrend and Behrend 1971). An infectious disease may also temporarily exert an aggravating influence on the progression of latent ankylosing spondylitis or on the beginning of a new attack of the disease. This applies also to dysentery (Mohr 1969) and to Reiter's disease, which is connected with Bechterew's disease and also causes obvious changes in the sacroiliac articulations. A specific treatment during the acute attacks and constantly repeated rehabilitation measures are indispensible for the reestablishment of the most extensive functional capacity (Bergsmann and Eder 1982). In severe cases, surgical straightening is considered (section 7.4). For additional information, see Miehlke (1975), and Schmidt (1980) (rehabilitation prognosis).

4.6.4 Metabolic Abnormalities

The extensive metabolic functions of normal bone tissue were discussed in section 2.3. Even though the skeleton is extensive, metabolic processes are more intense in the spine than in the long bones, since the blood-supplied red bone marrow in the spongiosa spaces of the vertebrae contacts the bone over a very large surface. This becomes especially obvious in several metabolic disorders. In addition to vertebral bones, intervertebral discs and ligaments may also be affected, with serious consequences for their stress resistance.

4.6.4.1 Diabetes and Gout

Spondylosis hyperostotica was first explicitly described by Forestier. There are still animated disputes concerning its origin. Overstressed prolonged posture is discussed as a possible origin. Since the icinglike bone accretion of scolioses and kyphoses is seen increasingly at the interior of the curvature, a certain relation to pressure stress seems to exist. The combination with a diabetic metabolic condition (50% of patients) and connections with hereditary and/or endocrine causes (which are often established in the literature) indicate a dominating significance of these causes.

Baader (1954) described the presence of meniscopathies in the knee joints in gout and diabetes. If this is true to a larger extent, then the suspicion that intervertebral discs (because of their similar structure) and the menisci in the vertebral arch articulations may be affected similarly is justified. Pathohistological studies are therefore recommended. They may lead to identification of the cause of any concomitant pain at the spine. For additional information, see Aufdermaur et al. (1980), Boos and Rehr (1969), Evans and Boda (1970), Forgacs (1974), Glick (1972), Pazderka et al. (1973), and Resnick et al. (1975).

4.6.4.2 Ochronosis (Alkaptonuria)

Metabolic disorders with serious effects on the spine include ochronosis (alkaptonuria). In this hereditary metabolic disorder, a specific enzyme is missing. Therefore, the cyclical amino acids are broken down only to homogentisic acid, which is deposited into the rather sluggishly nourished tissue and gives the tissue a black color. At the spine, the ligaments and especially the intervertebral discs are affected. In addition to the black discoloration, an obvious degeneration of the intervertebral disc tissue occurs at a young age and results in intervertebral osteochondrosis.

The typical changes of this clinical picture (height loss of the intervertebral spaces, sclerosis of vertebral body end plates, relaxed intervertebral motor segments) are accompanied by intervertebral disc calcification, which radiologically clarifies the syndrome. Intervertebral osteochondrosis coupled with incorrect mobility results in pain during each occurrence of stress. Thus, this disease affects physical activity and often prohibits it. In the final stage, bone bridges sometimes develop between the vertebral bodies. For additional information, see Schmorl and Junghanns (1968), Seliwanow et al. (1971), and Zimmermann et al. (1972).

In the case of severe destruction of the intervertebral disc tissue structure extending over wide areas of the spine, a reestablishment of a pain-free load-bearing capacity cannot be expected.

4.6.4.3 Other Intervertebral Disc Damage

There are several other changes in the tissue of the intervertebral disc that might be related to metabolic disorders (eg, the aging of bradytrophic tissue), which is determined by endogenous factors and depends greatly on metabolic processes. At the vertebral body–intervertebral disc boundary, various conditions may cause changes in the transitional layers (bony vertebral body end plate, cartilage layer in the intervertebral disc) and seriously threaten metabolism. This induces damage by wear or aggravates existing damage. Accompanying vibrations unfavorably affect the transitional layers or impair the normal fluid flow of supply and removal and cause stagnation.

4.6.5 Chemical Substances and Ionizing Rays

Bone tissue is a storage organ for various contaminants that invade not only through occupational exposure but also through environmental pollution (C.W. Schmidt 1976a) via the lungs or gastrointestinal tract. After passing into the blood stream, they finally arrive at the bone. Since the red bone marrow of the spine is especially well supplied with blood, well into old age, an overabundance of pollutants induces storage.

4.6.5.1 Fluorine

The best-known substance of the group of trace elements inclined to collect is fluorine.

Fluorosis of the vertebral bone may be seen in a relatively early state by spinal roentgenogram. Initially, a painful osteoporosis dominates the marble bones disease. With the progression of the disease, the spine undergoes increasing stiffness and motion and stress problems, as in ankylosing spondylitis [see Junghanns (1979a)].

4.6.5.2 Lead

Bone tissue is especially susceptible to the accumulation of an increased supply of lead. Since this is primarily true for growing bones, Stoefen (1975) pointed to the possibility of lead poisoning in children and adolescents caused by automobile exhaust. The involvement of the spine in chronic lead poisoning is discussed in detail in Chapter 7.

In the blood of adults, an increased lead content was linked with cigarette and alcohol consumption. The lead content in the blood of heavy drinkers was 30% higher than in the blood of nondrinkers or occasional drinkers. In heavy cigarette smokers (up to 40 cigarettes per day), the blood contained an average of 44% more lead than the blood of nonsmokers. The increased amount of heavy metal in the blood was primarily attributed to impaired liver function.

4.6.5.3 Cadmium

Because of increased industrial demand, cadmium, the rare heavy metal, now has a universal production of approximately 17,000 tons compared with 80 tons in 1911. Metallurgy and the burning of plastics release emissions into the air. Several types of grain and vegetables accept cadmium from the air as well as from the ground. Thus, cadmium reaches the human body by way of vegetables and meat products in the diet. In addition to this poisoning of the gastrointestinal tract, cadmium is also inhaled during manufacturing processes. Additional danger is inherent in cigarette smoke.

Because of this increasing environmental pollution, cadmium acts as a pollutant and the cause of several diseases that have a direct effect on the skeleton, especially the spine. Bone damage with pain in the pelvis, spine, and heel bone results. The bone damage caused by cadmium accumulation appears on a roentgenogram as severe osteoporoses, but should rather be counted as malacia. In the advanced stage, painful kyphoses and scolioses develop. For additional information, see Bittersohl (1976), Cumbrowski and Raffke (1975), Friberg (1960), Lachnit (1975a), and Rettig (1975).

4.6.5.4 Vinylchloride and Polyvinylchloride

Vinylchloride and polyvinylchloride cause bone damage, which has not been shown in the spine. The involvement of the sacroiliac articulations in the clinical picture deserves much attention. As in Bechterew's disease and Reiter's disease, the changes show irregular articular surfaces with marginal sclerosis. They are explained as arthritis (Buchter 1978; Dodson et al. 1971; Thiess and Versen 1974). The Bechterew's disease–like changes encourage a further examination of the spine since sacroiliac arthritis is often the initial symptom of a pathological process ascending in the spine. This might determine whether chemical influences are able to induce a spinal disease that resembles ankylosing spondylitis.

4.6.5.5 Ionizing Rays

Ionizing rays can cause damage in bone tissue and bone marrow. Emanations of radioactive substances as they occur in industrial manufacturing, with their incorporated radionucleides, may cause lung damage and simultaneous leukemias and similar damage of the blood. These diseases must be classified under those blood diseases that lead to osteosclerosis and are summarized under the term *osteomyeloscleroses*. They are similar to the marble bones disease caused by fluorine poisoning. Osteomyeloscleroses are characterized by an increase in the thickness of trabeculae with the external contours remaining the same. The spine is affected in an early stage (Schmorl and Junghanns 1968). In some cases, osteosclerosis of the spine in addition to changes in the blood is a sure diagnostic sign for damage caused by radioactive substances.

Radiation-induced leukemia in the form of chronic myeloid or acute leukosis, in spite of all precautionary regulations, is still a relatively frequent occupational disease of radiologists (Schuettmann 1974), who have a leukemic mortality rate three times higher than the general population (Lewis 1963).

Leukemia is 10 times as frequent in patients who have received radiation treatment for spondylitis ankylopoetica than in the general population. Radiation treatments for other reasons result in an increased leukemia rate, with involvement of the spine. For additional information, see R.E. Anderson (1971), Duncan and Howell (1970), and Oughtersen and Warpen (1956).

4.6.6 Tumors

In numerical terms, benign and malignant primary tumors play no important role in the bones and soft tissues of the spine. In contrast, tumor metastases are found much more frequently in the spine than in other bones. An extensive statistical study in this respect (1000 autopsies with tumor findings) was compiled in 1932 (Schmorl and Junghanns 1968). The spine is the primary site of metastases in men, with 66% of prostate carcinomas, 42% of sarcomas, and 33% of bladder tumors; in women, with 66% of carcinoma of the breast; and in men and women with 30% of lung and bronchial cancer.

It is not rare that the pain of vertebral metastases and their detection in roentgenograms lead to the search for primary tumors. Occasionally, the vertebral metastases with symptoms of paraplegia point to the previously unnoticed primary disease focus. Because of the pain, the performance capability of the spine is significantly impaired.

Tumors and metastases in the spine represent substantial impairments for the stability of bone tissue and therefore for stress resistance.

Radical surgery of a vertebra affected by a tumor, and its replacement with plastic or metal, is discussed in Chapter 7.

4.6.7 Space Flight

Acceleration and weightlessness are the two factors affecting the human body in various ways during high-altitude flight and space flight. They also result in spinal damage. A calcium loss leads to osteoporosis of the skeleton. In the intervertebral disc, the fluid content increases (see section 2.3). Both disorders affect performance capability in the job, daily life, and athletic performances, sometimes even for a long time after the damaging influences have ceased.

4.6.8 Injuries

After vertebral fractures, the former stress resistance returns, depending on the degree of bone healing and reconditioning of muscles attained through treatment and rehabilitation. The simple vertebral body compression fracture without a significant angle development may be gradually reintegrated soon after the bony stabilization.

In spinal injuries with paraplegia, the bone–intervertebral disc damage heals after corresponding conservative or surgical treatment to a point where they may be subjected to stress. The resumption of the former job or introduction into a new activity is difficult, but not impossible [see, eg, Meinecke (1976) and Paeslack (1975)].

Injuries of intervertebral disc, isolated or in connection with vertebral body and/or vertebral arch fractures, require a long healing process to recover a stable, functional condition. This is especially true for whiplash injury of the cervical spine (Erdmann 1973; Hinz 1970). The reason for this is the relaxation in the injured intervertebral disc tissue with accompanying damage in the adjacent soft parts, eg, hemorrhaging in the muscles. The majority of the injured will be able to perform in their previous job and to resume the stresses of daily life and suitable athletic activity. In general, a sufficient static and dynamic stress resistance returns, even though it may be limited to some extent.

In the case of severe compression fractures, surgical erection and stabilization are recommended (Chapter 7).

4.6.9 Surgery of the Spine

Surgery to repair prolapse of the intervertebral disc is the most common among the increasing number of operations for the spine. In many cases, the full stress resistance of the spine (according to age) returns. For additional information, see Braun and Maksoud (1980) (cervical spine); Schwaegerl (1980); and Shport et al. (1978).

An increasing number of operations to straighten kyphoses or scolioses are being performed (section 7.4) as well as operations to repair intervertebral instability (see Chapter 3). Such operations may result in painlessness and improved stress resistance. This applies also to operations for spondylolistheses (Baltschev and Schoolev 1978).

The majority of spinal surgery is performed after conservative treatment has failed. Because of the long duration of the disease with its painful conditions and impairments, a systematic postoperative rehabilitation is necessary and may frequently take some time. After successful rehabilitation, reintegration into the former life style becomes possible in most cases, as long as the primary disease does not progress or affect other areas of the spine. Regular checkups are recommended so that pseudoarthroses (which are not infrequent) (Suezawa 1980) may be discovered and immediately surgically removed. For additional information, see Beyeler et al. (1979), and Junghanns (1982).

Surgical stabilization of spinal sections results in the upper and lower portion of the reinforced section having new relations with regard to mobility and stress. This may occasionally lead to damage of the intervertebral discs and vertebral arch articulations, which lie immediately above or below the reinforced sections, and is manifested by renewed symptoms (Goymann and Konermann 1981).

Surgery for kyphosis is subject to special problems. Indications for surgery are freedom from acute recurrences for years, impairments, and psychological stress that affects the family and job.

4.7 PROGNOSIS OF SPINAL DISORDERS

Spinal disorders that are present or that begin in youth or develop in later decades of life have a tendency to worsen. However, the prognosis is decisively determined by the severity with which the disease begins, as well as the extent of accompanying exogenous influences. The individually determined resistance, individual behavior, timely beginning and continuation of suitable treatment, and cessation of detrimental exogenous influences determine the future progress. Prophylaxis is of essential significance. The partially hereditary constitution influences structure, function, and stress resistance in the spine to a degree that cannot be precisely established. This also applies to variations and malformations as well as vertebral displacement.

The percentage of genetically caused susceptibility to disorders of the intervertebral disc (eg, chondrosis in early life) remains disputed, even though juvenile kyphosis is considered a manifestation of endochondral dysostosis, which often runs in families. Berry (1961) demonstrated hereditary transmission of intervertebral disc changes in a species of mice. Because of the susceptibility of a "constitutionally weak" spine, individuals with this characteristic must be prophylactically treated.

In the prognosis concerning the stress resistance of a spinal column, attention must be paid to the loss of compensational ability with progressive age. This compensational ability to maintain muscle strength and ligament tautness lasts only for a few decades. For this reason, persons with weak muscles whose attitude prevents them from undertaking regular, continued reconstructive physiotherapy and enthusiastic athletic activity, must be evaluated differently than others. The further progress of a spinal disorder must be considered with special diligence if the patient is being examined after the age of 50.

4.7.1 Self-Protection/Adaptation

Fortunately, the self-protection inherent in the organs of the support and motor system offers certain capabilities in protecting the spine from detrimental mechanical influences. The adaptation to a required performance through changed bone structures, an increase in muscle strength, tightening of stressed ligaments, and a positive psychological attitude toward physical performance can prevent many kinds of spinal damage. However, compensation finds its limits where previous damage of the spine cannot be surmounted or where the lack of personal will has a hindering effect. Eitner (1975) accurately described how reactive, degenerative, and involutive aging processes (or their combination) affect the function of individual organ systems.

5

Strain Caused by External Influences

5.1 INTRODUCTION

5.1.1 Functions of the Spinal Column

The spinal column has primarily static and kinetic functions. It supports the head and shoulder girdle and transmits their weight and a large portion of the trunk weight onto the pelvis. In addition, the rib cage is anchored to the spinal column and the internal organs of the thorax and abdomen, which are in part suspended from the spinal column. However, the spinal column does more than support these weights. Because of the muscle and ligament connections beginning and ending there, the spine is continuously involved in the strains and movements of the extremities and head, as well as in the locomotion of the entire body. During this process it also makes possible sensory-physiological spatial orientation, eg, establishment of equilibrium and maintenance of the horizontal position of the eye contact line. All movements support the pump mechanism that is indispensable for the proper nutritional diffusion of the intervertebral disc (see section 2.3). Therefore, its biomechanical functioning regulates the biochemical conditions of the tissue in the intervertebral space.

In addition to these functions, the spinal column is also a protective organ of great importance. It encloses large parts of the central nervous system (CNS) with (1) nerve roots that exit at the top of each intervertebral motor segment through the intervertebral canals and (2) the accompanying blood vessels. These topographic conditions protect the spinal cord and nerve roots from endogenous and exogenous influences, but simultaneously leave enough room for movement within the framework of the range of normal motion possibilities: stretching, compressing, rotating, tilting, forward, and lateral and backward bending.

Nevertheless, because of the close interrelationship between the spinal column and the CNS, even insignificant impairments of the structure can produce significant pain.

5.1.2 Four Groups of External Influences

The most obvious exogenous strains affecting the spinal column are clearly mechanical influences, such as job strain and stress produced by the individual's shape and posture, walking, standing, running, jumping, bending, and athletic leisure activity; that is, essentially daily movements. This first group of influences has the most impact on the spinal column.

Because of our present lifestyle a second group of external influences has increased in significance: lack of exercise. Underexertion because of "comfortable" sedentary work which is compounded by additional long periods of sitting in leisure-time activities, threatens the natural functioning of the spinal column, especially the viability of the intervertebral disc: **the intervertebral disc thrives on motion, physical underexertion (lack of exercise) is more damaging to the spinal column than to other portions of the support and motor system.**

A third group of mechanical load stresses plays a very detrimental and ever-increasing role, also as a result of our modern lifestyle: vibrations. Vibrations especially stress the intervertebral discs that are avascular, depend on nutritional diffusion, and are important for movement and cushioning of many mechanical strains. Stress to the intervertebral discs causes a combination of biomechanical and biochemical problems (see section 2.3).

A fourth group—the effects of cold and heat, environmental influences, and chemical substances—has an impact on our daily lives on the job and in our leisure-time activities.

If they last long enough and have a certain intensity, these external influences may seriously threaten a healthy spinal column, especially a growing infantile or juvenile one. Also, they can significantly aggravate previously existing disorders of the spinal column that date back to youth or have developed in the third to fourth decade of life as a consequence of aging, especially in the tissue of the intervertebral disc. Knowledge of the progress of these disorders is important if the physician is to determine the stress resistance of the spinal column in order to suggest prophylactic measures or treatment. With this knowledge, the physician will be better able to prevent damaging transgressions of the functional tolerance of the spinal column.

For more information on the application of biomechanics to clinical practice, refer to the following literature (Andersson 1980, Erdmann 1968, Dupuis and Zerlett 1984, Junghanns 1979, Reuben et al. 1979, White and Panjabi 1976).

5.2 GENERAL BIOMECHANICAL FUNCTIONAL REQUIREMENTS

Biomechanics is the application of known rules, laws, and research procedures of mechanics to the study of the living body. It recognizes and researches interactions among physiological values (force, acceleration, etc.) and the living body for the purpose of deriving practical medical application. The cooperation of biologists, physicians, pathologists, and physiologists, with bioengineers, mathematicians, and finally computer analysts is necessary to advance knowledge in the field of biomechanics.

Because of its position as the central element of the body, the spinal column is the focus of much recent biomechanic research. Many new works have examined the mechanical stress resistance of the "resting" spinal column and the movement processes with their resulting stresses. In many cases, the researchers were concerned with the determination of threshold values between tolerable and excessive stress, the transgression of which would be followed by functional failure.

Biomechanical research has taken several paths. Stress-physiological research uses biological testing methods to ascertain the general stresses resulting from an individual's lifestyle and occupation, the damage to the spinal column caused by these stresses, and their prevention. Animal experiments are used to determine stress tolerance values. Basic ergometric data have been derived for certain postures and stresses that were then used to determine tolerance limits in daily life and athletic efforts.

Because the stress resistance of a limb chain (such as the spinal column) is no stronger than that of its weakest member, it is essential to determine where this weak point is located. In addition to biomechanical variations in the transition from soft tissues (intervertebral discs) to bones, a special susceptibility to strain lies in the transitional areas between the spinal column sections. The head-neck transition and lumbosacral transition are particularly susceptible to strain, as are the lower cervical spinal column and the transitional zone between the thoracic and lumbar spinal column. In addition, it must be established whether the intervertebral motor segments that lie between the compact bones and are functionally stressed to a special degree may be regarded as segmental units that resist mechanical impulses less well than the skeleton.

It is difficult to establish stress tolerance limits for the growing spinal column in childhood and for previously damaged or diseased spinal columns, eg, those with shape and posture abnormalities, intervertebral disc damage, bone diseases, etc. Because the question of "biomechanical value"—static, as well as dynamic—arises frequently in certain jobs, in daily life, and in sports, it is the responsibility of health care professionals and sports instructors to determine the stress tolerance limit of each individual to prevent transgressions of that limit.

Disparities between exerted stress and stress resistance, for the most part, will only be of pathological significance if congenital or previously acquired damage plays a role in the transition to disease. Vibrations also play a role in this context (see section 7.3).

5.2.1 Shape and Posture

The longest-lasting and most significant exogenous influence on the spinal column of humans occurred when the human straightened from quadruped to a two-legged position and began to walk (Fig. 2-1). This change took place many millions of years ago. It resulted in an admirable adaptation of the spinal column to its new spatial orientation and corresponding tasks. Nevertheless, it seems that the final stage of evolution from walking on all fours to standing has not yet been reached. Consider the many, very different variations and malformations at the two transitional zones—vertebral column/head and the lumbar spinal column/sacrum. These transitional zones are very unstable to this day. Variations in the number of vertebrae, abnormal vertebral body shapes, the fusing of individual elements, the absence of others, or their incorrect location are indications of a still ongoing developmental process (see section 4.3). These variations are linked to an increased pathological potential and frequent pain.

Anatomical, genetic, and orthopedic textbooks often contain contradictory opinions about the normal shape and posture of the spinal column. The question remains whether each spinal column has its own shape that is completely predetermined by genetic disposition or whether the upright walk determines the shape of the spinal column with its characteristic kyphotic and lordotic curvatures. In the opinion of Knese (1963),

> It is not possible for us anymore to regard the individual form of the spinal column as spinal curvature which resulted once from a very distinct stress. Each spinal column, as a variation of a basic type, has its own, individual form and displays its—unfortunately mostly unknown—developmental history.

5.2.1.1 Shape

The typical shape of the adult spinal column with two lordoses (cervical spinal column, lumbar spinal column) and two kyphoses (thoracic spinal column, sacrum) in the sagittal level and the obvious flexion between the last presacral vertebra and the base of the sacrum is adapted to an upright posture and walk, except for the exceptions mentioned in section 4.2. However, the curvature radius of each spinal column section can vary within a distinct range, even without pathological impairments.

In a frontal view, the spinal column should be straight and without curvature at the sacrum. However, often small scolioses exist that have only an insignificant impact on movement or stress capacity. Some authors attribute these scolioses to right- or left-handedness, as well as to the lateral aorta with its pulsating internal pressure (Schanz 1930, 1931).

The general consensus is that the spinal column gradually takes on an individual shape (Fig. 2-38) during a developmental process that is genetically influenced. However, the final shape of the spinal column is undoubtedly determined by vertical stress as well, ie biomechanical forces. Gravity also plays a role. The individual shape of each spinal column is determined by the influence of many muscles and by the shapes of the vertebrae and intervertebral discs, which are themselves genetically determined and modified during individual development (Knese 1963, Schulthess 1902). This final shape of the spinal column is the biomechanical base for the requirements of life.

The shape of the spinal column can be altered by prolonged mechanical stimuli. Neuromuscular diseases as well as lack of exercise (see section 7.3) can result in incorrect posture, eg, after a prolonged confinement to bed or weightlessness during space flight. In such situations the coordinated mechanical stimuli of gravity and muscle function and the discoligamental tension balance between the elasticity of the ligaments and the viscoelastic pressure of the intervertebral discs are absent.

The spinal column design and the maintenance of its shape are substantially determined by the inclination angles, which vary according to their location in the individual sections of the spinal column. The variously oriented joint surfaces of the vertebral arch articulations gradually change their inclinations and rotations at the transitions between the sections (Figs. 2-28 to 2-30 and 2-37). In addition, the articular surfaces are shaped differently and may differ on the left and right side. Therefore, the vertebral arch articulations exert an important (in part, impairing) influence on the static and dynamic functions of the spinal column.

The angle at the lumbosacral transition determines the shape of the entire spinal column to a particular degree, because its structure rests on the base of the sacrum. The sacral base's inclination in relation to the horizontal plane and the different anterior and posterior heights of the presacral intervertebral disc are the essential factors in determining the transmission of vibrations through the spinal column in the sagittal level up to the cervical spinal column/head transition. For this reason, the angle at the lumbosacral transition zone has been of interest to the fields of biostatics and biodynamics. It is difficult, however, to measure the angle at this location. Depending on the problem the person is attempting to solve, different points and lines of reference can be used (Figs. 2-41 and 2-42, Junghanns 1929, Whitman 1925).

The shape of the last presacral vertebral body, which is frequently malformed, significantly influences the promontory angle. A double promontory may develop (Figs. 2-41 and 2-42).

In addition to the variable angles at the lumbosacral transitional area, the numerous variations of the head articulations (transition between the head and cervical spinal column) are as responsible for the individual shape of the spinal column as the varied vertebral arch articulations at the other transitional areas—cervical spinal column/thoracic spinal column and thoracic spinal column/lumbar spinal column. Therefore, variations in the vertebral arch series and in the vertebral body/intervertebral disc column, as well as the accompanying muscle variations and the pelvic inclination, determine the distinct individual form of the axial organ (Davidowitsch 1976, Leger 1959, 1968). This shape provides an internal balance and is the foundation for posture and mobility of the entire support and motor system.

5.2.1.2 Posture

For humans, posture represents a striving for balance between gravity and the need for an upright position that is determined by the statics of the two-footed standing position. A normal posture is present when it may be maintained for a certain time with a minimum of energy and without active muscle use, without overexerting ligaments or several sections of the motor system. Any posture that does not fulfill those requirements may be regarded as pathological, whether it be the resting posture of a standing person or the sedentary position.

The purpose of the spinal column examination is to find the cause of each deviation from the postural harmony of the standing, walking, sitting, or resting position (see section 6.2).

The spinal column takes a leading part in the uniform posture system of the entire body. Each of the basic essential postures—standing, kneeling, sitting, lying—combines morphological-static and functional-dynamic elements that mutually influence each other in the close-knit posture system. Thus, posture is an individual result of form and function (Wagenhaeuser 1969).

Posture, for which the spinal column plays an important role as the central axial organ, may be defined from other aspects—from anatomy and biomechanics to orthopedics to behavioral psychology and the aesthetic view of the artist.

Many different methods have been used to portray the normal shape and posture of the spinal column. For example, Killus (1973 and 1976) produced studies on the curvature conditions of the spinal column in the sagittal level (Figs. 2-39 and 2-40). Groeneveld (1976) describes the necessary work to obtain comparable measurements of spinal column posture using the methods of photogrammetry, stereophotography, statokinesiometry, and electromyography. Matzdorf (1976) differentiates measurements of the thoracic spinal column according to race, gender, and age.

The axial organ spinal column is well organized, with fixed elements (vertebral bodies with vertebral arch and processes) and interposed motor segments (intervertebral motor segments) (Fig. 3-1). Mechanical influences may significantly alter its posture in its entirety and also in individual sections. Yet, the blocks that are part of the intervertebral motor segment permit only a limited effect of the exogenous influence on the individual segmental units because of the intervertebral discs that are bonded to the bony vertebral body epiphyses (Fig. 2-4), the limited mobility of the vertebral arch articulations, and the self-contained functional unit of the ligamental system and muscle corset (see section 3.2).

In daily life, leisure, and sports there are "utilitarian postures," such as the ramrod-stiff posture emphasized during military training, that deviate from the energy-saving rest condition. The more the spinal column deviates from the ideal resting form, the more unfavorable will be the influence of mechanical forces. Therefore, prophylactic measures (see section 7.3) have the objective of avoiding a too large or too long deviation from ideal posture or of alleviating the influence of this deviation by a change in posture or movement (see section 7.2). This objective may be achieved by individual postural training or by creating a seat that meets the requirements of the spinal column.

The threshold values of possible postural force combined with the always present muscular force must be considered in the calculation of stress influences and in seat design in home and school. This is especially important for avoiding additional stress damage to spinal columns with already existing growth- and age-related damages. (Kropp 1979, Landau and Reus 1979, Schoberth 1979).

The normal shape and posture of the spinal column is—in a lateral view—a more or less distinct S-shape (Figs. 2-40 and 5-1). This shape enables the spring-like absorption of all forces affecting the vertical body axis as it distributes these forces evenly among anterior and posterior sections of the limb chain. In addition, the S-shape acts as an elastic spring because the segmentally interposed elastic elements of the intervertebral motor segment absorb—though only within the tolerance range of bone and intervertebral discs—forces that have a vertical impact. Because of their lordoses, the cervical and lumbar spinal column are subject to a ventral extension and a dorsal pressure. At the thoracic spinal column the force distribution is the reverse.

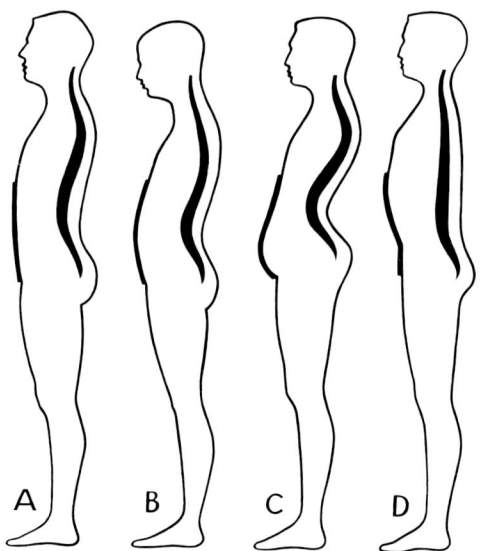

Fig. 5-1 Common back shapes with the corresponding abdominal silhouette (Junghanns 1963). **A,** Properly balanced back shape. **B,** Drawn-out thoracic kyphosis as in the juvenile kyphosis type. **C,** Lordotic curved back. **D,** Flat back.

Variations in individual shapes, excluding those caused by impaired development, often come quite close to the beginning of a pathological change in shape and posture of the spinal column. Most cases of the lordoses depicted in Figure 5-1 approach pathological significance. Even though they may be compensated for in youth, a stiffness of the large spinal column sections develops with increasing age.

It has not yet been sufficiently established which spinal column shape predisposes to damage from which type of strain. Is the drawn-out thoracic kyphosis (Fig. 5-1B) disadvantageous for prolonged sitting because the kyphosis in the lower portion of the cervical spinal column and the increased head slant resulting from it are subject to a special permanent strain? What is the stress resistance in a strong lumbar lordosis (Fig. 5-1C) or in the distinct flat back (Fig. 5-1D), both shapes that differ greatly from an "ideal back"? It is only possible to answer these questions after conducting long-term studies involving large numbers of test subjects. Beck (1973) and Killus (1973, 1976) believe that it is possible during the fitness examination of military flight personnel to determine from the computer-generated posture curves (Figs. 2-39 and 2-40) which persons with particularly aberrant curvatures would be especially susceptible to damage caused by such stresses as vibrations or destructive impacts (caused by special forms of flight service).

The close connection between the spinal column shape and pelvic inclination is depicted in anatomy textbooks (Fig. 2-20). Even a small change of pelvic inclination results in a shift of tension to other posture-stabilizing muscle groups.

It is very difficult to describe the ideal posture of the very mobile cervical spinal column. The curvature in the sagittal level varies, especially in children in the rest position between extension, sublordosis, lordosis, and hyperlordosis. Figure 5-2 shows several postural types as often seen in roentgenograms.

5.2.1.3 Psyche and Posture

There is a very close connection between psyche and posture. Such exogenous influences

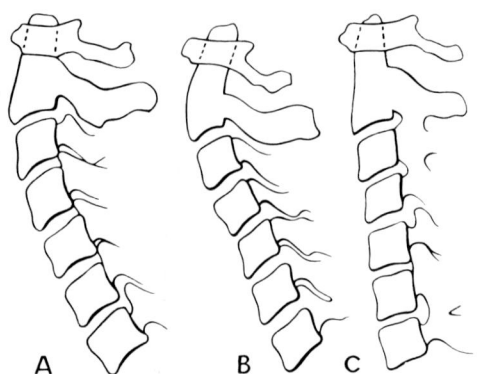

Fig. 5-2 Types of posture. The cervical spinal column. **A,** Slightly curved lordosis. **B,** Increased lordosis in the upper portion; slight kyphosis flexion at C-4 to C-5. **C,** Straight posture.

as fatigue resulting from exhausting physical activity or a trauma with a significant psychological impact, including direct psychological trauma, can change the spinal column posture. In addition, direct psychological influences or endogenously determined psychological reactions may, via nerves or muscles, severely impair the balanced biomechanics of the spinal column. Often, an individual's relationships with others may also affect posture (Crown 1978, Pongratz 1980).

Several authors have noted that a psychological factor may be observed in about one-third of all patients with spondylogenic syndromes. However, this probably depends significantly on the type of patient for whom a physician or hospital cares. When back pain develops, Bergsmann and Eder (1982) recommend that one clearly determine whether psychological or physical factors have more saliency in the spondylogenic disorder. They speak of a "psycho-barometer thoracic spinal column" (see sections 6.2 and 6.3).

Allport (1949) and Rowe (1922) have shown how deeply the psyche may affect mechanical functions. The posture of the trunk, the erect or inclined posture of the head, and therefore the overall impression of body posture depend on an individual's psychological state. Derbolowsky put it well: "Man reveals his soul in his posture" (Derbolowsky 1958, 1973). Body posture becomes body language, and the spinal column posture reflects the individual's internal posture.

The relationship between internal and external posture is illustrated in these popular colloquial expressions: Act in an upright manner!; Stay straight!; Show some backbone!; I am crushed; He is unstable; She is bent by grief.

There are many examples of the interrelationship of psychological strain and body posture in our daily lives. The sunken upper torso with drooping head is an expression of fatigue caused by strain or disease. A back that increasingly curves during the course of the day and often becomes increasingly painful has an adverse effect on the joy of living and therefore affects performance. In contrast, well-adapted persons have a straight body posture during which static and kinetic functions are in harmony with the organic spinal column structure and posture and motion systems (ligaments, muscles, nerves, etc) function properly.

The back becomes the expressive organ of a person impaired in personality or social relationships (Donner 1974, Vetter 1961, Weintraub 1971, 1977, 1979). Inhibited persons show movement and posture stereotypes, which accompany spasms, myogelosis of respective muscle groups, and hypotony of other muscle areas. These conditions are especially pronounced in feeble-minded persons because of the absence of intellectual stimulation, and they may lead to a large, curved functional total kyphosis. However, the high and stiffened thoracic kyphosis that is often explained as a "burden of age" is more a result of age-related muscle relaxation and damages at several intervertebral discs than direct psychological influences (see section 4.4).

Pain often results in a compensating posture that prevents motion, ie creates unfavorable conditions for the central axial organ.

Permanent deviations in posture, whether they result from physical strain or psychological influences, either cause various morphological damages or aggravate them. An initially desired posture, such as the military, ramrod-stiff posture, and one that is subsequently fixated may in the end result in a senile ankylosis: the straight, stiff back of the long-term soldier. Decades of hard physical labor, combined with pathomorphic damages and increased age-related damage often result in a fixation of the kyphotic thoracic spinal column to a large, curved total kyphosis. This posture may still be seen today in elderly farmers as the "farmer's back."

As shown by Riser (1962) in his work with the cervical spinal column, even pathological changes in sections of the spinal column can result in psychological problems. Back pain, even in the absence of specific vertebral symptoms or neurologically disturbed function, should not be dismissed as merely psychogenic or simulated. In order to avoid misdiagnoses, the physician should always be aware of the close interrelationship of the psyche with posture and motion of the spinal column (see section 7.2). This applies not only to severe chronic psychological disorders, as temporary postures or movement blocks may be caused by an individual's desires (escape into disease, desire for pension).

5.2.1.4 Posture and the Arts

The close connection between an individual's psychological state and body posture has been depicted by many artists. The "thinker" of Auguste Rodin sits bent forward, his chin supported on his hand, his view directed toward the ground in contemplation. Similarly, a sculpture by K.H. Krause from 1974 portrays a "thinker" in a sedentary position with a strongly curved back and lowered head. Psychologically ill persons are often portrayed as introverted and brooding with a curved back and lowered head.

The classic Greek and Roman sculpted figure has a head held high and the extended cervical spinal column of a self-confident individual. This artistic portrayal expresses an internal exuberance with the posture and look of the victor: an upright, lordotically emphasized torso posture and uplifted head.

In a copper etching of 1497 Duerer portrays "Four Witches" (Fig. 5-3). The figure on the left has a severe total kyphosis with lumbar lordosis. The back view of the witch in the center has a slight scoliosis.

"Nana" by Monet (Fig. 5-4), painted in 1877, shows how the fashionable high heels force, as they still do today, a tilted pelvis with an inevitable lordosis that is further increased by the tight bodice.

As does the painter or sculptor, the actor must, through posture and movement, find

Fig. 5-3 "The Four Witches" by Duerer, 1497.

Fig. 5-4 "Nana" by Monet, 1877.

forms of expression that will give vivid and realistic expression to psychological influences, often even serious psychological disorders.

5.2.2 Mobility/Movement

To date, attempts to establish conclusive norms of mobility have been unsuccessful, because differences are dictated by race, type (asthenic, pyknic), and individual shape and posture. Too, the norms of mobility are determined to a great extent by the condition of an individual's ligaments and muscles. In any case, the mobility of the spinal column of a newborn (Fig. 5-5) with its large range of motion cannot be considered the standard norm even for a toddler, as Virchow (1909) established with a ligament specimen (Fig. 5-6).

The early studies on the mobility of the spinal column (Braus 1921, Fick 1911) were based on measurements of (mostly macerated) spinal column specimens. Many later descriptions were based on roentgenogram studies, some of which were performed on living persons and some on isolated, but unmacerated spinal column specimens (Bakke 1931, Dittmar 1930, 1931, Leger 1959, Rizzi 1979).

5.2.2.1 Standing, Sitting, Lying

The ideal posture of the spinal column differs from the postures assumed in daily life by the average individual. The biomechanical strain that is inherent even in lying has biochemical consequences.

In contemporary society, the most frequently assumed position is sitting. While sitting, the spinal column may take many different postures, ranging from the very upright and often back-supported sitting posture to the unsupported, relaxed posture with rounded kyphosis (Fig. 5-7). The greater the inclination of the pelvis, the more the lumbar lordosis reverses into a kyphosis, which continues into the thoracic spinal column by increasing the normal thoracic kyphosis. The postural kyphosis of sitting is even increased when legs are crossed. This unfavorable sitting posture increases not only the strain on the lumbar muscles, but also creates a by far greater strain on the neck mus-

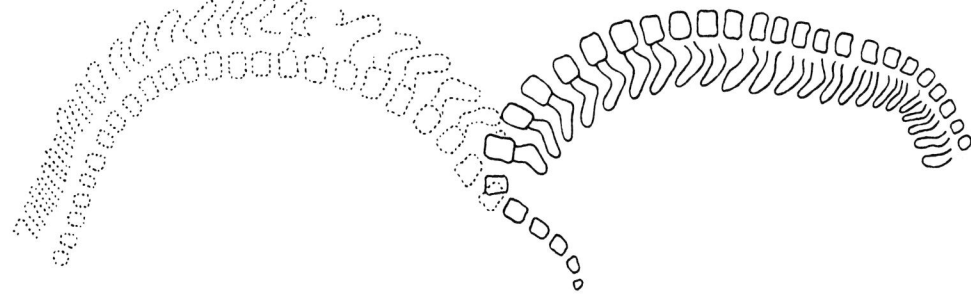

Fig. 5-5 Range of movement between the forward and backward bend of the isolated spinal column of a newborn. Sketch by Schoberth (1962) according to roentgenograms.

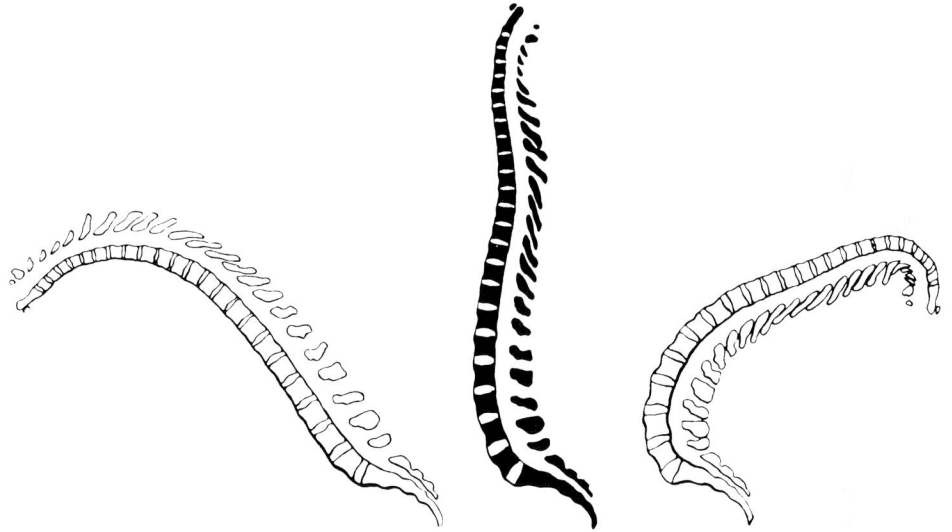

Fig. 5-6 Extreme forward and backward bend of the spinal column in a ligament specimen [from Virchow (1909)].

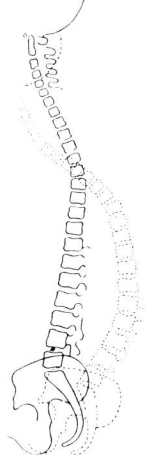

Fig. 5-7 Change of spinal column posture from the erect, taut position to a relaxed, unsupported sedentary position (from Schoberth [1962]).

cles. The neck muscles are forced to compensate in order to ensure an upright head position. Electromyographic findings demonstrate this strain (Fig. 5-8, illustrations 7–10). The more the spine curves, the faster the muscles tire and the more the stress rests on the anterior portions of the intervertebral discs. In addition, the abdominal muscles can exert no force in this position. Therefore, the abdominal bag, which gives hydraulic support and which Schanz emphasized so vividly in his studies (1930, 1931), slackens.

During prolonged sitting without back support, the spinal column posture deteriorates because of muscle fatigue caused by incorrectly contracted muscles and ligaments. This becomes especially obvious in the head and neck area when the head is inclined. However, sitting in the usual trunk posture requires a free movement

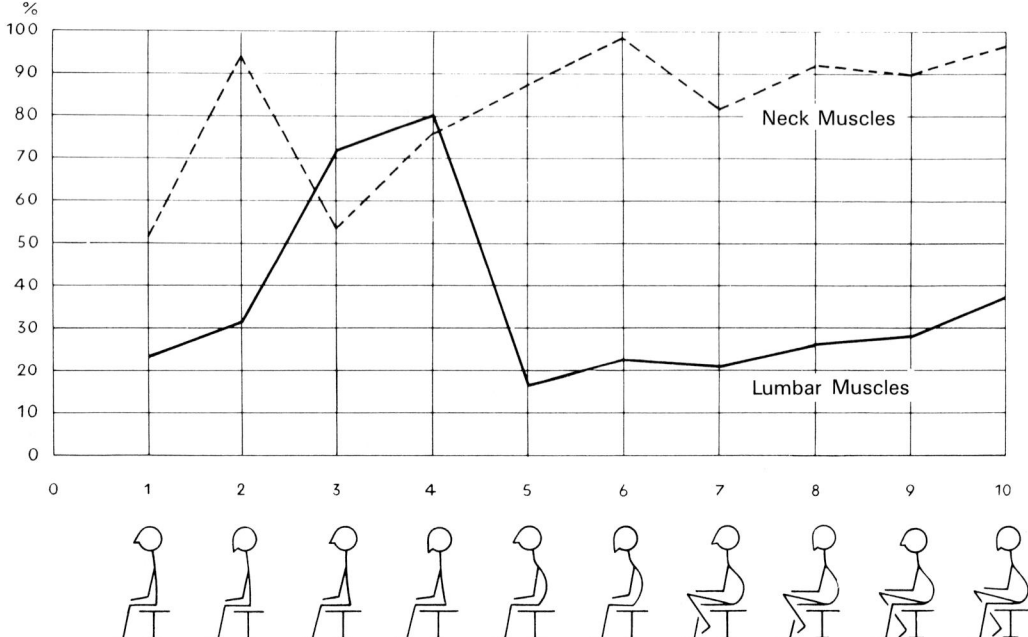

Fig. 5-8 Electromyographic findings at the neck and lumbar muscles in various sedentary postures with an upright head position and straight view (1, 3, 5, 7, 9) and with an inclined head in a reading and writing posture (2, 4, 6, 8, 10) [from Schoberth (1962)].

chain of the hip joint-pelvis-lumbar spinal column. Each impairment in this unit is connected with an especially stressful sitting posture.

Sitting is not only the most frequent utility posture but is also the most damaging. While sitting, pressure on the intervertebral discs of the lower lumbar spinal column increases by 30%. It creates more strain on the spinal column than any other posture because it interferes with the pump mechanism that is absolutely necessary for the intervertebral disc (see section 2.3). **The intervertebral disc thrives on movement.**

If prolonged sitting is accompanied by vibration stress, as when riding in motor vehicles, the potential for damage to the intervertebral disc tissue increases.

Figure 5-9 illustrates how muscles are exerted in various sedentary postures. In addition, pressure conditions in the intervertebral discs are graphically depicted in the figures in section 3.2.

In contrast to stressful sitting, lying is the best resting posture for the spinal column (see section 7.3). No measurable energy use is attributed to lying. However, merely raising the arms expends energy (Fig. 5-10).

Yet, the direct, mechanical strain of the spinal column cannot solely be judged by energy consumption; rather, it is necessary to measure the pressure developing inside the limb chain. Several research teams have measured the internal pressure of the intervertebral disc L-3/L-4 (see section 3.2). If the relative pressure in the spinal column in a standing position is designated as 100, it is 75 in the flat, lateral position and 25 in the prone position (Fig. 3-5).

Although there is a tension- and stress-free resting position for the articulations of the extremities, the pressure in the interior of the intervertebral hemiarthrosis—turgor of the nucleus pulposus (see section 3.2)—causes a countertension in the fiber ring layers, as well as in the ligamenta of each corresponding intervertebral motor segment: anterior and posterior longitudinal ligament, ligamenta flava, interspinal ligaments of the vertebral arch series, etc. These discoligamental tensions possess an inherent unrest that is partially determined by the changed

Strain Caused by External Influences 151

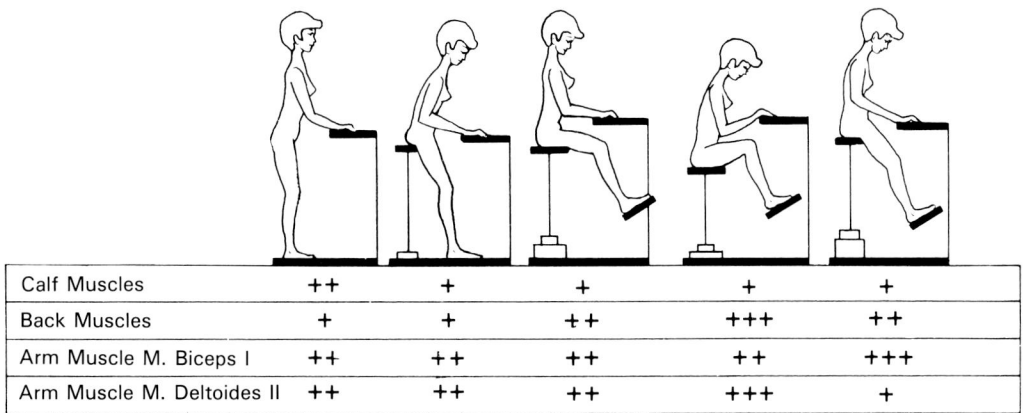

Fig. 5-9 Electromyographically determined muscle contraction in various body postures [from Laurig & Rohmert]. The number of crosses corresponds to the relative contraction force.

fluid content in the intervertebral discs in the resting position and in part by compensatory movements of the surrounding muscles. Therefore, **the spinal column is subject to mechanical strain in any position.**

5.2.2.2 Walking, Bending, Rotating

The left- and right-swaying movements connected with walking have the effect of strengthening the back muscles. At the same time, they support the metabolism of the intervertebral disc by way of the pump mechanism (see section 2.3). The strength of this important pump mechanism is also augmented with each step by additional, moderately strong vibrations that reach the spinal column via the legs and pelvis. However, only the relaxed walk in suitable shoes combined with a rolling of the foot can enable the proper coordination of these processes (see section 7.3). In contrast to normal walking, the unfavorable influences of athletic walking and athletic running disciplines for the spinal column are discussed in Chapter 8.

In 1975 Groh and Groh reported that a person living in a city walks about 20,000 steps daily. This means 10,000 steps for each leg and, at the same time, the transfer of the same number of

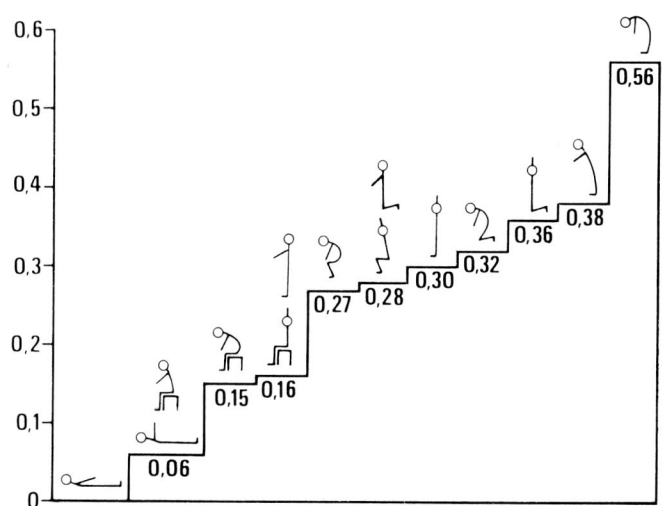

Fig. 5-10 Energy consumption in kcal/min in different body postures [from Saemann (1970)].

pressure impacts to the spinal column (vibration influences), which always results in a slight swaying toward the opposite side. Therefore, the lumbosacral transition must readjust itself about 20,000 times per day. A healthy spinal column not only endures this very well, but the impact even strengthens the stabilizing function of the dynamic muscle corset (see sections 3.2 and 4.8) and stimulates the pump mechanism necessary for the nutritional diffusion of the intervertebral discs.

Flexion and a prolonged flexed posture create several strain problems. During anteflexion the spinal column is transformed into a total kyphosis if it does not have any fixated curvatures while the pelvis is simultaneously rotated. In this utility posture, which is normal during flexion, the energy consumption increases to 0.56 kcal/min (from 0.16 kcal/min in a standing position) because of the necessary counterpressure forces of the muscles. This is the highest measured value for any commonly assumed posture (Fig. 5-10). At the same time, the anterior portions of the intervertebral discs are subjected to a high pressure, which may aggravate any pre-existing damage. Therefore, avoiding a total kyphosis while lifting (see sections 3.2, 7.3) is an important way to protect the spinal column.

Because it is so accessible the cervical spinal column has often been used to calculate averages of mobility. The tilt and rotation movements in the upper cervical area and at the head transition have received special consideration. Penning (1976, 1978), by measuring functional roentgenograms, determined the axes and movement potentials of the various segments to the front, side, and back. There is a frequent, slightly telescopic displacement of the cervical vertebrae during anteflexion that is especially obvious at the level of C-2 to C-3 and C-3 to C-4 in children. In addition, Penning calculated the decline in range of motions during the course of life: from 120° between ante- and retroflexion at age 10 to only 75° at age 70.

At the thoracic spinal column the anatomic conditions (vertebrocostal articulations, spinous processes, vertebral arch articulations) allow a much smaller retroflexion and anteflexion potential (Stofft & Ribka 1975). (The terms "extension" and "hyperextension," which are often used instead of backward bend and retroflexion are confusing; see section 7.3.)

Measurements of the mobility of the lumbar spinal column and the statically and dynamically important lumbosacral transition, the lumbosacral hinge, are almost as frequently made as for the cervical spinal column. They are part of any basic physical examination (see section 6.3) and are especially important because the lumbar spinal column is subject to powerful external influences.

In extensive studies, the rotation mobility of the individual spinal column sections has been determined by measuring the extent of mobility of needles inserted in the spinous processes. The findings of Dupuis and co-workers on the influences of vibrations improve our understanding of rotation and twisting movements of the vertebrae (Fig. 5-11).

The degree of rotation in the intervertebral motor segment, which is sometimes combined with a slight tilting, depends very much on the possibilities allowed by the vertebral arch articulations. The intervertebral discs, with their fiber ring layers bonded to the vertebral body epiphyses, have an additional, inhibiting influence. The rotation potential also varies by standing and sitting.

In addition to pure ante-, retro-, or lateral flexions or rotations in all segments, often there are compound movements (see section 7.3). For instance, ante- or retroflexion is combined with rotation or a slight tilting of individual vertebrae, as Jirout demonstrated in 1970 in roentgenogram measurements of 2955 vertebrae of the cervical spinal column in 326 test subjects.

5.2.2.3 Lifting and Carrying

Lifting and carrying are frequently performed actions in daily life, leisure-time activities, and performance sports. The forces necessary for lifting and carrying derive from three elements: (1) the spinal column with the turgor of the intervertebral discs, (2) muscles, and (3) the internal pressure of the abdomen and rib cage (as combined hydropneumatic chambers according to Schanz 1930, 1931).

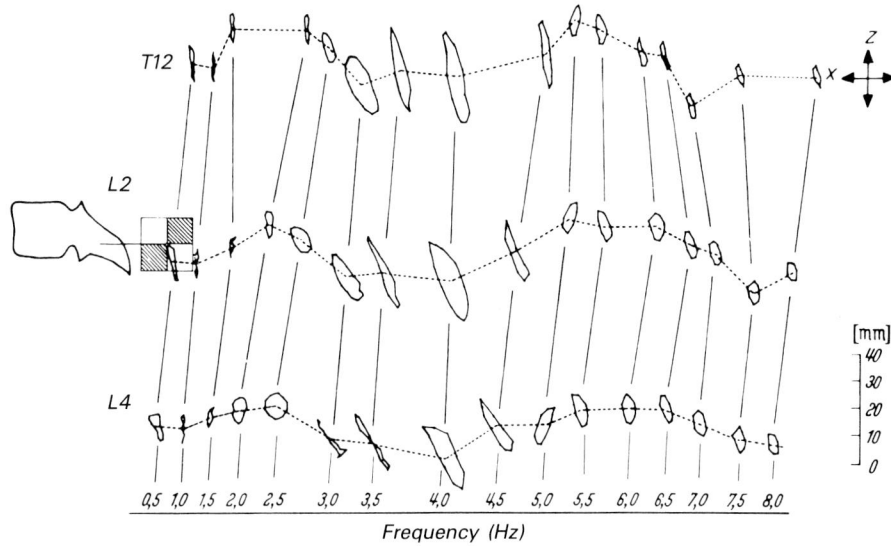

Fig. 5-11 Twisting movements of vertebrae T-12, L-2, and L-4 during vertical vibration stimulus (z-direction) of 0.5 to 8.0 Hz, recorded with the help of needles inserted in the spinous processes [from Dupuis (1975)].

Depending on the amount of muscle work, lifting and carrying produce an increased energy consumption. Anteflexion without lifting requires 0.56 kcal/min, which is the highest requirement of an unstressed posture (Fig. 5-10). If the flexion is accompanied by lifting of 10 kg, the erecting and balancing muscle force increases the pressure at the lumbosacral transition to 422 kg (Fig. 5-12, lower left). If the weight is lifted up from below the standing level, a pressure of 727 kg at the lumbosacral hinge results (Fig. 5-12, lower right).

Incorrect lifting with a curved back creates excessive pressure on the anterior portions of the intervertebral discs in the lower lumbar region (Figs. 3-3 and 3-4). A straight back while lifting and carrying enables the even distribution of pressure over the entire intervertebral disc. The lower lumbar spinal column and the transition to the base of the sacrum are best protected during lifting if a weight is lifted from a squatting position (Fig. 5-13). This figure shows especially clearly the great strain created by lifting with straight legs instead of from a squatting position (see sections 7.3 and 8.4).

In 1931, when Schanz described the abdomen as the auxiliary support organ of the spinal col-

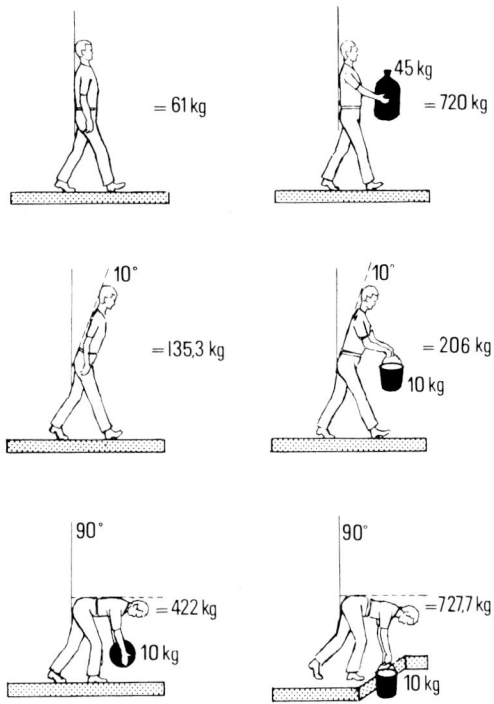

Fig. 5-12 Strain at lumbosacral transition during lifting. A weight of 45 kg held in front of the body (*upper right*) results in almost the same pressure strain as a weight of 10 kg lifted from below the standing level (*lower right*) [from Kucera & Charvat (1976)].

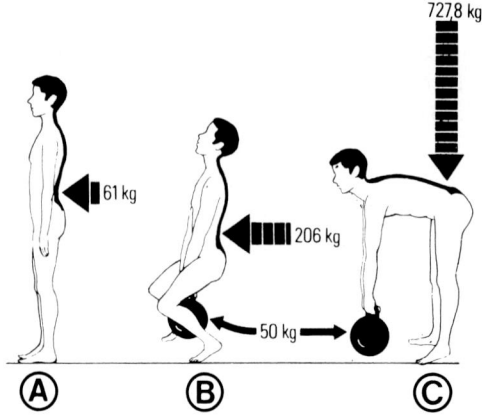

Fig. 5-13 Strain on the lumbosacral transition during (**A**) upright posture caused by the head-torso weight, (**B**) lifting of 50 kg with bent knees and straight back, and (**C**) incorrect lifting from anteflexion with straight legs.

umn, his description was not well understood. However, later studies showed that the internal abdominal pressure rises during the lifting of a weight by 150 mm Hg and the intrathoracic pressure by 50 mm Hg. The axial load-carrying capacity of the spine is supported by the increased internal pressure that, in other words, lowers the pressure of the weight—in the lumbar spinal column by 50% and in the lower thoracic spinal column by 30%. This observation is disputed by Farfan (1973) who holds that the posterior elements of the segment, essentially the vertebral arch articulations, absorb much of the load. In his opinion, the internal pressure of the abdomen only helps for a short time by decreasing pressure 5% to 10% during the tilting momentum that occurs in the lifting process. (see also Fairbank et al 1980, Grew 1980).

The studies of pressure strains on the intervertebral discs and the required muscular forces have resulted in practical reference points for lifting and carrying and for prophylactic measures (see section 7.3). Threshold values have been determined for on-the-job lifting and carrying. Only small loads are allowed for men and women under 18 years of age in order to protect the still growing spinal column (Tables 7-2 and 7-3).

Because lifting and carrying are often connected with a rotation of the body, Tichauer (1971) studied the rotation momentums at the lumbar spinal column and the hip articulations with myograms. This resulted in a "biomechanical profile" of the lifting process. The myographic measurements enable one to determine the corresponding performance for a lifted weight. Several ways of lifting the weight, as well as varying heel heights—all of which affect the lumbar lordosis—may be recommended with this profile (see section 7.3).

Carrying a book bag always under the same arm produces spinal column problems in childhood (see section 7.2). Carrying books in a book bag on the back causes fewer problems.

5.2.3 Involvement of Muscles, Nerves, and Blood Vessels

5.2.3.1 Muscles

The eminently important role of muscles is demonstrated in each body movement (see section 2.2). The spinal column is involved in each movement at least passively, and in a majority of instances actively, because of its central function as the axial organ of the support and motor system. The mechanical tasks are by no means the responsibility of only the muscles attached directly to the spinal column. Rather, each movement of the lower extremities, the rib cage, and the head requires the active participation of the trunk muscles, which not only assist or inhibit movement but also stabilize the posture. Those muscles that originate in the spinal column but attach far from it (eg, psoas and gluteus maximus) also participate actively in the straightening, posture, stabilization, and movement of the central axial organ. Additional tasks of muscles are to counter gravity and other mass forces, such as inertia.

The respiratory movements of the rib cage also affect the mechanical functions of the muscles. There are many functional connections among the muscles of the back, abdominal wall, and rib cage. The abdominal muscles have a special relationship to the rotation strain of the lumbar intervertebral disc (Farfan 1975, Figs. 2-18 and 2-19). The contraction of the exterior chest wall muscles reinforces the stabilizing effect of the rib cage on the spinal column. The chest and abdominal cavities act during muscle contraction as cylinders that keep their shape, ie as hydropneumatic chambers. As early as 1930 Schanz was prompted by the relationships among the rib cage, abdomen, and spinal column and by the internal pressure (air bubbles) present in the thoracic and abdominal cavity to consider the rib cage and abdominal cavity as auxiliary support organs of the spinal column.

The extent to which the abdominal muscles affect the internal pressure of the lumbar intervertebral discs was studied by Nachemson (1975). Isometric exercises of the abdominal muscles increase the pressure in the intervertebral disc L-3/L-4 to 110 kg. For comparison, the pressure in the resting position is 30 kg, and in an upright standing position, 70 kg.

Substantial functional impairments of the spinal column may result if individual muscles or muscle groups fail because of pathological paralysis or if a unilaterally stressed posture lowers the performance of certain muscle groups. Often, back discomfort draws attention to such muscular-mechanic misfunctions. Then the pain must be attacked at its origin by correcting the posture (see sections 7.2 and 7.3).

An important factor in the in vivo study of mechanical influences on the spinal column is the force of the back muscles used in conjunction with muscle groups of the trunk, neck, and cervix, as well as the arms and legs. It is very difficult to analyze these force ratios. In studies by Kroemer (1969) and other investigators, the forces developing directly at the spinal column or produced by it as a counterpressure cannot always be completely analyzed, as in the case of the tracts of the longissimi muscles, which have different lengths and which interweave with each other.

The force of the muscles that affect the spinal column directly is demonstrated by vertebral body fractures caused by tetanic muscle spasms occurring during tetanus and shock therapy (Schmorl 1932, Schmorl & Junghanns 1968). However, so far fractures of healthy vertebral bodies have not been shown to occur as a result of forceful, coordinated movements in daily life, ie consciously regulated forces. There are not even known instances of these fractures occurring during the dynamically balanced lifting of extreme weights in athletic weightlifting (see section 8.4).

The energy requirement, which is calculated in kilocalories per minute, is the most important criterion for any physical strain. In 1970, Saemann established energy consumption at 0.00 kcal/min for the relaxed supine position and determined the maximum value of 0.56 kcal/min for standing with a strongly flexed back (see Fig. 5-10). The muscles of the back, which have a very high mass, and those connecting the trunk with the head and extremities, consume the majority of energy.

However, the calculation of kcal/min values alone is not sufficient to determine spinal column strain. In order to obtain threshold values for damage-free stress resistance, several calculations must be performed. The relief of stress on the spinal column, which is provided by the internal pressure of the rib cage and abdominal cavity, was calculated by Morris (1973). At the main point of strain, the pivot joint of the lumbosacral transition, the strain measures 939 kg. It declines with muscle contraction of the abdominal walls and with the help of the internal abdominal pressure, to 672 kg.

Electromyography (EMG) is an excellent tool for assessing the use of muscles as they affect the spinal column. However, because it takes a long time to complete, EMG is not feasible for mass screenings. In its place, a simple procedure to assess muscle strength is to measure how long it takes to lift the trunk from a prone, overhanging position with outstretched arms.

The EMG does reveal the substantial changes that result from a relatively small change of support of the back and head in a sitting person, as shown in the "rest EMG" in Figure 5-14. More detailed information on the influence of the various angles of back rests on the intervertebral disc pressure and on EMG values of the sitting person is found in Figure 5-15. Intervertebral disc pressure (measured intradiscally between L-3 and L-4) and EMG values decrease with the increased angle between seat and back rest.

When the individual in a sitting position is subjected to vibration, as in a motor vehicle, a changed biochemical environment develops in

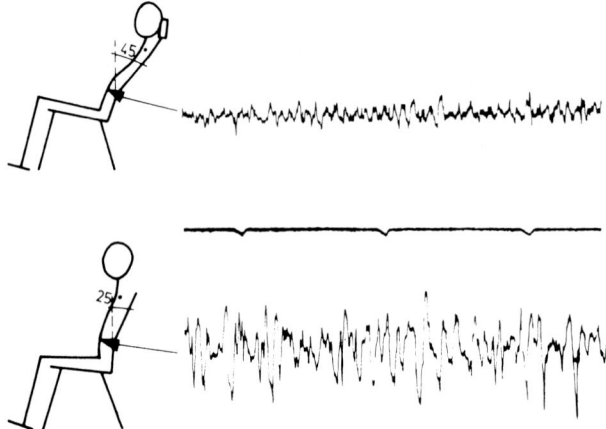

Fig. 5-14 Electromyograms of lumbar muscles (determined via skin electrodes) show that the strain on the "resting" back muscles varies according to back support with or without head support [Schmidtke (1973)].

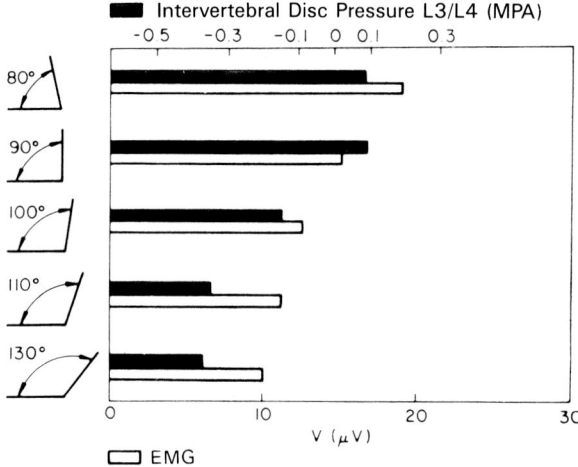

Fig. 5-15 Pressure in the intervertebral disc (*black*) and electromyogram (*white*) of the back muscles in relation to various inclination angles of the back rest [from Andersson & Oertengren (1974)]. (MPA = Megapascal)

the muscles (Junghanns 1979). Muscular weakness, muscle atrophy, and greater damages in the motoneuron have been described in that situation. The EMG is able to demonstrate these impact-related consequences in the back muscles.

Vibrations of at least 3 Hz in the x-axis (from front to back (and in the y-axis (from right to left)—that is, transverse from the spinal column—produce strong activity of the back muscles. Between 1.5 and 3 Hz, the EMG potential increases by 93%. This increase may be attributed to the resonance behavior of the upper torso (Dupuis 1972). For the spinal column of the sitting person, the excitement resulting from horizontal vibrations of 3 Hz (eg, through the back rest in an automobile) creates an especially great strain. The more the sinus vibrations change into stochastic vibrations, the greater the strain becomes. This strain causes static contraction with a high degree of muscle activity. Vibrations between 1 and 3 Hz that exert their influence in the horizontal y-direction cause much greater problems in motor control than vibrations of the x-direction, which are themselves stronger than those in the z-direction (of the vertical spinal column axis). Vibrations in the y-direction that appear in conjunction with rolling oscillations cause the most severe problems in muscle control. When an intervertebral insufficiency is present, these vibrations often cause back pain (see section 3.4). One of the reasons for the pain may be that the back muscles are unable to react quickly and to provide protection to the back because of the rapidity of the unexpected change of oscillation direction and amplitudes.

The various reactions of the lumbar muscles to sinus and stochastic oscillations that penetrate from the seat vertically as total body vibrations are impressively depicted in the vibration graphs in Figure 5-16. The vibrations generated in the dorsoventral direction take a slightly different course (Fig. 5-17).

The vibration-related biochemical processes in the metabolism of the muscles affect the load-bearing capacity of the trunk muscles. Continued vibrations result in fatigue and therefore in an incorrect posture of the spinal column. Thus, a vicious cycle manipulates the spinal column into a state of overexertion that results in disease. Therefore, muscles, ligament structures, and intervertebral discs require an intermediate stress change with a specific, refreshing movement. **Recovery through change is a basic biological principle** (see section 2.3).

Schoberth (1962) made conclusive comparisons of muscle reactions in the cervical and lumbar region in common sitting positions with the help of electromyographic studies. The findings, clearly arranged in Figure 5-8, show increased reactions in the cervical muscles if the head is inclined forward and the same back position is maintained. When this anteflexion is maintained for a prolonged period, it produces a tiring tensing of the cervical muscles. The maintenance of any head position, any movement of the head, and especially its forward inclination require exhausting, coordinated activity of the respective muscle groups in conjunction with the ligaments. If a tensing or fatigue of the muscles

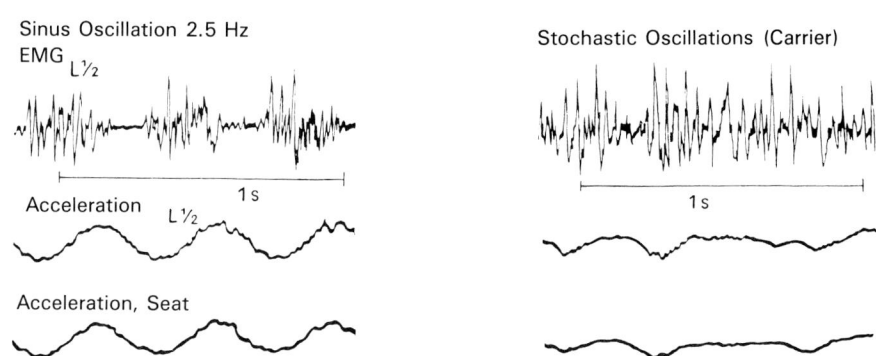

Fig. 5-16 "Programmed" muscle reaction of the lumbar muscles to stimulating sinus oscillations of 2.5 Hz (*left*). Reaction of the same muscle group without an existing behavioral pattern to stimulating, stochastic oscillations (*right*). EMG = electromyogram. L-½ = measuring point at the level lumbar vertebra L-1 to L-2.

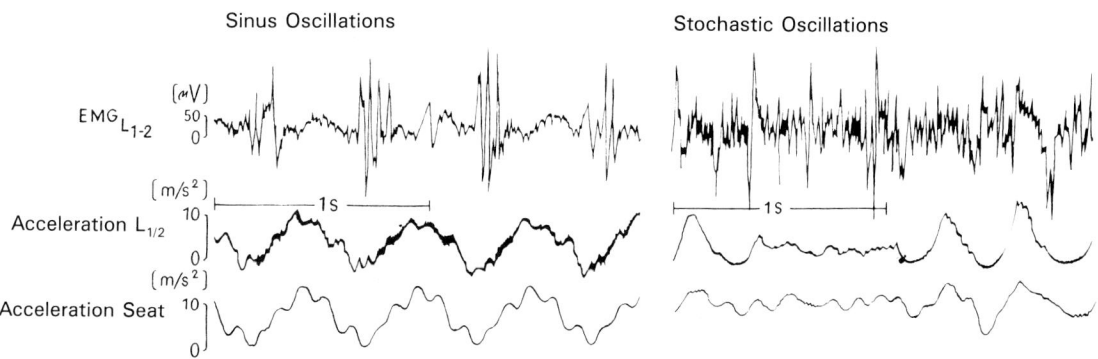

Fig. 5-17 Electromyograms of the m. erector trunci subjected to sinus oscillations (*left*) and stochastic oscillations (*right*) in the dorsoventral direction. Note the differences compared to the graphs in Fig. 5-16.

occurs as the result of maintaining a posture for a prolonged period—for instance because of incorrect inclination of a writing surface—there is the potential for serious damages. Prolonged work at the horizontal school desk often results in juvenile anteflexion headache (see section 7.2), which may produce a dislike of school. The use of slanted writing surfaces for school desks may alleviate this problem.

Because head-neck-shoulder-arm pain is so common, the cervical spinal column and its surrounding muscles have been studied often. Portions of the m. erector trunci alternately bridge several intervertebral motor segments with bundled fiber tracts. These portions ensure, even in the cervical region, differentiated, coordinated functions for various postures, as well as for static and kinetic requirements for the spinal column. Only an EMG examination can produce accurate findings concerning the cooperation and counterfunctions of the individual muscle portions during spinal column movements.

Many researchers have attempted to measure the counterpressure forces produced by the cervical muscles with the help of mathematical spinal column models and computer calculations (Junghanns 1979, Rizzi 1979). Figure 7-13 shows the pressure strain on the lower cervical spinal column if the forward inclined head must be stabilized by the strength of the cervical muscles. Compared to the resting position, the necessary muscle forces increase several times when the head is greatly inclined forward. Merely holding the functional head inclination during writing doubles the muscle forces required (see section 7.2) for the resting position. Thus, the muscles are extended far beyond the point of their ideal force development. The greatest amount of counterpressure must be assumed by the cervical ligaments. "This opposition of physical and biological factors tires the muscle system and leads to a permanent strain on the ligament structures" (Rizzi et al, 1976).

When the head is bent forward, the pressure on the lower cervical intervertebral discs also increases, especially on their anterior portions (Fig. 7-13). Instead of the average head weight of 6.7 kg, which in the normal posture rests on the transition from the cervical to thoracic spinal column, a pressure of 21.0 kg results because of the countertraction of the cervical muscles necessitated by the anteflexion.

The trunk muscles, as well as the muscles of the extremities, may become sore after prolonged strain. In the past the accumulation of lactate in the muscle substance was held responsible for this soreness. Currently, researchers believe that a microtraumatization in conjunction with reflex edema causes a painful muscle stiffness.

Because the tracts of the longissimus muscles cover each other and interweave with each other in individual fiber bundles, the power exercises of weightlifters, gymnasts, rowers, track athletes, and divers frequently result in small tears of individual muscle bundles and in painful muscle spasm. Often these tears are incorrectly interpreted as spondylogenic lumbago. With the help of appropriate therapy (heat, careful massage, etc.) the athletes should reattain their sports fitness after a few weeks.

5.2.3.2 Nerves

The close intertwining of the spinal cord and the nerve roots exiting the segments with the spinal column (see section 2.2) may produce mechanical impairments of these nerves. Fortunately, in a normally developed spinal column, the necessary penetration points in the vertebral and intervertebral canals are sufficiently wide and secured by block mechanisms (vertebral arch articulations, ligamenta flava, etc.) to prevent dangerous constrictions during normal spinal column movements and strains. However, even small variations in the spinal column shape or posture, the presence of a congenital vertebral canal constriction (see section 4.3), or damage in the area of the intervertebral motor segment may produce dangerous nerve constrictions (see sections 3.4, 4.3, and 4.5). In addition, partial or complete neural paralyses that are not related to the spinal column may still exert negative mechanical influences on it by producing muscular weaknesses or functional failure of muscles.

In addition to the larger nerve trunks with their described mechanical susceptibility, the smaller, segmentally organized nerve branches are also subject to mechanical influences that may produce a variety of damages (see section 3.4) in the intervertebral motor segment, such as intervertebral chondrosis and its consequences (see sections 3.2 and 4.6).

Prolonged vibrations also carry a potential for damage, especially for the peripheral nervous system. The central nervous system may be affected by both partial body and total body vibrations.

5.2.3.3 Blood Vessels

Blood vessels (see the description of their anatomy in section 2.2) are involved in many ways in the mechanical tasks of the spinal column.

The vertebral artery runs along the cervical spinal column to the transverse foramen. It is particularly susceptible to damage caused by external influences along its entire course (Meyermann 1982). There it may be constricted, similar to the nerve roots leaving the intervertebral canals, if special—mostly pathological—conditions are present. Even though the vertebral artery, because of its loops, adapts very well to the mechanical requirements of head movements in the suboccipital region, it is susceptible to constriction at this location if pathological or accident-related damage impairs the movement process or impedes the free play of the vascular loop. Such mechanical constrictions limit the blood flow in the artery either temporarily or for a long period and therefore may cause damage in the supply areas (brain, inner ear, etc.).

The segment arteries may occasionally affect the lower portion of the lumbar spinal column if they are mechanically impaired by a prolapse of the intervertebral disc. Compression occurs frequently and is a concomitant cause of sciatic symptoms and possibly also of paralyses. According to Schanz (1930), the taut, pulsating blood content of the aorta plays an auxiliary supporting role for the central axial organ.

A small artery enters the isthmus of the vertebral arch in its approximate center. This artery plays a significant role in the development of the spondylolysis at this location (see section 4.5). Is it possible that the artery canal is a risky weak point, or is the absence of the artery the cause of the development of the symphysis?

Blood vessels can adversely affect the spinal column in another way that has received little attention to date. Experiments and clinical observations have shown that in the presence of vibration disease (see sections 3.3 and 5.3) the blood flow is impeded in the neurovascular pathway, mostly in the end capillaries. Thus, nutritional impairments in the capillary supply area may develop, eg, the vasopastic disorder of the finger tips. If the vibrations of certain frequencies penetrate into the capillary areas of the vertebral body/intervertebral disc boundary (see section 2.2), which is probable though not experimentally proven, serious impairments of the intervertebral disc tissue, such as chondrosis and osteochondrosis, will develop (see section 4.6). These impairments result because the metabolism of the intervertebral disc tissue depends on the diffusion from these capillary areas.

The vertebral venous system in the interior of the vertebral canal runs from the caudal to the cranial pole of the axial organ. The closely woven venous plexus, which is made up of valveless venous plexi with sinusoid enlargements, encloses the dura and has many anastomoses with the vertebral body veins. These form many connections through the intervertebral canals with the numerous veins serving the spinal column. Thus, a connection from the pelvic veins up to the large cranial blood vessels enables blood to flow in both directions. These venous plexi permit an auxiliary circumvention in case of obstruction or surgical disruption of the upper or lower vena cava. However, they may permit the spread of infections or tumor metastases to other organs or into the brain without having to pass through the filtering lung (Batson 1957). In addition, the internal venous plexus is susceptible to many mechanical influences, such as prolapse of the posterior disc (see section 4.6) and tumors growing in the spinal cord canal that cause pressure.

In rare cases a prolapse of the intervertebral disc sequesters small tissue pieces. Encouraged by hormonal factors or traumas and supported by the abdominal muscle action, these pieces are finally transferred via the venous bone marrow sinus of the vertebral body to the expansive venous plexus in the vertebral canal and through vein-artery anastomoses. In 1979 Budka et al. described 12 cases in which myelomalacias in the posterior supply areas developed in this way.

5.2.4 Skeleton

The spinal column skeleton (vertebral bodies with vertebral arches and processes) is subject to the same laws as all other bones. That is, it undergoes the same accretion and transformation processes during growth and age, with the respective mechanical strains. In addition, it has both regulating or reacting metabolic functions (see sections 2.2 and 2.3).

5.2.4.1 Transformation of Bioarchitecture through Stress

The findings that Wolff deduced from his studies in 1892 are still valid today for the biomechanics of bone structure and its transformations. **Any change in bone function is followed by changed external bone shapes, all according to specific mathematical laws.**

There are two basic types of bone structures —network bone and lamellae bone—each with different internal structure, stability, and reactions to stimuli, including daily stresses. However, both types are important in performing the support function of the skeleton, as well as for metabolism. For instance, stimuli that are reactive to weightbearing and the genetic control of the bone tissue cell result via tropocollagen in a traction stability that surpasses the quality of even the best construction steel. Lamellae bone is especially responsive to static stimuli. In contrast, the network bone, which consists of uncoordinated, irregular fiber, does not respond to "static signals."

The skeleton is subjected constantly to normal mechanical forces that frequently change direction and intensity, such as body weight, muscle activity, exogenous forces, accelerations of gravitational force, vibrations, additional stress, etc. The reaction of the bone—the result of adaptation (see section 8.2)—to such mechanical influences depends on various factors: the point of action; intensity, duration, direction, and type of force; resistance capacity of the bone; and age, etc. In addition, the alternating influence of the forces acting from the exterior or interior is an essential variable. The sum of such one-time or prolonged acting forces determines whether the bone is deformed elastically or plastically or whether it breaks.

Therefore, the spinal column skeleton undergoes extensive transformation and adaptation processes. During these processes, the mineral components and the organic bone matrix increase or decrease, and bone regenerations (sclerosis, osteophytosis, etc.) or bone resorption, such as osteoporosis (see section 4.6), occurs.

Spongiosa structure and corticalis react to changed stress influences in a characteristic way (see Fig. 4-63). The compact corticalis cylinder is essential for the vertical stress resistance of the vertebral body. Also, the bony cover and base plates of the vertebral bodies (vertebral body end plates) act as "pressure absorption plates" (see section 2.2). For that reason, the trabeculae structure in the interior of the vertebral body does not possess a trajectory structure as "mechanically oriented" as the transition from the femur to the neck and to the head of the hip. The spongiosa tracts in the vertebral body that run in a head-rump direction are nevertheless important. For example, in osteoporosis, even though the number and thickness of the spongiosa lamellae are substantially decreased, a distinct trabeculae path remains in the head-rump direction.

Seyss (1967, 1968, 1969) notes that the fish vertebrae shape develops in osteoporosis because of the gradual restructuring in flexion lines corresponding to the elasticity module, rather than as a result of the direct pressure of the nucleus pulposus against the vertebral body end plates.

The bony spinal column structure can adapt to great changes in environmental influences, as seen in the state of weightlessness of the astronaut. Adaptation also occurs when there is physiological inactivity as a consequence of disease, such as muscular dystrophy, mental retardation, or brain and neural disorders for which bed rest is mandated.

Attention is increasingly being paid to the stress-related bioarchitecture of the bone, particularly the spinal column. Basic research in this area has advanced significantly during the last few decades. The precise analysis of bone conditions in the vertebrae has always included light microscopic studies, and more recently electron microscopic studies. Those procedures, in the form of a bone biopsy, offer the potential to determine the degree of bone substance loss in osteoporosis.

A relatively new procedure to determine growth, accretion, and transformation of bone substance (mineralization of the bone matrix) is marking with tetracyclines. Intravital marking with tetracyclines, porphyrins, and H_3 thymidine helps demonstrate the healing processes in bone fractures by showing the developed bone or cartilage callus in two different fluorescent zones. Such studies can be used to trace the healing processes of microfractures (see section 4.6) that are found in the area of the vertebral body end plate. The adjacent cartilage plate should also be studied because it has not been established yet whether damage at the hyaline cartilage plate may occur and what effect the healing processes in the bone and cartilage plates have on the diffusion metabolism of the intervertebral disc (see sections 2.2 and 2.3).

In this context, it must first be established via animal experiments whether breakdown or transformation in the bone or cartilage plates may develop as a consequence of prolonged permanent stress. Once this is known, tetracycline marking will probably be able to reveal the beginning of mechanically created bone structure changes at an early time in persons whose spinal column is especially susceptible to damage because of mechanical stress, athletic training, or vibrations. For instance, static and dynamic strains that the spinal column must undergo during various exercises and sports disciplines—often in a stereotypical succession—are able to cause gradual transformation processes in the skeleton. In weightlifters, a conspicuous, rough-streaked spongiosa structure in the vertebral bodies is identified as an adaptation to excessive axial pressure during the lifting (Neugebauer 1974). This early identification of damage will make the use of prophylactic measures possible.

5.2.4.2 Structural Analyses and Stability Studies

Research that penetrates deeper and deeper into the structure and stress resistance of the bones is essential in the field of biomechanics. Computer structural analyses can explain the qualitative relationships between mechanical requirements and the reaction of the living bone (Scholten 1976). Such studies may yield valuable findings regarding the structure of the vertebral body bone and the strain of the bioarchitectural angle structures at the transition from vertebral body to vertebral arch root and the articular process.

The density of the skeleton is easily recognized in the roentgenogram. Radiological substance analysis enables a classification of various osteoporosis stages according to severity. In addition to densitometry and the usual roentgenogram analysis, morphometry is another method to obtain comparable (standardized) values of osteoporotic changes.

Because the mass and composition of the bone substance are to a high degree related to age (Fig. 2-44), the loss of bone tissue volume is much greater in the vertebral body than in the femur and cranial bones (see Fig. 4-62). Similarly, the bone elements and total bone tissue in the vertebrae may decrease in younger persons as a result of underexertion due to lack of exercise (see sections 5.3 and 7.3).

The stress testing of the vertebral bone is a relatively easy biomechanical procedure. However, often it only indicates the stability of the isolated vertebral body, excluding the adjacent intervertebral discs and bony vertebral arches. Thus, such mechanical characteristics as pressure, traction, flexion, shearing, and rotation stress resistance are determined up to the stress tolerance limit. Table 5-1 establishes in its bottom half the decline of pressure resistance past the age of 45 to 50. The pressure resistance of the vertebral body for the square millimeter is shown in Table 5-2.

Sonoda (1962) determined the fracture tolerance of the vertebral bodies in different sections

Table 5-1 Vertebral Body Stress Tolerance (Messerer 1880)

56 Year-Old Male

	(kg)		(kg)		(kg)		(kg)
C-3	150	T-1	200	T-7	250	L-1	400
C-4	150	T-2	200	T-8	250	L-2	425
C-5	170	T-3	190	T-9	320	L-3	350
C-6	170	T-4	210	T-10	360	L-4	400
C-7	170	T-5	210	T-11	400	L-5	425
		T-6	220	T-12	375		

Age of Female	Values						
(years)	(kg)						
	C-4	T-1	T-6	T-10	L-1	L-4	L-5
25	—	300	360	480	620	—	740
30	275	450	600	850	1000	—	875
34	—	—	—	—	800	—	—
51	240	250	280	420	540	—	560
56	—	—	220	360	400	400	425
80	—	—	—	—	—	250	—
81	—	—	—	—	240	—	—

Table 5-2 Pressure Resistance of Vertebral Bodies

Author	Year	Vertebral Body	Pressure Resistance
			(kp/mm^2)
Messerer	1880	Fresh	0.22–0.84
G. Lange	1902	Fresh	0.15–0.56
Goecke	1928	Fresh	0.20–0.70
Sonoda	1962	Fresh	0.35–0.88
Bell et al.	1971	Macerated	0.402–1.335

Table 5-3 Stability Tolerances for Axial Pressure in the Fourth to Fifth Decade (Sonoda 1962)

	Cervical	Upper Thoracic	Lower Thoracic	Lumbar
	(kg)			
Intervertebral disc	320	450	1150	1500
Vertebral body	289	336	502	569

Table 5-4 Height Loss Caused by Axial Pressure until Collapse Compared with Pressure-Free Normal Height (Sonoda 1962)

	Cervical	Lower Thoracic	Lumbar
	(%)		
Intervertebral disc in the fourth to fifth decade of life	35.2	31.4	35.5
Vertebral body in the second to third decade of life	8.1	5.6	5.6

of the spinal column and at different ages with the help of spinal column specimens. In the middle-aged groups he found the following: 370 kg at the cervical spinal column, 431 kg at the thoracic spinal column, and 730 kg at the lumbar spinal column. He also noted that the height loss of the vertebral bodies was between 5.6% and 8.1% of vertebral body height until the fracture tolerance was reached (Tables 5-3 and 5-4). The elastic expansion of the vertebral body that was subjected to stress almost until the fracture tolerance was reached was 7% after the cessation of the strain and 11% after the conclusion of the elastic aftereffects. When the bone fractures after a prolonged pressure and an immediate height loss results, a continued pressure causes a slowly progressing deformation.

Sonoda (1962) also observed a traction strain of the vertebral bodies and the rupture tolerances, height increases, and elastic recontraction in that process (Table 5-5). The influence of forced horizontal rotations on vertebral bodies is shown in Table 5-6. The rotation deformation in middle age could be up to 13° in the upper thoracic spinal column and up to 5° in the lumbar spinal column before fractures occur.

Wyss and Ulrich performed studies in 1954 on fracture tolerance with similar results. In their studies, the fracture tolerance of the lumbar vertebral bodies was established at a pressure of about 400 kp (ie 40 kp/cm^2), which decreased after the age of 70 to 250 kp. New detailed studies were performed by Hannson et al. in 1980 and Piwernetz and Roehler in 1979.

In an interesting experimental set-up, Christ and Dupuis (1966) subjected a lumbar spinal column specimen to pressure and recorded the progress of the experiment cineradiographically. The force resulting in a fracture of the vertebral body was 822 kp.

Nachemson (1965, 1966) established the pressure strain on the lumbar intervertebral discs during normal everyday activities as 0.1 to

Table 5-5 Stability Tolerances in Axial Longitudinal Traction (Sonoda 1962)

	Cervical	Upper Thoracic	Lower Thoracic	Lumbar
Intervertebral disc	105 kg	142 kg	291 kg	394 kg
	0.33 kg/mm^2	0.24 kg/mm^2	0.26 kg/mm^2	0.30 kg/mm^2
Vertebral body	—	173 kg	336 kg	464 kg
		0.37 kg/mm^2	0.38 kg/mm^2	0.40 kg/mm^2

Table 5-6 Rupture Tolerances During Rotation Studies (Sonoda 1962)

	Cervical	Upper Thoracic	Lower Thoracic	Lumbar
Intervertebral disc	56 kg/cm	87 kg/cm	273 kg/cm	463 kg/cm
	0.52 kg/mm^2	0.46 kg/mm^2	0.48 kg/mm^2	0.51 kg/mm^2
Vertebral body	—	60 kg/cm	165 kg/cm	255 kg/cm
	—	0.37 kg/mm^2	0.34 kg/mm^2	0.32 kg/mm^2

0.2 kp/mm^2. Therefore, there is no danger of a further compression of a fractured vertebral body through pressure of the adjacent lumbar intervertebral discs. These findings encourage an early exertion and return to everyday life.

In 1957 Perrey described the peculiarity of the collapses of the bony vertebral body end plates, which are a frequent result of pressure studies on spinal column specimens. Many authors point out connections between those collapses and microfractures of the end plates (cribra) (see sections 2.2, 2.3, 3.2, and 4.6). They are also connected to tears and microfissures developing in the cartilage plates of the intervertebral discs during pressure studies. These tears are a first sign of pressure damage in the intervertebral disc and frequently develop even after stress influences that do not result in vertebral body fractures. It is not yet known whether a deterioration of posture results in an impairment of the diffusion flow between vertebral body and intervertebral disc (see section 2.3).

However, bone structures are not solely responsible for the mechanical stability of the vertebral body. The fluid pressure in the interior of the spongiosa spaces is also partially responsible. To a certain extent, the stress tolerance limit depends on this pressure, as was shown in measurements of the internal pressure of the bone marrow (Harrelson and Hills 1970, Hoffmann-Daimler 1974). With increasing—mostly age-related—osteoporosis the osmotic internal sure decreases, which is probably also caused by the decrease in fluid exchange in the capillary system with progressive age. Therefore, the deterioration of the mechanical resistance of the vertebral body is caused both by bone decomposition and a decrease of internal pressure. The hemodynamic-biostatic theory of osteoporosis by Krokowski et al. (1976) is important in this context.

Studies on the load-bearing capacity of the vertebral arch processes have been performed on human spinal column specimens. The stress tolerance limit before damage results is 15 kg for spinous and transverse processes and 100 kg for articular processes.

Frequently, experiments on pressure and flexion stability have been used to explain the development of spondylolysis—the cleavage of the compact bony interarticular portion in the vertebral arch (Fig. 4-29, sections 4.5 and 8.7). Roca and Jimeno maintained in 1980 that spondylolysis is the result of a fatigue fracture caused by traction during retroflexion. Farfan and his co-workers note the significance of anteflexion, in this process (see sections 4.5 and 8.7).

5.2.4.3 Stress Tolerance Values

The mechanical influences affecting the vertebral bones in everyday life and during leisure do not reach the stress tolerance level calculated to result in fractures. Therefore, those forces neither change the internal bone structure nor result in substance collapses (sintering). Even though unexpected, sudden overexertions—for instance, accidents—with a substantial transgression of the tolerance limit may occur in daily life or leisure, their discussion is outside the scope of this book.

The healthy vertebral bone will tolerate the initial stages of performance training without damage. Chapter 8 discusses to what degree training in high performance sports may pose danger for the vertebral bone, especially for the interarticular portion of the vertebral arch. For instance, only if the weightlifter uses an incorrect lifting technique in conjunction with a muscular misapplication will an athletic overexertion of the vertebral body result. However, when an individual has moderate skeletal damage that originated during the juvenile growth period and/or aging process, an individual stress tolerance limit should be determined prior to his or her participation in sports or conditioning programs.

Even coming close to the standard stress tolerance values poses a risk for persons with all forms of osteoporosis, especially senile osteoporosis and other disorders that affect the stress resistance of the bones (see section 4.6). Restraint in daily life is advised in such cases. It is obvious that such circumstances require individual consultations with an experienced physician. Before engaging in athletics, consultation with an experienced sport physician is absolutely necessary.

Exact stress tolerance limit for the bones of the spinal column may only be determined in experiments on individual vertebrae. However, these values are only of minor significance because the damaging overexertion of the spinal column is always caused by a number of additional factors. These include the resistance of the hemiarthrosis intervertebral disc and the numerous articulations and intervertebral motor segments (see Chapter 3).

5.2.5 Intervertebral Disc

Morphological characteristics distinguish the intervertebral disc from "genuine" articulations. The intervertebral disc bonds to adjacent vertebral bodies in the area of the vertebral body. It fulfills an important biomechanical function within the intervertebral motor segment.

5.2.5.1 Stress Tolerance Values

Just as stress tolerance values of vertebral bones were derived from the study of deceased specimens, the stress tolerance values of the intervertebral disc have been similarly calculated (see sections 3.2 and 3.4). Although such findings are not completely applicable to humans without any additional consideration, they do provide certain clues to those types of stresses that might pose a threat to the spinal column if they affect it violently, over a prolonged period, or in combination. Those stresses rarely occur in the normal course of everyday life or during light physical exertion in uncompetitive sports. However, they may often occur in athletic performance training, especially for high achievement in competition.

Often, stress tolerance limits for intervertebral discs gain significance at the time of transition between the third to fourth decade of life. At that time, the strength of the static-dynamic musculoligamentous corset in the trunk area decreases significantly because of the increase in time spent in sedentary activities at the expense of muscle-strengthening movements (sports, physical activities, fitness programs). This lack of exercise and the vibrations experienced during vehicle rides often cause the reappearance of intervertebral disc-related damages that originated during the growth period. The permanent functional limit that is the result of intervertebral insufficiency and its sequelae, which again depend on the condition of the intervertebral disc, will become more noticeable at this time (see section 3.4). An increase in muscle strength that may be attained through diligent, medically supervised treatment may increase this functional limit. However, when there is pre-existing damage, the functional stress limit will be lower than the standard value.

5.2.5.2 Models of Intervertebral Discs

Although models of the entire spinal column or of larger sections exist, models of individual intervertebral discs have been produced only in rare cases. In 1980, Bromberg and von Essen reported on such models that included the nucleus pulposus as a noncompressible fluid and 11 fiber layers in oblique, alternating directions. The intervertebral spaces of these ring fibers are filled with noncompressible fluid. Compression in the axial direction, rotation, oblique pressure, and combination stress have been studied. However, the model does not allow studies of extension. Based on such models, artificial intervertebral discs for surgical replacement have been constructed (Hoffman-Daimler 1974).

5.2.6 Ligament System

The numerous ligaments that are in direct contact with the sectioned spinal column (see section 2.2) form a biomechanical unit—a system of ligaments. The spine as a unit can perform its important functions because its elastic steering effect is transferred via the attachments at the larger bones (eg, the anterior longitudinal ligament at the vertebral bodies) and/or the numerous vertebral arch processes. It thus forms a self-contained functional sequence involving several segments. Together with the intervertebral discs this ligament chain acts as a stabilizing force for all mechanical influences. In addition to these general stabilizing functions, the ligaments also can control and inhibit unphysiological movements by the way in which their fiber tracts are structured and oriented. The elastic force inherent in the ligaments of the spinal column is demonstrated when the spinal column is extended by about 4 cm, and all ligaments at the level of each intervertebral motor segments tear, except for the ligaments of the intervertebral discs.

Because the ligaments possess a good nerve supply, they are assumed to play a role in the development of spinal column pain.

The ligament structures of the spinal column will be fully able to satisfy the necessary mechanical requirements only if they are properly coordinated with the relevant muscle groups. In the case of decreased muscle performance caused by poor training condition, advanced age, overexertion through unfavorable body postures, or paralysis, the ligament systems can exert a compensatory effect if there is no damage to their structures. However, constant use may result in excessive strain of certain ligament areas and thus may lower their functional capacity, thereby affecting the muscles adversely. On the other hand, damaged ligaments may impair the compensatory strength of the muscles in the long run, which will further decrease performance capacity. Such concomitant symptoms aggravate intervertebral instability (see section 3.4). At the appearance of the first signs of insufficiency symptoms, a muscle-strengthening therapy is urgently needed (see section 7.3). The connection between the ligament system and muscles is demonstrated by the anteflexion headache of school-aged children, a topic that receives too little attention (see sections 7.2 and 7.3).

5.3 SPECIAL MECHANICAL INFLUENCES

5.3.1 Lack of Exercise

A lack of physical exercise shadows life in our age. As a result, formerly unknown diseases now appear.

A severe and prolonged lack of dynamic and/or static exertion results in the degeneration of bone tissue in the skeleton, primarily at the spinal column. This so-called inactivity osteoporosis is characterized by a decrease in the number and diameter of the bone trabeculae. Well-known consequences of osteoporosis at the central axial organ are back pain; collapse of the vertebral body spongiosa into wedge, flat, or plane vertebrae (see section 4.6); decreased load-bearing capacity of the spongiosa; central indentations of the vertebral bodies; and an increased curvature of the spinal column caused by those indentations.

Significantly altered environmental conditions that impair the equilibrium of bone metabolism may lead to osteoporosis. One rare form develops as a result of weightlessness in outer space.

5.3.1.1 Illness

Osteoporosis may also be caused by hormonal changes. Estrogenic- and androgenic-deficiency osteoporosis present as senile and presenile bone decalcification. Drug use may also cause osteoporosis. Because bone disorders develop faster at the spinal column than at other bones, back pain is an initial symptom of osteoporosis. The frequent collapse of the vertebral body also significantly increases pain (see section 4.6).

Sitting or prolonged confinement to bed (see section 7.3) further aggravates osteoporosis. A vicious cycle may result in which bed rest due to pain aggravates the pathomorphic changes. The gradually developing muscular weakness that is the result of the absence of function is also part of the vicious cycle. In this way, the discoligamental tension loses its compensatory function.

Psychological disorders that restrict movement may cause an inactivity osteoporosis, which may result in the collapse of osteoporotic vertebral bodies. The adjacent intervertebral discs are frequently involved in this process because of a central swelling caused by fluid influx.

5.3.1.2 Bed Rest

Our normal nightly bed rest already has a stagnating effect on the fluid exchange of the intervertebral disc and therefore on its nutrition. This fluid retention results in an increase in height of the intervertebral disc spaces. As a result, body height, which measurably decreases during the course of the day, especially because of prolonged sitting or the carrying of heavy loads, returns to its normal value in the morning (Gritz 1975, Junghanns 1979).

Spinal column disorders caused by bed rest are not restricted to the intervertebral discs. Confinement to bed aggravates existing osteoporosis, and prolonged bed rest can result in an increasingly painful inactivity osteoporosis, even in the healthy vertebral bone. The calcium loss in the bone increases gradually until the eighth to ninth week of bed rest; thereafter, a constant calcium level is maintained (Vogel & Whittle 1975).

5.3.1.3 Sitting

In the past, lack of exercise combined with a prolonged forced posture (eg, during sitting) was held responsible for an osteoporosis of the spinal column with back pain. According to recent research, however, osteoporosis does not develop in this way. The inactivity osteoporosis of the spinal column appears only after a confinement to bed of several months.

Even though the lack of exercise during sitting does not result in any demonstrable damages in the skeleton, a long-lasting lack of exercise, however, does lead to unfavorable consequences for the intervertebral motor segments, especially for the intervertebral disc. These occur because the pump mechanism that is important for fluid exchange has been put out of use (see section 3.2). The ability to supply nutrients and remove waste is decreased. Therefore, **the intervertebral disc thrives on movement.**

The absence of movement during prolonged sitting does not only affect the intervertebral motor segments but also adversely affects the involved muscles at the trunk, neck, shoulders, and arms, as well as in the area of the pelvis and femur (see section 4.2). These muscles also require the change between rest and movement for their metabolism and maintenance of their strength. Thus, a vicious cycle of pressure caused by sitting and muscle relaxation damages the tissue of the intervertebral discs.

The oscillation strain on the spinal column is a part of many occupations and occurs when riding in motorized vehicles. The exposure to motorization is the second time period of susceptibility to damage for the growing spinal column of the child and adolescent (see sections 7.2 and 7.3). (The first time period of susceptibility is the transition from playing child to sitting child that occurs when he or she enters school. The third stage of susceptibility is the transitional period between the third and fourth decade of life.) Sitting on a vibrating surface is possibly damaging by itself and is multiplied by the detrimental influences of the strain of motionless sitting.

5.3.2 Total Body Vibrations

5.3.2.1 General Principles

As a consequence of our modern lifestyle, as well as requirements of work, sport, and exercise, the human body is exposed to different types of vibrations of different durations and different degrees of strength. The ever-increasing general mechanization of society and the widespread use of motor vehicles place a steadily increasing strain on the human organism through mechanical alternating forces that are transferred to the body and may result in damage. In the past, the cause for such damage was considered to be exclusively the direct impact of vibrations on the oscillation-sensitive spinal column and its corresponding muscle groups. Continued research has established, however, that a second, additional process may result in damage or may aggravate already existing, vibration-related damages. This process originates in the internal secretory organs. Nerves and blood vessels, as well as important tissue portions of regulatory organs of metabolism, react with pathological changes to the vibration stimuli (Janek et al 1964, Rakhimov et al 1970; Steplenski et al 1964). The larger neural structures are also subjected to damaging vibrations. The biochemical products of mechanically produced damage and of neural-vasal influences may, via these pathways, reach remote targeted organs. Impairments of the metabolism of muscles, bones, cartilage, and tendons may result. Because of their dependence on diffusion metabolism, the bony portions of the spinal column and of the intervertebral discs, as well as the cartilaginous surfaces of the vertebral articulations, are very sensitive to scillation-related damage.

The often complex characteristics of vibrations affecting the body in everyday life make research into vibration-related body damages more difficult. The transmission of oscillations among individual body tissues and body sections varies as well. Vibrations may gradually fade not only at the transitional surfaces of various tissues but also while passing through larger, uniform tissue sections. Under certain conditions, stimulating oscillations trigger a strong resonance with high amplitudes when they contact a co-vibrating system. Weak impulses may therefore, in conjunction with a suitable resonance frequency, be able to induce strong vibrations of an organ that is susceptible to oscillations.

Vibrations greater than 1000 Hz occur only rarely and only in the work environment. They are greatly attenuated in the topmost tissue layers of the body and do not affect deeper layers. The frequency range of those oscillations that affect the organs are much lower, ranging from less than 1 oscillation per second (1 Hz) to 100 Hz. Figures 5-18 and 5-19 show older research findings on subjectively perceived oscillations. More recent research has found that even vibrations below 4 Hz exert a strong influence on the human body. This fact requires special attention because vibrations caused by tractors and heavy construction machines are in this frequency range.

Depending on the direction from which the vibrations contact and penetrate the body, directional letters are used to designate them

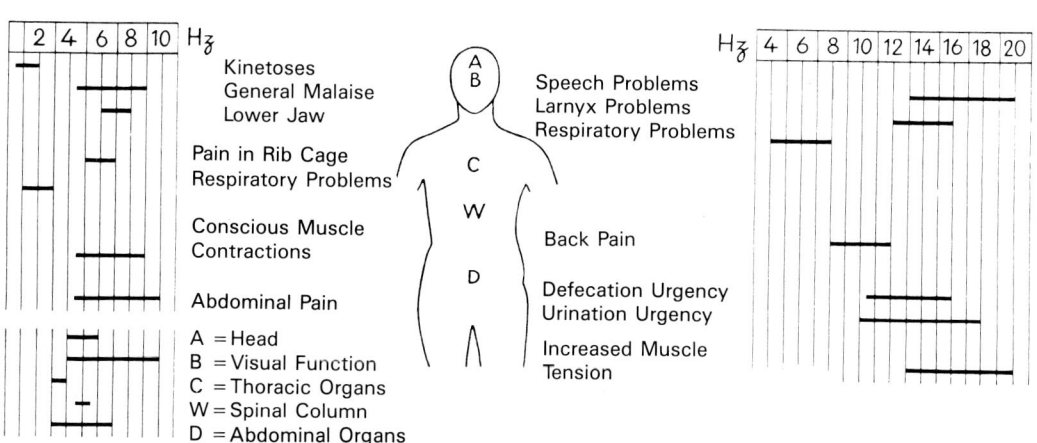

Fig. 5-18 Tolerance limits of various symptoms determined during vertical oscillating stresses in the sitting person.

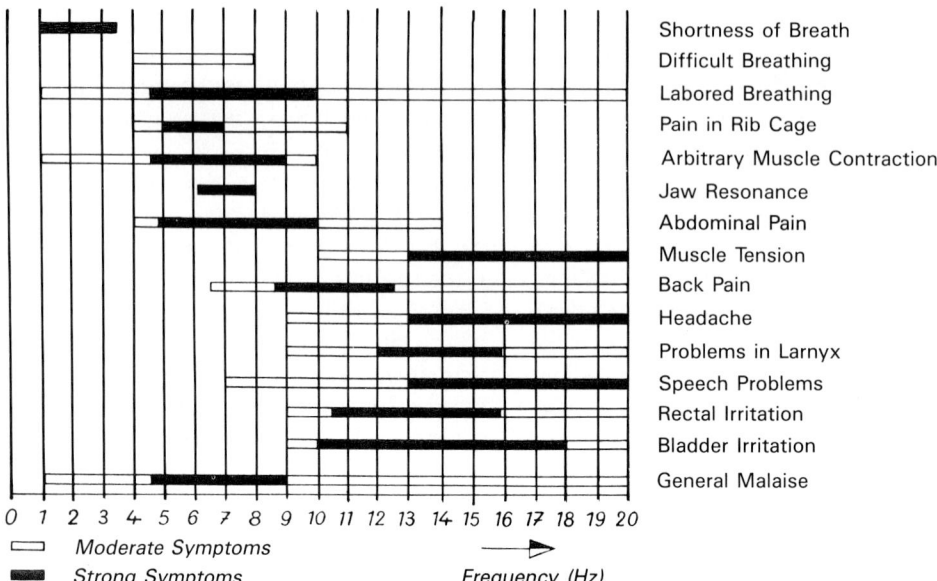

Fig. 5-19 Schematic on the perception of vibration-related symptoms. There are slight variations from Fig. 5-16 [from Magid].

(Fig. 5-20). Vibrations do not always reach the spinal column directly or after penetrating thin surface layers. Often, they use shorter or longer transmission pathways; for instance, arms or legs.

Some vibrations are subjectively perceived as especially bothersome and may decrease functional performance and even cause serious diseases. The vibrations transmitted to the cervical spinal column by blood vessels or nerves may impair the equilibrium in the middle ear, resulting in vertigo, indisposition, and even vomiting. Vibrations of under 1 Hz produced by long automobile, bus, or boat rides (seasickness) cause kinetosis, which impairs general well-being significantly (Fig. 5-18).

The influence of vibrations on human organs depends on self-resonance, which in most organs is 3 to 9 Hz. The predominant resonance frequency of the human body is 5 Hz (Dupuis & Zerlett 1984). Similarly, the spinal column has a resonance frequency of 5 Hz. The oscillation maximum of the cervical spinal column is 3.5 Hz, whereas the maximum resonance for thoracic organs is between 3 and 4 Hz and for abdominal organs between 3 and 7 Hz. The resonance of those organs is partially determined by their muscle tone. The value for the vertebral column/head unit is 6 Hz (Stech & Payne 1969, Terry & Roberts 1968). (Differences may be explained by the varying experimental set-ups.) During studies with an oscillating table, Cremona (1972) found the main strains on the spinal column to be at C-4 to C-6, T-10 to L-1, and L-4 to S-1. He determined that the vibrations of the

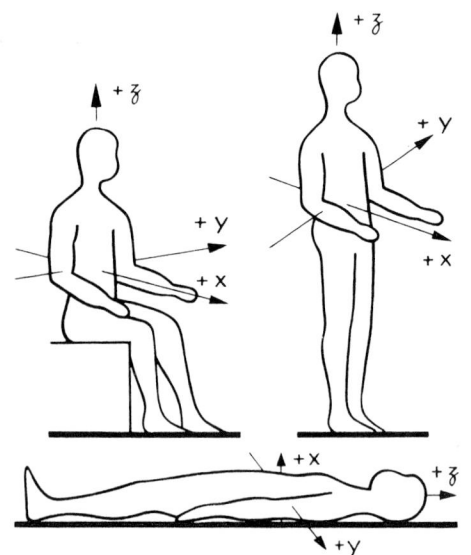

Fig. 5-20 Physiological coordinate system in various body postures used to designate the direction of oscillations.

head were three times as strong as those in the upper trunk area. An especially active muscle activity—between 4 and 8 Hz—exists in the resonance area of the trunk, as was proven in electromyographic studies. Pain occurred in the rib cage and shoulders at 4 to 6 Hz, in the abdomen at 9 to 10 Hz, and in the lumbosacral area at 8 to 12 Hz.

In a review of 29 epidemiological studies, Heide (1978) reported that total body vibrations between 0.1 and 20 Hz result in an increased risk for the spinal column (and in connection with it also for the peripheral nervous system) if their intensity exceeds the ''tolerance curve for health'' of VDI 2057 and ISO 2631.

The manifold transmission pathways by which vibrations travel directly to the spinal column or that, via other organs, influence the metabolism necessary for the viability of the intervertebral disc are able, in certain situations, to induce alterations in the structure of the intervertebral disc. Therefore, **vibrations are the secret destroyers of the metabolism of the intervertebral disc and in conjunction with lack of exercise, may become destroyers of the intervertebral disc structure.**

In some countries, spondylosis deformans, which results from vibrations of motor vehicles, heavy motorized work machines, or the operation of hand held compressed air equipment, has been designated as an occupational disease.

In sports, prolonged oscillations are found in only a few areas, such as motor biking or bicycling, car racing, horse racing, and sport flying. Participants in those sports should avoid additional, oscillating stresses in daily life.

However, in a considerable number of sports and exercise disciplines, severe and fast, repetitive, sterotypical vibrations may occur. Still unresolved are whether vibrations create or significantly aggravate spinal column damages and whether these problems should be recognized as ''sport damage'' or ''exercise damage'' similar to an occupational disease.

5.3.2.2 Vibration Sickness

Vibration sickness affects many organs and organ systems as an external, dynamic, alternating stress caused by oscillating forces. The consequences of organ involvement range from temporary subjective vexation (eg, kinotosis) to psychological impairment to a pronounced physiological effect. Decreased performance may be one consequence, or acute or chronic health damage may result.

In addition to the well-known damage to the ear produced by the noise of vibrations, oscillating forces also may harm the eyes. The critical frequency range for a decline in visual acuity lies between 2 and 10 Hz. Exciting oscillating frequencies around 20 Hz cause such a strong vibration of the eyeball that retinal detachment results. Exhausting water skiing may create such accelerations (see section 8.4). The cardiovascular system, respiration, and gastric juice production are also influenced by vibrations. Stomach ulcers may develop or be exacerbated by vibrations.

The influences of regular sinus-shaped, irregular (stochastic) oscillations, and mixed oscillations have been studied primarily for the muscles located immediately at the spinal column and for all muscles of the trunk: It is still unknown whether vibrations affecting bones, articulations, and soft tissue parts (eg, intervertebral discs or tendon attachments) may damage the spinal column directly or whether the spine is only affected secondarily by primary vibration-related damages of the nerves, blood vessels, ganglions, and regulatory organs of the metabolism. For example, a vibration-related metabolic disorder may threaten the viability of the sensitive bradytrophic intervertebral disc tissue. It is also not known whether the transmission pathway of partial body vibrations continues up to the cervical spine to affect neural structures or the capillaries at the hyaline cartilage plate.

The great extent of vibration-related damages in many organ systems has prompted numerous animal experiments to determine how damage is caused in different body tissues after prolonged vibration influences. In the course of these experiments, light microscopic and electron microscopic study procedures have been used.

Muscles. After a 4-week exposure to vibrations, Fassbender (1979) discovered an increase of mitochondria and giant cells. When he doubled the time of vibration exposure he observed the presence of stages of slight degeneration.

Witt and Fischer described in 1980 homogenized muscle cells with a lack of transverse striation. This damage was attributed to the vibration-related muscle hypertonus that is activated by reflexes.

Bones. After a prolonged exposure to vibrations, strongly enlarged blood spaces in the decreased spongiosa—blood pools—were found. They were interpreted as congestive impairments of the outflow and were also assumed to be an additional factor in the development of arthrosis (Witt & Fischer 1980).

Vibrations also caused an increase in nonorganic components while the level of calcium did not change. The bone became brittle and fragile as in senile osteoporosis; premature structural weakening was the result (Jankovich 1971).

Cartilage. In the study already mentioned, Fassbender (1979) also found generations of cartilage cells that could be interpreted as a precursor of osteochondrosis.

5.3.2.3 Effects on the Spinal Column

Persons riding in a vehicle are affected by vibrations from the seat, floor, and the co-vibrating backrest. The entire body is subjected to these vibrations; hence, the term "total body vibrations." The engine is the source of the sinus-shaped vibrations. Stochastic vibrations, which are irregular and of particular intensity and amplitude, are transmitted from the surface of the road via vibrating vehicle parts (wheels, axes, springs, vehicle cabin, etc.) and combine with the sinus-shaped total body vibrations. The driver is also affected by vibrations from the foot-operated pedals. In addition, he or she receives stochastic vibrations as partial body vibrations via the steering wheel and hand-operated levers. These vibrations penetrate the spinal column via the transmission pathway of the hand-arm-shoulder girdle. In these ways the central axial organ is affected by vertical and, less frequently, horizontal vibrations that continue either individually or in a combined manner (mixed vibrations). The vibrations are only seldom uninterrupted, harmonic sinus influences. More often they are irregular (stochastic) vibrations that combine with unexpected, additional pressure impacts of alternating, irregular vibration forms, that shake and flex abruptly, bend, and rotate (in curves). These vibrations with their unpredictable impacts have especially negative consequences. The muscles are unable to develop a sensible "behavior pattern" to protect against irregular, mixed vibrations and therefore are unable to sufficiently absorb and compensate for those impacts.

To apply the results of animal experiments to humans, increasingly realistic mathematical and biodynamic models, anthropomorphic dolls, and computer-simulation models have been used during the last decades. In many such models, the spinal column is depicted as a uniform, elastic column with a resonance frequency of 5 Hz that greatly attenuates the vibrations penetrating from the ground. In contrast, the spinal column is not actually a unit but is a sectioned organ composed of bone parts (vertebrae) and interposed soft parts (intervertebral discs) and with articular units (vertebral arch articulations) in each intervertebral motor segment. The individual intervertebral motor segment, or in most cases several or even all segments, serves as a "reacting system" to vertical stresses by engaging in movement, including rotation and tilting.

The substantial tissue portion of the intervertebral discs in the horizontally structured spinal column, which occupies one-third of the entire height of the spinal column, therefore plays a central role in determining the outcome of vibration influences. Several questions remain unanswered:

- What happens to vibration attenuation and resonance both at the caudal and at the cranial vertebral body/intervertebral disc boundary, ie, at the transition from bone to soft, elastic intervertebral disc tissue and also from intervertebral disc to the bone during vertical vibrations?
- The end capillaries of the vertebral body arteries (see section 2.2), which are of the highest importance for the nutritional diffusion of the intervertebral disc, are located at the transitions in the perforations of the bony vertebral body end plate. Are the vibrations affecting these end capillaries as

detrimental as those affecting the capillaries of the finger tips?
- What is the effect of horizontal vibrations, particularly rotation vibrations, on the border area of the vertebral body and intervertebral disc, as well as on such other susceptible areas as the bonding of the fiber ring in the bony epiphysis and connective fibers between the lamellae rings (see figures in section 2.2)?
- What is the connection between vertical, horizontal and rotatory vibrations and the microfractures in the area of the bony vertebral body end plate and the adjacent hyaline cartilage layer?

5.3.3 Partial Body Vibrations

In contrast to total body vibrations, which are a common part of our daily leisure and sports activities, partial body vibrations are primarily experienced in the occupational sector. When these vibrations are experienced both on the job and in everyday life, they may have clinical significance.

5.3.3.1 Diseases Caused by Partial Body Vibrations

The nervous system is the focus of study of partial body vibrations. When exposed to excessive vibrations, nerve receptors that are located in the sliding layers between individual organs and also between muscles may be stimulated to the point of destruction. Organs that depend on the affected nerves are thus inevitably affected. According to some researchers, the irritation of neural systems or nerve damages caused primarily by vibrations leads to blood vessel changes, which should be regarded as vibration-related vasospastic diseases: traumatic angioneurosis of the fingertips, traumatic vasospastic disease, Raynaud's disease, white finger disease, dead fingers, or vibration-related vasospastic syndrome (see section 3.3). Even after the damaging vibrations have ceased, further progress of these blood vessel damages can be observed. In such cases it is of urgent importance to avoid any further endangering vibrations in daily life, sports, or leisure activities.

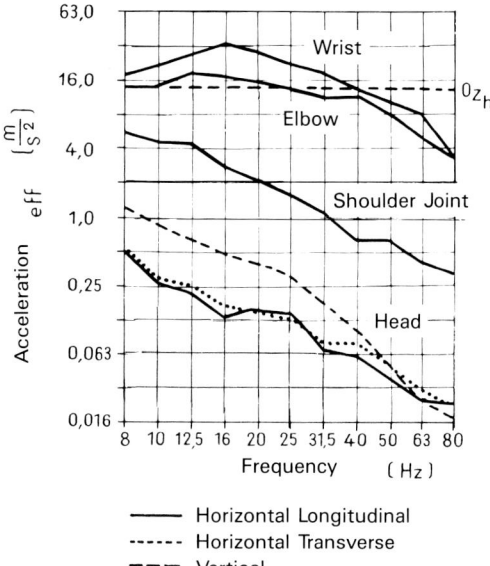

Fig. 5-21 Biomechanical vibration transmission from vibrating tools to the hand, elbow, shoulder, and head (8 to 80 Hz).

After blood vessel and nerve changes, vibration-related bone and articular damage is the most frequent consequence of partial body vibrations. Hand articulations, elbow, and the acromioclavicular articulation are especially subject to these potential damages: scaphoid bone fracture, lunate bone death, arthrosis deformans, and osteochondrosis dissecans.

5.3.3.2 Effects of Partial Body Vibrations on the Spinal Column

The main transmission pathway of partial body vibrations to the spinal column runs from vibrating, hand-operated equipment or from the steering wheel and operating levers in a vehicle over the hand, arm, and shoulder into the transitional area between the thoracic and cervical spinal column. On certain vibration intensities, this pathway continues via the cervical spinal column to the head and may also cause the head to vibrate. However, the reduction in intensity of the vibrations (Fig. 5-21) along the course of the pathway is responsible for the smaller influence of vibrations on the cervical spinal column. In the hand and shoulder area, influences on the muscles, as well as articular and blood vessel damages, also occur.

When partial body and total body vibrations combine, the increase in vibration intensities, the mixing of flexing and rotatory influences, and the development of significant (three-dimensional) roll oscillations may have serious consequences. If the equilibrium organ is involved and if vasospastic influences are present, sensations, such as kinetosis, may develop.

Thus in the racket sports—tennis, squash, badminton, and table tennis (see section 8.4)—substantial vibration intensities reach the cervical spinal column via the arm and shoulder when the ball hits the racket at 300 kilometers per hour. Often the stress resistance limit of an intervertebral disc is exceeded in this process so that initial damages (see sections 4.6 and 8.2) develop that may be the beginning of intervertebral chondrosis.

5.4 Biomechanical Behavior of the Entire Spinal Column

The biomechanical behavior of the spinal column is determined not only by the general stress conditions and the special mechanical characteristics of the spinal column, its bones, and intervertebral discs but also by the surrounding muscles, ligament systems, and blood vessels. Therefore, study of the form, posture, and mo-

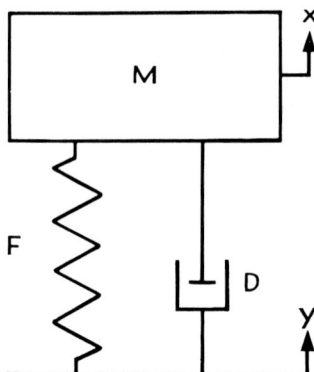

Fig. 5-22 Spinal column model with a degree of freedom [from King & Chou (1976)]. Mass = M, F = spring, D = attenuation, x,y = effective forces.

bility of the spinal column must be integrated with an examination of the mechanical relationships of the extremities and muscles connected with the spinal column.

The simple model of a unitary spinal column is inadequate to describe the effects of stress. It is necessary to evaluate the stress resistance of the spinal column by considering the weakest point for each type of movement and stress, including lack of exercise or vibrations.

For example, the intervertebral discs show a greater stress resistance than the vertebral bodies at the lumbar spinal column during axial pres-

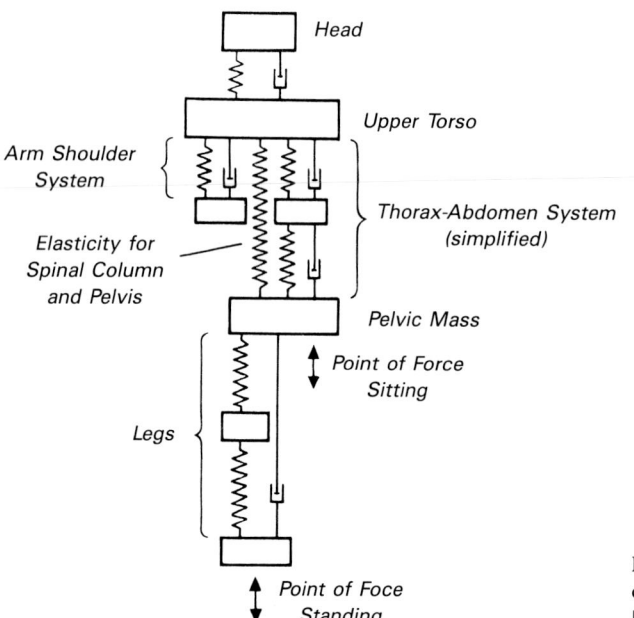

Fig. 5-23 Mechanodynamic replacement system of the spinal column in relation to the entire body [from Coermann (1961 to 1965)].

sure and also during rotation stress. However, the vertebral bodies are more stress resistant to longitudinal traction.

The study of the mobility and stress resistance of the spinal column has been based on increasingly more sophisticated models (Figs. 5-22 and 5-23). These have yielded useful data for the fields of occupational, sports, and aviation and space flight medicine. Computer-aided models are able to determine the stress tolerances for pressure, traction, and rotation, which of course is not possible with human volunteers (Belytschko et al 1973, Dupuis and Zerlett 1984, King and Chou 1976, von Gierke 1971).

6

Examination of the Spinal Column

By straightening to a two-footed posture and walk, human beings became severely encumbered with the lumbosacral curvature and the lumbar lordosis and therefore were subjected to new stress conditions at the lumbosacral transition (see Fig. 2-1). Changes also developed at the head-neck transition, resulting in transformed head articulations that support and move the head. Straightening also caused the multiple curves of the spinal column in the sagittal level, which have special tasks for mobility and the elastic cushioning of vertical stresses. However, the slow evolution to the present spinal column shape has not eliminated all the weak points of the spine. As a result, the spinal column is unable to cope with the ''unnatural'' stresses of the modern lifestyle.

6.1 EXAMINATION PRINCIPLES

6.1.1 Normal Mobility

The Zurich Convention of Manual Medicine of 1983 (Neumann 1983) provides a brief survey of examination techniques required to determine reversible functional impairments of the posture and motor system:

- Static and dynamic examination of the posture and motor system
- Palpation of the articular mechanisms
- Evaluation of muscle function and coordination
- Palpation of reflex reactions and changes in the substance of muscles, ligaments, subcutaneous tissues, and skin
- Evaluation of neurological and vascular findings, primarily in regard to segmental changes

The norms of mobility (without consideration of age) based on the neutral-0-method are shown in Table 6-1 and Figures 6-1 and 6-2.

6.1.2 Shape and Postural Impairments

A slight kyphosis or scoliosis cannot be called pathological without further consideration. However, if a patient cannot establish a normal spinal column curvature and maintain it for a longer period without pain, then one can assume that the proper muscle function is impaired as long as there are no significant damages in the skeleton or intervertebral discs. Medically supervised physiotherapy is required in order to re-establish permanently the normal posture or to avoid a deterioration.

If long-term therapy is unsuccessful, this case can no longer be considered an impaired posture caused by muscular insufficiency. Kyphosis,

176 CLINICAL IMPLICATIONS OF NORMAL BIOMECHANICAL STRESSES ON SPINAL FUNCTION

Table 6-1 Normal Mobility of the Spinal Column (Kapandji 1974)*

Movement	Degree
Ante-retroflexion (Fig. 6-3)	
Cervical spinal column	40-0-75
Thoracic and lumbar spinal column	105-0-60
Lumbar spinal column	60-0-35
	110-0-140
Right/left flexion (Fig. 6-4)	
Cervical spinal column	35-0-35
Thoracic spinal column	20-0-20
Lumbar spinal column	20-0-20
	75-0-75
Right/left rotation	
Cervical spinal column	45-0-45
Thoracic spinal column	35-0-35
Lumbar spinal column	5-0- 5
	90-0-90

*Data in neutral-0-method.

Fig. 6-1 Physiological lateral flexion of the spinal column [from Kapandji (1974)].

scoliosis, or kyphoscoliosis of various, mostly endogenous causes is then present (see section 4.4). Frequently, exogenous influences have already caused a deterioration (Fig. 6-3) including incorrect posture.

The spinal column shape is influenced by many factors, including the individual's psychological state. It can be affected as greatly by the internal pressure of the rib cage and abdominal cavity as by neural and muscular influences. In

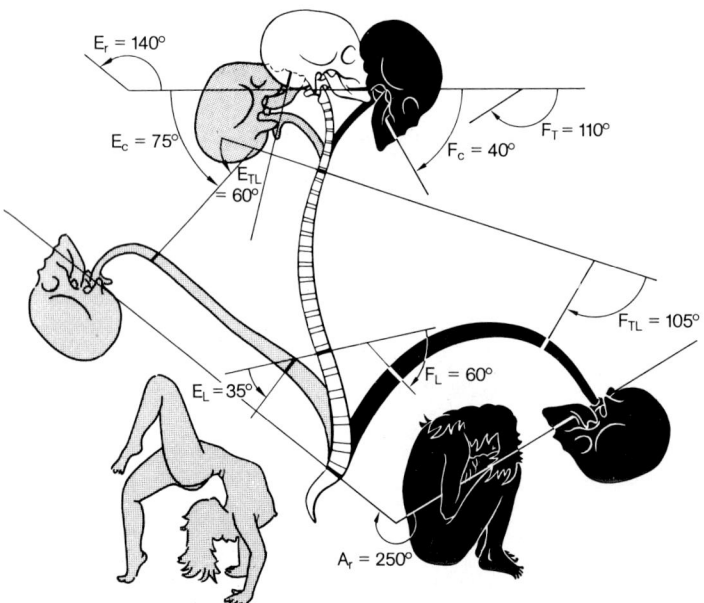

Fig. 6-2 Normal retro- and anteflexion potentials of the spinal column [from Kapandji (1974)].

Examination of the Spinal Column 177

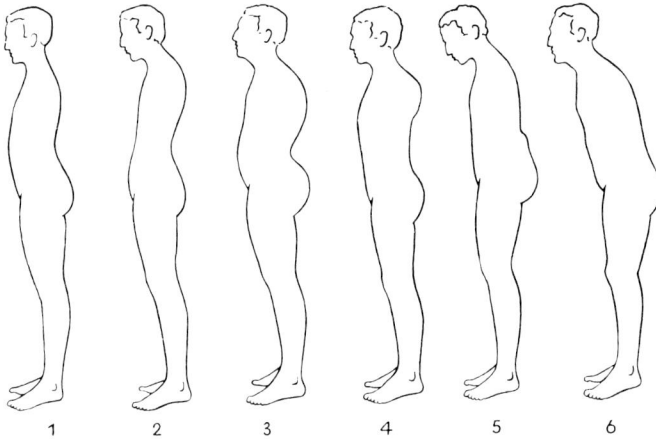

Fig. 6-3 Comparison of the normal body profile with pathological spinal column forms: (*1*) balanced back shape; (*2*) juvenile kyphosis in the thoracic spinal column area; (*3*) severely curved juvenile kyphosis in the thoracic and lumbar sections (total kyphosis), with static compensation through a flexed lumbar lordosis; (*4*) kyphoscoliosis of the thoracic spinal column; (*5*) spondylolisthetic stage through prolapse of the fifth lumbar vertebral body; (*6*) pain-caused posture in sciatica.

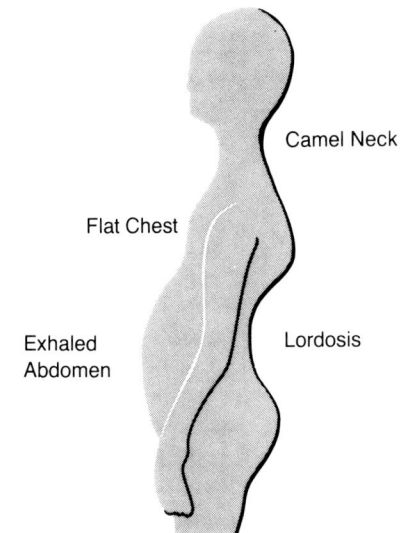

Fig. 6-4 Kypholordotic back caused by abdominal breathing.

clinical practice, it is sometimes difficult to differentiate an impaired posture from fixated damages of the spinal column, eg, the kypholordotic back of children (Figs. 5-3 and 6-4). Some authors attribute this back shape to persistent and overemphasized abdominal respirations and therefore evaluate it as a "behavioral disorder" (von Kuegelgen 1976). The spinal column shape can also be altered by wearing an overly high shoe heel, although the effect of the heel has been characterized differently by several authors (Hartenberg 1978, Weiss 1978).

"Bad posture," which is common among adolescents, can be differentiated from serious spinal column disorders by an examination method developed by Matthiass (arm-stretching attempt) (Fig. 6-5). One special form is the "relaxed" jeans posture of adolescents (see Fig. 6-6, section 7.2 and Fig. 7-1).

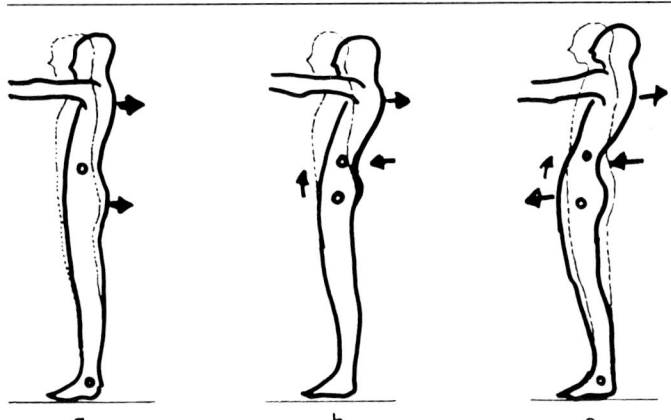

Fig. 6-5 Posture test using the arm-extension method of Matthiass (1966). By extending the arms the point of gravity is moved forward. A child with strong posture displaces his or her entire body only slightly backward (*a*), which sometimes reinforces the thoracic kyphosis and the lumbar lordosis (*b*). The child with weak posture pushes the pelvic forward and increases the lordosis significantly, hence, postural degeneration (*c*).

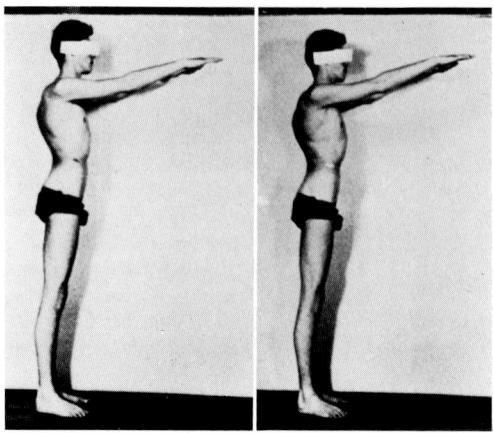

Fig. 6-6 Back with strong posture in spite of a severely curved total kyphosis (from Matthiass).

6.1.3 Mobility Impairments

The most frequent mobility impairment in the spinal area is decreased mobility. Yet, stiffness in the spinal area does not originate exclusively in the spinal column. At the thoracic spinal column, stiffness may be caused by congenital or infection-related rib fusions or by bone plates formed after pleuritis. The spasm of several smaller or larger muscle groups, which has either a neural or infectious origin, may be an exogenous cause of limited spinal column mobility. Stiffness may also develop because of congenital malformations or abnormal vertebral shapes (see section 4.3). When a localized stiffness appears suddenly and with great pain, a vertebral blockage should be suspected (see section 3.4).

Hypermobility is another, less common impairment of mobility. It may have many possible causes. The criteria for the diagnosis of hypermobility are as follows:

- Cervical spinal column
  1. Lateral inclination to ear-shoulder contact
  2. Head rotation of more than 180°
- Thoracic spinal column
  1. Unfolding of thoracic spinous processes (Ott's measurement) by more than 5 cm
- Lumbar spinal column
  1. Unfolding of lumbar spinous processes (Schober's measurement) by more than 6 cm
- Movement combinations
  1. Fingertip-floor distance in anteflexion with straight knee joints
  2. Lateral inclination of the trunk spinal column by more than 35° so that the perpendicular drops from the convex-lateral axillary fold to the contralateral pelvic half

Often, increased mobility originates at individual or multiple intervertebral motor segments, which are referred to as the "relaxed segment." This pathological condition in the intervertebral discs is especially likely to stiffen a spinal column section by myogelosis because of neural pain stimuli.

Hypermobility in the entire spinal column or in individual sections has a significant impact on participation in sports and acrobatics. Contortionists have an especially great mobility, often causing destruction of important bony vertebral arch portions. Yet, their success may be due to their deliberately created, pathological, painful condition (see section 8.6). The pelvic girdle relaxation that is frequently present in asthenic women may also be sought by instructors and coaches seeking talented athletes for training in floor exercises and other sport and gymnastic disciplines.

Only through observation of the body in various postures and with palpation diagnostics (manual examination) can clues to the causes of increased or decreased mobility be detected. At times, imaging techniques may be needed to find the causes.

6.2 MEDICAL EXAMINATION

Various diagnostic procedures, including the specific functional case history, are briefly described in the following sections. Special consideration must be paid to information about the patient's pain, not only while establishing the case history but in all stages of the physical examination. Often, the pain symptoms do not correspond to physical and radiographical findings, which may be because the examination techniques are not entirely suitable for the individual case. The physician should therefore exercise caution in making the final diagnosis.

Psychosomatic conditions warrant special attention because of the close relationship between psyche, simulation, dissimulation, and back pain (see sections 5.2 and 7.3). In 1979 Weintraub wrote:

> The physician calms himself and his patient with insignificant findings in the roentgenogram and disregards the emotional content of the syndrome: the person is being hanged on a spur of his own skeleton. The back pain which has thus been fixated and is carried by the patient with an exact vertebrae or intervertebral disc number is often hard to dissipate.

Figure 6-7 gives visual expression to this concept.

A psychologically oriented diagnosis frequently helps uncover the true origin of problems projected to the back. Spinal column pain may be an indication of the individual's psychological problems. Even the sympathetic talk at the beginning of an examination may uncover psychosocial factors that are the deeper causes of back pain. Table 6-2 categorizes psychosomatic back problems.

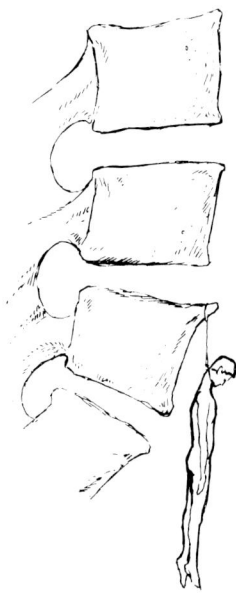

Fig. 6-7 The spinal column patient "hangs" at the spurs of the spinal column. The treating physician hangs the pain complex of the patient on the spur [from Weintraub (1979)].

6.2.1 Case History

In order to evaluate the stress capacity of the back, it is necessary to determine through the case history whether functional problems have already been observed. The patient should be asked whether he or she experiences motor disturbances or back problems at these times:

- After everyday stresses
- During household activities (which specific activities?)
- After physical leisure-time activities
- After prolonged sitting (in what types of chairs?)
- After walking, standing, lifting, and carrying (what type of carrying?)

In addition, students and adolescents should be questioned about these issues:

- Exercise and sports (occasional, regular, performance sports, etc.)

Table 6-2 Psychosomatic Back Problems (Weintraub 1979)

Classification	Lexical Content
Psychosomatic cervicodynia	Emotionally impeded assertion, stubborn "preservation of face"
Psychosomatic dorsalgia	Grief, desperation, discouragement, or compensating, upright forced composure
Psychosomatic sciatica	Psychological strain, moodiness, frustration, especially in cases of impaired sexuality

- Complaints while sitting at school (what type of school desk, slanted writing surface?)
- Dislike of certain exercises and sports because of back problems
- Problems during performance sports (what type of sport, training, or prolonged peak performance?)
- Discontinuing of athletic performance training (reasons?)

Detailed follow-up questions must be asked for any issues of concern.

In the case history, it is important for the physician to ascertain the patient's future athletic objectives. The physician can then conduct the subsequent examination in anticipation of expected stresses and can order the appropriate roentgenograms and imaging procedures to obtain the needed information.

6.2.2 Physical Examination

6.2.2.1 General Examination

In order to evaluate accurately those changes at the spinal column (eg, stiffness or movement or stress pain) that affect the spinal column externally from the extremities and muscles, the examination of the spinal column must be based on a general physical examination.

The radiologist Erdmann developed the concept of a "manual examination," which he considered to be an indispensable prerequisite for the subsequent specific radiological examination of the spinal column. The manual examination is based on palpation, which Sutter (1983) describes as "more than touching and fingering: palpation is feeling, questioning, grasping, taking hold of and understanding."

The examiner who wants to gain an understanding of the stress requirements placed on the central axial organ and also of the individual stress capacity of the back must possess basic knowledge in anatomy, physiology, biomechanics, and biochemistry. Structure and function as they are expressed in shape and posture during standing, sitting, walking, and other movement processes must be considered. In this respect, the "functional spinal column concept" described by Hinz and Erdmann in 1968 and Erdmann in 1968 is helpful. A visual and manual examination, palpation of pressure sensitivity, and the diagnostic pain generation through careful dislocation are three examination methods that can be useful in check-ups. Hinz advocated a three-part examination in 1977: mobility test, local manual palpation, and examination of the functional condition of the muscles.

The constitutionally relaxed spinal column should be looked for in the basic examination. The constitutionally relaxed spine poses potential danger for adolescent athletes in training and in sports participation. As mentioned previously, it may also play a role in the search for talented gymnasts.

A neurological general examination is necessary in all cases of neural damage, segmental radiation pain, serious cases with localized pain, and those with signs of paralysis. It is also a stringent requirement before all surgical procedures. Often, the evaluation of a neurologist is necessary.

6.2.2.2 Special Examinations

Because one purpose of the examination of the spinal column and the back is to establish a special stress capacity for participation in sports and high-performance training, the posture in the resting position must initially be observed. This posture is the result of the internal equilibrium of the limb chain spinal column and the external supporting forces, muscles, and ligaments (Rizzi 1973).

In addition, the sports medicine physician is justified in obtaining detailed information on the condition of the respiratory organs and the cardiovascular system by means of the functional lung test, electrocardiogram with and without the stress test, oscillogram, laboratory tests, etc. Where doubts arise about an individual's stress capacity, various mechanical procedures should be a part of the spinal column examinations, including electromyography of the back muscles and the use of a statokinesiometer and similar devices. The statokinesiometer can be used to test and document the coordination function that is important for the stress capacity of the spinal column (Groeneveld 1976).

To evaluate the increasing threat posed by vibrations, a procedure recommended by Debrunner and Graden in 1975 may be useful. They tested the dynamic function of the spinal column by introducing a pressure impact from the pelvis in the axial direction and measuring the transmission time to the head, as well as the oscillation attenuation at several points along the spinal column. A similarly sensitive instrument that would be suitable for mass screenings would be an important step in recognizing vibration-susceptible spinal columns.

Simpler procedures such as the back shapes in different postures in Figures 6-8 and 6-9, are primarily used in consultations and especially in check-ups. Another simple test procedure is the spinal column profile, which may provide an indication of an incorrect posture or pathological changes (see Fig. 6-3).

An examination oriented toward function requires measurements of the mobility of the entire spinal column, as well as of its individual sections. The most common procedure is to measure intervals between the spinous processes C-7 to T-12 and from T-12 to L-5 or S-5 for upright standing and anteflexion. Normal findings for this procedure are shown in Table 6-3 (Erdmann, 1979). The palpation of intervals between the spinous processes indicates mobility problems in the individual segments. Testing by turning and inclining the head (Table 6-4), as well as the documentation of rotation and flexion capacity with reporting of resulting pain, is also important.

Although it is still in favor, using the finger-ground distance as a criterion for the flexibility

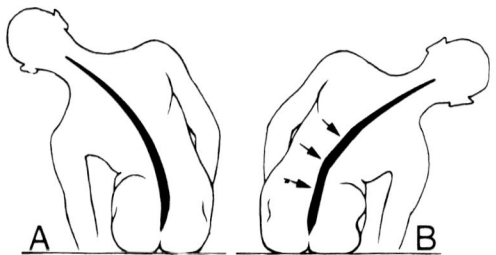

Fig. 6-8 (A) Balanced, curved lateral flexion; (B) sharp bend in lateral flexion, probably the result of the latent scoliosis.

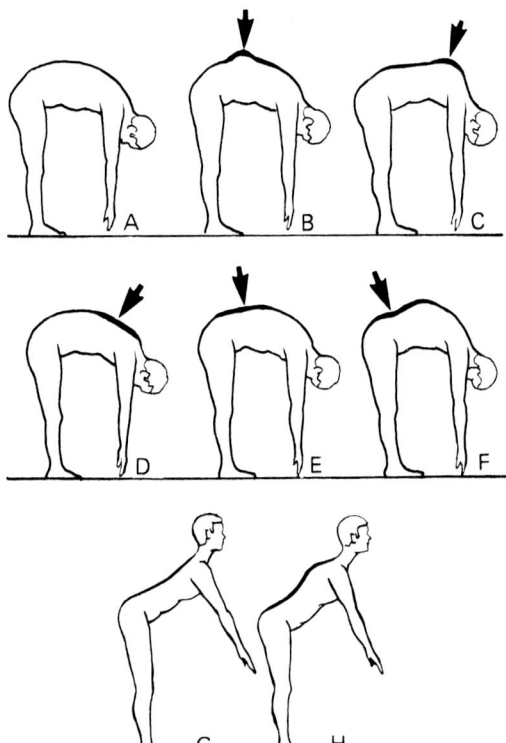

Fig. 6-9 (A) Anteflexion, balanced and curved. (B) Kyphosis in the lumbar portion. (C) Kyphosis in the thoracic portion. (D) Fixated straight posture in the thoracic portion. (E) Fixated posture in the lumbar portion. (F) Kypholordotic back with fixated lordosis. (G) Slightly curved lordosis in the thoracic and lumbar portion during straightening of a healthy, young spinal colmn. (H) Fixated thoracic lordosis during straightening.

of the spinal column should be avoided. Even when there is absolute spinal column stiffness, it is still possible to touch the ground with the fingertips if there is good hip mobility as Erdmann demonstrated (Fig. 6-10).

Table 6-3 Testing of Anteflexion: Norms for a Body Height of 1.60–1.70 Meters (Erdmann 1979)*

	Standing Upright (cm)	Anteflexion (cm)	Differential (cm)
C-7–D-12	33	35	2
D-12–S-5	27	35	8
C-7–S-5	60	70	10

*Anteflexion of the thoracic and lumbar column in a standing position. A measuring tape is used to determine the interval size.

Table 6-4 Head Rotation Mobility of the Cervical Spinal Column: Norms for Persons between 20 and 30 Years (Erdmann 1979)*

	To the Right	To the Left
From anteflexion	45°	45°
From middle position	90°	90°
From retroflexion	60°	60°

*Testing in a supine position.

In addition to using a simple measuring tape, several mechanized measuring procedures are available (Figs. 6-11 to 6-14). Yet, it remains questionable whether measurements of mobility and spinal column curvature should be part of the examination process of all check-ups. Only measurement procedures that are easy to implement and to document should be used. How difficult this is, is demonstrated by experiences from premilitary service fitness examinations. In 1974, Beck stated, "All formulas established so far are not sufficient to characterize satisfactorily and are particularly not sufficient to evaluate whether a curvature or angle changes the physiological stress value."

Measurements require norms, which should be classified according to age. However, norms become increasingly less valuable as points of reference for physical examinations when dealing with older patients. Differences in the three spinal column sections of older patients can only be approximated (Table 6-5).

Table 6-5 Differences in Mobility in the Three Spinal Column Sections*

	Cervical	Thoracic	Lumbar
Anteflexion, retroflexion	+++	+	+++
Lateral flexion	++	+	++
Rotation	++	+	++
Lateral flexion with rotation	+++	+	+++

*+++ large, ++ intermediate, + slight extent of mobility

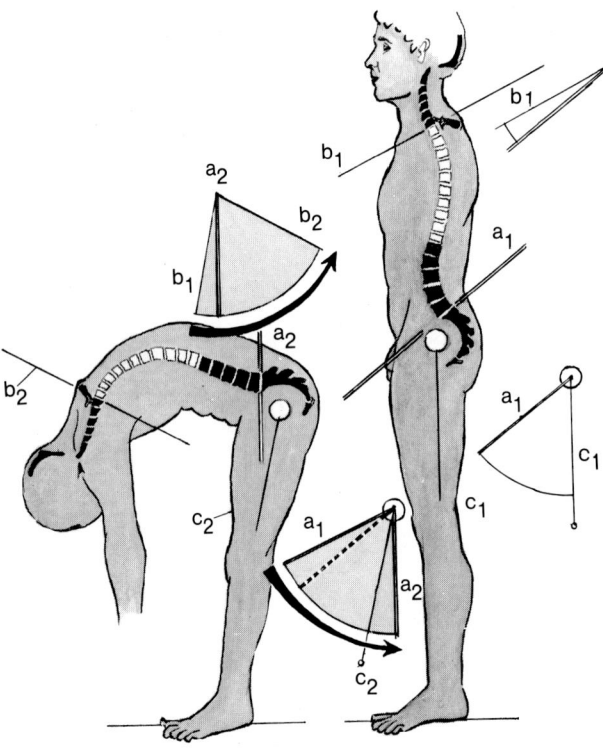

Fig. 6-10 Anteflexion from standing (own movement) as a joint performance. Not only the spinal column but also the hip joints are involved. The *top fan on left* represents the movement portion in the trunk axis (b_1 and b_2 = intervertebral disc level between C-7 and T-1; a_1 and a_2 = intervertebral disc level between L-5 and S-1). The *bottom fan* represents the movement portion in the two hip joints (c_1 and c_2 = femur support axis, standing upright and bent forward, respectively). The combination of the two individual performances (spinal column on one side, hip joints on the other) represents the decisive disadvantage in the measurement of the fingertip-ground distance for testing spinal column mobility [from Erdmann (1979)].

Examination of the Spinal Column   183

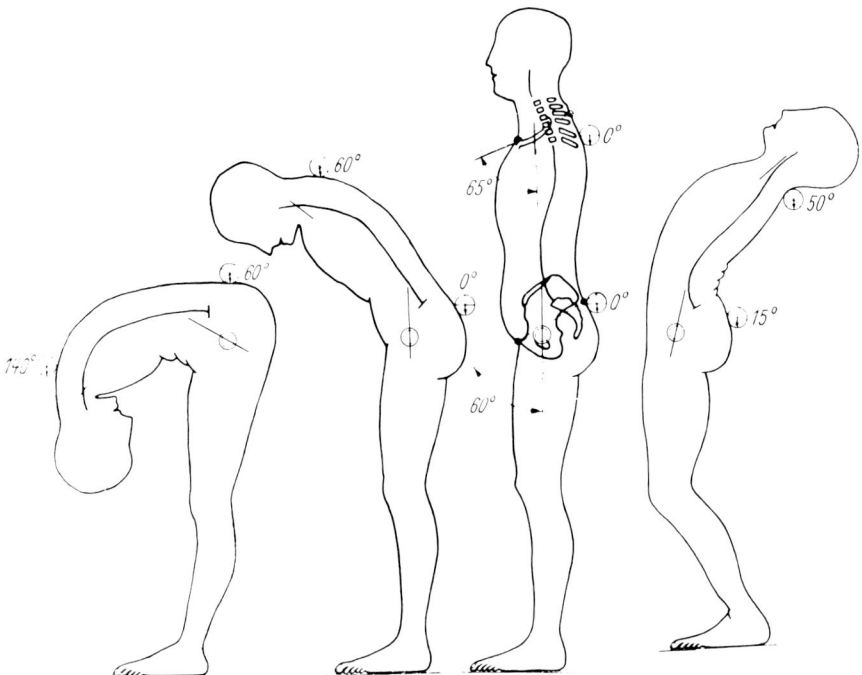

Fig. 6-11 Norms for anteflexion and retroflexion, measured with the elkameter from left to right. Anteflexion with pelvic movement, anteflexion without pelvic movement, neutral position, and retroflexion.

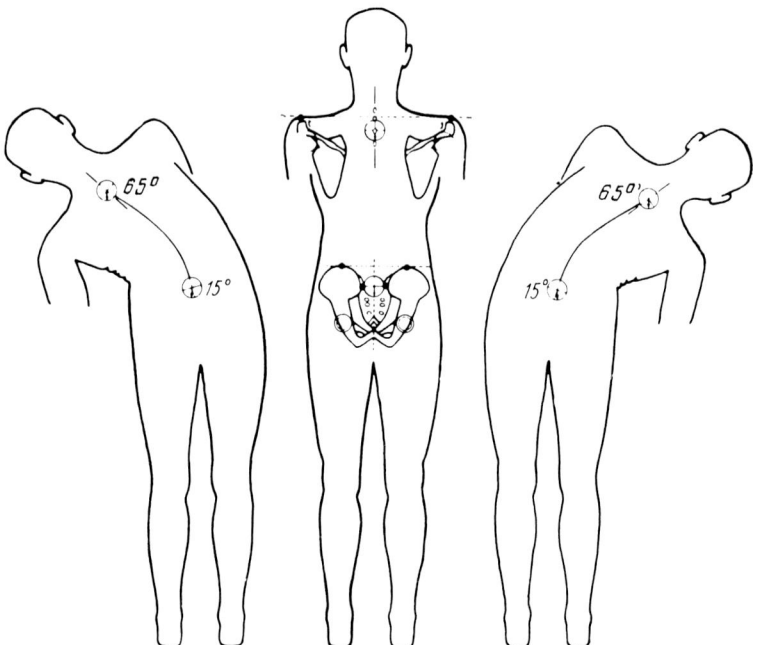

Fig. 6-12 Norms for lateral flexion to right and left, measured with the elkameter. The value between the two measuring points (15° and 65°) is the average flexion value of 50°.

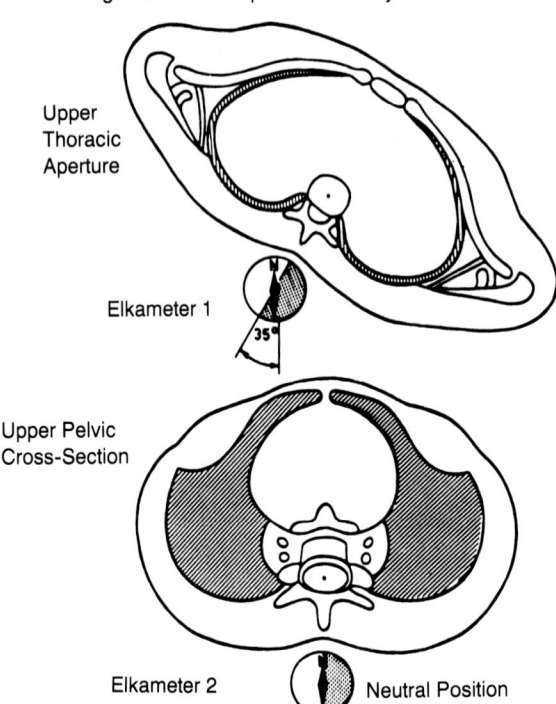

Fig. 6-13 Measurement of the upper torso rotation (*top*) in comparison with the neutral position of the pelvis.

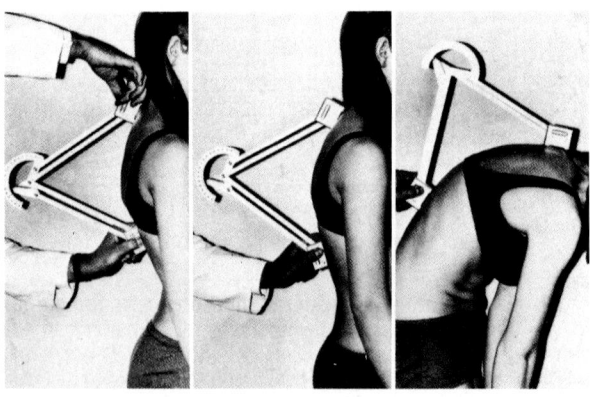

Fig. 6-14 Measurement of the thoracic spinal column mobility with the kyphometer. The curvature angle of the thoracic spinal column is measured in an upright standing position between the spinous processes T-2 to T-3 and T-12 to L-1 and then during maximum flexion and maximum extension. It is also possible to measure lordoses with the kyphometer [from Debrunner (1972)].

In addition to determining the presence of damage that would reduce the stress capacity, the assessment of muscle function is essential because insufficiency of the back muscles, for whatever reasons, affects the spinal column. A simple and inexpensive means of assessing the functional performance of back muscles is to measure how long an individual can lift the trunk from a supine position and maintain that position. A duration of at least 120 seconds is an indication of adequate muscle function. Any lesser duration is an indication of the functional insufficiency of the back muscles. In the examination series of Christ and Dupuis (1966), 36.7% of persons (with an average age of 29.3 years) had insufficient muscle function. A higher insufficiency rate of 43.2% was found in non-athletes.

Similar, simple studies of back muscle strength were described by Groeneveld in 1976. The simple arm-stretching test without additional strain (posture test in Fig. 6-6) demonstrates back insufficiency if there is a displacement of the body to the back with a simultaneously increased lumbar lordosis and advancing of the pelvis.

Only rarely will an existing or presumed pathological change in the spinal skeleton require a vertebral biopsy in order to clarify the character of the damage by light or electron microscopy. A test vertebrotomy is only seldom necessary.

Because patients with back and lower back pain often seek out various specialists, special diagnostic examinations are sometimes necessary. Diagnostic local anesthesia is a simple, successful procedure with few complications (Gerbershagen 1979). A detailed neurological diagnosis to differentiate vascular pain from radicular pain is often required in cases of neck-shoulder-arm pain. Urological, gynecological, or orthopedic examinations may sometimes be needed to determine the origin of pain. Thermal irritation in the area of the lumbar spinal column is a diagnostic help because it establishes the origin of radiation pain (Fig. 6-15). Figure 6-16 shows the pain zones that are significant in differentiating lumbago from radiating pain zones of the urogenital zone.

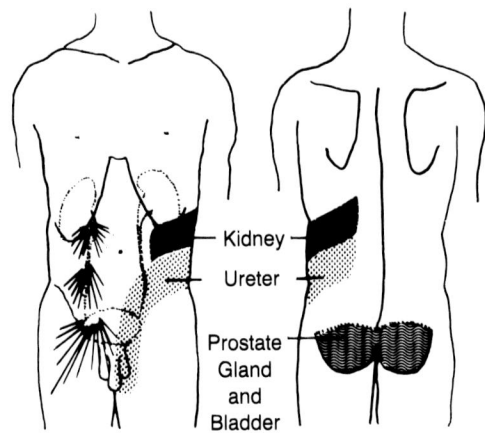

Fig. 6-16 Pain zones of the kidney, ureter, prostate gland, and bladder, as well as pain projection of the transferred, mostly colic-like pain [from Lutzeyer & Hild (1979)].

6.2.2.3 Documentation of the Physical Examination

During the basic examination the general practitioner should both obtain the most important information about the spinal column and record it in an easy-to-use documentation form. Unfortunately, many of the most commonly used forms provide insufficient space to record data about the support and motor system. Very little space is provided for the spinal column, whereas other organ systems often receive a disproportionate large amount of space. Often, these forms are designed to facilitate input into electronic data processing (EDP) systems.

A suggested documentation form for spinal column examinations is shown in Table 6-6. The physical examination of the axial organ may require supplemental technical procedures, eg, imaging procedures. Myograms (see section 5.2) and thermograms may also be used.

If documentation of examination findings is to serve therapeutic or research purposes, more data must be collected. From a neurosurgical perspective, Schirmer published in 1980 a form to document the problem of lumbosciatica. In great detail, it covers lumbosciatic symptoms, diagnoses the manifold pain and neurological failure syndromes, and supports the indications for the required therapy. More detailed forms are

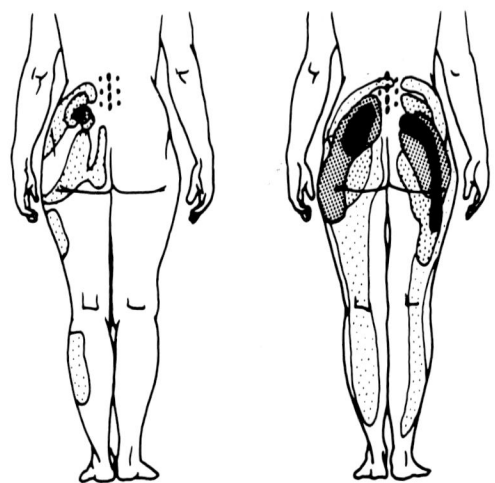

Fig. 6-15 Zones of radiating pain during thermal irritation (from Matthiass [1983]).

Table 6-6 Documentation Form for the Spinal Column Examination (Junghanns 1979)

I. Shape of the spinal column
  A. Normal
  B. Flat back
  C. Increased thoracic kyphosis
  D. Increased lumbar lordosis
  E. Scoliosis   Cervical   Thoracic   Lumbar
    1. With arch outside right
    2. With arch outside left
  F. Kyphoscoliosis

II. Functions of the spinal column sections (including the pain test)
  A. Cervical spinal column

	Movement	
	Limited	Painful
1. Longitudinal traction		
2. Anteflexion		
3. Retroflexion		
4. Lateral flexion to right		
5. Lateral flexion to left		
6. Rotations		
a. In normal posture — to right		
to left		
b. In anteflexion — to right		
to left		
c. In retroflexion — to right		
to left		

  B. Thoracic and lumbar spinal column

	Thoracic Movement		Lumbar Movement	
	Limited	Painful	Limited	Painful
1. Anteflexion				
2. Retroflexion				
3. Right rotation				
4. Left rotation				

  C. Spinous processes—pressure pain
    1. Cervical
    2. Thoracic
    3. Lumbar

  D. Measurement (in cm)

	T-1–T-12	T-12–L-5
1. Upright posture	cm	cm
2. Large anteflexion	cm	cm

III. Extension pain of the sciatic nerve   Right   Left

found in these references: Binzus (1978)—for rheumatological diagnoses, Thumb (1978)—a computer-compatible form, Tillman (1978), and Winkler (1979)—for the orthopedic examination.

A newer and somewhat more complicated procedure than myography is contact thermography (Riede 1978). After a special foil is placed on the skin, liquid crystals are applied to the foil. According to the skin temperature, the foil changes color from blue (warm) to green to yellow and red (cold). In this way the effectiveness of chirotherapy may be monitored.

Moiré photography (Fig. 6-17), by clarifying the back profile, can enable the examiner to follow the progress of scolioses and kyphoses. Other Moiré illustrations are found in section 4.4.

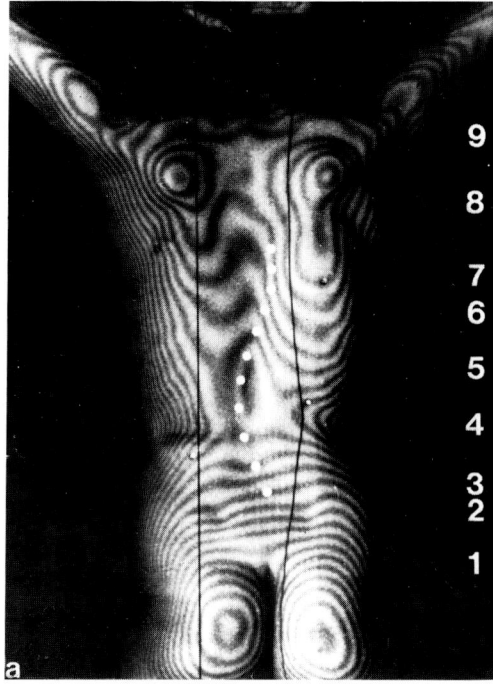 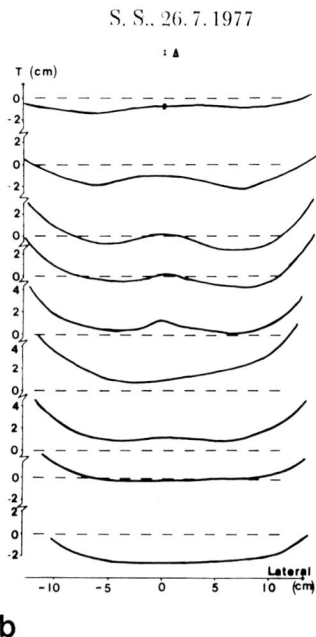

Fig. 6-17 (**A**) Vertebral body centers attained from stereoscopic roentgenograms are projected onto the Moiré photogram of the back (*a* = white dots). (**B**) The horizontal profiles are determined at the level of the transverse lines 1–9 designated in the left picture while using the Moiré picture [from Drerup (1978)].

6.2.3 Imaging Procedures for Diagnostics

6.2.3.1 Radiodiagnostics

The case history and physical examination are the foundation of a specific radio diagnosis. The roentgenogram provides additional basic information about pathomorphic damages and pathophysiological conditions that is required for the differential diagnosis of spinal column disorders. It is also possible to diagnose soft tissue damage from spinal roentgenograms, mostly in the intervertebral motor segment (see sections 3.4 and 4.6). Such damage is much more frequently the cause of temporary or permanent disorders and disables the spinal column more seriously than obvious, visible damages in the skeletal structure. The skeleton may be indirectly affected by damage of the soft tissues as well. Conclusions from the radiographically determined bone changes at the vertebral body-intervertebral disc boundary may be drawn with regard to the condition of the soft tissues.

In appropriate cases, roentgenograms taken in an upright standing position—and at the cervical spinal column also in a sitting position—may be standardized in such a manner that they permit comparisons regarding static conditions (Lewit 1982).

In most cases, the condition of the spinal column can be clarified by taking one roentgenogram picture in a standing position, either a lateral or front view. Often, roentgenograms in two levels are needed to clarify the condition of the spinal column. However, other radiodiagnostic procedures may be necessary, especially if the stress capacity of the spinal column must be ascertained, as in pre-employment examinations and testing before training begins for high-performance sports. In those instances, total roentgenograms of the spinal column are recommended. According to K.P. Fischer (1964), "The total picture epitomizes the compromise of specific posture influence and specific functional disablement" and shows on which level the disability originated. It shows spinal column curvatures in the sagittal and frontal level, as well as in the pelvis position. At the same time it can serve as the standard for a later comparison on the state of the spinal column under the stresses of everyday life.

If the stress capacity of the spinal column cannot be determined by the initial roentgenograms, further roentgenogram diagnostic procedures should be done according to a graduated plan, with a continuing consideration of symptoms and physical findings and by anticipating expected future stress. The danger of radiation exposure can be lessened by establishing and following a graduated plan of procedures. Such a plan is particularly necessary for the spinal column examination. Often, diagnostic dilemmas can only be solved by the use of special procedures that require multiple x-rays, whereas in other skeletal areas, it is often sufficient to take pictures in two levels. Therefore, it is necessary to apply restraint in ordering roentgenogram examinations of the spinal column and to follow a graduated plan from the outset, so that the least amount of roentgenogram pictures will be necessary.

In the first stage of this graduated plan, oblique roentgenograms may be considered. Most often they are necessary at the lumbar spinal column during the search for spondylolysis in the interarticular portion (see sections 2.1 and 4.5) or for a vertebral arch articulation arthrosis (see section 4.6). At the cervical spinal column, oblique pictures are an indispensable means of determining conditions at the intervertebral canals. Oblique pictures may also be used to take pictures of the vertebral arch articulations at the cervical spinal column (Erdmann 1979, Zsernaviczky et al 1981).

Tomograms and occasionally oblique tomograms are recommended as a second step if certain changes exist at certain sections of the spinal column. They are required to determine details of bone structures, to clarify conditions at the vertebral body-intervertebral disc boundary, and to depict telescopic displacements and/or arthroses of the vertebral arch articulations (see Fig. 3-20). In an emergency situation, a tomogram may be required to diagnose newly injured persons (Erdmann 1979).

The second stage also includes pictures taken with a tilted tube that uses special ray paths to portray conditions at the transition from the head to cervical spinal column and in the intervertebral space from the front, eg, at the cervical spinal column or in the last presacral intervertebral space (Decking 1977).

The third stage of radiodiagnostics comprises all other procedures that must be implemented by the radiologist according to the requirements of the individual case.

The recommendation of a graduated plan for roentgenograms represents in no way an endorsement for a multitude of roentgenograms. On the contrary, from the first examination on, the graduated plan enables the limited use of imaging diagnostics. If this plan is followed properly from the beginning, the collected documentation may be supplemented with more roentgenograms if needed. In this way too frequent radiation exposure may be avoided. If the use of miniature film gradually becomes more accepted, past pictures will be easier and faster to procure. Too, new imaging procedures, such as computer tomography and sonography, which are already used as an initial diagnostic aid in cases of accidental injuries, may modify the graduated plan in the future.

Because of the danger of exposure to radiation, the radiodiagnostics of the spinal column of adolescents is limited. Therefore, the suggestion of Stoddard and Osborn (1978) to begin radiodiagnostic procedures at the age of 12 and to repeat them regularly is questionable. It is not yet clear whether new noninvasive imaging procedures will be available to take pictures of larger sections or total pictures of the spine in the near future.

6.2.3.2 Special Radiodiagnostic Procedures

In some cases, special procedures may be used to supplement the graduated plan. Since the recommendation by Junghanns in 1937, function pictures taken in the final positions that the patient is able to attain have played an increasingly large role in radiodiagnostics. The importance of measuring the function roentgenograms at the cervical spinal column—biometric radiodiagnostics—is emphasized by Arlen (1978) and Lindner (1983). A functional analysis of the cervical spinal column is most often based on comparative function pictures of the cervical spinal column in anteflexion and retroflexion (Prantl 1982). The possibilities of lateral flexion to the right and left are still too little used to advantage. To recognize biomechanical problems in the area of transitional regions (eg, at the thoracolumbar transition), Rizzi et al. (1977) recommended comparative function pictures in anteflexion and retroflexion.

Stereoscopic roentgenograms may make possible the evaluation of pictures that are hard to diagnose (Olsson et al. 1977). Biplane stereoradiography is recommended to recognize a relaxation in the intervertebral motor segment (segmental instability) (Wilder et al. 1980).

To determine the need for a scoliosis operation and to monitor its success postoperatively, the measuring of roentgenograms is a strict requirement (metric diagnosis according to Steinhaus 1979).

Roentgenograms of the head and shoulders in a standing and sitting position are usually required only for certain sports medicine examinations and in scientific studies.

The radiological examination not only produces findings of the skeleton but may also uncover important damage to the soft tissues. For instance, a decreased height of the intervertebral space and a displacement position between the vertebral bodies point to causative or concomitant damages of the intervertebral disc. The clefts of the vertebral arch articulations that appear to be narrowed in oblique pictures may elucidate the cartilage loss of a beginning arthrosis deformans or may be concomitant symptoms of a blocked vertebra. "Telescopic displacements" in the vertebral arch articulations are symptoms of relaxed articular capsules (see Figs. 3-20 and 4-36). However, the determination of the cause and the time and manner of occurrence of soft tissue damage, which might be of essential importance for therapy, is much harder than the diagnosis of bone damage.

In many cases an angiography cannot be avoided. Arteriography, which is used to clarify the condition of the vertebral artery, is often essential (see Fig. 4-15). However, spinal phlebography and epidural venography only have limited diagnostic value (Tadie et al. 1979, Thelen and Burman 1979, Vogelsang 1979, Wilkie and Beetham 1980). Great caution must be used in performing an angiography because of its potential side effects of anesthesia and radiation paraplegia.

Only under certain conditions—for instance, to determine indications for surgery—are the following procedures recommended:

- Nucleography/discography, including discometry (Seifert 1979).
- Myelography, scintigraphy (Bessler and Feine 1979, Cording 1979, Hoer 1981), bone marrow scintigraphy (Schmidt and Schmidt-Brueggemann 1979, Schoeter and Wappenschmidt 1980), computer-assisted myelogram (Jackson et al. 1976), scintigraphy for impairments in the interarticular portion of the vertebral arch
- Myeloscintigraphy, function myelography, and similar procedures (Lotz & Cen 1978)
- Lumbosacral radiculography (Jepson et al. 1982, Tajima et al. 1980)

Cinematographic roentgenograms can be used to test movement processes after physical therapy and surgery. Because such pictures can be taken in vivo, they enrich our knowledge of movement sequences in the individual segments. Slow-motion analysis of the movement sequences is particularly valuable. With this procedure, Christ and Dupuis (1966) studied the influences of vertical vibrations and determined the maximum vibration at the cervical spinal column to be 3.5 Hz.

Roentgenogram computed tomography has already proved its value in medical archeology. Huebner and Pahl (1981) discovered vertebrae with osteolytic foci (probably metastases) in ancient Egyptian mummies.

6.2.3.3 Additional Imaging Procedures

The extensive number of imaging procedures permits the experienced physician to obtain a diagnosis with procedures that have been carefully chosen according to a graduated plan. Indiscriminate use of these procedures results in a wall of pictures and the recognition that less would have been more. Because of the great number of diagnostic procedures and the many new possibilities expected in the future, the physician must select the "right procedure at the right time."

Nuclear spin computer tomography—also called nuclear magnetic resonance computed tomography (NMR-CT)—makes it possible to obtain tomograms of the internal body without ionizing rays (Graul 1982, Stender 1983). NMR-CT facilitates the long-term observation of the disease process, which requires numerous repetitions of the magnetic field procedure, because there is no radiation exposure. It enables the determination of the performance requirements that the spine can safely meet. However, the possibility of side effects from NMR-CT has not been completely ruled out, so caution in its use is advised.

The NMR-CT differentiates clearly the fluid-filled nucleus pulposus from the fiber ring. In addition, the dissolution of the intervertebral disc tissue in nucleolysis/discolysis (see section 7.4) can be determined. Still unanswered is whether this procedure will be able to analyze biochemical processes in the soft tissues in a way that will be useful for clinical purposes. In the future, will it be possible to detect metabolic impairments in the intervertebral disc? Doing so would facilitate the early discovery of intervertebral disc damage and the early institution of such therapy as timely relief from pressure and the application of drugs to reestablish the metabolic equilibrium.

To date, sonography has been of little value in portraying the spinal column. Whether the further development of diagnostic ultrasound instruments will bring progress in this area remains to be seen in the future. It may be possible for the spinal column to be palpated in rest and movement and be documented on film in individual phases in the same way as internal organs are seen on sonography.

Thermography is useful in the detection of latent foci in the spinal column and the reaction of its surrounding area (Engel 1981). Figure 6-18 (left) shows a thermogram of the back of a healthy youth. Figure 6-18 (right) shows a prolapse of the intervertebral disc L-4/L-5, which was subsequently confirmed by surgery.

Recently roentgenogram stereophotogrammetry has been used to produce a more exact measurement of the back profile. It uses the projection of a line or grid net to calculate three-dimensional coordinates of any point.

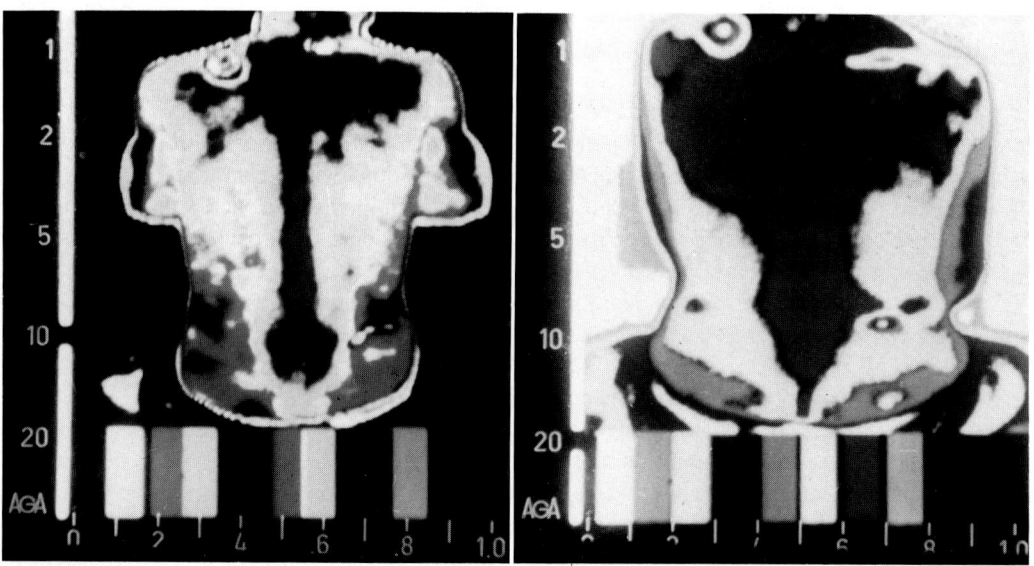

Fig. 6-18 *Left*, Color thermogram of the back (in a black and white picture) with normal heat distribution in which the spinal column is seen as an overly warm zone in black. *Right*, the overheating thermogram of the back shows a longitudinal, overheated zone at the lower lumbar spinal column, which was confirmed as a prolapsed disc L-4/L-5 by myelography and surgery [from Konermann & Koob (1979)].

6.2.3.4 Documentation of Imaging Diagnostics

The solution to the problem of storage of roentgenogram pictures seems to be the transfer of regular-sized roentgenograms to a miniature format. Doing so enables the miniature roentgenograms to be directly appended to the examination reports, making them readily available for follow-up examinations or consultation. Increasingly, images will be microfilmed, as written records are now.

In addition to the creation of miniature formats of roentgenogram pictures, the standard coding of the diagnoses may make roentgenogram documentation easier in the future. The location and form of pulmonary foci in silicosis and asbestosis (Bohlig 1977) are already coded on pulmonary roentgenograms. However, because of the multitude of pathological findings at the spinal column, a standardized evaluation classification schema that is suitable for computerization is very difficult to develop.

Moiré photography of the back (Fig. 6-17), in combination with stereoscopic radiograms of the spinal column, seems to be a promising new means of exact documentation, especially long-term comparative series. Although this procedure is presently used mostly for scientific purposes, its future technical development promises wider application (Adair et al. 1977, Drerup 1977 & 1978, Polster 1979, Willner 1979).

6.3 PREVENTIVE, FITNESS, AND FOLLOW-UP EXAMINATIONS

6.3.1 School Examinations

School examinations are among the most important preventive examinations. They cover a stage of development in which endogenous changes, such as growth acceleration, juvenile kyphosis, and scoliosis, and exogenous stresses created by prolonged sitting in school may cause serious damage. They are essential for the healthy development of the spinal column and the pertaining muscles by ensuring that children can handle the required physical activity in play and sports and that they will choose an occupation appropriate to their physical condition. Because children complain only rarely and their parents may neither recognize a slight deviation in the body posture nor regard it as a warning sign, regular school follow-up examinations should not be missed.

Changes in the spinal column curvature and body posture require special attention during the growth period of the child. The first manifestations of these changes—the deviation from normal posture and especially the discrete stiffness of certain sections of the spinal column during movement—are serious warning signs. Many painful back disorders in later life decades are a result of neglect during the juvenile growth period. Therefore, the medical care of school-aged children should follow a standard examination procedure and documentation of results so there can be a seamless transition to examinations in adult life.

6.3.2 West German Experience

Since 1960, the Juvenile Labor Law in West Germany has mandated an initial and follow-up medical examination for each youth seeking employment. The examination is not designed to serve as a job-specific occupational fitness test, but rather to provide guidelines for the choice of an occupation.

Usually, the general practitioner does the examination, without the use of sophisticated testing equipment or devices. Its goal is to recognize individual functional insufficiencies, such as postural insufficiency, incorrect posture and position, stiffness or partial stiffness, disorders of the axial organ (Scheuermann's disease), and pathological changes in the spinal column produced by an infectious disease or trauma.

If the general practitioner determines that the spinal column is susceptible to stress or damage, the youth is referred to an appropriate specialist—orthopedist, radiologist, possibly internist, or pathologist—and further testing is done. These findings are the basis for therapy and reinforcement of a correct behavior in everyday life, leisure, and sports to minimize further stress and damage.

A picture of the fitness and health of West Germany's youth can be formed from the data generated by these examinations.

- Of the 8.3% of patients with damage of the skeleton, the largest percentage (5.7%) have a deformed spinal column. Among the reported comments of susceptibility, visual problems were reported with the highest frequency, followed by impairments resulting from the spinal column condition.
- Of adolescents with deformed spinal columns, 49.8% were classified as susceptible to stress or damage.
- Based on the spinal column findings in follow-up examinations, 33.5% of youth were prohibited from entering certain occupations.
- There were 10,402 pathological findings concerning the spinal column compared to 4527 cardiopulmonary findings.
- Follow-up examinations after a probational period on the job resulted in a large number of additional occupational prohibitions because of spinal column damage, despite the fact that youths with susceptible spinal columns had already been restricted from certain jobs after the initial examination.

Remarkable data were obtained in regard to participation in sports. Active athletic involvement (62% of male youths and 45% of female youths) before taking up a job decreased by 50% in the first year after starting work. Another study showed that athletic involvement of youths declined from 43% to 35% between the ages of 14 and 17 and by the time of the first follow-up examination for the Juvenile Labor Law, this figure declined to 32%.

Unfortunately, not all the youths with susceptible spinal columns are detected during the physical examinations at school and for the Juvenile Labor Law. This is for instance true for Scheuermann's disease (see sections 2.3 and 7.2). Fifty percent of all youths show symptoms of this disorder, and half of them have serious complaints. The military fitness examination of more than 3 million conscripts born between 1942 and 1951 found changes at the spinal column in 54.3% of the soldiers. For those born between 1952 and 1955, the figure was even higher—68% (Gruschka 1976).

6.3.3 Mandatory Radiodiagnostics

The call for mandatory radiodiagnostic examination of the spinal column during preventive, fitness, pre-employment, and follow-up examinations is not new. Some authors base this demand on the positive experiences gained in fitness examinations for various types of sport: Beck (1973)—pilots, Refior (1970 and 1972)—sports.

In addition, the demand for a regular radiological examination of the spinal column during preventive and pre-employment examinations is increasingly being raised in the area of occupational medicine: Cremona (1972)—coal, iron, and steel industries; Mach et al. (1976)—dock workers; Redfield (1971)—forestry workers, Reiner (1958)—bus drivers, Stapleton (1978)—industry, Steinfeld (1970)—miners. Frequently x-rays in functional positions are recommended (Jirout 1967).

There are also dissenting voices. Many feel that roentgenograms should only be used to determine stress capacity when a high-performance sport and/or a physically stressful job is being considered (DiEmilio et al. 1969, Denman et al. 1961). This issue has yet to be resolved.

7

Effects of Daily Life on the Spinal Column

7.1 INTRODUCTION

Without exception, the functional requirements facing the limb chain spinal column from the beginning of life may only be met by a healthy organ whose functionally coordinated individual parts have an unimpaired functional capacity. Each congenital or acquired damage represents an endogenous weakening of the stress resistance; each changes the functional prerequisites to a varying degree.

Greater knowledge about spinal column damage will decrease the use of such common inaccurate diagnoses as back pain (undefined) structural disorders of the spinal column, or rheumatism of the back muscles. Such general statements neither help treatment, which must be based on a differential diagnosis, nor are they valuable for determining disability, school exemption, and participation in athletic and leisure-time activities. Conservative and surgical therapy, as well as rehabilitation, must be based on an accurate diagnosis of the damage to the spinal column. All medical counseling and therapeutic measures require the knowledge of the various spinal column damages, of their frequency, and the possibilities of diagnosis. Radiodiagnostic procedures are an invaluable means of assessing these damages.

Our modern lifestyle places unfavorable stresses on the spinal column. Although hard physical labor may have exerted the spinal column and muscles to a great degree, it also maintained the mobility of the axial organ and the strength of the trunk muscles through continuously repeated exercise. A more serious threat to the health of the spinal column is the increase in sedentary work and unfavorable sitting habits. Those unfavorable influences are exacerbated by vibration stress experienced during prolonged rides in motor vehicles, which increases the static and dynamic stresses exerted on the spinal column. These unfavorable consequences are not recognized and considered to their full extent by lay people. An increasingly important task of the general practitioner and specialists is to educate the public about the stresses posed by our modern lifestyle.

These stresses on the spinal column are found not only in the workplace but also at home, school, and in leisure-time activities. They thus not only affect workers but children and retirees.

Yet, even though the modern lifestyle has many hazards, damage to the spinal column has been found in human beings living millions of years ago. Deformed conditions at the spinal column, which can be classified as spondylosis deformans (see section 4.6), have been found in a 100,000,000-year-old dinosaur skeleton of the cretaceous period in Canada. Prehistoric primates have also been found with such impairments. Therefore, Grmek (1974, 1979) regards the evolution from the quadruped to biped walk (Fig. 2-1) as an important factor in the development of the spondylosis deformans.

7.1.1 Daily Life, Susceptible Periods, and Disorders Caused by Lack of Exercise

The term "daily life" encompasses activities apart from the job and prolonged leisure. It refers to the time that working persons spend in their home and during which the housewife performs her chores. It also includes the years that children and youth spend in play and school. When the child enters school, the spinal column is stressed in a new way that differs from the preceding years and that is similar or the same as some job-related stresses. During these early years, incorrect strains caused primarily by poor posture and a lack of compensating recovery time may create irrevocable damages at the spinal column to a greater extent than all later influences in the daily life and working life of the adult.

There are three time periods in daily life in which the spinal column is particularly susceptible to stress:

1. The first period is the transition from play child, which includes the preschool time (see section 3.2), to the sedentary child, ie, the beginning of school.
2. A second period of susceptibility begins with the involvement of the youth in activities involving motor vehicles (see section 5.3), which increases with progressive age and which affects leisure-time activities as well. The spinal column is affected by an unfavorable permanent posture, lack of exercise, and vibrations.
3. The third period of susceptibility starts at the transition from the third to fourth decade of life and continues in future years.

Unfortunately, the school-related negative influences on body posture are exacerbated by other impairment factors related to leisure activities. Sitting for hours in front of the television (again in an incorrect body posture) is a most significant negative influence. In addition, children have little room to play freely in crowded urban centers. Play is an essential element of human maturation and the prerequisite for the development of personality as well as the health maintenance of the spinal column.

During adulthood there is a shift from the enjoyment of movement during play with its benevolent effect on the spinal column to a monotonous lack of exercise. The typical modern adult moves more or less obviously into a state of functional insufficiency that will result in spinal column damage.

In the past, many physical activities were a necessary part of daily life:

- Walking or biking to school, work, or shopping, instead of sitting in the bus or automobile
- Walking up and down stairs, instead of taking the elevator or escalator
- Doing active and muscle-strengthening housework, such as washing with a washboard and/or hand-operated washing machine, instead of using a fully automatic washing machine
- Scrubbing and polishing floors and staircases, instead of vacuuming easy-care carpeting
- Beating carpets, instead of using chemical cleansers
- Carrying coal and wood to place in stoves, instead of using automatic oil or gas heat
- Exercising during work, at home, and in the yard and garden, such as hoeing, shoveling, and digging

These muscle-strengthening activities that also supported a good posture have been gradually replaced by "underexertion" with its negative effect on the spinal column. The physical activity level of most adults is now below the level of healthy movement and strain. This lack of exercise is often related to prolonged sitting, although the forced posture caused by prolonged standing also has a negative influence on the spinal column.

The connection between a lack of exercise and poor health has been made for the past two decades. In 1973 Mellerowicz noted that a lack of exercise causes cardiovascular disorders, vegetative dystonia, and obesity. Atherosclerosis and geriatric diseases with premature functional organic insufficiency are other probable results of underexertion. Von Ferber suggested in 1971 that a lack of exercise, as well as smoking and malnutrition, should be recognized and treated as a disease.

An individual's psychological state is also connected to body posture. A balanced posture is an expression of a stable mental attitude. In contrast, physical and mental fatigue, listlessness, and depression encourage a slack, stooped posture (see section 5.2).

A healthy support and motor system can be maintained by a lifelong striving to compensate for the lack of exercise and other damaging factors that endanger the central axial organ, ie, the spinal column and its muscles. Participation in leisure activities and popular sports can avert the dangers threatening the spinal column in our modern lifestyle (see section 8.2). It is the objective of this book to provide support for participation in those muscle-strengthening activities.

7.2 SPINAL COLUMN IN CHILDHOOD AND ADOLESCENCE

7.2.1 Introduction

In the past, such infectious diseases as scarlet fever, diphtheria, whooping cough, and tuberculosis threatened the health and function of children and adolescents. Those diseases have been eliminated for the most part by vaccinations and improved hygiene. In the last few decades, they have been replaced by new diseases and impairments of health, well-being, and functional and stress capacity. The spinal column as the central axial organ in the support and motor system is greatly affected by the significant increase of these so-called civilization diseases.

These and other symptoms should be considered an expression of maladaptation to the changed environment. The school-aged child and adolescent are today stressed differently and to a substantially greater degree to the point where they can no longer adapt to the changes in lifestyle. In addition, psychological strain is created by the knowledge explosion, which requires that children absorb an extraordinary amount of information. The necessary expansion of the school curriculum and overstimulation through television and other mass media significantly impede the total mental and physical development of the child by unnaturally restricting the children's striving for movement. The required study time at the schooldesk, possibly also in a bad posture, causes a serious postural degeneration. It is still not known to what degree muscle and ligament insufficiencies cause postural degeneration or whether they are only an additional influence on growth-related (possibly also genetically caused) spinal column changes.

During adolescence the negative influences of poor posture and underexertion increase because of the acceleration of growth occurring during puberty. The progress of spinal column growth is equated with the ossification of the iliac apophyses, which is visible on roentgenograms. They are firmly bonded with the iliac crest at the age of 16 for boys and 15 for girls. Therefore, no further increase of postural damages of the spinal column is expected in later years (Rathke and Buse 1963), although the histological studies of Schmorl (1927, 1930, 1932) showed growing cartilage at the vertebral body-intervertebral disc transition up to the age of 25. Therefore, the danger of postural damage to the spinal column must be combatted into the third decade of life— the time of university studies—by adapting seats and desks to support the spinal column and encouraging participation in muscle-strengthening leisure activities (see section 8.2).

Growth acceleration progresses in wave-like phases from early childhood on. This is in contrast to the growth pattern of children in the 18th century, which was steady. Too, several centuries ago, growth ended in the 21st year, in contrast to the present pattern of growth in years 17 to 18 (Neugebauer 1971). In some of the growth spurts, mostly during puberty, there is increased growth at the vertebral body-intervertebral disc boundary (see Fig. 2-4). During these periods an obvious sensitivity of the growth zones to pressure stresses exists (see section 4.6). Growth acceleration places an additional strain on the juvenile spinal column and is another impairment factor for the health of children.

The accelerated growth of the present young generation does not only result in damages of the back, but also lowers their psychological performance and stress capacity—Demirjian et al. (1971, 1972)—Canadians of French origin, Freyer (1979)—West Germany, Heath & Carter (1971)—Papua/New Guinea, Holibkova & Holibka (1968)—U.S.S.R., Juergens (1961)—West Germany, Kadanof (1969)—Germany, Kadanoff & Mutafov (1969)—Bulgaria, and Tiisala et al. (1971)—Finland. Growth acceleration, accompanied by bad posture with muscular insufficiency (jeans type), combines with the potential for damage at the vertebral body growth zones through overexertion in the kyphosisapex to form a vicious cycle. It can only be broken if prevention and therapy are coordinated by the physician as early as possible. How much the youth accepts responsibility for maintaining health will also affect his or her well-being. Unfortunately, this responsibility is frequently hard to instill. Therefore, the physician, parents, and school have the primary task of providing preventive and therapeutic services to children.

7.2.2 Preschool Age—Time of Mobility

In the healthy infant, the spinal column will develop without problems if the baby does carefully adapted infant gymnastics and exercises the mother was taught during the consultation of the pediatrician or orthopedist. Sit-ups from the abdominal position are appropriate exercises for strengthening the back muscles, which will during the coming years determine the transformation of the initially kyphotic curvature to the multiple curvature in the sagittal level (Fig. 2-38). The shape and posture of the back and trunk are the foundations for the shape of the entire body.

Parents must pay close attention to the spinal column posture of their very young children because deviations from the normal back shape may already be seen when the child is a toddler. If the parents are inattentive, these changes may evolve from a back insufficiency to an abnormal curvature, eg, juvenile kyphosis (see section 4.4, Figs. 4-6 to 4-9). Such problems may be prevented by strong back extensor muscles that have been strengthened by their use in a symmetrical way in exercises in the infant stage and early childhood. Weak back muscles lead to kyphotic posture, which places increased pressure on the anterior parts of the growing vertebral bodies. An increased kyphosis may be aggravated by processes taking place in their growth zones. In order to avoid such strains, children should be encouraged to play and read picture books while lying on the stomach, rather than while sitting in a chair (see section 4.4). Often sitting requires a prolonged kyphotic posture because of the incorrect ratio between the seating surface and table height. A child with poor back posture is not only susceptible to kyphosis but also to scoliosis (see section 4.4) and has a poor health foundation for the beginning of school (sedentary time). Unfortunately, about 25% of first-graders show a postural insufficiency even before the beginning of school, and some have an incorrect back shape—a sign that, more than in the past, exercises that strengthen the natural posture of the back by using the muscles in a symmetrical way should be pursued in early childhood.

Play is rightly called the "individual lifestyle of the child." Children train their muscles through play and learn to control them in encounters with the environment, especially with peers. Because in large cities there are few possibilities for free, uninterrupted play, more playgrounds are required (Grassl 1981).

The position of the infant during sleep is also of importance. Lying on a poorly designed mattress with weak springs damages the spinal column and may result in an incorrect posture. The pediatrician should recommend a suitable mattress.

7.2.3 School Age and Adolescence—Beginning of the Sedentary Period

7.2.3.1 Introduction

The beginning of school marks the transition from the mobile play child to the sedentary child and brings an abrupt change of influences on the spinal column. In the infant and toddler, exertion of the spine was balanced because of the varied activities of the muscles during play and movement. School replaces this exertion with sitting for hours, which continues during homework time. Thus, the child's daily life is more and more characterized by sitting as the youthful urge to move is choked. At the same time, the spinal column is held in an incorrect curvature because many schools use unphysiologically designed chairs with an incorrect ratio of height of chair to height of desk top. Together with the forced lack of exercise, this chair design determines the functional capacity or insufficiency of the spinal column for the rest of the child's life.

The physical ability of the child declines soon after the start of school. Maintaining that ability is a challenge to all schools and requires a greater emphasis on the sport activities and play of schoolchildren.

Yet, the juvenile spinal column is not only threatened by weak back muscles, incorrect posture, and a lack of exercise. Such environmental influences as poor nutrition and polluted air damage the growing bone; eg, cattle feed and cow milk contaminated by pesticides that, in turn, affect the growing child. Automotive exhaust is especially dangerous because it enables lead to reach the respiratory organs via the most frequent intoxication path and is also transferred into the gastrointestinal tract through saliva. In addition to traffic police, garage attendants, and road construction workers (see section 4.7), children are especially susceptible to excessive lead absorption because they inhale exhaust fumes that are concentrated near the ground as they play outdoors.

The maximum permissible value of lead in the blood is established at 40 µg/dL. Lead levels exceeding this value were found in more than 25% of children, in contrast to only 1% to 5% of adults.

Therefore, impairments of protein synthesis caused by excessive lead absorption are found in many children. Lead poisoning can play a major role in the pathogenesis of the spinal column as well (Stoefen 1975). In 1952 Mongelli reported on striking malformations of the spinal column and a high incidence of osteoporosis in young lead workers. During experiments with lead administration a delayed development of osteoid tissue and an increase of osteoclastic lacunar bone decomposition were found. In 1960 Deutschberger found osteosclerosis in lead-poisoned children. Feeding a powder containing lead to horses and a sheep resulted in swollen joints, thickened synovia, and the separation of articular cartilage from the bone (Guenther 1954).

Although those animal studies did not involve the spinal column, similar damage to the intervertebral discs, especially in the cartilage at the vertebral body-intervertebral disc boundary, may be assumed. Because the mucopolysaccharides—essential elements of the intervertebral disc tissue—contain sulphur, there is reason to suspect that they are susceptible to lead poisoning (Loisot 1971). In addition, lead may decrease the level of magnesium in the disc, which is important to its proper functioning.

Soviet investigators have reported that the negative influence of vibrations grows as lead content increases. They noted an increase in vibration-related dystrophic damages in the brain with a simultaneous lead absorption. This finding encouraged studies in which lead was fed to young animals whose spinal columns were subjected to prolonged vibrations. After an appropriate exposure time, the lead content of the vertebral bones and of the growth zones at the vertebral body-intervertebral disc boundary and the intervertebral discs should be tested.

The school medical examination plays a crucial role in the healthy development of the spinal column and related muscles by eliciting the first signs of shape and postural damage. During the growth period, the spinal column may change from one year to the next so examinations must be scheduled on a regular basis. Children susceptible to spinal cord damage require more frequent follow-up. As a result of these examinations, therapy is begun early and irreparable damages are prevented.

Despite a decade-long educational effort by orthopedists and school physicians, many parents are unaware of their responsibility for ensuring the healthy physical development of their children, particularly those susceptible to spinal column damage. Even though the numbers of spinal column growth disorders are increasing, the education about the possible sequelae of even slight spinal column damage has failed to spur many parents into action. Preventive measures, such as securing school furniture that is adapted to the needs of growing children and expanding gymnastics and sports in school, are needed to compensate for minor damage to the spinal column. In particular, a gymnastics program should be designed for those children who are susceptible to spinal column damage. Parents need to serve as advocates for their children, who themselves do not notice their poor posture or rarely complain about it. Often, the personal initiative of parents is not sufficient and slackens after a short time.

In summary, the impairment factors that have detrimental effects on the spinal columns of children and adolescents are as follows:

- Population concentration in cramped, urban conditions with insufficient space to move and play
- Formerly unknown (latent) environmental influences
- Premature and accelerated growth (growth acceleration)
- Leisure activities that damage the spinal column
- Prolonged sitting at school due to a more extensive curriculum which is combined with a lack of compensatory exercises that captivate the child's striving to move
- Poorly designed school furniture and other chairs
- Influences of motorization
- Overstimulation by television and other mass media
- Lack of exercise below the level of healthy stress
- Insufficient health consciousness

7.2.3.2 Postural Damage and Back Pain

From the time the child enters school (sedentary age) at age 6 and throughout his or her school years, active transformation processes are underway in the spinal column at about 50 growth zones (see Figs. 2-2 and 2-4). Growth does not take place uninterruptedly and uniformly, but in occasional, abrupt growth spurts. During these periods a constant observation of upper torso posture and the training of back muscles are required. Incorrect development that is supported by a kyphotic or scoliotic chronic posture forced by prolonged sitting (forced crooked posture) is later hard or even impossible to correct.

The visible large-curved kyphosis as unfortunately often assumed by school children can be compensated for easily in the beginning stages. If neglected, it will, however, grow into a fixed posture. The pressure on the anterior parts of the vertebral bodies impedes the uniform growth of the initially cartilaginous and later ossified vertebral body epiphyses (Figs. 2-2, 2-4, and 2-6). However, the potential for damage is not only restricted to the anterior portions of the ring-shaped vertebral body epiphyses but also can affect the entire growth layer at the transition from the bony vertebral body to the cartilage plate. If the kyphosis is augmented by other damages, such as the frequent indentations in the vertebral body end plate in the area of the former penetration point of the corda canal (Fig. 2-4) or minor chondrodystrophic damages (see section 4.6), then the beginning of a permanent juvenile kyphosis seems certain. The school physician and the parents must continue to test the compensatory possibilities of an increased thoracic kyphosis and must determine whether this crooked posture is perhaps the beginning of a kyphosis. If there is a well-founded suspicion of stiffness in the curved section, roentgenograms must be taken to confirm the diagnosis and determine the necessary therapeutic measures. The lateral picture, taken in the standing or sitting position but under no circumstances while lying down, most clearly shows the condition of the growth layers.

The same conditions that lead to kyphosis cause the development or aggravation of a scoliosis. The inclination of the torso to one side and the unilateral drooping shoulder during sitting, writing, standing, and while carrying a bookbag (Becker and Schlegel 1965), often also in connection with a kyphotic curvature, are warning symptoms deserving of attention (see section 5.2). The school medical examination is crucial for the early detection of this damage.

The extent of the scoliosis is determined by orientation frontal x-rays taken in the standing or lying position. The diagnosis is confirmed if no balanced, large-arched curvature during lateral flexion is present, but instead, over shorter or longer intervals, an interrupted curvature exists or if during anteflexion the characteristic rib hump can already be recognized.

However, conditions at the epiphyses are harder to establish. The first signs of impairments are difficult to identify because the ossification centers in the initially cartilaginous epiphyses (see Fig. 2-4) develop irregularly. In order to avoid high radiation doses, multiple oblique pictures are prohibited for children, except for rare and difficult cases. Therefore, the expert physical examination is still the primary tool of diagnosis.

Often, even with the bad posture of the school-aged child, that can still be compensated for, pain is experienced. It is caused by fatigue of the unilaterally strained muscles of the "back weakling." As the postural degeneration increases, the back pain grows, especially if there are no measures taken to correct the posture.

Numerous studies document the high incidence in schoolchildren of postural insufficiency and incorrect postures, as well as organic damage to the spinal column. In order to compare these data, a uniform classification system for posture, physical function, and strain capacity of the spinal column of children and adolescents is of primary importance. Berquet (1967, 1971) found that 20% of first-graders had bad posture of the back. According to Matthiass and Huennekens (1978), 35% of first-graders had postural insufficiency. During the examination of 60 children between the ages of 10 and 12, Noeh and Behnecke (1975) found a "conspicuous back form" in 57.1% and back pain in 25%. Especially frequent were complaints about headache (21.7%). During examinations of 1994 students, Wrede (1976) found evidence of minor postural insufficiency in 63.8% and conspicuous deformity or other orthopedic disorders in 2.9%. In another study of 233 students of all ages, only 40% had a spinal column with no radiologically determined symptoms, 40% had a clear kyphosis, and 15% had "true" Scheuermann's disease (Wespi 1969). This study was directed only to the thoracic spinal column. Therefore, the percentage of pathological changes in the entire spinal column would probably be much higher because the lumbar spinal column is frequently involved in juvenile kyphosis during adolescence; for instance in the "jeans type" kyphosis. According to Groh (1972), one-quarter of elementary schoolchildren have spinal column damages that warrant serious attention. The unsettling figure of 75% of schoolchildren with postural damage was reported by Breitenfelder (1963). Gamper and Vogt (1978) reported the frequency of postural damages as being 15% in preschool, 17% in third grade, and 35% in seventh grade.

Back pain was a prominent finding in several studies conducted in Switzerland (Wespi 1964). While grade-school students had an incidence of 12% to 14%, female grade-school students had 50% (Ulrich 1971) while middle-school students (Grenacher-Lutz 1979) had an incidence of 43%. Sixty-six percent of the reported back pain related to the low back. In the roentgenogram examinations of 1757 female students performed by Ulrich (1975), the case history revealed back pain in more than 50%; of these, 18% reported pain at the cervical spinal column, 20% at the thoracic spinal column, and 59.1% at the lumbar spinal column.

In addition to back pain, schoolchildren often suffer from the anteflexion headache, the so-called school headache (see section 5.2). It is caused by unfavorable writing and reading positions. The slanted desk and the attention of the teacher to poor posture during class time could prevent this condition.

Since the 1960s, the "jeans type" of bad posture has become increasingly prevalent among adolescents. In the standing position the adolescent has a compensated lumbar lordosis with a slight retroposition of the pelvis (Fig. 7-1). In the sitting position this posture is characterized by a C-shaped total curvature of the spinal column. In addition, tight-fitting blue jeans may create a partial hip contracture. Contemporary seating furniture has adapted to this posture to a great degree.

The balanced back shape with an appropriate pelvic position is seriously threatened by the

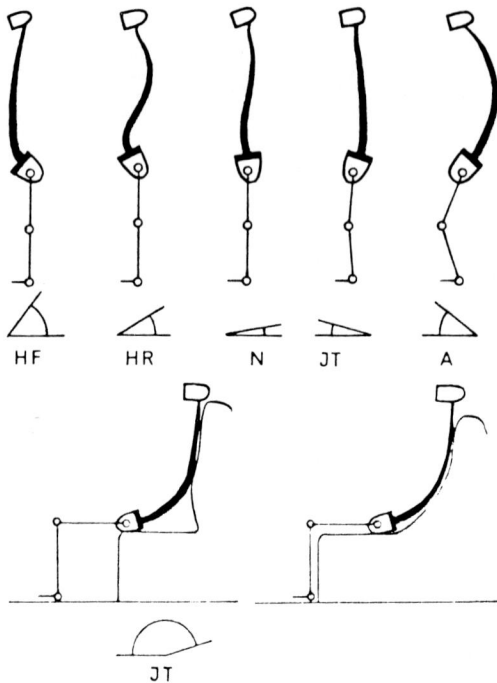

Fig. 7-1 The Jeans type of bad posture [from Ruetten (1978)]. *Top row*, Standing posture. HF = hollow flat back, HR = hollow round back, N = normal back, JT = jeans type, A = monkey. *Bottom row*, Sedentary posture of the jeans type in a straight-back chair and in the "comfortable" jeans chair.

---

jeans posture to the point where the S-shape of the spinal column is neutralized. The jeans posture aggravates or even causes an intervertebral chondrosis, which may be further exacerbated by the vibration influences of motorcycles or driving a truck with a poor suspension.

7.2.3.3 Chairs, Tables, and School Furniture

The sitting, writing, and reading habits of the school-aged sedentary child pose a significant hazard for the proper development of the spinal column during childhood and youth. Sitting in poorly designed chairs and reading and writing at tables that force an incorrect back and head posture are very detrimental to the spinal column (see section 5.2). Poorly designed school furniture can cause irreparable postural damage that is followed by symptoms with increasing disability in later years, long after school furniture has been forgotten as a possible cause.

The serious consequences of poorly designed school furniture have been recognized by physicians since the mid-nineteenth century. As early as 1881, Uffelmann urged that various designs of schooldesks, all with slanted writing surfaces, be used in the classroom (Fig. 7-2). The rather modern-looking back-support chair in Figure 7-2 was designed by Staffel in 1884 to go with a schooldesk with a slanted writing surface.

Writing on a flat surface causes the curvature of the back to increase after only 6 minutes in that position. Figure 7-3 graphically illustrates how posture worsens during the schoolday as a result of trunk muscle fatigue until the student is actually writing with his or her nose. Hourly exercise breaks may help alleviate muscle fatigue, which is significantly increased by flat writing surfaces (Figs. 7-4 to 7-6). **Long sitting is damaging; poor sitting is even more damaging.**

A slanted writing surface permits a more favorable posture even in older, taller students. (Figs. 7-7 and 7-8). The design and use of modern chairs and school furniture should be based on these factors: the shape and inclination of the chair surface and the indispensable back rest, the length of the extremities and the trunk of children of different ages, the appropriate combination of table and chair, the slant of the table surface, the ability to make the writing surface level as needed (Table 7-1). The chair and table should be considered as a unit, regardless of whether they are firmly attached as a chair-table system or whether they were planned as individual pieces. Such school furniture may be arranged in the classroom in such a way as to fulfill pedagogic requirements. Yet, even if school furniture does meet ergometric specifications, it will nevertheless continue to be the continuing responsibility of the teacher to reinforce the importance of good sitting posture and to draw the students' attention to their posture when they neglect it.

The ergometric considerations for sitting and writing furniture, which preclude damage to the growing spinal column, must not be limited to school furniture. Parents must provide well-designed furniture at home as well. Working at the ordinary kitchen table and sitting in a

Effects of Daily Life on the Spinal Column 201

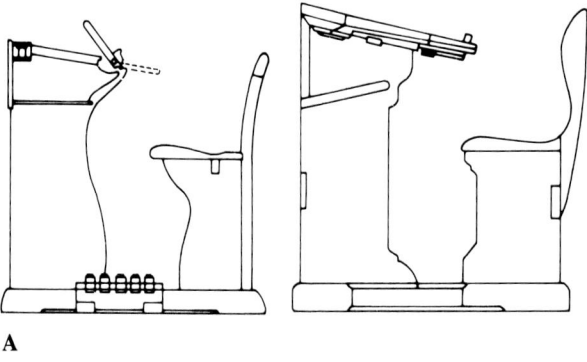

Fig. 7-2 Schooldesks of the 19th century with a slanted writing surface.

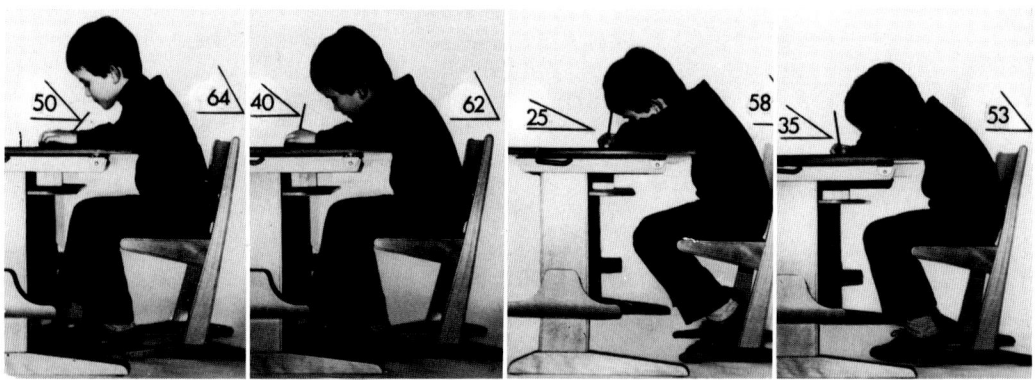

Fig. 7-3 The muscular decline of a student's back during the course of the schoolday, which is accompanied by a parallel decline of mental "freshness" and concentration [from Reinhardt (1983)].

Fig. 7-4 Six-year-old boy seated at a conventional schooldesk with a level surface. At the beginning of the writing assignment, the boy is upright. After 2 minutes, he begins to slump. After 4 minutes, his posture further declines. After 6 minutes he "writes with his nose" [from Hoefling (1972)].

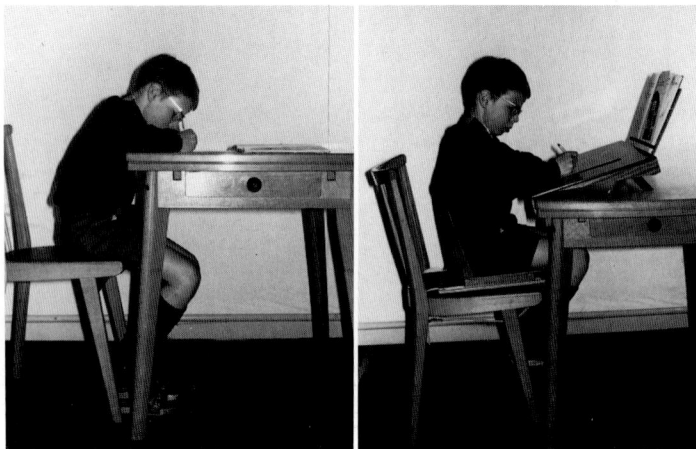

Fig. 7-5 *Left*, usual view of a student doing homework at a kitchen table. The angle of view onto the textbook, which is lying in front of the notebook, is very acute and unfavorable. For that reason children will stand up frequently in order to improve the distortion of the lines by widening the view angle. The chair, which is much too high, forces the child to sit at the chair edge so that the toes are just able to touch the floor. The table, which is also much too high, lifts the elbows and shoulders. *Right*, a children's high-chair with foot support and back rest allows relaxed sitting. The slip-proof desk top has at its top edge a retractable board with a lateral holder for textbooks. A series of notches enables the slant of the writing board to be adjusted. To read, the child must only lift the head while the torso may remain in a writing posture. Rotation and inclination of the torso are no longer necessary [from Hoefling (1972)].

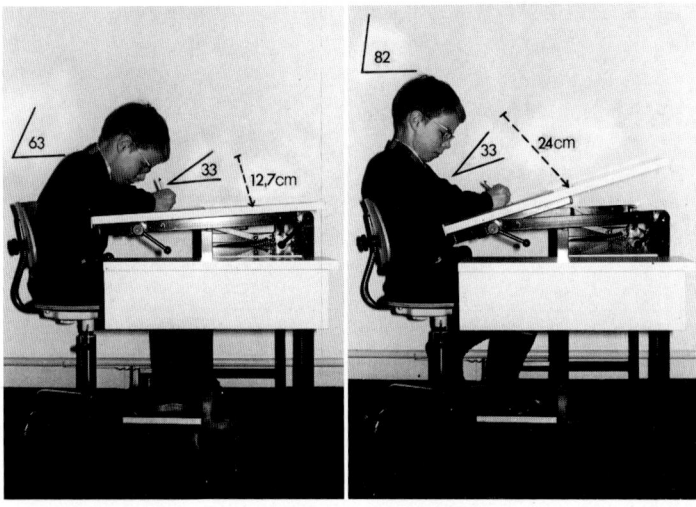

Fig. 7-6 A desk with adjustable height and a writing surface that can be inclined [from Hoefling (1972)].

straight-back chair aggravate the sitting posture during writing (Fig. 7-5). Office equipment must protect the spinal column as well (Schoberth 1979). Wotzka et al. (1969) encouraged substantial improvements in the auditorium seats of universities (Fig. 7-9).

7.2.3.4 Gymnastics, Sports, Play, and Break-Time Exercises

Over the last few decades the time allocated for gymnastics, sports, and play has been reduced in the first years of secondary schools and

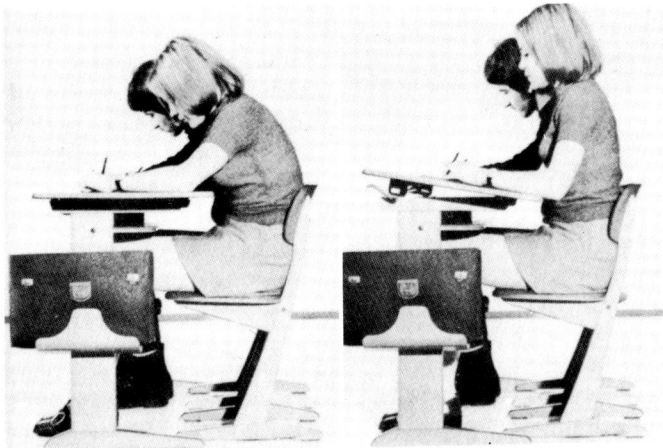

Fig. 7-7 *Left,* The flat writing surface creates a kyphotic posture in female students, which finally results in a permanent kyphosis. The forward inclined head may cause the school headache. *Right,* with a slanted writing surface a posture that is protective of the spinal column becomes possible; the head strains the spinal column in an axial direction.

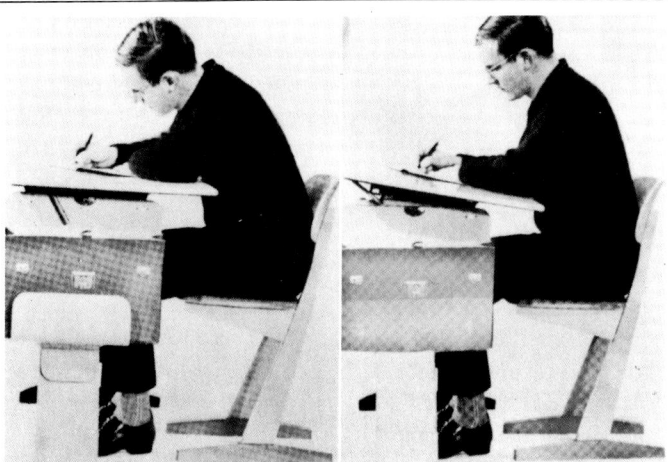

Fig. 7-8 *Left,* Incorrect "kyphotic posture" with inclined head and overexertion of neck muscles while writing on a flat desk surface. *Right,* The slanted writing surface straightens the back and improves the head posture.

even more so in the year or two preceding graduation. The after-school sports activities cannot themselves counteract the tendency of youths to "let go," even to a point of having the jeans-type posture (see Fig. 7-1). Some adolescents see organized sports as repressive (Jentschura 1972) and so spurn participation in them.

Performance gymnastics and performance sports have no place whatsoever in the school curriculum. Physical fitness must be achieved through activity in the gymnastic and sports classes and during break-time exercises. As students become physically fit, the muscular strength of the trunk increases, and the support and motor system that supports the posture, as well as the mobility and performance of the spinal column, is exerted. Physical activity relaxes the body and removes learning blocks, thereby enabling students to meet the intellectual demands of their classwork.

Students with developmental damages of the spinal column must participate in suitable gymnastic or sports classes or in specific physiotherapy. Often, they require treatment by a physician, because the postural insufficiency and damage to the spinal column stemming from

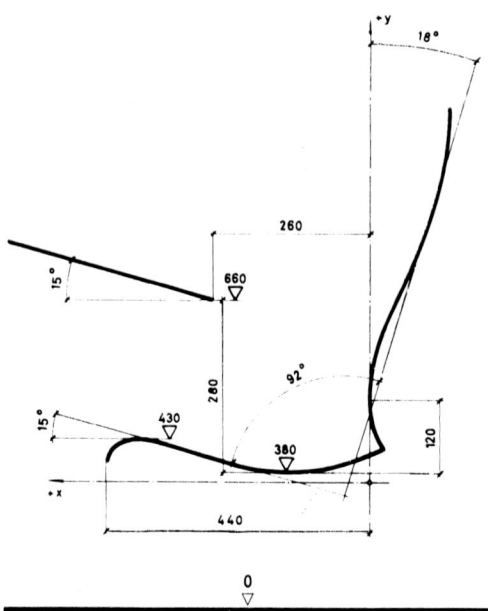

Fig. 7-9 An auditorium seat with spinal-adapted back rest and slanted writing surface [from Wotzka et al. (1969)].

early youth react differently to the stresses of school and the adolescent lifestyle. One impairment factor is prolonged and incorrect sitting. Too, the student may ambitiously seek athletic achievement, which must be constrained in order to prevent further spinal column damage. Exceeding the bearable limit either through underexertion or overexertion is not uncommon.

An effective form of compensation for prolonged sitting during the long schoolday is the regular break-time exercises that were introduced during World War I in German schools. The students performed the exercises either in the schoolyard or in the wide hallways during a prolonged break. A jog around the schoolyard, running in place, knee bends, movements of the trunk and arms with spread legs, head rolls, and similar exercises not only supported the cardiovascular system and respiration but also stimulated the general muscle circulation. Even in today's educational system in which students move from class to class, it should be possible to organize break-time exercises. If a scheduled break is impossible to implement, the short isometric exercise break suggested by Reinhardt in 1983 should be considered. It is performed in a sitting position (Fig. 7-10).

Schoberth (1979) described similar exercises for the legs, trunk, arms, and head that could be performed during an exercise break at the workplace without getting up from the chair. These exercises may be suitable for school, although it is preferable to schedule a break that enables children to leave the classroom.

In his book, *School Furniture*, Berquet (1971) argues for the importance of regular and frequent exercise during the schoolday:

> The German Orthopedic Society has for the last 50 years demanded daily physical education in order to compensate for damages caused by sitting. Today we are further from this objective than before. The best solution (ie, 20 minutes of teaching and 10 minutes of exercise play) is said to be allegedly impossible to implement in our present school system.
>
> Therefore we orthopedists will continue to repeat the demand for daily physical education or daily compensatory exercises. This is in no way an unrealistic modern demand. To the contrary, there have already been ministerial edicts which prescribed such physical compensation activity: The edict of the Prussian minister for Mental and Educational Matters of June 13th 1910 for all schools on all school days . . . [must include] a 10-minute exercise "in order to prevent damaging consequences and to achieve a general increase of physical and mental freshness of students which then may result in a positive effect on the body posture on the school bench."

Exemption from school sports must be limited to those few children who have damage to the spinal column or trunk muscles or corresponding radiation pain. All too often, there is a "refuge in the medical certificate" (sometimes with counterfeit certificates) allowing exemption from school sports due to back pain (Ehricht 1974).

During the past few years the minitrampoline has become a feature of school sports programs. Its use often results in serious spinal injuries and sometimes in paraplegia (Rompe 1980) (see section 8.4). Frequently, jumping on the trampoline causes initially latent damages to the still immature youthful spinal column, and there is serious doubt whether the young spinal column

Effects of Daily Life on the Spinal Column 205

Table 7-1 Basic Measurements of School Furniture (Berquet and Juergens 1972)

	Size Classification				
	120 (purple)	135 (yellow)	150 (red)	165 (green)	180 (blue)
	Body Height Group (cm)				
	112–127	128–142	145–157	158–172	172+
I. Chair					
A. Seat height[1]	30	34	38	42	46
B. Functional seat depth[2–4]	30	35	36	38	40
C. Minimum seat width, front	30	35	36	38	40
D. Slant angle of upper back rest portion	100–106°	100–106°	100–106°	100–106°	100–106°
E. Height of back rest bend	Max 15	Max 18	Max 19	Max 21	Max 22
F. Top of back rest	24–29	27–32	30–35	34–39	36–42
G. Bottom of back rest[5]	Max 12	Max 14	Max 15	Max 17	Max 19
H. Cord measure for back rest above bend for a radius of 35–40 cm[6]	28–31	30–34	32–37	35–41	36–41
II. Table					
A. Table top height	52	58	64	70	76
B. Table depth (min)	50	50	50	50[7]	60
C. Table length (table for two)	130	130	130	130[8]	150
at the work side (single table)	70	70	70	70	80
D. Slant of table top[8]	10–20°	10–20°	10–20°	10–20°	10–20°
E. Possible height for shelf[9]	6	6	6	6	8
F. Measurements for	30	30	35	40	40
G. Leg room	35	40	40	45	50
H. Foot room	25	30	30	35	35
I. Under the table	10	10	10	min 15	min 15

[1]Measured at highest point of the seat surface.
[2]A curvature of the legs at the front edge must be included in the depth measurement. The front curvature has a radius of 4.0 cm.
[3]For explanation of measurements, see Figure 7-2.
[4]The functional seat depth is determined by a line running sagittally through the middle of the seat surface. It starts at the front edge of the seating surface and ends in the foot of the perpendicular, which falls from the vertex of the back rest bend to the seat surface.
[5]The bottom edge of the back rest must not impede the sliding of the rump toward the back in a writing posture. Angle of bend against the top of back rest is 10–30°; degree depends on the respective angle of bend (see Fig. 7-2).
[6]The cord measure of the back rest is an approximate value that characterizes the measurement proportions of the back rest. This measurement should not be substantially fallen short off or exceeded at the top and bottom edge of the back rest.
[7]In smaller classes, the table size 60/150 should be chosen.
[8]An angle of 12° is recommended.
[9]K minus O is for sizes: 120-20, 135-20, 150-15, 165-10, 180-20.

---

should be subjected to those dangers. Therefore, **the minitrampoline cannot be used with a clear conscience in school sports programs.**

7.2.3.5 Dangers of Motorization

The excessive use of motorized bikes—different types of small mopeds or motorbikes—poses serious hazards for the spinal column. The time when adolescents start riding motorized vehicles is the second period of susceptibility for the well-being of the spinal column.

The forward-bent sitting position on motorized bikes neutralizes the normal S-shaped curvature of the spinal column and thus lessens its shock-absorbing capacity. Motor vibrations and impacts from irregularities in the road surface penetrate from the feet, seat, and arms to the back. Neck and back muscles, which are so important for the support of the spinal column, tire after being exposed for a prolonged period to vibrations. The relaxation of these muscles leaves the spinal column even more susceptible to the negative influences of vibrations. **Therefore, the motorcycle is a constant threat to the well-being of the youthful spinal column.**

The alternating, overlapping, and potentiating influences of partial body and total body vibra-

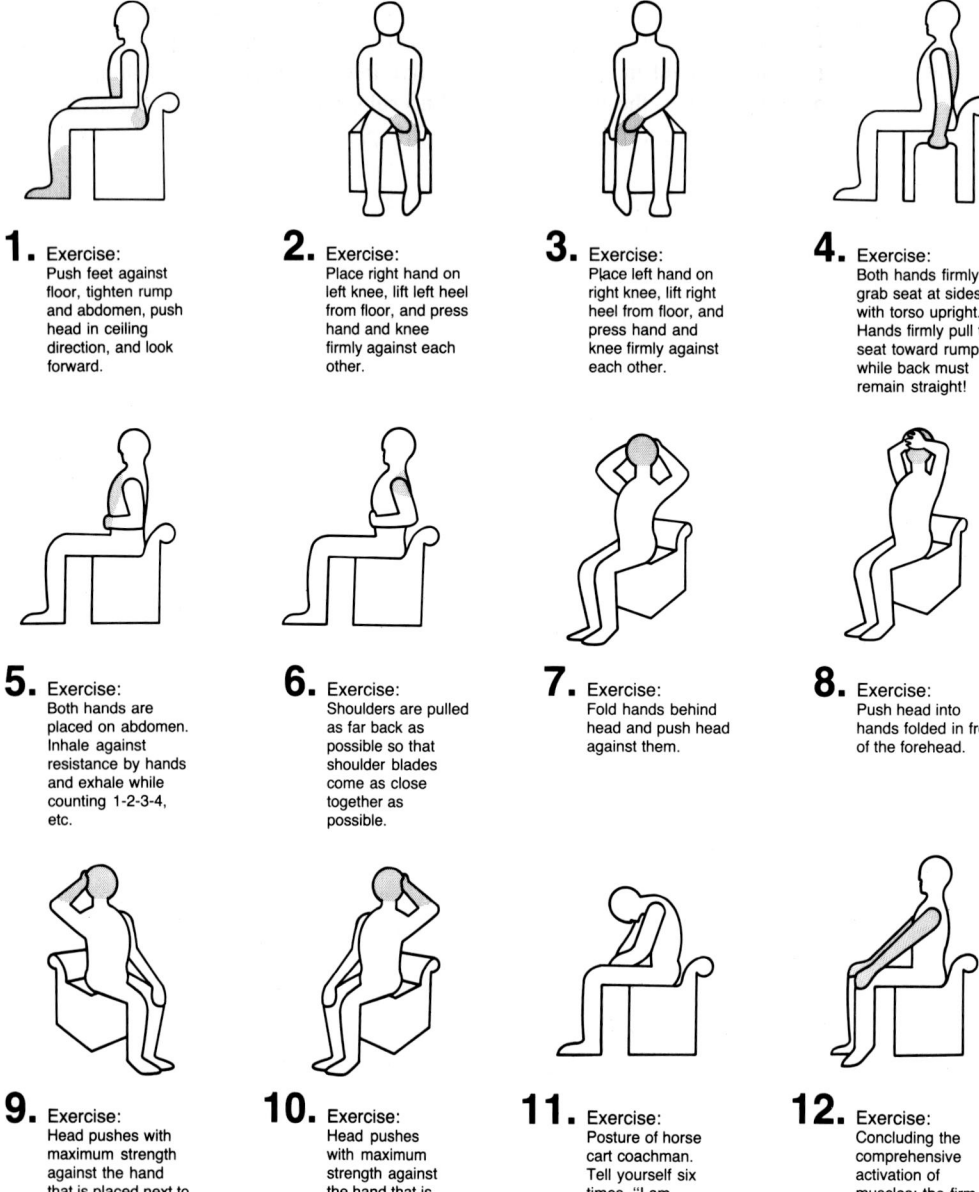

Fig. 7-10 Isometric exercise break resulting in progressive relaxation. These isometric exercises can be performed while sitting at the school chair [from Reinhardt (1983)].

tions from the different types of motorbikes form a vibration pattern that affects, to a varying degree of intensity, several locations along the still growing vertebral body-intervertebral disc boundary. At this point in the development of the adolescent, these growth zones are susceptible to impairment (see sections 2.7 and 5.3) and may suffer direct damage. In addition, the particular vibrations generated by motorcycles are able to induce hormonal growth damage, a fact that is known from studies of vibration disease (see section 5.3). If the daily use of the motorcycle is augmented by long vacation travel in a motorized vehicle, the spinal column of the youth is further exposed to detrimental vibrations.

Riding on increasingly bigger and heavier motorcycles has become a more popular form of recreation in recent years. This activity inevitably results in an increased overexertion of the spinal column. As the youth rides quickly around sharp curves, torsions occur at a few intervertebral motor segments. In conjunction with vibrations, they have an especially detrimental shearing effect on the fiber tissue of the intervertebral discs. The simultaneous traction and pressure damage the vertebral arch articulations, resulting in arthroses (see section 4.6). Reckless driving increases the potential for accidents and serious injury, including bone fractures, internal injuries, and paraplegia. The congregation of "reckless" motorcycle riders in groups and their "neck-breaking" driving style may be regarded as signs of the addictive character of motor-cycling.

Although motorcycle manufacturers have studied the degree of vibration stress emanating from several types of cycles, the effect of road surfaces and the transmission of vibrations to the rider have not yet been analyzed. Such studies are urgently needed in order to improve poor motorcycle designs; such an improvement in the design of the tractor was achieved as a result of research in that area (Dupuis 1956, 1959, 1963, 1974, 1976, 1980; Dupuis and Zerlett 1984).

7.2.3.6 Treatment for Existing Spinal Column Damage

Previously existing impairments of the spinal column in school-aged children and adolescents require constant observation. The nature and severity of the damage must be monitored by regular examinations. The time interval between examinations depends on the type of the disorder, with painful conditions receiving special attention.

Children with damage to the spinal column must be taught correct behavior and posture that will prevent further damage. This behavior and posture must be reinforced in activities outside school as well. Doing homework in the abdominal position on a wedge-shaped pillow is very effective in compensating for prolonged sitting, and no substantial problems in the neck, shoulders, or arms were reported even after lying in this position for hours (Gschwend 1978, 1981) (Fig. 7-11). To achieve this position, a posture board can be slanted against a table (Kolrausch 1958). Consulting with the parents and encouraging them to reinforce correct behavior is essential to the care of children with pre-existing damages of the spine.

The exemption of children with spinal column damage from play, exercises, and sports is a controversial issue. For some conditions, physical exercise and strain are actually healing therapy. Unfortunately, this fact is frequently not understood by worried parents. Exemptions should only be recommended on an individual basis after the present condition of the damage and the required strain have been evaluated. For instance, the exemption from school sports because of scoliosis is necessary only in severe cases. In the case of juvenile kyphosis an exemption becomes necessary only if the curving of the spinal column continues or when painful growth spurts occur (Groeneveld 1976; Schubert et al. 1978).

Long-term medically supervised physiotherapy and the referral of children and adolescents to sport clubs for the disabled are important components of treatment. Surgical therapy should only be recommended in serious cases of

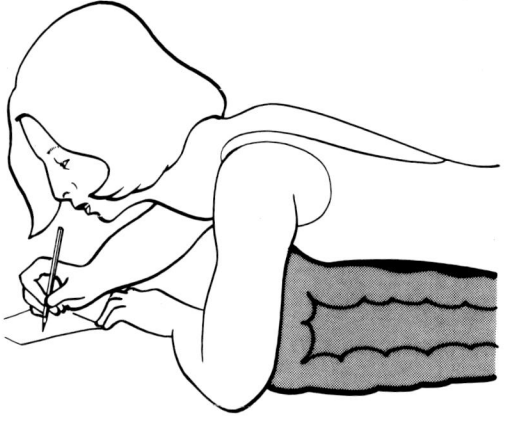

Fig. 7-11 Homework done in the abdominal position (from Gschwend [1978]).

pre-existing damages to the spinal column. For scolioses and kyphoses, straightening and stabilizing operations are appropriate depending on the extent and speed of progession of the curvature (Beyeler et al. 1979; Junghanns 1983; Matthiass 1959, 1979; Zielke 1978). The prolapse of intervertebral disc tissue to the posterior or lateral-posterior is rare in youths, but may be severe enough to require surgery (Billot and Bensahel 1980).

7.2.4 Transition to Adulthood

Between the end of school and the actual start of a job a large number of youths—for instance, university students—experience decisive and important years of physical maturation. During this period, the length of which varies from individual to individual, there is often no continuous medical observation of the spinal column. In part this interruption in medical care may be attributed to the adolescents' lack of interest and willingness to cooperate with health caregivers.

7.2.4.1 Posture

In late adolescence, the great majority of cases with spinal column damage stabilize. Only a few cases still show a tendency to aggravate significantly. It is the task of the physician to identify these especially susceptible adolescents.

Increasing back pain is a warning sign that requires an accurate diagnosis of its cause. The examination must be specifically oriented toward finding additional damage. For instance, the initial symptoms of Bechterew's disorder (see section 4.7) appear at this age and are often misdiagnosed because of their rarity. Perceptible problems of instability and slipping often occur in the first stages of spondylolysis, the true origins of which can only be determined in most cases by oblique roentgenogram pictures (or oblique tomograms) of the affected interarticular portions. Not only pain but just as frequently neck and back stiffness, which is disregarded by the adolescents themselves, are signs of impairment. The physician must use all of his or her persuasive powers to eradicate the jeans posture as well.

In this time of life in which spinal column growth is concluded, a decrease in back pain with a simultaneous increase of restricted mobility of the changed spinal column occurs more frequently than an aggravation of pain. Still, dangers exist in the vicious cycle made up of the decline of muscular strength and increasing stiffness. This is the starting point for therapy. Previously implemented prophylactic measures, such as participation in selected sports, games, swimming, or gymnastics, should be continued. If the curvature cannot be compensated for, therapy should emphasize the training of back muscles in order to prevent recurring episodes of pain. Even if the curvature does not worsen, the muscle atrophy that will develop without treatment will decrease the stress resistance of the spinal column. Many young adults express their striving for movement in discotheques and dance halls. However, such dancing is not a systematically controlled compensatory form of gymnastics that can counteract the damages of prolonged sitting. In fact, some dance movements strain the intervertebral motor segments of the lumbar spinal column severely, as Sollmann documented with radiocinematography.

7.2.4.2 The Disabled Young Adult

Spinal column damage and postural impairments may prevent a young adult from training for a job and hamper his or her integration into daily life and the leisure activities of the peer group. Disabilities may range from abnormal congenital curvature, muscular paralysis of the back caused by poliomyelitis with insufficiency and increasing curvature of the spinal column, problems caused by severe Scheuermann's disease, scoliosis or juvenile intervertebral disc prolapse (Kurihara and Kataoka 1980) and as consequences of vertebral fractures.

Disabled young adults need to be encouraged to engage in appropriate physical exercise. Systematic practice may improve their aptitude in various sports and their neuromuscular coordination; however, training has not been shown to increase endurance (Rieckert et al 1972), as these youths easily tire during prolonged efforts.

Encouraging these young adults to engage in leisure activities that incorporate medically controlled treatment (back gymnastics) may prevent the premature failure of damaged trunk muscles and the overexertion of the muscular corset of the spinal column. Participation in these activities may alleviate the damage that developed or was aggravated at the spinal column during puberty so that adult daily life and leisure are affected as little as possible.

In the past, disabled youths were almost regularly advised to take up a sedentary job. However, this recommendation should only be made for young adults with severe handicaps and after the consultation of a physician. In fact, a job that requires alternating periods of sitting and standing might be better suited to train the remaining stress potential and to protect the spinal column from further damage. When there is youthful muscle insufficiency that is not caused by serious, pathological damage, a muscle-strengthening exercise program should be started before the recommendation of sedentary work is made. In addition to swimming, such an exercise program could also include horseback riding as therapy (Riesser 1975). However, any program of exercise requires continuous medical supervision and must be performed over an extended period of time. Occasional massages are in no way sufficient!

Heavy lifting and carrying, as well as certain movements of the trunk, should be avoided by those who have spinal column damage originating in childhood that includes stress insufficiency and/or mobility impairment. In both the job and daily life, prolonged stresses, as well as abrupt muscle exertions in sports (eg, shot putting, vaulting) should be prohibited.

7.3 SPINAL COLUMN OF THE ADULT

The spinal column of the adult is characterized by the neglects of youth.

As the young adult enters the third decade of life, the "sins" of youthful carelessness and neglect of systematic training of the support and motor system, especially of the spinal column and its muscles, bear fruit. A "third period of susceptibility" to spinal column damage occurs as the adult moves from the third to fourth decade of life. During this period the spinal column is threatened by insufficient attention to the maintenance of its static and dynamic functional potential. The numerous opportunities for play and sports participation that are available for youth are replaced by work and family obligations. As a result, the spinal column with its ligaments and the trunk muscles with their connections to the neck, shoulders, and arms and over the pelvis to the legs are more than ever subjected to prolonged stresses: sitting in a forced posture, lack of exercise, and vibrations exposure. During this time, the functional potential of the healthy and even more so of the previously damaged spinal column must be supported and improved in order to counteract the age-related decline of muscle strength as long as possible, thereby preventing back pain, senile kyphosis of the spinal column, and premature retirement from an active lifestyle.

Taking responsibility for one's well-being is an essential challenge for each adult (Schaefer 1980). This challenge can take many forms: doing morning exercises or at work breaks, walking stairs, doing fitness exercises or the new aerobics, and participating in hiking, swimming, or winter sports. The result is a long-term compensation for the lack of exercise that unfortunately characterizes the modern way of life.

Many studies have been conducted on the postural stresses facing schoolchildren, and workers in various occupations. However, very little is known about the normal course of life of the adult outside the job, specifically:

- How long on average does an adult stand, sit, or walk each day?
- What relations exist between after-work postures and the same or similar postures of the spinal column on the job?
- What kind of compensatory measures are implemented in everyday life to regenerate neglected muscles, with special attention to the training of trunk muscles and to the posture of the spinal column?

The answers to these questions will help show adults how they can sensibly counteract the stresses of their jobs with a health-conscious after-work regimen.

7.3.1 Standing

The healthy spinal column adapts without difficulties to a prolonged standing position because of its S-shaped curvature with alternating kyphotic and lordotic sections, which provides elastic support (see section 5.2). The ideal vertical body posture can be maintained for a prolonged period if the muscles are sufficiently strong.

During the basic posture of standing the opposing muscle forces should be balanced so that the back muscles do not perform any active function. Only the compensating calves muscles should show activity on the electromyogram. The energy consumption during standing upright is small: 0.16 kcal/min. In comparison, in the supine rest position the energy consumption is 0.00 because energy consumption is determined essentially by muscular performance. The minimal energy consumption may not mean the absence of stress on the intervertebral column, however.

Frequently, when the shape and posture of the spinal column are considered, only the curvatures in the sagittal level (kyphoses, lordoses)—the lateral view—are referred to because of the dominant S-shape. When considering curvatures in the frontal level (scolioses), special biomechanical considerations arise. For instance, any change in the supporting leg/nonsupporting leg posture is followed by a change in spinal column flexion (Fig. 7-12). Often, the same supporting leg is exclusively used during prolonged standing. Doing so results in a unilaterally repeated posture scoliosis that stresses the back muscles unsymmetrically and may cause back problems, especially if there are fixated abnormal lateral curvatures. Therefore, a regular alternation of the supporting leg is very important. Even without an evidently altered back shape, back fatigue and increasing painfulness during upright standing may be the first warning signs of back muscle insufficiency. These warning signs must not go unnoticed because they require remedy by bending forward or, in serious cases, by specific treatment.

7.3.2 Walking

The spinal column is involved in the static and dynamic functions of walking. In each step, a rotation of the spinal column axis occurs. This rotatory motion of the spinal column (Gregersen and Lucas 1967) during walking is coordinated with the symmetrical right-left swayings of the spinal column axis. Each step thus strengthens the muscle corset of the spinal column. Together with the pump mechanism, walking is the most important element in maintaining the metabolism of the intervertebral discs (see sections 2.3 and 5.2).

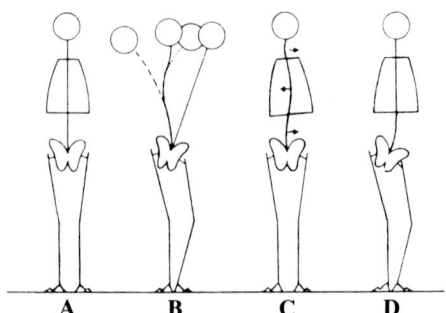

Fig. 7-12 Schematic portrayal of the spinal column in the supporting leg/nonsupporting leg posture (Knese 1963). (**A**), Normal posture. (**B**), Supporting leg left, nonsupporting leg right; development of compensatory curvatures through multiple back curvatures of the spinal column that bring the point of gravity of the total body above the supporting surface. (**C**), Physiological thoracic scoliosis right in normal posture; *arrows* indicate curvature direction for the development of compensatory curvatures. (**D**), Nonsupporting/supporting leg posture for lumbar scoliosis.

Muenchinger (1964) was able to record to what extent sinus-shaped vibrations penetrate from the feet to the spine during each step. The increase in vibration stress caused by wearing high heels is remarkable. When high heels are worn, vibrations have a stochastic character:

Walking (low heels)	0.5 g =	20 kp
Walking (high heels)	1.0 g =	40 kp
Walking down stairs (flat heels)	0.75 g =	30 kp
Walking down stairs (high heels)	2.58 g =	100 kp

The pressure differentials are also clearly portrayed in Figure 7-13. The data are based on the stress curves of the lumbar spinal column of a person weighing 70 kg. In this process, g = 9.81 m/sec^2 because the dynamic stress may be given as acceleration.

Adults walk an average of 20,000 steps daily. The much higher number of steps required by certain athletic disciplines results in the highest pressure strains of the spinal column, especially in the lumbosacral region, and are discussed in Chapter 8.

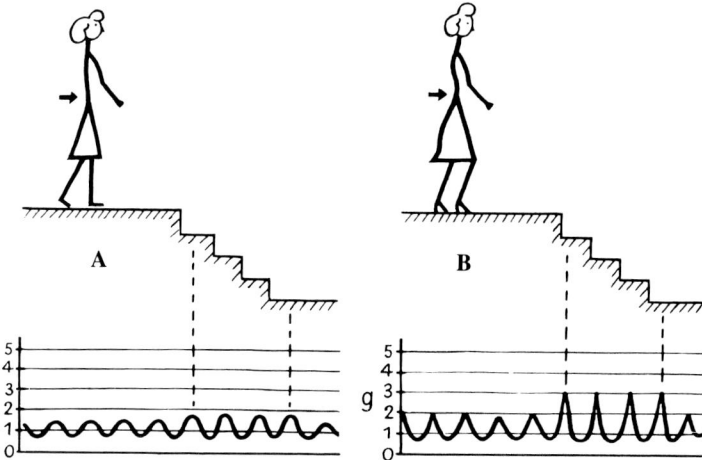

Fig. 7-13 Differences in accelerograms during walking and walking stairs with (A) low and (B) high heels [from Muenchinger (1964)].

The flexion potential for a newborn is very high, for anteflexion as well as retroflexion, but decreases with progressive age. With the exception of the thoracic spinal column portions, which remain obviously straight during retroflexion, all segments are almost equally involved in the development of a large curve. In the physical examination, the flexion capacity may be documented through measurement intervals or angular measurements (Stofft and Ribka 1975).

A note regarding nomenclature. Retroflexion is often called stretching or overstretching. In order to avoid confusion with the actual stretching of the spinal column (eg, the therapeutic extension in the longitudinal axis), the terms "retroflexion" or "backward bend" and their opposites, "anteflexion" or "forward bend," are recommended. The term "hyperlordosation" is only justified for lordotic sections, ie, for the cervical spinal column and lumbar spinal column.

The anteflexion of the cervical spinal column has practical importance because it is taken daily for a shorter or longer period of time as the reading posture at school or in everyday life. With an upright head posture, the pressure in the lower portion of the cervical spinal column is 6.8 kg. It increases about threefold during reading (21.0 kg), as shown in Figure 7-14. If a level writing surface requires an even greater anteflexion of the head, the pressure on the anterior sections of the intervertebral disc increases and the support muscles in the neck tire. The typical symptoms of school headache or reading headache develop. In adults these symptoms are often misdiagnosed, so that the correct remedy is not found.

Lateral flexion is greatly limited in the thoracic spinal column by blocks in the vertebral arch articulations and the restraint exerted by the lateral intervertebral disc fibers, which are firmly bonded in the bony epiphysis. Because these barriers to lateral flexion are not present in the cervical and lumbar spinal column, better lateral

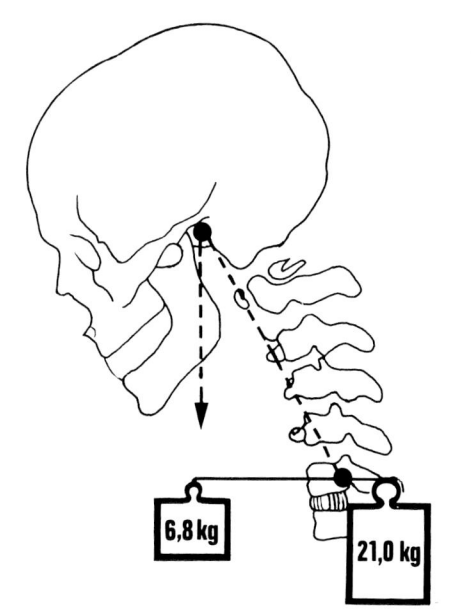

Fig. 7-14 Straining of the intervertebral disc C-6/C-7 caused by a forward inclined head posture during reading [from Matthiass (1956)].

flexion potentials exist in these sections. Lateral flexion, as does anteflexion and retroflexion, consists of a large curve because of the involvement of several intervertebral motor segments. Lateral sharp flexions with acute angles are prevented by the existing block mechanisms, as are sharp anteflexion and retroflexion.

Rotations to the left and right are only possible to a very small extent in the individual segments of the spinal column. However, they enable the rotation of larger spinal column sections when several or many segments are involved (rotation around the longitudinal axis). The thoracic portion is involved only to a small degree (see Table 6-5). The palpation of the proper, impaired or increased rotary mobility of individual segments is only possible in favorably located cases and with subtle chirodiagnostics.

Frequently, evasive compound movements occur during the examination of retroflexion and anteflexion, eg, lateral flexion with rotation (see section 5.2). When these occur, further diagnostic clarification is required, especially if pain is present.

7.3.3 Sitting

Too frequent sitting, especially continuous prolonged sitting, places a tremendous stress on the spinal column. Although some sitting postures use certain muscle groups that may actually alleviate pressure on the spine, most sitting postures increase this pressure, eg, on the anterior portions of the intervertebral discs during anteflexed sitting. Long sitting times frequently result in fatigue and muscle tension. The ligament systems lose their elasticity. Thus, the spinal column is trapped in a vicious cycle of strong, often unilateral pressure, overexertion of muscles and ligaments, and muscle fatigue. Pain during sitting and arising from the chair with an anteflexed stiff posture are distinct symptoms of a sitting insufficiency that develops when a spinal column undergoes pathological changes.

A large portion of these problems are caused by the forced lack of exercise when sitting. This more or less eliminates the pump mechanism (see section 3.2), which must maintain the fluid flow for the nutritional supply and waste removal of the intervertebral discs. The biomechanical and biochemical functions of the discs depend on the pump mechanism.

Pain caused by sitting is more likely to occur when an incorrect sitting posture is taken. Two sections of the spinal column are especially susceptible to painful sitting insufficiency: the cervical spinal column from where neck-head-arm pain may originate and the lumbar spinal column with its transition to the sacrum. From the lumbar area sitting-related pain radiates into the loin area and to the legs—lumbago, sciatica. Previously existing, frequently latent damage, such as chondroses, osteochondroses, and arthroses of the vertebral arch articulations, often cause pain as well.

The anteflexion headache, which occurs when reading and writing in a strongly anteflexed head position, is a serious warning sign of developing damage of the intervertebral discs, uncovertebral and vertebral arch articulations, and muscles and ligaments at the cervical spinal column. A change of reading chair, use of a slanted writing surface, and attention to a better sitting posture are required urgently. (Gschwend 1965; Kaiser 1977; Keegan 1953; Kropp 1979; Sund 1978).

An increased strain is placed on the spinal column if after-work hours are spent sitting, in addition to prolonged sitting while on the job. The problems of occupational sedentary strain must be compensated for by appropriate muscle-strengthening activities in daily life.

The potential damage caused by sitting is greater for older adults. They sit for long periods of time in seating arrangements that are not adapted to the spinal column. **The greatest danger for the spinal column of the adult is sitting furniture.**

Modern furniture—"comfortable" deep chairs with corresponding low tables—causes a great deal of back pain. When the ratio between the height of the chair and that of the table is incorrect, the problems caused by sitting are exacerbated. In contrast, office furniture has improved in recent years. It is ironic that the "chair in the parlor" no longer brings recovery for the back, but compensatory spinal column recovery must rather be sought in the office chair constructed according to ergometric considerations. Because it is impossible to eliminate sitting completely, it is essential to redesign domestic furniture to support the spinal column.

In a study by Grandjean (1967) on the frequency of physical complaints during sitting, only 15% of the study sample had no "sitting problems," 57% reported back problems, and 38% head-neck problems. In addition, 15% had problems in their arms and hands and 29% in their knees and feet. (These numbers add up to more than 100% since there were frequently multiple complaints).

Even with the best-designed chairs, sitting is a rest position that is susceptible to impairment. **The best chair does not replace the motion needed by every person for health prophylaxis and health maintenance.**

7.3.4 Correct Lifting and Carrying

Proper lifting and carrying techniques must not only be used at work but also in daily life, leisure, and sports because even occasional incorrect lifting and carrying may, in the case of a latent functional insufficiency (see section 3.4) result in neck, back, or lower back pain (frequently sciatica-like). Such pain is the sign of damage in the intervertebral motor segment, especially the intervertebral disc and vertebral arch articulation. The muscle and ligament system is also involved. That system's temporary and/or chronic failure during lifting and carrying closes the vicious cycle and results in intervertebral insufficiency (see section 3.4).

Using a proper lifting technique can alleviate the pressure affecting the sections of the intervertebral disc. Lifting with a straight back prevents overstraining the anterior intervertebral disc portions and pronounced spinal column anteflexion and lateral flexion, thereby enabling the damage-free lifting of much heavier weights (Fig. 7-15, see weightlifting in 9.4). The load ratio in relation to the intravitally measured intervertebral disc pressure is described in section 3.2 and in Figures 3-3 and 3-4.

Lifting and carrying do not only affect the support and motor system. In women the contraction of the abdominal muscles in lifting also affects the internal abdominal organs. Therefore the threshold stress values for men and women are different, especially in youth (Tables 7-2 and 7-3). Table 7-4 shows maximum weights for lifting and carrying that are used by the West German Department of Labor. In addition, the condition of an individual's intervertebral discs and/or vertebral arch articulations determines his or her stress resistance (see section 5.2).

While performing leisure and household activities, often lifting and setting down of weights are done with simultaneous rotation, particularly when there is a great height difference between the individual and the object (Figs. 7-16 and 7-17). Turning movements and lifting are especially stressful for the intervertebral disc; this combination stress must be avoided under all circumstances.

7.3.5 Spinal Column Stress Affecting Women

Even in the most modern households, women, who for the most part still have primary responsibility on the domestic scene, must perform a

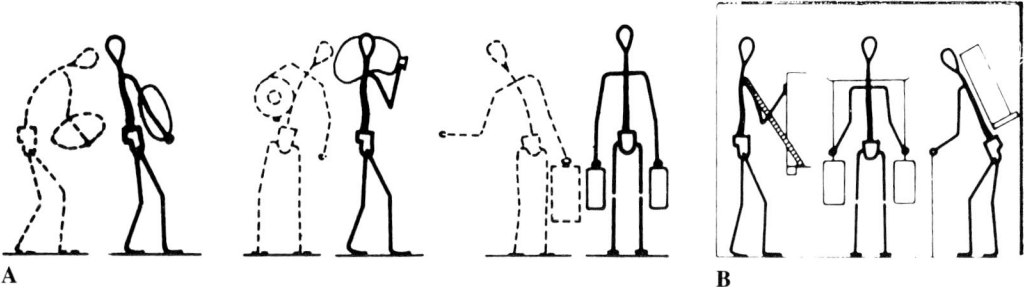

Fig. 7-15 (**A**), Incorrect and correct carrying of objects of various weights. (**B**), Carrying of heavy objects with auxiliary means, such as a shoulder strap, shoulder yoke, or carrier (from Muenchinger 1961).

Table 7-2 Threshold Stress Values for Lifting and Carrying (Junghanns 1979)*

	(Kg)
Young men	10–65, average of 16–20
Young women	7–25, average of 12–15
Men	30–100, average of 40–50
Women	7–30, average of 20–25

*Compiled from various regulations of different countries within and outside Europe.

Table 7-3 Maximum Threshold Stress Values in France

Age	Men	Women
	(Kg)	
Under 14 yr	10	5
14–16 yr	15	8
16–18 yr	20	10
Over 18 yr	—	25

Table 7-4 Limitations on Lifting and Carrying of Weights for Men and Women*

	Permissible Weight			
	Frequency of Lifting and Carrying			
	Occasionally		More Frequently	
	Women[1]	Men[1,2]	Women[2]	Men[2]
(yr)	(Kg)			
15–18	15	35	10	20
19–45	15	55	10	30
Over 45	15	45	10	25

*From Federal Minister for Labor and Social Order, West Germany.
[1]Not striated; threshold values that cannot normally be exceeded without endangering health.
[2]Striated; values recommended from an ergonomical viewpoint.

great deal of physical labor: caring for small children, carrying heavy shopping bags, doing the laundry, and cleaning floors. These tasks stress the spinal column for more than 8 hours a day. The household can be considered a high-risk and accident-prone workplace in regard to the stress resistance placed on the spinal column.

Stress can be caused in many ways. Too low worktables, found often in the kitchen, cause the individual to use a prolonged anteflexed trunk posture, whereas a table with a work surface of an adapted height protects the spinal column (Fig. 7-18). Figure 7-19 shows some of the many daily lifting and carrying household tasks. In addition, many activities are performed while sitting with a curved back, such as needlework and sewing. The many hours of leisure time spent watching television in poorly designed furniture add to the strain on the spinal column. Finally, the household is a source of additional stress for women who hold full- or part-time jobs outside the home because an incorrect body posture used doing household chores affects the spinal column that has already been stressed during several hours of sedentary work on the job.

For these reasons, women with back problems and cervical or lumbar spinal column syndromes represent a relatively large portion of the patient body of many physicians. Often, the mechanical spinal column stress alone is frequently not the decisive factor in seeking medical care. Often, hormone-related bone disorders, such as presenile osteoporosis, and also menopause are

Fig. 7-16 The dangerous swayback posture used during the transport of heavy objects.

Fig. 7-17 Incorrect lifting onto a too great height causes an anteflexed and laterally flexed spinal column. In each case occurs a torsion scoliosis that is under pressure.

Effects of Daily Life on the Spinal Column 215

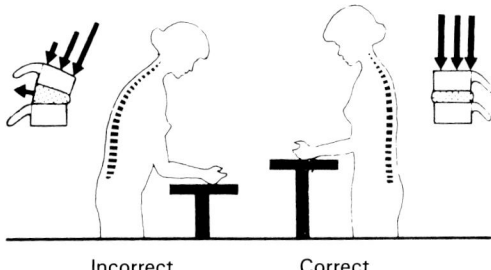

Incorrect   Correct

Fig. 7-18 Unfavorable (*left*) and correct (*right*) pressure distribution on the lumbar spinal column during standing work. The adapted height of the worktable (*right*) results in an adequate distribute of pressure.

Fig. 7-19 Examples of incorrect and correct lifting of a laundry basket, child, and child lying in bed.

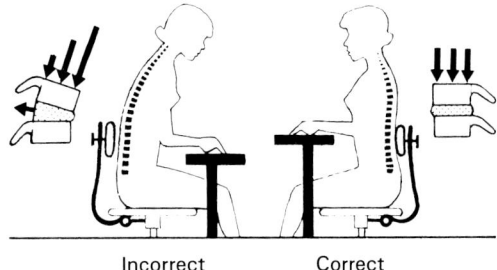

Incorrect   Correct

Fig. 7-20 Household work in a sitting position. The low height of the worktable (*left*) causes a curvature of the spinal column and places increased pressure on the anterior portions of intervertebral discs, in spite of the back rest. The correct working height (*right*) and the adapted back rest result in an evenly distributed pressure.

Fig. 7-21 Carrying techniques for the housewife. *Left*, Incorrect unilateral carrying results in a scoliotic posture. *Middle*, Straight posture of the spinal column through symmetrical carrying. *Right*, Carrying is replaced with rolling!

involved as well. Psychological problems often overlay spinal column problems, even though only insignificant objective findings can be determined at the axial organ and its muscles. Blécourt (1963) calculated that 30% of housewives suffer from a cervical syndrome, caused by bending with an anteflexed head, and 10% suffer from a lumbar syndrome.

Postural problems are more frequent in women than in men. The "postural degeneration of women" was called a "gender-specific orthostatic syndrome of women" by Martius as early as 1930 and 1931 (Schneider and Will 1958). It is closely linked with the shape of the female pelvis and the resulting excessive lordosis. In addition in the childbearing years, there is a general resistance insufficiency, a decline of muscle strength, and ligament insufficiency in the support and motor system.

Prophylactic measures can be taken in the "workplace household" and in the work habits of women to prevent damage to the spinal column by reducing the stress to which it is subjected. As mentioned, work surfaces for standing work can be made higher (Fig. 7-18), as well as those for sitting work (Fig. 7-20). Correct lifting and carrying techniques can be used as well (Fig. 7-21).

Muenchinger (1963) recommended use of a pendulum chair to enable good, straight spi-

Fig. 7-22 The pendulum seat for the housewife, eg, for ironing (*left*) or for longer sitting work at the sink (*right*).

nal column posture during various activities (Fig. 7-22). In a straight posture, the pressure is evenly distributed among the intervertebral discs. A weight-relieving standing chair works in a similar manner (Fig. 7-23). This standing chair is beneficial for use in factories as well.

7.3.6 The Adult at Home

Ideally, the home is a place for rest and relaxation and a refuge from demands of the job and other pressures. It should also be a place where the stresses on the spinal column of the workday are compensated for by limiting the amount of time spent sitting and, when it is necessary to sit, by doing so in ergometrically designed furniture. Deep, softly cushioned chairs with their matching low tables torture the back to a point that even the forward bending to the low table and, even more so, arising from them cause difficulties and back pain. Therefore, such sitting furniture should be banned from the home and replaced by such pieces as the old-fashioned standing desk of our forefathers. Instead of the slackening of muscles and ligaments, the standing desk promotes tautness of ligaments and muscle strength, ie, the static-dynamic musculo-ligamentous corset (see section 3.2).

Every back sufferer should engage in exercise to strengthen tensed and weakened muscles. The older person who already has suffered damage to the spinal column from youthful neglect is in particular need of exercise. Taking walks, jogging, and engaging in fitness exercises are recommended.

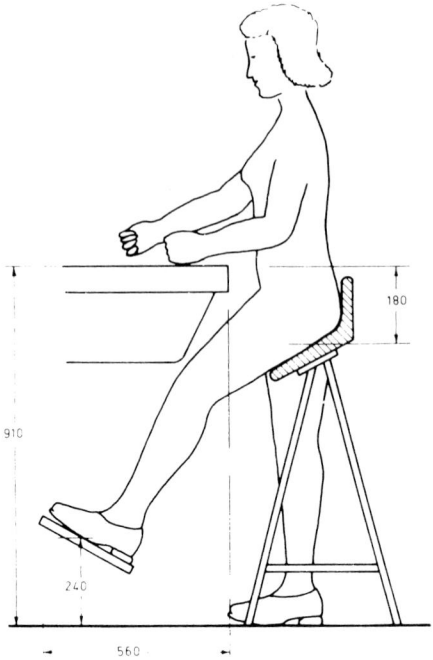

Fig. 7-23 The back-relieving standing seat.

After a prolonged, physical exertion, every back sufferer should take a rest at home by lying down in a supine position on a flat, firm mattress or in a suitable adjustable chaise with a padding that provides light support for the lumbar lordosis. A simple chair with sagging cloth does not provide the necessary relaxation for the back muscles.

7.3.7 Total Body Vibrations

As a motor vehicle is driven, several types of vibrations and oscillating mixtures reach the spinal column. The transmission pathways run either over the arms and shoulders, with a partial vibrating effect, or they penetrate from the pelvis and possibly also from the feet and legs, as vertically effective total body vibrations. In addition, the oscillation of the back rest may reach the spinal column horizontally. Such horizontal vibrations are frequently increased by abrupt acceleration moments occurring during starting or stopping the vehicle. The radial acceleration during curves and torsion with vibrations are additional unfavorable factors (Reischauer and Wagner 1959). Depending on the individual's body posture, one or the other of the crossing vibration pathways will have a more or less intense effect. On average, each person is affected by vibrations for several hours each day.

The increasing use of motorized vehicles for recreational activities greatly adds to the vibration stress of many individuals. The detrimental effect on the spinal column cannot be calculated by simply adding up the times of exposure, however. The additional exposure potentiates the damaging influence of vibrations on the central axial organ and muscles. In the same way, prolonged sitting has a potentiating effect because it is augmented by vibrations that are experienced everyday while riding in a vehicle.

The vibration tolerance of the spinal column is limited not only by the combination of exposure time and intensity but also by congenital or acquired damage and the aging of bones and soft tissue. Well-developed trunk muscles serve as a muscle corset to support the spinal column, but must be supplemented by compensatory prophylactic measures performed on a regular basis.

7.3.7.1 Kinetosis

Kinetosis or motion sickness affects passengers in trains, boats, airplanes, and motor vehicles. Elevators and carousels occasionally also cause the typical nausea of kinetosis. However, it rarely affects motorcyclists.

A kinetosis develops when rapid changes in direction are accompanied by changing rates of acceleration. The movement of the head affects the vestibular system of the middle ear. To date, the vibrations penetrating from the feet to the seat and back rest have received less attention as a causal factor. Those vibrations travel through the spinal column and continue to the head where they pass on the information of vibration accelerations of 1–2 Hz, which encourage the development of kinetosis. In especially susceptible persons, general indisposition may be caused by vibrations between 1–20 Hz (and increases between 5–9 Hz) and may result in vomiting. Serious kinetosis can result in the decline of an individual's general psychological functioning and curtailment of physical capacity (Table 7-5). The symptoms of headache and dizziness do not always occur during driving but may be observed hours after vibrations have ceased.

It is still unknown whether a pathologically changed cervical spinal column amplifies the transmission of vibrations. This seems probable because, in individuals with uncovertebral arthroses and/or osteochondroses of the cervical spinal column, the abrupt head movements are greatly increased. Impairment of the equilibrium organ may also increase kinetosis. Vertebral osteochondrosis, uncovertebral arthrosis, and vertebral arch articulation arthrosis may also constrict the vertebral artery and simultaneously exert pressure on the neural plexi (see Figs. 4-69 to 4-75). This greatly increases the possibility of an inner ear kinetosis because the end artery of the inner ear receives a large portion of its blood supply from the vertebral artery. Head movements and additional oscillations, primarily torsion vibrations, directly aggravate via the blood vessels or nerves the already constricted blood supply, therefore encouraging kinetosis.

Table 7-5 Degrees of Severity of Kinetoses (Dupuis and Zerlett 1984)*

Symptom	Degree Kanda et al. (1977)	Goethe (1957–1973)
Slight discomfort, fatigue, listlessness, loss of appetite, paleness, no incentive for mental work	1	1
Nausea, distinct weakness, indisposition, dizziness, decreased functional ability	2	2
Strong nausea and indisposition, vomiting	2	3
Strong vomiting, urge to defecate and urinate, distinct feeling of sickness	3	4
Constant vomiting, feeling of destruction, distinct adynamia and unresponsiveness	3	4

*No symptoms = 0.

Similar symptoms to those of motion sickness occur in daily life when sinus oscillations reach the cervical spinal column and head via the transmission pathway of the hand-arm-shoulder. They are intensified by stochastic impulses (partial body vibrations), which may occur during the operation of hand-operated grass mowers, electrical hedge trimmers, electric power tools, and rarely during the operation of hand-operated electrical kitchen appliances. Jogging during leisure, in addition to back pain, also causes the typical symptoms of kinetosis because of the penetration of stochastic oscillations from the feet, especially when a spinal column stiffness exists.

Even though the equilibrium organ in the ear is significantly involved in the development of kinetoses, the spinal column should be included in diagnosis and therapy, even for children who suffer from these uncomfortable complaints.

7.3.7.2 Bicycles

The recent rediscovery of bike riding as a form of recreation and transportation for both children and adults is welcome because it reduces environmental pollution, saves gasoline, and is an excellent form of exercise. However, it does cause stress on the spinal column, which must be clarified.

The racing bike with its low handle bar, which is a favorite of young people, provokes a strongly kyphotic posture, which is imitated from racing professionals (see Fig. 8-3). This posture places a damaging pressure on the anterior sections of the still immature intervertebral discs and the vertebral body-intervertebral disc transitional layers that are important to growth.

In addition, the road surface causes sinus-shaped vibrations and many, even stronger stochastic impacts. They penetrate the spinal column directly from the seat and combine with the vibrations transferred from the pedals over the legs to the pelvis to form total body vibrations. The transmission pathway for partial body vibrations runs from the handlebar over the arms to the shoulder girdle. Those partial body vibrations may reach the cervical spinal column and head in conjunction with the vibrations penetrating from the rump and pelvis. Thus, bike riders experience the same problems of motor vehicle drivers.

More and more adults are riding bicycles, both for recreation and as a form of pollution-free transportation. Nevertheless, riding a bicycle cannot be recommended for any adult with a previously damaged spinal column without further caution. Bike riding may cause back muscle strength to decline because of prolonged sitting and vibration stress, thereby resulting in increased problems in the neck and back if there are no compensatory measures. Such measures include back and trunk exercises that bike riders should practice just as do car drivers and passengers (see section 8.2, rule 5 of "10 rules for an active vacation"). A large number of bike racers suffer spinal column damage that may be attributed to prolonged forward bent sitting in a strongly kyphotic posture—biker's hump (see section 8.2).

7.3.7.3 Motorcycles

The warning regarding the excessive use of motor bikes or motorcycles by youths does not apply in the same manner to adults. First, only a few adults over the age of 25 ride a motorcycle frequently. Second, if the spinal column is healthy and supported by strong muscles, it does not suffer damages from safe motorcycle riding.

However, the situation is different, if a previous damage of the spinal column stemming from the adolescent growth period exists or if there are stress risks caused by other previous damages. In those cases it is essential to consult an experienced physician in order to determine the individual stress resistance of the spinal column. Back pain after riding a motorcycle is an indication of functional insufficiency of the spinal column that must not be overlooked.

7.3.7.4 Automobiles Including Transport in an Ambulance

It is not rare for a person to drive up to 500,000 kilometers in a decade and up to one million kilometers in the decades between the ages of 20 and 40, which are significant time periods for spinal column stress.

Prolonged sitting in a car—a lack of exercise in a forced position with prolonged tension of the muscle groups—weakens the back muscles significantly. Although the negative influence of vibrations varies according to vehicle type, seat surface, the back rest and its inclination, head rest, and operating levers, back and neck pain during or after a ride, back stiffness during exiting, and motion sickness syndromes (kinetosis) are all symptoms of these negative influences.

During the past few years, automobile manufacturers have devoted substantial attention in their research departments and laboratories to decreasing engine-related vibrations and improving the car body and seat so that oscillations from road surfaces affect the passengers, especially the driver, as little as possible. One focus of research and development has been the back-adapted car seat, which provides support to the spine. A back-adapted sitting posture is shown in Figure 7-24. Accelerograms indicating the results of poor posture are found in Figure 7-25, and Figure 7-26 shows a basic concept for an ergometrically designed car seat (Rosemeyer 1977).

The back rest deserves special attention. If possible, there should be an adjustable curvature in the area of the individual lumbar lordosis (Figs. 7-27 and 7-28). At the same time an

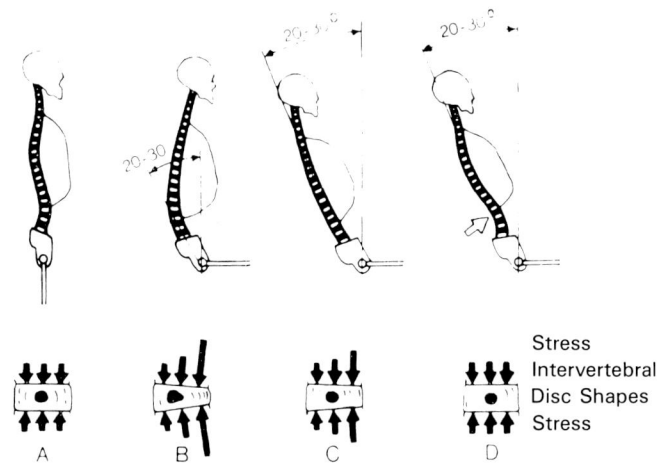

Fig. 7-24 Direction and amount of spinal column stress found in different sitting positions in vehicles.

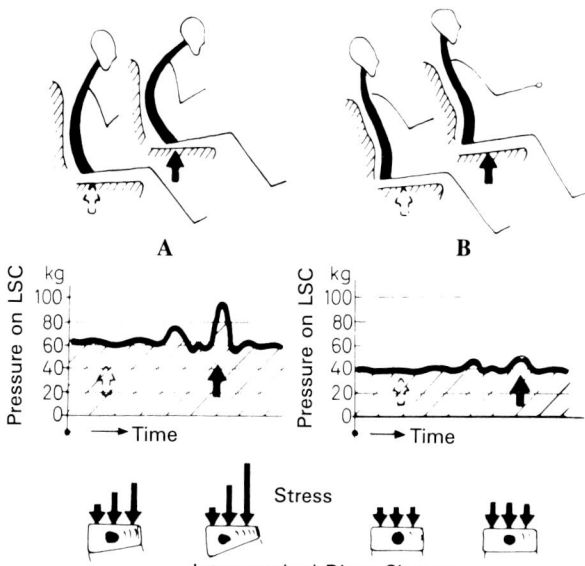

Fig. 7-25 Accelerograms indicating strain placed on the lumbar spinal column by slight impacts during incorrect (*left*) and correct (*right*) sitting posture in vehicles.

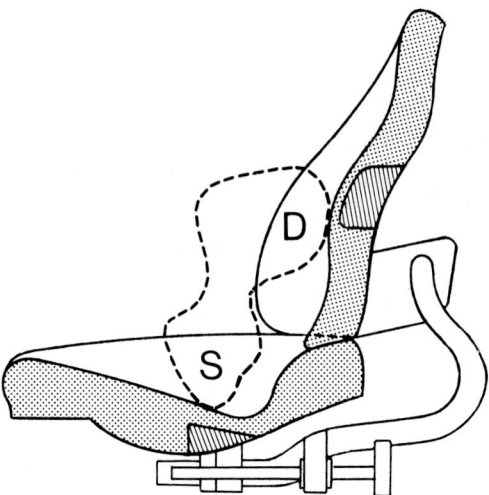

Fig. 7-26 Model of a car seat, which enables a stable pelvic impact between the ischial tuberosities and iliac crests. The sitting surface-back rest angle is 105°.

Beck (1974) developed a "dynamic car seat" made up of three narrow, horizontal, individually inflatable cushions for the lumbar lordosis: Ia, b, c. At the height of each shoulder there is a cushion: II a, b. Cushion III is located along the thoracic spinal column. Instead of the present diagonal belt, a seat belt and a shoulder belt are used. Persons testing this seat design reported less fatigue and a comfortable feeling caused by the slight cradling of the back, even after prolonged driving times. Those with minimal intervertebral disc damages considered the dynamic car seat to be beneficial. It is questionable, however, whether this somewhat complex construction will be adopted by automobile manufacturers and whether the complicated operation will be accepted by the users.

During the transport of sick persons, in ambulances, the transmission of vibrations of more than 1 Hz, which exceeds the vibrations in a car (0.5–0.8 Hz), cannot be avoided. The vibrations affect the lying person in various directions and result in "very high" strain (Dupuis et al. 1972). Frequencies between 20–50 Hz were found in all levels, especially in the spinal column longitudinal axis. Additional frequencies of 3–4 Hz were found in the chest-back axis. The permissible exposure times for such transport is less than 1 hour on an uneven road surface even for a healthy person; on concrete roads the time limit is 1.5 hours. Because the sick and injured are much more susceptible to damage than healthy persons, long driving times

inclination of the back rest with an average angle of 105° is necessary. Most cars enable the angle of inclination to be adjusted to meet the rider's perception of comfort.

A sitting posture that would relieve back strain was suggested by Kraemer (1973) for driving, as well as for watching television. The individual inclines at an angle of 135°, and the head is lifted with a neck cushion by 10° (Fig. 7-29). However, this position requires a longer back rest. Beck recommends the same rest position for pilot seats.

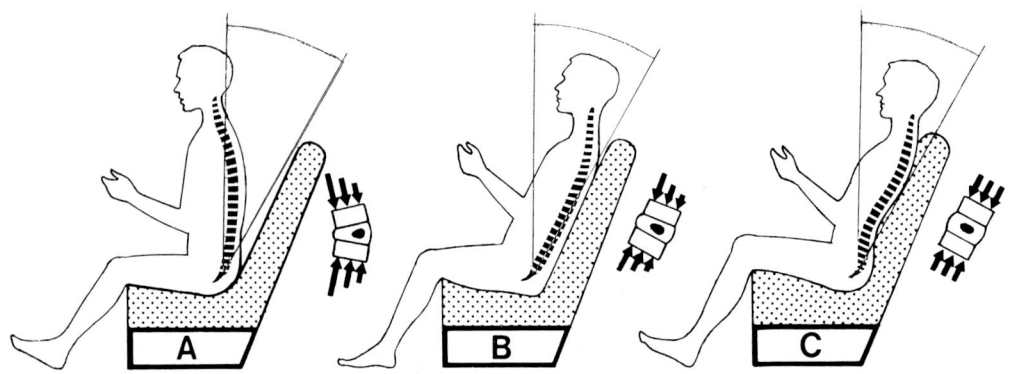

Fig. 7-27 Pressure conditions at the lumbar spinal column in the car seat. (**A**), In an anteflexed posture of the trunk excessive pressure is placed on the anterior portions of the intervertebral discs. (**B**), Resting of the back at the unshaped smooth back rest decreases the incorrect frontal strain only insignificantly. (**C**), A back rest that is adapted to support the lumbar lordosis and to provide sufficient room for the pelvis results in an even distribution of pressure.

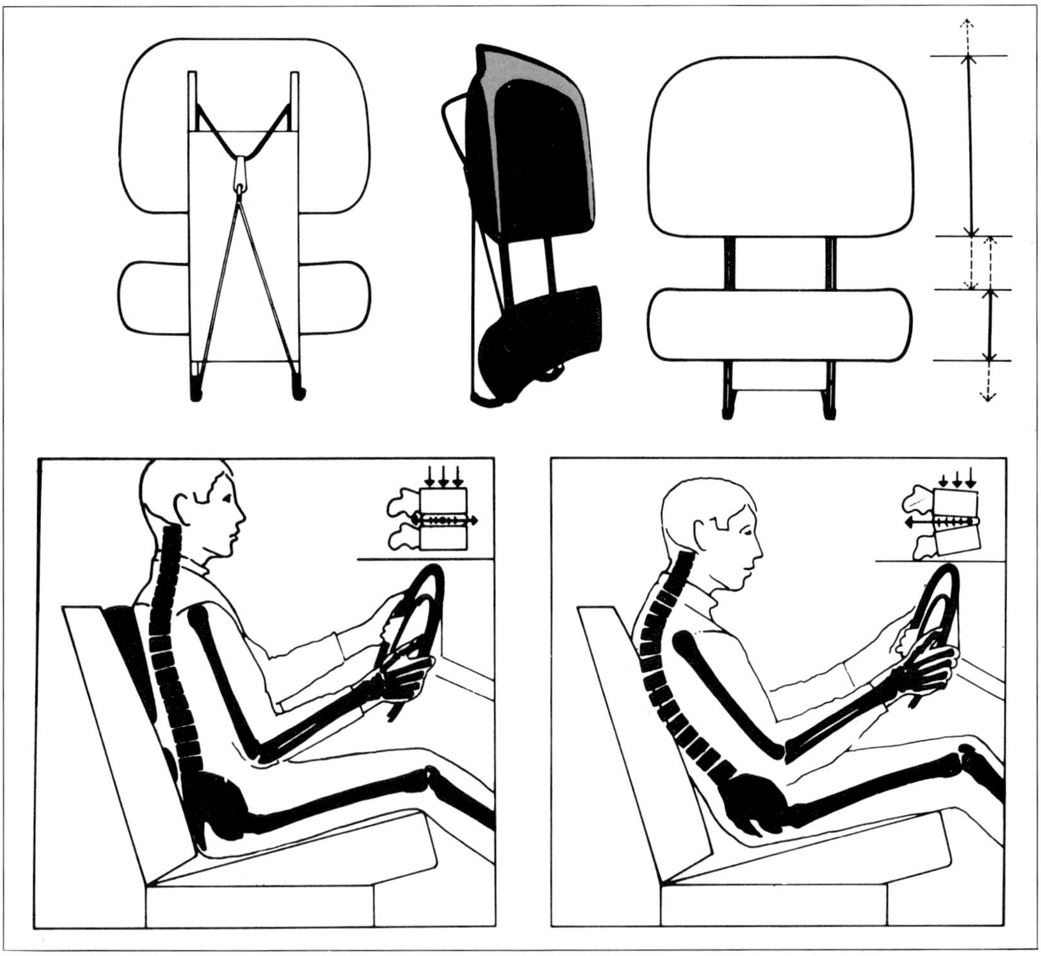

Fig. 7-28 Individually adjustable back rest for a car seat. It is made up of two adjustable cushions. The upper support receives the thoracic kyphosis and therefore supports the cervical spinal column. The lower support prevents the kyphotic changing of the lumbar spinal column section. This back rest could be mounted in any type of vehicle. The lower picture shows the spinal column of a driver in a corrected (*left*) and uncorrected posture (*right*) [from Rizzi (1969)].

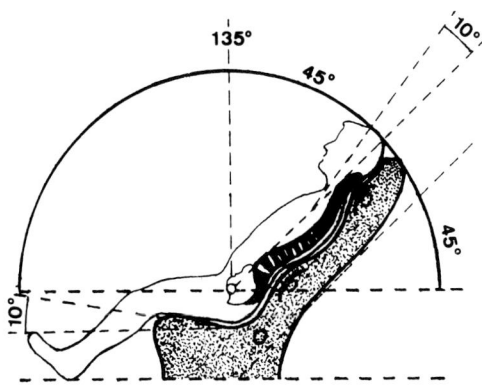

Fig. 7-29 Sitting posture that relieves back strain.

should be avoided. Instead transport by helicopter is recommended which causes 90% less vibration (Dupuis et al 1972).

7.3.7.5 Buses

Although the seat design in modern buses has been improved in recent years, even on good driving surfaces, sinus-shaped vibrations still penetrate from the seat and are transmitted via the spinal column. They are a significant factor in the development of kinetoses. Bumpy road surfaces and sudden braking and stopping cause additional stochastic alternating influences in passengers; these vibrations may reach the spinal column via the feet even in standing passengers. Vibrations that travel horizontally to the spinal column axis from the back rest or rotation influences from driving quickly around curves also occur. When those vibrations stress an already damaged spinal column, they may cause pain. In conjunction with the numerous other negative influences of daily life—prolonged car rides, lack of exercise, bad sitting posture—the vibrations of bus rides may exceed the permissible limit and may therefore aggravate age-related wear and pre-existing latent spinal column damages.

7.3.7.6 Trains

The syndrome of railway spine was observed during the early days of the railroad and was described as "disease after long railroad journeys" as early as 1896 (Kocher 1896). It was the first observation of intervertebral disc-generated back pain caused by prolonged vibrations.

Although the train ride today is much smoother than in the past, even modern trains do not operate completely free of vibrations. It has not yet been systematically established whether those vibrations reach the spinal column with high-oscillation amplitudes and energies from the seat or from the back rest and whether alternating stochastic forces have serious effects. Nor is it known how frequently kinetoses are caused by modern trains. The impact of new seat designs in reducing vibration stress must be studied further.

As in an ambulance, the passengers lying down in the sleeper compartment are exposed to sinus oscillations in the longitudinal body axis (z-axis), in the lateral direction (y-axis), and, frequently combined with impacts, in the back-chest direction (x-axis). Although data exist about the impact of sick transport, no such information is available about the effect of body position in regard to the direction of motion and the distance from the axes (upper bunk, lower bunk).

7.3.7.7 Airplanes and Helicopters

As long as the engines are running, vibrations affect flight passengers. During long flights, the passenger also suffers from lack of exercise, and vibrations frequently reach the spinal column as he or she is sitting in a forced posture with tense muscles. The narrow seats and small space between rows result in a twisted sitting posture. The lower back becomes stiff and painful for many passengers.

Improved seat design and more foot room can substantially reduce back strain. It has been reported that after such modifications in one airline, the cockpit crew achieved an 85% decrease in sitting-related susceptibility to back problems. The same reduction should be achieved for the airline passenger.

In helicopters that are used for sick transport, vibrations penetrate the spinal column from several directions. However, they are 90% lower than in an ambulance. The vibration stress varies according to the placement of the stretcher in the helicopter. Dupuis and Hartung (1966) determined that the middle one was subject to the lowest vibration—1 Hz. The vibration effect on the top one was 1.5 Hz and on the bottom one 1.34 Hz. On all three stretchers, the patients were least affected by vibrations in the rump area. The vibrations increased somewhat toward the shoulder and head along the spinal column and were largest at the heels and abdomen.

The vibration frequency of helicopters is between 3–6 Hz, a resonance range that has an especially detrimental effect on the spinal column. If there are previous damages—chondrosis disci, spondylosis deformans, intervertebral osteochondrosis, arthroses of the intervertebral articulations, or even unstable intervertebral motor segments—a special susceptibility to damage caused by vibrations must be feared. Therefore, a thorough physical examination should be conducted before pilot training is started, especially for helicopter pilots. In helicopters, vibrations directly penetrate from the seat to the spinal column in an axial direction, whereas jet pilots are much less affected by such seriously damaging vibrations (Fischer et al. 1980). The detrimental effect of helicopter vibrations is borne out by Fischer's findings that spondyloses and osteochondroses of the lumbar spinal column of the helicopter pilot tend to be aggravated after 1500 to 3000 flying hours. The special effect of the low-frequency vibrations is responsible for this aggravation and for the increasing lumbalgias.

7.3.7.8 Motorboats and Ships

The self-oscillations originating from propulsion engines have been decreased by modern structural and stabilizing measures, but have not been completely banished (Goethe 1976; Zorn 1973). Boat passengers are continuously subjected to hardly perceptible, fine, sinus-shaped total-body vibrations. In addition, large, irregular vibrations and occasional, uncoordinated sudden impacts, especially during the rolling of a ship, occur. Vibration and oscillation mixtures, including angular and arched accelerations and rotation oscillations, penetrate through the contact area of the feet or from the seat surface. They are then transmitted via the spinal column to the head. The head is held steady by unconsciously tensed neck muscles (reflex). Over a long period of time, the muscles tire.

The vibrations generated by the propulsion engines of the large passenger ships proceed vertically and gradually decrease in the upper decks. However, horizontal vibrations increase as they travel upward. In reports from 1978 and 1979, Goethe et al. showed that vibrations may be greater during sitting than during standing. However, when lying on the bunk the vertical acceleration under 10 Hz is greater than on the floor.

Despite this vibration stress, sea travel does not cause damage to the healthy spinal columns of adolescents or adult boat passengers. However, some passengers on long sea voyages who have previously damaged spinal columns may experience lower back and head-neck pain. The well-known sea sickness frequently is quite disabling for people afflicted with spinal column problems, depending on the type of ship and weather conditions.

7.3.8 Partial Body Vibrations

Partial body vibrations are transmitted through vibrating, hand-operated tools (compressed air tools or similar vibrating devices) over the hand-arm system to the cervical spinal column (see section 5.3). They are not as harmless as frequently assumed, but may damage bones, joints, blood vessels, and nerves when these devices are used on a prolonged basis at work and at home. In persons susceptible to kinetoses, problems often occur even after working with hand-operated vibrating tools for a short time. These problems are a sign to take a break and to start again only after a relaxing break!

7.3.9 Lack of Exercise

The mobile human being has been "immobilized" since the end of the last century. The share of human motion energy in the total energy yield since 1870 has decreased from about 90% to less than 1% (Murarov and Kiew 1978). Technical devices have replaced human energy to a degree not encountered since the transition from nomad to farmer. The continuous lack of exercise directly threatens many organs and organ systems of the body.

7.3.9.1 Confinement to Bed

Hormone disorders frequently cause painful osteoporoses, primarily at the spinal skeleton (see section 5.3). The early institution of therapy and its diligent application are essential. Long-term drug therapy (mostly with sodium fluoride) described by Jesserer in many publications from 1950 to 1982 must be combined with active and passive treatment of back muscles as far as pain allows. Exercise and improved circulation in the muscles also increase the blood supply to the vertebral bones and simultaneously support the metabolism of the intervertebral discs that are threatened by confinement to bed.

A flat, supine position is very relaxing to the spinal column, uses the smallest amount of energy and relaxes tense muscles and ligaments. Rest during the night regulates the fluid content of the intervertebral disc. However, prolonged bedrest is damaging to the skeleton because it may result in an inactivity osteoporosis. In addition, the impaired biochemical balance in the intervertebral disc fluid and the resulting damages in the fibers may result in significant structural changes (see section 2.3).

Continued bedrest always has an aggravating effect on osteoporosis as shown by increased pain and back stiffness. Treatment of a serious and very painful osteoporosis of the spinal column therefore requires, in addition to drug therapy especially when vertebral body fusions have already occurred, rest in a well-fitting cast. Soon, passive treatments of the longissimus muscles should begin. As soon as the decrease of pain permits, a gradual physiotherapy regimen is added. Chirotherapy is not recommended. Rotation and sitting in bed need to be gradually increased but not to the point of causing pain. The experienced physician must decide on a case-by-case basis whether a lightly supporting corset should be used.

Because back pain and the desire of the patient for bedrest often are based on an initially overlooked psychological component, it is necessary to determine the actual physical damage at the spinal column as clearly as possible. Only then may the psychological and somatic aspect of pain be treated expertly. If not, an invalid syndrome may develop in which the patient feels that prolonged bed rest is essential to his or her well-being.

7.3.9.2 Sitting

Sitting, no matter in which of the many positions it is performed, is and remains the worst posture for the human body. It always results in decreased exercise for the spinal column and increased stress with simultaneous, more or less vertical prolonged pressure. Although stress tolerances are not exceeded during sitting and even prolonged sitting does not result in bone damage or any direct destructive effect on the structure of the intervertebral disc, the disc metabolism is decreased in all sitting postures. This decrease seriously impairs the viability of the intervertebral disc. Long and frequent sitting disrupts the biochemical balance in the fluid metabolism, which eventually results in irreversible damage. Often, neck-shoulder-arm pain and chronic lumbago are aggravated by incorrect sitting habits in back-damaging chairs.

When a person first feels back pain and especially when lower lumbar back pain and stiffness occur on arising from modern sitting furniture, it is necessary to compensate for prolonged sitting by engaging in exercise.

7.3.10 Additional Exogenous Influences

To date, no valid studies have been conducted to determine whether cold or heat results in spinal column damage or to assess the alternating effects of cold and heat. Cold changes the water metabolism in the bradytrophic tissues (intervertebral discs) because heat from the deeper body layers (eg, from the back muscles) is distributed to the skin and evaporates. As long as cold exposure occurs only occasionally in daily life, it will have little effect. However, if there is previous damage at the spinal column, such as intervertebral chondrosis or intervertebral osteochondrosis, the cold may one day trigger lumbar back pain and neck-shoulder-arm pain. Recurrences of pain are warning signs for an examination of the spinal column and for instituting therapy. The physician should not be content with the unspecific diagnosis of rheumatism or muscular rheumatism (see section 4.7). The differentiation between inflammatory rheumatic diseases and chronic degenerative articular diseases is an important one (Sewering 1980). Frequent cold-related back pain may indicate a beginning Bechterew's syndrome.

Being soaked in connection with hypothermia, as well as a change between heat and cold, may evoke pain when there is previously existing damage in the area of the intervertebral disc. The pain draws attention to the basic problem in the spinal column and should always be a new reason for suitable behavior and medical treatment.

A large number of chemical substances damage the bone system through prolonged and excessive absorption into the body. These substances include fluoride, lead, phosphorus, cadmium, vinyl chloride, polyvinyl chloride, and chemical warfare agents (see section 4.7).

In addition to chemical substances, damages in the central axial organ are often caused by infections, inflammatory rheumatism, metabolic changes, injuries, surgery and its consequences, and primary tumors or metastases.

7.3.11 The Spinal Column in Old Age

Just as the spinal column is already characterized by the neglects of youth at the beginning of adulthood, the spinal column of the aging person is shaped by additional difficulties and problems encountered in the course of several decades of middle age.

Every person has both a chronological age and a biological age, which may differ greatly. The spinal column also has its own age determined by both environment and genetic foundations in a varying and complex manner. After all, each constitutional type (pycnic, asthenic, etc.) has distinct differences in the support and motor system that are visible even to the casual observer.

Successful prevention of age-related problems of the spinal column must begin in youth with a program of controlled movement and exertion. With progressive age, stress and relaxation for the spinal column must be brought into balance suitable for the individual's physical condition and age. The main concern for older persons is to avoid sitting whenever possible. Walking and hiking should be engaged in, as the aging person continues to live an active daily life and do leisure activities that benefit the mind and body.

7.3.11.1 Aging Disorders of the Spinal Column

The spinal column is affected by changes dating back to the embryonic period and early youth, as well as from later years, which are sometimes visible externally but are more frequently latent and only recognizable on roentgenograms. These damages vary in their severity and disabling nature. Some do not cause problems, some cause frequent problems, and some cause premature disability.

Increasing damage to the soft tissue, especially to the intervertebral discs, is the chief cause of spinal column disorders in later years. The most frequent disorders—spondylosis deformans, intervertebral chondrosis, and intervertebral osteochondrosis—cause the functionally impaired intervertebral motor segment, the intervertebral insufficiency described in Chapter 4. These disorders cause increasing pain for the aging person during both static and dynamic exertion. If stiffness develops in the affected segment through connective tissue or bony ankylosis, the pain recedes while mobility is lost. The "stiff senile back" develops, which endures static stress but which impedes mobility. Damages in the anterior portions of the intervertebral discs, increasing stiffness, and an increasingly painful curvature characterize the typical syndrome of senile kyphosis (see section 4.4).

The most prevalent disorder in the spinal skeleton is osteoporosis. In older age, senile osteoporosis frequently causes intense pain with fusion of vertebral bodies and hump back development in the middle section of the thoracic spinal column. The curvature vertex of senile kyphosis sits somewhat higher.

The arthrosis of the vertebral arch articulations may appear as an isolated syndrome, but more frequently accompanies wear and chondrosis of the intervertebral disc tissue in the same intervertebral motor segment. Serious, painful, and mobility-restricting problems may also be caused by arthroses of the uncovertebral articulations of the cervical spinal column and the sacroiliac, the head, and vertebrocostal articulations. Too frequently the diagnosis is not specifically confirmed, rendering the therapy less effective.

Even if there is a premature pronounced disability due to spinal column damage, it is rarely necessary to regard the condition of the spine a reason for physical inactivity in daily life or to induce further damage by an increased lack of exercise (sitting!). The remaining static and dynamic stress resistance should be maintained through muscle exertion and, in as far as the physical condition allows, should be improved through self-rehabilitation measures prescribed and monitored by the physician.

The aging of the spinal column begins in the fourth decade of life, mostly in the rather sluggishly nourished tissues. Depending on damages sustained in the growth period, the intervertebral discs are affected more or less by the aging process. The severity of the painful pathological conditions is determined primarily by the number of affected intervertebral motor segments. The condition of the spinal column is a major factor determining the individual's functional capacity.

7.3.12 Prophylactic Measures

7.3.12.1 Introduction

Prevention is the initial phase and follow-up is the concluding phase of medical care and treatment. Unfortunately, well-meant medical advice is not always implemented conscientiously, and follow-up care is not often pursued. The lack of a will to be healthy, coupled with an insufficient understanding of the necessity of self-help, is a barrier to the patient's cooperation in care. It is only possible to change this passive behavior if parents, teachers, and health care professionals work much more forcibly and convincingly than in the past to increase the health motivation of those with spinal column damage.

The skyrocketing costs of today's highly sophisticated medical care are forcing a reexamination of priorities. Rather than giving costly treatment for chronic diseases that could be avoided, resources should be directed toward improved health promotion. Yet, the eradication of smallpox was simple compared to the effort needed to eliminate the diseases of civilization, including chronic damage to the spinal column. Insufficiencies of the support and motor system, especially in the area of the spine, are tangible indications that the human ecosystem is no longer biologically balanced. This imbalance is expressed in the damages of the bradytrophic tissues of the intervertebral motor segment.

"Prophylaxis is better than healing." This old, but little-heeded proverb is particularly apt for the spinal column. Yet, maintaining the wellbeing of the spine is not easy. Prophylactic measures must be implemented continuously from early childhood on. As the individual matures, he or she must assume more and more responsibility for personal health maintenance. This responsibility requires the understanding that health risks are often caused by one's own behavior.

Many adolescents in particular have no understanding of the health risks posed by their behavior. They neglect their body posture and sit too much. Many ignore their increasing body fat and the decline of their muscle strength. They want to "enjoy" fully the achievements of civilization, from the automobile to television. Thus they avoid active participation in maintaining their health and take refuge when problems occur in passive measures, such as occasional massages, pills, injections, etc.

7.3.12.2 Individual Prophylactic Measures

The maintenance of a mobile and stress-resistant spinal column depends on the care—sensible exertion—of those muscles serving the spinal column. The entire static-dynamic musculoligamentous corset serving the spinal column has the task not only of moving the trunk but also controlling and stabilizing the spinal column in all postures.

Intervertebral disc wear, intervertebral osteochondrosis, and arthrosis in vertebral arch articulations cause functional insufficiency of the muscles and slacken the intervertebral motor segment. They cause muscles and ligaments to be used far more than normal until they become fatigued and enter a state of painful prolonged myogelosis that alternates with slackening. Thus, the musculoligamentous corset slows in performing the task of controlling the motion of the spinal column and thereby absorbing damaging external influences.

Therefore, the maintenance of healthy muscles must begin in early childhood. Healthy muscles are one of the most important defenses against the damaging influences of daily life.

Recurring fatigue and tension—with and without pain—of the muscles are the first serious warning signs of incipient damage to the spinal column. The physician must make clear the responsibility of the individual to undertake prophylactic measures in order to prevent the chronic aggravation of these symptoms. A change in the individual's life-style, replacing inactive leisure hours with muscle-strengthening activity, is essential. The commonly dispensed medical advice of "hot air and massage" is a necessary passive treatment of insufficient back muscles. However, only active (physiotherapeutically controlled) movement exercises are able to re-establish muscular strength. Therefore, only the combination of passive and active therapy is sensible. It is the physician's task to find combinations of therapy and prophylactic measures and to provide repeated reinforcement to the patient for engaging in those measures. The formation of self-help groups for back sufferers should be considered.

Prophylaxis should have these components:

- Consciously promoted participation in leisure-time sports activities according to one's capabilities and physical possibilities
- Hiking
- Jogging, including the exercises suggested along the jogging course
- Domestic sitting hygiene with the help of adapted chairs and tables
- Reading or watching television in an abdominal position
- Alternating use of a desk chair and standing desk and possibly a standing seat or pendulum chair
- Having regular exercise breaks at work or at home
- Doing break-time exercises at school
- Having exercise breaks during long rides in vibrating motor vehicles and during long bike tours
- Avoiding unnecessary motorcycle rides
- Reducing the use of vibrating vehicles

Exhibit 7-1 Exercise Break (Schoberth 1979)

Initial Position: Upright Sitting

Exercise 1: Walk in place while lifting toes from floor, alternating between right and left.

Exercise 2: From the same sitting position, stretch the legs forward, alternating between left and right, and bring them back.

Exercise 3: Lift knee from hip joints, alternating between right and left.

Exercise 4: Support both hands on seat and lift rump until it is completely removed from seat surface and back is slightly arched.

Exercise 5: Tilt the pelvis forward and backward during firm sitting, bounce back into a swayback, and arch back in subsequent alternations.

Exercise 6: Stretch arms out forward and angled. Lift and release rump from surface as in horseback riding.

Exercise 7: Circle the trunk to the right and left from an upright sitting position as if searching the ground for an object while flexing and extending the trunk.

Exercise 8: Relax by leaning backward. Arms hang relaxed, and muscles relax.

Exercise 9: Pull opposing shoulders forward and backward, alternating between right and left.

Exercise 10: Lift and release shoulders to the ear and back, first simultaneously and then alternating.

Exercise 11: Shadow box during sitting with the open hand. The muscles remain relaxed throughout. Additional relaxation is achieved by flinging the arms.

Exercise 12: Circle the head from upper right to lower left and in reverse, possibly also in a simple circle.

Exercise 13: Stretch arms out forward with elbows straight. Twist strongly from shoulder joints until the end point of movement.

Exercise 14: Stretch arms out forward with elbows in a right angle. Lower arms are vertical. Change rapidly the twisting of lower arms, ie, alternating between pronation and supination.

Exercise 15: As if playing a piano, move the relaxed fingers on a table top as preparation for return to work.

Implementing a fixed, standard exercise program at the workplace that is uniform for all employees is destined to fail. Only if the individual requirements of each employee are considered will the desired effect be realized. What is important is not the sequence of particular exercises but rather that breaks be built into the workday, even if employees only get up and walk about during these breaks. The foremost goal of all efforts is to make work more bearable for the individual, especially since the external circumstances often cannot be significantly changed.

When taking a long ride in a motor vehicle, it is important to take an exercise break every 1–2 hours. The suggested break exercises are simple. Relaxing exercises for the stiff neck and back muscles are especially necessary. For the tense muscles of the shoulder girdle, head rolls, shoulder rolls, arm movements, trunk flexions, and twisting to all sides are suitable. Jogging in place or back and forth over a 100-meter distance should be done. In accordance with the exercise rhythm a deep inhalation and exhalation pattern is important, which benefits the cardiovascular function. It would be wrong to abandon the car just to subject muscles that are already tense to additional sitting in restaurants or at home.

It is likely that quite a few professional truck-drivers or drivers of heavy motorized work vehicles, such as earth-moving equipment, regard car riding like sitting on a comfortable swing. However, the additional vibrations from riding in a car potentiate the damaging vibrations at work. Therefore, professional drivers should have regular exercise breaks.

Well-developed trunk muscles, especially in the area of the back, support the spinal column better, thereby decreasing the impact-related torsion and sharp flexion of the spinal column. Every muscle can be trained in a sensible, regular, leisure-time athletic activity and can serve as a defense against stresses. However, high-performance sports that increase wear because of stochastic impacts—extreme types of floor exercises, platform diving—are not suitable means of training muscles.

The body's center of gravity moves forward as the individual gains weight. This causes the back muscles to be continuously overstretched and to tire easily, exacerbating previously existing damages of the intervertebral disc. Weight loss is urgently recommended in order to retard the aggravation of back pain generated by the overstressed spinal column.

An important element of a personal prophylaxis program is the frequent interruption of static muscle strain (sitting, standing) by a dynamic exertion phase for the back muscles, such as walking to and from work. Walking up and down stairs at home and at work should also become a habit for the maintenance of the well-being of the spinal column muscles, as well as for cardiovascular training. Special attention should be paid to motion during social functions. Dancing has the effect of a dynamic exercise break for the back muscles after prolonged sitting. Cocktail parties should be used as a reason for walking about.

7.3.12.3 Technical Improvements

In recent years, sitting furniture has been redesigned to support and protect the spinal column. These innovative designs were first introduced in offices, but are as indispensable in the home (Figs. 7-30 and 7-31). The furniture industry has the responsibility to continue to apply the well-founded suggestions of ergonomic experts to the design of furniture.

The height of dining tables and desks matching the chairs needs to be adapted to the height increase of the spinal column that has been observed for the past several decades. Chair design must incorporate leg length and pelvic inclination considerations as well.

The usual built-in or portable chairs in conference or lecture rooms, theaters, concert halls, and restaurants are almost never adapted to the back. Even in newer facilities, elaborate seats with ear phone connections, folding tables, and reading lamps still lack a height-adjustable cushion for the lumbar lordosis. Probably because of space limitations, the fixed or folding seat surface is frequently too short in most facilities, and the space between rows leaves too little space for long thighs. Therefore, the sitting posture of the torso is forced to curve abnormally, similar to the situation in many commercial airplanes.

Effects of Daily Life on the Spinal Column   229

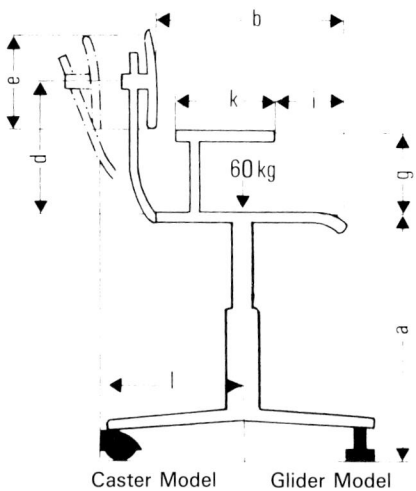

Fig. 7-30 Height-adjustable office chair with arm rests and adjustable back rest. Five legs prevent the chair from tipping and may be equipped with casters or gliders. Such a chair can also be used for work in the household or at the desk.

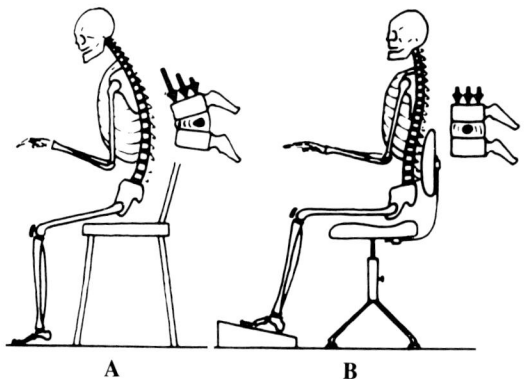

Fig. 7-31 Comparison of intervertebral disc stress in the lumbar spinal column during anteflexed sitting in an ordinary kitchen chair (*left*) and a back-supporting office chair (*right*).

Motor vehicle seats adapted to the spinal column can substantially reduce vibrations from the outside or the ones generated by the vehicle itself. However, these seats are still subject to simultaneous vibrations. Each new seat design must be tested to see how the vibrations penetrate over the seat, back rest, and operation levers into the spinal column; which transmission paths they use; and how they threaten the intervertebral discs. It also must take into account the changing body angles as arms and legs are used to drive and steer the vehicle.

Parents and educators must serve as advocates for their children's physical well-being by seeing that enough gymnastic and sport classes are provided and that they emphasize those exercises that increase the mobility of the spinal column and strengthen the back muscles. In addition, a regular exercise break should be scheduled in the schoolday. They should urge that ergometrically designed sitting and writing furniture be used.

7.4 TREATMENT AND REHABILITATION

7.4.1 Conservative Treatment

Conservative treatments are the procedures of choice for the greatest portion of back problems.

Improved physical examination methods and radiodiagnostic procedures make possible the accurate diagnosis of almost all disorders in the area of the spinal column. However, it is not always immediately possible to establish a clear diagnosis for complaints of recurring back problems. Incorrect static postures and excessive stresses on the central column may significantly affect the musculoligamentous corset of the spinal column, as well as the corresponding muscle tracts. The fatigued back responds with spastic painful stiffness. In such cases the physician must treat the affected muscles accordingly and must educate the patient about the possibilities of self-help and individual prophylactic measures.

If one or even several intervertebral motor segments are damaged, specific conservative treatment measures are required. However, neither the re-establishment of the normal anatomic and biomechanical conditions nor return to full functional capacity is possible.

The body may adapt to this damage in order to relieve pain and to achieve a certain stability, but without being able to attain anatomical regeneration. Thus, the initially cartilaginous and gradually ossifying vertebral body spurs bridge the slackened intervertebral space and stop the hypermobility in the segment with taut, bony clamping (Figs. 4-42 to 4-44). This clamping improves quite a few painful spondylogenic consequences or even completely eliminates them. The ingrowth of connective tissue fibers may stabilize pathological conditions of the instable intervertebral disc structure. Yet, even in those cases no functional intervertebral disc tissue develops, but rather intervertebral ankylosis, which represents the counterpart to the hypermobile articulation in intervertebral insufficiency, occurs. Such processes develop very slowly, often over years. Misunderstanding or impatience of the patient or misdiagnosis frequently results in therapeutic measures that counteract the natural healing process. Therefore, only few patients experience the inherent healing tendency of their body, which would result in intervertebral immobility.

In the case of some types of damage, the body possesses formerly almost unknown healing powers. For instance, the nerve pressure developing from a prolapsed disc (see section 4.6) may disappear when the prolapsed intervertebral disc tissue carves a new bed into the vertebral body back wall and when the nerve root itself moves into a newly formed bone bed (Fig. 7-32). This and similar self-healing processes reduce or eliminate pain by building a new static and functional balance of the affected spinal column section. However, it is accompanied by decreased mobility or complete stiffness.

Because of the interdependence of motion possibilities in the anterior and posterior portion of the intervertebral segment, therapy must consider both functional partners—the intervertebral disc and vertebral arch joint—although it is directed primarily to one or the other.

The question surfaces again and again to how to treat instable intervertebral motor segments that result, because of slight mechanical additional impulses (lifting, bending, rotating, prolonged postures, etc), in strong spondylogenic consequences, such as rotation stiffness with myogelosis, and radiating pain. Because healing of the pathological processes in the segment with restoration of the former anatomic form and normal function cannot be achieved, the treating physician must find different ways to eliminate the constantly recurring spondylogenic pain attacks in such patients. The simplest procedure is to avoid mechanical impulses that displace, rotate, or block the affected segment (see section 3.4). Many patients complain about morning pain or stiffness in the spinal column or nocturnal paresthesia in the neck and arms, a torturing affliction. A hard and flat mattress, no pillow (which places the cervical spinal column in a damaging position), and compensating, relaxing morning exercise are effective.

If motorcycle riding causes lumbago attacks or if prolonged sitting behind the steering wheel of a car or at the computer acts as an additional impulse for head-neck-arm pain, the physician must use all of his or her persuasive powers to encourage the patient to avoid or restrict these "additional impulses." The negative, external influences and body postures should be interrupted as often as possible and in regular intervals. The motorcyclist or car driver should take a break and relax the total body by walking about, swinging the arms, rolling the head, doing trunk flexions, and jogging for several hundred meters. Break-time exercises at school, at work,

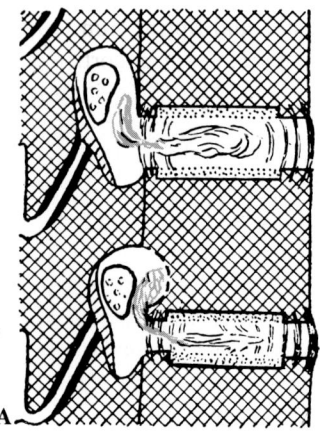
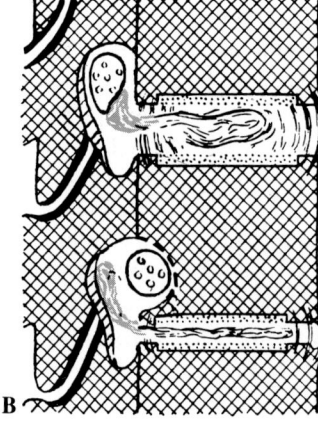

Fig. 7-32 (**A**), "Self-healing" of radicular irritation. Prolapse moves aside [from Burns & Young (1947)]. (**B**), Self-healing by evasion of the root [from Duus & Kahlau (1950)].

or in daily life relax the tense, unilaterally overstrained muscles and interrupt the pathological reflex sequences.

Conservative therapy is based on two principles. First, the basic cause of all problems—the slackened segment with its incorrect displacement and rotation possibilities that lead, in conjunction with additional impulses, from pathological disposition to the spondylogenic symptom—must be prevented from worsening so that its pathogenic effect is as little as possible. This treatment objective is achieved by treating the respective muscles. Chronically tense muscle groups must be relaxed, weakened muscles must be strengthened, and muscles incorrectly stressed because of incorrect spinal column curvature, scoliosis, or the like must be brought to proper function.

The second objective is to calm the overirritated (sensitive, motor, or vegetative) nerve so that any small irritation by pressure or traction will not immediately actuate the pathological reflex sequence with its inevitable consequences—myogelosis, pain, vegetative damages, and the like. Sometimes, this objective is achieved by strengthening the muscles. The restored muscle balance is able to absorb many additional impulses successfully so that such serious influences as torsion or displacement no longer affect the damaged segment. The irritated nerve may also be freed from its constriction by temporary traction (eg, Glisson sling or other extension procedures) or be calmed by the application of an anesthetic liquid at the location where it is subjected to constant or repeated pressure.

Many spas and health clubs advertise their treatment for spinal column disorders, articular problems, rheumatism, gynecological diseases, and many other ailments. However, often the treatments are given without any medical examination and are ineffective.

7.4.1.1 Drug Therapy and Diet

The impaired spinal column has been treated with drugs that are either swallowed, rubbed in, or absorbed transcutaneously since ancient times. In fact, some drugs used centuries ago are still part of today's armamentarium. Although new medications continue to be developed, no drug has yet been proven to result in true healing of the main cause of spinal column problems—the damages in intervertebral discs and articulations of the spinal column—or restoration of healthy anatomic structures to their full performance capacity.

Nevertheless, it is impossible to abandon drug therapy. If dosed accurately and given at the correct time, drug therapy can reduce pain and muscular and ligamentous tension and may eliminate spasms. Drugs are also able to alleviate spondylogenic symptoms and to further the beneficial effect of physical therapy and chiropractic manipulations. However, if incorrectly used, a drug may counteract the accompanying physical therapy.

Drug therapy may be a supportive measure in the systematic treatment of acute intervertebral disc prolapse (Joerg 1982). Surgery should be performed only after conservative therapy has proven to be unsuccessful, unless severe pain or paralysis develops as an unexpected initial symptom of the prolapse.

Drug therapy is an indispensable component of treatment for osteoporosis, which is the most prevalent disease of the skeletal system. The acute collapse of vertebral bodies at the thoracic spinal column results in wedged vertebrae, and collapse at the lumbar spinal column results in fish vertebrae. The resulting pain, which is often quite great, requires injection treatment at the location of pain and at the side walls of the affected vertebral bodies. Sodium fluoride is an important component of long-term therapy (Dambacher 1979; Jesserer et al 1975; Krokowski 1976). In addition, therapy also includes a range of physical measures (Bergsmann and Eder 1982; Kuester and Springorum 1980). Under no circumstances should cortisone be used because it exacerbates the osteoporotic symptoms.

The pain of osteoporosis of the vertebral skeleton results in a lack of movement and in confinement to bed. Unfortunately, a vicious cycle develops in which the bed rest further aggravates the osteoporosis. It can only be broken if the muscle atrophy can be counteracted by massages, bath treatments, and physiotherapy, in addition to palliative injections. The prescriptions of braces or firm corsets should be avoided.

A cast for the back may be of advantage during painful periods, but only for nightly rest. Although dietary treatment for damage at the intervertebral discs does not promise success, it is indispensable for osteoporosis.

7.4.1.2 Manual Medicine, Chiropractic, Extension Methods

Diligently chosen manipulations, but also forcefully attacking, pressuring, or extending methods to treat disorders at the spinal column, have been part of folk medicine for centuries. In Europe, manual therapeutic procedures with varied names—chiropractic, osteopathy, manipulation therapy—have been regarded as the domain of laypeople and occasionally medical pariahs.

However, after World War II, such forms of therapy have gained increasing acceptance by the medical community. Physicians using chiropractic techniques have become more involved in basic research into the spinal column, and researchers have become more open to exploring questions resulting from practice. As a result, many misconceptions about manual medicine have been eliminated in the past decade.

The International Federation for Manual Medicine (FIMM) created the Zürich Convention in 1983, which enumerates these important principles of manual medicine:

- Manual medicine deals with physiology and pathophysiology of functional impairments in the support and motor system.
- It comprises all diagnostic and therapeutic techniques at the spinal column and joints of the extremities that serve to uncover, eliminate, as well as prevent these impairments.
- Manual-medical therapy comprises manual treatment techniques that work to eliminate reversible functional impairments at the spinal column and extremities, as well as their local, regional, and reflexive effects.
- The following techniques are presently used: soft tissue techniques, mobilization techniques, and manipulation techniques—therapeutic measures at one or more joints that exceed the physiological limit but do not exceed the anatomical limit.

The reversible functional impairment of the intervertebral motor segment treated with manual medicine is called a segmental or peripheral articular dysfunction. It may be caused mechanically and/or as a reflex.

Manipulative therapy is effective in selected cases of spinal column-related disorders (Fig. 7-33). Various explanations are given for its mode of action, including the "thrust into the autonomic nervous system," manual shock on the

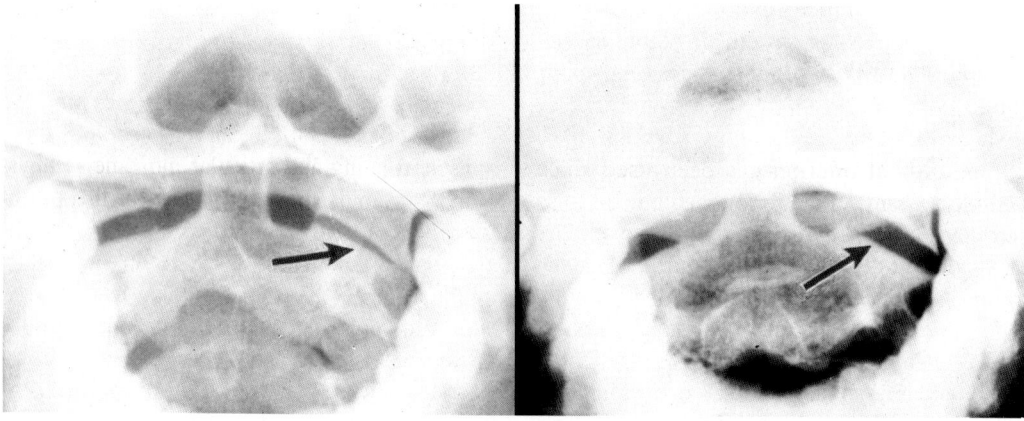

Fig. 7-33 Roentgenogram of the superior cervical spinal column through the open mouth in a 14-year-old male. *Left*, "Blockade" between atlas and axis with odontoid process (left) in the ring of the atlas and slanted articular surfaces between atlas and axis (right). Complete stiffness—"torticollis"—results. *Right*, Control roentgenogram to picture on left after manual spinal column therapy. The blockade is eliminated. Note the articular surface position.

muscles, repositioning of a displaced vertebra, relaxation of a pinched articular meniscus, or "de-blocking." According to the type of manipulations, a mechanical influence on the intervertebral motor segments of the spinal column can be assumed, but can only be radiographically confirmed in a few cases. The anatomical changes in the motor segment caused by the manipulations are still unknown. Often, the manipulations abruptly relieve pressure on a nerve or interrupt the incorrect reflex chain and lead in this way to an immediate reduction of the symptoms. Yet, they are just as unable as other procedures to result in a true anatomic and functional healing of vertebral damages.

Before manual therapy is begun, a diligent physical examination, laboratory tests, and x-rays must be done to determine whether such contraindications as tumors or tuberculosis exist to its use. The practitioner must be experienced in these techniques because incorrect maneuvers can cause a good deal of damage.

Manipulation therapy is important for all parts of the spinal column. Although it is most often used at the cervical or lumbar spinal column, it may also be successful at the thoracic spinal column, not only in the limited area of the intervertebral motor segment with its vertebral arch joints but also for arthroses of vertebrocostal joints (see section 3.4). Manual diagnostic and therapy can also be used for sacroiliac joints that play a central role in the loin-pelvis-hip region (Steinbrueck and Tilscher 1983).

Headaches may be an indication for successful manipulation therapy. The head joints may even be considered as an additional sensory organ (Wolff 1980).

Longitudinal traction has been used since antiquity as a manipulation procedure. Because it relaxes tense muscles and ligaments, especially at the cervical spinal column, it may be an excellent preparation for a medical manipulation and can be used in the movement bath. Rhythmic extensions not only relax muscles and ligaments but also support the necessary metabolic interplay of the intervertebral disc fluid with the pump mechanism. Many therapists prefer the hand-controlled longitudinal traction to the mechanized traction apparatus. Traction by hand enables the therapist to sense correct time for each specific therapeutic manipulation.

Rhythmic, alternating longitudinal traction in the Glisson sling traction apparatus is often used for the cervical spinal column. Prolonged traction in a lying position with the applied Glisson sling and hip belt distributes the traction over the entire spinal column. However, traction does not work equally on all spinal column sections, as its effectiveness depends on the respective level of tension in the trunk and cervical muscles. Therefore, its therapeutical effectiveness is difficult to determine. Extension therapy may not be indiscriminately performed during static longitudinal traction or rhythmic traction alternation and not without accurate diagnosis of the intervertebral disc conditions.

Nachemson (1975) determined the differences in intradiscal pressure during rhythmic traction treatment by measuring the pressure conditions in the intervertebral disc L-3/L-4. In the supine position a pressure of 30 kg rests on this intervertebral disc. During longitudinal traction it decreases to 10 kg.

Manual medicine plays an important role in athletic training and competition (Froehlich 1980), particularly in consideration of vertebral joint blockade. According to a report by Vortmann (1984), chirotherapy of the blocked cervical spinal column results in a significant freedom from pain, but does not improve mobility for anteflexion and retroflexion.

7.4.1.3 Physiotherapy, Massage, and Swimming

With its controlled and supportive, active muscle training and articular movement, physiotherapy holds great promise as a therapy of spinal column disorders. For many of the spondylogenic symptoms and syndromes described in Chapter 3, physiotherapy is the preferred healing procedure. It works by relaxing muscles that are painfully tense because of neural irritations from the impaired intervertebral motor segment. The frequent recurrence of tension and the resulting muscle insufficiency require additional measures of heat and bath therapy. The accompanying physiotherapy is always valuable. It is most effective when used in an early stage before the weakened muscles exert further influence on the instable intervertebral motor segment. The physician is encouraged to maintain the correct balance between relaxation and restoration of muscle strength and mobility.

In addition, physiotherapy is important in the treatment of beginning back problems and for recurring problems. After prolonged bed rest because of spinal column problems, physiotherapy is an effective means of muscle and movement training.

Physiotherapy also plays an important role in the therapy of incorrect back curvatures in adolescents, both kyphosis and scoliosis. The well-known creeping procedure (Klapp 1958) and the similar arched back-sway back exercise (Eder and Tilscher 1982) are helpful in this regard. Recently, the horse has also played a role in physiotherapy (Kuprian 1983).

The selection of physiotherapeutic treatment depends on the condition not only of the affected muscles and ligaments but also of the affected intervertebral discs, a fact that is frequently disregarded. The fluid content and thus the internal pressure of the discs are already reduced by minor damage. On average, the upright person shows a pressure of 70 kg and in the supine position, of 30 kg. During physiotherapeutic exercises the pressure increases to 180 kg (see Table 3-1). Figure 3-9 demonstrates how widely the pressure conditions can vary during different physiotherapeutic exercises.

Classic massage retains its place in the therapeutic armamentarium, despite the increasing use of physiotherapy in recent years. Today, massage procedures are specific to the particular motor segment that is the source of pain. Connective tissue massage works by finding the visceral reflex connections from the skin to the internal organs and so eliminating impairments (Teirich-Leube 1960). However, if it is performed too forcefully at the back of the neck, it may cause a headache.

Swimming in all its styles, strengthens back muscles and the connective muscles to the arms, legs, and neck, as well as the abdominal wall and rib cage muscles. At the same time swimming movements strengthen and relax all body muscles and benefit the cardiovascular system and respiration.

Swimming is an effective therapy for all forms of back problems if swimming is prescribed in accordance to the type of problem (Lekszas 1981). Alternating free-style is well suitable for therapeutical purposes because of the alternating left-right stretching and relieving of the longissimi muscles. However, the breast-stroke may cause tension of the cervical and back muscles because of the lifting of the head. Therefore, a long gliding phase with the head beneath the water is preferable for therapeutic swimming. One-sided freestyle requires lateral flexion of the head and results in a rotation of the spinal column, causing cervical pain. Back swimming is useful for posture and wear damages of the spinal column. The butterfly style often results in problems because of the inevitable lordosis.

7.4.1.4 Physical Therapy

Physical therapy, which has been practiced for centuries, is continually being improved by the development of increasingly more complicated technical equipment. Detailed knowledge is required of the possibilities offered by this equipment for treating back patients. The physician must consider the differential effect of the equipment in prescribing a therapy plan. He or she regularly scrutinizes the plan because a change in the character of the problems may occur during the course of treatment that might necessitate a change in therapy. Such a plan should specify how heat, applied through hot packs and baths, should be used in conjunction with underwater jet massages, as well as alternating cold-hot showers.

The therapy plan may also include the use of alternating mechanical forces (vibrations). Vibration treatment through tapping or hand vibration massages has been available for a long time, and more recently vibration equipment has been introduced. Therapeutically used vibrations have a short period of influence. As they transfer a minute amount of energy, they stimulate circulation and encourage by way of nerves mental activity. However, after a longer time they create a state of monotony, reduce activity, and result in adaptation and finally fatigue (Dupuis 1963).

Much of physical therapy consists of bath treatments and other forms of hydrotherapy that have been popular for centuries. During the therapy of back patients in water baths, one basic condition should always be followed: the water temperature should be about 32°C. The withdrawal of warmth is felt as unpleasant and causes increased, painful muscle stiffness in the back. Thus it often has an aggravating effect on the vicious cycle of spondylogenic problems. For this reason, cold therapy (cryotherapy), which is generally regarded as palliative and muscle relaxing by physical medicine, in no way always alleviates the most common back pain, ie, the pain caused by intervertebral discs.

Thermotherapy also includes mud and fango packs, infrared rays, short waves, and microwaves. A good combination of heat and movement therapy is the movement bath, which relaxes and strengthens spondylogenically impaired back muscles. Any hospital licensed to treat occupational disorders should have a movement bath.

7.4.1.5 Injection Treatments

Injection treatments should be integrated into a general plan of treatment in which other conservative procedures, such as drugs, physical healing methods, immobilization, and manual treatment, and even surgery have their rightful place. The simultaneous or alternating use of several injection methods is frequently practiced. Those procedures directed against neural spondylogenic impairments are the most important. Yet, none have so far been able to restore an intervertebral chrondrosis, intervertebral osteochondrosis, or arthrosis of the vertebral arch joints to a state of complete healing (regeneration).

Injections are usually regarded as conservative treatment. However, an injection that requires x-ray control for the positioning of the needle in order to avoid damages in the adjacent tissues may not be considered to be a conservative procedure; for instance, injection methods at the location of the disease, ie, in the interior of an intervertebral disc destroyed by chondrosis or within a spinal nerve root.

Injection treatments work by dissolving damaged intervertebral disc tissue. Fusing of the vertebrae to a point of pain-eliminating immobility is then expected to occur. Magnetic resonance imaging can monitor the dissolution process. The most effective injection sites are the pendural area, spinal cord roots, ganglias, vegetative nerve trunks, muscles, ligaments, and ligament attachments.

Some authors recommend that only the nucleus pulposus and the surrounding area (nucleolysis) be dissolved because the infiltration of injected fluid into the vertebral canal during the destruction of the lamellae ring damages the spinal nerve roots. Others advocate the complete destruction of the intervertebral disc—the nucleus pulposus and the lamellae ring (discolysis). During this process the cartilage plates of the intervertebral disc and bony end plates of the vertebral bodies are also damaged; hence, aseptic iatrogenic spondylodiscitis (see section 4.7).

The use of the enzyme chymopapain for discolysis has met with varying success (Kraemer 1973, 1978; Troisier et al. 1980; Wilkingson and Schuman 1980). Chymopapain was originally banned by the Food and Drug Administration in 1975 because of its side effects of serious spinal root damages and its unproven effectiveness, but a modified preparation was approved in 1982.

In recent years, the successful use of the enzyme collagenase has been reported (Brown 1976). Based on the results of intervertebral disc therapy, the use of collagenase of the bacterium, *Clostridium histolyticum*, is preferred. Nucleolysin is the registered trademark. In a preliminary report in 1983, Lenz described the successes of 130 injections.

The influence of chymopapain and collagenase on the neural and vasal structures surrounding the intervertebral disc has been compared (Rydevik et al. 1976). Chymopapain caused significant degeneration at nerve fibers and simultaneous development of intraneural fibrosis. In contrast, slight edema developed in the epineurium during experiments with collagenase, but the protective function of the

Schwann's sheath remained (Rydevik et al. 1982). The permeability of the endoneural intrafascicular microvessels was unimpaired.

Brock et al (1984) reported on their own experiences with injections of chymopapain and regard it as an alternative for a surgical procedure. Only a physician able to perform this surgery should use the injection method. Their experiences with collagenase were not encouraging.

During the past years, injections have been frequently used for painful conditions at the tips of the vertebral arch processes that are known to exist in insertion osteotendopathies (see section 4.6). Usually, anesthetic injections are used for that purpose. The injection of sclerosing compounds is recommended for stretched, slack ligaments in the area of the lumbar spinal column and at the cervical spinal column. Gutmann (1978) and Gutmann and Biedermann (1981) report on the return of ligamental tautness after sclerosing injections used in conjunction with therapy.

Percutaneous cervical facet denervation via injection is a new treatment of chronic cervical headaches (Hildebrandt and Argyrakis 1983). In one series, of 35 patients treated, 10 were completely or almost completely pain-free. There are no long-term studies of this procedure's effectiveness.

Of the direct injections performed for spinal column disorders or their spondylogenic sequelae, the injections into the peridural area come closest to the central nervous system. Peridural anesthesia is widely used to relieve spondylogenic pain, especially lumbalgia and sciatica. Twice- or thrice-weekly injection of pantocaine (with gelatin 1:10) is recommended, although many different injection compounds have been used at the cervical spinal column and against intercostal neuralgias.

In addition to injections with localized targets, general injections are commonly used for localized and radiating pain of a spondylogenic character. In these cases injections are made into the veins, subcutaneous tissue, or muscles outside the painful body area.

Even with the use of disposable needles, injection therapy poses the danger of iatrogenic infection. This occurs more frequently at the spinal column than in other areas of the body. Injections made for the purpose of discography, vertebral body biopsy, lumbar puncture, lumbar sympathetic trunk blockade, aortography, venography, and myelography are the most frequent cause of iatrogenic infection.

Incorrect insertion of the needle or the use of the inappropriate injected drug may cause direct injury to the spinal nerves and spinal cord, although this occurs rarely.

7.4.1.6 Segment and Neural Therapy

The simple schematics by Keegan (Fig. 7-34) and by Schliack (Table 7-6), have for decades served as the basis for documentation of the diagnosis of the location of a damage (segment diagnosis). The various possibilities of root constriction in the lumbar area caused by prolapsed nodes of various intervertebral discs are shown in Figure 7-35.

In the years just after World War II, the primary indications for segment therapy were nocturnal paresthesia and lumbosacral problems. Since then, intensive research and observation by neurologists, neuroanatomists, internists, and surgeons have placed a large complex of pseudoradicular pain into focus. Bergsmann and Eder (1982) suggest the term of "segmental reflexive complex" for these conditions, which include blockage-related lumbalgias, ligamentous insufficiency, pain syndromes of the hip joints, osteoporosis syndrome, scapulocostal syndrome, and pseudoradicular cervical syndromes. Impairments at the cervicocranial transition may cause distributed facial pain zones as shown in Figure 7-36.

7.4.1.7 Acupuncture

For more than 2400 years acupuncture has been used in China. Although it was described by Osler as early as 1909, it is only in the past two decades that physicians outside China have shown increasing interest in the theories and practice of acupuncture. There are many acupuncture procedures for spinal column disorders, especially for sciatica (Bischko 1975, 1980; Figar et al 1964; Michal and Synek 1963; Zimmermann 1979). Pain in the area of the vertebral arch joints is frequently treated with acupuncture combined with electrostimulation.

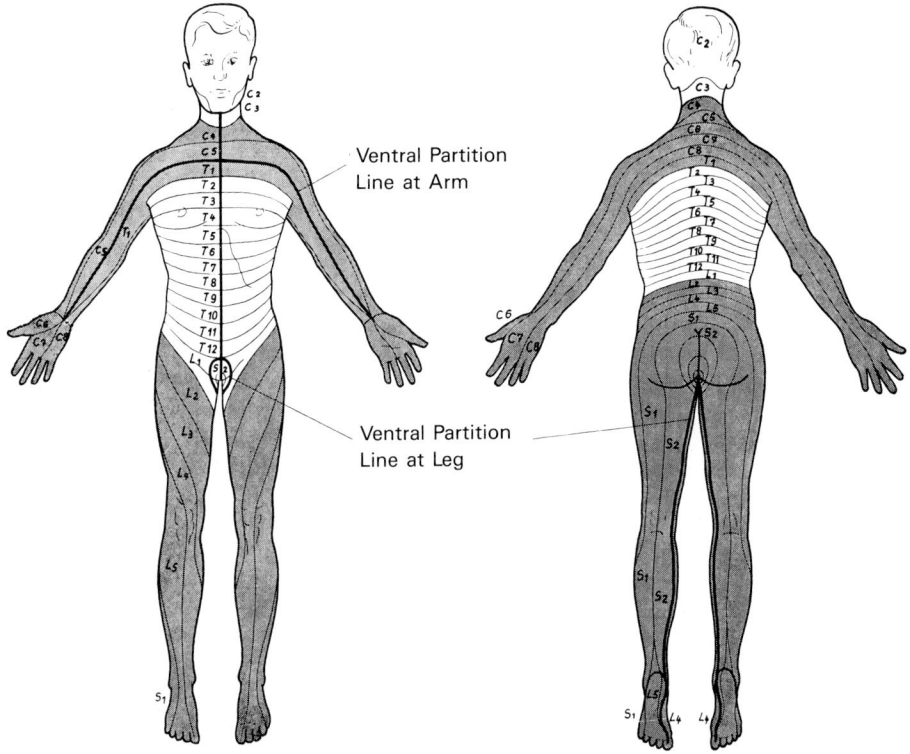

Fig. 7-34 Dermatome schematic [from Keegan (1953)].

It is very difficult to learn both the principles of the system and the proper methods of therapy. Only someone who has seriously studied and performed acupuncture should treat spinal column disorders with this method. Guidelines for its indications and therapy are evolving.

7.4.1.8 Orthotic Devices

The construction of orthotic devices for spinal column disorders has been improved significantly in recent years. Yet, not all prefabricated orthotic devices and made-to-order corsets as recommended by Wilhelm in 1980 may fulfill the expectations of the physician. Schmitt (1980) tested the effectiveness of the plaster corsets that can later be replaced by orthotic devices and various braces for individual spinal column sections. He concluded that a secure stabilization for the spinal arch joints is not always attained as required. Therefore, critical and continual observation is always appropriate.

In addition, prolonged wearing of orthotic devices or corsets decreases muscular activity. Physiotherapeutical treatments may therefore become necessary intermittently in certain cases.

For the special stress placed on the lumbar spinal column by motorcycle riding and certain occupations, wearing a tight loin-sacrum belt has proven beneficial and is even mandatory for certain military units. Such a garment is also used by load carriers. Wearers of such orthotic devices must do relaxing and strengthening physiotherapeutical measures periodically.

7.4.1.9 Additional Conservative Treatments

The role of the physician is to do those manipulations at the spinal column (manual therapy, chirotherapy, etc.) and to supervise other treatment methods done by ancillary health personnel and the patients themselves. The physicians should teach their patients how to do these personal prophylactic measures as follow-up measures after conclusion of conservative therapy or after surgery. Periodic reinforcement of these measures will be necessary.

Table 7-6 Radicular Symptoms (Schliack 1955)

Segment	Sensitivity	Primary Muscle	Proprioceptive Reflex of Muscle	Comments
C-4	Pain or hypalgesia in shoulder area	Partial or total diaphragm paresis	No typical reflex impairments	Partial diaphragm paresis may be caused by C-3, more rarely by C-5 with the change of dermatomes
C-6	Dermatome from exterior of shoulder to radial side of upper and lower arm downward to thumb	Biceps & brachioradialis	Failure of biceps reflex	
C-7	Dermatome dorsolateral of C-6 starting about the middle of upper arm and running to middle finger	Ball of thumb, especially abductor pollicis brevis	Failure or reduction of triceps reflex	Often the m. pronator teres is also paretic (pronation insufficiency)
C-8	Dermatome following dorsal at C-7, running to little finger	Ball of small finger, abduction of fifth finger weakened	Failure or weakening of triceps reflex	Differential diagnosis for ulnaris paralysis may be difficult (note other hand muscles)
L-3	Dermatome from trochanter major over extensor side of thigh to inner side of knee	Paresis of quadriceps femoris	Failure of quadriceps reflex	
L-4	Dermatome from outside of thigh over knee to inside of lower leg to inner ankle and inner foot edge	Paresis of femoris quadriceps and often the anterior tibial muscle	Impairment of quadriceps reflex (patellar tendon reflex)	
L-5	Dermatome starting from above knee at lateral articular protuberance, running to the lateral anterior at lower leg to back of foot and large toe	Extensor hallucis longus, often with involvement of extensor digitorum brevis	Failure of posterior tibial reflex; can only be used if this reflex exists at the other side	
S-1	Dermatome from the gluteal fold at the dorsal side of the thigh along the postero-exterior of the lower leg down behind the outer ankle, affecting the heel from the third to the fifth toe	Short fibular muscle, occasionally with involvement of the medial gastrocnemius head	Failure of the triceps surae reflex (Achilles tendon reflex)	
L-4/L-5	Dermatome L-4 and L-5	All extensors of lower leg, except the fibular muscles	Weakening of the quadriceps reflex, failure of the posterior tibial reflex	In contrast to fibular paralysis, fibular muscles are intact
L-5/S-1	Dermatome L-5/S-1	Paralysis of all muscles supplied by the tibial nerve, except, the anterior tibial muscle	Failure of the posterior tibial reflex and Achilles tendon reflex	In contrast to fibular paralysis, the anterior tibial muscle remains intact; consideration of Achilles tendon reflex helps prevent misdiagnosis

The proven prophylactic and treatment measures that prevent or heal damage to the spinal column and back pain include movement exercises under water, which should be preceded by physiotherapeutic movement therapy, and swimming. Guidelines are to maintain the water temperature at about 32°C, to do the breast stroke, and to avoid diving or intensive swimming. Calisthenics is another prophylactic measure that can be preceded by physiotherapeutical treatment (Loeckle 1982).

Self-help groups are an effective means of promoting adherence to this prophylactic regimen by chronic back patients. The use of self-help groups will become more widespread in the future (Schauwecker 1982).

Some unconventional procedures have been developed by patients from their own experi-

Effects of Daily Life on the Spinal Column 239

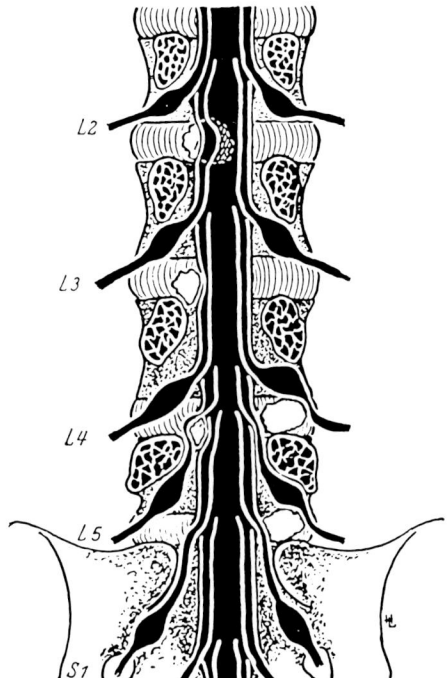

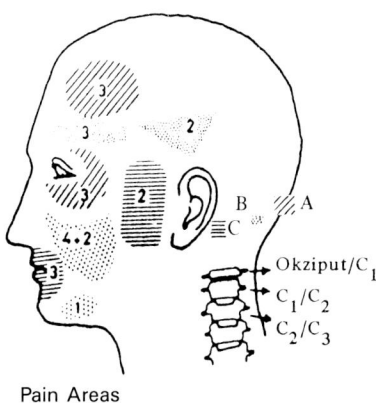

Fig. 7-36 Painful facial areas with corresponding infiltration points [from Tilscher et al. (1982)].

Pain Areas

A = Frontal (3) + Periocular (3)
B = Supraorbital (3) + Temporal (2)
C = Preauricular (2)
 Buccal + Palate (6) – (C_1/C_2)
 Peroral (3) – (Occiput/C_1)
 Chin (1) – C_2/C_3

Fig. 7-35 Relationship of prolapsed nodes of intervertebral discs to spinal cord roots. Medial intervertebral disc prolapse (L-2) results in few characteristic complaints and may affect several roots of the cauda equina. Unilateral prolapse (L-3, *left*) constricts root L-4 from the outside. The prolapse matter may also push itself between the lateral edge of the dura and the exit of the root so that it affects two roots simultaneously (L-4, left). Larger lateral prolapses exert simultaneous alternating pressure against two roots (L-4 and L-5, *right*).

ences and are becoming part of the armamentarium. Because prolonged sitting subjects the intervertebral discs to pressure, which leads to loss of fluid, as well as of their buffer function, hanging from a crossbar is one suggested method. Upside-down hanging with buckled feet requires specialized equipment. This restores the fluid in the intervertebral discs, but the hanging must be followed by subsequent exercise so that the pump mechanism necessary for the viability of the intervertebral discs begins again and the muscles resume their functions.

7.4.2 Surgical Procedures

This section describes the indications for surgery, the principles of surgical procedures, and the results of surgery. It should enable the treating general practitioner, internist, or other specialist to explain the necessity of an operation to the patient and to refer the patient to an experienced spinal surgeon who is equipped with the most up-to-date knowledge and equipment.

Back pain, radiating pain from the neck to the head or into the shoulders and arms, and lumbosciatica are not indications for immediate surgery. If such problems recur again and again in spite of intensive therapy or if the patients are never free from pain and work is missed frequently, an extensive examination by an orthopedist, neurologist, radiologist, or neuroradiologist with the help of computed tomography and new imaging procedures is in order. Only then can the decision to proceed with surgery be made.

The primary indications for back surgery are those spondylogenic diseases that are closely linked with the intervertebral motor segment: intervertebral chondrosis, vertebral osteochondrosis, prolapse of the intervertebral disc, insufficiency or instability of the intervertebral motor segment, and arthroses of the genuine articulations at the spinal column. In cases of sufficiently severe impairment, other damages at the spinal column are also suitable for surgery, including vertebral slippage, vertebral displacement, fractures, luxations, luxation fractures, spondylitis, spondylodiscitis, and tumors.

7.4.2.1 Basic Surgical Plan

A basic surgical plan has been established for a large number of surgically treatable spinal column damages, primarily those diseases and injuries that result in instability (slackened intervertebral motor segment). The objective of surgery is to re-establish the shape and load-bearing capacity of the affected spinal column section.

Basic surgical techniques include the evacuation of an impaired intervertebral disc from a lateral anterior or anterior approach with the spoon, tweezers, or vacuum drill; partial removal of adjacent vertebral body end plates to form a block bed; the search in the vertebral canal for penetrated intervertebral disc or bone sequesters; and application of a bone peg that spreads the intervertebral space and thus also the two spinal root canals (intervertebral foramina) (Figs. 7-37 and 7-38). Occasionally metallic fixation aids are required to provide support quickly, although plastic bone cement may sometimes be helpful. Permanent fusion is achieved by the rapid incorporation of bone. Spondylodeses that are added at the same time or later are suitable if pain-generating arthrotic spurs of the vertebral arch articulations must be removed or if an arch articulation arthrodesis is required.

Under certain conditions the operation should be performed under longitudinal traction in a Crutchfield clamp or Glisson sling.

In the case of uncovertebral and vertebral arch articulation arthroses of the cervical spine distinct bony protuberances are found in addition to osteochondrosis. They greatly constrict the intervertebral foramen and/or the penetration space of the vertebral artery. Frequently they cause serious pain and paralysis, as well as decreased blood circulation in the ear and brain (see section 4.6). Then, surgery becomes necessary; one such procedure is the uncoforaminectomy (Fig. 7-39, Biehl and Thomas 1982; Jung and Kehr 1974; Kehr 1982; Kehr et al. 1981).

Microsurgical procedures facilitate surgery at the cervical spinal column using a transoral approach (Saleman et al. 1979, Spetzler et al. 1981).

When operating on vertebral body fractures or luxations not only at the cervical spinal column but also at other spinal column sections, the

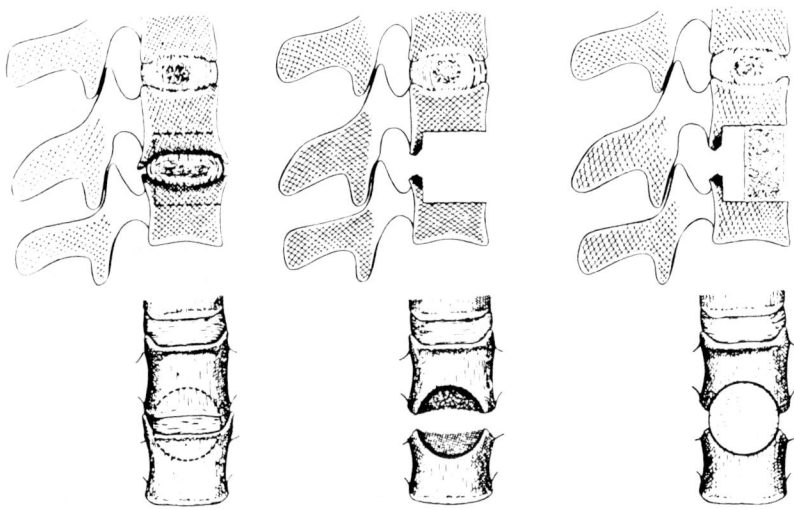

Fig. 7-37 Model of a bone-chip blocking operation at the cervical spinal column (intercorporeal spondylosis) for intervertebral osteochondrosis (from Cloward [1959]). *Top row left*, Marking of drill channel. *Top row middle*, After removal of intervertebral disc tissue, a drill channel is established, and the uncovertebral spurs are removed. *Top row right*, Bone-chip block is set in after spreading the intervertebral space. *Bottom row*, Respective views from the front.

Effects of Daily Life on the Spinal Column 241

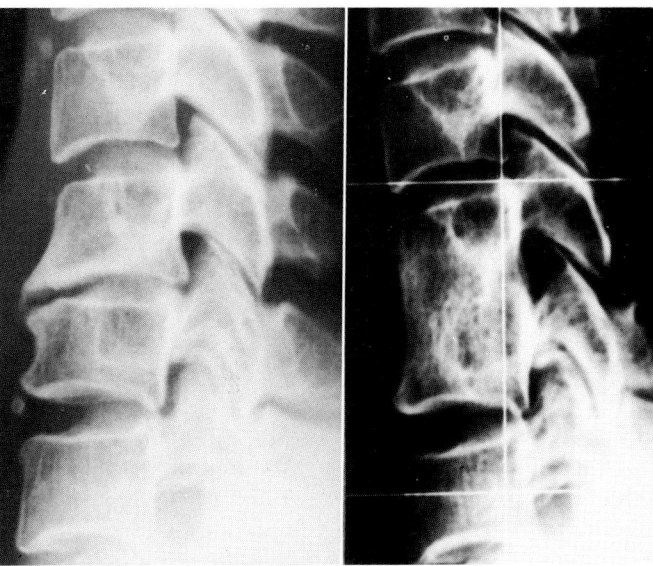

Fig. 7-38 Bone-chip blocking operation (see Fig. 7-37). *Left*, Intervertebral osteochondrosis in C-4/C-5 level in a 40-year-old female. *Right*, Follow-up after 5 symptom-free years showing incorporation of block and an increased intervertebral canal.

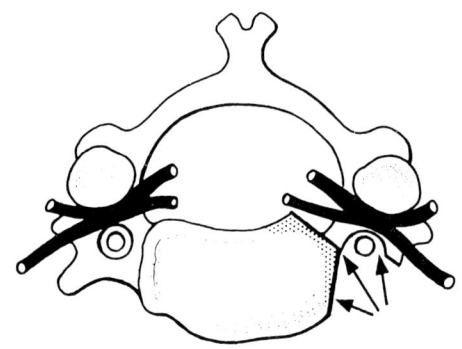

Fig. 7-39 Sketch from Jung and Kehr (1974) on the gradual exposure of the intervertebral canal at the cervical spinal column. The three arrows designate the transversotomy, uncusectomy, and anterior foraminotomy.

straightening extension in the longitudinal axis pulls apart the fragmental zone of the vertebral body. Many cases may require the space to be filled by spongiosa or small bone-chip blocks or preferably the insertion of a firm, stabilizing bone peg that supports both at the top and bottom and the use of an external metallic, stabilizing brace or screws. If there are simultaneous adjacent upper and/or lower collapsed vertebral body end plates with tears in the intervertebral disc, an increased, stabilizing intercorporal fusion over one or two segments is required (Boehler 1978; Junghanns 1970b, 1971a, 1973).

7.4.2.2 Prolapse of the Intervertebral Disc

After World War II intervertebral disc prolapse came to be considered an indication for surgery. However, before the development of such imaging procedures as discography, myelography, and computed tomography (CT) too often the surgeon's suspicion of prolapse as the cause of back pain was not confirmed by surgery. Fortunately, these imaging procedures enable accurate diagnoses, so that it is now possible to operate with greater certainty. In order to avoid the recurrence of back pain and to remove the always present instability, the procedure not only removes the prolapsed portion of the intervertebral disc but also clears the intervertebral space and fuses the segment that is slackened because of intervertebral disc damage with bone pegs (Figs. 7-40 and 7-41).

For many severe spinal column injuries with and without paraplegia, an immediate operation is performed if a sequestered portion of the intervertebral disc reaches the vertebral canal and presses on the spinal cord (Fig. 7-42). The decision to proceed with an immediate operation is facilitated today because the new imaging procedures enable an accurate diagnosis; for example, displaced intervertebral disc or bone portions can be seen in the CT scan (Fig. 7-43).

242   CLINICAL IMPLICATIONS OF NORMAL BIOMECHANICAL STRESSES ON SPINAL FUNCTION

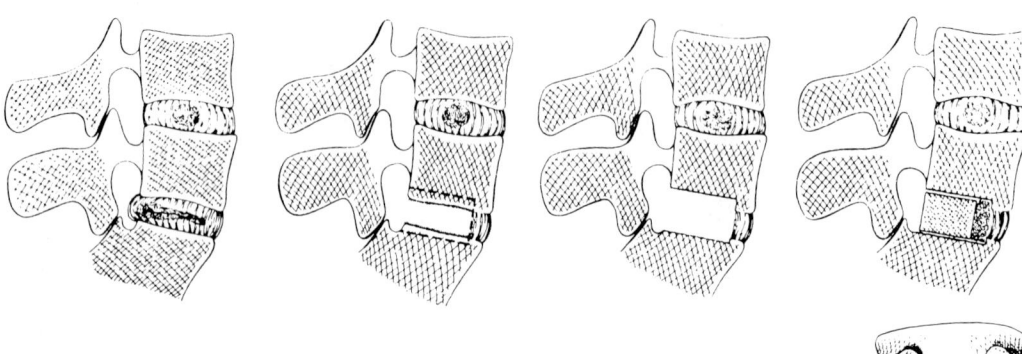

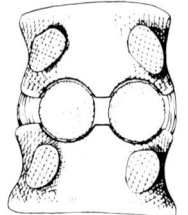

Fig. 7-40 Model of a bone-chip operation in the lumbar spinal column for intervertebral disc prolapse of L-5/S-1 with constriction of the intervertebral canal. Evacuation of the disc is done through the back as the exterior lamellae layers of the fiber ring remain intact. The canal is drilled so a round block can be inserted. In the drilling canal, **drill dust** is inserted in the front and the block is forced in. The lower picture shows the round bone pegs that have been pushed in from behind (right and left, each after the dura was pushed aside).

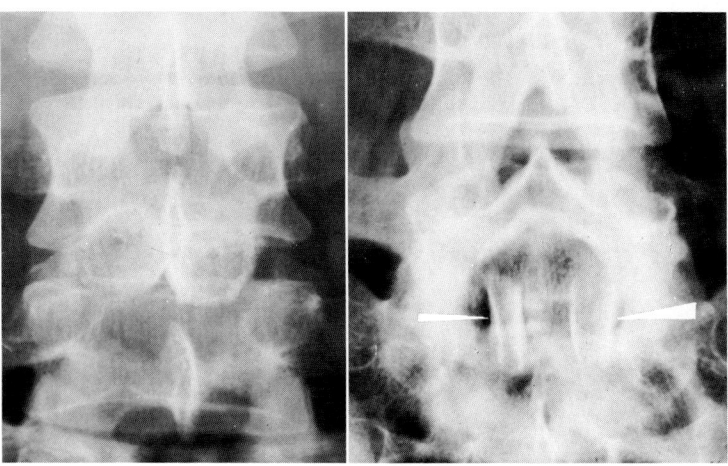

Fig. 7-41 Follow-up roentgenogram after operation on a prolapsed disc. *Left*, Round blocks between L-4 and L-5 in a 40-year-old male. *Right*, Two square pegs between L-5 and S-1 in a 35-year-old female.

The initial operation for intervertebral disc prolapses is more successful if microsurgical procedures other than macrosurgical technique are used (Gilsbach et al 1981; Oldenkott and Roost 1980; Weltbrecht et al 1980; Williams 1978). These operations are being done more frequently in children (Schuler et al 1982).

7.4.2.3 Painful Intervertebral Disc Disorders and Arthroses

Intervertebral chondrosis (wearing of the intervertebral disc), and intervertebral osteochondrosis are responsible for the frequent, painful syndrome of invertebral instability (the slackening of the intervertebral motor segment) (Junghanns 1959). The pain, and thus the necessity for surgery, increases if this syndrome is connected with discopathy/vertebral arch articulation arthroses. The preferred location of osteochondroses are the cervical and lumbar spinal column.

The goal of the surgical procedure is to stabilize the slackened intervertebral motor segment. Penetration from the front offers the best opportunities for success.

Because intervertebral discs and vertebral arch articulations work together closely in the interver-

Effects of Daily Life on the Spinal Column 243

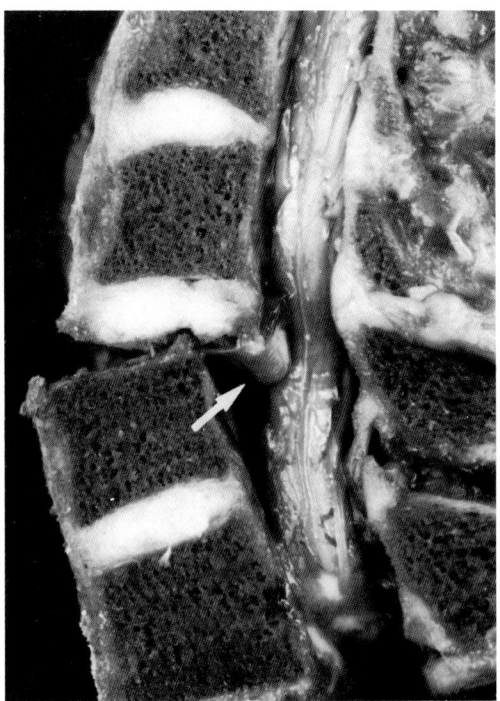

Fig. 7-42 Sagittal section of a cervical spinal column in a 38-year-old female pedestrian hit by a truck. Tear off of the intervertebral disc C-6/C-7 from the cover plate of the seventh cervical vertebral body with tearing of the anterior and posterior longitudinal ligament. Pressing of an intervertebral disc sequester into the peridural space with spinal cord contusion, fracture, and ligament tears in the vertebral arch area, eg, ligamentum flavum in the two next lower intervertebral motor segments.

tebral motor segment, pathological impairments in one part always also influence the other partner. This requires for instance an additional resection or screwing of arthrotic vertebral arch articulations. Recently, various surgical procedures have been recommended for the pseudoradicular pain generated by the vertebral arch articulations (facet syndrome): facetectomy (Getty et al 1981), denervation (Hickey and Tregonning 1977; Lora and Long 1976; Ogsbury 1977), thermocoagulation (Shealy 1976) and electrocoagulation (Vanderlinden and Salter 1978).

7.4.2.4 Vertebral Slippage and Displacement

Intervertebral osteochondrosis with retrolisthesis occurs frequently at the cervical spinal

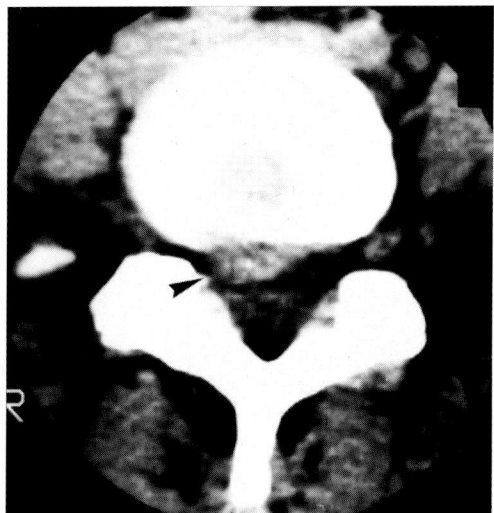

Fig. 7-43 Medium-sized posterolateral prolapse of the intervertebral disc at L-4/L-5 in a CT scan [from Schubinger (1984)].

column. In addition to spinal radicular pain it may cause permanent damages at the spinal cord if arthrotic spurs of the vertebral arch articulations constrict the vertebral canal by the pincers mechanism (see section 4.5). Surgery with frontal and occasionally with dorsal access becomes necessary.

The lumbar spinal column and the lumbosacral transition have become increasingly more interesting operation areas for spondylolysis or spondylolisthesis, for anterior pseudospondylolisthesis without lysis (pseudospondylolisthesis), and for retrolisthesis. A fusion operation is urgently needed in the case of an intervertebral osteochondrosis with very painful instability, if there are paralyses, or if roentgenograms show additional displacement. The presence of strong pain requires the exposure of the nerve roots by removing portions of the vertebral arch and the vertebral arch articulations. In those cases, an additional dorsal spondylodesis is required.

7.4.2.5 Scolioses, Kyphoses, and Kyphoscolioses

A variety of new methods for straightening and stabilizing back curvature have been developed in recent years (Fig. 7-44). The large-curved Bechterew's kyphosis at the thoracic or

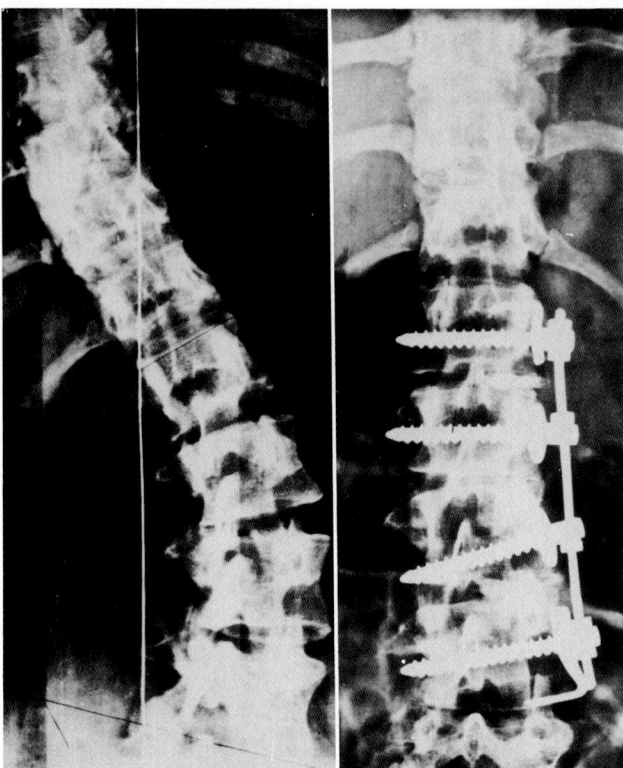

Fig. 7-44 X-ray of a scoliotic spinal column before and after ventral derotation spondylodesis (VDS) [from Zielke (1978)].

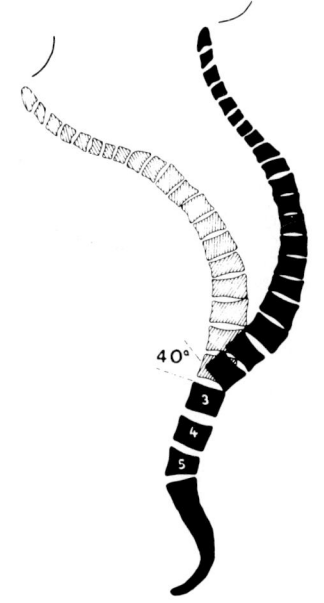

Fig. 7-45 The result of a straightening operation for ankylosis spondylarthritis of a 36-year-old male patient.

cervical section of the spinal column (Figs. 7-45 to 7-48) has its own special concerns. (Brussatis 1981; Junghanns 1968, 1970c, 1971c). Either a dorsal or anterior approach can be used to straighten kyphoses, even severe juvenile kyphosis.

7.4.2.6 Fractures, Luxations, and Luxation Fractures

The surgical re-establishment of the anatomical shape of the fractured spinal column is difficult to achieve because of the many individual parts in the fracture area and the connections among the spinal cord, spinal roots, blood vessels, and the involved intervertebral discs.

At the cervical spinal column, fractures with intervertebral disc injuries or especially unstable luxation fractures most often occur. The removal of the intervertebral disc with a concomitant search for intervertebral disc material shifted into the vertebral canal is essential after a careful longitudinal traction. Normally, an anterior

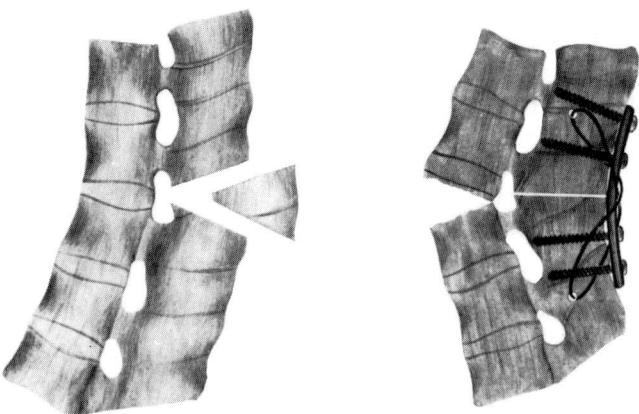

Fig. 7-46 A straightening operation of a severely curved "Bechterew spinal column." *Left*, At the level of the upper lumbar spinal column a wedge of about 40° is removed from the rod-like ossified vertebral arch series up to the vertebral canal. *Right*, After a slow straightening of the spinal column the vertebral body series gaps in an accordingly sized wedge in the front. The now-joined vertebral arch series is stabilized with a plate, several screws, and an additional harelip wire suture.

intercorporal fusion is done according to the basic surgical plan. Figure 7-37 shows the evacuation of disc material and stabilization at the cervical spinal column in a case of intervertebral osteochondrosis; the surgical result is shown in Figure 7-38. The same surgical technique is suitable for injuries (Fig. 7-49).

At the thoracic and lumbar spinal column the main treatment problem for fractures and luxations is to determine which kyphotically bent compression fractures should be straightened. There is a tendency toward doing an immediate operation to achieve the best load-bearing stabilization possible (Fig. 7-50). The fusion in the vertebral body-intervertebral disc series is the primary method, even if a spinal spondylodesis must sometimes be added. There is still doubt whether straightening and fusion should be performed also for those vertebral body fractures that do not involve the intervertebral disc and are less than one-third compressed. Surgical technique and the types of metallic stabilizers used still differ widely.

Figure 7-51 illustrates a stabilizing fusion operation at the lumbar spinal column performed from the anterior or lateroanterior approach. The surgery removes intervertebral disc portions and fills the vertebral body with bone pegs and spongiosa.

Since World War II, the positioning treatment has been the model for traumatic paraplegia because of the good results achieved by "the father of paraplegics," Sir Ludwig Guttmann.

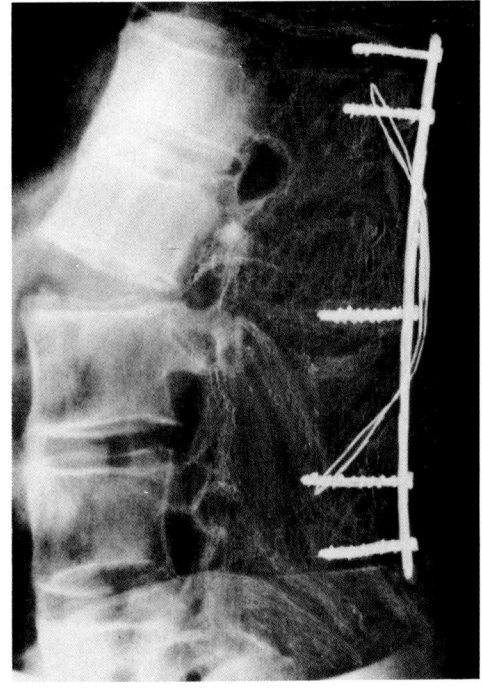

Fig. 7-47 Roentgenogram taken 1 week after straightening operation in a 36-year-old male with ankylosis spondylarthritis ankylosans.

However, there is reason to believe that immediate surgical straightening and stabilization may be helpful. Most likely, however, a return of spinal cord function is less expected than a facilitation for care and physiotherapy (Meinecke 1976).

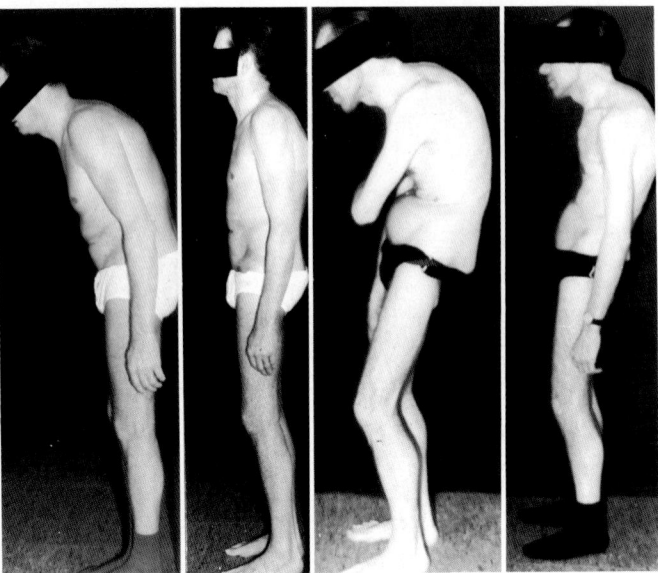

Fig. 7-48 Two examples of straightening operations in Bechterew's disease. *Left*, 48-year-old male; *right*, 54-year-old male.

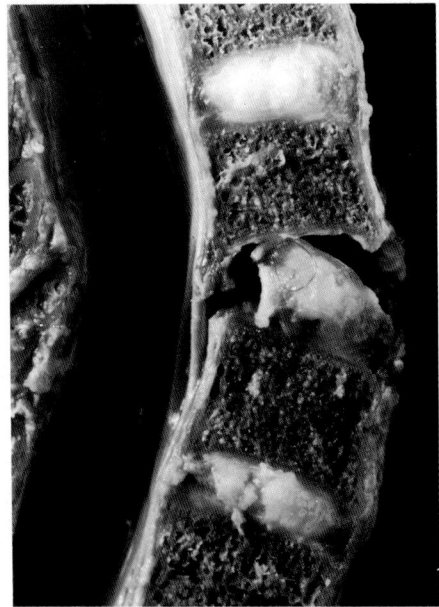

Fig. 7-49 In the cervical spinal column, a tear off of an intervertebral disc with its cartilaginous cover plate from the upper vertebral body and contusion of the anterior-inferior portion of the intervertebral disc with edge fracture of the vertebral body.

7.4.2.7 Spondylitis and Spondylodiscitis

Until the middle of this century the therapy for tubercular spondylitis was almost entirely conservative. After World War II surgical-tuberculostatical focal therapy was developed from either an anterior or lateral approach. The removal of the infectious focus and the introduction of the new antibiotics made it possible to treat the infection foci of the spinal column caused by different bacteria, such as vertebral osteomyelitis, according to the same principles. In this context, in 1976 Klemm introduced gentamicin-PMMA-balls. Arranged in septopal chains they are easy to remove. Figure 7-52 shows the position of such a chain in intercorporal osteomyelitis.

Spondylodiscitis is often caused by rheumatic, iatrogenic, or chemical influences on the intervertebral disc. Urgent removal of the focus is essential. As it progresses, a firm, connective tissue and/or bony healing process may take place, supported by metallic stabilization aids. An additional dorsal spondylodesis cannot always be avoided.

7.4.2.8 Tumors and Metastases

The complete removal of surgically accessible benign or malignant tumors or metastases is indicated (Fiedling et al 1979). In addition, since 1960 radical therapy of malignant tumors and their metastases at the spinal column is done with the insertion of replacement. Metallic vertebral

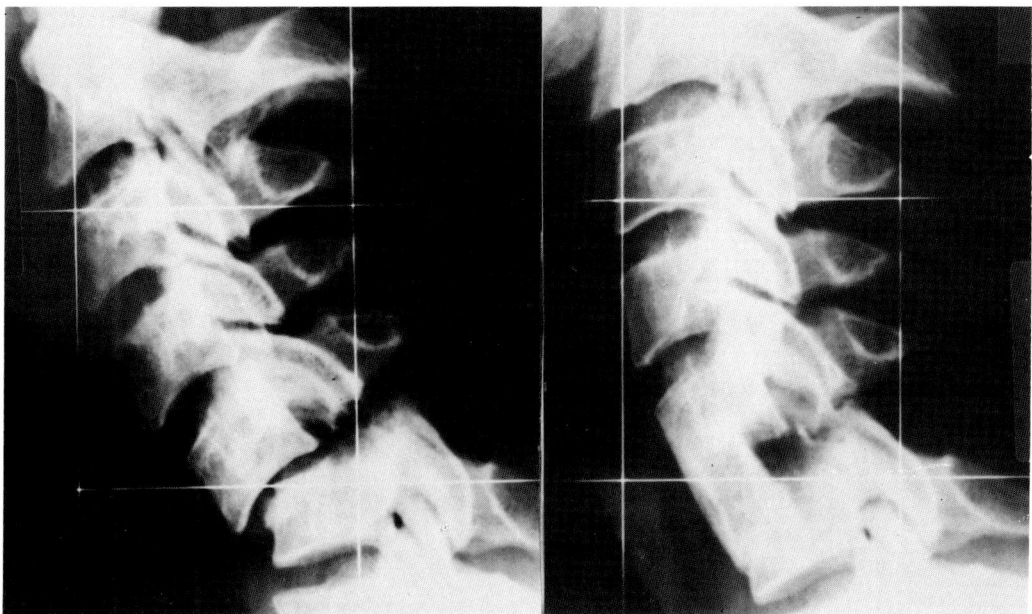

Fig. 7-50 New luxation fracture at C-5/C-6 of a 28-year-old female with fracture of the vertebral arch. *Right,* Intervertebral disc torn on May 27, 1965. Immediate operation under longitudinal traction and insertion of bone peg from pelvic crest were done according to the basic surgical plan. *Right,* Control roentgenogram on September 3, 1965 showing firmly incorporated bone peg and bony healing of vertebral arch fracture. Note the large penetration space for spinal root and blood vessels.

bodies or total vertebral prostheses may be used to fill the defects and support the spinal column; occasionally bone cement is indicated. The type and extent of additionally required stabilization must be planned on a case-by-case basis. Better adapted replacements and improved surgical technique will result in better successes in the future (Salzer 1977; Wolter et al. 1983).

7.4.2.9 Additional Surgical Indications

In rare cases large marginal spurs of the vertebral body of spondylosis deformans/osteochondrosis cause swallowing problems at the cervical spinal column (Fig. 7-53). If it causes great inconvenience, surgical removal may be helpful.

A stenosis of the vertebral canal may be observed at the cervical and lumbar spinal column and often appears in conjunction with a stenosis of the recessus lateralis. Surgery should be considered for changes in the spinal canal that cause a localized stenosis and myelopathies or radiculopathies. Other similar indications are projecting nodes of cartilage, calcium, or bone in the posterior longitudinal ligament, and more frequently in the ligamentum flavum (Chahal et al. 1982). In those cases it must be decided whether the removal of the nodes is sufficient or whether narrowed intervertebral spaces must be simultaneously widened and blocked (Igari and Miura 1980).

The pincers mechanism poses a difficult surgical task. Not only is the damage to the spinal cord caused by displacements in the intervertebral motor segment with spurs at the posterior vertebral body edges but also the thickened yellow ligament or bone eminences at the vertebral arch articulations are significantly involved in causing the stenosis from the posterior. In such cases an operation from the anterior and posterior approach may be indicated.

Vertebrocostal joint arthroses cause strong, intercostal radiation pain and in most cases are treated with injections or manual therapy. If there is a stubborn recurrence of pain, surgical removal may be indicated.

In Baastrup's disease an operation is indicated when pain becomes unbearable. The chiseling of the two surfaces of the nearthroses between the spinous processes is a possible option. Because

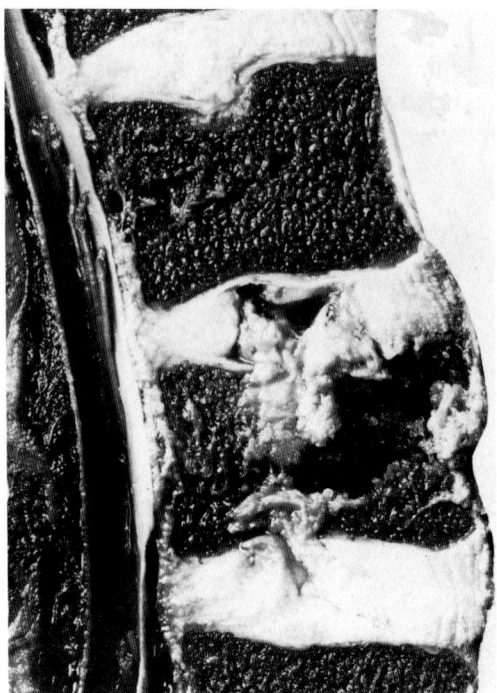

Fig. 7-51 Sagittal section surface of lumbar spinal column of a 25-year-old male. Fragmented fraction of vertebral body with prolapse of intervertebral disc tissue from both adjacent intervertebral discs. Note the small Schmorl's node with bone capsule in upper vertebral body.

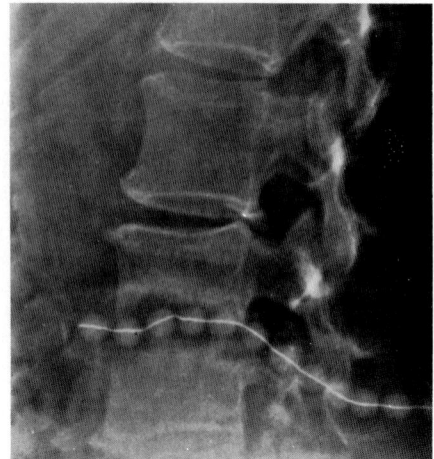

Fig. 7-52 Septopal chain after removal of focus in the lumbar spinal column [from Klemm (1976)].

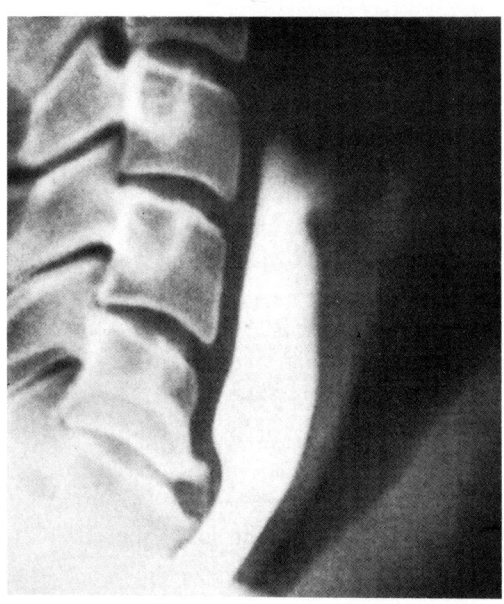

Fig. 7-53 Lateral roentgenogram of the cervical spinal column of a 42-year-old female. Radiopaque filling of the esophagus. The height of intervertebral space C-5/C-6 is decreased. Slight sclerosis of vertebral body end plates and slight retrolisthesis are present. Although these symptoms are signs of intervertebral osteochondrosis, the size and location of the edge spurs are equivalent to spondylosis deformans. They constrict the esophagus, causing substantial swallowing problems with occasional esophageal spasm.

almost always a simultaneous intervertebral osteochondrosis of the segment exists, the removal of the destroyed intervertebral disc with fusion surgery is recommended for severe cases.

7.4.2.10 Future Tasks for Spinal Column Surgery

Advancements in spinal column surgery continue to be made, enabling the rapid restoration of the support capability of the spinal organ. A new technical procedure, microsurgery, is used in operations for such conditions as intervertebral disc prolapse and for the transpharyngeal access path. More frequently required is the relief of pressure on spinal roots and blood vessels of the cervical spinal column through uncoforaminectomy, which is now a successful surgical procedure.

Although promising initial successes were obtained with a vertebral endoprosthesis, an intervertebral disc endoprosthesis still does not exist.

The objective of a replacement intervertebral disc must be the imitation of the complex functions of the disc in the intervertebral motor segment so that intercorporal fusion operation may be avoided. Metal balls that Fernstroem (1972) used in the lumbar spinal column to replace osteochondrotic or traumatically destroyed intervertebral discs were unsuccessful. They used a gelatin substance as the nucleus pulposus that was surrounded by synthetic fibers in a manner adapted to the structures of the fiber ring lamellae. The technical problems of bonding the replacement disc in the bony epiphyses of the two adjacent vertebral bodies remain to be solved. Perhaps the bonding of an intervertebral disc prosthesis between a bony vertebral body and a replacement body of metal or synthetic material could one day be a technical solution.

7.4.3 Rehabilitation

7.4.3.1 Introduction

Rehabilitation is the full or at least partial retraining for a lifestyle with a high degree of self-sufficiency. It is very difficult to reintegrate chronic back pain sufferers into their everyday activities. Unfortunately, medical treatment and a patient's own self-help are frequently followed by such prolonged pain, and treatment that the reintegration into home, family, and work is often in question. Controlled rehabilitation encourages adaptation and may be a key to regaining joy in motion and even in the exertion of the body (Saunders and Jacobs 1976). Self-help groups facilitate the rehabilitation process.

Rehabilitation targeted to the pathological spinal diagnosis and the psychological state of the patient should be implemented as soon as possible. It should be monitored by the physician and physiotherapist and combined with the use of specific occupational therapy. The rehabilitation of paraplegia caused by vertebral fractures requires specialized equipment, architectural modifications to the individuals' homes, wheelchairs, and many adaptive aids for coping with everyday needs (Lindemann and Blohmke 1964; Meinecke 1976).

Many of the patients in today's rehabilitation centers suffer from chronic back pain. An "especially good retraining result" is possible for this group of patients who have an average age of 30 years (Kollmeier and Wehmeier 1977). Therefore, it is very important not to classify these young patients as permanently disabled without taking advantage of all available rehabilitation aids and therapies.

The effectiveness of rehabilitation can be augmented by the patient's performance of self-help measures. Yet, self-help must not be limited to a once- or twice-weekly class in a self-help group. Self-help comprises daily exercise that supports heart function and blood circulation regulation as well. Even for the back sufferer, exercise includes walking up and down stairs and swimming in warm water (32°C) as often as possible, without diving but with underwater exercises for the back muscles.

All self-help measures—individual as well as group measures—should in no way be abolished after resuming work and the usual daily schedule. To prevent the return of pain generated by intervertebral disc damage, as well as back insufficiency, the continuation of the measures that were found beneficial is of utmost importance.

8

Stresses on the Spine in Sports, Gymnastics, and Leisure

8.1 INTRODUCTION

Sports-generated influences may not only aggravate previously existing damage but may also damage the healthy spine. In some sports, insofar as the goal is peak performance through extensive training, the bones and soft tissues of the intervertebral disc are stressed to their stress capacity and beyond. The intervertebral motor segment is quite susceptible to impairments because of its structure and thus plays a decisive role in all studies of sports-related damage potentials.

During the last decade, important findings were obtained from studies on the development of specific damage in the support and motor system of athletes. The following seem especially significant:

- Training systems are oriented to a limited physical performance in addition to general training.
- Hard and specific training begins even before the conclusion of the growth period to produce top athletes.
- The immature spine is overexerted through stereotypical motions and stresses.
- The fact that the spine still continues to grow even after the conclusion of puberty and that immature tissues at the epiphyses of the vertebral body–intervertebral disc boundary are especially susceptible to damage is disregarded.
- The fact that previous latent damage frequently exists at the spine is disregarded.

The unfavorable process of developmental damage and the development of premature wear of the spine of young athletes has serious implications for the affected person. Sports medicine has been able to determine important evaluation principles for the development and progress of overstrain damage through long-term studies of the spine: eg, sport-specific intervertebral chondrosis, arthrosis of the uncovertebral articulations, arthrosis of the vertebral arch articulations, damage at the sacroiliac joints, and causes and aggravations of spondylolisthesis. Only results confirmed in this way guarantee the necessary foundation for promising preventive measures.

8.2 LEISURE SPORTS AND FITNESS PROGRAMS

8.2.1 Leisure Sports

Sports and exercises have always been important aspects of leisure. Leisure sports should not emphasize one particular sport and in the process be expanded to performance or even high-performance sport. In spite of general physical preparatory training and suitable compensation exercises, damage at the spine still develops in varying frequencies.

During leisure, the athlete is not limited to sports clubs. Vacations, trips, and family weekend trips provide a large range of opportunities for athletic activities. Unfortunately, they are not utilized to the desired degree. During longer vacations, the practice of only one particular sport should be avoided. Additional, different physical activities may compensate for the increasing sedentary time at work: hiking in noise-free environments, jogging, and many other possibilities.

During the leisure time of families with children, the offering of only one sport should be an exception. The primary concern in this situation is to encourage essentially playful, physical activity of the individual or group while considering the age of the children. The activities should as much as possible take place outdoors and satisfy the children's desire for playing. For psychological reasons, it is advantageous for the parents to participate as much as possible. A variety of stimulating leisure programs is recommended for children.

Sports during leisure should be undertaken with the following motto in mind: During leisure, athletic performance competition is not the issue, but rather athletic play. From this point of view, sports offer an endless number of possibilities from which everyone may select a suitable physical activity. According to personal circumstances (age, diseases, prevention of diseases, etc.), each person should choose an activity together with his or her physician.

Sports should benefit health and represent joy in exercise. Sports during leisure may take its clues from performance sports but should in no case demand intensive training for high performance. Endurance activities should be included in the leisure plan. They are urgently required for everyone but are rightly preferred by older persons because of physiological necessity. In contrast, speed and power training appeals more to the physiological capacity of youth and their psychological attitude toward sports. Naturally, endurance activities must also be adapted to the performance capacity of the individual. However, the objective of a slow increase should always be observed.

Also important is the simultaneous dynamic prolonged stress of large, function-related muscle groups: back muscles, with their relation to the neck-shoulder-arm areas and the pelvis-leg muscles. Long-distance performances best achieve the desired muscular activity and the urgently needed oxygen intake: jogging with interposed gymnastics and exercises, running rallies, longer hiking distances, etc. Such long-term training of muscles increases their blood circulation by 15% to 20%. This benefits all organs of the body, especially since cardiovascular function and respiration are improved. The spine benefits greatly because of the prolonged and even application of the "pump mechanism": encouragement of intervertebral disc metabolism (see section 3.2).

A medical examination before taking up a sport is not only sensible at any age, but necessary. This includes the compilation of a medical examination report (see section 6.3) that documents data for the evaluation of the physical condition. In cooperation with the patient, the suitable possibilities for athletic leisure activities can be suggested.

A few comments should be made concerning swimming during leisure time. High performance should not be aspired to, no matter whether the classical swimming styles or the more difficult swimming disciplines are preferred. Some of these disciplines overstress the spine. Swimming during leisure should be regarded as enjoyable play and should be practiced in this way by the individual or family (Loeckle 1982). Swimming daily or several times a week is an excellent way to maintain general health, especially as training for all muscles, especially the muscles attached to the spine and the connecting muscles to head and extremities. Swimming also belongs in physical therapy of the support and motor system (see section 7.4). It is both prophylactic and healing for back sufferers. With a few reservations, symmetrical swimming styles can be recommended for older persons.

Statements from three investigators can serve as summary statements because of their general meaning:

1. "A person is as old as his [or her] blood vessels" (Uhlig).
2. "A person is as young as his [or her] joints" (Cotta 1979a).
3. "A person is physically as functionally young as his [or her] spine" (Junghanns).

Subsequent sections discuss sports for leisure activities in further detail.

8.2.2 Fitness Programs

The achievement of general physical fitness was the incentive for the introduction of fitness programs. They are based on different precepts and have the maintenance, improvement, or restoration of unimpaired health as a goal. Whatever the goal, the basic procedure applied to the present condition is always "exercise." The support and motor system are exerted, and its central organ, the spine, is always statically and dynamically stressed. This applies to exercising in place as well as to walking, running, hiking, play, and all possible combinations of measures that strengthen the body.

Many fitness programs cannot be wholeheartedly supported with regard to the spine. Beginners of such programs who are over the age of 35 are urgently advised to undergo a medical examination of the spine, including suitable imaging procedures, before they become involved. The same applies if neck-back problems develop.

During medical counseling regarding exercise and jogging, both beneficial and negative influences on the heart, circulation, and respiration are the primary concern. In the support and motor system, the muscles receive special attention since longer exercise of large muscle groups (eg, jogging) stimulates their metabolism and thus favorably influences the entire metabolic process of the body. The joints of the extremities are considered only when the static and dynamic effect of exercise/running causes problems.

The spine often remains in the background, even though it must fulfill important tasks as the central organ of the support and motor system. During each walking or running step, impact is alternately transferred on the left and the right to the spine via the leg and pelvis. The acceleration and force in this process have been described in many studies. The swaying of the pelvis alternately stresses the lateral portions of the lower lumbar intervertebral discs. If they lack fluid and their internal turgor is already reduced, longer running results in lower back pain. It is the task of a well-trained musculoligamentous corset to prevent this: it limits the swaying motion of the spine and absorbs damaging stresses. This must be especially considered with higher age groups so that chronic problems in the back do not interfere with the enjoyment of fitness programs. Medical counsel about necessary therapy accompanying the program will be helpful. Table 8-1 gives ten guidelines for participation in fitness programs.

8.2.2.1 Jogging

For many decades, the slow, long-distance run, now called jogging, has been practiced as an additional or compensatory sport. As aerobic endurance training, it improves circulation and respiration and challenges the muscle groups of the extremities and the important muscles of the trunk. The additional oxygen intake benefits all organs. The diffusion fluid that supplies the bradytrophic tissue of the intervertebral disc attains the most beneficial biochemical and hormonal composition and therefore decreases the susceptibility of the intervertebral disc tissue to damage. Jogging also strengthens the back muscles and ligaments and develops endurance. Pelvic swaying is decreased and therefore the adverse influences on the lower lumbar intervertebral discs are decreased as well.

Jogging creates better static and dynamic muscle activity so that the back muscles are better able to fulfill their role for the spine. The impacts that exist in spite of running shoes and soft running surfaces reach the spine via the legs and pelvis. If weak muscles are unable to react quickly enough to the rapid sequence of impacts, back pain results, especially after longer, downhill distances. This warning sign requires the search for causes with the help of a physical and radiological examination by a physician experienced in spinal damage. If damage in the spine exists, the fitness program may have to be redesigned. Back pain during running may be caused

Table 8-1 Ten Guidelines for Fitness Programs

1. **Shaping up is fun.** Look for a sport you like and enjoy. It is never too late—even if you have not practiced a sport for many years.
2. **Shaping up benefits your health.** If you are healthy, you may shape up without reservations but also without false ambitions. If you are in doubt or have not exercised for a long time, consult your physician, especially if you are 35 or older.
3. **Shaping up together is enjoyable.** Get fit with your family, friends, and neighbors—while hiking, bicycling, or playing ball.
4. **Shaping up is a part of leisure.** Dedicate a certain part of your leisure time to shaping up: after work, on the weekend, during vacation. Gain endurance, strength, and mobility.
5. **Endurance is essential to survival.** Shape up daily for 10 minutes until your pulse reaches at least (but not much more than) 180 beats per minute minus your age (for 40 years, eg, 180 − 40 = 140 beats). Your heart will be grateful! Especially suitable are jogging, bicycling, swimming, cross-country skiing, and dancing.
6. **Keep your strength.** You should exercise the most important muscle groups on a daily basis, at least once for a short period and with strength, but do not overexert. Suitable are knee bends, body circling, arm flexion, and stretching against counterforce.
7. **Stay flexible.** Once a day, consciously move your joints to the fullest extent, eg, through bouncing and stretching and flexing and stretching. Extreme overstretching or anteflexion of the spine is not called for.
8. **There are opportunities everywhere.** Interrupt any prolonged sitting (work, television, travel), and use the opportunity to stand and walk. Ride your bicycle more often and your automobile less. Take the stairs instead of the elevator.
9. **Eating and shaping up must both be done correctly.** Eat a variety of foods, but in moderation. Avoid heavy foods and drinking. Additional calories can be burnt up only through increased exercise and physical activity.
10. **Once is not enough.** Consistency and endurance are important. Start with a little, but stay consistent. Then increase gradually. The joy in shaping up grows with your improved condition.

Source: Federal Medical Council and German Sport Association, 1976.

---

by different leg lengths, a scoliotic pelvis, and other damage at the lower extremities.

During the third decade of life, the intervertebral discs are often the cause of problems during jogging and other athletic running disciplines. If the pathological symptoms go unnoticed (ie, the program is not interrupted when these warning signs appear), the initial symptoms in the intervertebral disc tissue progress to an initially latent functional insufficiency that eventually progresses to perceptible disease. The ambitious insistence on increasing jogging performance may cause the progression of the intervertebral disc disorder. The physical training, which should in no case be discontinued, should initially be redirected (strengthening physiotherapy, swimming, etc.) to strengthen the back muscles. The back muscles regain their static and dynamic function better through these types of exercise than through jogging, where the inherent impacting vibrations would further affect the muscles. Walking in a hiking step may be helpful. Abstinence from physical activity is an incorrect reaction to neck and back pain. A life characterized by lack of exercise leads to muscle insufficiency of the spine.

8.2.2.2 Short Fitness Program

A few minutes in the morning, during working hours, or during a break from driving a long distance may be used for a short program for fitness (Hollmann 1976) as illustrated in Figure 8-1.

8.2.2.3 Active Vacation

Fitness programs may be transferred to a long vacation, which then becomes an active vacation. Ten guidelines for an active vacation are listed in Table 8-2. These guidelines essentially suggest active physical activities. The goal is exercise that includes the spine and pertinent muscles.

8.2.2.4 Hiking, Alpine Hiking, Mountain Climbing, and Cross-Country Skiing

Hiking, alpine hiking, mountain climbing, and cross-country skiing are popular as self-contained fitness programs for the entire body. They are suitable for all age groups and can be performed even in old age. The fresh air benefits respiration and the cardiovascular system and increases the oxygen content in the muscles.

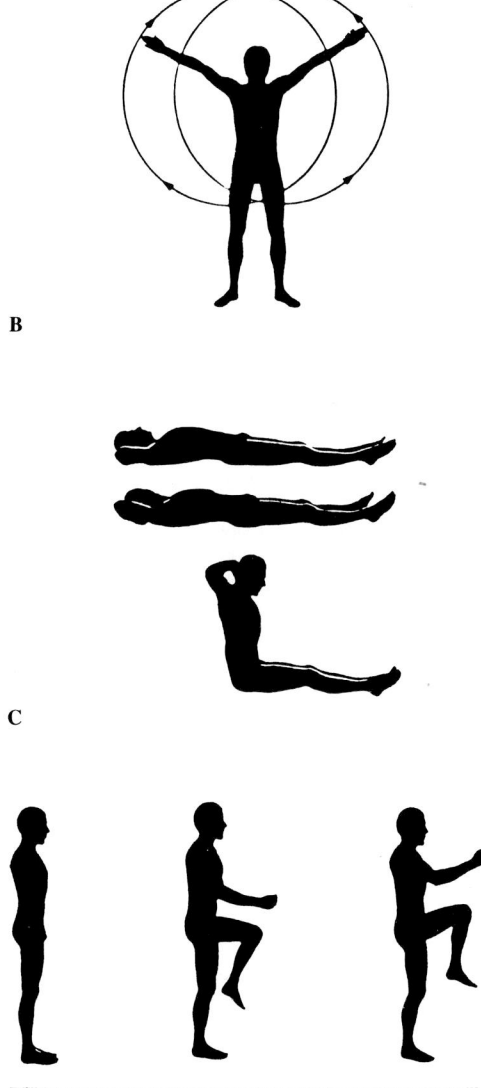

Fig. 8-1 Short fitness program. (**A**) With straddled legs, lifted arms, and anteflexion of the torso, touch the ground with the hands; stand up, stretch, and feather backward. Purpose of exercise: improve spinal column and hip joint mobility. Duration of exercise: 15 to 30 seconds. (**B**) Stand upright, lift the arms; circle the arms as fast as possible in opposing directions. Purpose of exercise: improve elasticity and shoulder mobility. Duration of exercise: 20 to 30 seconds. (**C**) Assume the supine position with the legs stretched and closed and the arms crossed behind the head. Move the head from side to side. Quickly sit up several times to a straight sitting position; lie down; sit up. Flex the head slightly forward and press against crossed hands 5 or 6 times without stretching the head backward. Purpose of exercise: strengthen abdominal, lumbar, rump, and thigh muscles; improve mobility of cervical spine. Duration of exercise: 15 to 30 seconds. (**D**) Alternately pull up the right then the left knee to the waistline as in running, with corresponding rhythmic arm movements. Purpose of exercise: speed training. Duration of exercise: 15 to 30 seconds [according to Hollmann (1976)].

Hiking also supports a well-coordinated use of the trunk muscles and relaxes chronic tensions. Someone who is planning a hiking vacation should hike beforehand.

Hiking in subalpine and alpine ranges is especially beneficial for the spine since the ascent and descent provide both static and dynamic exercise of the legs. The bouncing absorption with the longissimi muscles alternating with the steps from left to right are sources of strength for the movement and posture of the torso, which last a long time after the hiking has ended.

Long periods of hiking necessitate the use of a backpack. It was only in this century that the backpack was developed from a simple sack with two carrying straps into a backpack with a high-tech carrying frame. During its gradual

Table 8-2 Ten Guidelines for an Active Vacation

1. **Choose a suitable vacation destination.** Plan early and diligently. A relaxing vacation should last at least two weeks. Consider what your wishes are regarding a vacation and what is suitable for you.
2. **Prepare correctly for the vacation.** Actually, a vacation begins some time before the actual travel. Persons who get in shape before a vacation will enjoy themselves more. The hiker will be in better condition and less sensitive to the weather, the swimmer will have more endurance, and the skier will enter the slopes with more strength. Take along a travel emergency kit. If you are on constant medication, take along a sufficient supply: you may not be able to resupply yourself. This applies especially to persons with diabetes, heart and high blood pressure problems, asthma, or rheumatism. Prepare yourself for your destination by reading about it ahead of time. If you know in advance what awaits you, you will see and experience more.
3. **Play and sports equipment belong in the luggage.** Play brings joy, especially with your family. Bring along your sports equipment from home. Athletes need good equipment. Unsuitable equipment may spoil the vacation enjoyment and the good mood. Get good advice when you buy. You don't need the brand name the world champion uses, but you do need equipment to fit your size, weight, and performance level.
4. **Take active breaks on the way.** Driving an automobile may be heavy labor. Don't drive home harassed from work and continue into your vacation. Leave well rested and after plenty of sleep. Schedule enough time for the drive. Take a break every two to three driving hours and relax well: stretch, walk about, or run. Take time for a light meal: perhaps an enjoyable picnic. The traveling should be part of the vacation! Railroad and plane passengers should also get some exercise. If you travel with children, try to reach the destination in the afternoon. Then you will be able to recover somewhat from the drive, take care of formalities unhurriedly, and explore the area a little.
5. **Avoid unhealthy ambition.** The first day at the destination should be a day of rest! The body requires several days to adapt to high altitude, a great change in climate, or a significant time change. Explore your new surroundings restfully. After you have acclimatized, you can undertake some things or even start with a sport—but in moderation, without false ambition and overexertion. Don't throw yourself into new stress. Leisure or vacation stress is no remedy for work stress! False ambition damages health and spoils the vacation mood!
6. **Eat well without problems.** Don't let your enjoyment of food be spoiled during a vacation, but avoid vacation weight gain. A person exercising more during a vacation can eat a little more. A day spent hiking, in the mountains, in the water, or on a bicycle permits a somewhat more substantial menu. But be careful, and don't overestimate the calorie requirement!
7. **Learn sports with fun and patience.** Get to know yourself from a different side during the vacation, for instance in a sport new to you or in a new hobby. You'll then be able to bring something back home that will enrich your life. Try a sport you enjoyed in the past. Be patient, and especially have fun. Practice makes perfect, but you don't have to be perfect!
8. **Strengthen your heart and circulation.** Take a frequent "oxygen shower" in the form of a hike, bicycle tour, swim or jog, or endurance sport. The body changes much more oxygen into energy during these activities than during sitting, prolonged lying down, or strolling.
9. **Get closer in play.** Even children need leisure and freedom during a vacation. Nevertheless, this is an especially good opportunity to demonstrate family unity in play, sports, and fun. Play brings people closer together and overcomes age, language, and cultural differences.
10. **Stay active when the vacation ends.** A hurried, tiresome ride home can cost you in a few hours the entire relaxation you gained during your vacation! Schedule at least one day at home to acclimatize again. Make room for relaxation even after your vacation, and practice the hobby that provided so much enjoyment, stimulation, and contemplation during your vacation. Consider joining an athletics club.

Source: German Sport Association, 1978.

---

design, attention was fortunately paid to the form best suited for the back. Nevertheless, one question remains unanswered: What is the permissible weight of a backpack for a young hiker so that damage of a still immature spine can be avoided? There are opposing answers by physicians. Some recommend that any vertically stressing load on the spine of youths (up to age 16) should be avoided so that no overstress damage develops. Others recommend that young hikers have a modern backpack that lies on the back, is belted firmly at the pelvis, and has the capacity to load on top: only load carrying in this way is suitable for the axis of the spine.

The question of permissible load still remains unanswered. Table 7-2 shows the loads a healthy spine is able to carry regularly and over a long time for 8 hours a day. According to the legal regulation in France (Table 7-2), a youth under 14 years of age is permitted a load of 10 kg (5 kg for girls). However, Kohlback (1982) had the opinion that such a load was linked with the risk of spinal damage. For men, the damage-free load potential is 40 to 50 kg (see Table 7-2). Such loads are not rare among high-mountain hikers. The group should relieve the young participants by carrying their equipment so that the backpack weight exceeds the limit of 10 kg only as an exception (well-trained youths). If back problems develop, medical counsel must always be sought.

8.3 GENERAL INFORMATION ON SPORTS-RELATED SPINAL DISORDERS

8.3.1 Limits of Biomechanical Stress Resistance

The maximum stress of an athletic movement does not have to be damaging in its absolute extent. But its continuously repeated influence tires the resistance capacity of certain tissue types. If not enough attention is paid, the stress tolerance is exceeded too easily, eg, in the susceptible tissues of the intervertebral disc. Finally, after one or more initial "impacts," the initial damage develops. The shorter the interposed relaxation time is, the bigger this danger is. "Recovery through change" is a basic principle for maintaining the life of the intervertebral disc.

Extensive studies established in the past that the heart muscle can be trained just as body muscles: increase in mass, function capacity, and resistance capacity. Sports-related damage could be determined only in a fraction of 1%. Unfortunately, such positive results cannot be reported regarding sports stress on the spine—with the exception of the pertinent muscles.

There are some assumptions that the avascular cartilage tissue and especially the intervertebral discs become more resistant through stresses attributable to systematic sports training, but this is unconfirmed. The results of training success in these tissues cannot be measured in the same way as is possible for skeletal muscles and the heart. Exercise and exertion of the spine within physiological limits improve the diffusion exchange of the intervertebral disc metabolism, which is required to maintain health. However, the rapidly repeated or even singular stresses in certain sports are unphysiological. They result in reactions in the intervertebral disc tissue that cannot be completely understood given the present state of knowledge but that in no way increase the resistance capacity of the tissue. The pressure of these impacts not only displaces fluid in the tissue layers but probably also lowers the fluid content of the intervertebral disc and, therefore, has an unfavorable effect on the biochemical processes in the intervertebral disc. Based on past studies of spinal specimens, it may be assumed that pressure and in many sports accompanying spinal torsions are the initial impulses for microdamage and increasing tissue destruction. This is also known from practical experience.

The differentiated studies by Kuriyama (1973) support these opinions. Over a period of two years, young monkeys were fixated on a daily basis for 30 minutes at a rotation angle of the spine of 90 degrees. (At this angle, a substantial resistance was determined.) The studies included four groups: (1) without resection, (2) after resection of the interspinal and supraspinal ligaments in the lumbar spine, (3) after injection into the intervertebral discs, and (4) after laminectomy. The roentgenograms taken each month showed decreased intervertebral spaces in groups 2 and 4 after 6 months. Groups 1 and 3 showed only minor degenerative changes. In groups 2 and 4, posteromedial intervertebral disc prolapses occurred. The studies showed that 90-degree torsion overstresses the fiber tissue of the intervertebral discs. Damage developed and progressed rapidly.

These studies, which could be supplemented by others, show that prolonged mechanical stresses may damage the intervertebral disc tissue, including tearing of annular fibers, and also aggravate the progression of the damage once it has developed, including intervertebral osteochondrosis.

The stress capacity of the important intervertebral motor segments depends mostly on the anatomic structure in the boundary of the vertebral body and intervertebral disc. Koeller et al. (1981), in a study on the flexibility of the intervertebral discs under pressure, confirmed the damage already found in earlier pathoanatomic examinations. They were able to show that the increased impact stress on the vertebral body epiphyses and the epiphyseal annulus results in sclerosis of the end plate and simultaneous fissures in the annulus and vertebral body epiphysis. Such conditions were described for the first time in the studies of the Schmorl School (Dresden, 1929–1932).

During high performance sports training, the mechanical resistance force inherent in the intervertebral disc structure may be overstrained. This can be expected when the same stress affects the disc like percussion and when there is insufficient recovery time, eg, the continuously repeated bouncing during flips. Slowly progressing tissue wear follows. Finally, the latent insufficiency becomes a perceptible disorder with recurring pain. The stress capacity should be established in cooperation with a sports physician and trainer before this state is reached. It is therefore important to study athletic training procedures with regard to the stress tolerance of the intervertebral disc tissue with regard to pressure, flexion, and twisting in order to deduce altered motion processes for training and competition.

Previous damage from the embryonic period or the adolescent growth period, or damage that develops during the course of life, lowers the stress tolerance below the normal value. This happens when the resistance capacity is exceeded too rapidly during training. Only a well-trained musculoligamentous corset of the trunk is able, to a certain extent, to alleviate damage or prevent its progression for a certain time. These cases require the special attention of a sports physician.

Reports on sports damage attributable to chronic stresses are rare and show diverging results. Such complex studies cannot consider "sports" as such. Individual sports or groups of sports in which similar effects on the spine can be expected must be selected, and the training participants must be examined regarding the consequences of increased use of the spine.

A spine that is greatly stressed in its mechanical functions in many sports does not always measure up to the high requirements of performance sports in spite of regular, interposed compensation gymnastics and "interval training." This applies especially to children and youths. Thus functional damage may result if the stress tolerance limit is repeatedly and continuously exceeded. This applies not only to the bradytrophic tissue of the intervertebral disc and the cartilage of the vertebral arch joints but in the case of certain strains also to the bone, eg, spondylolysis/spondylolisthesis in the vertebral arch. Similar observations have been made for many sports in dissections of vertebral arch processes.

The beginning of arthrosis in the vertebral arch joints and uncovertebral joints, which is mostly connected with damage in the intervertebral disc, the biological partner of the segment, can be discovered only with oblique roentgenograms, oblique tomographs, or computerized tomography. This form of arthrosis, which is discovered more frequently because of specific studies, causes progressive pain. The symptoms continue to worsen and are controlled by the training-related exceeding of the stress tolerance, which is already lowered because of beginning cartilage damage. The young, ambitious athlete initially will not complain and frequently dissimulates. It has not been shown whether arthrosis of the vertebral arch joints results in sports disability, and thus leads to the end of the athletic career, and how the problems and decreased work ability progress in the years afterward. Only extensive studies can clarify whether certain sports instigate problems and damage during training and competition.

Some sports that subject the spine to special stress are listed in Table 8-3. In these disciplines, the danger lies in the frequent exceeding

Table 8-3 Sports with Special Stress on the Spine

Basketball	Rollerskating
Bicycle racing	Rowing
Butterfly swimming	Slalom skiing
Competitive skiing	Throwing sports
Floor exercises	Trampoline sports
Gymnastics	Triple jump
Iceskating	Weight lifting
Karate	Wrestling
Platform diving	

of the tolerance limits of bradytrophic tissues such as intervertebral discs and articular cartilage. The training impacts that affect the spine in the stereotypical, percussion manner, particularly in gymnastic disciplines, are responsible for the resulting damage:

- anteflexion, lateral flexion, and retroflexion, frequently with excessive lumbar lordosis
- short but rapidly repeated axial stresses such as jolts, jumps, and flips during hand and foot position changes
- varied figure combinations with forceful torsions

Special attention should be paid to the previously damaged spine and the spines of children and youths involved in performance sports.

Since physiological stress tolerances are different for each athlete, the sports physician must conduct a thorough physical examination (and follow-up examinations) with imaging procedures to determine the maturity of the spine, congenital abnormalities, and previously existing changes from the adolescent growth period. Nevertheless, the assessment will often still be difficult. If there are problem cases, they must be referred for observation to a specialist in the particular sport. There is always the danger that ambitious juveniles may impede the work of the sports physician.

Overstraining in sports affects primarily the bradytrophic tissue of the intervertebral discs. In addition, the hyaline cartilage of the joints may be affected: head joints, uncovertebral joints, vertebral arch joints, vertebrocostal joints, and sacroiliac joints.

8.3.2 Statistics

As in most statistics regarding spinal damage, reliable data in sufficient quantity on the connection between the individual sports and related damage of the spine do not exist. Gender-specific data do not exist. There are insufficient data to compare specific age groups. Frequently, data for various sports are combined. Of the large number of statistics on the relationship between sports and the spine, a report by Steinbrueck (1983) should be mentioned. Seven percent of the examined athletes reported spinal problems. They were distributed differently among various sports (see Table 8-4). The report also contained additional information regarding diagnoses and causes.

A serious problem can be recognized in all statistics: beginning training of performance sports during early childhood or youth. In these age groups, the spine has just started giving its vertebral bodies their final shape. The vertebral body bones and the covering cartilage plates are immature. In the cartilaginous epiphyses, the dot-shaped bone epiphyses gradually develop and finally fuse into rings, which bond with the vertebral body bones. The last growth processes continue until puberty and beyond. These findings are based on statistically confirmed studies of thousands of spines and have been confirmed anatomically and radiographically (see section 2.1). It seems strange that certain performance sports are promoted for preschool and young children even though it has been shown that the still growing spine is subjected to excessive requirements with regard to stresses and mobility. Damage is inevitable.

Two important questions have hardly been addressed statistically: How many athletes "drop out" after beginning performance training or the competition phase because of back problems? What damage has developed in the spine of top athletes who had to give up their high-performance sport after great success because of age (or other reasons)? Some high-performance athletes end their athletic career without significant cervical-back-sacral problems. But if prob-

Table 8-4 Percentage of Spinal Problems Distributed among Individual Sports

Sport	%
Spear throwing	42.1%
Swimming	37.9%
Weight lifting	34.5%
Trampoline	28.6%
Rowing	27.8%
Sport students	23.1%
Horseback riding	21.8%
Gymnastics	19.4%
Biking	17.1%

Data from Steinbrueck (1983).

lems develop later when the back muscles with their connective shoulder-arm muscles, pelvis and leg muscles, and abdominal-thoracic muscles lose their former strength, they are not attributed to sports-related causes. Only well-documented follow-up statistics can clarify these relationships.

In the future, it will be necessary to clarify the possible sports-related influences on the spine through statistics and systematic long-term studies of athletes involved in particular high-performance sports. This should include the initial examination (with radiological tests), which must be referred to when problems occur. Damage in the intervertebral motor segments should be noted, ie, primarily the height and outline of the intervertebral space and arthrosis at the vertebral arch joints and sacroiliac joints. In the lower lumbar spine and lumbosacral boundary, conditions at the interarticular portions of the vertebral arch and spinous processes should be ascertained. Attention should be paid to sports that are already performed at a young age before the conclusion of growth and to the style of high-performance training: gymnastics, floor exercises, platform diving, rowing, trampoline sports, acrobatics, ballet, etc. Comparable figures on the development and progression of damage should be compiled only within a certain age group and for the same duration of training and intensity of the athletic training.

The classification by Groher (1971) into a level I for the first five years of training and a level II for the additional years of intensive high-performance training for 325 athletes can be recommended for future studies. The beginning of sports training in level I was approximately between the ages of 7 and 20 (with an average of 12 years). After approximately five years of training in the performance sport (level I), the athlete chose the intensive high-performance training followed for nine years (level II). The results of the studies by Groher and other investigators are used for comparison in the following sections on individual sports.

Groh [cited in Chapchal (1983)] compiled statistics from the data of various investigators that show the great differences in the incidence of the same pathological symptoms in various sports (Table 8-5). Later, Groh and Groh (1975) compiled more statistics (Table 8-6) that clearly show that a certain top group of high-performance athletes can fulfill the training and competition requirements in spite of spinal damage. In the examined athletes, the existing damage was merely the memorial to acute conditions that had occurred earlier. It is very probable that these conditions comprised bony, ligamental, and/or muscular damage.

Braun (1969) reported on patients he operated on for prolapsed discs. He concluded that there was proof that sports should be held partially responsible for the development of lumbar prolapsed discs. Only horseback riding was participated in by a larger number in his group of patients who had undergone surgery than in a control group. However, Braun pointed out that these results should be considered with reservation because of the small number of patients.

Because of many unanswered questions, an attempt should be made to determine the extent of the stresses that affect the spine for each sport. Based on such statistical foundations, it would then be possible to examine and clarify the relationships between a particular sport and damage of the spine. Such results could lead to improved training methods, including identification of the recovery phases that are essential for the cartilage of the vertebral arch and uncovertebral joints.

8.4 STRESS AND DAMAGE POTENTIAL IN VARIOUS TYPES OF SPORTS

8.4.1 Introduction

The following sections group sports (including ballet, dancing, and acrobatics) that are assumed to stress the spine in the same manner. The system is oriented toward the spine and frequently deviates from medical or Olympic groupings. Some groups, despite a common generic name, have different influences on the central axial organ. This applies, for instance, to winter sports, which include, in addition to sledding and cross-country skiing, complicated jump disciplines such as ski jumping. Speed skating is also a winter sport but exerts stresses on the spine, through an especially unnatural

Table 8-5 Pathological Spinal Symptoms in X-Ray Films of Athletes

Author	Year	Sport	No. Athletes	Symptoms			
				Diverse	Osteochondr.	Vertebral Dislocation	Scheuermann's
Querg	1958	Rowers (m)	59	0%	0%	0%	30 (51%)
Jäger	1959	Competitive gymnasts (m, f)	24	0%	3 (12.5%)	33.7%	25%
Refior and Zenker	1970	Young gymnasts	50	Spina bifida 28 (56%)	0%	0%	25 (50%)
Tütsch and Ulrich	1974	Competitive gymnasts (m, f)	22	0%	0%	7 (30%)	13 (59%)
Groher	1970	Platform divers (m, f)	17	Vertebral arch arthrosis 14 (82%)	0%	5 (29%)	0%
Jaros and Cech	1965	Weight lifters	20	0%	0%	0%	0%
Hördegen	1974	Riders	115	Vertebral arch arthrosis 60 (52%)	20 (17.5%)	5 (4.4%)	57 (49.5%)

Data from Groh, cited in Chapchal (1983).

Table 8-6 Spinal Symptoms in Athletes Whose Performance Was Not Affected

Author	Year	Sport	No. of Athletes	Diverse	Osteochondr.	Vertebral Dislocation	Scheuermann's	Cause
Loder and Amsler	1961	Average population					30%	
Rübe and Hemmer	1962	Average population					30%	
Refior and Zenker	1970	Youths	25				28%	
Jäger	1969	Gymnasts (m, f)	24	0%	3 (12.5%)	4 (16%)	3 (12.5%)	Microtrauma
Rücker and Kobbe	1965	Sports club	340	0%	0%	0%	86 (27%)	Overstress
Querg	1958	Competitive rowers	59	0%	0%	0%	30 (51%)	Overstress
Refior and Zenker	1970	Young gymnasts	50	Spina bifida 28 (56%)	0%	0%	25 (50%)	Overstress
Groher	1970	Platform divers (m, f)	17	Spina bifida 6 (35%) Baastrup's 10 (59%) Vertebral arch arthrosis	0%	5 (29%)	0%	Trauma
Tosatti and Gavioli	1950	Weight lifters	10	0%	0%	0%	0%	
Jaros and Cech	1965	Weight lifters	20	0%	0%	0%	0%	
Bozdech	1966	Top athletes	20	0%	0%	0%	0%	
Beuker et al.	1966	Weight lifters	254	No clinical symptoms	No x-rays	20 (100%)		

Data from Groh and Groh (1975).

body posture, that are very different from those exerted in the usual winter sports or ice skating (dancing). Sports that can be performed without any significant damage to the spine are not discussed.

In some groups of sports, the spine is very frequently subjected to risky excesses of performance tolerances since this is the only way the athlete can attract attention: weight lifters, contortionists, catapult acrobats, ski acrobats, gymnasts, trapeze acrobats, trampoline athletes, etc. Many sports are suitable as club sports or athletic leisure activities for any healthy athlete but can also be performed as Olympic sports with a highly stressful use of the spine: swimming, horseback riding, rowing, and many others. These broad opportunities in many sports make it difficult to evaluate the spinal risk. The range of severity is extensive, especially since the time interval of athletic activity is an indispensible factor for the evaluation. A serious problem for the development of sports-related damage of the spine is the abuse of beginning training in some sports in earlier and earlier years of childhood.

8.4.2 Driving Sports

Even though there are large differences in driving sports between motorized high-performance machines and "leg-propelled" bicycles, the possibly damaging mechanical influences in driving sports affect the spine to a significant degree. Unfortunately, no sufficient control studies exist. Sports medicine must establish the biomechanical effects of various vibrations on the bony, cartilaginous, and connective tissue elements of the spine.

8.4.2.1 Car Racing

The sinus-shaped, stochastic or jolting vibrations generated by the road surface and structure of the vehicle are transferred to the drivers of race cars in very different directions because of the varied seat designs. The stress on the spine depends on whether the driver takes a more sitting or lying position and is also influenced by the design of the back support. Since 1956, Dupuis et al. (1956, 1959, 1963, 1972, 1966) have studied basic questions regarding agricultural tractors and automobiles. Similar study procedures would be suited to studies of race cars. In any case, detailed examinations of the spine of race car drivers would have to be available first so that the technical questions and studies could be specifically applied.

8.4.2.2 Motorbike Racing

The dangers of motorbike racing apply espeically to youths, whose spines are still growing. The danger is increased by the fact that youths prefer to ride their small mopeds on difficult race courses. These courses contain many deliberately uneven areas that transfer a very large number of jolting vibrations to the immature spine. The most susceptible parts of the growing spine, the vertebral body–intervertebral disc boundary in the thoracic spine, including the boundary with the lumbar spine, are seriously damaged. Motorbike riding should be taken seriously because of the predictable spinal damages that are often disregarded by parents.

The stress on the trunk, especially on the spine with its muscles and ligaments, through stochastic and jolting vibrations is substantial with all motorbikes. The vibrations have a drum fire effect. The vibrations and irregular jolting of the machines are obvious to the spectators on dirt tracks and other difficult courses. Drivers who have previous damage, such as juvenile kyphosis and scoliosis, should pursue this sport only after a consultation with an experienced racing sport physician. Any pain must be discussed with a physician before substantial, irreversible spinal damage develops, which may result in life-long pain. The wearing of a wide and firm loin-pelvis belt is urgently recommended to every motorbiker, even if no back pain or stiffness has occurred.

8.4.2.3 Bicycle Racing

As in many other sports, total kyphosis (Fig. 8-2) is an inevitable status symbol of bicycle racers. The negative effects of sinus vibrations and jolting vibrations are intensified by hard training: road training requires weekly distances of 300 to 500 km including steep inclines

Fig. 8-2 Total kyphosis of a bicycle racer [from Kukla (1982)].

from biking athletes in the top performance class.

Initially, general complaints about back pain are common. They recede gradually with progressing stiffness, as in other disciplines with a similar development of the athletic hump. Increasing problems develop in the areas above and below the stiffness. The frequent, compensatory lordosis of the cervical spine leads to cervical migraine and cervical syndromes, such as neck-shoulder-arm pain. Starting from damage at the lower transition of the kyphosis, lumbago and ischialgia develop.

Neugebauer studied the development and progression of the biker's hump in 1961. The kyphotic forms with the strongest curvature occur at the spinous process of the 10th thoracic vertebra but are frequently continued to the lumbar spine. Neugebauer discovered osteochondric damage in bike racers at an earlier age than usual. In his opinion, the forceful traction work of the arms has an additional aggravating effect on the rounding of the back. As compensation sports, field and track athletics, swimming, and gymnastics are suitable. For further information, see Jani (1981), Kohlrausch (1961), and Seyfarth (1957, 1962a).

8.4.3 Track and Field Sports

In the past, training for track and field disciplines was mostly oriented toward the discipline itself. Today, the competition has become harder and requires time-consuming physical training, including power training with workout machines. With regard to muscle training, the muscles of the trunk, including the abdominal and thoracic walls, play an especially important role, since they may to a certain extent be able to control and alleviate the impacts on the spine generated by running and jumping.

Each style of walking, running, and take-off runs before jumping results in impacts. With each step, they are initially transferred from the foot, over the leg and pelvis, to the lumbosacral boundary, and then to the lumbar spine. The intervertebral discs of this region must absorb the arriving sinus-shaped vibrations and stochastic impacts. The musculoligamentous corset of the trunk is also involved in important tasks. The rapid, consecutive steps in training and competition in walking, running, and jumping disciplines stress the intervertebral discs like an ongoing percussion. The effect is increased if twisting, torsion, or even lateral slipping is added.

Even normal walking influences the central axial organ with its right-left swaying motion of the pelvis. In the process, the lumbar spine performs slight torsions in addition to alternating lateral flexions. Muenchinger (1960 to 1964) recorded accelerograms according to which a person with a weight of 70 kp stresses the lumbar spine during walking with flat heels with 20 kp (½ g). Walking in high heels results for each step in a load of 40 kp. The wave-shaped stress process during walking and climbing stairs is illustrated in Figure 7-12.

Overstresses of the spine attributable to incorrect performance of running steps and swing stresses that approach overexertion may cause lumbagolike and sciaticalike pain in running and jumping athletes, especially when the back muscles and connecting muscles to the pelvis and legs tire. Not infrequently, blockades in the sacroiliac joints or vertebral arch joints develop. In contrast to other sports, spondylolysis and spondylolisthesis are only rarely observed in runners.

The sinus-shaped or stochastic vibrations transferred into the lumbar spine result in great demands on the intervertebral discs of this area. Fluid reduction of all tissue elements of the affected intervertebral discs must be expected. This is connected with an adversely changed metabolism. During longer running distances, the rest periods needed for the recovery are absent. In this way, chronic damage may develop that will prevent further athletic involvement.

Athletes of many track and field disciplines are susceptible to spine-related damage with corresponding pain such as lumbago, sciatica, and vertebral blockades (which may start from the intervertebral space, vertebral arch joints, or sacroiliac joints). This susceptibility is not infrequently caused by previous damage that is located not only at the spine but at the lower extremities. Even a very slight abnormal curvature of the spine (kyphosis, scoliosis) that is not obvious in daily life and that causes no problems diminishes the high performance capacity required for the athlete. The same applies to differences in leg lengths, hip joint disorders, a scoliotic pelvis, etc. Even if such damage results in only slight load differences between the left and right during the athletic strain, the danger of premature sequelae in the spine exists, which hampers the athletic career. During the fitness test, special attention must therefore be paid to the question of whether the beginning of a career as a track and field athlete can be medically justified. Running and jumping disciplines require a proper, symmetrically distributed pressure load on the spine. In the case of unilaterally emphasized loads, lumbosacral problems, sciatic root irritations, and possibly blockades occur. There are no extensive studies that provide a survey of long-term observations.

Figure 8-3 (Scheele et al. 1979) is based on the examination of 149 track and field athletes. In addition to walking, running, and jumping, the throwing sports (ball, discus, hammer, vault) and decathlon are included. The high incidence (62.7%) of trunk damage is striking. However, the spine was not mentioned separately. Accord-

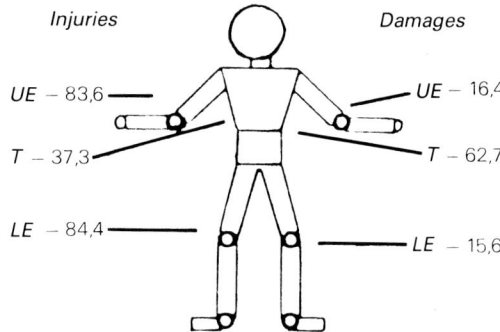

Fig. 8-3 Percentage distribution of damage and injuries in track and field athletes (Scheele et al. 1979). UE = upper extremities; LE = lower extremities; T = trunk. Note the most damage at the trunk, ie, the spine.

ing to general experience, a high percentage of damage occurs at the spine.

8.4.3.1 Walking

The lumbar spine of walkers is subject to a special stress during the 20-km Olympic course because it causes swaying of the pelvis that excessively stresses the motor segments of the lumbar spine (see Fig. 8-4). No long-term studies regarding the spine of walkers have been conducted. Scheele et al. (1972) described arthrosis of the hip joints in walkers.

The lumbar spine of tractor operators moves in a similar swaying manner but is subject to

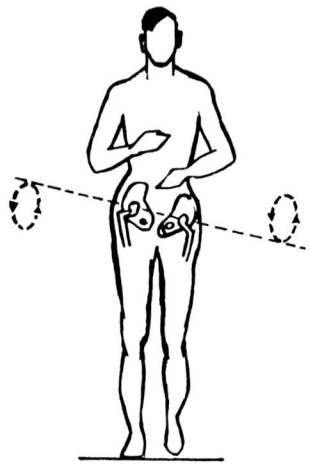

Fig. 8-4 Swaying motion (rotation) of the pelvis during athletic walking [according to Whitblock].

even more jolting. Dupuis (1974) produced clear pictures in which the rolling of the spinous processes of the lumbar vertebrae was made visible (Fig. 5-8). This test procedure is also able to determine the rolling of the lumbar vertebrae in walkers, possibly on a tread mill. The rolling figures that have been recorded during the lateral motions and the ascent and descent of the spinous process tips will be able to establish at what level of the lumbar spine the swaying is concentrated in walkers, ie, which intervertebral discs are primarily affected by stresses and torsion. These segments should be examined with X-rays for damage in the intervertebral spaces (intervertebral osteochondrosis) and arthrosis of the vertebral arch joints. Radiocinematography could also supply more detailed information on the movement processes in the spine. These results could help establish less damaging training and walking methods.

Rompe and Rieder (1976) recommended the avoidance of walking as a sport (also tennis and gymnastics) when chronic lumbago or myostatic insufficiency existed. For additional information, see Gregersen and Lucas (1967) and Wyndham et al. (1961).

8.4.3.2 Running

During each athletic running step, an impact force results that is almost twice the starting acceleration (2 g) and alternately affects the left and right leg. Therefore, the overstress damage of runners was examined in the leg area. However, the vibrations that penetrate over the transmission path (foot-leg-pelvis) to the lumbar spine must be absorbed from the intervertebral discs of the lumbosacral region.

Sprinters. Sprinters, who first remain in the rest position (Figs. 8-5 and 8-6) in the starting box, go for the starting position into an arm-supported squat with a tilted pelvis and total kyphosis. At the instant of the start, the kyphosis straightens in the initial rise and changes into a straightened trunk position with the forward stance of the body. Because of a slight lordosis of the cervical spine, the head is slightly inclined toward the back of the neck. The sprinting distance is run in the same posture with large steps. The wideswinging arms are accompanied by twisting of the spine. The low start of the sprinter is depicted in Figure 8-6.

It has not been determined what kind of vibrations and/or impacts affect the lumbosacral boundary during the alternating steps from left to right in short-distance running. It is known that they affect the intervertebral discs in the lower lumbar section as well as their partners in the intervertebral motor segment, vertebral arch joints, and sacroiliac joints.

Medium-Distance Runners. Medium-distance runners have a slightly different running

Fig. 8-5 Start in sprinting.

Fig. 8-6 Drawings of the low start of the sprinter [according to Wehlen (1976)].

style compared to short-distance runners (Fig. 8-7). The trunk is inclined less forward. They look straight ahead since the head is held in the axial direction of the upper body. To what extent the influences of this trunk and head posture result in stresses on the lower lumbar intervertebral discs and pertaining joints remains to be determined. This also applies to the cervical spine and the stresses on the spine.

Long-Distance Runners. During each 10,000-m course, the runner (with 6,000 running steps) stresses each leg 3,000 times. The long-distance runner runs 70 km per week. During strict precompetition training, such runners run between 100 and 200 km per week. If this distance is run over a period of 10 years at competition speed, this results in 10,950,000 impacts for each side of the transmission path to the lumbar spine (Groh and Groh 1975).

In the lumbar area, each running step results in a lateral flexion with a short arch that changes almost 11 million times. This means that every time the jolting unilateral stress on the lower lumbar intervertebral discs occurs, a simultaneous slight torsion also occurs because of the long running step. Depending on the mobility of the spine, the torsion may be increased through the additional torsion between the horizontal axis of the shoulders and pelvis that develops from the alternating arm movements. The resulting consequences for intervertebral discs, vertebral arch joints, and sacroiliac joints were discussed in the sections on sprinters and medium-distance runners.

Brueggemann and Koring (1980) examined problems and pathological symptoms of the support and motor system of 100-km runners that led to withdrawal from the sport. The runners were between 13 and 75 years of age. The interest of the investigators was limited to the lower extremities.

A surprisingly large number of trained long-distance runners are in high age groups: 122 runners with an average age of 68.8 years were examined by Pufe and Hilmer (1980) but only from a sports medicine/internal medicine point of view. Nothing was reported on the condition of their spine.

The 42-km marathon has always been regarded as the crowning performance of any long-distance runner. It is regarded as the domain of middle-aged runners. More recently, sport physicians have supported the participation of children in marathon races. What damage is done to the juvenile spine that receives such rapid and repeated impacts during training and competition? This question can be answered only with the help of initial and follow-up examinations, including radiodiagnostics. How many children who began long-distance running training had to stop because of spinal problems? When will the time come when this action is condemned?

Relay Racers. Relay races have no peculiar influences on the spine since the length of the steps corresponds essentially to those of other running disciplines.

Hurdle Sprinters and Hurdle Runners. The stresses on the spine are completely different during hurdle sprinting and hurdle running than during long-distance running. This is because of the forward stance of the body, the force application of the jumping leg (Fig. 8-8), and the stress

Fig. 8-7 Phase pictures of medium-distance running.

268 CLINICAL IMPLICATIONS OF NORMAL BIOMECHANICAL STRESSES ON SPINAL FUNCTION

Fig. 8-8 Women's 100-m hurdle run. (**A**) Motion drawings. (**B**) Running over a hurdle, frontal view [according to Jonath et al. (1977)]. The picture corresponds to No. 6 in **A**.

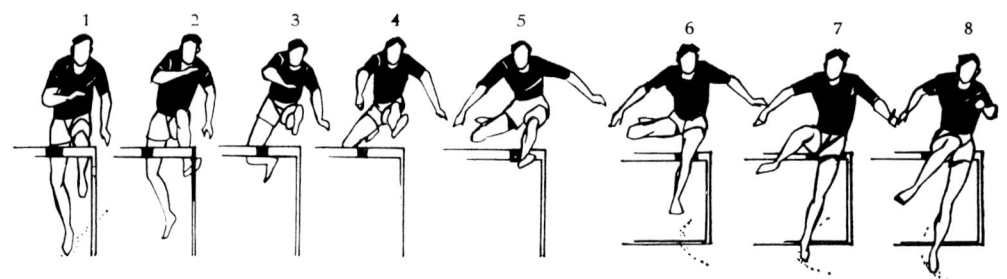

Fig. 8-9 The hurdle step in a curve [from Schmolinsky, 1974].

against the pelvis through the landing leg. In addition, there is a slight tilting and torsion of the pelvis during the jumping process, especially in curves (Fig. 8-9). The rapidly alternating stress influences are the causes of lumbago and sciatic pain, as well as the painful blockades of the vertebral arch articulations or sacroiliac joints.

More than half of all top hurdle runners complain of prolonged back pain, which is called hurdle runners' disease by the runners themselves (Cotta and Krahl 1977). The investigators described osteochondrotic and spondylarthrotic damage in 17% of the examined runners, which was attributed to the innumerable repetitions of the hurdle step. Because of the many problems, and also damage at the spine, of hurdle runners, the sports physician is advised not only to treat the "back pain" but to diagnose the existing

Fig. 8-10 Drawings of jumping during an obstacle race.

symptoms so that a specific therapy can be prescribed.

Obstacle Course Runners. Running the obstacle course is very different from hurdle running because of the prolonged jumping phase (Fig. 8-10). During the approach to the obstacle, a completely neutralized lordosis dominates while the trunk is flexed forward. During the jumping phase, the spine is gradually straightened and is finally in the upright position. During the landing in the water ditch after the stretched-out jump, the landing leg is subject to a hard impact that is transferred to the lumbosacral boundary. (A bad landing frequently results in partial tears of the Achilles tendon.)

8.4.3.3 Jumping

There are many relationships between jumping and the spine. Depending on the discipline, they exist primarily in the jump-off pressure of the jumping leg, which affects the lumbosacral boundary unsymmetrically; during the landing on both feet, during which the pressure continues over both legs to the spine; or through the rotating motion of the trunk in the longitudinal body axis. A strong curvature that results in total kyphosis also takes place during the down jumps (long jump, triple jump).

Muenchinger (1964) produced accelerograms on acceleration and stress during down jumps from a height of 50 cm (Fig. 8-11) in which the differences between a soft (bouncing) and a hard (stiff) landing on the ground are portrayed. The calculations from his studies are based on a person weighing 70 kg:

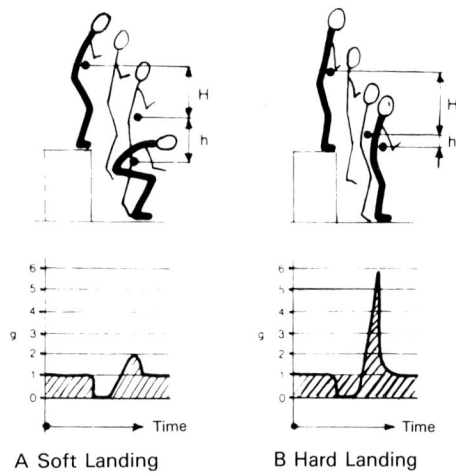

Fig. 8-11 Jump accelerogram (described in text).

Down jump from a 50-cm height	
Soft, bouncing landing	2 g = 80 kp
Hard landing	6–8 g = 240–320 kp
Fall from a 4-m height	9–11 g = 360–440 kp
Fall on buttocks	10–20 g = 400–800 kp
For comparison	
Impacts during riding a tractor	5 g = 200 kp
Anteflexed posture while lifting 50 kg	= 700 kp

These accelerograms cannot be applied to athletic jumping disciplines without reservations because the many new jumping techniques (straddle, flop) avoid higher down jumps. Even though polevaulting requires a high start, the fall on the back on a soft surface results in different stresses on the spine than the down jump does on the feet.

The stresses on the spine, which vary in the jumping disciplines, with regard to direction and force cannot be tolerated by a previously changed spine. Therefore, a fitness test should include a thorough physical and radiological examination of the spine. A florid juvenile kyphosis should prohibit jumping training. Other disorders of the spine such as scoliosis and spondylosis/spondylolisthesis must also be critically considered with regard to possible athletic involvement.

Long Jump. During the long jump (Fig. 8-12), the jumping-off pressure of the jumping leg initially plays an important role with regard to the spine. It was measured with the dynamogram at 500 kp and exists with approximately the same force at the lumbar spine–pelvis-hip area (LPH area). For a discussion of the significance of this pressure on the intervertebral discs in this region, see section 3.2.

During the final landing phase of the long jump curve (Fig. 8-12), the straightened, upright trunk posture turns into an anteflexion, with kyphosis and lifting of the legs. This forcefully executed "folding up like a pocket knife" creates stresses with a tendency to shift to the intervertebral discs of the lumbosacral boundary. This applies to several long jump styles, eg, the running, stepping, and floating jump.

Down Jump. The down jump is associated with similar problems since in the final phase of the jump there are substantial forces that reach the LPH area. In addition, the upper body and pelvis must be straightened. Thus the load is distributed unevenly, the nucleus pulposus may be displaced, and unsymmetrical stresses on the fiber rings of the intervertebral discs may result. The consequences of these processes are discussed in section 4.6.

Triple Jump. In the triple jump (Fig. 8-13), which is composed of hop, step, and jump stresses, the jumping leg alternates between the right and left several times, in contrast to the long jump, and therefore subjects the spine to several impacts. The special landing technique of the final jump, during which the thoracic and

Fig. 8-12 Long jump [from Krahl and Riemer (1981)].

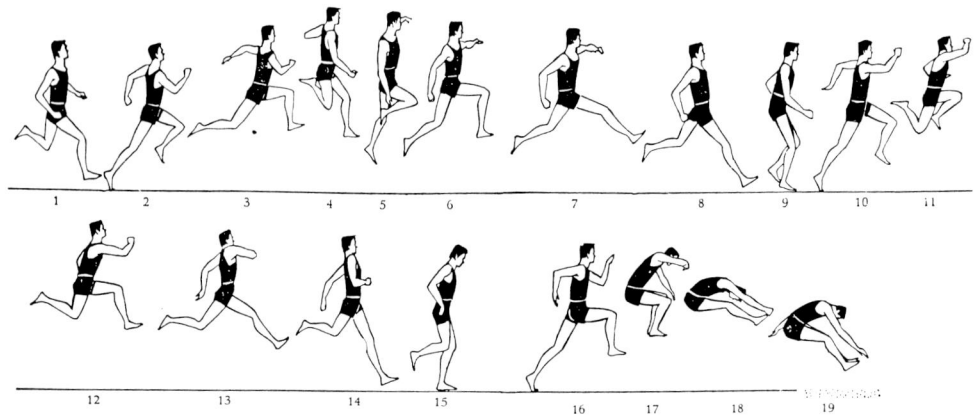

Fig. 8-13 Triple jump from a "hop, step, and jump" position [from Schmolinsky (1984)].

lumbar spine initially form a total kyphosis, results in problems for the spine in addition to those described for the landing impact of the long jump.

High Jump. In high jumping, the straddle style has recently been almost abandoned (Fig. 8-14). After the great stress on the jumping leg, which is greater than in any other type of sport, the pole is overcome by a rotation of the body in the longitudinal spinal axis in an abdominal position. The jump-off force and body rotation have a significant influence on the lumbar spine.

In the Fosbury flop (Fig. 8-15), the body in a lordotic posture pushes itself by rotating around the longitudinal axis backward over the pole. The rolls common in the high jump have a very adverse effect on the mechanics of the lumbosacral boundary because of the torsion of the spine.

Donskoi (1961) found vertical pressures between 50 and 450 kg during the jump-off phase, as ground pressure (Fig. 8-16). Such forces are always transferred as stochastic impacts to the lumbar spine from step to step, in changing force, over the transmission path of the leg. The impact forces reaching the lumbar spine have not

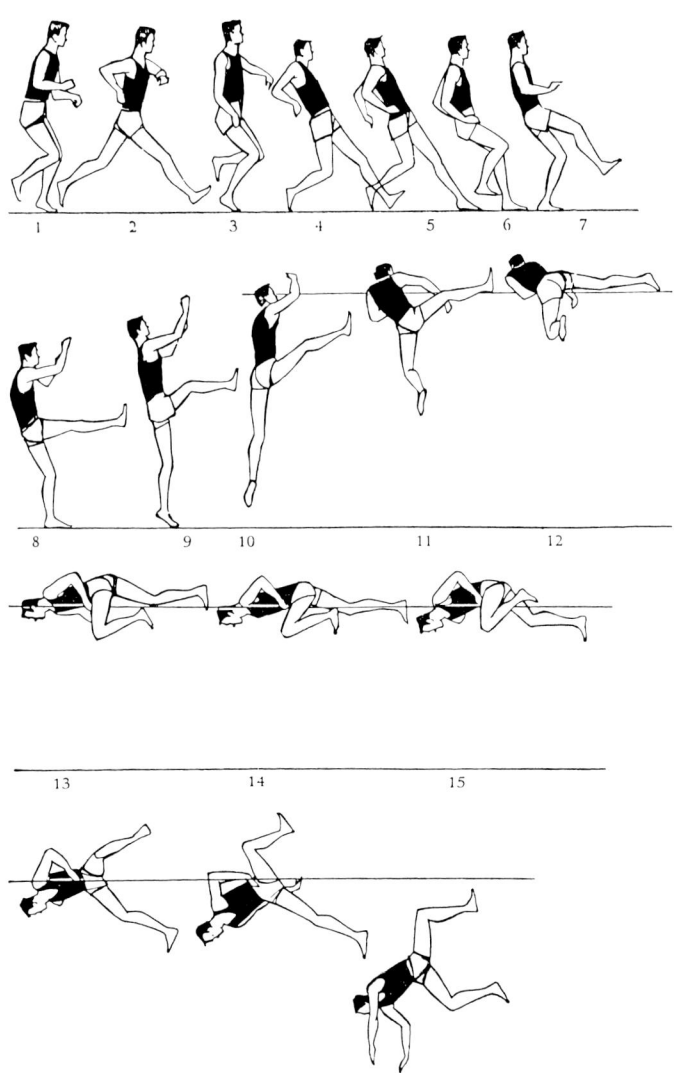

Fig. 8-14 High jump in the straddle style [from Schmolinsky (1974)].

272 Clinical Implications of Normal Biomechanical Stresses on Spinal Function

Fig. 8-15 High Jump with the Fosbury flop [from Krahl and Riemer (1981)].

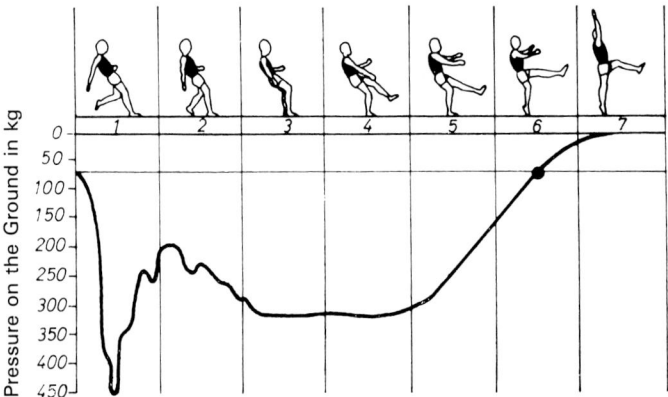

Fig. 8-16 Vertical pressures affecting the spine (primarily axially) during the jump-off phase of high jumping [from Donskoi (1961)].

been systematically determined for high jumping.

Krahl (1975b) studied the damage caused by the flop jump. Spinal damage increases, especially if there is posture damage and structural disorders. It has not been determined whether posture damage and structural disorders existed before the start of training or whether they were a result of training. The mostly dynamic power training takes up approximately one half of the total training time.

Pole Vaulting. Pole vaulting with metal or fiberglass poles (Fig. 8-17) subjects the athlete to the most difficult task during the transition from the jump-off to the suspension phase. Pole vaulting is one of the disciplines with the greatest damage potential. Theiss (1980) reported on the follow-up examination of 46 athletes: 58.7% complained of recurring problems in the lumbar spine, which were mostly noticed during the jump-off phase and during the use of fiberglass poles. Scoliosis was found in 48% of 46 athletes. Spondylolysis, in part with olisthesis, affected 39.1%. Jungmichel and Gabler (1970) reported an increased incidence of Baastrup's disease.

8.4.3.4 Decathlon/Quintathlon

The men's decathlon consists of an interesting combination of several running and jumping disciplines as well as several throwing sports. The men's quintathlon is of only minor significance in competitions. The women's quintathlon consists of two jumping disciplines, two running disciplines, and shot putting.

Scheele et al. (1979) reported the results of a poll of decathlon athletes. The investigators expressed their surprise that in spite of the strength, speed, and endurance required of the athletes, relatively few injuries or damages were reported. They suggested that the variety of movements in training and competition were accountable for

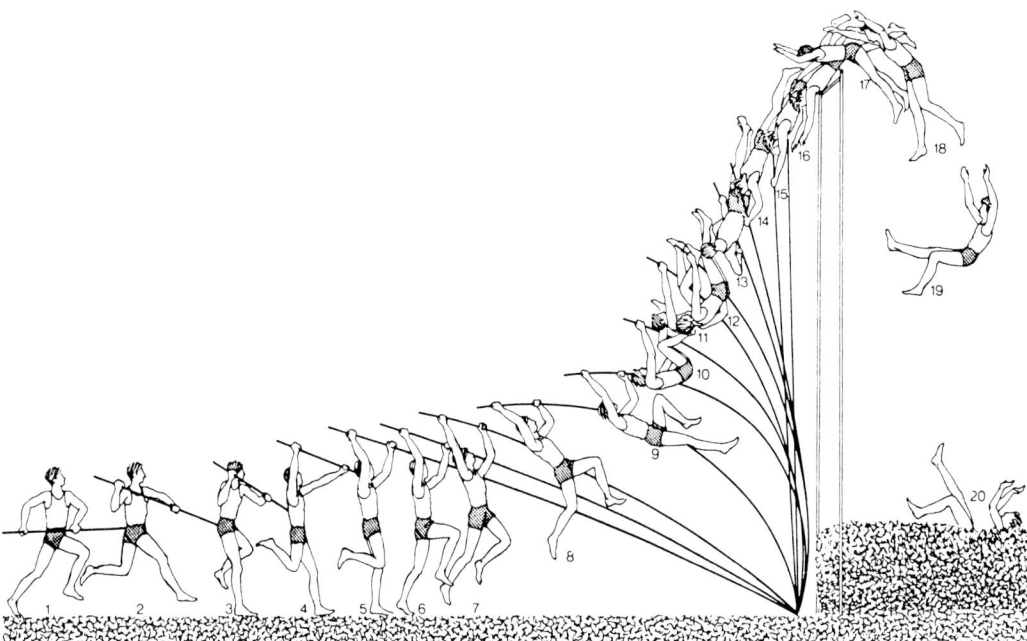

Fig. 8-17 Motion analysis of pole vaulting [according to Bauersfeld, Schroeter]. The stress on the arms and trunk can be seen in phases 6–16.

---

this finding. Several well-documented studies regarding these questions will be required before a final judgment is possible.

8.4.4 Golf and Racket Sports

It is an unfortunate fact that the spine has not been given the consideration it requires with regard to golf and racket sports. There are no systematic long-term studies. However, Hess (1980) demonstrated premature osteochondrosis, spondylolysis, and spondylarthrosis in racket athletes above the age of 30.

8.4.4.1 Golf

Golf players perform a lateral flexion with a rapid and very forceful trunk rotation. During the hit, they hold the club with both hands, in contrast to ''one-armed'' tennis players and throwers. Because of the uplifted initial position of the club, the hit follows in conjunction with a rotation of the shoulder girdle and a simultaneous twisting of the trunk. In spite of this fact, the literature has only rarely referred to damage at the spine attributable to the torsion momentum in the trunk [see Ito et al. (1970) and Fischer (1976)].

Zettel (1960) discussed functional damage with severe, acute pain in throwing sports and similar sports, which they attributed to vertebral blockages. These could be an incarceratio intercorporalis sive intraarticularis and/or blocked vertebrocostal joints. The frequency of these conditions in golfers, the influence of previous damage of the spine, and the question of whether permanent damage will develop have not been sufficiently studied. Only long-term studies will be able to determine the relationship between golfing and lumbar osteochondrosis, vertebral arch joint arthrosis, spondylolysis/spondylolisthesis, and separations of the spinous processes. For further information, see Rompe et al. (1971).

8.4.4.2 Racket Sports

All racket sports especially stress the hitting arm, which is subject to injuries and spot damage (eg, tennis elbow). The cervical spine is continuously subjected to strong, dynamic stresses, such as rotation and flexion, because of the frequently rapid head movements. The lumbar spine is also affected: rotation, flexion, and especially lordosis. In addition, during jumps, the spine must absorb the sinus vibrations and very frequent stochastic impacts that are transmitted from the legs via the pelvis. This happens not infrequently during a simultaneous lateral flexion in torsion and hyperlordosis. This can cause cervical syndromes, which lead finally to frequent and permanent problems: precursors of osteochondrosis. The stress-related damage of the lumbar spine may result in lumbago. Blockades occasionally develop in the thoracic spine and vertebrocostal joints. In racket players, the thoracic spine–vertebrocostal joints boundary shows hypermobility, and the area above may be painfully stiff. According to Pfoerringer et al. (1980), there is an increased incidence of osteochondrosis, spondylosis, and spondylarthrosis in racket players over the age of 30. It has not been established if the jumping stresses at the lumbosacral boundary are the cause for the development or aggravation of spondylolysis/spondylolisthesis. The spines of older athletes will rarely be able to endure high-performance competition in racket sports.

Tennis. The hitting arm of the tennis player must return the ball weighing 56.7 g, which arrives at a high speed, with force. Recent measurements showed that a ball hit by 17-year-old Boris Becker left the racket after a force expenditure of nearly 1 ton. The vibrations resulting from the hit doubtlessly traveled to the shoulder and into the cervical spine, which is mostly flexed and additionally twisted. Biomechanical studies are needed, especially since racket sports have the third highest number of active players (after soccer and gymnastics) in the Western world.

Similar to the thrower, the tennis player requires a swing arm, which, together with the shoulder, scapular area, and pertinent neck and cervix muscles, is subject to special stresses and whose muscles are being strengthened through training. In spite of compensation training, the competition depends on the dominating importance of one arm. This has effects on the cervical spine and, to a certain extent, on the entire spine. Flexing and twisting of the spine is a part of the motion process of the tennis player.

Sports literature has dealt explicitly with the syndrome of the tennis elbow. Pfoerringer and Keyl and their co-workers (1978 to 1983) discussed it in detail and compiled literature references. The "tennis shoulder" was also discussed, and the overextension of the shoulder muscles was mentioned. In the opinion of some researchers, changes in the electromyographic curves of neck muscles and radiographical findings at the cervical spine confirm the relationship between spondylogenic irritation and tennis elbow. It can be assumed that the intervertebral osteochondrosis at the cervical spine, which generates the irritation, is a consequence of long-term tennis training and athletic competition.

Squash. Squash is the hardest and fastest competitive racket sport. The ball, which hits the racket at 300 km/h requires in addition to the high dynamic performance of the hitting arm large tension forces in the muscle chain from the neck to the lumbar spine. The lumbar syndrome (lumbago) is the most frequent overexertion damage. There are also significant rotary tensions in the cervical spine (Fig. 8-18).

Badminton. Badminton is the third most frequent racket sport and is a very fast game. It leads only rarely to injuries and more frequently to overexertion damage. In addition to the Achilles tendon, the shoulder joint is subject to great stresses because of the rapid hitting sequence. This probably affects the cervical spine, which is twisted or held in a very tensed position (Fig. 8-19).

An excessive lordotic posture in the lumbar spine is regarded as typical for the sport. Figure 8-19 suggests a lordosis and clearly shows a scoliotic posture, with the cervical spine twisted in the opposite direction. Players frequently complain about lumbago pain, which can probably be attributed to the hard floor of the competition halls. Because of these circumstances, it seems advisable that badminton players should be examined by a sports physician with regard to their spine and that long-term studies should be performed. Compensation sports such as swimming and light weight training are recommended. For further information, see Pfoerringer and Keyl (1983).

8.4.4.3 Table Tennis

In comparison with other athletes, the table tennis player suffers relatively few injuries. Most frequently, the legs are affected (70%). The trunk is involved with only 6% of injuries. The incidence of vertebroradical symptoms was given as 10% by Biener and Oechslin (1979). This is not surprising. The same damage as with other racket sports is possible with table tennis. The playing arm, including the shoulder girdle and its boundary with the cervical spine, is substantially stressed in this sport because of smash hits that hit the racket at a speed of 160 km/h.

In addition, table tennis players take a prolonged, anteflexed, slightly twisted, and laterally flexed trunk position. This results in frequent scolioses, which are fixated in a position that is convex to the hitting arm. Cotta and Steinbrueck (1979) thought that these scolioses were sports related.

Because of the fast play with simultaneous jumps alternating between the left and right, the LPH region is subject to rapid, consecutive, and strong stochastic motions. It has not been deter-

Fig. 8-18 Squash. During a squash competition, the cervical spine is often greatly stressed by the sudden turning back against the shoulder, which is led forward [from Pfoerringer and Keyl (1983)].

A B

Fig. 8-19 Badminton. (**A**) Badminton player during a jump: arm rotation up to the shoulder joint; muscles of the cervical spine greatly tensed; slight lordosis of the lumbar spine. (**B**) Badminton requires fast reactions: the shoulders are turned, and the head is moved to the upper back in a countermovement to the scoliosis of the spine [from Pfoerringer and Keyl (1983)].

mined how strongly they affect the intervertebral motor segments of the lower lumbar spine in the axial and horizontal direction and what kind of force they develop.

Not only youths but also a surprisingly large number of older persons play table tennis in competition. According to Biener and Oechslin (1979), an increasing number of problems at the cervical and lumbar spine must be expected in older players. It will be difficult, however, to determine whether radiographically confirmed damage such as osteochondrosis and vertebral arch joint and sacroiliac arthrosis should be regarded solely as age-related damage or whether athletic stresses of the spine have substantially contributed to them.

8.4.5 Contact Sports

Contact sports, which according to Williams (1973) include rugby, soccer, and judo, cause 45% of all sports injuries. A portion of these can be attributed to chronic overexertion (23%). Kewalramani et al (1981) expressed the opinion that contact sports should be called collision sports, which include wrestling, boxing, soccer, and especially football.

8.4.5.1 Boxing

The literature with regard to boxing is mostly concerned with skull-brain injuries (Unterharnscheidt 1970). They are the most obvious of the serious boxing injuries, with often lengthy and sometimes irreversible consequences. Even death caused by bleeding in the brain or spinal cord or carotid sinus shock occurs (almost 400 cases in England since World War II). The danger of boxing was explained by Groh (1962).

Too little attention is paid to the fact that upper cuts and facial cuts always affect the cervical spine. In spite of the instinctive countertension of the neck muscles (Fig. 8-20), there is frequent, abrupt twisting with simultaneous sharp flexion. Similar damage can be expected as with the snap injury of the cervical spine caused by a frontal collision with an automobile when the chin hits the dashboard or steering wheel (Fig. 8-21). This should not be confused with the whiplash injury of the cervical spine caused by the abrupt flinging back of the head (Fig. 8-21).

Boxing cuts against the chin and head, with their strong, flexed lordosis of the cervical spine and abrupt twisting, occur repeatedly during training and the match. The single cut does not result in immediately perceptible damage at the cervical spine. It is highly likely that such repeated influences (Fig. 8-20) lead to distortions because of the exceeding of the resistance capacity of the intervertebral disc tissue in the sense of an initial impulse. In this way, the smallest, repeated fissures may cause damage.

Fig. 8-20 Hard upper cut in boxing.

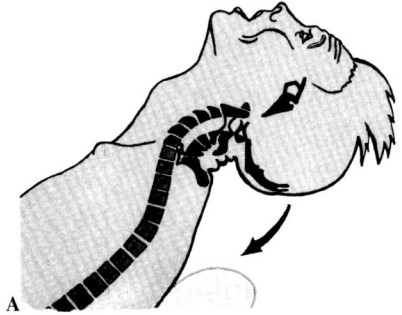 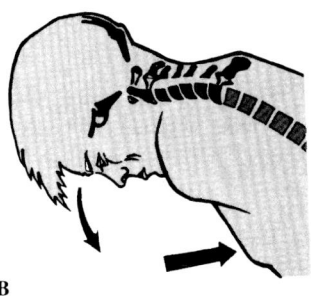

Fig. 8-21 Whiplash and snap injury. (A) Whiplash injury of the cervical spine when the automobile is hit from the back; (B) snap injury of the cervical spine when the automobile is hit from the front against a resistance [from Erdmann (1973)].

Table 8-7 Wear Damage at the Cervical Spine in Boxers Compared to General Population

Age	Boxers (%)	General Population (%)
20–29	33.3	13.7
30–39	50.5	36.8
40–49	100.0	67.5
50–59	100.0	82.3
60–69	100.0	94.5
70+	100.0	100.0

Data from Jung and Schumann (1975).

Table 8-7 shows wear damage at the cervical spine (radiodiagnostically confirmed) for boxers in comparison with the general population. There is no other sport with such a high incidence of damage between the ages of 20 and 50.

It is unknown whether damage affects only the intervertebral discs (osteochondrosis), lateral vertebral body joints of the cervical spine (uncovertebral arthrosis), or vertebral arch joints (arthrosis) or whether these three elements in the intervertebral motor segment are equally affected. Damage at the head joints requires special attention. Unfortunately, the differential diagnosis is not always accurate. For additional information, see Brennan and O'Connor (1968), Rompe and Krahl (1972), and Strohal (1965).

There are occasional references to the boxer's hump in sports literature, with the vertex in the middle thoracic spine. The cause is assumed to be the constant bent posture with increased tension of the intercostal muscles during training and the match. It still must be determined whether impaired spinal growth (eg, juvenile kyphosis) as a previously existing damage plays a role or whether the hump constitutes a direct, sports-related damage.

The serious, sometimes even deadly, dangers threatening the boxer have resulted in sharp criticism from the medical profession. The World Medical Association recommended that boxing be outlawed. Boxing is already outlawed in Sweden and Norway, and Britain wants to follow suit.

8.4.5.2 Wrestling

Wrestling consists of repeated flexions, twisting, and torsions of all sections of the spine and forcefully executed forced positions (bridge, neck hold, etc.) or throwing techniques in which lordosis with simultaneous torsion occurs. There is frequent damage at the cervical spine.

Youths start this sport between the ages of 14 and 18. Serious osteochondrosis (often at different levels) and frequent uncovertebral arthrosis were discovered in examinees between the ages of 23 to 29 (Buetti-Baeuml 1954). Multiple, slight traumatic stresses were suggested as the cause. These stresses probably develop during the "bridge" that is common in this sport (Krayenbuehl et al. 1967b). The athletes were unaware of injuries and had no complaints. The functional roentgenograms of the cervical spine showed limited mobility. This limitation was more pronounced than was expected based on the usual roentgenograms in two levels.

Koehler (1959) examined 30 wrestlers of which 14 had moderate to serious damage at the cervical spine: intervertebral osteochondrosis with spurs and uncovertebral arthrosis, primarily

Fig. 8-22 Wrestling phases that subject the spine to significant stresses [according to Wehlen (1976)].

at intervertebral motor segments 5-6 and 6-7. On the average, the wrestlers had begun the sport between the ages of 19 and 21. The oldest examinees were 27, but the described damage was also found in 17-year-olds. This damage belongs in the group of causes of the occipitocervical syndromes that are frequent in wrestlers. Franke (1974) reported on disorders that affect wrestlers to a greater degree: cervical osteochondrosis, shoulder-arm syndrome, and vertebral arch joint blockades.

Arthrosis and the resulting painful blockades in the vertebrocostal joints of the thoracic spine are frequently reported by wrestlers. There are no long-term studies regarding this special problem. As with other articular blockades, chiropractic manipulations may be required.

The various and frequent forces affecting the spine of wrestlers (Fig. 8-22) may not immediately result in serious problems. But one of these forces may be the initial impulse for the first damage of the intervertebral disc structure that introduces the slow progression of an intervertebral disc disorder (see Chapter 4). In addition, an excessive kyphosis can be observed in wrestlers, just as in boxers: the athlete's hump.

The lumbar spine of the wrestler is frequently in the center of medical concerns since here, and even more in the entire LPH region, serious problems develop that frequently put an end to a wrestling career. Initially, the cause of the pain is thought to be harmless distortions since the lumbar spine is greatly stressed during the wrestling match by frequent, excessive anteflexion and retroflexion. In addition, there are axial pressures and/or simultaneous traction forces on the fiber rings because of torsion. This situation applies not only to the match but also to the continuous, additional, and varied power training. A simple "distortion," however, is not the final stage. Sooner or later, the initial impulse for damage in the intervertebral disc tissue occurs.

The torsions in the LPH area also result in blockages of the vertebral arch joints and sacroiliac joints. The incidence of spondylolysis is 23.8%. This percentage is far above normal for the general population: 5% to 7%.

The damage so frequently found in wrestlers is primarily sports related. It is the consequence of overexertion of the articular cartilage or the intervertebral disc. In order to prevent spinal damage, Koehler (1959) and several others have suggested changes in the competition rules, renunciation of free-style wrestling, and the start of training after the conclusion of spinal growth.

8.4.5.3 Japanese Wrestling

Japanese wrestling belongs in the group of aggressive sports with body contact. Training puts great stresses on the spine. Sports physicians and trainers should attempt to structure the individual fighting phases so that the spine, which is stabilized by well-trained muscles, suffers as little damage as possible. Although Menge et al. (1980) reported that no sports-related damage had been demonstrated with judo and karate, they found stress problems at the spine in 25% to 26% of participants. Other investigators have also reported a high number of back problems under stress. Such problems should be diagnosed with manual and radiographical diagnostics. The discovery of the damage (eg, chondrosis of the intervertebral discs, vertebral arch joint arthrosis, spondylosis/spondylolisthesis) is the only basis for specific changes in training or the development of specific therapy.

There is much information regarding the increasingly popular sport of judo. Damage at the soft tissue of the spine, in addition to many injuries that primarily affect the extremities, has been reported. The highest percentage of damage is in the soft tissue (10%). This damage may be caused by the pressure that develops during the hyperlordosis of the lumbar intervertebral discs. The hyperkyphosis that develops during certain defensive maneuvers affects the lower portion of the thoracic spine and its boundary with the lumbar spine. In judo, the lumbosacral region is even more subject to pressure with rotation (Brueggemann 1978). Brueggemann (1978) expressed a serious warning regarding the early specialization of adolescents in this sport. Collaud (1970) described the consequences of judo training: ankylosed lumbar spine, decreased height of the intervertebral spaces in 63%, and spondylolysis/spondylolisthesis in 12% and 60%, respectively, of lumbar osteochondroses in participants above the age of 25. According to Lethuillier (1979), the frequent necessary lifting of the training partner creates increased and damaging pressure in the lumbar intervertebral discs. Participants frequently suffer cervical syndromes (Steinbrueck and Tilscher 1983). According to Lekszas (1973), cervicobrachialgias can easily develop during floor fighting phases and result in head rotation pain and a blockade in the intervertebral motor segment.

Godt and Vogelsang (1979) reported on injuries at the cervical spine in 26- to 28-year-old participants with tetrapareses. The existence of previously existing damage in these cases was noteworthy: isolated osteochondrosis in intervertebral motor segment 5-6, often combined with 3-4 and 5-6 at the cervical spine, and retrospondylosis. Because of the young age of these persons, it is likely that the practice of the sport for years was responsible rather than singular traumatic influences. Brueggemann (1978) recommended that older participants (ie, beginning at age 40) forego certain training techniques and throws in order to avoid chronic damage or increased injuries.

Many experts believe that judo training should start at about the age of 12. If it is begun much earlier, the risks for the juvenile spine increase, even though they are not immediately manifested in back pain during training. The person notices pain only unconsciously and often disregards it because of ambition. Finally, the participant no longer enjoys this time-consuming and tiring sport even before reaching the age of 12, which is when training should begin.

8.4.5.4 Soccer

In soccer, the entire support and motor system is moved and stressed, especially the spine. Serious accidental spinal injuries are rare. But according to Kerjean (1970), intervertebral disc damage at the cervical and lower lumbar spine is more frequent in soccer players than in the general population of the same age.

In the case of children and youths with previous damage of the spine, Schoberth and Heidensohn (1975) warned against soccer training and competition. This warning applies to those with juvenile kyphosis or more serious hip joint damage. Another sport should be chosen in these cases (eg, swimming).

One peculiarity of soccer players is the frequently detected large kyphosis of the thoracic spine. Of 266 soccer players, 88% showed a fixated kyphosis (Schoberth 1972). In 210, the curvature continued into the lumbar spine. It has been noted that an abnormally curved kyphotic spine exists in many top athletes of various disciplines. There is a connection to juvenile kyphosis.

The lumbar spine, especially the lumbosacral boundary, is a remarkably frequent location of pain and damage for soccer players: intervertebral chondrosis, intervertebral osteochondrosis, vertebral arch joint arthrosis, and arthrosis of the sacroiliac joints. The cause of such pain may be damage that developed unnoticed during the early growth period and that was aggravated by the substantial stresses of soccer. Occasionally, pain may be caused by numerous microtraumas during play.

For soccer players, the LPH region is directly exposed to sports-related stresses. During training and competition, these stresses can be absorbed only if the connective muscles between the trunk, hip joint, and legs are specifically trained and if the bones and joints (vertebral arch joints, sacroiliac joints) and soft tissues (intervertebral discs, ligaments) are intact in their anatomic structure and physical resistance capacity. Nevertheless, sudden events during the course of the game can substantially impair the function of the LPH region: a sudden stop with a change in stress distribution, a forced change of direction during dribbling, and slipping with pelvic torsion. If such and other similar forces interrupt the flowing, preplanned motion process, a pelvic torsion develops. This results in a very painful blockade in the sacroiliac or vertebral arch joints. Expert manual examination together with chirotherapy may frequently bring fast relief.

The head ball in soccer hits the head with a speed of up to 95 km/h. Strong longitudinal compression and sharp bending of the cervical spine, frequently with abrupt torsion, are the consequences. The team physician of the British National Team reported wear of the cervical spine in his protegees, which was much further advanced in 30-year-olds than was usual at this age. Kerjean (1970) reported intervertebral disc damage at the cervical spine of soccer players that was much too frequent for the age of the athletes.

While referring to extensive experience with soccer players, Schoberth (1972) reached a remarkably opposing conclusion. He concluded that playing head balls was not dangerous and did not cause premature wear damage at the cervical spine. Schoberth (personal communication 1983) based this on the fact that soccer players can resist the advancing ball with correspondingly controlled muscles. It will remain the task of future long-term studies to clarify the contradictions in the findings of different investigators.

8.4.5.5 Other Team Sports

The active team sports of children and youths are valuable in training for general mobility and therefore also for developing strong muscles. Strong muscles are especially necessary in the trunk to ensure the strong, internal structure of the spine and support its continued, normal growth. Unfortunately, just when youths begin team sports, a frequent disorder of the thoracic spine prevents their participation: juvenile kyphosis. Although it has internal causes, it may be seriously aggravated by athletic activity during the acute disease spurts. If it is accompanied by back problems, the susceptible zone at the vertebral body end plates becomes more "unstable," and the back curvature increases. At this point, medically supervised therapy is mandatory. This therapy is oriented toward a radiographically confirmed diagnosis. Short-term or long-term interruption of participation in team sports may be necessary. Medically supervised physiotherapy, also in water, and swimming must be adapted to the severity of the kyphosis. The gradual resumption of school, team, and leisure sports is usually possible.

Ball games put specific stress on the trunk and spine, in addition to several joints of the extremities. Free, loose mobility of the lumbar spine is important in ball players. However, the hypermobility that is frequent in tall persons and desirable for ball players can cause damage. The excessive torsion potential of the intervertebral disc causes an especially sudden tension on the bondings of the intervertebral disc fibers in the bony vertebral body epiphyses and the boundary with the hyaline cartilage of the vertebral body end plates. Only very strong muscles at the spine–pelvis boundary are able to absorb the dangerous traction during the moment of turning, and only if they react in time.

The force and frequency of mechanical influences vary greatly in the individual disciplines of team ball sports. The combination of pressure and torsion especially affects team players who must be in a bending position frequently or for a prolonged period, as in hockey and ice hockey. They are frequently subject to torsion at the lumbosacral boundary. The same applies to the high jumps of volleyball players who perform torsions before and after jumping. In addition, there are frequent, unexpected, and fast reactions to defend against a body contact. In nearly all team players, the sacroiliac joints are chronically changed by frequent torsions of the pelvis, and they frequently block. Steinbrueck and Tilscher (1983) assumed that one important cause of this was the uncoordinated power training phases of ball players.

Basketball. Basketball takes second place after soccer in the frequency of injuries. An essential part of the reason for this is the frequent, hard body contact in the fight for the throw into the basket. Injuries occur on the arms as well as the legs. The jumping up with outstretched arms, frequently with forceful, tense rotation of the trunk, and the subsequent downjump onto the feet create a damaging situation for the spine. Because of the continuous repetition of these activities, tendinosis at the pelvic brim and the tips of the spinous and transverse processes develops.

A problem frequently discussed in the literature concerns the height of basketball players. According to the studies of Rompe (1980), the question of whether tall players who have a weak spine and generally weak ligaments and are hypermobile are more susceptible to injury remains unanswered. During examinations, attention should be paid to the intervertebral discs of the lumbosacral area, vertebral arch joints, and sacroiliac joints. For additional information, see Cady (1970), Haefner (1982), and Kraemer and Berns (1980).

Volleyball. Volleyball is a fast game that is characterized by jumping and stretching in order to get the ball over the net. The ball coming from the opponent may reach a speed of 120 km/h. Frequently, the vertical high jump with outstretched arms is combined with rotation of the trunk (Fig. 8-23). During training and competition, these play situations are frequently and rapidly repeated. This results in abrupt traction at the muscle and tendon attachments of the pelvic crest, as well as at the tips of the vertebral arch processes in the area of the lumbar spine, that finally causes tendinosis in many volleyball players. This can be regarded as a sports-related damage of this discipline. According to Franke (1974), cervical osteochondrosis, shoulder-arm syndrome, and vertebral arch joint arthrosis are frequent. However, the injuries at the extremities of volleyball players are of primary concern [see also Fiedler (1975)].

Handball. In this hard competitive sport, contusions and contortions of the extremities are frequent, but serious injuries are rare. The high stress during jumping is held partially responsible for the development of spondylolysis/spondylolisthesis. Since training and competition frequently require sudden, deep anteflexion, frequently accompanied by torsions, intervertebral disc damage in the lumbar area and at the lumbosacral boundary should be expected. Complaints of lumbago are frequent. The hard indoor floors and unsuitable shoes may also be causes of lumbago.

Hockey. Field hockey in summer and indoor hockey in winter require a distinct, aggressive physical involvement and fast reaction ability. The hard-hit, small ball has a higher speed than a

Fig. 8-23 Movement sequence in volleyball. This sequence only suggests the strong rotation at the loin-pelvis boundary (from Fiedler [1975]).

soccer ball. The play situations change rapidly. Prolonged, stereotypical postures and constantly repeated monotonous movements are absent. Therefore, the muscles in general and the trunk muscles specifically are strengthened. Because of the stick position, however, running during the play requires a slightly forward bend of the trunk. During the hitting of the ball, there is an additional inclination to the right, with slight torsion. Pain in the sacral area, vertebral arch joint arthrosis, intervertebral disc damage, and spondylosis, which are frequent in other sports, are not substantially increased. However, there are no long-term studies that confirm this finding.

Water Polo. Water polo is considered the hardest competitive sport after ice hockey. But in contrast to ice hockey, no serious injuries have been reported.

Rugby. Rugby involves a great deal of hard body contact. The scrimmage and the penetration into the open lane of the two teams are the high points of the game. There are additional physical contacts during the course of the game, during which cuts in the head, knocked-out teeth, nose fractures, and concussions occur. However, the spine is primarily affected: separations of transverse processes or of vertebral arch processes attributable to chronic damage and intervertebral disc damage at the cervical spine. A report by Schumacher (1982) provided pictures of competitive situations.

8.4.5.6 Roller Skating

Roller skating is a popular leisure activity for many. Only a few will become involved in competitive roller skating. There are close similarities to ice skating, but roller skating requires the use of more physical strength since the roller skates are heavy and must overcome more friction on rougher surfaces.

The running style of roller skate racing, with its greatly forward bent upper body and wide swinging arms, corresponds to ice racing. The dangers for the spine resulting from this are discussed in section 8.4. Figure roller skating corresponds in its technique and dancing/artistic figures to ice skating (Fig. 8-24).

8.4.5.7 Fencing

Literature on the relationship between fencing and the spine is rare. Menge et al. (1980) found scoliosis in 85% of 45 performance fencers. Radiodiagnostics showed that scolioses of more than 10 degrees accounted for 25% of scolioses in 28 fencers. Attention was primarily paid to the lumbar spine. Although growth damage of the young spine attributable to external stresses during fencing seem possible, it was impossible to show that the fencing subjected the growth of the spine to damaging influences. But the physical examinations of 18 of 45 fencers who had been involved in the sport for an average of 10 years (average age of 20 years) revealed seg-

Fig. 8-24 Roller skating figure [from Siegfried (1981)].

mental irritation symptoms, mostly at the boundaries between the spinal sections: 50% had a scoliotic pelvis, mostly to the right. In about half of the fencers, the thoracic kyphosis could not be compensated for. The investigators did not consider a compensation sport necessary because of the insignificant abnormalities and had no objections to further practicing of the asymmetrical training.

Since the training that emphasizes one arm begins in childhood, between age 7 and 10, the spine in its immature state is subject to dangerous overstressing. Overstressing it is increased by the training methods, which are becoming increasingly harder. Almost all sports performed with one arm stress the shoulder joint with its pertaining muscles, which include the cervical muscles. This has a unilateral effect on the spine. Osteochondrosis may develop in susceptible intervertebral discs. In connection with this, uncovertebral arthrosis and/or vertebral arch joint arthrosis frequently develops in the same intervertebral motor segment.

Serious damage should not be expected in all fencers. The susceptibility of the intervertebral discs depends on the endogenously predetermined tissue stability but is also affected by the overstress in early youth. This susceptibility should be determined with the help of long-term studies of performance fencers, using general and radiographical diagnostics. The results could necessitate changes in training procedures and the introduction of a special compensation sport and gymnastics.

The scoliosis and scoliotic pelvis described in fencers make it seem likely that this sport subjects the lumbar and cervical spine to similar stresses as in other one-armed disciplines. Ehlert (1978) reported his biomechanical analyses of the spine of juvenile and adolescent fencers. He stated that the cartilaginous epiphyses of the spine are damaged in adolescents by excessive loads during training.

8.4.6 Weight Training

Weight training is often recommended as a compensation sport. It should rather be regarded as a supplemental sport or accompanying training. In such cases, it is not necessary to increase weight training to the level of the rules of competitive weight lifting. High-performance weight lifting subjects the spine to loads at the limit of stress tolerance and may result in damage.

Dumb-bell training is an excellent initial and conditioning training for many sports to strengthen the neck and shoulder muscles with the transition to the back, thoracic, and abdominal muscles. It should be performed in a flat, supine position or while inclined. This enables the development of adequate strength for swimming, gymnastics on the apparatus, field and track athletics, and other disciplines.

8.4.6.1 Weight Lifting

The opinions on spinal damage in weight lifters vary. Tuetsch and Ulrich (1973) found no noteworthy intervertebral disc damage, not even spondylolisthesis. (Differing results are discussed in this section.) The pressure on the intervertebral discs, which is vertical if the correct technique is used, is tolerated without damage since the intervertebral disc is able to bear pressures up to 1,500 kp. The damage-free pressure tolerance decreases to 500 kp during great anteflexion and rotation to 100 kp during lordosis. Accuracy in training methods must be stressed, especially if training with heavy dumb-bells is a coordination training for other disciplines. Errors in the method occasionally lead to incorrect stress or overstress. This may be serious and may prevent the continuation of training.

According to Schanz (1931), weight lifters are able to use the abdominal cavity and rib cage as support for the spine through contracting the abdominal wall and holding their breath. Schanz referred to Oriental load carriers who regularly used abdomen-loin belts. Recently, the wearing of additional supporting hip belts or lower back support belts was recommended for better competitive results in weight lifting (Kraemer and Brenner 1978; Neugebauer 1974). In this way, the best weight lifters are able to lift 200 kg up high (Muenchinger 1960). The strongest athletes carry loads of 800 kg distributed over the shoulders and hips. For pictures portraying the lifting of weights and the stresses on the spine, see Figures 3-3, 3-4, 3-7, 3-8, and 5-9.

Top weight lifters train for 30 to 40 hours a week and lift up to 70 metric tons each day. Jaros and Cech (1965) reported on 20 weight lifters with an average age of 28 years. They had trained three times a week for eight years and had lifted 6,000 to 10,000 kg each training day. Every individual exercise exceeded 120 kg. A third of them complained of lower back pain at the beginning of the training, which improved as the muscles strengthened. Wear damage such as osteochondrosis could not be confirmed radiologically, but separated spinous processes and transverse processes are known to occur.

The technique of weight lifting has changed greatly. "Snatch" and "clean and jerk" are now competitive techniques (Fig. 8-25). Figure 8-26 shows a typical weight lifting phase. Figure 8-27 shows the result of incorrect technique that causes damaging stress on back muscles and intervertebral discs. The main stress on the longitudinal spinal axis is on the intervertebral discs and vertebral arch series. A decline in spinal damage can therefore be expected with the new techniques. However, there are insufficient statistics concerning spinal damage in weight lifters who have trained only with the new techniques.

Rompe and Rieder (1976) reported damage at the lumbar intervertebral discs of weight lifters but no spondylolysis/spondylolisthesis or vertebral arch joint arthrosis. In contrast, Groher (1975), in his statistical studies of spondylolysis/spondylolisthesis, described other athletes (who included primarily weight lifters) in whom there were 14 double-sided spondylolyses (including 3 spondylolistheses) in 45 examinees of group II (intensive training for more than five years) and vertebral arch joint arthroses in 39.

In addition to the increased incidence of spondylolysis/spondylolisthesis, other investigators found Baastrup's disease and overstress tendopathy. Kraemer and Brenner (1978) found Baastrup's disease (Fig. 4-60) in 22 of 40 exam-

Fig. 8-25 Weight lifting. **Top row:** Two-armed snatch, the technically most difficult competitive exercise. It requires not only strength but also perfect technique, quickness, mobility, and the right "attitude." The weight must be lifted in one motion, without pause, vertically over the head, until the arms are fully stretched. A change in the position of the feet or bent legs are permitted. **Bottom row:** Two-armed clean and jerk, the exercise that allows the highest performance. The weight first rests on the collar bones or the completely flexed arms. The athlete then bends the legs somewhat and suddenly straightens. At the same time, the weight is pushed over the head with completely outstretched arms [from Neugebauer (1974)].

ined weight lifters. Neugebauer (1974) also reported on the occurrence of Baastrup's disease.

Weight lifters frequently suffer strong, lumbagolike pain. According to present opinion such lumbago attacks are caused by incarceratio intradiscalis or intra-articularis (see Chapter 3). They result from a depletion of muscle strength and ligament elasticity caused by sloppy lifting techniques (Fig. 8-27). This causes excessive shearing forces at the lumbosacral boundary with an increased danger of exceeding the tolerance limit of the intervertebral disc. This ensues in the development of new and the aggravation of existing intervertebral disc damage. The sports physician should immediately treat this pain, which is a frequent result of arthrosis of the vertebral arch joints or sacroiliac joints. Rotation under pressure from the lifting, often unintentional during training, subjects the loin-pelvishiphip boundary to especially detrimental stresses and causes blockades in the sacroiliac joint. Chiropractic manipulations can eliminate the pain instantly. For more details, see Steinbrueck and Tilscher (1983) and section 7.4. According to Neugebauer (1974), weight lifters have a strikingly large-stranded spongiosa structure in the vertebral bodies, which can probably be attributed to adaptation to the excessive and frequent axial pressure during lifting.

The start of weight training by increasingly younger athletes poses a problem. In some countries, even 10-year-olds are trained. Their imma-

Fig. 8-26 Typical phase in weight lifting [from Doerr and Pfoerringer (1981)].

ture spine is subject to the dangers described in section 8.9. There are no known radiologically controlled long-term studies on the results. The sports physician must be a critical counselor in this regard. Mironova et al. (1969) warned women not to take up weight training because of the high spinal stress. The potential damage that

Fig. 8-27 Error during weight lifting (from Steinbrueck [1983]).

may be caused by lifting heavy weights must also be considered for sports that have integrated weight lifting into their general training program.

Grube and Mueller (1973) mentioned the noise level in the training halls of weight lifters: 92 db. Various vegetative reactions develop at a noise level between 60 and 80 db and strongly affect the concentration of the person training. Trainers in this sport may develop hearing losses caused by the daily effect of this noise. For additional information, see Wood and Hayes (1974).

8.4.7 Air Sports

8.4.7.1 Parachuting

There are several injuries that occur during parachuting. In the French military, 10,333,525 jumps resulted in 11,533 accidents with 155 vertebral fractures, frequently with intervertebral disc involvement (Teysandier 1967). The fractures mostly involved the upper lumbar vertebral bodies (Gubser 1976). Tittel (1962) found fractures of the anterior edges of the cervical vertebrae.

In addition, chronic damage at the spine was reported, which develops without a distinct trauma, and is regarded as the "vertebral syndrome of parachuters" (Richaut et al. 1967). Teysandier (1967) and Horsky and Dite (1965) assumed microtraumas to be the cause of these problems. Microtraumas, which are caused by many landings, lead to damage of the intervertebral discs and ligament system at the lumbar spine and result in progressive wearing of the intervertebral discs. Kusmitsch and Ylitowski (1968) described degenerative-dystrophic damage with spondylosis deformans and anterior height reduction of the intervertebral spaces. In addition, they found distinct arthrosis of the vertebral arch joints. The frequency of articular arthrosis should be studied in more detail because it may play a major role in the pain.

Kleinod and Wilke (1973) attributed osteochondrosis of the lumbar spine in a national parachuting team to the landing impact, which can be considered the impulse for the constantly repeated microfissures at the lumbar spine. The opening of the parachute affects the cervical spine, frequently in the form of a whiplash injury, and causes progressive osteochondrosis in the lower intervertebral discs of the cervical spine. Eight of 11 parachuters with an average of 2,100 jumps complained about back problems and had radiographically confirmed osteochondrosis, which was shown to be progressive in later comparisons.

Schlitt (1976) described the most frequent cervical pain as being caused by the strong head retroflexion, which is caused by the opening of the parachute, which reduces the falling speed from 200 to approximately 17 km/h. The process is similar to that of a whiplash trauma. This causes an initial damage in the intervertebral disc tissue, similar to the one in the lumbar intervertebral discs.

Volek (1963) reported on parachuters with an average age of 30 years. He found the incidence of chronic-degenerative damage at the spine to be 27.8%, clearly higher than in the general population of the same age group. The lower cervical spine was the most affected.

In a radiographically supported study, Mustajok et al. (1978) found the cervical spine of parachuters in almost all cases to possess distinct characteristics of intervertebral osteochondrosis. The thoracic spine was less affected, and the lumbar spine was not significantly affected.

These studies cannot be compared since roentgenograms were not regularly performed and described. Nevertheless, it seems justified to conclude that frequently repeated small traumas are the cause of slowly developing problems, mostly at the cervical and/or the lumbar spine. There are insufficient study results regarding damage and problems affecting the head joints of parachuters. These questions should be systematically researched in larger studies, especially with respect to changes in training procedures and equipment. Further, these studies did not discuss how many parachuters had to give up jumping because of spinal damage and how the damage developed in later years. For further information, see Boeger and Kirchhoff (1965) and Murray-Leslie et al. (1977).

8.4.7.2 Gliding

The higher the demands on the glider, the more the spine suffers. Stedtfeld (1976) came to this conclusion as the result of his studies, which extended over decades. Gliding results in a much higher degree of stress and susceptibility than other kinds of flying. Aerodynamic requirements are inevitable law in the design of glider planes, and the pilot must abide by them while essentially forgoing his freedom to move and to sit comfortably. In some glider designs, the pilot is forced to lie on the stomach with the head bent back excessively and the chin supported. Modern development went from sitting to half-sitting to lying positions, which were equally detrimental in terms of spinal statis. World-record, high-performance machines necessitate a supine position with a strongly flexed lumbar spine and additional kyphosis of the upper thoracic spine with an anteflexion of the cervical spine up to 90 degrees. This subjects the thoracolumbar boundary of the spine to special stresses so that even small, additional impulses lead to fractures in this region. The strong anteflexion of the head is not without influence on the cervical spine.

However, no studies exist on damage of the intervertebral discs, which are greatly stressed in the cervical area and at the thoracolumbar boundary. But damage should be expected since the forced position must be held for more than five hours during long flights. During this time, the necessary pump mechanism is absent, and the intervertebral discs have no stimulation for metabolism. The rigid lying position and the cold in high altitudes also cause myogelosis. There are frequent g-stresses, especially during the takeoff (thermal circling). Sometimes, long-distance flyers must be helped off the plane because of painful spinal stiffness.

Those adverse stress conditions especially affect gliding teachers, who are subject to prolonged stresses on the intervertebral discs and the inevitable pressure and shearing traumas during landings many thousands of times. The teachers examined by Stedtfeld (1976) had begun gliding during their early adolescent years. None of them suffered Scheuermann's disease, but without exception, there were ventral recessions of several vertebral bodies in the thoracolumbar boundary (the most stressed area). The roentgenograms showed severe osteochondrosis at the lumbosacral boundary. Stedtfeld did not report damage at the cervical and thoracic intervertebral discs. Tittel (1962) observed separations of spinous processes from the 12th thoracic to the 2nd lumbar vertebral arch. Pilots who have flown for many years are also affected by wear disorders of the spine. They increasingly complain of radicular irritation syndromes. Top athletes frequently suffer from intervertebral disc disorders that require surgery.

8.4.8 Equestrian Sports

8.4.8.1 Horseback Riding

Horseback riding has become increasingly popular. For many riders, sitting on top of a horse is an occasional or frequent hobby. Sitting on a horse, and even more riding in the various paces, stresses the spine and the connective muscles to the pelvis, legs, shoulder girdle, and cervical region. These stresses are partially static and partially dynamic. In riding, as in swimming, the entire body is stressed. But the swimmer, who also benefits from the water's buoyancy, is able to control and direct the use of muscle strength, whereas the rider depends on the horse and its movements.

During systematic riding lessons, the correct sitting position on the horse is taught first (Fig. 8-28). Figure 8-28C shows the classic posture for the rider: a drawn-up sacrum and a retroflexion angle of 20 to 30 degrees. The similarity of the backward inclined sitting posture in riding with the spine–supporting inclined position of the back rest in an automobile is remarkable (see Figs. 7-24 through 7-26). In this position, the axial stress affects the intervertebral discs gently, whereas a lordosis distributes the stress poorly.

In the interactive relationship between the rider and horse, the spine plays an essential role. The sitting position of the rider, the reactions to the movements of the horse, and the guiding of the horse with pelvic movements and thigh pressure require the uninterrupted active-dynamic use of the muscles. In addition, the spine in its entirety is axially stressed as a static element. The stresses are total body vibrations, mostly in the sinus form, that are from time to time interrupted by unexpected impacts. Thus the spine of

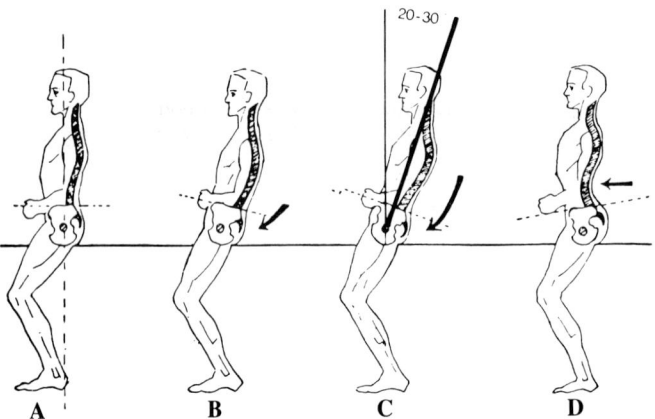

Fig. 8-28 Sitting positions of a rider. (**A**) normal sitting; (**B**) drawn-up sacrum; (**C**) further drawn-up sacrum; (**D**) lordosis. The lordosis causes an incorrect stress on the intervertebral discs in the lumbosacral area. This results in pain (lumbago in the sacrum, radiating pain in the sciatic nerves) [from Hoerdegen (1975)].

a rider is subject to similar stresses as that of an automobile passenger (see section 5.3).

Gottwald (1980a) reported on the movement processes of the spine during riding. Because of the relatively loose connection of the swinging shoulder girdle with the spine, he found hardly any influences on the upper spine. The rotation angle is between 2 and 3 degrees. In contrast, the lumbar spine shows a large, laterally alternating flexion with a rotation angle of 16 degrees. In addition to vertical movements of the spine during riding, there is a left-right swaying torsion of the spine. The torsion angle is almost 19 degrees. In addition, the kyphosis of the thoracic spine is straightened, but the normal lordosis in the lumbar region is increased. The three-dimensional riding movement of the spine requires constant movement coordination by the rider.

Riding injuries are at about the tenth place on the list of sports injuries. Riders have the highest number of sports-related fractures: 38.2%. Paraplegias caused by riding accidents are in the second place for paraplegias caused by sports.

According to Steinbrueck (1979a), riders frequently complain of occasional back pain: 23.8% during riding, 55.2% after riding. In his study series, no striking spinal damage attributed to the sport was found. Hoerdegen (1975) found back problems and intervertebral disc damage, which he explicitly classified.

The literature does not agree on the question of prolapsed discs related to horseback riding. Braun (1969) reported prolapsed discs requiring surgery, which were more frequent in riders than in a control group (14:7). For riders who were performance athletes, the ratio was 14:2. New statistical findings prompted Braun to report in 1972 that riding could be regarded as a factor for the development of prolapsed discs. In addition, he found an increased incidence of sciatica and spinal problems in riders, especially female riders.

Hoerdegen (1975, 1976) found no increased incidence of prolapsed discs in the riders he examined. He regarded the development of prolapsed discs as unlikely since the lumbar spine was stressed axially during riding. He concluded that prolapsed discs are basically caused by sudden retroflexion. (The causative mechanism of prolapsed discs is controversial, as is discussed in section 4.6). The detailed statistics of Hoerdegen provide interesting information concerning the existence of intervertebral disc damage in riders (Tables 8-8 and 8-9).

Painless and successful athletic riding also depends to a great degree on correct sitting in the saddle (Figs. 8-28 and 8-29). Horse trainers are in first place in the statistics on lower back pain and on the list of radiographically confirmed spinal damage. The interested person should read the studies of Hoerdegen for more details.

Persons contemplating riding, even as a healthy leisure time activity, should undergo an examination by a sports physician who is experienced in this discipline. Attention should be paid especially to the spine. If back pain develops, the causes should be determined by the physician with radiographic diagnostics. If damage is discovered, riding should not necessarily be prohib-

Table 8-8 Analyses of Lower Back Pain in Riders

Development of Pain	No.	%
During riding	12	23.5
During and after riding	11	21.5
Before, during, and after riding (chronic pain)	4	0.8
Before riding	2	0.4
After riding	22	43.0
No pain during riding	24	47.0

Data from Hoerdegen (1975, 1976).

Table 8-9 Dependency of Pain According to Rider Groups and Duration of Riding Activities

Riding Activity in Years	Horse Trainers		Sports Riders		Hobby Riders	
	No.	%	No.	%	No.	%
10–19	4	57	15	41.5	7	46.5
20–29	5	50	7	54	1	33.2
30–39	4	57	4	44.5	1	14.2
40–60			2	50	1	25

Data from Hoerdegen (1975, 1976).

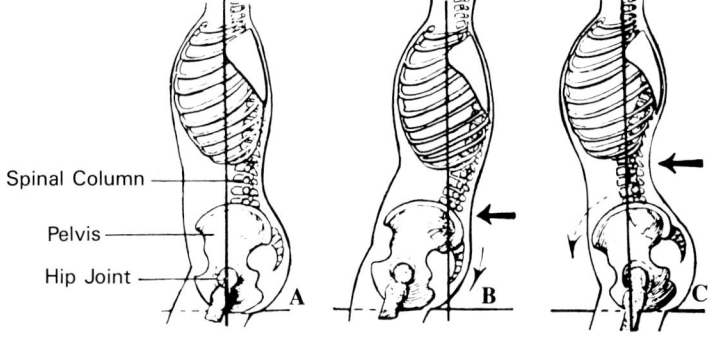

Fig. 8-29 Riding postures. (**A**) Good riding posture. Incorrect postures that may cause pain are the (**B**) slack sitting position and (**C**) the tense sitting position [from Dahmen and Haesen (1979)].

ited. This decision is up to the physician and depends on the type and extent of the damage. In suitable cases, therapeutic riding may be recommended. Riding as therapy is discussed in Chapter 7 and later in this chapter.

8.4.8.2 Polo

In polo, the body posture is always slightly inclined to the right and affects the spine. The swing from the shoulder also stresses the cervical muscles. Continued play, therefore, could have a serious effect on the lumbar and cervical spine. The movement of the spine during the frequently changing sitting and movement processes is an additional factor impeding the study of these combined movement processes.

8.4.8.3 Horse Jumping and Dressage

During horse jumping, falls from the horse or with the horse are relatively rare but result frequently in vertebral fractures, often with serious consequences (paraplegia). There is little information in the literature on particular spinal damage in horse jumpers. Further, it is not known whether dressage riders are affected by special spinal damage.

8.4.8.4 Trotting Races

Jockeys are affected by significant vibrations and interposed hard impacts in the light and swaying sulky. Glick and Katsch (1970) reported frequently developing lumbar syndromes, but there are insufficient long-term studies of spinal damage.

The average stress in trotting training and competition is also unknown.

8.4.8.5 Galloping Races

Jockeys standing in the stirrups absorb the developing vibrations to a certain degree with their well-trained leg muscles by cushioning in the joints, similar to the downhill skier. Nevertheless, vibrations reach the spine via the foot-leg-pelvis pathway. It has not been shown how far they penetrate via the spine toward the head of the jockey. The problems are similar as with vibrations in motorized vehicles (see Chapter 5).

8.4.9 Gymnastics

In all types of gymnastics, the spine is in the center of motions and various stresses. Temporary problems and even serious damage are not infrequent and affect the juvenile or adolescent gymnast strikingly often. They span from cervical syndrome, lumbago, sciatica, and blockades in the intervertebral motor segment to radiographically determined damage of varying severity at singular or multiple intervertebral motor segments: in the soft tissues (intervertebral discs, ligaments) and the pertinent vertebral arch joints and sacroiliac joints. In addition, bone damage develops and progresses.

The trunk muscles, with their boundaries with the neck, shoulders, arms, pelvis, and legs, and the extensive ligament systems can suffer damage during exercises (eg, strains with small fissures) that are initially hardly recognized but that result in chronic myogelosis and thus stiffness of spinal sections. Repeated articular distortions have a similar effect and are the cause of frequently latent articular ankylosis.

The gymnast's hump is often mentioned. It has been called the status symbol of gymnasts. It is a distinct, round-arched kyphosis in the thoracic spine that occasionally involves the upper sections of the lumbar spine. The kyphosis remains stiff during all gymnastic and athletic exercises, even during retroflexion. This is obvious during competition and demonstrations. Training for these disciplines normally starts during early youth, when the spine is still maturing.

The transition between ankylosed kyphosis and mobile lumbar lordosis should receive special attention. Since kyphosis in youths develops during the early growth period of the spine, gymnastics and sports have an additional detrimental influence on the progress of the disease. Children suffering from serious forms of Scheuermann's disease (see Chapter 4) should not participate in gymnastics unless medically supervised physiotherapy is successful. If it is successful, the gradual resumption of sports and gymnastics may be possible.

Tuetsch and Ulrich (1973) found a high number (more than 50% of 13 gymnasts) of juvenile kyphoses in gymnastics. The average for youths is only 30%. Other statistics on gymnasts show similar figures. Refior and Zenker (1970) found juvenile kyphoses in 50% of 50 young performance gymnasts and in only 28% of the control group. Refior (1970) determined that the kyphoses of young gymnasts (9 and 19 years) had significantly increased to the gymnast's hump three years after the initial examination. There were also more fixated spinal sections. Refior recommended that youths with radiographically confirmed damage at the spine be excluded from performance training.

Even running causes high-pressure impacts that affect the spine via the leg-pelvis-sacrum pathway. This is even more the case for gymnastic and athletic jumps. A jump from an apparatus 4 m high results at the time of landing in a shock of 9 to 11 g which frequently reaches the stress tolerance limit. Teutsch and Ulrich (1974) measured acceleration forces in the landing phase after the downswing from the apparatus with a pressure tension of more than 66 kp/cm^2 at the intervertebral discs. In order to distribute this high pressure on the entire intervertebral disc, the lumbar lordosis must be as straight as possible during the downswing from the apparatus and the landing. Unfortunately, the downswing with a hyperlordosis is preferred in competition. Thus the main stress is on the posterior parts of the lumbar intervertebral discs (Figs 8-30 and 8-31). Unfortunately, excessive lordoses are required in many figures of sports and gymnastics.

To prevent damage (eg, by previous disorders), a fitness test with roentgenograms of the spine is indispensible before the start of training for high-performance sports and gymnastics. During the test, attention should be paid to signs of intervertebral disc damage and conditions at the vertebral arch joints and interarticular portions.

High-performance training causes many problems for the spine in nearly all gymnastic disciplines and sports. Tuetsch and Ulrich (1974) found and discussed in detail 7 cases of spondylolisthesis in 22 high-performance gymnasts. Ulrich, in his appendix to the detailed report of Krayenbuehl et al. (1967b), reported on the frequency of problems in the cervical and lumbar spines of gymnasts. Olympic high-performance

Fig. 8-30 Exit from the even bar. Young gymnast with excessive lumbar lordosis.

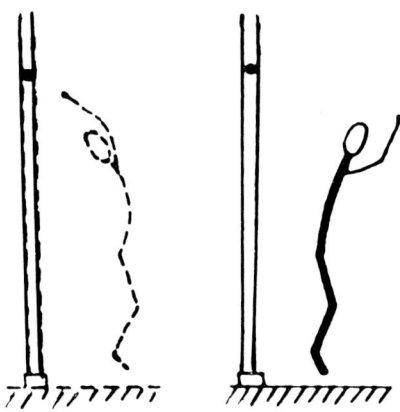

Fig. 8-31 Exit from the horizontal bars. **Left:** Damaging lordosis; **right:** correct straight posture in the lumbosacral area.

gymnasts from Switzerland, Italy, and Japan had a strikingly large number of prolapsed discs in the lumbar spine, some of which required surgery. Two of four members of Switzerland's 1964 Olympic gymnastic team ended performance gymnastics because of spinal disorders. The cause of these difficulties was assumed to be the excessive stress attributable to the strongly emphasized lumbar lordosis in many gymnastic disciplines.

The lumbar lordosis plays a considerable part in many sports and gymnastic disciplines. The lordotic posture in some figures and in thousands of training hours is constantly repeated and is deliberately gradually increased through a relaxation of the intervertebral motor segments in the lumbar area. This posture is unphysiological since it results in a strong pressure on the posterior portions of the lumbar intervertebral discs. The nucleus pulposus is pushed forward. This results in the excessive contraction of the fibrils running from the lamellae rings into the vertebral body epiphyses (Fig. 2-4). This predetermines damage in the internal structure of the intervertebral discs. In addition, there is a special pressure in the vertebral arch joints. Cartilage damage in the articular surfaces leads to the well-known painful arthrosis. The excessive lumbar lordosis should be eliminated from gymnastic and athletic positions as soon as possible. The downswings from the apparatus have an especially adverse effect on the pelvis–lumbar spine boundary. The vibration impact takes place even with a soft floor surface and is transferred from the feet via the legs and pelvis to the intervertebral disc tissue. This results in the abrupt backward dislocation of at least the lower and usually several vertebrae. This process exceeds the stress tolerance of the intervertebral disc structure. The lumbar lordosis is a typical example of incorrect and excessive stress caused by sports-related and training peculiarities.

The unstable pelvic girdle, which is found primarily in young women and occasionally in children and youths of both sexes, is often connected with a hypermobility of the spine. It may have endogenous causes but is in some disciplines achieved or increased only after partner training or softening. The combination of a hypermobile spine and an unstable pelvic girdle is a prerequisite for several gymnastic and athletic disciplines.

8.4.9.1 Floor Exercises

Pictures of figures and processes demonstrate the intensive stresses in training and high-performance competition on the entire spine of the floor gymnast, especially on the lumbosacral boundary. The frequently required rapid change from an excessive lumbar lordosis over straightening into a kyphosis, which continues into the lumbar and thoracic spines, is very detrimental. Although these figure processes flow into one

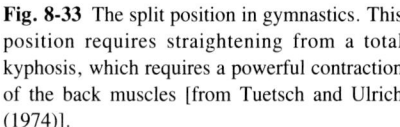

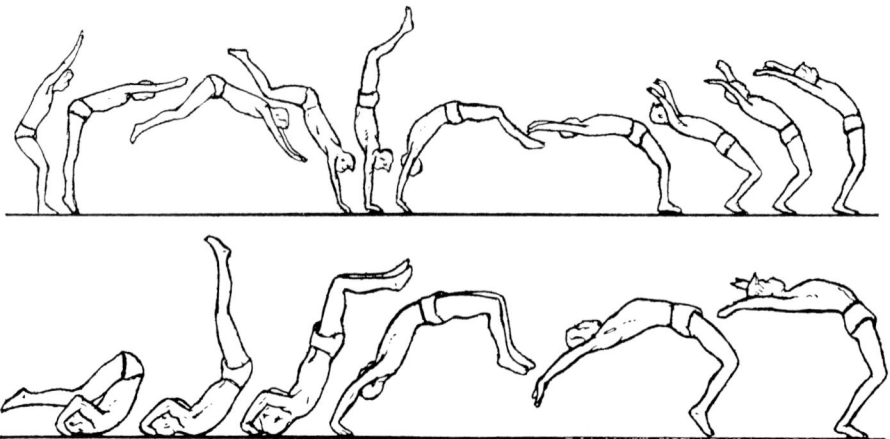

Fig. 8-32 Common phases in floor exercises.

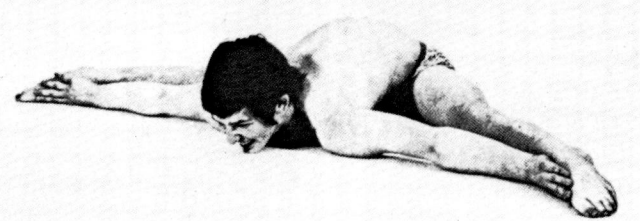

Fig. 8-33 The split position in gymnastics. This position requires straightening from a total kyphosis, which requires a powerful contraction of the back muscles [from Tuetsch and Ulrich (1974)].

another in well-trained athletes, significant stress remains. The interposed forward and backward saltos in the air with additional body screws or floor rolls also primarily affect the lumbar spine and its boundary with the sacrum. Figure 8-32 shows common phases in floor exercises. The entire range of figures in an optional or obligatory program causes various stresses in different directions and leads to an uninterrupted percussion that greatly stresses the lumbosacral boundary. These rapidly alternating stresses on the spine also result in impacts in the lower back of 2 to 8 g.

The straightening of the trunk, which was bent forward during a split, results in strong pressure against the lower lumbar intervertebral discs because of the required muscle strength. During the kyphotic position shown in Figure 8-33, the discs are initially stressed in the front. During straightening to a lumbar lordosis, the muscle-controlled pressure shifts over the middle intervertebral disc portions to the posterior portions. In order to protect the intervertebral disc tissue, the athlete and trainer should make sure that the movement is executed smoothly and not abruptly.

Floor exercises also require other spine-stressing influences, such as the neck stand (Fig. 8-34), during which almost the entire weight of the body rests on the sharply flexed cervical spine. During the head stand, the slightly flexed cervical spine carries an excessive load in spite of the arm support. The hand and the lower arm stand require a hyperlordotic cervical spine. Many of the basic floor exercise figures cross over to the wide artistic spectrum of competitive gymnastics on the apparatus.

8.4.9.2 Gymnastics on the Apparatus

Training and competition on the apparatus stress the lower lumbar spine with its boundary to the pelvis, especially during the exit with 80 to 320 kg of pressure, depending on whether the landing is soft or hard (ie, depending on the quality of the floor and the degree of elastic cushioning with the hip and leg joints). Additional screws have been increasingly imple-

Fig. 8-34 Selected figures and figure groups from floor exercises.

mented into the exit, and the anteflexion and retroflexion of the lumbar spine are especially large stresses during flips or saltos. Frequently, there are multiple, rapid changes between lordosis, kyphosis, lateral flexion, and torsion. There are no detailed measurements of the stresses caused by the various figures in gymnastics on the apparatus that affect the spine.

Gymnastics on the apparatus include a large number of unique figures (Fig. 8-35) that exert the same influences as with floor exercises on the spine in many aspects. Damage of the soft tissues (intervertebral discs, ligament systems, articular cartilage) may result since their elastic reserves (defense mechanisms) are unable to react sufficiently because of the rapid change in movements. The next change with its new impact follows immediately. The effects of these rapid changes on the intervertebral disc metabolism are discussed in Chapter 3.

Abel and Witak (1977) studied 18 female apparatus gymnasts. They found relatively little spinal damage, even though the observation time was during the especially sensitive period of susceptibility during the growth of the spine (between the ages of 12 and 14). Only 4 of the gymnasts reported back problems. All 18 girls had a clearly improved mobility after several years of training: the retroflexion ability was increased to 90 degrees. The average is only 30 degrees. In 2 gymnasts, spondylolisthesis at L-4/S-5, which had not been present at the beginning of training, was detected on roentgenograms. The investigators attributed the low incidence of damage, which they described in detail, to the initial physical fitness test that included roentgenograms and a strict selection on two levels.

During saltos, the odontoid process of the 2nd cervical vertebra may break off. It has not been determined whether the fractures are a result of one trauma or whether they are fatigue fractures caused by repeated athletic-gymnastic training or competition.

Fig. 8-35 Basic exercises in gymnastics on the apparatus. The many stresses to which the spine is subject are suggested in these drawings.

Fig. 8-36 Young gymnast on the balance beam: severe lordosis.

It is not surprising that spondylolysis and spondylolisthesis are frequently discovered. The characteristic problems appear in most cases soon after the start of training. Finally, spondylolysis/spondylolisthesis is found on the roentgenogram (Schwerdtner and Schoberth 1973). If the excessive lordosis must be repeated again and again by juvenile and adolescent gymnasts (Figs. 8-36 and 8-37) during thousands of training hours and in competition, the spine at the lumbosacral boundary will be damaged, in spite of the congenital hypermobility that has been improved through training. However, well-trained muscles may through timely fixation of the susceptible spinal section alleviate the impacts but will scarcely be able to eliminate them. Damage at the intervertebral discs, spondylolysis/spondylolisthesis, vertebral arch joint arthrosis, sacroiliac arthrosis with pain, and mobility impediments are the consequences that become obvious only in later life.

Many trainers believe that the bodies of adult women look too awkward in gymnastic figures. Therefore, almost only children (girls) are being accepted for performance training at a preschool age. Some of them train in vain. But it has not been systematically recorded whether they leave because of back problems and how the development of their spine progresses. Others, after seven to ten years of hard training, attain championships at an age of 13 or 14 years. But what does their spine look like?

8.4.9.3. Competitive Gymnastics

Modern gymnastics can be performed competitively. This requires a planned structure for the program of figure sequences that must be performed accurately. Elements of floor exercises are frequently integrated into competitive gymnastics. A dancelike graciousness is seen in the figure sequences. Typical figures of competitive gymnastics are shown in Figures 8-38 and 8-39.

Stresses on the Spine in Sports, Gymnastics, and Leisure 295

Fig. 8-37 Exercises on the balance beam. Excessive lordosis of the lumbar area with simultaneous torsion; hypermobility of the hip joint [from Schneider (1976)].

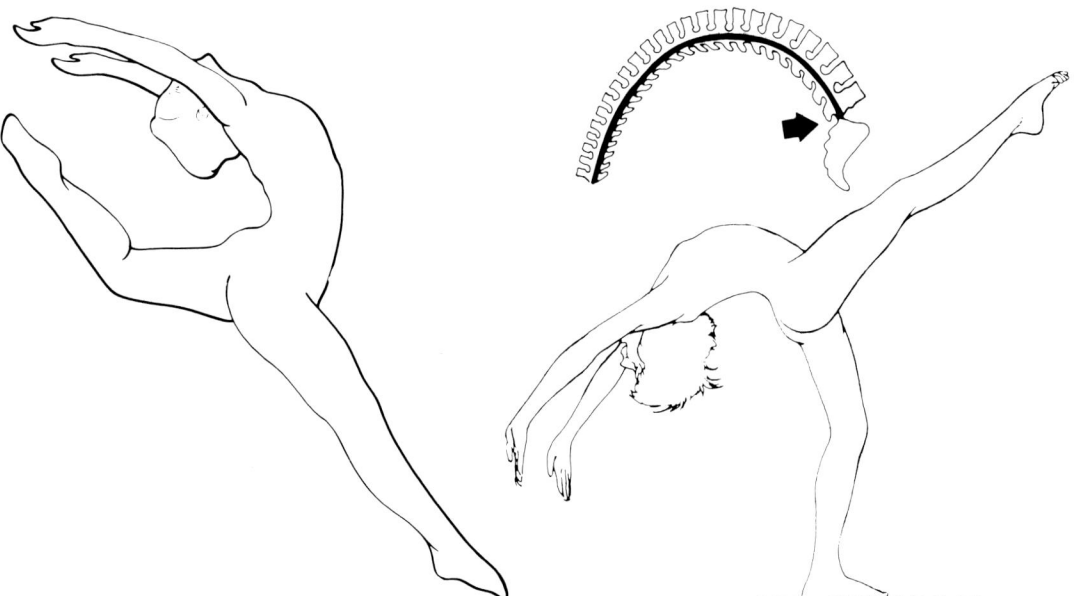

Fig. 8-38 A frequent jumping figure as it is interposed between other figure sequences in competitive gymnastics. Note the excessive lordosis.

Fig. 8-39 Flip in competitive gymnastics. The **arrow** indicates the susceptible point and the anterior cleaving in the intervertebral space L-5/S-1.

The movements and pauses in the middle of a figure, as well as the change between retroflexions and anteflexions, stress the intervertebral motor segments in the same manner as floor exercises and gymnastics on the apparatus. Exceeding stress tolerance limits cannot always be avoided. Such damaging individual causes can become the initial impulse for sequelae in the intervertebral discs and the articular cartilage of the many spinal joints. The often uninterrupted repetition of similar figure sequences may be an even greater cause of damage. As with other spine-stressing sports and gymnastic disciplines, the problems that manifest themselves in back and radiating pain should be taken seriously early.

During the softening in competitive gymnastics, the spine, in addition to the joints of the extremities, is in the center of partner training (Fig. 8-40). Certain similarities to the stresses of contortionists can be observed. But since there are no long-term studies, it is not known whether damage at the spine of competitive gymnasts is as widespread as in contortionists.

8.4.9.4 Competitive Gymnastics on the Apparatus

Competitive gymnastics on the apparatus may be called artistic gymnastics (Fig. 8-41). During compulsories, the athlete must perform predetermined figures on the apparatus accurately. Because of the numerous pieces of equipment, it is not possible to discuss details here. But in competitive gymnastics on the apparatus, as in other gymnastic disciplines, pressures, flexion stresses, and traction forces combine with a varying degree of tension in the spine and exert combined or rapidly changing forces.

Competition in gymnastics on the apparatus requires coordination between the extremities and trunk since many individual exertions must in each figure combine to form an entity. Damage at the spine (intervertebral discs, vertebral joint cartilage) caused by the repetition of stereotypical motion and stress phases are frequent because of the initial damage following the damaging initial impulse.

8.4.9.5 Trampoline Gymnastics

Trampoline gymnastics is becoming increasingly popular. Unfortunately, it often leads to serious injuries of the spine. Paraplegias are not infrequent (Rompe 1980; Steinbrueck 1979b; Steinbrueck and Paeslack 1978). Gradually developing damage at the spine is rather common. This is understandable since during the landing and jumping from the trampoline, the jumping height and falling height create a maximum force of five times the body weight:

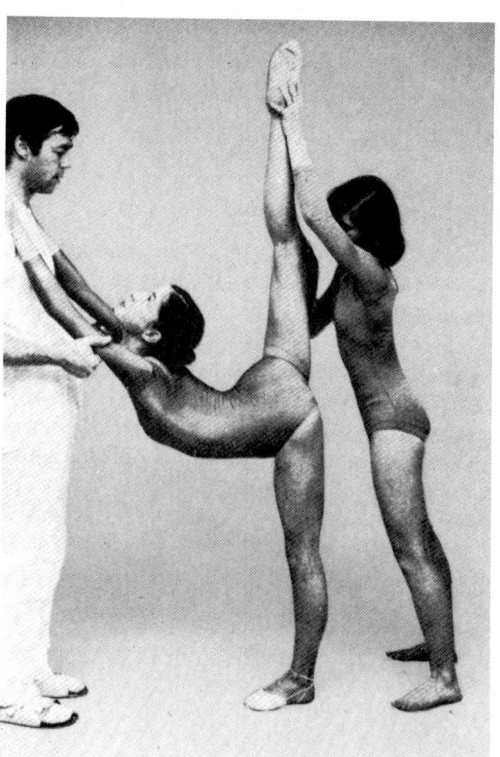

Fig. 8-40 Softening in partner training of young competitive gymnasts [from Steinbrueck and Rompe (1980)].

Fig. 8-41 Artistic high performance of a female athlete in competitive gymnastics on the apparatus achieved through an excessive lordosis [from Krahl (1975)].

between 250 and 350 kp (Fig. 8-42). But the intervertebral discs are stressed not only by these weight forces but also by various jumping figures, where they are subject to torsions alternating with high axial or shearing pressure. The resulting damage in the soft tissues of the intercorporal space (fiber ring, nucleus pulposus) is serious.

The mechanical stress on the spine during trampoline gymnastics is significant and repetitive. It is concentrated on the lower lumbar spine and the lumbosacral boundary. Unexpected pressures affect these areas through retroflexion and anteflexions that do not flow into one another smoothly enough. During an unexpected incorrect innervation, the contracted muscles suddenly relax or are brought in a poor contraction direction. Additional stresses are torsions during screwjumps, especially the stress during forward and backward saltos and the lateral flexions in certain jumps. Failed jumps have an especially adverse effect, with the abrupt force concentration on the lower back, and may also affect the cervical spine.

Because of the abrupt change between landing and bouncing, trampoline gymnastics create an unphysiologically rapid and forceful pressure on the intervertebral discs. The discs are also stressed if the jumper turns the body in this moment or if there is a sudden break in a body screw during the landing. Schwerdtner and Fohler (1974) attributed the increased incidence of reduced physiological curvatures in trampoline gymnasts to torsions and the axial pressure, which frequently affects the spine with 5 g (ie, five times the force of gravity). Riehle (1971) calculated acceleration values of 8 g for the axial jolting during the jump of trampoline gymnasts and pressure tensions in the intervertebral discs of up to 66 kp/cm^2.

Trampoline jumping stresses the lumbar spine to a great degree. During the landing, it must absorb the forces. This is possible only with the help of well-trained muscles, which must be contracted in this instant. In contrast, the jumping figures with torsions, flexion, and jolting forces require a localized hypermobility of the lower spine.

In spite of efforts in training to train the necessary muscles and structure the figures accordingly, Groher (1969, 1974a) reported serious damage. Of 41 trampoline gymnasts of level I, 3 showed spondylolysis/spondylolisthesis (7.3%). Of 27 of level II, 7 showed spondylolysis/spondylolisthesis (25.9%). Spondylolysis was assumed five times in level I and six times in level II. The increase in the incidence of damage after longer, intensive training is obvious. Many investigators have reported similar incidences of spondylolysis/spondylolisthesis.

Groher discovered a striking number of vertebral arch joint arthroses in a study series of trampoline gymnasts and platform divers in spite of their young age: 4 of 22 in group I (18.2%) and 59 of 66 in group II (89.4%) in platform divers. In trampoline gymnasts, roentgenograms detected in level I in 13 of 41 (31.7%) and in 22 of 27 in level II (81.5%) in part severe vertebral arch joint arthroses in the two lower intervertebral motor segments of the lumbar spine. Limited mobility and severe back pain were also noted in some of these athletes. Reduced lumbar lordosis with limited mobility, as well as osteochondrosis, has been reported several times.

The cervical spine should not be neglected in trampoline gymnasts. Serious injuries may lead to paraplegias.

Apart from serious injuries, a less forceful but similar stress on the spine (eg, through the steady

Fig. 8-42 Dangerous trampoline gymnastics [from Steinbrueck and Paeslack (1978)].

repetition of the head roll) may result in the development of damage that may cause wearing of the intervertebral disc, instable intervertebral motor segments with potential dislocations, and vertebral arch joint arthrosis. Such damaging consequences of common training and competition figures have not been given enough attention.

Trampoline gymnastics is not only an independent sport, it also accompanies other sports (eg, gymnastics on the apparatus, platform diving, trapeze acrobatics, tightrope acrobatics, ski acrobatics, and air acrobatics). It is suitable as conditioning training for many general athletic and gymnastic training groups.

8.4.10 Aquatic Sports

8.4.10.1 Rowing and Canoeing

The first reports of studies of rowers were by Koehler (1959a), Querg (1958), and Querg and Schroeter (1958). In accordance with the main stresses, which affect the lower area of the thoracic spine, the investigators found pain and radiographically continued intervertebral disc damage with consecutive osteochondrosis from the 5-6th to the 11-12th motor segment. The damage determined in the thoracic spine was serious in 30% of men and 17.5% of women affected. To a lesser extent, damage was found in 20% of men and 30% of women. Therefore, obvious pathological symptoms existed in an average of 50% of these athletes between 20 and 25 years, which is unusual at this age. The frequency of damage in the middle to lower thoracic spine was attributed to the fact that the thoracic spine is fully matured only two years after the lumbar spine. During athletic rowing, the thoracic spine is therefore affected during the last growth periods of such youths, who started specific rowing training too early—and probably without the correct basic physical training. The lumbar spine showed no significant damage.

Ulrich (1972) and other investigators found the lower lumbar spine to be the center of damage (osteochondrosis), but insufficient data are available to support this finding. According to Ulrich (1972), the differing involvement of the thoracic and lumbar spines in the damage is probably attributable to the different rowing styles: the Fairbairn style with a kyphotic posture and mostly leg work and the orthodox style with a straight back. Future studies should pay attention to these differences (Fig. 8-43). Endler et al. (1980) presented force calculations for the various rowing styles (Fig. 8-44). The force lines in shoulder height, which run to the sternum and spine, are shown in Figure 8-45. The yearly rowing performance of top athletes (5,000 to 6,000 km) is remarkable. For the athletic high-performance years, this is at least 50,000 km in the boat.

Blietz (1967) reported on performance diagrams produced by rowers in part in training modules, in part in the boat. The back muscles perform most of the work. The spine is stressed through flexion. But the straightening of the spine, which is flexed at the beginning of the rowing motion, does not cause compression of the intervertebral discs. On the contrary, it alleviates the burden on the discs. Blietz believed that fears that rowing would result in damage at the spine were unjustified. Similar studies are needed to reconcile this opinion with the results of roentgenogram examinations by other investigators.

Liebau and Wulkenhaar (1974) studied Scheuermann's disease with respect to rowers. They found insufficient evidence that juvenile kyphosis was caused or significantly aggravated by rowing. The stress during the forceful straightening of the formerly strongly anteflexed body during rowing is distributed over the vertebral arch joints, whereas the vertebral body–intervertebral disc series is unburdened by the spreading out of the anterior portions of the intervertebral space. This supposedly counteracts the damage of Scheuermann's disease, which mostly affects the anterior portion. But some criticism is in order here. Growth damage is most frequently found in the anterior portions of the vertebral body–intervertebral disc boundary, but it may also affect the entire epiphysis. Prophylaxis requires unburdening the anterior portions of the vertebral body–intervertebral disc series. But forceful contraction of the back extensor muscles during rowing results in a pulling apart of the anterior intervertebral disc por-

Stresses on the Spine in Sports, Gymnastics, and Leisure 299

Fig. 8-43 Drawings of the Fairbairn style (**left**) and the orthodox style (**right**) of rowing [according to Ulrich (1972)].

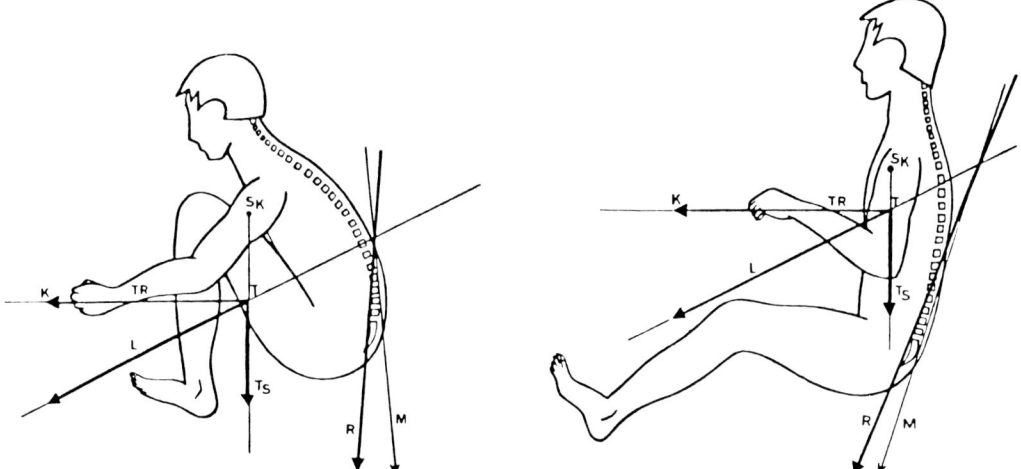

Fig. 8-44 Force conditions during the stroking phase in rowing [calculated by Endler et al. (1980)]. **Left:** Beginning of stroke. Assuming a partial force (T_r) of 50 kp exerted by the rower and a partial force of body gravity (T_s) of 26 kp (total body weight 70 kg), the stress (L) was constructed, which must be balanced by the muscle force (M) of the erector trunci. With the help of vectorial addition, the direction of the resulting stress affecting the first lumbar vertebral body is found. It runs approximately axially to the vertebral body. **Right:** End of stroke phase. Even though the stress (L) is brought close to the spine, the direction of the resulting force (R) remains approximately the same.

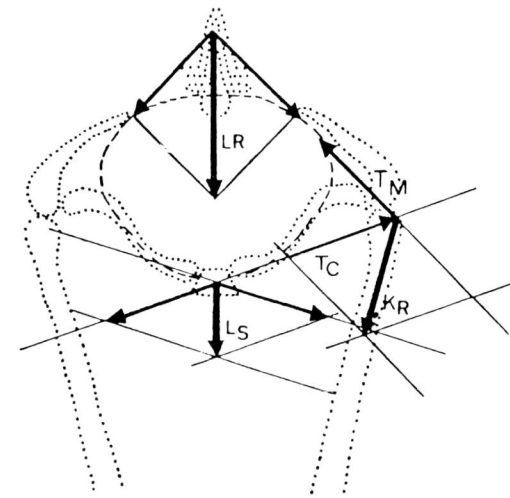

Fig. 8-45 Description of force employment at shoulder height during rowing. The rowing force (K_r) is accepted at the shoulder by the dorsal drawstring and the clavicula and must then be transferred in two partial forces: T_c and T_m. The anterior component (T_c) affects the sternum via the clavicula; the posterior component (T_m) works as drawstring over the spinoscapular and spinohumeral muscles on the spinous processes. With the help of vectorial addition of the partial forces of the two sides, the distribution of the force affecting the sternum (L_s) and the spine (L_r) can be portrayed.

tions with substantial traction force in the anterior parts of the fiber ring. With Scheuermann's disease in a florid phase, this may result in an equally damaging pressure as increased anterior pressure.

Liebau and Wulkenhaar (1974) examined 46 young rowers and found moderate or questionable damage from Scheuermann's disease in 12 (less than 30%). This percentage corresponds to the usual figures that have been reported in the literature. In 2 of the 6 youths who had a follow-up examination, the symptoms had worsened. Two remained unchanged; 2 had improved. These results cannot confirm the conclusion that rowing neither causes nor aggravates juvenile kyphosis.

For youths with minor symptoms of juvenile kyphosis, rowing may have a beneficial effect on the back muscles, as long as there is no intensive training program. But young rowers require observation since their spinal growth is by no means concluded. Back pain during or after training is a warning sign.

Endler and coworkers (1980) found symptoms of juvenile kyphosis in 68.8% of 45 rowers. They attributed the high percentage to unphysiological, frequent maximum stresses on the lower portions of the thoracic spine to which rowers are subject. The large differences in percentages that exist in the literature can to a large degree be attributed to differences in nomenclature and the difference in value the individual investigators give to roentgenogram criteria.

Endler et al. (1980) reported on spinal changes in performance rowers. They concluded that the stress during the proper rowing style corresponds to a physiological, axial stress on the vertebral bodies and intervertebral discs (Fig. 8-44). Nevertheless, the investigators believed that the stereotypical, forceful and prolonged rowing motions frequently result in spinal stress that is too high. The pathogenetic influences of top performances are a result not only of their forces, but primarily of their repetition. This may result in damage. An endogenous inferiority of the intervertebral disc tissue (eg, in the case of juvenile kyphosis) lowers the stress resistance. This increases the possibility of damage at the intervertebral discs.

According to Blietz (1967), the rowing motion is a harmonic, forceful straightening of the crouched body. But according to Endler et al. (1980), the straightening of the body is limited by the turning moment of the counterforce. The substantial, average force moment of the extensor muscles was calculated by Chapman and Troup (1979) to be 4,000 kg/cm^2 in the segment L-4/L-5. In rowing, the critical pressure points are in the middle and lower thoracic vertebral area and in the lower lumbar spine. Endler et al. described more than 45 rowers with reduced mobility in the lower thoracic spine and upper lumbar area and frequently recurring lumbago and sciaticalike problems. Their incidence was much higher in rowers than in nonathletes.

Endler et al. (1980) found spondylolysis in four of the examined rowers. This is a percentage of 8.9%, which is only slightly above the average for the white population. No spondylolisthesis was found, in spite of the stressful rowing training. The investigators concluded that rowing does not result in slippage, even in the case of an inferior interarticular portion, since the stress in this sport does not significantly affect the interarticular portion.

There have been no radiological studies on the question of whether intensive one-sided oar training causes concentrated spongiosa structures at the vertebral bodies that are excessively stressed in the center of the motion. Vertebral bodies with concentrated spongiosa have been described in other sports with unilateral, prolonged, and repetitive pressure stresses.

Since biking causes kyphosis, it is not sensible to recommend biking as a combination training for rowers. Both sports have an adverse effect on the young, immature spine. If a rower regards bicycle training as necessary, it can be undertaken only in the supine position on a bicycle trainer.

The lack of information regarding the cervical spine is striking. Endler et al. (1980) described how the rowing force distributes itself over the shoulder girdle (Fig. 8-45). In a diagram, they portrayed the directions of the partial forces. The cervical muscles are closely connected with the shoulder girdle and are bonded at various vertebral arch processes with ligaments. In oar rowers, a unilateral elevation of the shoulder results, and thus an inclination to scoliosis. After prolonged high-performance training for oar rowers, damage at the lower cervical spine and its boundary with the thoracic spine should be expected. If this should be confirmed, an attempt must be made to remedy the situation by changing the rowing style. As in many other performance athletes, there is a large, fixated kyphosis, known for rowers as the rower's hump. It probably develops in addition to juvenile kyphosis.

Canoeing also causes a fixated kyphosis because of the prolonged kyphotic position. Damage at the intervertebral discs in the lumbosacral area can be frequently observed. It is caused by the sport or is aggravated through the demands of the sport on the spine. Such damage is related to the painful and inhibiting vertebral blockages that occur in wet and cold weather, as described by Steinbrueck and Tilscher (1983).

Kayaking results in spondylolysis/spondylolisthesis because of the stress of retroflexion with torsion (Stewart 1953).

During the unilaterally controlled Canadian rowing, rolling of the pelvis is obvious. It causes pressure on and rotation of the sacroiliac joints, alternating between right and left and unsymmetrically distributed in its force. Fixated scoliosis is often observed.

8.4.10.2 Sailing

Sailing is a popular, nonstressful sport. During training for competition, a slightly twisted forced posture of the trunk and head is frequently required over a prolonged period. This leads to functional damage with acute pain through vertebral blockages. The cause of the blockages is damage at the intervertebral discs, vertebral arches, or uncovertebral joints in the cervical area.

8.4.10.3 Swimming

Swimming is rightly said to be not only beneficial to the spine but also therapeutically important for improving spinal disorders by improving the back muscles. This applies to swimming motions with symmetrical movement of the bilateral longissimi muscles, as well as the muscles that connect with the neck, shoulders, arms, and legs and the muscles of the abdominal wall and rib cage. Other positive influences that benefit the entire body are:

- the buoyancy of the water, which carries nine tenths of the body weight
- the relief of the support function of the spine and its musculoligamentous corset
- the reduced pressure on the intervertebral discs
- the external hydrostatic pressure, which improves the return of the blood and tissue fluid

However, there are some types of swimming that overstress the spine unilaterally in athletic high-performance training and cause problems. These include the butterfly because of the required lordosis. Figure 8-46 shows a 15-year-old female swimmer, a world champion in synchronized swimming, with an excessive lordosis that greatly stresses the posterior portions of the lumbar spine.

Unilateral free-style swimming requires a prolonged lateral flexion with rotation of the spine

Fig. 8-46 Female swimmer in a figure of conditioning training, which includes an excessive lumbar lordosis.

and stresses the cervical spine, which is stressed just as much during the usual symmetrical breast stroke because of the lordosis. The development of cervical syndromes is a sign of this and requires diagnosis by a sports physician. In certain cases, athletic back swimming should be temporarily interrupted (with suitable treatment by a physician) or should be discontinued in the case of serious intervertebral disc or articular damage. Ross (1974) reported on the painful swimmer's neck and recommended free-style swimming with goggles and snorkel to avoid it. However, this suggestion will be of no use for athletic performance training. The swimmer's hump is probably connected with juvenile kyphosis (Fig. 8-47).

8.4.10.4 Scuba Diving

Although in the past, diving could be performed for only a short time and in shallow depths, it can now be performed using equipment. Diving became highly popular when new equipment made the penetration of depths of several hundred meters possible. Unfortunately, damage developed in the process that was connected mostly with surfacing too rapidly: barotrauma.

The scientific and practical principles of barotrauma have been described by many investigators. Wuensche and Scheele reported on it in detail from 1974 to 1976. Literature concerned with sports medicine deals primarily with damage at the internal organs and only touches the development of damage at the skeleton (Groh 1962; Metz and Huellemann 1976). The radiomorphology of bone marrow infarct was described by Horvath (1978) for long bones. Damage in the subchondral zones of large joints, such as hip or shoulder joints, attributable to decompression sickness (dysbarism) has received special attention. If scuba divers surface too quickly, they complain of pain in the joints, the so-called bends. Roentgenogram studies of the painful joints are urgently required in these cases. If back pain develops, roentgenogram studies of the affected sections are also necessary. Repeated roentgenogram studies are required if the problems persist, so that the destruction of joints can be recognized in time. If the problems are untreated, the most severe articular damage develops: barotraumatic arthrosis.

The most important role in these processes is played by hydrogen, which is dissolved in the blood and tissues. If the external pressure changes suddenly, the general symptoms of acute barotrauma develop: shortness of breath with a feeling of suffocation, sweating, collapse, and unconsciousness. Their cause is the suddenly excessive pressure of the hydrogen. If the pressure increases significantly, the hydrogen can no longer be excreted through the alveolar membranes. Hydrogen bubbles develop. Tissues with a high fat content, such as bone marrow and the lipoid organs (eg, central nervous system), have a special tendency to develop gas bubbles since they contain more hydrogen than other tissues.

These consequences of decompression sickness cause frequent bone-joint pain in the acute state. This pain is caused by the hydrogen bubbles that have developed in the fatty bone marrow and those that have traveled to the capillary areas of the bone-cartilage boundary as gas

Fig. 8-47 Swimmer's hump in a seven-times Olympic champion.

emboli. The bone pain develops during the acute decompression phase because of the deformation pressure of the growing gas bubbles. The initial pain subsides in most cases, but impaired nourishment of the infarcted areas frequently results. This leads to chronic damage at the bone areas close to the joints (less frequently in metaphysis or diaphysis). It is most frequently located in the subchondral layers of the upper arm and/or hip head but also affect other bones. In roentgenograms osteolysis with cysts can be seen and, occasionally, calcifications. Under the influence of the stress, the bone centers break and/or cartilage pieces break off. Articular deformations (arthrosis) follow. The roentgenogram provides much information on the start and progress of these diseases, which become perceptible only at a later time as barotraumatic arthrosis, often only after the diver has long forgotten the barotrauma.

Even though avascular bone necroses caused by decompression damage are frequently observed and described, there are still many unanswered questions, especially regarding the etiopathogenesis. Details may be found in Junghanns (1979).

During the acute phase of the decompression stress, there is, in addition to bone and joint pain, spinal pain (Klotzbuecher 1972). However, chronic damage at the spine has only rarely been described (Holstein 1971). This is remarkable, because the high fat content of the spinal marrow and the fine capillaries at the vertebral body–intervertebral disc boundary, which can be compared to the anatomic conditions in the bony joint head and joint cartilage, predispose gas bubble emboli with the described consequences for the large joints. The pain in the spine during acute decompression sickness points to such phenomena.

According to present knowledge, the spine is seriously threatened by decompression stresses. Regular roentgenogram studies during follow-up examinations of divers may be able to reveal decompression-related damage at the spine. Bogetti (1965) observed vertebral osteosclerosis as a consequence of decompression sickness. Genadinnik and Dumkina (1969) described a 30-year-old diver who after a serious decompression accident was temporarily able to work as he had before. Radiologically, the typical symptoms of aseptic necrosis at the thigh bone existed. Gradually, he suffered increasing back pain with radiating pain into the legs. Several years after the painful conditions had started, the roentgenograms showed fusing of the 7th and 8th thoracic vertebra. According to the case history and diagnosis, the assumption of an avascular osteonecrosis in the vertebral bodies attributable to serious decompression stress was justified.

It is hoped that sports physicians will give their attention to the spine of scuba divers. This includes the search for radiographically perceptible vertebral arch joint arthrosis, which can develop after decompression stress, just as impairments at the vertebral body–intervertebral disc boundary.

8.4.10.5 Platform Diving

Diving is performed from the platform in a special, artistic manner that requires a long and intensive training: 175,000 dives from the platform during a training and competition period of approximately 12 years.

The number of training dives of a female athlete described by Jaster (1963) increased within three years from 9,453 to 11,652, and then to more than 22,505. Among them were 1,650 dives from the 10-m platform. Jaster pointed out the susceptible spine of competitive and platform divers. The spine is adversely affected by difficult diving figures, especially during the learning period of new movement processes.

Young board and platform divers train before and during puberty, when the great elasticity and resilience of the spine permit artistic dive sequences. But this results in an even greater danger for the spine. The soft tissues in the intervertebral motor segments, especially the intervertebral disc and its cartilage plates and ligaments, are unphysiologically slackened during the frequently repeated dives because of their youthful elasticity. The result is a deliberate, sports-related intersegmental hypermobility. The stretched ligaments of the vertebral arch joints allow increasingly greater mobility. The resulting opening of the joints facilitates an excessive total kyphosis, but with substantial pressure on and tension stress of the LPH region (Fig. 8-48) or lumbar lordosis (Fig. 8-49). This is the reason for the frequent arthrosis of the vertebral arch joints in the lumbar area observed by several investigators.

In a small number (14) of radiologically examined platform divers, Groher and Heidensohn (1970) found vertebral arch joint arthrosis in 82%. Jaster (1963) and Groher and Heidensohn (1970) found frequent, reduced, fixated lumbar lordosis in young competitive platform divers. This was the result of sports-related overstrain of several lumbar intervertebral discs and the pertinent vertebral arch joints and muscles. Feared among platform divers are the hyperlordoses that can occur during the learning period of new dives through an incorrect movement process by immersion into the water. They are caused by insufficiently prepared muscle contraction and cause frequent problems, often probably attributable to vertebral blockades.

Well-trained platform divers can avoid serious damage at the cervical spine through correct diving techniques. Nevertheless, initially, distortion damage at the cervical spine occasionally develops during incorrect dives or the training of new dives in spite of outstretched arms. Such incidents will be forgotten, and the consequences will finally add up to permanent damage through the pressure that affects the spine, even during technically well-performed dives. Although this happens rarely, platform divers with problems at the cervical spine should be medically examined immediately, and roentgenogram studies should be performed to look for intervertebral chondrosis and/or intervertebral osteochondrosis and uncovertebral arthrosis.

Since the various saltos forward and backward and body rotations during the artistic dives stress the lumbar spine and especially the boundary with the sacrum, it is not surprising that Groher and Heidensohn (1970) found spondylolysis/spondylolisthesis in approximately 34% of platform divers. Groher (1969, 1974a) found spondylolysis/spondylolisthesis in the vertebral arches L5-L2, in part unilateral, in part bilateral. At level II (66 examinees), he showed the radiological proof of 17 spondylolysis and 3 spondylolisthesis (20 of 66 cases; 30.3%). In addition, spondylolisthesis was suspected in 18 more cases. In level I (22 examinees), spondylolysis was suspected in 2 cases. The large number of vertebral arch arthroses and spondylolyses/spondylolistheses found in platform divers points to the high stress on the osteoligament-muscle partnership in the intervertebral motor segments of the lumbosacral area. The causes comprise a group of factors in which excessive stress may play an important role. Based on his experiences with young platform divers, Jaster (1963) formulated a critical conclusion: A previously damaged spine is an indication to prohibit any kind of performance sport. Almost the same conclusion was reached by Zippel and Pfeil (1980).

Diving from the board presents special problems, which are connected with jumping from the bouncing board. The takeoff pressure creates vibrations that reach the spine in spite of the

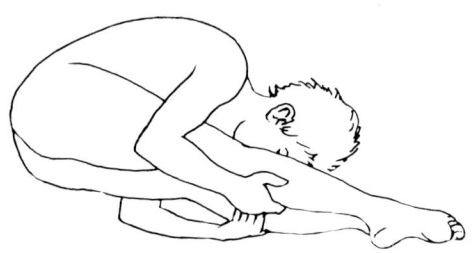

Fig. 8-48 Total kyphosis during platform diving with great stress on the LPH region [from Groher (1970)].

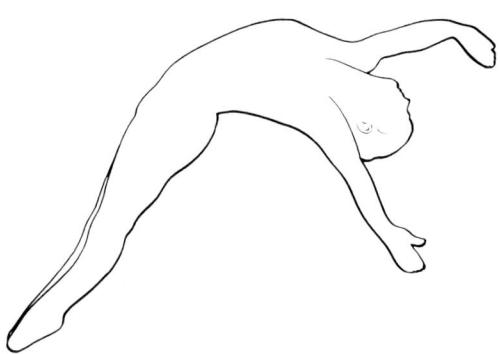

Fig. 8-49 Excessive lumbar lordosis of a 22 year-old female platform diver.

well-developed leg muscles, at least partially over the transmission path over the leg and pelvis. Insufficient biomechanical studies of divers have been undertaken. The body posture during the immersion is very important for the spine, both for the dive from the platform and from the board (Fig. 8-50). The body must immerse straight, with the head between the arms. Only with this diving technique is the pressure evenly distributed over the entire surface of the intervertebral disc. If a lordosis exists during the immersion, overstraining of the lamellae fibers occurs in the anterior intervertebral disc portions. Damaging stretching or small tears may occur in the front. In contrast, the posterior portions are subject to a high pressure, which may exceed the stress tolerance limit of the tissue. Pain in the sacral area after such an incorrect dive should be reported to a sports physician.

8.4.10.6 Water Skiing

Water skiing causes great stresses on the support and motor system. The high speed and hard impact with the waves transmit high vibration frequencies over the spine to the head, in spite of efforts to absorb them in the knee and hip joints. At the head, Dupuis (1976) measured 17 to 20 Hz during studies on the mechanical causes of amotio retinae, which is observed after water skiing. Commandre et al. (1974) studied 27 male water skiers (15 to 37 years of age). Twelve of them participated in competitions: slalom, figure skiing, and jumping. The investigators described lumbago, lumbago-sciatica, and arthrotic damage. For children and youths whose spine is still immature, water skiing may overstrain the spine.

8.4.10.7 Surfing

Surfing has attracted more and more fans. Occasionally, injuries of the spine occur during bad falls. Even soft riding over the waves requires a continuously changing balance, which must be maintained through appropriate movements of the entire body. The spine must compensate for these changing stress distributions with its muscles and ligaments.

Differences in pressure, mostly connected with torsions and shearing, affect the intervertebral discs. In addition, the vertebral arch joints with their cartilage surface and ligaments are also affected through traction, pressure and displacement. The lumbar spine, with its boundary with the sacrum, is stressed the most. Similar to water skiing, sinus-shaped, irregular (stochastic) vibrations or shock vibrations of various intensities penetrate into the spine. For further information, see Rosemeyer (1980/81a).

8.4.10.8 Wind Surfing

In wind surfing, surfboards equipped with a hand-operated sail reach speeds up to 45 km/h. The physical stress on the entire support and motor system is substantial. The spine, with its muscles and ligaments, plays the central role in the support, constraint, and balancing work. Long regattas in high winds require prolonged static support from the spine with a uniform forced posture. This causes high pressure with torsion, which affects many, mostly lower, intervertebral motor segments (i.e., intervertebral discs, vertebral arch joints, and sacroiliac joints). Painful myogelosis and sciatica are frequent as are probably vertebral blockages. Attention should also be paid to the influences of vibrations caused by waves.

The motion and support work of the spine probably substantially exceed those in water skiing and surfing. Unfortunately, there are insufficient studies regarding those questions. There is one study on the stress on the cardiovascular system, hypothermia, and static muscle exertion (Schoenle et al. 1981).

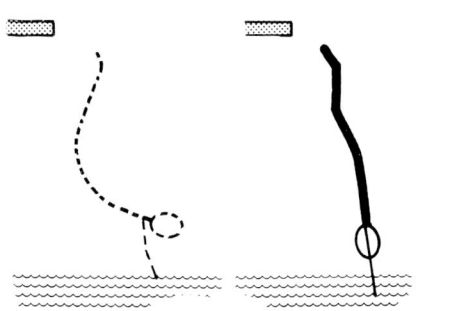

Fig. 8-50 Diving form. **Left:** Incorrect lordosis; **right:** correct straightening posture.

According to Schoenle (personal communication), several wind surfers complained of sudden lumbago attacks and back pain after practicing their sport. In one case, after the neurological symptoms were considered, surgery became necessary because of a prolapsed disc. Although these are only individual cases that are not necessarily connected with wind surfing, such symptoms should be clarified with the help of radiodiagnostics. Sports-related stresses during surfing could be damaging.

Menge and Rind (1982) concluded that wind surfing was not damaging to the support and motor system. This conclusion should be confirmed since the investigators reported stress problems in the lumbar spine in 26.5% of their subjects. Other areas of the body were much less affected: hands, 19.0%; knees, 14.7%; and shoulders, 13.4%. For additional information, see Krueger and Mang (1979) and Rosemeyer (1980/81b).

8.4.11 Winter Sports

8.4.11.1 Sledding and Bobsledding

Competitive sledding is regulated by international regulations. The tracks, which have been designed with curves, have an artificial ice surface. Top speeds of up to 117 km/h, with an average of approximately 95 km/h, can be reached. Competitive sledding allows one-seaters and two-seaters. Intensive summer training is necessary, which affects the cervical and back muscles.

During bobsledding, hourly speeds of up to 130 km/h are reached. Active athletes require extensive power training during the summer, similar to but much more intensive than that of sledding athletes (C. Schmidt, 1981a,b). There are no detailed long-term studies on the effects on the spine.

Such studies seem urgently needed. In high-performance bobsledding, the spine is subjected to substantial stresses during the pushing phase, the jump, and the ride. In addition, there is the stress caused by the power training. Examinations of bobsled athletes by a sports physician should therefore include the spine. Damage at the intervertebral motor segments of the lumbar section and the L5-/S-1 boundary should be looked for. In the course of examinations, intervertebral osteochondrosis should also be considered, as well as arthrosis in the vertebral arch joints and sacroiliac joints and spondylolysis/spondylolisthesis.

8.4.11.2 Skiing

Skiing is a demanding sport, even if the skier has taken skiing classes for beginners and advanced skiers over several winters. Skiing requires not only strong leg muscles but also a well-trained musculoligamentous corset of the trunk, which is able to stabilize the spine, even in difficult situations. If such a stabilizer is absent, the stress limit for youths and adults can easily be exceeded so that intervertebral discs and vertebral arch joints may suffer damage attributable to several initial impulses.

Pain during leisurely skiing develops less because of peculiarities of the skiing technique than because of incorrect technique, insufficient muscle strength and mobility, and previous spinal damage. Leisure skiers, especially older skiers, should always consider if their leg and trunk muscles are in condition for downhill skiing. If there are doubts, the transition to cross-country skiing or ski hiking is a good alternative.

The typical symptoms of the neck-shoulder-arm syndrome develop rather frequently because of the arm work with the poles during cross-country skiing and ski hiking. The physician must determine whether these problems are caused by intervertebral disc damage or by changes in the vertebral arch or uncovertebral joints of the cervical spine. Just as for lumbago, lumbalgia, and sciatica, the correct therapy is essential.

Even though children, youths, and middle-aged enthusiastic winter vacationers prefer downhill skiing because of its speed, cross-country skiing should not be left aside even at these age levels. Cross-country skiing trains endurance of the cardiovascular system and respiratory organs and results in the oxygen shower whose significance is discussed in section 8.2. In addition, the regular steps achieve a coordinated use of the shoulder-trunk-leg muscles.

Thus cross-country skiing forms a part of the program for sensible fitness.

Ski hiking should receive more attention than the more exhausting and athletic cross-country skiing. In addition to all muscles of the body, the increased supply of oxygen benefits the soft tissues at the spine: intervertebral discs, ligaments, and cartilage surfaces of the spinal joints.

8.4.11.3 Competitive Skiing

Skiing is performed competitively in several disciplines. Athletes who perform this high-performance sport require long years of preparatory training. The spine is subject to great stress in all types of competitive skiing. It is not true, as many leisure athletes believe, that skiing involves mostly leg work. Although the legs must be diligently trained, the training of the trunk muscles is not less important. In all disciplines of competitive skiing, the trunk muscles are subject to very high static and kinetic force demands.

Downhill Racing. In competitive downhill racing, there is a very high axial pressure on the lumbar spine. This axial pressure reaches or exceeds the stress resistance limit of the intervertebral disc tissue and exerts a pressure of 1,500 kg with the addition of the skiing momentum and torsion during the flexion (Friedrich 1969). This is an excessive, frequently damaging force for the young, but even more for the aging, intervertebral discs. It is experienced several times a day during skiing and is caused especially by mistakes in technique. Lower back pain and attacks of lumbago and sciatica are the consequences and warning signs to pay attention to one's performance limits. This also applies to ski jumpers. Prokoop (1966) simulated the skiing technique in spinal specimens. The intervertebral discs of young people ruptured in a laterally twisted spine (hip flexion) under a pressure of 300 kg; those of older people ruptured under a pressure of 100 kg.

The downhill skier does not always have a strong, stabilizing musculoligamentous corset. Insufficient (accompanying) coordination training of the back muscles, fatigue, and inattention may lead to failure of the supporting forces so that hard pressures affect the soft tissues of the spine in the intercorporal space (intervertebral disc) or vertebral arch joints (cartilage surface). Such an initial impulse may cause microdamage that results in progressive tissue damage.

Dupuis and Zerlett (1984) had without a doubt the image of a perfectly trained downhill skier in mind when they concluded that larger vibration stresses can be borne even during certain body postures. But even the top athlete during a competition rarely finds a long, uniform downhill slope. Downhill racing includes jumps and especially frequent swings that do not always allow the uniform and easily absorbed gliding assumed by these investigators. Slalom and giant slalom (Figs. 8-51 through 8-53) require the highest concentration and the rapid changing of the stabilizing direction of the musculoligamentous corset in the lumbosacral area. The detrimental effects of the failure of these stabilizing potentials were described in the previous section. For additional information, see Pankratz (1971).

8.4.11.4 Ice Sports

Among ice skating disciplines, speed skating and competitive ice skating have at least as many potential damaging influences as competitive skiing (slalom) and gymnastics.

Speed Skating. According to E. Keller (1981), this sport is considered the fastest non-mechanical sport. During the 500-m sprint runners reach top speeds of 60 km/h, and on the 10,000-m long distance course, an average speed of 44 km/h.

The far anteflexed body posture and the swinging arms in right-left alternation lead to swaying of the central axial organ (Fig. 8-54). The arm swings change unilaterally during the running of curves. This results in a distinct turning of the spine to one side. This alternating use of the swinging arms has an effect down to the intervertebral motor segments of the lower lumbar spine and its boundary with the sacrum. It has not been established to what extent the sacroiliac joints are affected.

As can be seen from the runners, competitive racing and the additional conditional and muscular power training develop strong back and connective muscles to the pelvis-thigh area. This

Fig. 8-51 Downhill skier during jump [from Baer (1981)].

Fig. 8-52 Slalom skier during swing with body rotation and lumbar-pelvic flexion [from Baer (1981)].

Fig. 8-53 Movement process during slalom swing [from Baer (1981)].

Fig. 8-54 Two phases of speed skating. **Top:** Starting phase; **bottom:** running phase.

extensive muscle corset reduces the motion and stress influences on the susceptible portion of the intervertebral disc caused by competition. According to E. Keller (1981), the crouched jumps with load stresses practiced during training are the cause of degenerative damage at the lumbar spine.

Figure Skating. This balletlike sport requires constitutional hypermobility. If it is not present to the full extent, it may be deliberately improved by training and, in certain cases, even acquired. Because of lax articular ligaments and capsules, the joints with constitutional or trained mobility tend to hyperflexion or luxations. Specific training can strengthen the muscles so that no "ugly" hyperflexion of the joints occurs during the figures. The same applies for the necessarily lax lumbar spine. The frequent, excessive lordosis can be stabilized and held in the necessary arch only through a properly trained static-dynamic musculoligamentous corset. In spite of correct muscle control, the intervertebral motor segments of the lower lumbar spine and its boundary with the sacrum are subject to substantial stresses. During high and far jumps, loads of up to 600 pounds affect the spine and the leg joints. In addition to the frequent, excessive lordosis of the lumbar spine, there is excessive lordosis of the cervical spine during some skating figures (Figs. 8-55 and 8-56). However, there are no long-term studies on pain, ankylosed cervical lordosis, or verifiable chronic damage.

Fig. 8-55 Frequently performed ice skating figure. Note the lumbar lordosis and the lordotic, slightly twisted cervical spine.

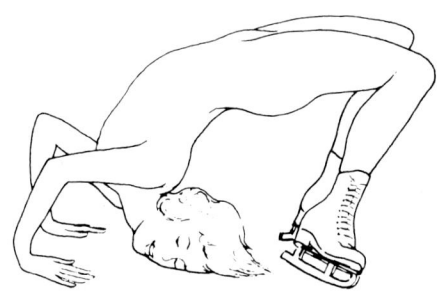

Fig. 8-56 Female ice skater separated from her partner during a swing. The lordosis of the cervical spine is also twisted to the side.

The pliable bodies of children are especially suited for figure skating training. Therefore, talent searches frequently begin at the preschool level with the justification that ten years of training are required to achieve championship titles at the age of 17 or 18. But many ice skaters withdraw from the sport years before then at 14 years of age. Medical counselors have found insufficient, thin cartilage layers in the stressed leg joints of these children in intensive training. During overstressing by ice skating training, the excessive and premature wear of the intervertebral disc tissue (intervertebral chondrosis) could progress to intervertebral osteochondrosis, which is followed by lifelong problems.

In competitive juvenile and youthful ice skaters, muscle pain in the lumbar spine (hyperlordosis) and cervical area are reported and are mostly diagnosed as distortions, myalgias, and myogeloses. It should be determined whether they involve radiating pain that masks beginning damage of the intervertebral discs, vertebral arch joints, and sacroiliac joints.

During partner skating, the female skater is especially subject to the described dangers for the spine. During many dancing figures, the partner is subject to the same stresses on his spine. In addition, as the "bottom man," he must absorb high static stresses with axial pressure, and often simultaneously the torsions generated by the centrifugal force, with his trunk muscles. For further information, see Siegfried (1981/82).

Ice Hockey. Ice hockey, the fastest and hardest team sport, is played with a puck, a small hard rubber disc. In contrast to field and indoor hockey, it requires an especially far anteflexed trunk and a reduced lumbar lordosis. However, this posture is frequently interrupted by sudden stopping during the run and rapid straightening. Anteflexion and straightening, frequently with forceful turning moments, subject the intervertebral discs and vertebral arch joints to damaging stresses. The LPH region must therefore bear great stresses. There have been no reports on specific damage in the LPH region attributable to ice hockey.

8.4.12 Throwing Sports and Shooting Sports

The throwing of the javelin, shot, and hammer stresses the spine through the trunk rotation with

Fig. 8-57 Figure sequence during the discus throw [from Schmolinsky (1974)].

lateral flexion and the swinging during the throw. Therefore, a high percentage (up to 70%) of s-shaped scolioses can be found in throwers, most of them concave to the throwing side. Rompe and Dreyer (1972) suggested unilaterally increased trunk muscles as the reason since approximately 6,000 throws are common during a sports season. In addition, 14% of the examined throwers had spondylolisthesis.

The forces required by the trunk muscles are substantial. They are necessary to stabilize the stressed sections of the spine in order to protect the intervertebral discs from damage by impacts, torsion, and twisting. The pelvis-leg muscles are necessary aids for stability, as are all muscles in the shoulder–upper arm area. All mentioned muscle groups require intensive training adapted to throwing disciplines.

Together with high pressures, the twisting in the LPH area is often damaging for throwers. It may result in blockades in the vertebral arch and sacroiliac joints. The fact that in many throwers the special pressure that affects the spine on the throwing side results in a unilateral adaptation through concentrated spongiosa has received little attention in the literature.

8.4.12.1 Discus Throw and Hammer Throw

During the multiple rotation movement before the discus is released, the acceleration of the throwing arm with the disc is faster than the body

Fig. 8-58 Discus thrower (statue by Myron; approximately 450 B.C.).

rotation (Figs. 8-57 and 8-58). This results in a twisting of the transverse axes between the shoulder and pelvic area with pressure and torsion in the intervertebral motor segments of the

Fig. 8-59 Movement sequences during the hammer throw [from Schmolinsky (1974)].

lower lumbar spine. Frequently, the stress tolerance of the affected intervertebral discs is exceeded. If the trunk muscles are unable to stabilize the rotation at the right moment in the LPH region, the intervertebral discs in the central rotation area are endangered.

Extraordinary forces result during the hammer throw: 1,500 training hours per year and up to 40 throws per training day cause frequently repeated spinal stress. Tons of pressure affect the knee joints when the hammer is brought to its throwing speed of 100 km/h after the forceful and rapid triple rotation of the body (Figs. 8-59 and 8-60). At the same time, this results in a tremendous traumatic force on the spine, which is subject to the stress of the strongly contracted back muscles and the rotation pressure during alternating lateral flexion. According to Scheele

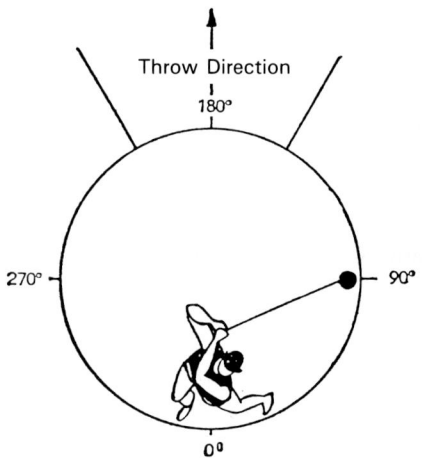

Fig. 8-60 Schematic drawing of the hammer throw [from Schmolinsky (1974)].

Stresses on the Spine in Sports, Gymnastics, and Leisure 313

Fig. 8-61 Figure sequence for shot putting [from Schmolinsky (1974)].

et al. (1979), the thrower forces the hammer during the last throw phase with a force increasing to approximately 300 kp. The investigators attributed the damaging stress on the intervertebral discs of the lumbar area (ie, spondylarthrosis and intervertebral osteochondrosis) to this force. Even the frequent spondylolistheses may be attributed to the stress on the interarticular portions, where the stability of the vertebral arch is determined.

During the discus throw and the hammer throw, insertion osteotendopathies are frequent. However, they are only rarely observed in the spine. But they should still be looked for if back pain develops so that a suitable therapy can be initiated. Occasionally, separations of the spinous processes are reported for both disciplines.

8.4.12.2 Shot Putting

The shot weighs 7.25 kg for men and 4 kg for women and youths. During the acceleration phase (upper body bent forward, simultaneous hip and knee flexion), the shot is brought to shoulder height. While the thrower straightens the trunk, the rotation in the front follows into the throw phase, during which both legs straighten instantaneously and with maximum strength while the throwing arm straightens simultaneously in a flowing, forceful movement to propel the shot to the top front (Fig. 8-61).

The main stress of the rotating and stretching trunk motion is on the lumbar spine. During training and competition, the soft tissue structures of the spine are stressed to such an extent that intervertebral chondrosis, intervertebral osteochondrosis, and prolapsed discs result.

8.4.12.3 Javelin Throwing

The javelin weighs 800 g for men and 600 g for women. It is propelled on its course at a release speed of 30 m/s. This occurs approximately 6,000 times in each sports season. During the average training and competition time of approximately eight years, this amounts to 48,000 throws. In addition, there is weight training of 40 to 60 tons per training day. The spine is subject to an arched contraction (Fig. 8-62) with a simultaneous, large scoliosis of the thoracic spine, concave to the throwing arm side (Fig. 8-63).

Together with this scoliotic posture, the shoulder on the throwing side is further retracted during the take-off run and the throwing phase. The subsequent rotation of the trunk requires the systematic execution of a motion sequence while the muscles are strongly contracted. Only this provides the prerequisite for reaching the necessary speed of at least 30 m/s for the release of the javelin.

The pressure and rotation forces not only stress the intervertebral motor segments of the lumbar spine but result in twisting from the lumbosacral boundary to the sacroiliac joints. This is the reason that a relatively large number of javelin throwers suffer from arthrosis of the vertebral arch joints and sacroiliac joints, which frequently leads to painful blockades. According to statistical data by Rompe et al. (1971), the force and movement concentration the javelin thrower must develop in the LPH area lead to radiographically perceptible spondylolysis, in part also with spondylolisthesis, in 50% of the top athletes. Considering the described stresses, it is understandable that osteochondrosis in the lumbar region can frequently be found.

In 70% of javelin throwers, the postural scoliosis that can frequently be observed during training and competition results in a fixated chronic scoliosis in the thoracic spine of approximately 15 degrees (Cobb 1948). If throwers

Fig. 8-62 Javelin thrower during the release phase. Excessive lumbar lordosis with a schematic drawing of the essential muscle tracts from Tittel.

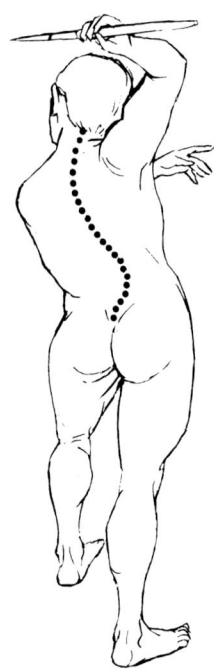

Fig. 8-63 Javelin thrower in the release position. The lordosis (Fig. 8-62) is connected with a scoliotic posture.

complain about lumbago, overstrain tendinosis of the spinous or transverse processes should be looked for. This has a different pain character and requires different therapy than neural or muscle-related lumbago.

Condensed spongiosa in the stressed vertebral bodies develop unilaterally on the throwing side. These cases are an especially interesting adaptation of bones to unilateral stresses.

8.4.12.4 Shooting and Archery

Loesel (1981) reported extensively on the stress on the spine during shooting sports. He made extensive measurements of the vibration stress on the arms and shoulders during the firing of various weapons. The acceleration components were 1.4, 4, and 14 kHz. Measurements taken at the forehead and acromion revealed no risk factors for the shooter. Measuring points at the tips of the spinous or transverse processes could possibly result in interesting data concerning the evaluation of vibration influence on the spine that probably develops during firing as a strong impact of postpulse vibration.

The early recognition of existing or gradually developing posture and stress damage in all areas of the spine is important since training and competitive shooting require frequent, prolonged, static aiming positions with rotation and flexion positions of the spine. More than 27% of all shooters suffer from spinal problems. There is insufficient information on how many and what type of damage actually exists at the spine of high-performance shooters.

The aiming position of the various shooting disciplines have very different effects on spinal sections. For instance, shooting (standing aim) is a rather unphysiological position since it requires a strong lordosis of the lumbar spine and additional torsion in the lateral flexion (ie, a scoliotic posture). Therefore, the standing aim is not a suitable position for youths and adolescents. Shooting (kneeling aim) requires a distinct kyphosis of the thoracic and lumbar spines. Shooting moving targets requires spinal torsion. During shooting clay pigeons, torsion and probably the slight lordotic posture affect the spine. Archery causes torsion with high, static stress on the upper spinal sections. All shooting postures are scoliotic postures convex to the inherent supporting arm.

Shooting requires the constitution of a high-performance athlete with the performance and stamina capacity of a trained athlete. Therefore, suitable strengthening, fitness, and power training of the entire body is necessary. Compensatory motions are necessary during the training and competition hours so that the tense muscles of the shoulder area and the trunk are relieved and relaxed.

8.4.13 Teachers and Trainers

The back pain of which sports and gymnastic teachers in many disciplines complain so frequently occasionally prevents the flowing demonstration of some exercises. Various spinal problems are so frequently found in teachers and trainers that they are considered an occupational disorder. Differentiated data should be collected on the conditions at the spine causing this pain (eg, proportional frequency, radiologically perceptible damage, and distribution of the special symptoms at the spine). In addition to such general statistics, it is necessary to study individual criteria for each case. This would include previously existing spinal damage, duration of work, former active involvement in high-performance sports, and the reasons for the transition from active sports to trainer/teacher activity.

Commandre et al. (1974) reported on sports teachers, who are subject to a chronic, severe stress in the lumbosacral spine. They described problems such as lumbalgia and sciatica and many other pathological symptoms and thus demanded roentgenogram studies and stricter fitness requirements in connection with pre-employment fitness tests. Spondylolisthesis and other serious changes (eg, attributable to intervertebral disc damage) were regarded as absolute criteria for the unsuitability of an applicant. The findings of deSeze et al. (1960) on 1,000 applicants for sports teacher jobs are interesting in this context: 55% were rejected because of spinal damage.

8.5 BALLET AND DANCE

8.5.1 Classical Ballet

Ballet training in its artistic structure of constantly changing body movements, postures, and positions demands great skills in commanding the expressive ability of the back. The spine can be called the center of rest and motion. During the dance phases, a high mobility and stress capacity is demanded of the spine.

During training, which begins in early youth, the spine is trained together with all other parts of the motor system. The goal is an improved stress capacity of ligaments and strengthening of muscles. But the spine is subject to great stresses. The basic position of the dancer requires a tilting of the pelvis, with reduced lumbar lordosis and thoracic kyphosis. Unfortunately, literature on spinal damage attributable to specific dancing positions and the special demands of acrobatic portions of many ballet figures is sparse. Figure 8-64 shows the demands on the spine during ballet training for modern artistic-acrobatic ballet figures.

Hesse (1972) studied the spinal postures of 50 members of a ballet troupe and an opera ballet group. Although the observed rest position of the dancers approached normal posture, there was still a tendency toward lumbar lordosis. Functional studies showed that 42% of dancers had a disposition to poor posture that remained in spite of classical training.

Baudysova and Harnach (1960) determined a reduced thoracic kyphosis in 59 ballet troupe members: in 58% of men and 71% of women. These numbers clearly exceed the average values for the general population. Radiographically perceptible damage at the cervical and lumbar spines was more frequent than at the knee joints. However, because of the low number of subjects, these and several other findings do not allow conclusive statements with regard to whether intervertebral osteochondrosis, uncovertebral arthrosis, and arthrosis of the vertebral arch joints develop more frequently or are more severe with ballet training. Hesse (1972) found only one case of double-sided spondylolysis in the X-ray films of 59 dancers.

Fig. 8-64 Acrobatic-artistic training for classical ballet [from Berquet (1980/1981)].

Nikolaev and Najdenov (1970) described in detail chronic damage at the joints of the feet, knees, and hips of 33 male and female dancers. They did not examine the spine. Miller et al. (1975) also reported on body damage caused by ballet, including damage at the spine. They described a changed thoracic spine in a 36-year-old dancer (who began dancing at age 10) that was the result of a juvenile kyphosis. The pelvic roentgenogram showed serious arthrosis of both sacroiliac joints.

Marti (personal communication 1983) reported that only a few young girls at the Orthopedic Hospital in Amsterdam were found with spondylolysis/spondylolisthesis among 500 observed professional dancers. They were advised not to continue their ballet career only in cases of distinct listhesis. Marti considered degenerative damage even during the later professional years of dancers to be no more frequent than among the general population.

Thomasen (personal communication 1983) observed osteochondrosis of the intervertebral discs 5-6 and 6-7 at the cervical spine. Such damage was absent in the area of C-1 and C-2, where the movements of pirouettes take place. He considered the lumbar spine to be a problem for older dancers. The reduced lumbar lordosis (flat back without lumbar lordosis) is preferred by teachers during selection for ballet training. Thomasen found osteochondrosis of the lumbar spine in 48 dancers with an average age of 30 years and considered it to be a common disorder. Only 1 of the 48 dancers had to undergo surgery (bone-chip blocking), and he was able to dance again. In addition, Thomasen found intervertebral disc prolapse in 53 dancers. In spite of spondylolisthesis, the majority of 17 dancers performed their job without impairments.

Damage at the spine in ballet novices is probably not observed early enough because the primarily small children who are already in stressful training during the growth period of the spine continue in spite of substantial and frequently recurring problems because of their ambition—and even increase the training. They dissimulate in order not to be rejected. The early medical examination is missed, and the counseling of the physician is ignored—frequently because of the influence of ambitious ballet teachers who do not want to lose gifted ballet students. The reduced thoracic kyphosis and lumbar lordosis required for the basic position in ballet are not without pain. The future training requires hyperlordosis with excessive stresses on the intervertebral discs, vertebral arch joints in the lumbar area, and sacroiliac joints. Changing symptoms, interrupted by pain-free periods, may gradually result in chronic problems at the intervertebral discs, including the vertebral arch joints. Pain is frequently disregarded. For additional information, see Berquet and Hesse (1979), Gelabert (1964), Gluecksmann et al. (1957), and Lepihov and Rokhlin (1967).

8.5.2 Other Dances

Dancing is suited for perfecting the basic, essential, motoric characteristics of the body, especially if appropriate training is undergone regularly. The spine is less stressed during the standard dances and more during the Latin American tournament dances. The frequent change between a rhythmic gliding movement and the sudden stop of the dance figure in the middle of a torsion (when the static stress turns into a dynamic one) results in significant strain on and tension in the ligament systems of the vertebral arch joints and the hemiarthrotic connection of the two sacroiliac joints. In the latter, a deliberately trained laxity frequently exists, if not a constitutional hypermobility in the sense of a pelvic girdle hypermobility.

This may be an advantage for the female dancer but becomes a disadvantage if painful arthrosis develops. The same applies to the vertebral arch joints. Such gradually developing damage can cause painful blockades of these joints during the course of a dance, and the dance must occasionally be interrupted. Dancing with a hyperlordosis (in women) often leads to aggravation of the damage and pain. In the partner, the statically fixated right-sided muscles of the neck-shoulder-arm series are strongly contracted. This may lead to neuromuscular pain.

Since dancing sports show a tendency toward increasingly more difficult dancing-acrobatic training and increased competition, stress damage at the spine should be expected to rise in number. Since dancing is primarily practiced by the younger generation, the spine should be examined before the beginning of training, either with roentgenograms or the newer imaging procedures. For additional information, see Boehmer and Ambrus (1981/82).

8.6 ACROBATICS

8.6.1 Contortionists

The artistic work of contortionists requires not only extraordinary movements for many joints, with stretching of ligaments and muscles, but also an unnatural mobility of the spine. Contortionists use either the rubber technique (hyperlordosis) (Fig. 8-65) or the Klischnigg technique (kyphosis) (Fig. 8-66). As is known from many studies, such acrobatics result without fail in serious damage at the spine.

Contortionists practice their skill only professionally. The profession of contortionists is fre-

318   CLINICAL IMPLICATIONS OF NORMAL BIOMECHANICAL STRESSES ON SPINAL FUNCTION

Fig. 8-65 Rubber contortionists during two exercises. The unnatural, excessive lordosis cannot be achieved without serious damage at the lumbosacral boundary after years of painful training [from Steinbrueck (1983)].

Fig. 8-66 Klischnigg artist during a circus performance.

quently a family tradition. These are probably families with genetic hypermobility or laxity of the joints of the extremities or the spine. The stretching exercises (softening) frequently start in early childhood, mostly in partner training of family members, which is practiced on a daily basis for many hours and is continuously increased in time and difficulty. For 20% of contortionists, this is already the case between the ages of 3 and 6 years. Therefore, the spine is already subject to damaging mechanical stresses during the early growth period.

The rubber technique (Fig. 8-65) is the most common among contortionists. The hyperlordosis especially stresses the lumbar and cervical spines.

Peak performances are connected with severe damage at the intervertebral discs. For example, the intervertebral disc L-5/S-1 suffers through the anterior cleavage of the spatium intercorporale separations from the upper sacral end plate. This is confirmed by the characteristic gas bubble (vacuum phenomenon) in the lateral roentgenogram, as shown by Brauer (1967). In one third of the studied cases, Brauer also found avulsions of the anterior vertebral body margins and marginal lesions as well as retrolisthesis of lumbar vertebrae (Figs. 4-35 and 4-36). The roentgenograms are of young artists in whom the ossification centers of the vertebral body epiphyses are not yet fused with the vertebral margins. It is likely that the ossification processes are impaired or delayed by the strong tractions at the anterior vertebral body margins. This causes the distinct development of the marginal lesions and separations (avulsions) of the margins. During retroflexion, the avulsion fragment is lifted like a lid from the vertebral body margin. Because of the continuously repeated training, the damage at the intervertebral disc tissue finally causes unstable segments intervertebral instability, with telescopic slipping of the vertebral bodies to the back. Unstable capsules at the vertebral arch joints and stretched adjacent ligaments are unavoidable. Arnold (1956) classified the damage at the vertebral body epiphyses in contortionists as vertebral ossification impairments.

Rubber contortionists also show articular process fractures. They must be considered fatigue fractures and do not heal because of the continuation of the stress. They become nearthroses. Brauer (1967) reported crumbling of the separated bone portions so that only stumps of the articular processes remained.

Clefts in the interarticular portion of the lumbar spine frequently develop (spondylolysis). In one case, Brauer (1967) described them at the arches of L-2 and 3; in another case at L-1, 2, 3, and 5. At L-5, a substantial spondylolisthesis developed. At L-1, 2, and 3, clefts could be seen in the roentgenogram, but no ventral listhesis was visible. Steinbrueck (1983) conducted a follow-up examination of a rubber artist 25 years after she was described by Brauer. Although there had been four earlier spondylolyses, only two could be found 25 years later. Erdmann illustrated the spinal damage visible on roentgenograms (Fig. 8-67).

Contortionists who impress many spectators with their artistic skill have always admitted that they feel strong spinal pain in the lumbosacral area during daily softening and performances. They finally become disabled because of their spinal disorder, which had its origin in childhood. Schroeter (1961) described a female contortionist who had been introduced to the

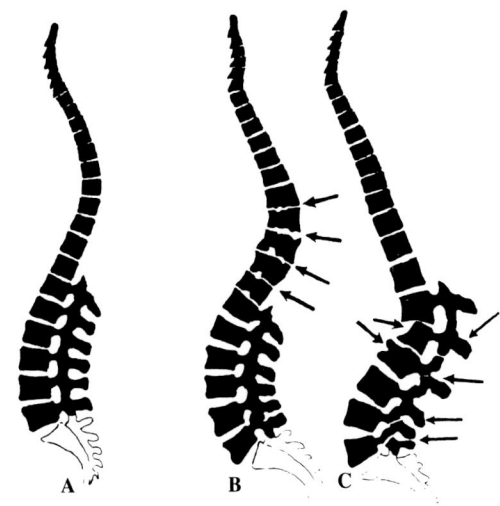

Fig. 8-67 Sketches of spines of contortionists. (**A**) Healthy; (**B**) changed by Scheuermann's disease; (**C**) typical damage characterized by abnormal damage locations, multiple spondylolysis, and "riding" articular processes (with mostly destroyed vertebral arch joints) [from Erdmann (1966)].

profession at the age of 3 by her father and was unable to perform at the age of 31 because of spondylolisthesis at the 2nd, 4th, and 5th lumbar vertebra. For additional information, see Krayenbuehl et al. (1967b), Lederer (1972), and Steinbrueck and Springorum (1980).

8.6.2 Trampoline Acrobatics

The piece of equipment for the trampoline artists that has now been developed to high technical perfection is named after a famous acrobat from the last century: Trampoline. He used a catapult for his acrobatic performances.

Trampoline acrobats are mostly professionals, even though they begin as trampoline gymnasts. They are often family groups in which the children participate in performances at an early age and train extensively and hard for many hours per day.

Trampoline acrobats perform approximately 225,000 jumps in five years, in which many figures are integrated (eg, forward and backward saltos and screws around the vertical body axis). Many maneuvers increase the jumping height. The many figure combinations stress the LPH region through alternating contracting and relaxing of muscles.

The development or aggravation of damage (such as vertebral arch joint arthrosis, sacroiliac arthrosis, and intervertebral disc damage) and stiffness in reduced lordosis are as unavoidable for trampoline artists as for trampoline gymnasts because of the continuous stressing and overstressing in the lumbosacral region (including sacroiliac joints). Damage at the cervical spine is the same as for trampoline gymnasts.

8.6.3 Ski Acrobatics

This sport is so risky that the Swiss Accident Insurance (SUVA) excludes accidents attributable to ski acrobatics from their coverage (Bronz 1978). The usual disciplines of ski acrobatics are ballet, hot dogs (acrobatic hump slope skiing), and jumps.

There are no systematic long-term studies on spinal damage in ski acrobats. Ligaments and muscles of the back are subject to strong stresses during jumps and figures. Many severe spinal injuries are caused by jumps. Sudden rotation with strong axial pressure, lateral flexion, and hard landings often result in stresses on the spine, in addition to those on the joints of the lower extremities, that regularly approach the tolerance limit and probably frequently exceed it. The soft tissues such as intervertebral discs, ligaments, and cartilage surfaces of the vertebral arch joints and sacroiliac joints are not able to bear this without damage.

The location and extent of such sports-related damage in ski acrobats must still be systematically determined. The question of whether there is an increased incidence of spondylolysis/spondylolisthesis remains unanswered.

8.7 DETRIMENTAL STRESS ON THE VERTEBRAL ARCHES THROUGH SPORTS AND GYMNASTICS

8.7.1 Spondylolysis and Spondylolisthesis

Spondylolysis and spondylolisthesis are increasingly discovered in high-performance athletes. In certain sports, the percentages reported in the literature greatly exceed the incidence of such damage in the average European population, which is 5% to 7%. An increased incidence of damage in the bone structure of the interarticular portions occurs in divers, trampoline gymnasts, gymnasts on the apparatus and the floor, javelin throwers, weight lifters, wrestlers, football players, and other athletes. Rossi (1972) found spondylolysis in more than 20.7% of 474 examined athletes ranging from age 18 to 26. Of 80 female performance athletes, 25% showed spondylolisthesis (Knobling as noted in Schwerdtner and Schoberth 1973). In a study series of 160 athletes and circus acrobats, Maltschenko (1973) found spondylolistheses in 81 (50%).

Schwerdtner and Schoberth (1973) reported in detail on the progress of spondylolysis in two female high-performance apparatus gymnasts who had started training between the ages of 12 and 13. Since lumbosacral problems developed, tomographies of the lumbar spine were performed between the ages of 14 and 16. There were no impaired interarticular portions. After further intensive sports training, clefts in the 3rd lumbar vertebral arch were found with the help of tomograms in one gymnast, and clefts at the 5th lumbar vertebral arch in the other.

Rompe and Dreyer (1972) studied ten javelin throwers with more than eight years of training (up to 15 years) and found four spondylolistheses (14%); 19 javelin throwers with less than 8 years of training showed no spondylolisthesis. These findings agree with study results of female gymnasts in whom spondylolisthesis could be discovered only after more than 5 years of training. The "backward roll" was named as the cause. Because of strong, progressive pain, some athletes had to discontinue the competitive sport (Schwerdtner and Schoberth 1973).

Groher (1974a) reported spondylolisthesis in 16% of 24 gymnasts, 29% of 17 platform divers, and 100% of 20 top athletes.

Jackson et al. (1976) reported on 100 female athletes between the ages of 14 and 24 (average age 15.1) who were radiographically examined. Eleven showed damage in both interarticular portions of the 5th lumbar vertebral arch, and in 6 of these 11, spondylolisthesis in the first degree existed. The incidence of spondylolysis/spondylolisthesis in these athletes was approximately four times as high as in a control group without athletic training. Of the 89 athletes not affected by spondylolysis, 23% complained of lumbosacral problems that necessitated training pauses. The investigators thought the essential cause for damage in the lamina to be repeated overstressing and strong retroflexion and anteflexion. In the opinion of the investigators, a bone scintigraphy may discover imminent danger in the interarticular portion earlier than other examinations.

Roick and Albrecht (1973) found spondylolysis and spondylolisthesis in 5.1% of 452 young athletes between the ages of 9 and 17 (ie, within the limits of normal incidence). Because of the danger of increasing listhesis, which must be expected from intensive training, the investigators did not consider individuals with spondylolisthesis to be suited for performance sports. They also recommended that performance sports be discontinued in cases of spondylolysis without listhesis. Rompe and Krahl (1975) had reservations with regard to full performance capacity in sports that required frequent retroflexions and recommended that the general progression in children and youths be constantly observed. Some cases of spondylolisthesis in young athletes can be attributed to the common damage at the interarticular portions during the growth period.

Damage at the interarticular portion of athletes is usually discovered only in roentgenograms after problems have developed. In most cases, a progression of a previous condition occurred, which probably would have remained stable without the added stress of athletic activity. In many known cases without effects of athletic stresses, perceptible and disabling problems develop only in later decades of life because of the slackening ligaments and decreasing muscle strength (ie, the loss of compensatory forces). Some athletes with spondylolysis/spondylolisthesis never feel impaired.

H. Schmidt (1979) reported on ten athletes who were examined for evidence of spondylolysis and spondylolisthesis. The sports disciplines varied widely: sled racing, canoe racing, biking, gymnastics on the apparatus, platform diving, volleyball, track and field athletics, and handball. In five of these cases, the initial roentgenograms showed no evidence of spondylolisthesis. However, damage was discovered two to three years later at follow up. Because of these results, Schmidt believed that the development of spondylolysis/spondylolisthesis attributable to athletic stresses can be considered confirmed. A review of the literature on the development of spondylolyses/spondylolisthesis attributable to athletic training was reported in 1975 by Rompe and Krahl. For additional information, see Barash et al. (1970), Baumgartner and Taillard (1971), Henssge (1980), Jaeger (1969), and Jani (1981).

Stewart (1953) and Rompe and Krahl (1975) considered retroflexion to be a decisive influence for the development of spondylolisthesis. In contrast, Farfan et al. (1976) emphasized the special significance of torsion with anteflexion for the development of spondylolisthesis and pointed to the circumstances in soccer [see also Lamy et al. (1975)]. They described in detail three factors that caused changes in the interarticular portion: overstressed flexion, unbalanced shearing movements, and forced rotation. They considered the rotating force to be the most destructive stress on the interarticular portion.

Tuetsch and Ulrich (1973) studied forces that combine during athletic training to stress the lumbosacral area: forcefully executed abrupt retroflexion, rotation of the lumbar spine opposite to the pelvic direction, and lateral tilting and shearing forces to the front or side.

The sum of microtraumas in the interarticular portions of the vertebral arch during the large number of training hours must be considered for the development of spondylolysis in high-performance athletes of the susceptible sports. Figures on the stress dimensions may be found in Groher (1974a). Especially dangerous is constantly repeated hyperlordosis such as in floor exercises and gymnastics on the apparatus (Figs. 8-29, 8-31, and 8-36), competitive gymnastics (Fig. 8-38), and platform diving (Fig. 8-47).

8.7.2 Separations (Avulsion Fractures) of Vertebral Arch Processes and the Odontoid Process

Spinous process separations (Fig. 8-68) occur mostly at the lower cervical and upper thoracic

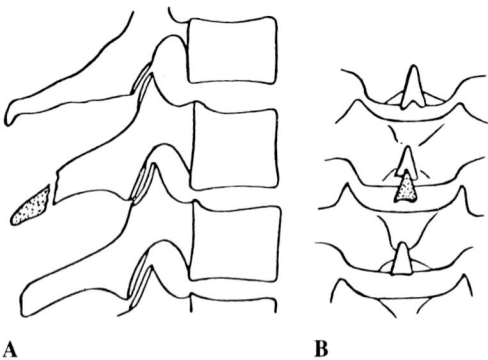

Fig. 8-68 Spinous process separations.

spines and are found as specific sports damage in weight lifters, discus throwers, hammer throwers, and golfers (Ito et al. 1970). Tittel (1962) found them in glider pilots. However, in these cases, they developed from the 12th thoracic to the 2nd lumbar process. No long-term studies exist on sports-related spinous process separations.

Groh and Groh (1975) reported on transverse process separations attributable to athletic stress in gymnasts, wrestlers, weight lifters, and fencers.

8.7.3 Tendopathy, Tendinosis, and Baastrup's Disease

Tendopathy/tendinosis may appear together with pain at all end points of the vertebral arch processes as well as at the attachment points of the longissimi muscles at the pelvis. It is considered to be distinct overstress damage and develops especially frequently in certain sports: volleyball, racket sports, and discus and hammer throwing.

The simultaneous jumping up, stretching, and rotation in some team sports (eg, basketball and volleyball) cause a sudden, strong traction stress at the tendon attachments in the loin-pelvis area, and therefore tendinosis. Therapy becomes necessary, and the sport that caused the damage must be discontinued for a long period of time. A simultaneous injection therapy must be added (see section 7.4).

Tendopathy/tendinosis should not be disregarded because primarily young people are involved in the damaging sports. In most cases, the athletes terminate the high-performance sport before the age of 30. When pressure and traction pain in the spinal muscles and their attachments occurs repeatedly in later life, between the ages of 40 and 50, who will remember that an athletic overstress damage during youth was the cause for the chronic damage at the spine? For additional information, see Groher and Heidensohn (1970), and Scheele et al. (1979).

Baastrup's disease also belongs into the group of sports damage at the vertebral arch and was reported in statistics by Groher (1970). Baastrup's disease was found 28 times (42.4%) in 66 platform divers and 9 times (33.3%) in 27 trampoline gymnasts of level II. These numbers are far above the numbers for the average population. The disease is also seen in pole vaulters and weight lifters and is a serious impairment for competition. Occasionally, surgery is indicated.

8.7.4 Articulations

In a series of lectures, Refior reported in detail on the reactions of the lumbar vertebral arch joints during performance sports. His studies of a number of performance athletes showed, for instance, that arthrosis developed less frequently in the upper vertebral arch joints of the lumbar spine than in the lower ones. A 24-year-old performance gymnast already had double-sided vertebral arch joint arthrosis, which aggravated until the age of 34. There was little pain. This is generally attributed to the adaptation of the diseased cartilage surfaces. Training and competition were possible.

8.8 SPORTS FITNESS IN THE CASE OF A PREVIOUSLY DAMAGED SPINE

The evaluation of performance capability for sports and gymnastics in the case of existing spinal disorders is crucial. Such an evaluation is necessary not only for high-performance athletes but also for participants in school and leisure sports. The specific sport or gymnastic discipline must also be considered. Ehricht (1978) compiled extensive overviews in this context (see Tables 8-10 through 8-13).

8.8.1 Juvenile Kyphosis

Juvenile kyphosis can lead to further spinal damage if the spine is stressed excessively and

Table 8-10 Evaluation and Athletic Activity of Patients with Spinal Damage Attributable to Malformations, Assimilation, and Vertebral Arch Abnormalities

Spinal Symptoms	Sports Fitness	Recommendations for Athletic Activity
Multiple malformations of vertebrae	PS −	
Spinal dysraphism with neurological involvement	SS +	Swimming; gymnastics
Severe spondylolisthesis, severe assimilation with unilateral support	LS +	
Isolated but fully formed malformations of vertebrae	PS −	
Multiple fissurations in arch section without neurological failure; dysplasia	SS + +	All sports without stresses on spine after counseling by specialist; follow-up examinations
Unilateral, distinct assimilations	LS + +	
Minor dysplasia of lumbosacral boundary; minor assimilation; isolated fissuration in arch section	PS possible SS + + or + + + LS + + or + + +	Activity after evaluation by specialist; follow-up examinations

Legend: PS = performance sport; SS = school sport; LS = leisure sport; − = not fit to participate in sports; + = limited fitness; + + = fit with supervision; + + + = fully fit.
Data from Ehricht (1978).

Table 8-11 Evaluation and Athletic Activity of Patients with Scolioses Attributable to Vertebral Malformations, Conditions after Infections and Traumas, and Paralyses

Spinal Symptoms	Sports Fitness	Recommendations for Athletic Activity
Scolioses (short)	PS + SS + + + LS + +	Only after extensive examination by specialist
Scolioses (long)	Minor PS − SS + + LS + +	Progress control relief for spine
	Distinct PS − SS + LS + and + +	Progress control relief for spine
	Severe PS − SS + LS + and + +	Progress control relief for spine
Conditions after vertebral trauma and infections with or without neurological failures	Individual evaluation according to specialist's recommendations	

Legend: See Table 8-10.
Data from Ehricht (1978).

Table 8-12 Evaluation and Athletic Activity of Patients with Spinal Damage through Pelvis-Leg Changes, Systemic Diseases and Osteopathies after Metabolic Disorders and Growth Disorders, and Aseptic Necrosis at Vertebral Bodies

Spinal Symptoms	Sports Fitness	Recommendations for Athletic Activity
Scolioses after pelvis-leg changes	Minor	
	PS++	No activity in gymnastics on apparatus, throwing disciplines, or weight lifting
	SS+++	Exemption: gymnastics on apparatus
	LS+++	
	Severe	
	PS−	
	SS+	Swimming; gymnastics
	LS++	Tourism; gymnastics; swimming
Hyperkyphosis and hyperlordosis; kypholordotic and total kyphotic back	PS+	Hardly fit for gymnastics on apparatus, weight lifting, rowing, or throwing disciplines
	SS++	Not too high stress on spine
	LS+++	Full activity
Spinal changes during systemic diseases and osteopathies after metabolic disorders	Bland diseases	
	PS++	Specialist evaluation regarding performance ability
	SS+++	Specialist evaluation regarding performance ability
	LS+++	Full activity
	Distinct diseases	
	PS−	
	SS+	Counseling by specialist
	Conditions after systemic diseases and osteopathies after metabolic disorders: LS++	Spinal stress must be considered in follow-up examinations
Scheuermann's disease	Minor involvement of vertebral bodies	Full activity with medical supervision
	PS+++	
	SS+++	
	LS+++	
	Larger involvement of vertebral bodies with proof of floridity	
	PS−	
	SS+	No activity in florid state
	LS+	Gymnastics with avoidance of kyphotic spine; breast stroke swimming during reconstruction of defects according to specialist's evaluation
	Condition after Scheuermann's disease	
	PS++	Activity according to static complaints
	SS+++	Full activity
	LS+++	Full activity

Legend: See Table 8-10.
Data from Ehricht (1978).

Table 8-13 Evaluation and Athletic Activity of Patients with Wear Symptoms at Intervertebral Motor Segments and Hip-Loin Extension Stiffness

Spinal Symptoms	Sports Fitness	Recommendations for Athletic Activity
Dyschondrosis	PS temporarily −	Possible full activity after healing
	SS temporarily +	After treatment + + +
	LS temporarily +	After treatment + + +
Structural slackening; vertebral blockage	Minor or one-time	
	PS temporarily −	Activity possible after treatment
	SS temporarily +	After treatment + +
	LS temporarily +	After treatment + +
	During recurrences	
	PS −	Discontinuation of PS
	SS temporarily −	After treatment + and + +
	LS temporarily −	After treatment + and + +
Intervertebral disc protrusion; prolapse (conservative and operative); hip-loin extension stiffness	PS −	Discontinuation of PS
	SS temporarily −	After treatment +
	LS temporarily −	After treatment +

Legend: See Table 8-10.
Data from Ehricht (1978).

unphysiologically. Such unfavorable stresses can have two essential and frequent causes: incorrect sitting at school and very stressful gymnastic or athletic activity that is begun too early in life. The spine grows in spurts during the entire growth period. During such growth accelerations, the epiphyseal layers between the vertebral body and intervertebral disc are especially susceptible to stress.

For the evaluation of the stress danger in individual cases, the list of the five stages of conditions in section 4.4 offers a helpful comparison of radiological symptoms. However, the roentgenogram findings or other imaging procedures are insufficient to determine sports fitness. The knowledge of the sports physician with much experience in this area is needed. The athlete must be under constant medical supervision. Trunk flexions and jumping and endurance training should be avoided until growth has been concluded.

Groher (1980) compiled the positive and negative influences of athletic activity regarding the various stages of Scheuermann's disease (Table 8-14). Groher et al. (1983) described the important criteria for the possibilities of stressing the spine during athletic and school activity (Table 8-15). If signs of juvenile kyphosis can already be determined during the grade school years (8 to 10 years of age), leisure sports should also be avoided. If discomfort appears, sports with high impact, pressure, and rotation stresses should be temporarily discontinued under the supervision of a physician.

- basketball
- bicycle racing
- boxing
- butterfly swimming

Table 8-14 Positive and Negative Influences on Scheuermann's Disease

Positive Influences	Negative Influences
Gymnastics to strengthen trunk muscles (I–III)	Weight lifting (I–III)
Swimming (I–III)	High and long jump (I–III)
Skiing (alpine, cross-country) (I–III)	Gymnastics as performance sport (I–II)
Jogging in forest (II–III)	Basketball as performance sport (I–II)
School sports (only in rare cases a temporary exemption from certain exercises) (I–II)	Biking (I–II)

Legend: Classification into stages: I = recession; II = progression; and III = chronic changes.
Data from Groher (1980).

Table 8-15 Criteria for Evaluation of Sports Fitness of Persons with Scheuermann's Disease

- The respective degree of severity of the disease is established by answering the following four questions:
  1. Which spinal section is affected?
  2. How far has it spread?
  3. How old is the patient?
  4. In what stage is the disease (recession, progression, final state)?
- In the sports disciplines, the degree of possible stress to which the spine is subject is important.
  1. light stress: swimming
  2. primarily dynamic stress: cross-country skiing
  3. primarily static stress connected with dynamic stress: weight lifting
  4. primarily static stress: biking
  5. combination of all stress types, including impact stress: most sports
- the intensity of athletic stress must be differentiated.
  1. school sports
  2. leisure sports
  3. performance sports

Note: Various criteria that refer to the syndrome itself, the athletic discipline, and the intensity of athletic activity are essential in the evaluation of sports fitness in cases of existing Scheuermann's disease.
Data from Groher et al. (1983).

- canoeing
- competitive gymnastics
- competitive rowing
- gymnastics on the apparatus
- handball
- ice hockey
- figure skating
- jumping disciplines
- platform and board diving
- roller skating
- speed skating
- team ball games
- trampoline gymnastics
- weight lifting
- wind surfing

If these and similar sports must be avoided during florid spurts of Scheuermann's disease, medically prescribed and continuously supervised physical activities are necessary, such as physiotherapy, back stroking in alternating semi-lateral positions, and slow biking with high handle bars. This maintains the metabolism required for muscle and bone accretion as well as for the maintenance of the health of the intervertebral discs. The abdominal position is recommended for reading and writing.

Steinbrueck et al (1980) considered a number of sports to be unsuitable if Scheuermann's disease was present (Table 8-16).

Schmitt (1984) compiled a list of permitted or even desirable sports for persons with juvenile kyphosis: basketball, soccer, free-style swimming, biking with high handle bars, tennis, and volleyball. This applies only to healed and painless stages of the disease. Athletes with completely ankylosed total kyphosis may attain top performances in many disciplines.

Table 8-16 Unsuitable Sports for Persons with Scheuermann's Disease

- Weight lifting
- Butterfly swimming
- Gymnastics
- Trampoline gymnastics
- Platform diving
- Rowing
- Biking
- Sailing
- Jumping disciplines (field and track)

Data from Steinbrueck et al (1980).

8.8.2 Scoliosis

If a person with scoliosis wishes to participate regularly in sports or gymnastics, unilateral-monotonous stresses must be avoided: rowing, shooting, unilateral throwing sports, tennis, and table tennis. Pain necessitates medical counseling.

8.8.3 Bone Damage (General)

If sports or gymnastic fitness is affected by back pain, the diagnosis today is mostly targeted toward soft-tissue damage (muscles, tendons, intervertebral discs, or articular arthrosis). Damage in the skeletal structure still remains unrecognized or underevaluated in spite of imaging diagnostics. The most frequent causes for bone-related painful stress insufficiency are various forms of osteopathy, especially osteoporosis. Today, the formerly frequent spondylotides are rare. Attention should be paid to tumor metastases, which develop in the skeleton of the spine often earlier and more numerously than in other bones.

8.8.4. Spondylolysis, Spondylolisthesis, and Vertebral Dislocations

The evaluation of sports and gymnastic fitness in cases of possible displacements is one of the most difficult tasks for a sports physician. A physical examination and knowledge of the changing pathological picture are required to determine whether a complete or temporary exemption from sports is indicated and the appropriate type of therapy. In this process, it should be considered how often an athlete's ambition leads to dissimulation.

If the fitness examination uncovers spondylolysis or other forms of beginning or existing vertebral dislocations, starting sports should be urgently advised against. However, regular physiotherapy under medical supervision is necessary so that these children will not grow up with weak muscles.

8.8.5 Damage Caused Mostly by Intervertebral Discs or Articulations

Damage caused by intervertebral discs or articulations is the most frequent disease of the spine. It must be looked for in fitness examinations, even if only insignificant back muscle pain seems to be present. The back muscles often act as an indicator of a deeper cause by way of radiation.

Since all intervertebral disc damage and articular diseases (arthrosis) have a tendency to aggravate, a previously existing damage can be activated through excessive stresses and motions during sports. In these cases, it must be determined whether further practice of the sport is possible, whether training should be temporarily discontinued in favor of treatment, or whether a different sports discipline should be chosen.

In some sports, lumbagolike pain attacks are the first warning signs that intervertebral disc or joint-related disorders are developing. It is necessary to recognize and determine the causes, which are often latent. Protrusions or prolapses of intervertebral disc tissue are the most frequent causes. Continued sports fitness must be determined. Very sudden and usually strong, knifelike pain is caused by blockades in the area of the intervertebral motor segment but may also be caused by small joints (eg, vertebrocostal joints or uncovertebral joints). In most cases, sports fitness can be restored through chirotherapeutic treatment. In cases of frequent recurrences, surgery must finally be considered in order to restore sports fitness.

8.8.6 Surgery

Surgery does not prevent the starting or resumption of sports and gymnastics. The resumption of a performance sport can be successful even after extensive intervertebral disc surgery. Those who want to be athletically active after a spinal operation should choose swimming, preferably swimming in the abdominal or back position. Butterfly, one-sided, and alternating free-style swimming are not suitable since they subject the back muscles to unsymmetrical traction and tensile forces.

8.9 THE JUVENILE SPINE AND PERFORMANCE SPORTS

The frequently stated opinion that the conclusion of growth for boys is around age 16 and for girls is around age 15 (ie, at the end of puberty) applies to the spine only with reservations. Even in the case of normal development, a complete stress capacity of the "adult" spine can often be expected only at the transition from the second to the third decade of life. Therefore, until this age, every athlete should be under the supervision of a sports physician with regard to the spine. With regard to the athletic stress capacity of the youthful spine, it must be considered that the mechanical resistance of the epiphyses at the upper and lower end plates of the vertebral bodies decreases toward the end of the growth period. This increases the danger during school sports and performance training for students in higher grades.

In order to determine whether youthful growth damage of the spine is present, a radiodiagnosis of the spine should be performed in all cases before the start of athletic training. Examinations that are required before the start of and during athletic training should include the support and motor system and especially the spine. However, such examinations should not lead to a generic rejection of participation in sports based solely on a diagnoses of Scheuermann's disease or scoliosis. In certain cases, a sport that is acceptable to the sports physician and adapted to the momentary state of the spine can be suggested, even though it may not correspond to the sport desired by the youth. This is especially important for juvenile kyphosis since the various progressive stages are susceptible to a different degree.

Refior and Zenker (1970) demanded an exact limit for the mechanical stress capacity of young athletes in the growth period. Close cooperation between the sports physician and coach is necessary for this individual care in order to make a selection among young athletes based on their spine and to avoid the progression of spinal damage. Enthusiastic athletes require continuous observation of their health, especially since youths usually do not often complain and because back pain is often regarded as harmless.

The diligent health care of young athletes includes regular examinations of the spine. The prolonged, increasing stresses on the spine through training and competition are the reason for this necessity. Their consequences are much more serious than the rarer sports injuries. In long-term studies, incorrect postures are found much more frequently in young athletes than in nonathletes. This was confirmed for young performance gymnasts by Tilscher and Oblak (1973, 1974). It is also important in sports medicine to consider the developmental stages, especially in the structure of the spine during maturation, before deciding on the beginning of training for a specific sport.

The results of long-term follow-up examinations of former young performance athletes were reported by Tilscher and Oblak (1974) (Table 8-17).

Table 8-17 Results of Examinations of 46 Former Young Performance Athletes

	Men	Women	Total
Survey of problems			
Present problems	29	8	37
Problems caused by			
performance sports	10	7	17
Problems earlier in sports			
or training	24	7	31
Pain at the spine (19 of			
23 examinees)			
Lower back			14
Thoracic spine and thorax			8
Neck and head			4
Changes in posture and			
static in 17 of the 19 cases			
with spinal problems			
Excessive kyphosis			
or lordosis			11
Flat back			2
Scoliosis			8
Scoliotic pelvis			6
Head vertical outside			
base vertical			3

Data from Tilscher and Oblak (1974).

8.10 PROPHYLACTIC EXAMINATIONS IN SPORTS MEDICINE

The potential sports damage discussed in the various chapters of this book indicate the importance of prophylactic measures. This is especially true for the spine since general sports and training for performance and high-performance sports start during a period when the spine has not yet reached its final maturation. The stresses of sports affect the active epiphyses at the vertebral body–intervertebral disc boundary, which in many sports and gymnastics is subject to special, prolonged stresses: traction, pressure, and torsion. If this results in damage at the epiphyses of the vertebral body–intervertebral disc boundary and/or in the cartilage layers of the joints, then the future damage results in impaired growth and an abnormal vertebral body shape.

This damage is always connected with the danger of increasing difficulties in the metabolism of the intervertebral disc with its high fluid content. The consequences of the impaired diffusion process range from intervertebral chondrosis to intervertebral osteochondrosis. The cartilages of the numerous spinal joints are affected in a similar manner. Also endangered during the growth period are the paired interarticular portions of the vertebral arch.

Based on this knowledge, the prophylactic examination has taken a special place in sports medicine. The prophylactic care of athletes from the start of athletic activity to the discontinuation of active sports must be continued, especially if sports damage exists. A long-term picture of the athlete or the sport can thus be obtained and damage can be discovered earlier in its development.

8.10.1 Examinations for Sports Fitness

The general fitness test with the addition of imaging procedures for the spine has become indispensible before the start of serious athletic activity and especially before the start of performance training. This applies especially to children and youths. The initial examination must establish sports fitness and the degree of severity of previously existing damage. Further negative factors in the spine of children and youths must also be considered. If such damage is present, careful exercises in gymnastics and sports should be started if abstinence from sports is not recommended. These problem cases must be supervised by a physician in short intervals.

The physician should give maximum attention to the spine even before performance sports become an issue. All data obtained in sports fitness tests show an unexpectedly high percentage of previous spinal damage. Rompe and Steinbrueck (1981) reported previous damage in 47.8% of those examined.

8.10.2 Medical Observation of Young Athletes

There is a necessity for children and youths to be under constant observation by a sports physician. The experienced sports physician knows the extent to which ambitious young athletes neglect warning discomforts and how ambitious coaches play down the problems of their protégés. Therefore, the sports physician will regularly examine these athletes and pay special attention to the spine.

8.10.3 Follow-Up Examinations and After Care

Sports influences on the spine lead to a forced, premature discontinuation of athletic activity when undiagnosed or insufficiently considered previous damage progress unfavorably. In general, such damage has a progressive character. Many persons affected by such symptoms notice the increasing disability only after years, by which time they might not look for the cause in earlier athletic activity. The follow-up observation of athletes should be suggested not only because of scientific reasons (determination of further progression of damage) but also for medical reasons. Back pain frequently appears only after sports have been discontinued. This happens when the musculoligamentous corset of the spine is no longer active enough and thus loses its stabilizing influence.

The importance of follow-up examinations of former performance athletes was demonstrated by the results of a poll conducted by Tilscher and Oblak (1974) that involved 46 former performance athletes (see Table 8-17).

8.11 PROPHYLAXIS, REHABILITATION, AND REINTEGRATION

8.11.1 Prophylaxis

Prophylaxis starts with birth. Practical prophylaxis becomes more comprehensive and requires more attention when the wishes of children and youths turn away from playing and toward the more regulated gymnastics and sports. This is also the time when spinal problems start, resulting in the too frequent, initially unnoticed, latent damage.

Many chapters of this book describe the great difficulties that appear when athletic stresses affect bones and especially soft tissues of the spine up to the stress tolerance limit. Suitable prophylaxis (eg, through thorough conditioning training) may prevent damage. Specific, prophylactic training is necessary for the absorption of damaging forces as they result from traction, pressure, and torsions. The natural corset of trunk muscles must be turned into a hyperphysiological musculoligamentous corset, a static-dynamic musculoligamentous unit.

Prophylactic and preventive measures also have a very individual character where the spine is concerned. They have a long-lasting effect only if the person concerned participates during his or her entire life (see section 7.3).

8.11.2 Rehabilitation and Reintegration of Adolescents and Persons with Disabilities

The question of whether athletes, especially youths, will be able to resume athletic training after accidental injuries or sport damage at the spine must be answered individually. Certain sports demand performances a damaged spine cannot tolerate. The gradual and diligently observed reintegration is the responsibility of the sports physician. In the process, the dissimulation of the enthusiastic athlete must be recognized in time in order to prevent relapses. On the other hand, specific sports that train existing capability and at the same time improve mobility and muscular strength without causing damage must be supported. A previously injured spine is a very exact indicator. Back pain and radiating pain must be observed by the sports teacher and be reported to the sports physician so that new damage will be avoided.

8.11.3 Sports for Older Persons

Sports, gymnastics, physical leisure activities, and participation in fitness programs can be continued into even the highest age levels if they have been practiced for a long time and do not cause any problems at the support and motor system—and especially if there is no back pain. With progressive age, a stiff spine (ankylosed senile kyphosis) must be expected, which may be a hindrance to physical activity. But this alone is no reason to give up sports or other activities that are stressful for the spine. The desire for athletic-gymnastic activity at a higher age should in each case be the cause for prophylactic, age-adapted, muscle-strengthening measures that especially involve the trunk muscles.

As soon as back pain develops, a physician must be consulted. After examining the cardiovascular and pulmonary system, including respiratory function, the physician will determine whether and to what degree physical activity is possible or seems necessary to maintain or restore health. However, if sports or other physical activity is resumed at retirement age after lifelong sedentary work, then a thorough search for disabling damage, primarily at the spine, is mandatory.

The older athlete must pay attention to symptoms of physiological age degeneration at the spine and even more to damage that becomes more and more perceptible. This includes essentially the negative transformation balance in the skeleton, which leads to decreased stress resistance (ie, osteoporosis, arthrosis in the vertebral arch joints and in other articular connections, and the very frequent intervertebral chondrosis). The older athlete should immediately report all back problems to the physician, who will decide whether physical activities should be temporarily discontinued or replaced with therapeutic measures.

During middle age (ie, the fourth and fifth decades of life), a person is generally in top shape mentally, whereas top athletic performances are attained only as an exception, especially in running disciplines. Good performances may still be attained in general sports. The attempt to achieve ultimate performances would accelerate the physiological course of aging of the spine or even cause damage. Even, harmonic stress on the spine should be sought.

Only a few older athletes will be able to maintain the majority of their athletic and gymnastic capabilities. Others should be content with physical activities without athletic ambition. Preferable are activities that older persons suffering from senile kyphosis can perform as prolonged activities in fresh air. In addition to long-distance running, cross-country running, and jogging, these include cross-country skiing, hiking, and alpine hiking. Certain symmetrical swimming styles can also be recommended, but not the butterfly style. Gymnastics should be specifically adapted to the "senior back." In an exercise bath with a water temperature of 32°C, they relax the tense back muscles and alleviate the pain of senile kyphosis.

Biking is of great importance for heart and respiratory training until old age. However, back problems are often aggravated because of the vibration impacts from the seat and because of the curved posture of the back. Problems may be improved somewhat if raised handle bars neutralize the lumbar lordosis or at least reduce it and thus reduce the pressure on the anterior portions of the intervertebral discs.

Several investigators regard golfing as an opportunity for exercise at a higher age. Older persons with a previously damaged spine must be careful since the hits stress the lumbar spine significantly. Consultation with a physician is recommended in order not to create damage additional to the age degeneration of the spine.

Tennis is not the best sport for the harmonic, systematic movements the aging spine requires. In general, the ankylosed and frequently painful spine of the aging person cannot tolerate the much harder and quicker racket sports (eg, squash and badminton). Table tennis must be evaluated similarly because of the prolonged kyphotic posture in the lower spine and because of the rapid jumps to both sides. They cause very adverse stochastic and jolting vibrations, which are not beneficial for the aging skeleton.

Grass and inside hand ball games require sudden sprints, frequent rotation, and jumps. They should not generally be recommended for the spine that is already handicapped by physiological aging since the abrupt movement has a damaging effect. Although some individuals will be able to participate in these movement games without any remarkable back problems, caution is in order.

Bowling presents problems for the aging person. The spine is affected by flexion and the fast throwing of the ball and reacts with pain. Bowling may increase the aggravation tendency of spinal disorders. In addition, there are pauses in bowling that are bridged with sitting. This behavior also damages the aging spine.

Attention should be paid to muscle-tendon-attachment pain. This overexertion pain is unfortunately frequently disregarded. It develops at the end points of the vertebral arch processes and at the attachment points of the back muscles at the sacrum and pelvic rim. Massages of the back muscles and especially of the painful locations aggravate the pain. Short rest, heat, and injections alleviate the pain.

Even more than the younger person, the older person must consider the fact that any motion alternating with stressing and relieving actuates important biochemical reactions in the muscular metabolism that benefit the total metabolism since it improves the circulation everywhere. Varied exercise stimulates the circulation and maintains the viability of the cartilage layers in the joints and intervertebral discs, which depend on diffusional nutrition. This creates conditions that control the development and progression of senile osteoporosis, senile arthrosis (also in spinal joints), and intervertebral chondrosis.

8.11.4 Sports As Therapy

Sports and gymnastics offer many possibilities for the therapy of spinal disorders. However, the specific therapy plan must be established by an experienced sports physician.

The extent to which swimming and other water sports are suitable as therapy for back sufferers depends on the force and movements they demand of the spine. An experienced sports physician should always be consulted.

Ski hiking (cross-country) strengthens the musculoligamentous corset along the spine and the connective muscles to the neck/shoulder girdle as well as to the pelvis and legs. The aerobic function connected with cross-country skiing is also an important factor for muscular metabolism. The slow, alternating gliding stimulates the pump mechanism that regulates the metabolism of the intervertebral disc fluid.

Horseback riding as therapy (hippotherapy) has rightly been recommended more and more. Riesser (1975) compiled an extensive list of diagnoses for which hippotherapy may be used. However, with regard to the spine, he mentioned only postural damage, which certainly has a special significance for riding. But other spinal damage may also be improved by riding (eg, with caution, intervertebral disc damage). Although riding alone will not heal the damage, it may restore the muscular strength in the back and tighten the ligaments. The prerequisites and the special forms of riding as a healing sport are discussed by Riede (1976). However, hippotherapy can be helpful only if it is performed with the greatest caution and because of an explicit order by an experienced physician. The physician will evaluate in detail the damage at the spine and test the stress capacity of the back of the patient undergoing rehabilitation.

Bibliography

Adair, I.V., Van Wijk, M.C., Armstrong, G.W.D., Moire topography in scoliosis screening. Clinical Orthopedics and Related Research 129 (1977) 165.

Adams, P., Muir, H., Biochemical studies of individual lumbar discs., Ann. Rheumatol. Dis. 34 (1975) 467.

Adams, P., Muir, H., Qualitative changes with age of proteoglycans of human lumbar discs, Ann. Rheum. Dis. 35 (1976) 289.

Adams, P., et al., Biochemical aspects of development and aging of human lumbar intervertebral discs, Rheumatol. Rehabil. 16 (1977) 22.

Adorno, T.W., nach Jetschura 1972.

Ahlinder, S., et al., Metabolism and distribution of IgG in patients confined to prolonged and strict bed rest, Acta med. scand. 187 (1970) 267.

Akerblom, B., Standing and sitting posture, Nordiska bokhandeln stockholm 1948.

Akerblom, B., Ein neuer Sitzstuhl, Die Wirbelsauele in Forschung und Praxis 5 (1958) 94.

Akerblom, D., Zur Wirbelsaeulenhygiene des zivilisierten Menschen, Hippokrates 29 (1958) 251.

Akerblom, D., Anatomische und physiologische Grundlagen zur Gestaltung von Sitzen, Proc. Symp. "Sitting Posture," ed. by Grandjean, E., London 1969, Taylor & Francis.

Akeson, W.H., Woo, S.L.Y., Taylor, T.K.F., et al., Biomechanics and biochemistry of the intervertebral disks: the need for correlation studies, Clinical Orthopedics and Related Research 129 (1977) 133.

Aleksejew, A.P., Lenden-Kreuzschmerzen bei Fallschirmspringern, Wojenno-medizinski Schurnal 2 (1971) 70.

Allport, F.W., Persoenlichkeit, Klett, Stuttgart 1949.

Ambrus, A.P., et al., Boxsport. Aus: Sport. Trauma und Belastung, Hrsg. Pfoerringer et al., Perimed Verlag (1985).

Anderson, J.A.D., Rheumatism in industry: a review, British Journal of Industrial Medicine 28 (1971) 103.

Anderson, R.E., Leukemia and related disorders, Human Pathology 2 (1971) 505.

Andersson, B.J., Jonsson, B., Oertengren, R., Myoelectric activity in individual lumbar erector spinae muscles in sitting, Scandinavian Journal of Rehabilitative Medicine (1974) 91.

Andersson, B.J., Oertengren, R., Myoelectric back muscle activity during sitting, Scandinavian Journal of Rehabilitative Medicine 6 (1974) 73.

Andersson, B.J., Oertengren, R., Nachemson, A., et al., Lumbar disc pressure and myoelectric back muscle activity during sitting, Scandinavian Journal of Rehabilitative Medicine 6 (1974) 104, 122, 115, 128.

Andersson, B.J., Oertengren, R., Nachemson, A.L., et. al., The sitting posture: an electromyographic and discometric study, Orthopedic Clinics of North America 6 (1975) 105.

Andersson, G., Low backache in working life, Lakartidningen 73 (1976) 1305.

Andersson, G.B.J., Biomechanics of the lumbar spine, Clinics in Rheum. Dis. 6 (1980) 37.

Andersson, G.B.J., Oertengren, R., Nachemson, A., Quantitative studies of back loads in lifting, Spine 1 (1976) 178.

Andersson, G.B.J., Oertengren, R., Nachemson, A., Intradiscal pressure, intra-abdominal pressure and myoelectric back muscle activity related to posture and loading, Clinical Orthopedics 129 (1977) 156.

Andreeva-Galanina, T., Artamanova, D., Die Begutachtung der Arbeitsfaehigkeit bei Schwingungskrankheit (Russian) (ESK), G.I.M.L. 98 (1963).

Andrian-Werburg, H. Frhr. v., Spondylarthrosen, Osteochondrosen und Arthrosen der Rippengelenke, Die Wirbelsaeule in Forschung und Praxis 83 (1979) 141.

Apel, J., Witak, G., Wirbelsaeulebefunde bei 12-14 jaehrigen Turnerinnen nach mehrjaehrigem, Training Med. und Sport 17 (1977) 117.

Arct, W., Zervikalsyndrome auf der Grundlage kostovertebraler Arthrosen, Kongressband 25. Tagung Ges. Orthop. der DDR, 4-6 June 1978 in Dresden.

Arct, W., Lumbale Wirbelkoerperkantenabtrennung-Ueberlegung zur Aetiologie und Differentialdiagnose, Orthop. Praxis 16 (1980) 739.

Arct, W., Zur Aetiologie der Spondylolyse und Spondylolisthesis, Orthop. Praxis 16 (1980) 743.

Arlen, A., Messverfahren zur Erfassung von Statik und Dynamik der Halswirbelsaeule in der sagittalen Ebene, Manuelle Medizin 16 (1978) 25.

Arnim, D. von. Hoecherl, G., Die Bedeutung der nichtberuflichen Erkrankungen am Arbeitsplatz aus der Sicht des Rheumatologen, Arbeitsmedizin, Sozialmedizin, Praeventivmedizin 11 (1976) 245.

Arnold, K., Kritisches zu den vertebralen Deutungen SCHMORLs unter dem Blickwinkel des Kontorsionistenschadens, Z. Orthop. und Grenzgeb. 87 (1956) 186.

Assman, H., Besel, R., Lumbo-thorakale Dimer-X-Myelographie unter erweiterter Indikationsstellung in Verbindung mit Tomographie und Myeloszintigraphie, Dt. Gesundh.-Wesen 33 (1978) 883.

Atomic bomb casualty commission (ABCC), Pathology studies, Hiroshima und Nagasaki 1945-1970, Human Pathology 2 (1971) 269.

Auberlen, M., Renten statt Arbeitsplaetze, Aerzteblatt Baden-Wuertt, 31 (1976) 248.

Aufdermaur, M., Die pathologische Anatomie der Spondylitis ankylopoetica, Docum. rheumatol. Geigy (1953) 2.

Aufdermaur, M., Wirbelsaeulenbefunde bei der chronish-entzuendlichen Polyarthritis, Z. Rheumaforsch, 17 (1958) 177.

Aufdermaur, M., Pathologische Anatomie und Pathogenese der Scheuermann-Kyphose., Die Wirbelsaeule in Forschung und Praxis, Hippokrates Stuttgart 60 (1975) 55.

Aufdermaur, M., Pathologische Anatomie und Pathogenese der Scheuermann-Kyphose, Die Wirbelsaeule in Forschung und Praxis, Hippokrates Verlag 60 (1976) 55.

Aufdermaur, M., Regressive Veraenderungen der Wirbelbogengelenke und ihre Folgezustaende, Die Wirbelsaeule in Forschung und Praxis Bd. 87 (1981) 85.

Aufdermaur, M., Fehr, K., Lesker, P., et al. Quantitative histochemical changes in intervertebral discs in diabetes, Explorator Cell Biology 48 (1980) 89.

Auquier, L., Mignot, J., Paolaggi, J.B., et al., Application de mesures histomorphometriques a des disques intervertebraux lombaires normaux et pathologiques, Rev. Rhumat. 41 (1974) 509.

Azouz, E.M., Chan, J.D., Wee, R., Spondylolysis of the cervical vertebrae, Radiology 111 (1974) 315.

Baader, E.W., Gewerbekrankheiten, 4. Aufl. 1954, Urban und Schwarzenberg, Munich.

Baastrup, C., On the spinous processes of the lumbar vertebral and the soft tissues between them, Acta radiol 14 (1933) 52.

Baastrup, C., Le lumbago et les affections radiologiques des apophyses epineuses des vertebres lombaires, J. Radiol. Electrol. 19 (1936) 78.

Baehler, A., et al., Korsett-Typen und ihre Wirkungsweise, Orthop. Techn. 33 (1982) 164.

Baer, H.W., Alpiner Skilauf. in Pfoerringer et al. (Hrsg.) Sporttraumatologie, perimed Verlag (1981).

Baetzner, Sport- unde Arbeitsschaeden, Thieme, Leipzig (1936).

Baginski, A., Schulbaenke, Enke, Stuttgart (1889).

Bakke, S., Roentgenologische Beobachtungen ueber die Bewegungen der Wirbelsaeule, Acta Radiol. Suppl 13 (1931).

Baltshev, G., Scholler, D., Zur Entwicklung der chirurgischen Behandlung der Spondylolisthese, Orthop. Praxis 14 (1978) 424.

Banzer, D., et al., Eine neue Methode zur Messung des Rotationswinkels der Wirbelskoliose, Fortschr. Roentgenstr. 132 (1980) 403.

Barash, H.L., et al., Spondylolisthesis and tight hamstrings, Journal of Bone and Joint Surgery 52-A (1970) 1319.

Barbieri, L., de Franceschi, L., Considerazioni sulla biomeccanica del disco intersomatico interpretato come un sistema visco-elastico, Chir. Organi Mov. 61 (1975) 705.

Bargon, G., Roentgenologische Messmethode der Wirbelsaeule, Roentgen-Bl. 33 (1980) 2.

Barnett, E., Nordin, B.E.C., The radiological diagnosis of osteoporosis, Clin. Radio. 11 (1960) 166.

Batson, Oe. V., Das vertebrale Venensystem, American Journal of Roentgenology 78 (1957) 195.

Baudysova, J., Harnach, Z., Die Veraenderungen des Bewegungsapparates bei Berufsballettaenzern und Versuch zur Wuerdigung der Auswahl der Jugend fuer das Ballett, Act chir. orthop. traumat. Czechoslov 27 (1960) 238.

Baumgartner, R., Taillard, W., Die Beanspruchbarkeit der spondylolisthetischen Wirbelsaeule, Die Wirbelsaeule in Forschung und Praxis, Hippokrates Verlag Stuttgart 52 (1971) 80.

Bausewein, J., Conradty, M., Gutachten zu Fragen des therapeutischen Reitens, Publications of the Bundesminister for Youth, Family, Health, Vol. 21, Kohlhammer Verlag, Stuttgart (1974).

Bechtoldt, W., Zur Frage von Ueberlastungsschaeden der Wirbelsaeule bei Bandscheibendegeneration, Z. Orthop. 106 (1969) 5.

Beck, A., Radiologische Beurteilung der Wirbelsaeule aus fliegeraerztlicher Sicht, Wehrmed. Mschr. 17 (1973) 267.

Beck, A., Dynamische Autositze koennten Bandscheibenschaeden verhueten, Arztl. Praxis 26 (1974) 548.

Beck, A., Wirbelsaeule und Flugmedizin-Einfuehrung in die Thematik, Die Wirbelsaeule in Forschung und Praxis, 68 (1976) 9.

Beck, A., Killus, J., Mathematisch-statistische Methoden zur Untersuchung der Wirbelsaeulenhaltung mittels Computer, Biomed. Technik 19 (1974) 72.

Beck, G., Ein Fall von echter Spondylolisthesis im Halsteil, Fortschr. Roentgenstr. 136, 1 (1982) 93.

Becker, F., Orthopaedische Probleme im Rahmen des Jugendarbeitsschutzgesetzes, Fortschr. Med. 80 (1962) 133.

Becker, M.C., Schlegel, K.F., Schultasche und Haltung, Z. Kinderhk. 92 (1965) 7.

Becker, W., Krahl, H., Die Tendopathien, Georg Thieme Verlag, Stuttgart (1978).

Beekman, C.E., Hall, V., Variability of scoliosis measurement from spinal roentgenograms, Physical Therapy 59 (1979) 764.

Behrend, T., Behrend, H., Aetiologie und Pathogenese von Erkrankungen des rheumatischen Formenkreises bei Arbeitnehmern, Arbeitsmedizin, Sozialmedizin, Arbeitshyg. 6 (1971) 192.

Behrends, Margot, Bandscheibenoperationen, Frankfurter Allgemeine Zeitung 2.9. (1981).

Bellamy, R., Lieber, A., Smith, S.D., Congenital spondylolisthesis of the sixth cervical vertebra, Journal of Bone and Joint Surgery 56-A (1974) 405.

Belytschko, T.B., et al., Analog studies of forces in the human spine: computational techniques, J. Biomechanics 6 (1973) 361.

Benini, A., Das kleine Gelenk der Lendenwirbelsaeule, Huber, Bern (1978).

Bennet, H.E., School posture and seating, Boston, Ginn & Company (1928).

Benson, D.R., Schultz, A.B., Dewald, R.L., Roentgenographic evaluation of vertebral rotation, Journal of Bone and Joint Surgery (American) 58 (1976) 1125.

Bente, D., Das vegetative Reizsyndrom des oberen Koerperviertels, insbesondere bei Osteochondrose der HWS, Mschr. Psychiatr. 125, 141 (1953).

Berger, W., et al., Haltung und Bewegung, Springer Verlag Heidelberg (1984).

Bergsmann, O., Eder, M., Funktionelle Pathologie und Klinik der Brustwirbelsaeule, G. Fischer Verlag Stuttgart (1982).

Berquet, K.H., Sitzschaden und Autositz, Med. Welt 23 (1967) 1419.

Berquet, K.H., Schulmoebel-Geschichte-Auswahl-Anpassung, Monogr., Bonn (1971), Duemmler.

Berquet, K.H., Die Bedeutung der Moebel am Arbeitsplatz fuer statische und degenerative Veraenderungen des Haltungs- und Bewegungsapparates, ASP 9 (1974) 144.

Berquet, K.H., Klassisches Ballett aus Aporttraumatologie Hrsg. Pfoerringer et al., Perimed Verlag Erlangen (1980/81).

Berquet und Hesse., Ballettaenzerinnen und -taenzer, Medical Tribune 32 (1979).

Berquet, K.H., Juergens, H.W., Grundmasse von Schulmoebeln, Oefentl. Gesundheitwesen 34 (1972) 51.

Berry, R.J., Genetically controlled degeneration of the nucleus pulposus in the mouse, Journal of Bone and Joint Surgery 43-B (1961) 387.

Bessler, W., Feine, U., Die szintigraphische Untersuchung der Wirbelsaeule, Die Wirbelsaeule in Forschung und Praxis, Hippokrates Stuttgart Bd. 83 (1979) 107.

Beyeler, J., Reichmann, B., Schneider, W., Schweizer, A., Thorakaler Morbus Scheuermann: 10-und Mehr-Jahresresultate operativ und konservativ behandelter Patienten, Orthopaede 8 (1979) 180.

Biehl, G., Das Arteria vertebralis-Kompressionssyndrom-Klinik, Diagnostik und operative Behandlungsergebnisse der Foraminotomie nach JUNG kombiniert mit der ventralen Spondylodese nach Robinson, Z. Orthop. 119 (1981) 622.

Biehl, G., Schmitt, J., Die Insertionstendopathie an den Extremitaeten als Sportschaden, Orthop. Praxis 18 (1982) 940.

Biehl, G., Thomas, W., Die operative Behandlung des zervikoenzephalen Syndromes oder Arteria vertebralis-Syndromes, Contr. to Orthop. und Traumatol 29 (1982) 199.

Biener, K., Oechslin, M., Sportmedizinisches Profil des Tischtennisspielers, Dtsch. Zeitschr. f. Sportmedizin 30 (1979) 406.

Billot, C., Bensahel, H., La hernie discale lombaire chez l'enfant, Rev. Chir. Orthop. 66 (1980) 43.

Bilow, H., Weler, S., Halswirbelsaeulenverletzungen-Die konservative Behandlung und ihre Ergebnisse, Unfallheilkunde, H. 149 (1980) 77.

Binzus, G., Methoden zur Dokumentation und Auswertung rheumatologischer Befunde in Funktionspruefungen und Befunddokumentation des Bewegungsapparates, Hrsg.: G. Josenhans, Thieme Verlag Stuttgart (1978).

Bischko, J., Akupunktur und ihre Anwendung in der modernen europaeischen Therapie, Die Heilkunst 4 (1975) 1.

Bischko, J., Akupunktur-Grundlagen, Indikation und Grenzen, Orthop. Prax. 10 (1980) 887.

Bittersohl, G., Literaturbericht Kadmium, text part, Arbeitsmed.-Information 3 (1976) 49.

Blaesig, W., Die bisherige Praxis der Erziehung und Bildung des mehrfachbehinderten Schuelers, Rehabilitation 18 (1979) 150.

Blecourt, J.J., de., Einige Bemerkungen ueber die Bedeutung von Wirbelsaeulenschaeden anhand von Untersuchungen ganzer Bevoelkerungen, Rheumat. Forsch. Prax. II, Bern/Huber (1963) 149.

Blietz, R., Leistungsdiagramm und Bewegungsanalyse des Ruderns im Uebungsbecken und im Boot, Z. Orthop. 103 (1967) 214.

Blohmke, F., Wohnungen, Heime und Oeffentliche Einrichtungen fuer Koerperbehinderte, Year book Dtsch. Vereinigg. fuer Rehab. Behinderter (1965/66) 114.

Blow, J., Some factors influencing the duration of morbidity in industry, Proc. R. Soc. Med. 63 (1970) 1158.

Blumer, W., Bleivergiftung durch Autoverkehr und ihre Behandlung in der Praxis, Schweiz. Rundschau Med. (Praxis) 66 (1977) 491.

Boeck, G., Andersch, H., Schmidt, H., Standardisierte roentgendiagnostische Urteilsbildung bei degenerativ bedingten Schaeden der Wirbelsaeule als Beitrag zur Erhaltung der Tauglichkeit, Verkehrsmed, 26 (1979) 18.

Boeger, J., Kirchhoff, H.W., Wirbelsaeule und Wehrfliegerverwendungsfaehigkeit, Wehrmedizin 3 (1965) 143.

Boehler, J., Fehldeutung einer zervikalen Spondylolisthese als Luxationsfraktur, Z. Orthop. 104 (1968) 609.

Boehler, J., Erfolgversprechende Techniken fuer Aufrichtung und Stabilisierung bei Wirbelsaeulenverletzungen, Die Wirbelsaeule in Forschung und Praxis 55 (1972) 131.

Boehler, J., Konservative und operative Behandlung der Verletzungen der Okzipitozervikalregion, Die Wirbelsaeule in Forschung und Praxis, 76 (1978) 99.

Boehler, J., Wirbelsaeulenverletzungen, Hefte Unfallheilk. 148 (1980) 216.

Boehler, L., Eine einfache Methode zur Bestimmung der Beweglichkeit der Wirbelsaeule, Munich Med. Wschr. 80 (1933) 1826.

Boehmer, D., Die Bedeutung der biochemischen Leistungsdiagnostik fuer den Schul- und Vereinssport, Therapiewoche 28 (1978) 5434.

Boehmer, D., Ambrus, A.P., Tanzsport, in Sporttraumatologie, Hrsg.: Pfoerringer et al. Perimed Verlag (1981/82).

Boerner, M., et al., Der gefallene Ikarus oder der schwerverletzte jugendliche Motorradfahrer, Unfallchirurgie 8 (1982) 1.

Bogetti, B., Wirbelosteosklerose durch Caissonkrankheit, Lavoro e medicina 19 (1965) 83.

Bohl, W.R., Steffee, A.D., Lumbar spinal stenosis, Spine 4 (1979) 163.

Bohlig, H., Probleme und Ergahrungen mit der EDV-gerechten Roentgenbefundung von Pneumokoniosen, Radiologie 17 (1977) 2.

Boos, O., Die Bedeutung exogener Faktoren fuer Erkrankungen des degenerativen Rheumatismus aus der Sicht des Klinikers, Med. Sachverst. 61 (1965) 96.

Borgesen, S.E., Vang, P.S., Herniation of the lumbar intervertebral disk in children and adolescents, Acta orthop. scand. 45 (1974) 540.

Boss, R., Rehr, I., Hyperostotic spondylosis and diabetes mellitus, Verh. Dtsch. Ges. Rheumatol. 1 (1969) 244.

Bozdech, Z., Spondylisthese der Halswirbelsaeule, Beitr. Orthop. Traumatol. 14 (1967) 158.

Bradford, D.S., et. al., Surgical stabilization of fracture and fracture dislocations of the thoracic spine, Spine 2 (1977) 185.

Bradford, D.S., Ahmed, K.B., Moe, J.H., et al., The surgical management of patients with Scheuermann's disease, Journal of Bone and Joint Surgery 62-A (1980) 705.

Brauer, W., Das Krankheitsbild des Kontorsionistenschadens bei den Artisten der "Kautschuk"-Gruppe, Med. Wiss. Ges. Roentgenol. DDR Leipzig Akademie Verl. 1955.

Brauer, W., Zur Kasuistik der Kontorsionistenschaeden, Z. Orthop. 86 (1955) 140.

Brauer, W., Wirbelsaeulenschaeden bei Klischnigg-Kontorsionisten, Z. Orthop. 93 (1961) 46.

Brauer, W., Wirbelsaeulenschaeden bei Kontorsionsschaeden, Medizin und Sport DDR 7 (1967) 33.

Brauer, W., Ueberschaer, K.H., Ein Kontorsionistenschaden, Fortschr. Roentgenstr. 79 (1953) 524.

Braun, W., Ursachen des lumbalen Bandscheibenvorfalles, Die Wirbelsaeule in Forschung und Praxis 43 (1969), Hippokrates Verlag, Stuttgart.

Braun, W., Sport und lumbaler Bandscheibenvorfall, Sportarzt und Sportmedizin 9 (1972) 238.

Braun, W., Maksoud, M., Zur operativen Behandlung des zervikalen Bandscheibenvorfalls, Orth. Praxis 9/80.

Braus, H., Anatomie des Menschen I, Vogel Berlin (1921).

Breitenfelder, J., Bestehen Beziehungen der koerperlichen Haltung Jugendlicher zu ihrer geistigen Leistungsfaehigkeit? (1963).

Brennan, T.N., O'Connor, P.J., Incidence of boxing injuries in the Royal Air Forces in the United Kingdom, British Journal of Industrial Medicine 25 (1968) 326.

British Standards Institution, Part 3, Pupils, classroom chairs and tables, B.S. 3030 (1959).

Brocher, J.E.W., Die Prognose der Wirbelsaeulenleiden-Eine berufsprophylaktische Betrachtung, Thieme Stuttgart (1973).

Bromberg, K.B., Essen, H.O. von, Modeling of intervertebral discs, Spine 5 (1980) 155.

Bromley, J.W., et al., Collagenase—an experimental study of intervertebral disc dissolution, Spine 5 (1980) 126.

Bronz, G., Die Skiakrobatik, D. Ztschr. Sportmed 29 (1978) 334.

Brook, M., et al., Chemonukleolyse mit Chymopapain, Dtsch. Aerztebl. 81 (1984) 2965.

Brown, M.D., Chemonucleolysis with disease, technique, results, case reports, Spine, 1 (1976) 115.

Brown, T., Hansen, R.J., Yorra, A.J., Some mechanical tests on the lumbosacral spine with particular reference to the intervertebral discs, J. Bone It. Surg. 29-A (1957) 1135.

Brueggemann, G., Sportverletzung und Sportschaeden beim Judo, Orthop. Praxis 5 (1978) 396.

Brueggemann, G., Koring, W., Fussdeformitaeten bei 100-km-Laeufern und ihre Veraenderungen unter der Belastung des 100-km-Laufes sowie Beschwerden und krankhafte Befunde am Haltungs-und Bewegungsapparat, die zur Aufgabe bei 100-km-Laeufen fuehrten, Berichtsband Sportaerztekongress 1980, ed. Kindermann und Hort, Hippokrates Verlag Stuttgart (1980).

Brune, G., Halswirbelsaeule (Koerperliche Untersuchung), Die neurologische Untersuchung bei Erkrankungen der Halswirbelsaeule, Z. Orthop. 119 (1981) 574.

Brussatis, F., Elektromyographische Untersuchungen der Ruecken-und Bauchmuskulatur bei idiopathischen Skoliosen, Die Wirbelsaeule in Forschung und Praxis, Bd. 24, Hippokrates Stuttgart (1962).

Brussatis, F., Zervikale Aufrichtungsosteotomie bei Morbus Bechterew, Orthopaede 10 (1981) 178.

Buchmann, F., Heinzerling, J., NMR-Tomographie, GIT. Lab. Med. 6 (1983) 102.

Buchter, A., Der Arbeiter in der PVC-Industrie, in Aerztliche Berufskunde, Arbeitsmedizin, Sozialmedizin, Praeventivmedizin (1978) Beilage 133.

Buckwalter, J., Cooper, R., Maynard, J., Elastic fibers in human intervertebral discs, J. Bone Joint Surg. 58 (1976) 73.

Budka, H., Perneczky, A., Pusch, St., Bandscheibengewebsembolien in Spinalgefaessen als Ursache von Myelomalazien vorwiegend in Spinalis posterior-Versorgungsgebieten, Vienna Klin. Wschr. 91 (1979) 578.

Buesing, E.W., Indikation und Technik der Spondylodese bei der Spondylolisthesis, Orthop. Praxis 13 (1977) 622.

Buetti-Baeuml, C., Funktionelle Roentgendiagnostik der Halswirbelsaeule, Thieme Stuttgart (1954).

Buran, I., Novak, I., Der Psychische Faktor bei schmerzhaften vertebragenen Syndromen, Manuelle Medizin 22 (1984) 5.

Burgstein, L., Netolitzky, A., Das Schulzimmer, in Handbuch d. Schulhygiene, Fischer Jena (1902).

Burton, A.C., Edholm, O.G., Man in a cold environment, Arnold Publishers (1955).

Burton, C.V., Computer tomographic scanning and the lumbar spine, part 1: economic and historic review, Spine 4 (1979) 353.

Burton, C.V., et al., Computed tomographic scanning and the lumbar spine, Part II: Clinical considerations, Spine 4 (1979) 356.

Bush, H.D., Horton, W.G., Smare, D.L., et al., Fluid content of the nucleus pulposus as a factor in the disk syndrome, British Medical Journal 445 (1956) 81.

Bushell, G.R., et al., The collagen of the intervertebral disc in adolescent idiopathic scoliosis, J. Bone Joint Surg. B-61 (1979) 501.

Busse, O., Stolke, D., Seidel, B.U., Die postoperative Discitis intervertebralis lumbalis, Nervenarzt 47 (1976) 604.

Cady, J., Basket-Ball et Rachis, Med. Sport. Paris, 33 (1970) 13.

Caillard, J.F., Thilliez, A., Problemes poses au medecin du travail par les lombalgies, Arch. mal. prof. 36 (1975) 773.

Caille, J.M., Acquisitions recentes de la radiologie du rachis cervical, Bordeaux Chirurgical, 41 (1970) 110.

Capandji, J.A., The physiology of the joints, Livingstone, Edinburgh (1974).

Caplan, A., Certain unusual radiological appearances in the chest of coal miners suffering from rheumatoid arthritis, Thorax 8 (1953) 29.

Caplan, A., Payne, P.B., Withey, I.L., A broader concept of Caplan's syndrome related to rheumatoid arthritis, Thorax (London) 17 (1962) 205.

Caplan, P.S., Freedman, L.M.J., Connelly, T.P., Degenerative joint disease of the lumbar spine in coal miners, Arthr. Rheumat. 9 (1966) 693.

Caroit, M., Perignon, M. de, Seze, S. de, Contribution au diagnostic etiologique des spondylodiscites, Rev. Rhumat. 42 (1975) 145.

Caroit, M., Perignon, M. de, Levernieux, J., et al., Contribution au diagnostic etiologique des spondylodiscites, Rev. Rhumat. 42 (1975) 153.

Carrera, G.F., Haughton, V.M., Syvertsen, A., et al., Computed tomography of the lumbar facet joints, Radiology 134 (1980) 145.

Chahal, A.S., Jyoti, S.P., The radical treatment of tuberculosis of the spine, Int. Orthop. 4 (1980) 93.

Chahal, S., et al., Lumbar canal stenosis, Paraplegia 20 (1982) 288.

Chaiton, A., et al., Disappearing lumbar hyperostosis in a patient with Forestier's diease: an ominous sign, Arthritis and Rheumatism 22 (1979) 799.

Chapman, A.E., Troup, J.D., Prolonged activity of lumbar erectores spinae, Ann. Phys. Med. 10 (1979) 262.

Charles, P., Le Rachis chez le nageur (The spinal column during swimming), Med. Sport, Paris 44 (1970) 3.

Charlton, O.P., Gehweiler, J.A. Jr., Morgan, C.L., et al., Spondylolysis and spondylolisthesis of the cervical spine, Skeletal Radiol. 3 (1978) 79.

Christ, W., Dupuis, H. (Ueber die Beanspruchung der Wirbelsaeule unter dem Einfluss sinus-foermiger und stochastischer Schwingungen, Z. angew. Physiol. Arbeitsphys. 22 (1966) 258.

Christ, W., Dupuis, H., Untersuchung der Moeglichkeit von gesundheitlichen Schaedigungen im Bereich der Wirbelsaeule bei Schlepperfahrern, Max-Plank-Inst. for agricultural work and technology, Bad Kreuznach (1966) 52 und Med. Welt 19 (1968) 1919.

Clara, M., Das Nervensystem des Menschen, J.A. Barth, 3. Aufl. Leipzig (1959).

Clark, B., Stewart, J.D., Tresholds for the perception of angular acceleration about the three major body axes. Acta Otolaryngol. 69 (1970) 231.

Clemens, H.J., Intraossale (transspinale) Angiographie der Vertebralvenensysteme mit der Bildverstaerker-Roentgen-Kinematographie, Die Wirbelsaeule in Forschung und Praxis Vol. 34 (1966) 88.

Clement, J.D., et al., Minimum standards of physical fitness required of candidates for collision sports at the University of Maine, J. Maine Med. Ass. 58 (1967) 121.

Cloward, R., The treatment of ruptured lumbar intervertebral disc by vertebral body fusion III. Method of use of banked bone, Arch. Surg. 136 (1952) 987.

Cloward, R., Operative technique cervical disks, description of instruments and operative technique, American Journal of Surgery 98 (1959) 722.

Cloward, R.B., Treatment of acute fractures and fracture-dislocations of the cervical spine by vertebral-body fusion: a report of eleven cases, Journal of Neurosurgery 18 (1961).

Cloward, R.B., Buzard, L.L., Discography, American Journal of Roentgenology 68 (1952) 552.

Coan, R.M., et al., The acupuncture treatment of low back pain: a randomized controlled study, American Journal of Chinese Medicine 8 (1980) 181.

Cobb, J.R., Outline for the study of scoliosis instructional course lectures, American Academy of Orthopedics (1948) 261.

Coermann, R., Comparison of the dynamic characteristics of dummies, animals and man, in: Impact Acceleration Stress Proc. Brooks AFB, Texas, NAS-NCR-977, Washington (1961).

Coermann, R., Die Wirkung mechanischer Schwingungen auf den Menschen und seine Arbeitsleistung, Werkstattstechnik 52 (1962) 18.

Coermann, R., The mechanical impendance of the human body in sitting and standing at low frequencies, ADS-TR-61-492, Aeronautical System Division, WPAFB Ohio (1961) and Human Factors (1962) 227.

Coermann, R., Biologische Wirkungen mechanischer Schwingungen auf den Menschen, Zbl. Verkehrsmed 9 (1963) 2.

Coermann, R., Physiologische Schwingungsprobleme in Fahrzeugen, Zentralbl. Verkehrsmedizin 3 (1965).

Coermann, R., Uebertragung von Fahrzeugerschuetterungen auf den Organismus, Der Mensch im Verkehr, Beiheft 3, Mainz (1965) Krausskopf.

Coin, C.G., et al., Diving-type injury of the cervical spine: contribution of computed tomography to management, Journal of Computer Assisted Tomography 3 (1979) 362.

Colachis, S., Strohm, B., A study of tractive forces and angle of pull on vertebral, interspaces in the cervical spine, Arch. Phys. Med. Rehab. 46 (1965) 820.

Collaud, D.: Die Wirbelsaeule beim Judoka, Med. Sport, Paris 44 (1970) 20.

Commandre, E.I., et al., Rachis lombo-sacre et ski nautique (Lumbar spinal column and water skiing). Cinesiologie, Paris 13 (1974) 173.

Commandre, F., et al., Le devenir du rachis lombosacre chez les enseignants d'education physique et sportive (A propos de 23 observations). The development of the lumbar spinal column in athletes, 23 observations), Med. Du Sport, Paris 48 (1974) 73.

Commandre, F., et al., Sportverletzung/Lendenwirbelsaeule, Cinesiologie, Paris 13 (1974) 52, p. 163.

Cording, R., Der Stellenwert der Szintigraphie bei der Fruehdiagnose des Morbus Bechterew, Orthop. Praxis 15 (1979) 746.

Cotta, H., Der Mensch ist so jung wie seine Gelenke (mit Angabren zu Uebungen fuer die Wirbelsaeule), R. Piper und Co., Verlag Munich (1979).

Cotta, H., Ergebnisse zue Entstehung von Spondylolyse und Spondylolisthese, Z. Orthop. 118 (1980) 435.

Cotta, H., Krahl, H.: Degenerative Veraenderungen der Wirbelsaeule und sportliche Belastung, Sportarzt und Sportmedizin 28 (1977) 114.

Cotta, H., Steinbrueck, K., Wirbelsaeulenschaeden beim Leistungssportler, Langenbeck Arch. Chir. 349 (1979) 385.

Coventry, M.B., Introduction to symposium, including anatomy, physiology and epidemiology, instructional course lecture on the symposium low back pain and sciatic pain, Journal of Bone and Joint Surgery 50-A (1968) 167.

Cremona, E., Die Wirbelsaeule bei den Schwerarbeitern der Eisen-und Stahlindustrie sowie des Bergbaus, Kommiss. Europ. Gem. Generaldir. Soz. Angelegenheiten Dok Nr. 1911/72 d (1972).

Cremona, E., La colonne vertebrale chez les travailleurs de force de la siderurgie et des mines, personally provided manuscript from 1972, in possession of the commission of the European associations, general directorate for social matters, Doc. 1911/72.

Crown, S., Die psychologischen Aspekte der tiefsitzenden Rueckenschmerzen, Rheumatol. Rehabil. 17 (1978) 114.

Crown, S., Psychosocial factors in low back pain, Clinics in Rheumatic Disease 6 (1980) 77.

Cumbrowski, J., Raffke, W., Cadmium-Ein Schadfaktor in der menschlichen Umwelt, Z. ges. Hyg. 21 (1975) 1.

Dahmen, G., Beurteilung und Behandlung von Haltungsschaeden bei Kindern und Jungenlichen, Materia Medica Nordmark 30 (1978) 237.

Dambacher, M.A., et al., Die Osteoporosen, Aktuelle pathogenetische und therapeutische Ueberlegungen, Therapiewoche 29 (1979) 6868.

Davidowitsch, P., Ueber die Beziehungen zwischen Becken und Wirbelsaeule und ihr Verhaeltnis zur Haltung und zum Haltungsindex, Manuelle Medizin 14 (1976) 112.

Dawley, J.A., Spondylolisthesis of the cervical spine, Journal of Neurosurgery 34 (1971) 99.

Debrunner, H.U., Die klinische Untersuchung der Wirbelsaeule, Z. Unfallmed. Berufskrankh. 4 (1971) 260.

Debrunner, H.U., Das Kyphometer, Z. Orthop. 110 (1972) 389.

Debrunner, H.U., Graden, R., Objektive Kriterien der Wirbelsaeulenmechanik. Ortho. Praxis 11 (1975) 479.

Dechelotte, J., Doury, P., Pattin, S., Nouvelle Etude sur l'Evolution a moyen terme des syndromes de Fiessinger-Leroy-Reiter observes en milieu militaire, Rev. Rhum. Mal. Osteoartic, 42 (1975) 497.

Dechous, J., Aspects radiologiques pulmonaires observes chez les mineurs atteints de polyarthrite rhumatoide, Arch. Mal. Prof. Med. Trav. Sec. Soc. Paris, 33 (1972) 347.

Decking, D., Die Bedeutung des Atlas im seitlichen Roentgenbild der Halswirbelsaeule, Orthop. Praxis 13 (1977) 874.

Decking, D., ter Steege, W., Roentgenologische Parameter der Halswirbelsaeule im seitlichen Strahlengang, Die Wirbelsaeule in Forschung und Praxis, Hippokrates Verlag Stuttgart 64 (1975).

Deeb, Z., Frayha, R.A., Multiple vacuum-discs and early signs of ochronosis, Journal of Rheumatology 3 (1976) 82.

Degenhardt, K., Tierexperimentelle Untersuchungen zur Aetiologie und Phaenogenese (frueherworbener) axialer Fehlbildungen. Z. menschl. Vererb.- und Konstit.-Lehre 34 (1958) 509.

Delank, H.W., Zervikale und thorakale Syndrome aus neurologischer Sicht, Die Wirbelsaeule in Forschung und Praxis, Hippokrates Verlag Stuttgart 83 (1979) 159.

D'Emilio, M., Di Gregorio, M., Die Roentgenuntersuchung der Wirbelsaeule bei der Beurteilung der Arbeitsfaehigkeit, Securitas, Rome 54 (1969) 203.

Demirjian, A., Dubuc, M.B., Jenicek, M., Etude comparative de la croissance de l'enfant canadien d'origine francaise a Montreal, Canadian Journal of Public Health 62 (1971) 111.

Demirjian, A., Jenicek, M., Dubuc, M.B., Les normes staturoponderales de l'enfant unbain canadien francais d'age scolaire, Canadian Journal of Public Health 63 (1972) 14.

Denman, F.R., Candy, J.R., Hampton, W.R., Zur Roentgung der Wirbelsaeule bei der Einstellungsuntersuchung, Texas State Journal of Medicine 57 (1961) 704.

Dennert, R., Muenzenberg, K.J., Zur roentgenologischen Unterscheidung zwischen pathologischer Osteoporose und altersbedingtem Knochenabbau. Z. Orthop. 113 (1975) 1097.

Deplante, J.P., Queneau, P., Contassot, J.S., et al., Vertebre noire isolee d'origine staphylococcique bacteriologiquement confirmee a propos d'un cas. Lyon Med. (1974) 65.

Derbolowsky, U., Gibt es psychogene Erkrankungen der Wirbelsaeule, Hippokrates Stuttgart 29 (1958) 345.

Derbolowsky, U., siehe Manuelle Medizin (1973) 73.

Deutschberger, O., Report on the increase of lead poisoning as revealed by laboratory and x-ray examinations, Proc. Rudolf Virchow Med. Soc. 19 (1960) 13.

Deutscher Sportbund, Trimming 130, Redaktion H. Pieper.

Devas, M., Stress fractures, Spondylolisthesis, Churchill Livingstone, Edinburgh (1975).

Dewald, et al., Severe lumbosacral spondylolisthesis in adolescents and children, Journal of Bone and Joint Surg. 63-A (1981) 619.

DGMM-Memorandum, Verhuetung von Zwischenfaellen bei gezielter Handgrifftherapie an der Halswirbelsaeule, Unfallchir. 6 (1980) 199.

Diamant, B., Karlsson, J., Nachemson, A., Correlation between lactate levels and pH in discs of patients with lumbar rhizopathies, Experimentia 24 (1968) 1195.

Dick, W., Die konservative und operative Behandlung der idiopathischen Skoliose bei Jugendlichen, Swiss Rundschau Medizin (Praxis) Nr. 3 (1980) 69.

Dieckmann, D., Die Einwirkung mechanischer Schwingungen bis 100 Hz auf den Menschen, Ultraschall in Medizin und Grenzgeb. 9 (1956).

Dieckmann, D., Die Wirkung mechanischer Schwingungen auf den Menschen, VDI Berichte 25 (1957).

Dieckmann, D., Die Wirkung mechanischer Schwingungen in Kraftfahrzeugen auf den Menschen, ATZ 10 (1957).

Dieckmann, D., Einfluss vertikaler mechanischer Schwingungen auf den Menschen, Int. Zschr. angew. Physiol. 16 (1957) 519.

Dieckmann, D., Die Minderung der Schwingbelastung der Menschen in Kraftfahrzeugen, VDI-Berichte 8 (1957) Forschungsber. des Wirtschaftsund Verkehrsministerium Nordrhein-Westfalen Nr. 635 (1958).

Dieckmann, D., Einfluss horizontaler mechanischer Schwingungen auf den Menschen, Internat. Z. angew. Arbeitsphysiol. 17 (1958) 83.

Dieckmann, D., Mechanische Modelle fuer den vertikal schwingenden menschlichen Koerper, Internat. Z. angew. Physiologie 1 (1958).

Dieckmann, D., A study of the influence of vibration on man, Ergonomics, 1 (1958) 345.

Dieckmann, D., Einwirkungen mechanischer Schwingungen auf den Menschen, In Handbuch der gesamten Arbeitsmedizin, Band 1, Urban & Schwarzenberg, Berlin, Munich, Vienna, 1961.

Dieckmann, D., Einige Methoden zur Untersuchung des Schwingverhaltens von Kraftfahrzeugsitzen, ATZ 3 (1962).

Dieckmann, D., Einige Untersuchungen zur Entlastung des Gahrers von Kraftfahrzeugen, Der Mensch im Verkehr Beiheft 3 Arbeitswissenschaft, Krasskopf Mainz (1965).

Dieckmann, D., Schwingungen in Kraftfahrzeugen, Hefte Unfallhik. 87 (1966) 214.

Dieckmann, D., Scheffler, H., Untersuchungen von Schwingungen in einem Omnibus und ihre Einwirkung auf den Menschen, Arbeitsschutz 6 (1956) 129.

Dieckmann, H., Basilare Impression, Atlasassimilation und andere Skelettfehlbildungen der Zervikookzipitalen-Region, Die Wirbelsaeule in Forschung und Praxis, Hippokrates Verlag 32 (1966).

Dieckmann, H., Basilare Impression, Atlasassimilation und andere Skelettfehlbildungen der Zerviko-Okzipital-Region. Wirbelsaeule in Forschung und Praxis, Hippokrates Verlag, Stuttgart Vol. 32 (1966).

Diener, W., Die Arzneimittelbehandlung der Chondrosis intervertebralis und ihrer Folgezustaende, Die Wirbelsaeule in Forschung und Praxis Hippokrates Verlag Stuttgart 8 (1958) 7.

Diethelm, L., Kastert, J., Die entzuendlichen Erkrankunden der Wirbelsaeule, Hand. Med.

Radiol. Band VI/2 Springer Berlin-Heidelberg-New York 1974.

Dihlmann, E., Funktionelle Roentgenuntersuchungen der Wirbelsaeule, in Funktionspruefungen und Befunddokumentation des Bewegungsapparates, Hrsgb. G. Josenhans, Thieme Stuttgart 1978.

Dihlmann, W., Ueber die typischen sakroiliakalen Ueberlastungsschaeden, Therapiewoche 25 (1975) 3925.

Dihlmann, W., et al., Sakroiliakale Computertomographie, Fortschr. Roentgenstr. 130 (1979) 659.

Distelmaier, P., Zur Bedeutung der Funktionsaufnahmen der Halswirbelsaeule bei der Diagnostik zervikaler Syndrome, Fortschr. Roentgenstr. 126 (1977) 160.

Dittmar, F., Die Beziehungen der Wirbelsaeule zur Segmentdiagnostik und -therapie, Naturheilverfahren III Stuttgart, Hippokrates Verlag, Stuttgart (1955).

Dittmar, F., Die Segmentdiagnostik als Massnahme zur Objektivierung von Wirbelsaeulenschaeden, Die Wirbelsaeule in Forschung und Praxis, Hippokrates Verlag, Stuttgart 9 (1959) 76.

Dittmar, F., Wirbelsaeulenleiden, Musik und Medizin 11 (1980) 7.

Dittmar, O., Die sagittal- und lateralflexorische Bewegung der menschlichen Wirbelsaeule im Roentgenbild. Zur Mechanologie der Wirbelsaeule, Z. Anat. Entwickl. Gsch. 92 (1930) 644.

Dittmar, O., Roentgenstudium zur Mechanologie der Wirbelsaeule, Z. Orthop. Chir. 55 (1931) 321.

Dodson, V.N., Dinman, B.O., Whitehouse, Ileosacral Arthritis, Arch. Environmental Health 22 (1971) 83.

Doerfler, R., Probleme d. Kurindikation bei Werktaetigen der Schwerindustrie, Arch. Phys. Ther. 22 (1970) 389.

Donaldson, C.L., et al., Effect of prolonged bed rest on bone mineral, Metabolism 19 (1970) 1071.

Donisch, E.W., Trapp, W., The cartilage end plates of the human vertebral column (some considerations of postnatal development), Anat. Rev. 167 (1971) 705.

Donner, N., Psychische Aspekte bei vertebralen Stoerungen, Manuelle Medizin 12 (1974) 73.

Donskoi, D.D., Biomechanik der Koerperuebungen, Sportverlag Berlin 1961.

Dorn, W., Zur Segmentbehandlung in der Chirurgie, Die Wirbelsaeule in Forschung und Praxis Hippokrates Verlag, Stuttgart 28 (1957) H 6.

Dornike siehe bei Haffner.

Drasch, G., Meyer, L.v., Kreglinger, R., Untersuchungen zum Bleigehalt menschlicher Knochen, Arbeitsmedizin, Sozialmedizin, Praeventivmedizin 14 (1979) 32.

Drasche, H., Die orthopaedischen Berufskrankheiten aus arbeitsphysiologischer und arbeitsmedizinischer Sicht, Z. Orthop. 113 (1975) 625.

Drerup, B., Anwendungen der Moire-Topographie zur Diagnose und Dokumentation von Fehlbildungen des Rumpfes, Z. Orthop. 116 (1978) 789–794.

Drerup, B., et al., Bestimmung der Formcharakteristika der Rueckenoberflaeche bei Kyphose und Skoliose durch optische Vermessung, Z. Orthop. 120 (1982) 577.

Drerup, B., et al., Oberflaechenvermessung bei Wirbelsaeulendeformitaeten, Vorabdruck, 69. DGOT conference, Mainz 1982, Reports from the Dept. of Biomechanics of the Orthop. University Hospital Muenster Nr. 8.

Drerup, B., et al., Computerized evaluation of surface measurements of kyphosis and scoliosis, More Fringe Topography and Spinal Deformity (ed. 1983 by Drerup, Frobin, Hierholzer), G. Fischer Verlag, Stuttgart, New York 155–162.

Dul, J., et al., Bewegungen und Kraefte im oberen Kopfgelenk beim Vorbeugen der Halswirbelsaeule, Manuelle Medizin 20 (1982) 51.

Duncan, K.P., Howell, R.W., Health of workers in the United Kingdom Atom Energy Authority, Health Physics, Pergamon Press 19 (1970) 285.

Dunsker, S.B., Colley, D.P., Mayfield, F.H., Kinematics of the cervical spine, Clin. Neurosurgery, Proc. 1977, 174, Williams & Wilkins Co. Baltimore 1978.

Du Pan, R.M., Widmer, H., Das akute kindliche Iliosakralgelenksyndrom, MM 17 (1979) 79.

Dupuis, H., Die menschliche Beanspruchung bei der Bedienung von Kraftfahrzeugen insbesondere landwirtschaftlichen Schleppern Automobiltechn. Ztschr. 7 (1956).

Dupuis, H., Schlepperschwingungen am Menschen gemessen, Landarbeit, Stuttgart 7 (1959).

Dupuis, H., Senkrechte Schwingungsbeschleunigungen von Fahrern in Kraftfahrzeugen, auf Ackerschleppern und selbstfahrenden Arbeitsmaschinen, Grundlagen d. Landtechnik 16 (1963).

Dupuis, H., Belastung durch mechanische Schwingungen und moegliche Gesundheitsschaedingungen im Bereich der Wirbelsaeule, Fortschr. Med. 92 (1974) 618.

Dupuis, H., Belastung und Beanspruchung der Wirbelsaeule durch Vibration, Die Wirbelsaeule in Forschung und Praxis, Hippokrates Verlag, Stuttgart 68 (1976) 48.

Dupuis, H., Einwirkung berufsbedingter Vibrationen auf die Wirbelsaeule, Die Wirbelsaeule in Forschung und Praxis, Hippokrates Verlag, Stuttgart 92 (1980) 45.

Dupuis, H., Christ, W., Untersuchung der Moeglichkeit von Gesundheitsschaedingungen im Bereich der Wirbelsaeule bei Schlepperfahrern, Max-Planck-Inst. for agricultural work and technology, Bad Kreuznach, Vol. A (1972) 2.

Dupuis, H., Hartung, E., Schleppersitz-Untersuchungen mit Hilfe eines servohydraulischen Schwingungssimulators, Landtechn. Forschung 16 (1966) 163.

Dupuis, H., Hartung, E., Louda, L., Zur Wahrnehmung und Ertraeglichkeit von gemischten mechanischen Sinusschwingungen in vertikaler Richtung, Arbeitsschutz 3 (1971) 72.

Dupuis, H., Hartung, E., Louda, L., Vergleich regelloser Schwingungen eines begrenzten Frequenzbereiches mit sinusfoermigen Schwingungen hinsichtlich der Einwirkung auf den Menschen, Ergonomics 15 (1972) 237.

Dupuis, H., Zerlett, G., Beanspruchung des Menschen durch mechanische Schwingungen-Kenntnisstand zur Wirkung von Ganzkoerperschwingungen, Publications of the chief association of occupational associations, May 1984.

Dvorak, J., Dvorak, V., Neurologie der Wirbelbogengelenke, Man. Med. 20 (1982) 77.

Dvorak, J., Dvorak, V., Manuelle Medizin-Diagnostik, Georg Thieme Verlag Stuttgart 1983.

Ebersbach, W., Sozialmedizinische Bedeutung der Wirbelsaeulensyndrome und des Weichteilrheumatismus, Hippokrates 47 (1976) 287.

Echeverria, T., and Lockwood, R., Lumbar spinal stenosis, NY State Journal of Medicine 79 (1979) 72.

Eckel, H., Die roentgenologische Funktionsdiagnostik der Halswirbelsaeule, Roentgen-Bl. 33 (1980) 11.

Eckert, H.F., Decker, A., Pathological studies of the intervertebral disc, Journal of Bone and Joint Surgery 29 (1947) 447.

Edelmann, P., Schmerzursache und Therapie der schmerzhaften juvenilen Kyphose, Die Wirbelsaeule in Forschung und Praxis 89 (1980) 63.

Eder, M., Tilscher, H., Zur Pathogenese und Klinik pseudoradikulaerer Schmerzbilder, Manuelle Medizin 19 (1981) 54.

Eder, M., Tilscher, H., Schmerzsyndrome der Wirbelsaeule-Grundlagen, Diagnostik, Therapie-Die Wirbelsaeule in Forschung und Praxis (2. Aufl. 1982) Hippokrates Verlag, Stuttgart.

Edgar, M., Ghadially, J.A., Innervation of the lumbar spine, Clinical Orthopaedics (1976) 35.

Eger, W., Rheumatische Beschwerden im Bereiche der Wirbelsaeule und ihre morphologischen Grundlagen, Die Wirbelsaeule in Forschung und Praxis, Hippokrates Verlag Stuttgart 34 (1966) 25.

Ehalt, W., Haltungsfehler und Haltungsturnen im Kindes-und Jugendalter, Landarzt 42 (1966) 815.

Ehlert, V., Die biomechanische Analyse der statischen Wirbelsaeulenbelastung bei jugendlichen Fechtern durch die Fechtwaffe, siehe in Waterloh et al.

Ehricht, H.G., Wirbelsaeulenentwicklung und Sport, Therap. Umschau 31 (1978) 243.

Eichler, J., Einstellungsuntersuchungen fuer Berufe der Schwerarbeit, Die Wirbelsaeule in Forschung und Praxis, Hippokrates Stuttgart 55 (1972) 15.

Eisenstein, S., Spondylolysis—a skeletal investigation of two population groups, Journal of Bone and Joint Surgery 60-B (1978) 488.

Eitner, S., Der alternde Mensch am Arbeitsplatz, Verlag Tribuene, Berlin 1975.

Elhabali, M., Scherak, O., Seidl, G., Kolarz, G., Tomographic examinations of sacroiliac joints in adult patients with rheumatoid arthritis, Journal of Rheumatology 6 (1979) 417.

Ellwanger, E., Die Bedeutung der Scheuermann-Krankheit fuer die Rentenversicherung, Die Wirbelsaeule in Forschung und Praxis, Hippokrates Stuttgart 60 (1976) 95.

Ellwanger, E., Berufliche Rehabilitation aus der Sicht der Rentenversicherung, Z. Allgemeinmedizin 53 (1977) 208.

Elsner, Lehrlingskyphose, Z. Orthop. Chir., 32 (1913).

Emminger, E., Die Gelenkdisci an der Wirbelsaeule, Hefte Unfallheilk. 48 (1955) 142.

Emminger, E., Anatomie und Pathologie des Bewegungssegmentes (Junghanns) der Wirbelsaeule, Die Wirbelsaeule in Forschung und Praxis 10 (1958) 7.

Endler, M., et al., Wirbelsaeulenveraenderungen und ihre Mechanopathologie bei Leistungsruderern, Z. Orthop. 118 (1980) 91.

Engel, J.M., Quantitative Thermographie in der Diagnostik-und Therapiekontrolle der manuellen Medizin, Manuelle Medizin 20 (1981) 36.

Erdmann, H., Endogene Ursachen bei der Wirbelsaculcn-Osteochondrose des Lendenabschnittes, Arch. orthop. Unfallchir. 45 (1953) 415.

Erdmann, H., Die Verspannung des Wirbelsaeulensockels im Beckenring, Die Wirbelsaeule in Forschung und Praxis, Hippokrates Verlag Stuttgart 1 (1956) 51.

Erdmann, H., Die angeborenen Veraenderungen der Halswirbelsaeule, Therapiewoche 13 (1963) 453.

Erdmann, H., Auf welche Fragen kann das Roentgenbild der Wirbelsaeule Antwort geben? Die Wirbelsaeule in Forschung und Praxis, Hippokrates Verlag Stuttgart 36 (1965) 668.

Erdmann, H., Vergleichende anatomische Untersuchungen zum Verstaendnis der Statik und Dynamik vom Becken und Lendenwirbelsaeule bei verschiedenen Beckentypen, Diaetetik, Phys. Med. Rehab. 6 (1965).

Erdmann, H., Gesichtspunkte zur Begutachtung von Antraegen auf Entschaedigung von Wirbelsaeulenschaeden "wie eine Berufskrankheit," Schriftenreihe des Hauptverbandes der Gewerbl. Berufsgenossenschaften 1 (1966) 155.

Erdmann, H., Grundzuege einer funktionellen Wirbelsaeulenbetrachtung, Man. Med. 5 (1967) 55, Pt. 1. 6 (1968) 32, Pt. 2. 6 (1968) 79, Pt. 3.

Erdmann, H., Die Schleuderverletzung der Hals-Wirbelsaeule Erkennung und Behandlung, Die Wirbelsaeule in Forschung und Praxis Hippokrates Stuttgart 47 (1973).

Erdmann, H., Die koerperliche Untersuchung, Die Wirbelsaeule in Forschung und Praxis, Bd. 83 (1979) 13, Hippokrates Stuttgart.

Erdmann, H., Traumen, Die Wirbelsaeule in Forschung und Praxis, Bd. 87 (1981) 103.

Erlacher, P., Direkte Kontrastdarstellung des Nucleus pulposus, zugleich ein Beitrag zur Pathologie der Bandscheibe, Z. Orthop. 80 (1949) 40.

Eshougues, J.R. de, Wachemacker, R., Das Bewegungssegment der Wirbelsaeule, ddb 66 (1975) 667.

Eskenasy, J., Das zervikale wirbel-radikulaer-medullaere Leiden der Schwingungen ausgesetzten Arbeiter in den grossen metallurgischen Werken, Sympos. Neurologic. Sighisoara (1967).

Eskenasy, J., La myelopathie vertebrale vibratoire cervicale, Arch. Mal. Prof. 30 (1969) 121.

Eskenasy, J., Die Schwingungsneurose, Internat. Arch. Arbeitsmed. 26 (1970) 263.

Eskensasy, J., La syncope peripherique par vibrations, Arch. mal. prof. Paris 33 (1972) 31.

Esmarch, J. von, Zur Belehrung ueber das Sitzen der Schulkinder, Lipsius und Tischer (1884).

Eulderink, F., Meijers, K.A., Pathology of the cervical spine in rheumatoid arthritis, J. Pathol. 120 (1976) 91.

Eulert, J., Die sportliche Belastungsfaehigkeit der gesunden und der kranken Wirbelsaeule, Therapiewoche 29 (1979) 4159.

Eulert, J., Differentialdiagnose des Kreuzschmerzes, Z. Allg. Med. 55 (1979) 1962.

Evans, J.W., Boda, J.M., Glucose metabolism and chronic acceleration, American Journal of Physiology 219 (1970) 893.

Evans, W.E. III, Barron, C. I., Medical care of aircrew men in an industrial environment, Journal of Occupational Medicine (1968) 688.

Exner, G., Moeglichkeiten und Grenzen der Manualmedizin (Chirotherapie), Deutsches Aerzteblatt 80 (1983) 44.

Eylau, O., Zur Aetiologie, Pathogenese und Therapie des Schulter-Arm-Syndroms, Med. Klin. (1956), 1951.

Faerber, D., Orthesen beim Kreuzschmerz aus der Sicht des niedergelassenen Orthopaeden, Orthop. Praxis 18 (1982) 236.

Fahlbusch-Wendler, C., Die Zulaessgikeit der staatlichen Forderung des Kinderhochleistungssportes in der Bundesrepublik Deutschland, Ahrensburg bei Hamburg: Czwalina, 1982 Sportwissenschaft und Sportpraxis, Bd. 44.

In addition, lecture on same topic: Herbsttagung des Konstanzer Arbeitskreises fuer Sportrecht.

Fahrner, W., Konstruktion des Schultisches, Jb. Kinderheilk. 6 (1963) 151.

Fairbank, J.C.T., O'Brien, J.P., Davis, P.R., Intraabdominal pressure—Rise during weight lifting as an objective measure of low-back pain, Spine 5 (1980) 179.

Falter, E., Hellerer, O., Hochleistungsturnen im Wachstumsalter, Morpho. Med. 2 (1982) 39.

Farfan, H.F., Mechanical disorders of the low back, Lea & Febiger, Philadelphia, 1973.

Farfan, H.F., Muscular mechanism of the lumbar spine and the position of power and efficiency, The Orthopedic Clinics of North America 6 (1975) 135.

Farfan, H.F., Biomechanische Probleme der Lendenwirbelsaeule, Die Wirbelsaeule in Forschung und Praxis, Hippokrates Verlag Stuttgart 80 (1979), Uebersetzung von H. Erdmann, Original Title: Mechanical disorders of the low back.

Farfan, H.F., The pathological anatomy of degenerative spondylolisthesis, Spine 5 (1980) 412.

Farfan, H.F., et al., The effects of torsion on the lumbar intervertebral joints: the role of torsion in the production of disc degeneration, Journal of Bone and Joint Surgery 52-A (1970) 468.

Farfan, H.F., et al., The mechanical etiology of spondylolysis and spondylolisthesis, Clin. Orthop. No. 117 (1976) 40.

Farfan, H.F., Huberdeau, R.M., Dobuw, J.H., Lumbar intervertebral disc degeneration, the influence of geometrical features on the pattern of disc degeneration, a post-mortem study, Journal of Bone and Joint Surgery 54-A (1972) 492.

Fassbender, H.G., Symposion "Therapie der rheumatoiden Arthritis," Berlin 1973.

Fassbender, H.G., Pathologie der Spondylitis ankylopoetica, Med. Welt 26 (1975) 2039.

Fassbender, H.G., Pathologie rheumatischer Erkrankungen, Therapiewoche 28 (1978) 8776.

Fassbender, H.G., Tierexperimentelle licht- und elektronenmikroskopische Untersuchungen ueber die Entstehung um den Charakter von Vibrationsschaeden, unpubl. research report, Mainz (1979).

Fast, J., Body language, M. Evans and Company, New York 1970.

Felbiger, J., Schulgebaeude auf dem Lande, Ch. G. Hilschern 1783.

Felten, H., Anordnung und Bedeutung der intraspinalen Rueckenmarkaufhaengung, Die Wirbelsaeule in Forschung und Praxis Hippokrates Verlag Stuttgart Bd. 5 (1958).

Felten, R., Zur medizinischen Bedeutung von Sport, Bewegung und koerperlicher Taetigkeit in unserer Umwelt heute, Ernaehrungs-Umschau 24 (1977) 17.

Fenollosa, J., Spondylites metitococciques, Rev. Chir. Orthop. 61 Suppl. 2 (1975) 214.

Ferguson, R.J., et al., Low back pain in college football linemen, Sports Medicine 2 (1974) 63.

Fernstroem, U., Der Bandscheibenersatz mit Erhaltung der Beweglichkeit, Die Wirbelsaeule in Forschung und Praxis 55 (1972) 125, Hippokrates Verlag Stuttgart.

Fessler, W., Die Bedeutung der nichtberuflichen Erkrankungen am Arbeitsplatz, Arbeitsmedizin, Sozialmedizin, Praeventivmedizin 12 (1976) 254.

Fick, R., Handbuch der Anatomie und Mechanik der Gelenke unter Beruecksichtigung der bewegenden Muskeln, Fischer Jena 1911.

Fiedler, J., Volleyball, Sportverlag DDR Berlin (1975).

Fielding, J.W., et al., Anterior cervical vertebral body resection and bone-grafting for benign and malignant, The Journal of Bone and Joint Surgery 61 A (1979) 251.

Figar, S., et al., Vazomotoricke reakce pri akupunkture u. lumbosakralnick syndromu, Zs Neurol 27 (1964) 251.

Finkbeiner, G.F., Thiel, K., Krankengymnastik in der Rehabilitation Bandscheibenoperierter, Rehabil. 19 (1980) 13.

Fischer, H., Traumatologie der Wirbelsaeule und ihre Behandlung, Die Wirbelsaeule in Forschung und Praxis Bd. 57 (1973) 13.

Fischer, H., Spaetschaeden nach Atombombendetonationen und Strahlenunfaellen, Munich med. Wschr. 117 (1975) 1983.

Fischer, H., Sport und Wirbelsaeule, (Literaturuebersicht), Die Wirbelsaeule in Forschung und Praxis Hippokrates Stuttgart 65 (1976) 10.

Fischer, K.P., Wirbelsaeulenganzaufnahme und Statik, Die Wirbelsaeule in Forschung und Praxis, Hippokrates Verlag Stuttgart 28 (1964) 52.

Fischer, V., et al., Vibrationsbedingte Wirbelsaeulenschaeden bei Hubschrauberpiloten, Arbeitsmedizin, Sozialmedizin, Praeventivmedizin 15 (1980) 161.

Floeel, H., Der psuedoanginoese Herzschmerz im Rahmen des kostovertebralen Syndroms, anatomische Gegebenheiten, Z. Allg. Medizin 56 (1980) 15.

Floyd, W.F., Ward, J.S., Posture of schoolchildren and office workers, Ergonomics, Proc. 2nd I.E.A., Congress Dortmund (1964) 351.

Floyd, W.F., Ward, J.S., Anthropometric and physiological considerations in school, office and factory seating, Proc. Symp. "Sitting Posture," London 1969, 18, Taylor & Francis.

Fochem, K., Klumair, J., Zur Problematik der Wirbelkoerperdarstellung im Computertomogramm, Roentgen-Bl. 32 (1979) 533.

Foehr, R., Mayer, R., Vogt, J.J., Minderung der Arbeitsbelastung der Buendler von Feinblechen, Z. Arbeitswiss. 29 (1975) 41.

Ford, L.T., Postoperative infection of lumbar intervertebral disk space, Southern Medical Journal 69 (1976) 1477.

Forgacs, S., Knochenveraenderungen bei Diabetikern, Med. Klin. 69 (1974) 1971.

Frank, D., Ein Beitrag zu geroarbeitshygienischen Fragen bei Hitzearbeitern, J. Aerztl. Fort. (Jena) 64 (1970) 1119.

Frank, P., Gleeson, J.A., Radiology now, destructive vertebral lesions in ankylosing spondylitis, British Radiology 48 (1975) 755.

Franke, D., Fenn, K., Hennig, K., Die gezielte Wirbelbiopsie, Chir. Praxis (1978) 385.

Franke, K., Typische Sportschaeden und Sportverletzungen, Ztschr. Unfallmedizin und Berufskrankh. 67 (1974) 176.

Franke, K., Traumatologie des Sportes, Verlag Volk und Gesundheit, DDR Berlin (1977).

Franke, K., Gesundheitstraining-eine form der "Selbstbeteiligung," Dtsch. Aerzteblatt Vol. 44 (1980) 2631.

Freyer, H.U., Der Gesundheitszustand unserer Schuljugend (Zschr. Nordmark, 1979).

Friberg, L., Vergiftungen durch Kadmium, Handbuch d. ges. Arbeitsmedizin Bd. II, S. 218, Urban und Schwarzenberg, Berlin (1960).

Friedrich, F., Spaetschaeden am Bewegungsapparat durch Skilaufen, Materia Medica Nordmark 21 (1969) 651.

Frisch, H., Chirodiagnostik, Die Wirbelsaeule in Forschung und Praxis, Hippokrates Verlag Stuttgart 83 (1979) 21.

Frisch, H., Programmierte Untersuchung des Bewegungsapparates-Chirodiagnostik-Springer Verlag Berlin (1983).

Frisch, H., Programmierte Untersuchung des Bewegungsapparates, Springer Verlag, Heidelberg (1983).

Fritze, E., Lungenveraenderungen bei rheumatoider Arthritis, Dtsch. med. Wschr. 99 (1974) 19.

Fritze, E., Gundel, E., Reisch, A., et al., Zur Bedeutung in der Berufsarbeit gelegener Einfluesse fuer Aetiologie und Pathogenese entzuendlich-rheumatischer Krankheiten, Arbeitsmed., Sozialmed., Praeventivmen. 6 (1971) 197.

Froehlich, E., Manual-medizinische Aspekte der Wirbelsaeule bei Belastung durch Training und Wettkampf in Sport- und Leistungsmed. Hrsg. Kindermann und Hort, Demeter Verlag, Graefefing 1980.

Fuermaier, A., Die Begutachtung und Beurteilung der degenerativen Wirbelsaeulenerkrankunge vor allem im Rahmen der Sozialversicherung, Med. Mschr. 8 (1954) 274.

Funk, J., Wells, R., Injuries of the cervical spine in football, Clinical Orthopaedics and Related Research 109 (1975) 50.

Gaizler, G., Madarasz, J., Funktionelle Roentgendiagnostik der Halswirbelsaeule, Manuelle Medizin 17 (1979) 82.

Gamper, U., Vogt, H., Haltungsstoerungen bei Schulkindern, Krankengymnastik 30 (1978) 142.

Ganssen, A., Ruesch, D., Die Erkennung von Wirbelsaeulenleiden mittels Thermographie, Die Wirbelsaeule in Forschung und Praxis, Hippokrates Verlag Stuttgart 55 (1972) 75.

Garbe, J., Einfluesse von Beschleunigungen auf den Menschen, Aerztl, Dienst (DB) 36 (1975) 96.

Gargano, F.P., Transverse axial tomography of the spine, Crc. Crit. Rev. Clin. Radio. Nucl. Med. 8 (1976) 279.

Gauer, O.H., Henry, J.P., Behn, C., The regulation of extracellular fluid volume, Annual Review of Physiology 32 (1970) 547.

Gehweiler, J.A., et al., Spondylolisthesis of the axis vertebra, American Journal of Roentgenology 128 (1977) 682.

Geiger, T., Herz und Wirbelsaeule, Z. Allg. Med. 55 (1979) 1955.

Gelabert, H., Anatomy for the dancers with exercises to improve technique and prevent injuries, as told to W. Como, Dance Magazine, New York 36 NY 268 West 47th Street (1964).

Gelehrter, G., Umwandlung der Nukleographie durch Ausweitung der Untersuchungsmethodik, Zschr. Roentgenstr. 122 (1975) 517.

Genadinnik, I.S., Dumkina, G.Z., Schaedigung der Wirbelkoerper bei Caisson-Krankheit, Gig. truda prof. Zabol. 13 (1969) 55.

Genadinnik, I.S., Dumkina, G.Z., Schaedigung der Wirbelkoerper bei Caisson-Krankheit, Gig. truda prof. Zabol. 13 (1969) 55.

Gerbershagen, H.U., Der diagnostisch reproduzierund koupierbare spondylogene Schmerz, Die Wirbelsaeule in Forschung und Praxis, Hippokrates Verlag Stuttgart 83 (1979) 225.

Gerner, J.H., Funktionelle Anatomie der Wirbelsaeule, Bericht Unfallmed. Tagung Mainz Nov. 36 (1978) 143.

Gertzbein, S.D., Degenerative disk disease of the lumbar spine, Clinical Orthopedics 129 (1977) 68.

Gertzbein, S.D., Tait, J.H., Devlin, S.R., The stimulation of lymphocytes by nucleus pulposus in patients with degenerative disk disease of the lumbar spine, Clinical Orthopaedics 123 (1977) 149.

Getty, C.J.M., et al., Partial undercutting facetectomy for bony entrapment of the lumbar nerve root, British Editorial Soc. Journal of Bone and Joint Surgery 330 (1981).

Ghosh, P., et al., Distribution of glycosaminoglycans across the normal and the scoliotic disc, Spine 5 (1980) 310.

Gierke, H.E. von, Biodynamic models and their application, Journal of Account. Soc. Am. 50 (1971) 1397.

Gilsbach, J., et al., Vor- und Nachteile der vorderen zervikalen Bandscheibenoperation ohne Verblokkung, Z. Orthop. 119 (1981) 600.

Gingras, G., Warren, J., Die posttraumatische Rehabilitation, Folia traumatologica Geigy 1971.

Glenn, W.W., et al., Multiplaner display computerized body tomography applications in the lumbar spine, Spine, 4 (1979) 282.

Glick, E.N., Hyperostotische Spondylosis, Internat. Kongress, Physik. Med. Barcelona (1972) 17.

Glick, J.M., Katch, V.L., Musculoskeletal injuries in jogging, Arch. Phys. Med. 51 (1970) 123.

Gluecksmann, J., et al., Morphological lesions and functional aberrations of the vertebral column and on the hands in members of the Czech philharmonic orchestras, Divadelni Ustav Prague (1973).

Gluecksmann, J., et al., Klinicko-rentgenologicke zmeny pohyboveho ustroji u baletnino souboru (Clinical-radiographical changes at the locomotor system in ballet) Acta chir. orthop. traumat. boh. 24 (1957) 312.

Gluecksmann, J., Streda, A., Zmeny kloubni a slachove u orchestralnich hracu (Veraenderungen von Gelenken und Baendern bei Orchestermusikern), Pyakt. lek. 2 (1953) 23.

Goald, H.J., Herniated lumbar disc treated by a new surgical procedure, Advances in Pain Research and Therapy, 3 (1979) 719.

Godt, P., Vogelsang, H., Seltene Verletzungen beim Budosport, Unfallheilkunde 82 (1979) 215.

Goecke, C., Das Verhalten spongioesen Knochens im Druck- und Schlagversuch, Verh. dtsch. Orthop. Ges. 20 (1925).

Goecke, C., Beitraege zur Druckfestigung des spongioesen Knochens, Bruns Beitr. klin. Chir. 143 (1938) 539.

Geothe, H., Der Einfluss von Kinetosen auf die Leistungsfaehigkeit, In: Mensch und Schiff, III. Marinemed.-scient. symposium in Kiel, Schiffahrtmed. Inst. d. Marine im Auftr. d. Inspektion des Marinesanitaetsdienstes Kiel, Schmidt & Klannig, Kiel (1972).

Goethe, H., Kinetosen, in Hdb. d. Ergonomie, Ed. H. Schmidtke, Luftfahrt Verlag (1976).

Goethe, H., Kinetosen-Reisekrankheiten, In: Innere Med. in Praxis und Klinik, Hrsg. H. Hornbostel et al., 2. Aufl. Bd. 3 Thieme, Stuttgart (1977) S. 14–39.

Goethe, H., et al., Untersuchungen zum Problem niederfrequenter mechanischer Schwingungen und deren Auswirkung auf den Menschen an Bord von Schiffen, 1. und 2. research report of the Bernhard-Nocht Institute for nautical and tropic diseases, Abt. Schiffahrtsmedizin, Hamburg (1978 and 1979).

Goethe, H., Fischer, G., Ueberlegungen zur Erfassung der physikalischen Groessen, die zur Entstehung der Seekinetose fuehren, Zbl. Verk. Med. 3 (1957) 148.

Goetze, H.G., Rompe, G., Empfehlungen zur gutachtlichen Bewertung von Personen mit Skoliosen, Z. Orthop. 115 (1977) 239.

Geotze, H.G., et al., Indikation und Technik der ventralen Aufrichtungsosteotomie bei Morbus Scheuermann, Die Wirbelsaeule in Forschung und Praxis, Hippokrates Verlag Stuttgart 89 (1980) 111.

Gottwald, A., Reittherapie bei skoliotischer Haltung und Osteochondrosis deformans juvenilis (Scheuermann). In: Baumann, J.U., Therapie auf dem Pferderecken, Helyas Verlag, Beromuenster (1978) 106.

Gottwald, A., Bewegungsablaeufe beim Reiter unter besonderer Beruecksichtigung der Wirbelsaeulenbewegung, Deutsche Zeitschr. Sportmedizin 31 (1980) 172.

Gottwald, A., Biewald, N., Bewegungsablaeufe geuebter, ungeuebter und wirbelsaeulegeschaedigter Reiter, Kongressband Dt. Sportaerztekongr. 1980 Hrsg. Kindermann und Hort, Demeter Verlag Graefelfing (1980).

Goutallier, D., Chirurgie der lumbosakralen Spondylolisthesis mit erheblichen Wirbelverschiebungen, Rev. Rhum. Mal. Osteo-AA. 44 (1977) 231.

Goymann, V., Konermann, H., Nachbarschaftsreaktionen nach spontanen und operativen Versteifungen und Lockerungen, 11. Arbeitstagung der Gesellschaft f. Wirbelsaeulenforschung 1979: Die Wirbelsaeule in Forschung und Praxis, Hippokrates Verlag Stuttgart 87 (1981) 129.

Grabias, S., Current concepts review, the treatment of spinal stenosis, Journal of Bone and Joint Surgery 62-A (1980) 308.

Grandjean, E., Physiologische Arbeitsgestaltung, Leitfaden der Ergonomie, Oct. Thun and Munich, 2. Aufl. (1967).

Grandjean, E., (Herausgeber) Sitting posture, Sitzhaltung, Posture assise, Taylor & Francis, London (1969).

Grandjean, E., Boeni, A., Kretzschmar, H., The development of a rest chair profile for healthy and nostalgic people, Ergonomics 12 (1969) 307.

Grandjean, E., Burandt, U., Die physiologische Gestaltung von Ruhesesseln, Bauen und Wohnen (1964) 233.

Grandjean, E., Huenting, W., Ergonomics of posture—review of various problems of standing and sitting posture, Applied Ergonomics 8 (1977) 135.

Grandjean, E., Huenting, W., Sitzen Sie richtig? Bayerisches Staatsministerium fuer Arbeit und Sozialordnung, Reg. Nr. 10/77/12, Munich (1978).

Grassl, E., Mehr und bessere Kinderspielplaetze in der Bundesrepublik schaffen, Deutsches Aerztebl. (1981) 354.

Graul, E.H., Mikroelektronik und Computer revolutionieren die Technik bildgebender Verfahren in der Medizin. Dtsch. Aerztebl. 79 (1982) 40.

Grebe, H., Aerztliche Verantwortung beim Boxsport Deutsches Aerzteblatt 80 (1983) 455.

Grebe, S.F., Szintigraphie im Bereich der Wirbelsaeule, Die Wirbelsaeule in Forschung und Praxis, Hippokrates Verlag Stuttgart 55 (1972) 48.

Gregersen, G.G., Lucas, D.B., An in vivo study of axial rotation of the human thoracolumbar spine, J. Bone Joint Surg. 49-A (1967) 247.

Grew, N.D., Intraabdominal pressure-response to loads applied to the torso in normal subjects, Spine 5 (1980) 149.

Grewe, H., Vergleichende Untersuchungen ueber die Wirkung der gezielten Novocainblokade des Grenzstranges mit der Ausschaltung der sympathy. Nervenendigungen der Sympathicolytika Zbl. Chir. (1955) 1428.

Griss, J., Pfeil, Ergebnisse rein dorsaler und kombiniert ventraldorsaler Aufrichtungsoperationen bei der juvenilen Kyphose, Eine vergleichende Untersuchung am eigenen Krankengut, Z. Orthop. 121 (1983) 369.

Griss, P., Der Rueckenschmerz des Jugendlichen, Orthop. Praxis H. 4 (1979) 260.

Griss, P., Ergebnisse dorsaler Aufrichtungsoperationen bei juvenilen Kyphosen, Die Wirbelsaeule in Forschung und Praxis, Hippokrates Verlag Stuttgart 89 (1980) 117.

Gritz, H.A., Die physiologischen Laengenaenderungen der menschlichen Wirbelsaeule im Verlaufe eines Tages sowie der Einfluss von Be- und Entlastung auf den Intervertebralabschnitt, Diss. 1975 Med. Fak. Dusseldorf.

Grmek, M.D., Die Wirbelsaeule im Zeitgeschehen, Manuelle Medizin 17 (1979) 69, Med. Welt 25 NF (1974) 70.

Grobler, L.J., Simmons, E.H., Barrington, T.W., Intervertebral disc herniation in the adolescent, Spine 4 (1979) 267.

Grobovschek, M., Fischbach, R., Enger zervikaler Wirbelkanal als Ursache chronischer Schulter-Armschmerzen, Fortschr. Roentgenstr. 131 (1979) 332.

Groeneveld, H.B., Die Scheuermann-Kyphose, Bedeutung fuer den Schulsport, Die Wirbelsaeule in Forschung und Praxis, Hippokrates Verlag Stuttgart 60 (1976) 67.

Groeneveld, H.B., Metrische Erfassung und Definition von Rueckenform und Haltung des Menschen, Die Wirbelsaeule in Forschung und Praxis, Hippokrates Verlag Stuttgart 66 (1976).

Groeneveld, H.B., Wert und Unwert der Orthesenbehandlung beim Morbus Scheuermann, Die Wirbelsaeule in Forschung und Praxis, Hippokrates Verlag Stuttgart 89 (1980) 77.

Groh, H., Boxsport und Arzt, in: Sportmedizin, Hrsg.: Groh Ferdinand Enke Verlag Stuttgart (1962).

Groh, H., Sportmedizin, biologische und medizinische Grundlagen der Leibesuebungen, Enke, Stuttgart (1962).

Groh, H., Sportschaeden am Bewegungsapparat, Med. Welt 41 (1964) 2185.

Groh, H., Wirbelsaeulenschaeden beim Leistungssport, Sportarzt 21 (1971) 221.

Groh, H., Leistungssport und Wirbelsaeule, Selecta 4 (1972) 324.

Groh, H., Sportschaeden am Bewegungspparat insbes. an der Wirbelsaeule, Munich Med. Wschr. 114 (1972) 1377.

Groh, H., Zur Biomechanik von Koerperuebungen, Zschr. Orthop. 110 (1972) 823.

Groh, H., Groh, P., Sportverletzungen und Sportschaeden, Luitpold-Werk Munich (1975).

Groher, W., Kreuzschmerzen und Wirbelsaeulenveraenderungen bei Kunst- und Turmspringern, Sportarzt, Sportmedizin 11 (1969) 444.

Groher, W., Muskulaere und knoecherne Veraenderungen im Bereich der Wirbelsaeule beim Kunstund Turmspringen, Westfaelisches Aerzteblatt 24 (1970) 1296.

Groher, W., Belastung kindlicher und jugendlicher Lendenwirbelsaeulen beim Sport (Turnen, Kunstspringen, Trampolinspringen), 24, Sportaerztekongress, Wurzburg 14.10., 17.10. (1971).

Groher, W., Spondylolyse und Spondylolisthesis als erworbener Spaetzustand nach staendig einwirkenden Microtraumen bei Sportlern, Habilitationsschrift Berlin (1974).

Groher, W., Sportmedizin aus orthopaedisch-chirurgischer Sicht, Hefte Unfallheilk. 117 (1974) 166.

Groher, W., Auswirkungen des Hochleistungssportes auf die Lendenwirbelsaeule, Wiss., Publications of the German Sport Association 12 (1975) Verlag Hofmann Schorndorf.

Groher, W., Ueberbeweglichkeit als Auslesefaktor im Sport, Leistungssport 9 (1979) 244.

Groher, W., Sport im Rahmen der Vorsorge orthopaedischer Erkrankungen, Der Kassenarzt 20 (1980) 850.

Groher, W., et al., Welche Einschraenkungen erfordert das Scheuermann-Syndrom im Hochleistungssport sowie Schul- und Breitensport, in: Sportverletzungen und Sportschaden, Hrsg. G. Chapchal Georg Thieme Verlag, Stuttgart (1983).

Groher, W., Heidensohn, P., Rueckenschmerzen und roentgenologische Veraenderungen bei Wasserspringern, Z. Orthop. Grenzgeb. 108 (1970) 51.

Groher, W., Noack, W., Spaetschaeden durch Leistungssport, Medizin 5 (1977) 2013.

Gross, D., Sympathalgien des Nacken-Schulter-Arm-Bereiches, Munich Med. Wschr. 121 (1979) 1167.

Grube, M.R., Mueller, R., Untersuchungen ueber die Laermbelaestigung beim Gewichthebertraining, Medizin und Sport DDR 113 (1973) 281.

Gruenewald, B., "Sport" als Praevention: Ist Bewegungsmangel als Risikofaktor gesichert? Therapiewoche 30 (1980) 5205.

Gruschka, G., Wirbelsaeule und Scheuermann-Kyphose-Bedeutung fuer die Bundeswehr, Die Wirbelsaeule in Forschung und Praxis, Hippokrates Verlag Stuttgart 60 (1976) 79.

Gschwend, N., Die Bedeutung der Scheuermannschen Krankheit, Med. und Hyg. 23 (1965) 612.

Gschwend, N., Sitzschaeden der Wirbelsaeule, Z. Praeventivmedizin 10 (1965) 106.

Gschwend, N., Schulgestuehl und Haltungsschaeden, Z. Praeventivmedizin 14 (1969) 187.

Gschwend, N., Die Bedeutung des Vorzustandes als Ursache von Kreuzschmerzen, Orthopaedie 1 (1972) 141.

Gschwend, N., Die degenerativen Erkrankungen der Wirbelsaeule: Klinische Bedeutung, Ursachen. Therapie, Therapeut. Umschau, Revue Therapeutique 35 (1978) 165.

Gschwend, N., Persoenliche Mitteilung 1978. "Schularbeiten in Bauchlage," "Pausengymnastik."

Gschwend, N., Der Patient und sein Kreuz, Man. Med. 21 (1983) 114.

Gschwend, N., Scherer, M., Munzinger, U., Entzuendliche Veraenderungen der Wirbelsaeule bei der chronischen Polyarthritis, Orthopaede 10 (1981) 155.

Gubser, A., Wirbelsaeulenfrakturer: Entstehung-Erkunnung-Beurteilung, Die Wirbelsaeule in Forschung und Praxis, Hippokrates Verlag Stuttgart 68 (1976) 19.

Guenther, H., Fuetterungsversuche mit Flugstaub einer Metallhuette an Pferden und einem Schaf, Dissertation, Tieraerztl. Hochschule, Hannover (1954).

Guentz, E., Beitrag zur pathologischen Anatomie der Spondylarthritis ankylopoetica, Fortschr. Roentgenstr. 47 (1933) 683.

Guentz, E., Die Kyphose im Jugendalter, Die Wirbelsaeule in Forschung und Praxis, Hippokrates Verlag Stuttgart 2 (1957).

Guentz, E., Die Kyphosen, ihre klinischen Erscheinungen und therapeutischen Gesichtspunkte, Die Wirbelsaeule in Forschung und Praxis, Hippokrates Verlag Stuttgart 5 (1965).

Gueth, V., Elektromyographie bei Wirbelsaeulenerkrankungen, Die Wirbelsaeule in Forschung und Praxis, Hippokrates Verlag Stuttgart 83 (1979) 31.

Gueth, V., Abbink, F., Vergleichende elektromyographische und kinesiologische Untersuchungen and kongenitalen und idiopathischen Skoliosen, Z. Orthop. 118 (1980) 165.

Guillaume, L., Die Gesundheitspflege in den Schulen, Christen, Aarau 3. Aufl. (1865).

Gutmann, G., Schulkopfschmerz und Kopfhaltung, Zschr. Orthop. 105 (1968) 497.

Gutmann, G., Spezielle Roentgendiagnose zur Chirotherapie, Orthop. Praxis 6 (1970) 43.

Gutmann, G., Chirotherapie-Grundlagen, Indikationen, Gegenindikationen und Objektivierbarkeit, Med. Welt 29 (1978) 653.

Gutmann, G., Das ligamentaere Schmerzsyndrom-Grenzen seiner krankengymnastischen Behandlung, Krankengymnastik 32 (1980) 261.

Gutmann, G., Manuelle Medizin und Roentgendiagnostik, Manuelle Medizin 18 (1980) 26.

Gutmann, G., Funktionelle Pathologie und Klinik der Wirbelsaeule, Band 1 Die Halswirbelsaeule, Gustav Fischer Verlag Stuttgart-New York (1981).

Gutmann, G., et al., Arteria vertebralis/Traumatologie und funktionelle Pathologie, Springer-Verlag Berlin (1985).

Gutmann, G., Biedermann, H., Sklerosierungstherapie im Bereich der Wirbelsaeule, Die Wirbelsaeule in Forschung und Praxis, Hippokrates Verlag Stuttgart 87 (1981) 167.

Gutmann, G., Vele, F., Das aufrechte Stehen, Forschungsber. d. Landes Nordrhein-Westf. Nr. 2796, Westdtsch. Verlag Opladen (1978).

Gutmann, G., Wolff, H.D., Die Wirbelsaeulenschaeden als volkswirtschaftlicher Faktor, Hippokrates Verlag 30 (1950) 207.

Gutzeit, K., Anamnese und Klinik der vertebragenen Erkrankungen, Die Wirbelsaeule in Forschung und Praxis, Hippokrates Verlag Stuttgart 1 (1956) 482.

Gutzeit, K., Der vertebrale Faktor im Krankheitsgeschehen, Die Wirbelsaeule in Forschung und Praxis, Hippokrates Verlag Stuttgart 1 (1956) 22.

Gutzeit, K., Der vertebrale Faktor im Krankheitsgeschehen (Nachdruck), Manuelle Medizin 19 (1981) 66.

Hacohen H., Bandscheiben-Aufloeser: kein Ersatz fuer Operation, Aerztl. Prax. 33 (1981) 2589.

Hacohen, H., Ueber Chemonuklcolyse als ergaenzende Diskushernienbehandlung, Ther. Umschau 39 (1982) 22.

Haefner, H., Basketball, in: Sporttraumatologie, Hrsg.: Pfoerringer et al., Perimed Verlag Erlangen (1982).

Haeublein, H.G., Belastbarkeit und Spaetreaktionen in der Arbeitsmedizin, Die Wirbelsaeule in Forschung und Praxis, Hippokrates Verlag Stuttgart 87 (1981) 77.

Haeublein, H.G., Braeunlich, A., Weitere Ergebnisse aus Vorsorgeuntersuchungen im Berliner Bauwesen, Z. ges. Hyg. 17 (1971) 361.

Haffner, S., Wenn der Spitzensport zum Spritzensport wird, Frankfurter Allgemeine am 5.7.85 S.3.

Hajkova, Z., Streda, A., Skrha, F., Spondylosis kyperostotica und Diabetes mellitus, Ann. Rheumat. Diseases 24 (1965) 536.

Hall, G., Seltene und problematische berufsbedingte Zoonosen, Arbeitsschutz, Arbeitsmedizin 13th Kongress (1973) 529.

Hall, G., Zoonosen als Berufskrankheiten, Homburg-Inf. Werksarzt 21 (1974) 122.

Hallermann, W., Die Ostitis derformans Paget der Wirbelsaeule, Fortschr. Roentgenstr. 40 (1929) 999.

Hamerman, D., Rosenberg, L.C., Diarthrodial joints revisited, Journal of Bone and Joint Surgery 52-A (1970) 725.

Hansson, T., Roos, B., Nachemson, A., The bone mineral content and ultimate compressive strength of lumbar vertebrae, Spine 5 (1980) 46.

Harms, J., Rolinger, H., Die operative Behandlung der Spondylolisthese durch dorsale Aufrichtung und vertrale Verblockung, Z. Orthop. 120 (1982) 343.

Harrelson, J.M., Hills, B.A., Changes in bone marrow pressure in response to hyperbaric exposure, Aerospace Medicine 41 (1970) 1018.

Harris, P., Cervical spine stenosis, Paraplegia 15 (1977/78) 125.

Harrington, P.R., Treatment of scoliosis, correction and internal fixation by spine instrumentation, Journal of Bone and Joint Surgery 44-A (1962) 291, Zit. nach Hirsch C. and Waugh, T., The introduction of force measurements guiding instrumental correction of scoliosis, Acta orthop. scand. 39 (1968) 136.

Harrington, P.R., The etiology of idiopathic scoliosis, Clin. Orthop. No. 126 (1977) 17.

Hartenberg, V., Der Einfluss der Absatzhoehe auf Wirbelsaeule und Becken (Entgegnung zu Weiss), Z. Kr. Gym. 30 (1978) 262.

Hartung, C., Anna, O., Biomechanische Eigenschaften weicher Gewebe, Die Wirbelsaeule in Forschung und Praxis, Hippokrates Verlag Stuttgart 68 (1976) 87.

Hartung, K., Zur Frage der Haeufigkeit von Haltungsfehlern und Fusschaeden bei Berufsschuelern, Zbl. Chir. 90 (1965) 867.

Harvey, A.M., McKusick, V.A., Osler's Textbook Revisited, Meredith Publ. Co., New York (1967) 158.

Hatt, M.U., Hoehenlokalisation der cervikalen Diskushernie in Klinik, Elektromyographie und Myelographie, Dtsch. Z. Nervenheilk. 197 (1979) 56.

Hattori, S., et al., Cervical intradiscal pressure in movements and traction of the cervical spine, Z. Orthop. 119 (1981) 568.

Havelka, S., Neuere Erkenntnisse ueber die Aetiopathogenese der Altersosteoporose, Orthop. und Traumatol. 22 (1975) 583.

Hawkes, C.H., Roberts, G.M., Lumbar canal stenosis, British Journal of Hospital Medicine (1980) 498.

Heath, B.H., Carter, J.E.L., Growth and somatotype patterns of Manuas children, territory of Papua and New Guinea: application of a modified somatotype method to the study of growth patterns, American Journal of Physical Anthropology 35 (1971) 49.

Heide, M., Das Zervikalsyndrom und physiokotherapeutische Moeglichkeiten, Die Heilkunst 81 (1968) 184.

Heide, M., Zur Differenzierung des Zervikalsyndroms, Allg. Therapeutik 8 (1968) 423.

Heide, M., Praekardiale Beschwerden haeutig Teil der Schmerzsymptomatik eines Irritationszustandes im Zervikalbereich, Phys. Med. und Rehab. 13 (1972) 6.

Heide, M., Praekordialbeschwerden koennen vertebragen sein, Aerztl. Prax. 31 (1979) 3093.

Heide, M., Rueckenschmerrzen ueberwinden, Hippokrates Verlag Stuttgart (1983).

Heide, R., Zur Wirkung langzeitiger berutlicher Ganzkoerpervibrationsexposition, Diss. Zentralinst. fuer Arbeitsmed. d. DDR Berlin (1978) 151.

Heide, R., Seidel, H., Folgen langzeitiger berutlicher Ganzkoerpervibrationsexposition, Z. ges. Hyg. und Grenzgeb. 24 (1978) 153.

Heindel, W., Huck, W., Gewebsdifferenzierung im Bereich des zentralen Nervensystems mit der Kernspintomographie: erste klinische Erfahrungen, electomedica 51 (1983) 2.

Heine, J., Spondylarthrose bei Kyphosen und Skoliose, Die Wirbelsaeule in Forschung und Praxis, Hippokrates Verlag Stuttgart 87 (1981) 91.

Heine, J., et al., Die Prognose der Scheuermannschen Erkrankung, Z. Orthop. 119 (1981) 812.

Heine, J., Rodegerdts, U., Histologische Untersuchungen der kleinen Wirbelgelenke bei Patienten mit Lumbalskoliose, Z. Orthop. 117 (1979) 600.

Heipertz, W., Die Rolle des Bewegungsapparates im Sport, Oeffentl. Gesundh.-Wesen 35 (1973) 675.

Heipertz, W., Turnen, Schulsportbefreiung und Schulsonderturnen bei Skoliose, Z. Orthop. 114 (1976) 470.

Heipertz, W., Therapeutisches Reiten, Sport, Franckhsche Verlagsbuchhandlung, Stuttgart (1977).

Heipertz-Hengst, C., Reitsport fuer Behinderte, Sporttherapeutische Praxis 6 (1980) Verlag Schmidt-Roemhild, Luebeck.

Helbing, R., Das Iliosakralgelenk nach Hueftarthrodese, Z. Orthop. 116 (1978) 113.

Hellinger, J., et al., Wirbelsaeulenstabilisation bei Spondylitis mit der Harrington-Instrumentation, Zbl. Chirurgie 107 (1982) 885.

Hellner, H., Allgemeine Krankheiten der Knochen, In Klinische Chirurgie fuer die Praxis, IV (1961) Thieme Stuttgart.

Hellstadius, A., Some cases of paradiscal defects, Acta Orthop. Scand. 18 (1949) 377.

Henderson, R.J., Hill, D.M., Vickers, A.A.M., et al., Brucellosis and veterinary surgeons, British Medical Journal 5972 (1975) II 656.

Henschel, A., Effects of age on work capacity, American Industrial Hygiene Association Journal 31 (1970) 430.

Henssge, J., Liegeschale und Korsett bei der Adoleszentenkyphose pathogenetisch begruendete Behandlungsverfahren? Die Wirbelsaeule in Forschung und Praxis, Hippokrates Verlag Stuttgart 89 (1980) 75.

Herman, G.T., Coin, C.G., The use of three-dimensional computer display in the study of disk disease, Journal of Computer Assisted Tomography 4 (1980) 564.

Hermann, A., Ueber die Einrichtung zweckmaessiger Schultische, Brauschweig, Hotbuchhandlg. Leibrock 1868.

Hermann, H., Gesundheitliche Probleme bei Jugendlichen waehrend der Ausbildungszeit, Homburg Informationen fuer d. Werksarzt 21 (1974) 188.

Hermann, H., Goethe, H., Vibrationen an Bord unter dem Gesichtspunkt der Einwirkung auf den Menschen, Schiff & Hafen 27 (1975) 126.

Hess, H., Anpassungsvorgaenge am Haltungs- und Bewegungsapparat und ihre Grenzen, in Sportmedizin fuer Breiten- und Leistungssport, Hrsg. Kindermann und Hort Demeter Verlag Graefelfing (1980).

Hess, R., Die Mitwirkung von Aerzten bei der Einleitung von Rehabilitationsmassnahmen nach dem Rehabilitationsangleichungsgesetz, Z. Allgemeinmed. 53 (1977) 208.

Hesse, H., Ist das klassische Ballett eine Haltungsschulung? Diss. Med. Fakultaet Dusseldorf (1972).

Hesse, H., Anpassungsvorgaenge am Haltungs- und Bewegungsapparat und ihre Grenzen, in Sportmedizin fuer Breiten- und Leistungssport, Hrsg. W. Kindermann, W. Hort Demeter Verlag Graefelfing (1980).

Hettinger, T., Verhuetung von Schaeden durch Heben und Tragen von Lasten, Die Berufsgenossenschaft 36 (1984) 96.

Heuck, F., Die radiologische Erfassung des Mineralgehaltes des Knochens, Handbuch Med. Mineralogie IV/1, Springer, Berlin-Heidelberg-New York (1970).

Heuck, F., Morphologische und biochemische Untersuchungen ueber den normalen Alterungsprozess der Wirbelkoerper, Die Wirbelsaeule in Forschung und Praxis, Hippokrates Verlag Stuttgart 60 (1976) 7.

Hickey, D.S., Hukins, D.W.L., Relation between the structure of the annulus fibrosus and the function and failure of the intervertebral disc, Spine 5 (1980) 106.

Hickey, R.F.J., Tregonning, G.D., Denervation of spinal facet joints for treatment of chronic low back pain, New Zealand Medical Journal 85 (1977) 96.

Hierholzer, E., Der Display-Stereokomparator, ein neues Geraet zur Auswertung von Stereo-Roentgenaufnahmen, Interner Bericht-SFB 88/CI Nr. 10, Arb. Gruppe Biomechanik Muenster, Juni (1977).

Hierholzer, E., Die Rekonstruktion der raeumlichen Form der Wirbelsaeule aus Stereo-Roentgenaufnahmen, Fortschr. Roentgenstr. 126 (1977) 22.

Hildebrandt, J., Argyrakis, A., Die perkutane zervikale Facettdenervation-ein neues Verfahren zur Behandlung chronischer Nacken-Kopfschmerzen, Manuelle Medizin 21 (1983) 45.

Hinz, P., Die Verletzungen der Halswirbelsaeule durch Schleuderung und durch Abknickung, Die Wirbelsaeule in Forschung und Praxis, Hippokrates Verlag Stuttgart 47 (1970).

Hinz, P., Normen der Tragfaehigkeit, Belastungsfaehigkeit und Beweglichkeit der Brust- und Lendenwirbelsaeule, Hefte zur Unfallheilk, 129 (1977) 287.

Hinz, P., Die koerperliche Untersuchung der Wirbelsaeule im Rahmen der Begutachtung, Schriftenreihe Unfallmed. Tagungen, Landesverbd. d. Gewerbl. Berufsgen. 36 (1979) 273.

Hinz, P., Erdmann, H., Zur manuellen Untersuchung der Halswirbelsaeule in der Gutachterpraxis, Zschr. Orthop. 104 (1968) 28.

Hipp, E., Hackenbruch, W., Funktionelle Roentgendiagnostik der Wirbelsaeule, Die Wirbelsaeule in Forschung und Praxis, Hippokrates Verlag Stuttgart 83 (1979) 61.

Hirsch, C., et al., Biophysical and physiological investigations on cartilage and other mesenchymal tissues: VI characteristics of human nuclei pulposi during aging, Acta Orthop. Scand. 22 (1952) 175.

Hirsch, C., Ingelmark, B., Miller, M., The anatomical basis for the low back pain, Acta Orthop. Scand. 33 (1963) 1.

Hirsch, C., Lewin, T., Lumbosacral synovial joints in flexion-extension, Acta Orthop. Scand. 39 (1968) 303.

Hochheim, W., Lehrlingsjahre und Fruehschaeden am Bewegungsapparat, Schrift. Zentralverb. d. Aerzte fuer Naturheilverfahren 8 (1962) 24.

Hoefling, G., Schlechte Haltung beim Schreiben (Ursache und ihre Beseitigung), Hippokrates Verlag Stuttgart (1972).

Hoelzl, H.R., Riedler, L., Wirbelsaeulenosteomyelitis nach lumbaler Grenzstrangblockade, Zbl. Chir. 101 (1976) 807.

Hoer, G., Tumoren der Wirbelsaeule-Szintigraphie, Vortrag auf d. 12, Arbeitstagung d. Ges. fuer Wirbelsaeulenforschg. Tuebingen 25/26 (Sept. 1981).

Hoerdegen, K.M., Wirbelsaeule und Reiten, Schweiz. med. Wschr. 105 (1975) 668.

Hoerdegen, K.M., Der Einfluss des Reitens auf die Wirbelsaeule, Sportarzt und Sportmedizin 27 (1976) 189.

Hoffman-Daimler, S., Die Wirbelsaeule unter typischen Arbeitsbelastungen, Orthop. Praxis 10 (1974) 210.

Hoffmann-Daimler, S., Zur Frage des Bandscheibenersatzes, Z. fuer Orthop. 112 (1974) 792.

Hohmann, D., Die degenerativen Veraenderungen der Kostotransversalgelenke, Beil. H. Z. Orthop. 105 (1968).

Hohmann, D., Pathologisch-anatomische und roentgenologische Befunde an den Kostotransversalgelenken, Manuelle Medizin 19 (1981) 25.

Holdorff, B., Lumbale Syndrome aus der Sicht des Neurologen, Die Wirbelsaeule in Forschung und Praxis, Hippokrates Verlag Stuttgart 83 (1979) 183.

Holibkova, A., Holibka, V., Die koerperliche Entwicklung der Kinder der Olomoucer laendlichen Umgebung, Acta Universitatis Palackianae Olomucensis 51 (1968) 127.

Hollman, W., Fitnessprogramme, in Leistungsmedizin, Sportmedizin, Hrsg.: K.D. Huellemann, Georg Thieme Verlag Stuttgart (1976).

Hollmann, W., Aufgaben und Bedeutung der Sportmedizin im Hochleistungssport, Deutsches Aerzteblatt 76 (1979) 2135.

Hollman, W., Breitensport-physiologische und biochemische Grundlagen, in: Sportmedizin im Breiten- und Leistungssport, Hrsg.: Kindermann und Hort, Demeter Verlag, Fraefelfing (1980).

Hollmann, W., Lienen, H., Beurteilung und Groesse der Koerperlichen Leistungsfaehigkeit, in Leistungsmedizin, Sportmedizin, Hrsg.: Huellemann, Georg Thieme Verlag Stuttgart (1976).

Holstein, E., Melde- und Entschaedigungspflicht bei Berufskrankheiten, J.A. Barth, Leipzig 1951, 4. Aufl. (1971).

Hoppenfeld, S., Physical examination of the spine and extremities, Appleton-Century-Crofts, New York (1976).

Hoppenfeld, S., Orthopaedische Neurologie, Aus dem Amerik. uebers. von D. Vollkammer (Buecherei des Orthopaeden, Bd. 24) Stuttgart: Enke (1980).

Horsky, V., Dite, B., Resultate der Wirbelsaeulen-Untersuchung bei einer Gruppe von Fallschirmspringern, Voj. zdravotn. Listy 34 (1965) 197.

Horst, M., Mechanische Beanspruchungen der Wirbelkoerperdeckplatte, Die Wirbelsaeule in Forschung und Praxis, Hippokrates Verlag Stuttgart 95 (1982).

Horst, M., et al., Langzeitergebnisse von Rezidivoperationen nach Nukleotomie, Orthop. Praxis 16 (1980) 71.

Horst, M., Drerup, B., Die Moeglichkeiten der Moire-Topografie fuer die Dokumentation juveniler Kyphosen, Die Wirbelsaeule in Forschung und Praxis, Hippokrates Verlag Stuttgart 89 (1980) 27.

Horvath, F., Roentgenmorphologie des Caisson-bedingten Knochenmarkinfarktes, Fortschr. Roentgenstr. 129 (1978) 33.

Hoske, H., Reifungszeit und Jugendsport in Sportmedizin, Hrsg.: Groh, Ferdinand Enke Verlag Stuttgart (1962).

Houston, C.S., Pre-employment radiographs of lumbar spine, Journal of the Canadian Association of Radiology 28 (1977) 170.

Howald, H., Morphologische und funktionale Veraenderungen der Muskelfasern durch Training, Manuelle Medizin 22 (1984) 86.

Howald, H., Morphologische und funktionale Veraenderungen der Muskelfasern durch Training, Manuelle Medizin 22 (1984) 86.

Huebener, K.H., Pahl, W.M., Computertomographische Untersuchungen an altaegyptischen Mumien, Fortschr. Roentgenstr. 135 (1981) 213.

Hulley, S.B., et al., The effect of supplemental oral phosphate on the bone mineral changes during prolonged bed rest, Journal of Clinical Investigation 50 (1971) 2506.

Hult, L., Dyndrome des vertebres cervicales dorsales et lombaires, Acta orthop. scand. Suppl. 17 (1954).

Igari, T., Miura, Y., Zervikale Radikulomyelopathie infolge Verkalkung des leg. flavum, Z. Orthop. 119 (1981) 739.

Inoue, H., Three-dimensional architecture of lumbar intervertebral discs, Spine 6 (1981) 139.

International Labour Organisation, ILO/Genf, Maximum permissible weight to be carried by one worker, International Labor Organisation, Preparatory Technical Conference on Maximum Weight, Report I (1966), Report II (1966).

International Labour Organisation, ILP/Genf, Kinetic methods of manual handling in industry, occupational safety and health series No. 10 (1972).

Internationales Arbeitsamt, IAA/Genf, Die hoechstzulaessige Traglast je Arbeitnehmer, Internationales Arbeitsamt, Internationale Arbeitskonferenz (1967) Bericht VI (2).

Irvine, D.H., Foster, J.B., Newell, D.J., Klukvin, B.N., Prevalence of cervical spondylosis in a general practice, Dissertation, University of Newcastle upon Tyne 1964.

ISO 2631, Guide for the evaluation of human exposure to whole-body vibration, 1978.

Ito, A., et al., Two cases of the spinal process caused by golf swings, Orthopedic Surgery Tokyo 21 (1970) 811.

Jackson, D.W., et al., Spondylolysis in the female gymnast, Clinical Orthopaedics and Related Research 117 (1976) 68.

Jackson, H.C., et al., Nerve endings in the human lumbar spinal column and related structures, Journal of Bone and Joint Surgery 48-A (1966) 1272.

Jaeger, K., Geraeteturnen und Wirbelsaeule bei Leistungssportlern, Sportarzt und Sportmedizin 10 (1969) 110.

Jamiokowska, Angefuehrt nach ARCT, Orthop. Praxis 16 (1980) 743.

Janek, I., et al., Histologische und klinische Untersuchungen ueber das Verhalten einiger Enzyme der Nebennieren nach Schwingungen, Int. Arch. Gewerbepath. Gewerbehyg. 20 (1964) 411.

Jani, L., Haltungsfehler-Scheuermann, Eine Ueberdiagnose und Uebertherapie, Therapeutische Umschau 33 (1976) 175.

Jani, L., Indikation und Kontraindikation, sportlicher Betaetigung bei Erkrankungen des Bewegungsapparates im Wachstumsalter, Therapiewoche 31 (1981) 25.

Jankovich, J.P., Structural development of bone in the rat under mechanical vibration, NASA CR-1823 (1971).

Jaros, M., Cech, M., Die Wirbelsaeule bei Gewichthebern, Beitr. Orthop. 12 (1965) 653.

Jaster, D., Klinik von Wirbelsaeulenschaeden beim Kunst- und Turmspringen, Beitr. Orthop. Traumatol. 10 (1963) 745.

Javid, M.J., Treatment of herniated lumbar disk syndrome with chymopapain, Journal of American Medical Association 243 (1980) 2043.

Jelinek, J., Malinsky, J., Inervace bedernich meziobratlovych plotenek cloveca, Cs. Morfol. 4 (1956) 205.

Jenkner, F.L., Das Cervicalsyndrom, Springer Verlag Vienna (1982).

Jentschura, G., Haltungsschaeden und Schulsport, Z. Orthop. 110 (1972) 738.

Jentschura, G., Haltungsschaeden bei Kindern und Jugenlichen, Enke Verlag Stuttgart (1977).

Jepson, K., et al., The role of radiculography in the management of lesions of the lumbar disc, Journal of Bone and Joint Surgery B.64 (1982) 405.

Jesserer, H., Die Knochenaufbaustoerungen der Wirbelsaeule, Die Wirbelsaeule in Forschung und Praxis, Hippokrates Verlag Stuttgart 16 (1960).

Jesserer, H., Osteodystrophia deformans. (Morbus Paget), Therapiewoche 27 (1977) 3818.

Jesserer, H., Prinzipien der Osteoporosetherapie, Fortschr. Med. 95 (1977) 387 und 466.

Jesserer, H., Diagnose und Prognose der Osteomalazie, Lebensvers. Medizin 32 (1980) 83.

Jesserer, H., Diagnose und Prognose der Osteodystrophia deformans (Morbus Paget), Lebensvers. Medizin 33 (1981) 197.

Jesserer, H., Die sogenannte idiopathische Osteoporose, Therapiewoche 31 (1981) 5395.

Jesserer, H., Fortschritte in der Behandlung der Osteoporose, Vienna Klin. Wschr. 94 (1982) 135.

Jesserer, H., et al., Medikamentoses, physikalische, manuelle und operative Moeglichkeiten der Behandlung von Wirbelsaeulenerkrankungen, Therapiewoche 25 (1975) 3981.

Jesserer, H., Kirchmayer, W., Die praesenile und senile Involutionsosteoporose, Docum. rheum. Geigy 8 (1955).

Jirout, J., The normal mobility of the lumbosacral spine, Act. Radio. 47 (1957) 345.

Jirout, J., Studien der Dynamik der Halswirbelsaeule in der frontalen und horizontalen Ebene, Fortschr. Roentgenstr. 106 (1967) 236.

Jirout, J., Die Kippung der Halswirbelsaeule in der sigittalen Ebene bei Seitneigung der Halswirbelsaeule, Fortschr. Roentgenstr. Nuklearmedizin 112 (1970) 793.

Jirout, J., The influence of postural factors on the dynamics of the cervical spine, Neuroradiology 4 (1972) 239.

Jirout, J., Vliv statiskych faktoru na dynamiku kroni patere, Czech Neurol. Neurochir. 35 (1972) 14.

Joensson, M., Einstellungsuntersuchungen bei Berglehrlingen unter besonderer Beruecksichtigung der Wirbelsaeule, Dtsch. Gesundheitsw. 21 (1966) 1809.

Joerg, J., Therapie des akuten "Bandscheibenvorfalls," Dtsch. med. Wschr. 107 (1982) 465.

Joerg, Schlegel, Funktionsstoerungen des Bewegungsapparates bei Erkrankungen des Nervensystems, in Witt, Rettig, Schlegel, Hackenbroch, Hupfauer (Hrsg.: Handbuch fuer Orthopaedie in Praxis und Klinik, Bd. IV, Thieme Verlag).

Jonath, U., et al., Leichtathletik I, Rowohlt Taschenbuch Reinbek (1977).

Josenhans, G., Funktionspruefungen und Befunddokumentation des Bewegungsapparates, Thieme Verlag Stuttgart (1978).

Juergens, H.W., Welchen Einfluss haben akzelerationsbedingte Formaenderungen des menschlichen Koerpers auf die angewandte Anthropologie, Zbl. Arbeitswiss., 15 (1961) 149.

Jumashev, G.S., Operationen mit anteriorem Zugang bei Erkrankungen und Verletzungen der Halswirbelsaeule (Russian), Ortoped. travmatol. protez. 11 (1975) 19.

Jumashev, G.S., et al., Chirurgische Behandlung von Verletzungen der Halswirbelsaeule (Russian), Ortoped. travmatol. protez. 7 (1976).

Jumashev, G.S., et al., Chirugisches Vorgehen bei Schaedigungen des Halsbereiches der Wirbelsaeule (Russian), Khirurgija 12 (1978) 28.

Jung, A., et al., The cervical spine. Primary and posttraumatic disorders: advances in surgical management, H. Huber, Bern (1974).

Jung, A., Brunschwieg, H., Recherches histologiques sur l'innervation des articulations des corps vertebraux, Presse medicale 40 (1932) 316.

Jung, A., Kehr, P., Anterolateral cervical operations using direct lesional approach (transversotomies, uncusectomies, uncoforaminoetomies according to Jung), The Cervical Spine, Hans Huber Verlag Bern (1974).

Jung, A., Schumann, E., Korrelation zwischen Beschwerden im Sinne eines vertebragenen Syndroms und roentgendiagnostisch nachweisbaren Veraenderungen der Halswirbelsaeule, Vienna Med. Wochenschrift, 125 (1975) 79.

Jung, H.D., Beruflich bedingte, generalisierte, vom Wildschwein uebertragene Erypsipeloid-Infektion mit Subklaviavenenthrombose und Polyarthritis, Dt. Desundh.-Wesen 32 (1977) 860.

Jung, Marlis, Steinke, T., Koerperbehinderte in der Regelschule-Erfahrungen aus dem "Modell lichtenau," Rehabilitation 17 (1978) 188.

Junghanns, H., s.a. Schmorl und Junghanns.

Junghanns, H., Der Lumbosakralwinkel, Dtsch. Z. Chir. 213 (1929) 322.

Junghanns, H., Spondylolisthese, Bruns Bestr. klin. Chir. 159 (1930) 423.

Junghanns, H., Spondylolisthesen ohne Spalt im Zwischengelenkstueck, Arch. orthop. Chir. 29 (1930) 118.

Junghanns, H., Ueber Wirbelgleiten, Arch. klin. Chir. 159 (1930) 423.

Junghanns, H., Die Zwischenwirbelscheiben im Roentgenbild, Fortschr. Roentgenstr. 43 (1931) 275.

Junghanns, H., Altersveraenderungen der menschlichen Wirbelsaeule,
1. Die Altersosteoporose, Arch. klin. Chir. 165 (1931) 303;
2. Die Alterskyphose, Arch. klin. Chir. 166 (1931) 106;
3. Haeufigkeit und anatomisches Bild der Spondylosis deformans Arch klin. Chir. 166 (1931) 120.

Junghanns, H., Blutgefaesschaedingungen durch Dauererschuetterungen infolge Arbeit mit Pressluftwerkzeugen als Berufskrankheit, Arch. Klin. Chir. 188 (1937) 466.

Junghanns, H., Die funktionelle Pathologie der Zwischenwirbelscheibem als Grundlage fuer klinische Betrachtungen, Arch. klin. Chir. 267 (1951) 393.

Junghanns, H., Wirbelsaeulenschaeden und Benutzung von Kraftfahrzeugen, Zbl. Verkehrsmedizin 1 (1955) 106.

Junghanns, H., Rudern und Wirbelsaeule, Medizinische 42 (1956) 1516.

Junghanns, H., Einspritzungsbehandlungen bei Wirbelsaeulenleiden und spondylogenen Symptomen, Die Wirbelsaeule in Forschung und Praxis, Hippokrates Verlag Stuttgart 6 (1958) 7.

Junghanns, H., Einspritzbehandlungen bei Wirbelsaeulenleiden und spondylogenen Symptomen, Die Wirbelsaeule in Forschung und Praxis, Hippokrates Verlag Stuttgart, Ref. Band I (1958).

Junghanns, H., Gezielte Beeinflussung der vegetativen Nerven durch Einspritzungen, Die Wirbelsaeule in Forschung und Praxis, Hippokrates Verlag Stuttgart 6 (1958) 8.

Junghanns, H., Die Insufficiential intervertebralis und ihre Behandlungsmoeglichkeiten, Die Wirbelsaeule in Forschung und Praxis, Hippokrates Verlag Stuttgart 13 (1959) 18.

Junghanns, H., Einheitliche Namengebung auf dem Gebiete der Wirbelsaeule, Die Wirbelsaeule in Forschung und Praxis, Hippokrates Verlag Stuttgart 25 (1962).

Junghanns, H., Chirurgie der Wirbelsaeule, in Klinische Chirurgie fuer die Praxis Bd. 4 Thieme, Stuttgart (1963).

Junghanns, H., Der Wirbelsaeulenverschleiss als soziales Problem, Therapiewoche 10 (1963) 415.

Junghanns, H., Aufrichtungsoperation bei Spondylitis ankylopoetica (Bechterew), Dtsch. med. Wschr. 93 (1968) 1592.

Junghanns, H., Correction quirurgica de la Espondilitis anquilopoetica (Bechterew), Medicina alemana, Buenos Aires 9 (1968) 1194.

Junghanns, H., Korrigierende und stabilisierende Operationen an den Extremitaeten sowie and der Wirbelsaeule unter Verwendung von Metallen und von Knochenkitt, Bulletin de la Societe International de Chirurgie 1 (1970) 1.

Junghanns, H., Operative Behandlung schwerer Kyphosen und Hueftarthrosen bei Ankylosierender Spondylitis, Rheumatologie 1 (1970) 171.

Junghanns, H., Operative Behandlung von wirbelsaeulenbedingten Wurzelsyndromen, Therapiewoche 20 (1970) 3038.

Junghanns, H., Verblockungsoperationen bei Frakturen der Halswirbelkoerper, Mschr. Unfallheilk. 73 (1970) 443.

Junghanns, H., Verblockungsoperationen bei Frakturen der Halswirbelsaeule, Die Wirbelsaeule in Forschung und Praxis, Hippokrates Verlag Stuttgart 93 (1970) 24.

Junghanns, H., Operative Behandlungen fuer die Schleuder- und die Abknickverletzungen der Halswirbelsaeule, Mschr. Unfallheilk. 74 (1971) 485.

Junghanns, H., Operative Rehabilitation bei Spondylitis ankylopoetica, Therapiewoche 24 (1971) 1835.

Junghanns, H., Die sozialmedizinische Bedeutung von Wirbelsaeulenschaeden, Arb. med. Sozialmed.-Arb. Hyg. 7 (1972) 29.

Junghanns, H., Die Wirbelbogengelenke, Manuelle Med. 100 (1972) 1.

Junghanns, H., Introduction a l'etude des articulations interapophysaires, Ann. Med. Phys. 25 (1972) 171.

Junghanns, H., Die Behandlung der Bandsheibennoete unserer Zeit, Tagung d. Hufeland-Stiftung, Cologne 28.3.1973.

Junghanns, H., Metallfixation von Knochenblocks an der Halswirbelsaeule, Chirurg. 44 (1973) 87.

Junghanns, H., Die Bedeutung der Insufficientia intervertebralis fuer die Wirbelsaeulentherapie, Erfahrungen aus 50 Jahren Wirbelsaeulenforschung, Manuelle Medizin 12 (1974) 93.

Junghanns, H., Fuenfzig Jahre Wirbelsaeulenforschung, Die Wirbelsaeule in Forschung und Praxis, Hippokrates Verlag Stuttgart 63 (1975) 10.

Junghanns, H., Berufsbedingte Abtrennungen von Wirbelbogenfortsaetzen, Arbeitsmedizin, Sozialmedizin, Praeventivmedizin 11 (1976) 111.

Junghanns, H., Arbeitsmedizinische Vorsorge bei Wirbelsaeulenschaeden, Arbeitsmedizin, Sozialmedizin, Praeventivmedizin, 12 (1977) 49.

Junghanns, H., Nomenclatura Columnae Vertebralis-Woerterbuch der Wirbelsaeule, Die Wirbelsaeule in Forschung und Praxis. Hippokrates Verlag Stuttgart 75 (1977).

Junghanns, H., Wiedereingliederung des "Rueckenleidenden" in die Arbeit-Eine Aufgabe der Rehabilitation, Kompass 88 (1978) 221.

Junghanns, H., Die Wirbelsaeule in der Arbeitsmedizin, Teil I Biomechanische und biochemische Probleme der Wirbelsaeulenbeslastung, Teil II Einfluesse der Berufsarbeit auf die Wirbelsaeule, Die Wirbelsaeule in Forschung und Praxis, Hippokrates Verlag Stuttgart 78 und 79 (1979).

Junghanns, H., Wirbelsaeule und Jugendarbeitsschutzgesetz, Arbeitsmedizin, Sozialmedizin, Praeventivmedizin, 14 (1979) 116.

Junghanns, H., Erkrankungen der Wirbelsaeule, Pathogenese, Klinik, Therapie, Klinik der Gegenwart, Urban & Schwarzenberg, Munich, Bd. IX (1982).

Junghanns, H., Chirurgie der Wirbelsaeule (zum 100. Kongress der Deutschen Gesellschaft fuer Chirurgie), in: Chirurgie im Wandel der Zeit 1945, 1983, Hrsg.: Schreiber, Carstensen, Springer Verlag Berlin (1983).

Jungmichel, D., Gabler, U., Wirbelsaeulenuntersuchungen bei Sportlern, Beitr. Orthop. 17 (1970) 690.

Kaben, H., Lafrenz, M., Ziegler, K., Sanger, R., Klinische Erfahrungen mit der Bruzellose des Menschen, Zschr. ges. Hyg. und Grenzgeb. 22 (1976) 97.

Kadanoff, D., Ueber die Unterschiede in der koerperlichen Entwicklung von Kindergruppen verschiedener oder gleicher Koerperhoehe zu Beginn der longitudinalen Untersuchung, Aerztl. Jugendkunde 60 (1969) 440.

Kadanoff, D., Mutafov, S., Ueber das Wachstumstempo und die koerperliche Entwicklung von

Kindern und Jugendlichen von 3 bis 18 Jahren, Z. Morph. Anthrop. 61 (1969) 258.

Kaiser, E., Loch, E.G., Die lumbalen Syndrome aus der Sicht des Gynaekologen, Die Wirbelsaeule in Forschung und Praxis, Hippokrates Verlag Stuttgart 83 (1979) 193.

Kaiser, G., Das normale und krankhafte Altern der Wirbelsaeule, American Journal of Physiology 223 (1972) 319.

Kaiser, G., Das normale und kranhafte Altern der Wirbelsaeule, Orthop. Traumatol. 22 (1975) 546.

Kaiser, G., Gedanken zur Gestaltung von Sitzmoebeln, Beitr. Orthop. und Traumatol. 24 (1977) 461.

Kamieth, H., Roentgenbefund von normalen Bewegungen in den Kopfgelenken, Die Wirbelsaeule in Forschung und Praxis, Hippokrates Verlag Stuttgart 101 (1983).

Kapandji, J.A., Physiologie articulaire, Paris 1972, Vol. III Maloine.

Karvonen, M.J., Koskela, A., Noro, L., Preliminary report on the sitting posture of school children, Ergonomics 5 (1962) 471.

Kastert, J., Die Spondylitis tuberculosa und ihre operative Behandlung, Die Wirbelsaeule in Forschung und Praxis, Hippokrates Verlag Stuttgart 3 (1957).

Kastert, J., siehe bei Diethelm und Kastert (1974).

Kazmin, A.I., et al., Ob effektivnosti lecheniya poyasnichnogo osteokhodroza vnutridiskovym vvedeniem papaina, Orthop. Travmatol. Protez 10 (1977) 12.

Keegan, J.J., Alterations of the lumbar curve related to posture and seating, Journal of Bone and Joint Surgery 35-A (1953) 589.

Kehr, P., Die Chirurgie der Arteria vertebralis bei unkarthrotischen und posttraumatischen Zervikal-Syndromen, Manuelle Medizin 20 (1982) 115.

Kehr, P., et al., Die Unkusektomie und Unkoforaminektomie nach Jung mit oder ohne intersomatische Fusion-Indikationen und Resultate, Z. Orthop. 119 (1981) 612.

Keller, E., Eisschnellauf, in Pfoerringer et al., (Hrsg.) Sporttraumatologie, perimed Verlag 1981.

Keller, K., Reiten als Therapie, Zeitschr. Allgemeinmed. 52 (1976) 10.

Kellgren, J.H., Lawrence, J.S., Rheumatism in miners, British Journal of Industrial Medicine 9 (1952) 197.

Kempf, G., Ein Beitrag zur Bekaempfung des Haltungsschadens, des Schulkopfschmerzes, der Schulmuedigkcit, Orthop. Praxis 8 (1972) 108.

Kerdiles, Y., et al., Les complications osseuses de l'aortographie lombaire, A propose d'un case de spondylodiscite L 2-3, J. Chir. (Paris) 109 (1975) 333.

Kerjean, J., Le rachis du footballeur, Med. Sport, Paris 44 (1970) 10.

Kersten, E., Ueberlastungsschaeden bei Hochseefischern und ihre Beurteilung im Sinne der VO ueber Melde- und Entschaedigungspflicht bei Berufskrankheiten, Z. ges. Hyg. 13 (1967) 179.

Kestler, O.C., Spondylolysis and spondylolisthesis, New York State Journal of Medicine 79 (1979) 700.

Kewalramani, L.S., et al., Cervical spine injuries resulting from collision sports, Paraplegia 19 (1981) 303.

Kibler, M., Segment-Therapie, Hippokrates Verlag, Stuttgart (1950).

Kienzler, G., Experimentaltraining bei wirbelsaeulenerkrankten und -verletzten Sportlern, Z. Orthop. 110 (1972) 801.

Kietz, H., Der Ausdrucksgehalt des menschlichen Ganges, Barth Leipzig (1956).

Killus, J., Statistische Untersuchungen an Roentgengannzaufnahmen menschlicher Wirbelsaeulen zur Entwicklung exakter medizinischer Beurteilungsgrundlagen, Luftfahrtmed. und Grenzgeb. 32 (1973) 4.

Killus, J., Technik und Moeglichkeiten der Computeranalyse der Wirbelsaeule, Die Wirbelsaeule in Forschung und Praxis, Hippokrates Verlag Stuttgart 68 (1976) 73.

Kimberly, P.E., Bewegung, Bewegungseinschraenkung und Anschlag, Manuelle Medizin 4 (1980) 53.

Kindermann, W., Hort, W., Anpassuungsvorgaenge am Haltungs- und Bewegungsapparat und ihre Grenzen, Berichtsband Deutscher Sportaerztekongress, Saarbruecken 1980, Demeter Verlag, Graefelfing 1981.

King, A.I., Chou, C.C., Mathematical modelling, simulation, and experimental testing of biomechanical system crash response, Journal of Biomechanics 9 (1976) 301.

Kinzl, L., Operative Therapie der thorakalen Wirbelfrakturen, Hefte Unfallheilk. 149 (1980) 161.

Kitzinger, E., Akupunktur und Manualtherapie-Ergaenzung oder Alternative? Dtsch. Z. Akup. 6 (1980) 126.

Klapp, B., Die Stellung des Klappschen Kriechverfahrens in Prophylaxe und Therapie der Wirbelsaeulenerkrankungen, Krankengymnastik 10 (1958) 138.

Klaus, E., Ein Fall von echter Spondylolisthese mit Spondylolyse der Halswirbelsaeule, Fortschr. Roentgenstr. Nuklearmedizin 110 (1969) 277.

Klavehn, S., Beziehungen zwischen Koerpergewicht und degenerativen Gelenk- und Wirbelsaeulenveraenderungen, Dissertation 1976, Berlin, Humboldt-University.

Klein-Vogelbach, S., Funktionelle Bewegungslehre, Springer Verlag Heidelberg (1984).

Kleinod, G., Wilke, M., Ursachen und prophylaktische Massnahmen bei Rueckenbeschwerden der Fallschirmspringer, Med. Sport. Berlin 13 (1973) 224.

Klemm, K., Die Behandlung chronischer Knocheninfektion mit Gentamycin-PMMA-Kugeln und-ketten, Sonderheft Unfallchirurgie 1977, Symposium Munich 1976, VLE-Verlag, Erlangen.

Klose, U., Ueber Wirbelsaeulenveraenderungen der Ruderer, unter besonderer Beruecksichtigung der Skoliose bei Riemenruderern, Med. Diss. Magdeburg (1966).

Klotzbuecher, E., In Koelschs Handbuch der Berufserkrankungen, 4. Aufl. G. Fischer Jena (1972).

Klumair, S., Fochem, K., Zur Problematik der Wirbellochmessung in der Computertomographie, Radiologe 20 (1980) 203.

Knese, K.H., Bau und Mechanik der Wirbelsaeule, Die Wirbelsaeule in Forschung und Praxis, Hippokrates Verlag Stuttgart 26 (1963) 9.

Knese, K.H., Kristallisation und Aufloesung von Kollagenfibrillen waehrend der Histogenese der Zwischenwirbelscheibe, Acta anat. 100 (1978) 328.

Knobling, H., See under Schwerdtner.

Knoch, H.G., Das Baastrup-Phaenomen aus klinischer Sicht, Zentralblatt fuer Chirurgie, 87, 1962, 17 Johann Ambrosius Barth Verlag Leipzig.

Knoll und Matties, See under Tittel.

Kocher, T., Die Verletzungen der Wirbelsaeulen zugleich als Beitrag zur Physiologie des Menschlichen Rueckenmarkes, Mitt. Frenzgeb. Med. und Chir. 1 (1896) 415.

Koehl, U., Les dangers encourus par les conducteurs de tracteurs, Arc. Mal. prof. 36 (1975) 145.

Koehler, G., Vertebrale Dekompensation durch Sportschaeden, Die Wirbelsaeule in Forschung und Praxis, Hippokrates Verlag Stuttgart 9 (1959) 81.

Koehler, G., Noack, H., Zur Frage der Wirbelsaeulenveraenderungen bei Rederern unter besonderer Beruecksichtigung weiblicher Leistungsruderinnen, Sportarzt 3 (1959) 62.

Koeller, W., et al., Das Verformungsverhaten von lumbalen menschlichen Zwischenwirbelscheiben unter langeinwirkender axialer dynamischer Druckkraft, Z. Orthop. 119 (1981) 206.

Kohlbach, W., Ueberlastungsschaeden der Wirbelsaeule-Folge der Evolution, Orthop. Praxis (1979) 871.

Kohlback, W., Rucksack schadet Jugendlichen, Medical Tribune 21.5.82 Nr. 21.

Kohlrausch, W., Teirich-Leube, H., Lehrbuch der Krankengymnastik bei inneren Erkrankungen, Fischer, Stuttgart (1958).

Kohlraush, W., Ueberlastungsschaeden am Bewegungsapparat, Leibesuebung und koerperliche Erziehung (1961) 193.

Kolar, J., Jirasek, L., Vrabec, R., Berufsbedingte Knochenveraenderungen durch aeussere Strahlenbelastung, Fortschr. Roentgenstr. Nuklearmedizin 103 (1965) 584.

Kolar, J., Stasek, V., Palecek, L., et al., Beitrag zur Symptomatologie der strahlenbedingten Wachstumsstoerungen an der Wirbelsaeule, Fortschr. Roentgenstr. Nuklearmedizin 103 (1965) 319.

Kollmeier, H., Wehmeier, G., Datenquerschnitt und Rehabilitationsmedizinischer Bereicheiner Berufstoerderungswerkes, Rehabilitation 16 (1977) 25.

Konermann, H., Koob, E., Die Untersuchung der Wirbelsaeule, Thermographie, Die Wirbelsaeule in Forschung und Praxis, Hippokrates Verlag Stuttgart 83 (1979) 47.

Konu, S., Hayashi, N., Kasharara, C., et al., A study on the etiology of spondylolysis with reference to athletic activities, Journal of the Japanese Orthopedic Association 49 (1975) 3.

Kosnik, E.K., Johnson, J.C., Scoles, P.V., Rossel, C.W., Cervical spondylolisthesis, Spine 4 (1979) 203.

Kotz, R., Ramach, W., Salzer-Kuntschik, M., Nadel-biopsie-Die Wirbelpunktion als diagnostische Massnahme, Die Wirbelsaeule in Forschung und Praxis, Hippokrates Verlag Stuttgart 83 (1979) 115.

Kraemer, J., Exchange of substances and fluids in the intervertebral disc, Z. Orthop. 111 (1973) 557.

Kraemer, J., Biochemie der Zwischenwirbelscheiben, Die Wirbelsaeule in Forschung und Praxis, Hippokrates Verlag Stuttgart 59 (1976) 10.

Kraemer, J., Stoffaustauschvorgange in der Bandscheibe des alternden Menschen, Die Wirbelsaeule in Forschung und Praxis, Hippokrates Verlag Stuttgart 60 (1976) 21.

Kraemer, J., Pressure dependent fluid shifts in the intervertebral disc, Orthopedic Clinics of North Amcrica 8 (1977) 211.

Kraemer, J., Bandscheibenbedingte Erkrankungen, Thieme Verlag Stuttgart 1978.

Kraemer, J., Grundlagen zur funktionellen Fruehbehandlung beim Morbus Scheuermann, Die

Wirbelsaeule in Forschung und Praxis, Hippokrates Verlag Stuttgart 89 (1980) 69.

Kraemer, J., Physikalische Therapie und Orthesen, Die Wirbelsaeule in Forschung und Praxis, Hippokrates Verlag Stuttgart (1980).

Kraemer, J., et al., Die entlastende Sitzhaltung beim Autofahren, Med. Welt 30 (1979) 238.

Kraemer, J., Berns, J., Schaeden am Bewegungsapparat bei Baskettballspielern, Dtsch. Z. Sportmedizin 1 (1980) 16.

Kraemer, J., Brenner, H., Gefahren fuer die Wirbelsaeule beim Gewichtheben, Orthop. Praxis 14 (1978) 43.

Kraemer, J., Gritz, A., Koerperlaengenaenderungen durch druckabhaengige Fluessigkeitsverschiebungen im Zwischenwirbelabschnitt, Z. Orthop. 118 (1980) 161.

Kraemer, J., Laturnus, H., Instillation of pressure-reducing substances into the lumbar disc, Verhandl. SICOT, Copenhagen (8 July 1975).

Kraemer, J., Laturnus, H., Intradiscale Instillationstherapie mit quelldruckreduzierenden Substanzen beim lumbalen Bandscheibensyndrom, Ztsch. Orthop. 113/6 (1975) 1031–1038.

Krahl, H., Aspekte der Tauglichkeitsbeurteilung im Lesitungssport, Orthop. Praxis 11 (1975) 56.

Krahl, H., Sportverletzungen und Sportschaeden bei Hochspringern in ihrer Beziehung zu Training und Technik, Medizin und Sport 15 (1975) 277.

Krahl, H., Sporttauglichkeit bei M. Scheuermann und Spondylolisthesis, Therapiewoche 27 (1977) 9170.

Krahl, H., Physiologische und pathophysiologische Aspekte des Breitensportes aus orthopaedischer Sicht, Therapiewoche 28 (1978) 7635.

Krahl, H., Die Belastungstoleranz des Bewegungsapparates, Deutsches Aerzteblatt 81/6 (1980) 318.

Krahl, H., et al., Klinische Kriterien der Floriditaet bei M. Scheuermann, Die Wirbelsaeule in Forschung und Praxis 89 (1980) 33.

Krahl, H., Steinbrueck, K., Traumatologie des Sports-Grundbegriffe und Analysen, Orthop. Praxis 14 (1978) 28.

Krajina, L., Versuch einer Praevention vertebragener Erkrankungen bei Bergarbeiterlehrlingen, Prakt. lek. 46 (1966) 815.

Kraus, H., et al., Quantitative tabulation of posture evaluation, Physiother. Rev. 26 (1946) 1.

Krayenbuehl, H., et al, Ueber die Dedeutung von testigkeitstechnischen Untersuchungen fucr die Beurteilung, Behandlung und Prophylaxe von Bandscheibenschaeden, Sportarzt, Sportmedizin 2 (1967) 2.

Krayenbuehl, H., et al., Bandscheibenschaeden durch Leibesuebungen und ihre Verhuetung, Sportarzt, Sportmedizin 18 (1967) 51 and 92.

Krayenbuehl, H., Benini, A., Die Enge des Recessus lateralis im lumbalen Bereich der Wirbelsaeule als Ursache der Nervenwurzelkompression bei Bandscheibenverschmalerung, Z. Orthop. 117 (1979) 167.

Kreei, L., Osborn, S., Transverse axial tomography of the spinal column: a comparison of anatomical specimens with EMI scan appearances, Radiography, 42 (1976) 73.

Krezel, T., Die jugendliche Wirbelsaeule unter sportmedizinischem Aspekt, Munich med. Wschr. 117 (1975) 71.

Kroemer, K.H.E., Push forces exerted in 65 common working positions Aerospace Medical Research Laboratory-TR-68-143 (1969).

Krokowski, E., Die quantitative Bewertung der Osteoporose, Z. Orthop. 101 (1966).

Krokowski, E., Die postmenopausische Osteoporose-ein Zeitabschnitt im normalen Knochenumbau, Med. Klin. 69 (1974) 2100.

Krokowski, E., Langzeitbeobachtung nach Natriumfluorid-Behandlung der Osteoporose, Munich med. Wschr. 116 (1974) 1845.

Krokowski, E., Die Osteoporose aus radiologischer Sicht: Entwicklung einer neuen Theorie, Radiologe 16 (1976) 54.

Krokowski, E., Prophylaxe der Osteoporose-eine sportmedizinische Aufgabe, Sportarzt und Sportmed. 28 (1977) 180.

Krokowski, E., Peter, E., Muskelinsuffizienz als Teilursache der Osteoporose, Munich med. Wschr. 119 (1977) 555.

Krokowski, E., Polonyi, S., Fricke, M., Interpretation der Osteoporosezeichen im Roentgenbild als Teilaspekt der neuen haemodynamisch-biostatischen Theorie der Osteoporose, Fortschr. Geb. Roentgenstr. Nuklearmedizin 125 (1976) 310.

Krone, A., Oldenkott, P., Der akute Kreuzschmerz: Im Mettelpunkt steht die neurologie Untersuchung, Notfallmedizin 8 (1982) 30.

Kropp, H., Neurologische und neurophysiologische Aspekte des Cervikalsyndroms und verwandter Schmerzzustaende unter Beruecksichtigung pathogener Arbeitsbedingungen, insbesondere monotoner Sitzhaltungen, ASP 14 (1979) 137.

Krueger, P., Mang, W., Verletzungen beim Windsurfen, Langenbecks Archiv. Chir. 349 (1979) 396.

Kruse, H.P., Grundlagen der Therapie der Osteomalazie, Therapiewoche 27 (1977) 3794.

Krywicki, H.J., Consolazio, C.F., Johnson, H.L, et al., Water metabolism in humans during acute high-altitude exposure (4,300 m), Journal of Applied Physiology 30 (1971) 806.

Kubat, R., et al., Sportschaeden bei Kindern, in: Sportverletzungen und Sportschaeden, Hrsg.: G. Chapchal, Georg Thieme Verlag, Stuttgart (1983).

Kucera, M., Charvat, A., Koerperueberlastung bei Jugendlichen und ihr Einfluss auf die chronischen Schaeden des Bewegungssystems, Sportarzt und Sportmedizin 6 (1976) 130.

Kuegelgen, H. von, Ein Beitrag zur Genese des hohlrunden Rueckens durch persistierende Bauchatmung (pBA), Z. Orthop. 114 (1976) 247.

Kuehhirt, M., Voll, J., Aufgaben der Rehabilitation bei der Behandlung von degenerativen Wirbelsaeulenerkrankungen, Rehabilitation 13 (1974) 43.

Kuester, H.H., Springorum, H.W., Die Wirbelkoerperspontanverformung und ihre therapeutischen Konsequenzen, Orthop. Praxis 4/81 416.

Kuhlenbaeumer, C., Familienuntersuchungen beim Morbus Scheuermann, 64, Tagung d. Dtsch. Ges. Orthop. und Traumatol. 14/17 Sept. 1977.

Kuhlendahl, H., Stoerungen des Nervensystems von der Wirbelsaeule her. In Funktionelle Pathol. der Wirbelsaeule, Hrsg. K.H. Heine, Berlin 1957, S. 117.

Kukla, D., Radsport, aus Sporttraumatologie, Hrsg. Pfaerringer et al., Perimed Verlag 1982.

Kummer, B., Funktionelle und pathologische Anatomie der Lendenwirbelsaeule, Orthop. Praxis 18 (1982) 84.

Kunert, W., Wirbelsaeule und Innere Medizin, Stuttgart 1975.

Kunert, W., Zervikobrachiale und thorakale Syndrome aus der Sicht des Internisten, Die Wirbelsaeule in Forschung und Praxis, Hippokrates Verlag Stuttgart 83 (1979) 165.

Kunert, W., Wirbelbogengelenke-Fernwirkungen auf innere Organe, 11, Arbeitstagung d. Ges. fuer Wirbelsaeulenforschung 1979: Die Wirbelsaeule in Forschung und Praxis, Hippokrates Verlag Stuttgart 87 (1981) 125.

Kuprian, W., Die Rolle des Pferdes in der Krankengymnastik, Z. Physik. Therapie 35 (1983) 18.

Kurihara, A., Kataoka, O., Lumbar disc herniation in children and adolescents, Spine 5 (1980) 443.

Kuriyama, S., Experimentelle Studie ueber das Ergebnis von wiederholten Torsionen auf die Zwischenwirbelscheibe, Journal of the Japanese Orthopedic Association 47 (1973) 101.

Kusmitsch, Y., Ylitowski, Veraenderungen im Stuetz- und Bewegungsapparat und peripheren Nervensystem bei Fallschirmspringern, Wojennomedizinski Schurnal 11 (1968) 56.

Laarmann, A., See under Lederer.

Laarmann, A., Der Pressluftschaden, Leipzig (1944).

Laarmann, A., Berufskrankheiten nach mechanischen Einwirkungen, Enke Verlag Stuttgart (1977).

Laban, R. von, Coreographie, Diederichs, Jena 1926.

Lachenal, B., Korrigiertes Sitzen bei chronischer Lumbalgie, Dtsch. Badabetr. 70 (1979) 604.

Lachnit, V., Berufliche Nierenschaeden, Arbeitsmedizin, Sozialmedizin, Praeventivmedizin 10 (1975) 160.

Lachnit, V., Ueber die Schaedlichkeit von Blei fuer den Menschen, Sichere Arbeit 28 (1975) 9.

Lafferty, J.F., Winter, W.G., Gambaro, S.A., Fatigue characteristics of posterior elements of vertebrae, Journal of Bone and Joint Surgery 59-A (1977) 154.

Lagier, R., Mac Gee, W., Erosive intervertebral osteochondrosis in association with generalized osteoarthritis and chondrocalcinosis, Z. Rheumatol. 38 (1979) 405.

Lamy, C., et al., Bazergui, A., Kraus, H., Farfan, H.F., The strength of neural arch and the etiology of spondylolysis, Orthopedic Clinics of North America 6 (1975) 215.

Lancourt, J.E., et al., Multiplanar computerized tomography in the normal spine and in the diagnosis of spinal stenosis, Spine 4 (1979) 379.

Land Nordrhein-Westfalen, Landesamt fuer Datenverarbeitung und Statistik, Jahresbericht (1973).

Land Nordrhein-Westfalen, Erkrankungen durch Vinylchlorid, Jahresbericht 1974 der Gewerbeaufsicht.

Landau, K., Reus, J., Koerperhaltungen bei Taetigkeiten aus Industrie, Verwaltung, Landwirtschaft und Bergbau. International Arch. of Occupational and Environmental Health 44 (1979) 213.

Lang, G., et al., Die unkarthrotisch bedingten unteren HWS-Syndrome, Z. Orthop. 119 (1981) 608.

Lange, C., Untersuchungen ueber Elastizitaetsverhaeltnisse in den menschlichen Rueckenwirbeln mit Bemerkungen ueber die Pathogenese der Deformitaeten, Z. Orthop. Chir. 10 (1902) 47.

Lange, M., Die Wirbelgelenke, Enke, Stuttgart 1934.

Langer, E., Vethacke, W., Gefaessveraenderungen nach rhythmischen Erschuetterungen, Mschr. Unfallheilk. 60 (1957) 129.

Laschner, W., Bewegungserziehung im Vorschulalter, Z. Orthop. 112 (1974) 1131.

Lawrence, J.S., Molyneux, M.K., Dingwall-Fordyce, J., Rheumatism in foundry workers, British Journal of Industrial Medicine 23 (1966) 42.

Leatherman, K.D., Radiation deformities of the spine, Journal of Bone and Joint Surgery 52A (1970) 405.

Leavitt, S.S., Johnston, T.L., Beyer, R.D., The process of recovery patterns in industrial back injury, Industrial Medicine and Surgery 40 (1971) 1.

Lee, C.K., Hansen, H.T., Weiss, A.B., Developmental lumbar spinal stenosis, Spine 3 (1978) 246.

Lederer, E., Degenerative Erkrankungen der Wirbelsaeule und der Gelenke, Koelschs Handbuch der Berufserkrankungen Fischer, Jena 4, Aufl. (1972).

Leger, W., Die Form der Wirbelsaeule mit Untersuchungen ueber ihre Beziehungen zum Becken und die Statik der aufrechten Haltung, Z. Orthop./Beiheft 91 (1959) 1.

Leger, W., Jugendarbeitsschutzgesetz in orthopaedischer Sicht, Therapiewoche 20 (1966) 623.

Leger, W., Die Wirbelsaeulenhaltung und ihre krankhaften Stoerungen, Die Wirbelsaeule in Forschung und Praxis, Hippokrates Verlag Stuttgart 40 (1968).

Leistner, K., Epidemiologische Aspekte der Osteoarthrosen und Bandscheibenschaeden, Beitr. Orthop. und Traumatol. 27 (1980) 11.

Leithead, C.S., Lind, A.R., Heat stress and heat disorders, Casell London 1964.

Lekszas, G., Sportartspezische Verletzungen im Judo-Kampfsport, Med. und Sport 13 (1973) 79.

Lekszas, G., Heilsport in der Orthopaedie, Enke Verlag Stuttgart (1981).

Lenhardt, P., Die Muskeln des Rueckens, Dtsch. Badebetr. 68 (1933) 348.

Lenhardt, P., Die alternde Wirbelsaeule und ihre Probleme, Dtsch. Badebetr. 68 (1977) 348.

Lenz, W., Zur Aetiologie des Morbus Scheuermann, Die Wirbelsaeule in Forschung und Praxis, Hippokrates Verlag Stuttgart 89 (1980) 11.

Lepihov, E.B., Rokhlin, G.D., Einige Charakteristiken des Skelettes bei Ballettartisten, Arkh. anat. USSR 53 (1967) 42.

Lessing, G., Ultraschall und Erschuetterung, in Koelschs Handbuck der Berufserkrankungen, 4, Aufl. Fischer, Jena (1972) 83.

Lethuillier, G., Der Ruecken des Judoka, Dtsch. Badebetr. 70 (1979) 12.

Lewin, T., Osteoarthritis in lumbar synovial joints, Munksgaard, Kopenhagen (1964).

Lewin, T., Foramen intervertebrale und Wirbelbogengelenke im Lendenabschnitt der Wirbelsaeule, Die Wirbelsaeule in Forschung und Praxis, Hippokrates Verlag Stuttgart 40 (1968) 74.

Lewis, E.B., Leukemia, multiple myeloma, and aplastic anemia in American radiologists, Science 142 (1963) 1492.

Lewit, K., Manuelle Therapie im Rahmen der aerztlichen Rehabilitation, Leipzig (1973).

Lewit, K., Manuelle Medizin im Rahmen der medizinischen Rehabilitation, Urban & Schwarzenberg, Munich (1977).

Lewit, K., Roentgenologische Kriterien statischer Stoerungen der Wirbelsaeule, Manuelle Medizin 20 (1982) 26.

Leyshon, G.E., Franis, H.W., Lifting injuries in ambulance crews, Public Health (London) 89 (1975) 71.

Liebau, J., Wulkenhaar, H., Die Scheuermannsche Erkrankung bei Rederern, Beitr. Orthop. 21 (1974) 220.

Liebeskind, D., Berufskrankheiten im Roentgenbild, J.A. Barth Verlag, Leipzig (1970).

Lindblom, K., Technique and results in diagnostic disc puncture and injection (discography) in the lumbar region, Acta Orthop. Scand. 20 (1950) 315.

Lindemann, H., Kuhlendahl, H., Die Erkrankungen der Wirbelsaeule, Enke Stuttgart (1953).

Lindemann, K., Blohmke, F., Die Behindertenwohnung, Rehabilitation 3 (1964) 139.

Lindner, H., Die biometrische Roentgenfunktionsdiagnostik nach Arlen in der Praxis der neidergelassenen Arztes, Manuelle Medizin 21 (1983) 123.

Lipson, S.J., Muir, H., Vertebral osteophyte formation in experimental disc degeneration, Arthritis and Rheumatism 23 (1980) 319.

Llopis, F.B., Biomecanica de la columna cervical, Rev. Esp. Reumat. 12 (1968) 18.

Loch, R.C., et al., Sport und Leistungsmedizin, Deutsches Aerzteblatt 40 (1980) 2342.

Loeckle, W.E., Schwimmen wie noch nie-besinnlich, angstfrei und gesund, EVO-Verlag Frankfurt/M. (1982).

Loesel, H., Die Belastbarketi der Wirbelsaeule Jugendlicher und Heranwachsender, Deutsche Schuetzenzeitung 2/1981, 32 und 8/31, 46.

Loesel, H., Schiessport-Sporttraumatologie, in Beitr. Sportmed. 15 (1981) 119 Hrsg.: Pfoerringer et al., Perimed Fachbuch, Erlangen.

Loesel, H., Schiessportspezifische Schwingungsbelastungen, Deutsche Schuetzenzeitung 6/1981, 42 und (1981) 32.

Loesel, M., Sportmedizinische Aspekte in Schiessport, Dtsch. Zeitsch. Sportmed. 32 (1981) 299.

Loisot, P., Connective tissue mucopolysaccharides and glycoproteins, Lyon Med. 226 (1971) 33.

Lora, J., Long, D., So-called facet denervation in the management of intractable back pain, Spine 1 (1976) 101.

Lotz, W., Cen, M., Die Szintigraphie bei roentgenologisch unklaren Wirbelkoerperverletzungen, Fortschr. Roentgenstr. 129 (1978) 228.

Louis, R., The anatomic basis of surgery on the thoracolumbar junction, Anatomia Clinica 1 (1978) 73.

Louyot, P., Girault, Malraison, Le rachis des arrimeurs, Revue Rhum. 4 (1956) 1.

Louyot, P., Jouret, De Ren, G., Le rachis des chauffeurs de locomotive, Revue Rhum. 21 (1954) 727.

Ludin, H.P., Praktische Elektromyographie, Enke Stuttgart 1976.

Lumsden, R.M., Morris, J.M., An in vivo study of axial rotation: immobilization at the lumbosacral joint, Journal of Bone and Joint Surgery 50-A (1968) 1591.

Luschka, H.V., Die Nerven des menschlichen Wirbelkanales, Laupp Tuebingen 1850.

Luschka, H., Die Halbgelenke des menschlichen Koerpers, Berlin 1858.

Luther, R., Legal, N., Spondylolyse durch Leistungssport, 22, Kongr. Vereinig. Sueddtsch. Orthop. Baden-Baden 1.5.1974.

Lutzeyer, W., Hild, F., Der urologisch bedingte Kreuzschmerz, Die Wirbelsaeule in Forschung und Praxis, Hippokrates Verlag Stuttgart 83 (1979) 197.

Mach, J., Heitner, H., Ziller, R., Die Bedeutung der beruflichen Belastung fuer die Entstehung degenerativer Wirbelsaeulenveraenderungen, Z. ges. Hyg. und Grenzgeb. 22 (1976) 352.

Magnus, P., Physiologie of posture, Lancet, 2 (1926) 531.

Magora, A., Investigation of the relation between low back pain and occupation, Industrial Medicine 39 No. 11 (1970) 465.

Maigne, R., Wirbelsaeulebedingte Schmerzen und ihre Behandlung durch Manipulationen, Die Wirbelsaeule in Forschung und Praxis, Hippokrates Verlag Stuttgart 45 (1969) Neue Aufl. (1983).

Maigne, R., Wirbelsaeulebedingte Schmerzen und ihre Behandlung durch Manipulationen, Die Wirbelsaeule in Forschung und Praxis, Hippokrates Verlag Stuttgart (1970) 45.

Maigne, R., Das Symptom der Uebergangszonen der Wirbelsaeule, Manuelle Medizin 22 (1984) 122.

Majdecki, T., Lukomski, Z., Piekarski, J., Angeborene Wirbelsaeulenanomalien und Ischias bei Eisenbahnbeschaeftigten, Verkehrsmedizin 24 (1977) 180.

Majoch, S., Krankengymnastik bei Scheuermann's scher Krankheit (Adoleszentenkyphose), Dtsch. Badebetr. 74 (1980) 508.

Maltschenko, O.W., Besonderheiten des Spondylolyse-Verlaufes bei Sportlern, Ortopedija (1973) 71.

Manani, G., Melanotte, P.I., et al., Spondylosdiscite cervicale post-operatoire, Ann. l'anesth. Franc. 21 (1980) 153.

Marcuse, H., nach Jentschura 1972.

Markuske, H., Untersuchungen zur Statik und Dynamik der kindlichen Halswirbelsaeule: Der Aussagewert seitlicher Roentgenaufnahmen, Die Wirbelsaeule in Forschung und Praxis, Hippokrates Verlag Stuttgart 50 (1971).

Markuske, H., Zur funktionellen Roentgendiagnostik der Halswirbelsaeule unter besonderer Beruecksichtigung des Kindesalters, Beitr. Orthop. Traumatol. 22 (1975) 671.

Maroudas, A., Stockwell, R.A., Nachemson, A., et al., Factors involved in the nutrition of the human lumbar intervertebral disc: cellularity and diffusion of glucose in vitro, Journal of Anatomy 120 (1975) 113.

Maroudas, A., Stockwell, R.A., Nahemson, A., et al., Nutrition of the human lumbar intervertebral disc, Journal of Anatomy 120 (1975) 133.

Marsh, Rombold, angef. n. Brocher 1973.

Martel, W., Pathogenesis of cervical discovertebral destruction in rheumatoid arthritis, Arthritis and Rheumatism 20 (1977) 1217.

Marti, R., et al., Traumatische Lasionen des Fusses in der Supinationslinie in: Sportverletzungen und Sportschaeden, Hrssg. G. Chapchal, Thieme Verlag Stuttgart 1982.

Martius, H., Umbauformen und andere Anomalien der unteren Wirbelsaeule und ihre pathogenetische Bedeutung, Arch. Gynaek. 139 (1930) 581.

Martius, H., Klinik und Pathologie der Lumbosakralregion, Zbl. Chir. 40 (1931) 2518.

Mathie, F., Schaeden am Bewegungsapparat von Jugendlichen im alpinen Leistungssport, Z. Orthop. 115 (1977) 866.

Mathie, F., Schwaiger, B., Schaeden am Haltungs- und Bewegungsapparat bei jugendlichen Hochleistungssportlern, Z. Allgemeinmedizin 52 (1976) 1417.

Mathiass, H., Rheumatismus und Arbeitsplatz, Arbeitsmedizin, Sozialmedizin, Praeventivmedizin, 9 (1974) 129.

Mathiass, H., Langzeittherapie von Erkrankungen des Bewegungsapparates, Therapiewoche 25 (1975) 51.

Matthiass, H.H., Haltung und Haltungsschaeden in den Entwicklungsphasen des Wachstumsalters, Sportarzt 10 (1959) 102.

Matthiass, H.H., Reifung, Wachstum und Wachstumsstoerungen des Haltungs- und Bewegungsapparates im Jugendalter, S. Karger, Basel-Freiburg-New York (1966).

Matthiass, H.H., Die Fruehtherapie von Wirbelsaeulendeformitaeten, dargestellt am Beispiel der Skoliose, Therapiewoche 29 (1979) 1936.

Matthiass, H.H., Klinische Messmethoden an der Wirbelsaeule, Die Wirbelsaeule in Forschung und Praxis, Hippokrates Verlag Stuttgart 83 (1979) 25.

Matthiass, H.H., Die Klinik der Osteochondrosis spinalis adolescentium (Morbus Scheuermann), Die Wirbelsaeule in Forschung und Praxis, Hippokrates Verlag Stuttgart 89 (1980) 15.

Matthiass, H.H., Die Objektivierung manualtherapeutischer Untersuchungen, Manuelle Medizin 21 (1983) 131.

Matthiass, Huennekens, nach Schwarz (1978).

Mattson, S.B., Caplan's syndrome in association with asbestosis, Scandinavian Journal of Respiratory Disease 52 (1971) 153.

Matzdorf, J., Das aeussere Winkelprofil der Brustwirbelsaeule des Menschen in rassen-, geschlects- und altersspezifischer Differenzierung, Die Wirbelsaeule in Forschung und Praxis, Hippokrates Verlag Stuttgart 70 (1976).

Mau, H., Wesen und Bedeutung der enchondralen Dysostosen, Thieme Stuttgart (1958).

Mau, H., Die Scheuermannsche Krankheit, Landarzt 42 (1966) 811.

Mau, H., Die sozialmedizinische Bedeutung der Wirbelsaeulendysplasien, Arbeitsmedizin, Sozialmedizin, Arbeitshygiene 7 (1972) 32.

Mau, H., Skoliose und Spondylolyse-Listhese, Z. Orthop. 115 (1977) 803.

Mau, H., Klassifikation der Kombination Skoliose, Spondylolyse/Spondylolisthese, Z. Orthop. 118 (1980) 434.

Mau, H., Die Aetiopathogenese der Skoliose, Ferdinand Enke Verlag, Stuttgart (1982).

McCulloch, J.A., Chemonucleolysis, Journal of Bone and Joint Surgery (BR) 59 (1977) 45.

McPhee, I.B., O'Brien, J.P., Scoliosis in symptomatic spondylolisthesis, Journal of Bone and Joint Surgery 62-B (1980) 155.

McSweeney, T., Injuries of the spine in operative surgery, 3. Aufl. Butterworth & Co., Ltd., London-Boston (1978) 348–373.

Med, M., Variability of intervertebral articulations with regard to the movement of the spine: Rehabilitacia (Bratislava) 8 (1975) 36–41.

Med, M., Anatomiske typy meziobratlovcho skloubeni (The anatomic types of vertebral joint connections-czech.), Lekar a teles, vychova (Prague) (1979) 60–63.

Meinecke, F.W., Behandlung und Rehabilitation Querschnittverletzter (Literaturuebersicht), Die Wirbelsaeule in Forschung und Praxis, Hippokrates Verlag Stuttgart 67 (1976) 12.

Meinecke, F.W., Spinal cord lesions after diagnostic and therapeutic procedures, Paraplegia 17 (1979/80) 284.

Mellerowicz, H., Situation der Sportmedizin in der Bundesrepublik Deutschland, Hefte Unfallheilk. 117 (1973) 163.

Menge, M., et al., Auswirkungen asymmetrischer Belastungen auf die Wirbelsaeule jugendlicher Fechter, in: Sportmedizin fuer Breiten- und Leistungssport, Eds.: Kindermann und Hort, Demeter Verlag Graefelfing (1980).

Menge, M., et al., Sportverletzungen und Sportschaeden bei zwei Budosportarten (Judo und Karate), Sporty und Leistungsmedizin, Eds.: Kindermann und Hort, Demeter Verlag Graefelfing (1980).

Menge, M., Rind, R., Verletzungen und Ueberlastungssyndrome des Bewegungsapparates beim Windsurfen, Sport: Leistung und Gesundheit in Kongressband Dtsch. Sportaerztekongr. (1982) Cologne.

Mennet, P., Wagenhaeuser, F., Boeni, A., Degnerative Erkrankungen der Lendenwirbelsaeule und ihre sozialwirtschaftlichen Folgen in einer Schweizer Stadt, Swiss Med. Wschr. 101 (1971) 293.

Mergold, D.P., Das klinische Bild und die Diagnose der durch Brucellose bedingten Sakroiliakal-Arthritis in der Endphase der Erkrankung, Soviet Medicine Moscow 27 (1963) 51.

Messerer, O., Elastizitaet und Festigkeit von Knochen, Cotta Stuttgart 1880.

Metz, J., Huellemann, K.D., in Tauchen in Leistungsmedizin, Sportmedizin, Hrsg.: Huellemann, Georg Thieme Verlag Stuttgart (1976).

Metz, P., Zielke, K., Erste Ergebnisse der Operation nach Luque, Z. Orthop. 120 (1982) 333.

Meuli, H.C., Skeletterkrankungen und Sport, Therap. Umschau. 31 (1974) 253.

Meyer, E., Wirbelsaeulenuntersuchungen bei jugendlichen Kunstturnerinnen, Swiss Z. Sportmedizin 23 (1975) 189.

Meyer-Burgdorff, H., Untersuchungen ueber das Wirbelgleiten, Leipzig (1931).

Meyermann, R., Moeglichkeiten einer Schaedigung der Arteria vertebralis, Manuelle Medizin 20 (1982) 105.

Michal, D., Synek, V., Zkusenostis lecbou radikularnich spondylogemich syndromu akupunktorou Plzensky lek, Sborn, 22 (1963) 139.

Michel, Cl.R., Dwyer contre Harrington.

Micheli, L.J., Risenborough, E.D., The incidence of injuries in rugby football, Journal of Sports Medicine 2 (1975) 93.

Miehlke, K., Aetiologie der Spondylitis ankylopoetica, Vortragsmanuskript 1975.

Miles, S., Medical criteria in the selection of athletes, Proc. Royal School of Medicine 62 (1969) 921.

Miller, E.D., et al., A new consideration in athletic injuries, Clinical Orthopaedics and Related Research 3 (1975) 181.

Miller, E.F., Graybill, A., Motion sickness produced by head movement as a function of rotational velocity, Aerospace Medicine 41 (1970) 1180.

Mironova, Z.S., et al., Lumbo-sakrale Schmerzzen bei Sportsleuten und ihre Behandlung, Die Wirbelsaeule in Forschung und Praxis, Hippokrates Verlag Stuttgart 44 (1969) 47.

Mittelmeier, H., Feuerstake, G., Ein neues Geraet zur vertikalen Patientenextension, Med. Orthop. Techn. 101 (1981) 183.

Mitzkat, K., Das Beschwerdebild der Scheuermannschen Erkrankung in Abhaengigkeit von den Behandlungsmassnahmen und der beruflichen Beanspruchung, Die Wirbelsaeule in Forschung und Praxis, Hippokrates Verlag Stuttgart 89 (1980) 67.

Mladenovic, V., Mihajlovic, M., Ochronotic spondylopathy, Acta rheumat. Belgradensa VII (1977) 69.

Modelia, A., et al., Klinika i pathomorph. ja sejnoga vegetat. gang. pri vibracionni bolezni, Klin. Med. Moscow 48 (1970) 78.

Moehrle, R., Manuelle Therapie an den Wirbelbogengelenken, Die Wirbelsaeule in Forschung und Praxis, Hippokrates Verlag Stuttgart 87 (1981) 159.

Mohing, W., Die sogenannten physikalischen Berufskrankheiten, Landarzt 33 (1957) 93.

Mohing, W., Sportverletzungen und chronische Schaeden an der Wirbelsaeule, Hefte Unfallheilk 91 (1967) 155.

Mohr, U., Schimek, I.I., Fusionsstoerungen des Auges als Folgen vertebragener Funktionsstoerungen, Manuelle Medizin 22 (1984) 2.

Mohr, W., Spondylitis bei Tropenkrankheiten, Dtsch. Ges. Rheumatologie 1 (1969) 70.

Mohr, W., Begutachtung bei Malaria-Erkrankungen, Med. Klin. 70 (1975) 1326.

Montgomery, C., Preemployment back x-rays, Journal of Occupational Medicine 18 (1976) 495.

Moritz, W., Das zervikale Sympathicus-Syndrom und seine praktische Bedeutung, Zschr. Laryng. 12 (1953) 270.

Morris, J.M., Biomechanics of the spine, Archives of Surgery 107 (1973) 418.

Morscher, E., The spinal column and sports in youth, Swiss Z. Sportmed. 17 (1969) 151.

Morscher, E., Pubertaet und Leistungssport, Swiss Z. Sportmedizin 23 (1975) 7.

Morscher, E., Korrektur der Hyperkyphose bei frischen und alten Wirbelkompressionsfrakturen, Orthopaedie 9 (1980) 77.

Moseley, I., Neural arch dysplasia of the sixth cervical vertebra, congenital cervical spondylolisthesis, British Journal of Radiology 49 (1976) 81.

Mueller, M., Der psychogene Schmerz, Praxis 50 (1961) 169.

Muenchinger, R., Gewichtheben und Bandscheibenbelastung, Swiss Z. Sportmedizin 8 (1960).

Muenchinger, R., Arbeit und Bandscheibenbeanspruchung, Medizin und Hygiene Geneva 19 (1961) 333.

Muenchinger, R., Hebe richtig, trage richtig, Merkbl. 1001/61 Schweiz. Unf. Vers. Anst. Lucerne.

Muenchinger, R., Lastentransport von Hand, Schweiz. Blaetter, Arbeitssicherheit 41 (1961) 14.

Muenchinger, R., Physiologische und medizinische Gesichtspunkte zur Arbeit der Hausfrau, Schweiz. Ztschr. Gemeinnuetzigkeit 102 (1963) 19.

Muenchinger, R., Die Funktionsstoerungen der Wirbelsaeule, Rheumatismus, Die Wirbelsaeule in Forschung und Praxis, Hippokrates Verlag Stuttgart 2 (1964) 136.

Muenchow, Albert (1969) angef. nach Rompe und Steinbrueck.

Muhr, G., DGB-Programm: Chancen der Aelteren im Betrieb verbessern, Die Quelle 26 (1975) 462.

Muhr, G., et al., Operative Therapie bei Halswirbelsaeulenverletzungen, Die Wirbelsaeule in Forschung und Praxis, Hippokrates Verlag Stuttgart 93 (1981) 17.

Mumenthaler, M., et al., Der Schulter-Arm-Schmerz, Verlag Huber Bern (1980).

Murarov, Kiew, angef. n. Palm (1978).

Murray-Leslie, C.F., et al., The spine in sport and veteran military parachutists (Fallschirmspringer), Ann. Theum. Dis. 36 (1977) 332.

Mustajok, P., et al., Permanent changes in the spines of military parachutists, Aviation Space Environment Medicine 49 (1978) 823.

Nachemson, A., Lumbar intradiscal pressure, Acta Orthop. Scand. Suppl. 43 (1960).

Nachemson, A., Some mechanical properties of the lumbar interveretebral discs, Bull. Hosp. Joint Dis. 23 (1962) 130.

Nachemson, A., The influence of spinal movements on the lumbar intradiscal pressure and on the tensile stresses in the anulus fibrosus, Acta Orthop. Scand. 33 (1963) 183.

Nachemson, A., In vivo discometry in lumbar discs with irregular nucleograms, some differences in stress distribution between normal and moderately degenerated disc, Acta Orthop. Scand. 36 (1965) 418.

Nachemson, A., The effect of forward leaning on lumbar intradiscal pressure, Acta Orthop. Scand. 35 (1965) 314.

Nachemson, A., The load on lumbar discs in different positions of the body, Clinical Orthopaedics and Related Research 45 (1966) 107.

Nachemson, A., Intradiscal measurements of pH in patients with lumbar rhizopathies, Acta Orthop. Scand. 40 (1969) 23.

Nachemson, A., Towards a better understanding of low-back pain: review of the mechanics of the lumbar disc, Rheumatology and Rehabilitation 14 (1975) 129.

Nachemson, A., The lumbar spine, an orthopaedic challenge, Spine 1 (1976) 59.

Nachemson, A., Bjure, J., Grimby, G., Results of intravital dynamic pressure measurement in lumbar disc, Proc. 5 International Congress on Physical Medicine, Montreal (1968).

Nachemson, A., Elfstroem, G., Intravital dynamic pressure measurements in lumbar discs, Almqvist und Wiksell, Stockholm 1970 und Scandinavian Journal of Rehabilitative Medicine, Suppl. 1 (1970).

Nachemson, A., Lewin, T., Maroudas, A., et al., In vitro diffusion of dye through the end plates and the anulus fibrosus of human lumbar intervertebral discs, Acta Orthop. Scand. 41 (1970) 589.

Nash, C.L., Moe, J.H., A study of vertebral rotation, Journal of Bone and Joint Surgery 51-A (1969) 223.

Nathan, H., Osteophytes of the vertebral column, an anatomical study of their development according to age, race and sex, Journal of Bone and Joint Surgery 44-A (1962) 243.

Nau, H.E., Atlas der Computertomographie, Die Wirbelsaeule in Forschung und Praxis, Hippokrates Verlag, Stuttgart (1983).

Nauwald, G., Ein Erfahrungsbericht zur gesundheitlichen Problematik bei Einstellungsuntersuchungen von Lehrlingen in der Schiffbauindustrie, Z. aerztl. Fortbild 70 (1976) 974.

Naylor, A., Changes in the human intervertebral disc with age, Proc. Royal Society of Medicine 51 (1958) 573.

Naylor, A., The biochemical changes in the human intervertebral disc in degeneration and nuclear prolapse, Orthopedic Clinics of North America 2 (1975) 343.

Naylor, A., Happey, F., Turner, R.L., et al., Enzymatic and immunological activity in the inter-

Naylor, A., Shentall, R.D., Micklethwaite, B., An electron microscopic study of the segment long spacing collagen from the intervertebral disc, Orthopedic Clinics of North America 8 (1977) 217.

Naylor, A., Smare, D.L., Fluid content of the nucleus pulposus as a factor in the disc syndrome, British Medical Journal 2 (1953) 975.

Neugebauer, H., Radsport und Rundruecken, Sportaerztl. Praxis 4 (1961) 110.

Neugebauer, H., 1971, angef. n. Gschwend 1978.

Neugebauer, H., Sportschaeden beim Gewichtheben, Austrian Journal of Sport Medicine 4/4 (1974) 5.

Neugebauer, H., Haltungsstoerungen der Wirbelsaeule, in Erkrankungen der Wirbelsaeule, Hrsg. Bauer, Thieme Verlag Stuttgart (1975).

Neugebauer, H., Kyphose-Index fuer Reihenuntersuchungen, Orthop. Praxis 11 (1975) 482.

Neugebauer, H., Prophylaxe der Haltungsschaeden bei Jugendlichen, Z. Allgemeinmedizin 52 (1976) 135.

Neumann, H.D., Die Zuercher Konvention, Manuelle Medizin 21 (1983) 109.

Neumann, H.D., Wolff, H.D., Theoretische Fortschritte und Erfahrungen der Manuellen Medizin, Vortraege vom 6th Internat. Kongr. d. Interat. Ges. Man. Med. von 18.-22.4.1979 in Baden-Baden, Herausg. DGMM Hamm.

Nicklas, K., Freizeit im Krankenhaus, Schriften der Deutschen Sporthochschule 8 (1981), Richarz Verlag St. Augustin.

Niedner, F., Zur Kenntnis der normalen und pathologischen Anatomie der Wirbelkoerperrandleisten, Fortschr. Roentgenstr. 46 (1932) 628.

Niethard, F.U., Die Form-Funktionsproblematik des lumbosakralen Ueberganges, Die Wirbelsaeule in Forschung und Praxis, Hippokrates Verlag Stuttgart 90 (1981).

Niethard, F.U., Gaertner, B.M., Die lumbale Symptomatik der thorakalen juvenilen Kyphose, Die Wirbelsaeule in Forschung und Praxis, Hippokrates Verlag Stuttgart 89 (1980) 37.

Niethard, F.U., Rompe, G., Das lumbale Facettensyndrom, Manuelle Medizin 19 (1981) 49.

Nikolaev, J.A., Najdenov, S., Osteo-arthropathies professionnelles et danse classique, Arch. Mal. Profess. Med. Trav. Sec. Soc. (Paris) 31 (1970) 39.

Nitz, H.T., Presber, W., Beitrag zu Sportschaeden bei Hochleistungstraining, Sportmedizin (1958) 313.

Noack, W., Gaudin, P., Sportliche Belastbarkeit bei Morbus Scheuermann, Die Wirbelsaeule in Forschung und Praxis, Hippokrates Verlag Stuttgart, Band 89 (1980).

Noeh, E., Behnecke, U., Der Wirbelsaeulenschmerz des Schulkindes, Orth. Praxis 11 (1975) 564.

Nordby, E.J., Brown, M.D., Present status of chymopapain and chemonucleolysis, Clincal Orthopaedics and Related Research 129 (1977) 79.

Novotny, A., Dvorak, V., Manuelle Med. 1 (1973) 1.

Oblak, O., Tilscher, H., Zur Ursache und Prophylaxe von Schaeden am Stuetz- und Bewegungsapparat durch Leistungssport, Sportarzt Sportmedizin 25 (1974) 101.

Oerthengren, R., et al., Studies of relationships between lumbar disc pressure, myoelectric back muscle activity, and intra-abdominal (intragastric) Spine 6 (1981) 98.

Oest, J., Ueber Spaetfolgen von Gefangenschaft am Skelettsystem, Aerztl. Praxis 14 (1962) 1179.

Ogata, K., Whiteside, L.A., Nutritional pathways of the intervertebral disc, Spine 6 (1981) 211.

Ogsbury, J.S., et al., Facet denervation in the treatment of low back syndrome, Pain 3 (1977) 257.

Oldenkott, P., Roost, D.V., Traitement microchirugical de la hernia discale lombaire, Neurochirurgie 26 (1980) 229.

Olsson, T.H., Selvik, G., Willner, S., Mobility in the lumbosacral spine after fusion; studied with the aid of roentgen stereophotogrammetry, Clinical Orthopaedics and Related Research 125 (1977) 181.

Ortmann, H., Konstitutionsbiologische Untersuchungen ueber den Gesundheitszustand Berliner Berufsschueler, Oeffentl. Gesundheitsdienst 18 (1956) 289.

Osler, W., angef. n. Harvey und McKusick.

Ott, R., Wurm, H., Spondylitis ankylopoetica, Steinkopf Darmstadt (1957).

Ott, V.R., Spondylosis hyperostotica, Aktuelle Probleme d. Geriatrie 3 (1970) 200.

Ott, V.R., Possner, R., Schmidt, K.L., Mueller-Eckhardt, C., Die Spondylosis hyperostotica in der Differentialdiagnose der versteifenden Wirbelsaeulenerkrankungen, Verh. Dtsch. Ges. Rheumatol. 5 (1978) 396.

Otte, P., Sport bei Stoerungen im Bewegungssegment, Jahresberict Rehabilitation Behinderter, Thieme Verlag 1972.

Oughterson, A.W., Warpen, S., Medical effects of the atomic bomb in Japan, Division III vol. 8 National Nuclear Energy Series, Manhattan Project Technical Section, McGraw-Hill Book Co., Inc. New York (1956).

Oxford, H., Are you aware of the danger of sitting incorrectly? Namco, Australia (1966).

Oxford, H., The problem of misfit furniture, Department of Education, Sydney (1968).

Paeslack, V., Zur Frage der beruflichen Eignung und Einsatzfaehigkeit des Tetraplegikers, Orthopaed. Praxis 11 (1975) 12.

Palm, J., Der sanfte Weg zur Fitness, D. Aerztebl. 81 (1978) 2915.

Panjabi, M.M., Brand, R.A. Jr., White, A.A., Mechanical properties of the human thoracic spine as shown by three-dimensional load-displacement curves, Journal of Bone and Joint Surgery Am 58 (1976) 642.

Panjabi, M.M., Krag, M.H., White, A.A., Soutwick, W.O., Effects of preload on load displacement curves of the lumbar spine, Orthopedic Clinics of North America 8 (1977) 181.

Panjabi, M.M., White III, A.A., A mathematical approach for three-dimensional analysis of the mechanics of the spine, Journal of Biomechanics 4 (2972) 203.

Pankratz, P., Die Wirbelsaeule wedelt nicht mit, Du und die Welt, Cologne 22 (1971) 32.

Parsch, K., Eulenburg, F., Der Bandscheibenvorfall beim Jugendlichen, Z. Orthop. 121 (1983) 398.

Pavelka, K., Rotationsmessungen der Wirbelsaeule, Z. Rheumaforsch, 29 (1970) 366.

Pazderka, V., et al., Spondylosis hyperostotica, Csl. Radio. 27 (1973) 228.

Peerebom, M., Copius, W., Age-dependent changes in the human intervertebral disc: fluorescent substances and amino acids in the anulus fibrosus, Gerontologie (Basel) 16 (1971) 352.

Penning, L., Normale Bewegungen der Halswirbelsaeule, Die Wirbelsaeule in Forschung und Praxis, Hippokrates Verlag Stuttgart 62 (1976) 102.

Penning, L., Normal movements of the cervical spine, American Journal of Radiology 130 (1978) 317.

Penning, L., Blickman, J.R., Instability in lumbar spondylolisthesis: A radiologic study of several concepts, American Journal of Radiology 134 (1980) 293.

Penzholz, H., Die radikularen Symptome, Med. Sachverst. 60 (1964) 41.

Perrey, O., Fracture of the vertebral end plates in the lumbar spine: an experimental biomechanical investigation, Acta Orthop. Scand. Suppl. 25 (1957).

Perrey, O., Resistance and compression of the lumbar vertebrae, Handbuch Med. Radio. Roentgendiagnostik der Wirbelsaeule, Springer Berlin-Heidelberg Bd. 6 (1974) 141.

Petry, Silikose und Polyarthritis, Arch. Gewerbepath. 13 (1954) 3 and 221.

Pfeil, E., Experimentelle Untersuchungen zur Frage der Entstehung der Spondylolyse, Z. Orthop. Grenzgeb. 109 (1970) 231.

Pfoerringer, W., Keyl, W., Traumatologie im Racketsport in: Sportverletzungen und Sportschaeden, Ed. G. Chapchal, Georg Thieme Verlag Stuttgart (1983).

Pfoerringer, W., Mueller-Wohlfahrt, H.W., Skelettveraenderungen bei Hochleistungssportlern, in Sportmedizin, Eds.: Kindermann und Hort, Demeter Verlag Graefelfing (1980).

Pieper, H., Palm, J., Trimming 130, Deutscher Sportbund, Frankfurt/M. (1983).

Piwernetz, K., Roehler, R., Elasticomechanical properties of trabecular bone from the human vertebral body, Holography in Medicine and Biology, Springer New York 18 (1979) 15.

Platzer, W., Funktionelle Anatomie der Wirbelsaeule, Bauer, R., Ed. Erkrankungen der Wirbelsaeule, Thieme Stuttgart (1975).

Plaue, R., et al., Das elastomechanische Verhalten menschlicher Bandsheiben unter statischen Druck, Art. orthop. Unfallchir. 79 (1974) 139.

Pohl, H.J., Humanisierung der Arbeit fuer altere Arbeitnehmer, Soziale Welt 27 (1976) 278.

Polster, J., Die Probevertebrotomie, Die Wirbelsaeule in Forschung und Praxis, Hippokrates Verlag Stuttgart 83 (1979) 119.

Polster, J., Roentgenuntersuchungen mit Hilfe von Stereoaufnahmen und der EDV, Die Wirbelsaeule in Forschung und Praxis, Hippokrates Verlag Stuttgart 83 (1979) 37.

Pongratz, J., Leitsymptom: Wirbelsaeulenschmerzen, Eine psychosomatische Studie, Zschr. psychosom. Med. 26 (1980) 12.

Pope, M.H., Rosen, J.C., Wilder, D.G., Frymoyer, J.W., The relation between biomechanical and psychological factors in patients with low back pain, Spine 5 (1980) 173.

Pope, M.H., Wilder, D.G., Matteri, R.E., Frymoyer, J.W., Experimental measurements of vertebral motion under load, Orthop. Clinics of North America 8 (1977) 155.

Portmann, angef. n. Palm (1978).

Potter, H., Sicher Sport treiben, SUVA und Winterthurversicherungen.

Poulsen, E., Back muscle strength and weight limits in lifting burdens, Spine 6 (1981) 73.

Prange, G.H., Rehabilitation nach dem Sozialhilfegesetz, Deutsches Aerzteblatt 8 (1972) 423.

Prantl, L., Halswirbelsaeulen-Roentgen-Untersuchung mit Funktionsaufnahmen, Manuelle Medizin 19 (1982) 112.

Present, A.J., Radiography of the lower back in pre-employment physical examinations, Radiology 112 (1974) 229.

Prestar, F.J., Morphologie und Funktion der Ligamenta interspinalia und des Ligemantum supraspinale der Lendenwirbelsaeule, Morphol. Med. 2 (1982) 53.

Prioleau, G.R., Wilson, C.B., Cervical spondylolysis with spondylolisthesis, Journal of Neurosurgery 43 (1975) 750.

Pritzker, K.P.H., Aging and degeneration in the lumbar intervertebral disc, Orthopedic Clinics of North America 8 (1977) 65.

Pschirrer, M., Vermessungen an der Halswirbelsaeule, Diss. Frankfurt (1968).

Pueschel, J., Der Wassergehalt normaler und degenerierter Zwischenwirbelscheiben, Beitr. z. path. Anatomie und allgem. Pathologie 84 (1930) 123.

Pueschel, J., Zielke, K., Korrekturoperationen bei Bechterew-Kyphose, Indikation, Technik, Ergebnisse, Z. Orthop. 120 (1982) 338.

Pufe, P., Hilmer, W., Langzeitbeobachtungen bei intensiv trainierenden Langzeitstreckenlaeufern im hoeheren Lebensalter, Berichtsband Sportaerztekongress 1980, Hrsg.: Kindermann und Hort, Hippokrates Verlag Stuttgart (1980).

Puhl, W., Weber, M., Wetzel, R., Laengsschnittuntersuchungen beim Morbus Scheuermann zum Krankheitswert roentgenologischer Veraenderungen, Die Wirbelsaeule in Forschung und Praxis, Hippokrates Verlag Stuttgart 89 (1980) 41.

Putz, R., Zur Morphologie und Rotationsmechanik der kleinen Gelenke der Lendenwirbel, Z. Orthop. 114 (1976) 902.

Putz, R., Funktionelle Anatomie der Wirbelgelenke, Normale und Patholog. Anatomie Bd. 43, Thieme (1981).

Querg, H., Schroeter, G., Roentgenologisch-klinische Untersuchungen der Wirbelsaeule an Rederern, Sportmedizin 7 (1958).

Querg, M., Les resultats radiologiques et cliniques des ramerus (et ramerures) juveniles et des jeunes adultes, Kongressband XII, Internat. Kongr. Sportmedizin, Moscow (1958).

Radiological Health Handbook, Revised Edition (Jan. 1970), U.S. Department of Health, Education and Welfare, Rockville, Maryland.

Rakhimov, J.A., Bilkin, V.S. Morphology of vessels of certain endocrine glands in dogs to whole-body vertical vibration, Archiv anatomii gistologii iembryologii 59 (1970) 43.

Ramazzini, B., Untersuchungen von denen Krankheiten der Kuenstler und Handwerker, Weidmann-Verlag Leipzig 1718.

Rathke, F.W., Die juvenilen Rueckgratverkruemmungen, Thieme Stuttgart (1961).

Rathke, F.W., Der jugendliche Rundruecken, Dtsch. med. Wschr. 90 (1965) 520.

Rathke, F.W., Die Therapie der juvenilen Wachstumsstoerungen der Wirbelsaeule, Die Wirbelsaeule in Forschung und Praxis, Hippokrates Verlag Stuttgart 89 (1980) 51.

Rathke, F.W., Buse, H., Erkennung und Beurteilung jugendlicher Haltungsschaeden, Aertzl. Sammelbd. 52 (1963) 85.

Rauber, A., Seltene Wirbelanomalie, Morph. Jb. 36 (1907) 603.

Ravichandran, G., Multiple lumbar spondylolyses, Spine 5 (1980) 552.

Ravichandran, G., Zygapophysical Arthropathy, Intervertebral apophyseal joint arthropathy, Arch. Orthop. Traumat. Surg. 96 (1980) 149.

Razumov, J.K., Denisov, E.J., Posdnjakova, R.Z., Der energetische Charakter der Vibrationswirkung auf den menschlichen. Organismus, Gig. trud. prof. Zabol. 11 (1967) 3.

Reason, J.T., Brand, J.J., Motion sickness, Academic Press, London (1975).

Redfield, J., Die Roentgenaufnahme der Lendenwirbelsaeule als Bestandteil fuer die Forst- und Holzwirtschaft, Journal of Occupational Medicine 13 (1971) 219.

Refior, H.J., Vergleichende Untersuchungen zur Frage von Wirbelkoerperveraenderungen bei jugendlichen Hochleistungsturnern, Orthop. Praxis 6 (1970) 160.

Refior, H.J., Die Wirbelsaeule des Leistungsturners, Biobacktungen zur Entwicklung bei Kindern und Jugenlichen, Z. Orthop. Grenzgeb. 110 (1972) 741.

Refior, H.J., Die Wirbelbogengelenke-Belastbarkeit und Spaetreaktionen in der Sportmedizin, Die Wirbelsaeule in Forschung und Praxis, Hippokrates Verlag Stuttgart 87 (1981) 63.

Refior, H.J., Zenker, H., Wirbelsaeule und Leistungsturnen Jegendlicher und Kinder, Munich Med. Wschr. 112 (1970) 463 (118).

Rehberg, H., Die Segment-Therapie mit Hautemphysem, Med. Klin. (1957) 1927.

Reindell, H., Die Situation der Sportmedizin in der Bundesrepublik Deutschland, Therapiewoche 30 (1980) 3093.

Reiner, L., Pre-employment x-ray survey of the lumbosacral spine in bus drivers, Industrial Medicine 27 (1958) 15.

Reinhardt, B., Die Stuendliche Bewegungspause, Die Wirbelsaeule in Forschung und Praxis, Hippokrates Verlag Stuttgart (1983).

Reinhardt, K., Spondylosis rheumatica cervicalis juvenilis, Dtsch. med. Hschr. 99 (1974) 1073.

Reinhardt, K., Roentgendiagnostik der Wirbelsaeule, Skoliosen und Kyphosen, in Handbuch med. Radiol. VI, 3 (1976).

Reinhold, H., Tillmann, R., Der Morbus Scheuermann als soziales Problem bei schwerer koerperlicher Berufsarbeit, Deutsch. Gesundheitswesen 23 (1968) 1469.

Reischauer, F., Die Begutachtung der Wirbelbandsheibenschaeden, Mschr. Unfallheilk. Berheft 42 (1951) 7.

Reischauer, F., Lumbago, Ischialgien und Brachialgien in ihrer Beziehung zur Bandscheibe, Langenbecks Arch. klin. Chir. 267 (1951) 418.

Reischauer, F., Ueber die Behandlung des zervikalen Vertebral-Syndroms, Dtsch. med. J. (1956) 554.

Reischauer, F., Wagner, R., Autofahren und Wirbelsaeule, Dtsch. med. Wschr. 84 (1959) 617.

Resnick, D., Shaul, S.R., Robins, J.M., Diffuse idiopathic skeletal hyperostosis (DISH) Forestier's disease with extraspinal manifestations, Radiology 115 (1975) 513.

Rettig, H., Berufsbhaengige Erkrankungen in der Orthopaedie, Z. Orthop. 113 (1975) 633.

Reuben, J.D., Brown, R.H., Nash, C.L. Jr., Brower, E.M., In vivo effects of axial loading on healthy, adolescent spines, Clinical Orthopaedics and Related Research 139 (1979) 17.

Richaut, et al., Les accidents et les fractures dus au parachutisme, Rev. Med. Aeronaut. Spatiale 1967 Nr. 24.

Rieckert, H., et al., Vergleichende Untersuchungen im Schul- und Leistungssport, Aerztl. Forschung 26 (1972) 32.

Rieckert, H., Hesse, B., Der Schulsport in der reformierten Oberstufe, Materia Medica Nordmark 30 (1978) 188.

Riede, D., Therapeutisches Reiten, in: Lekszas, G.: Heilsport in der Orthopaedie Berlin: Volk und Gesundheit 14 (1976) 178.

Riede, D., Versuch der Objektivierung manueller Therapie an der Halswirbelsaeule mit Fluessigkeitskristallen, Kongressband 25, Tagung Ges. Orthop. der DDR, 4–6 June 1978 in Dresden.

Riehle, A., Die Beanspruchung der Wirbelsaeule bei Trampolinturner, Diplomarbeit, Deutsche Sporthochschule Cologne 1971.

Rienzo, S. di, Die Brucelloese Spondylitis, Fortschr. Roentgenstr. 73 (1950) 333.

Riesser, H., Therapie mit und auf dem Pferd., Rehabilitation 14 (1975) 145.

Rinaldi, I., et al., Computerized tomographic demonstration of rotational atlanto-axial fixation, Journal of Neurosurgery 50 (1979) 115.

Rinck, P.A., et al., NMR-Ganzkoerpertomographie-Klinische Anwendungen, Deutsches Aerzteblatt 80 (1983) 27.

Rippstein, J., Vom Schaetzen und Messen mit neuen Hilfsmitteln, Orthopaede 6 (1977) 81.

Rippstein, J., Pluri-Meter, Werbeprospekt 1979.

Riser, M., Psychiatric disturbances of patients with osteoarthritis of the cervical spine, Clinical Orthopaedics and Related Research 24 (1962) 64.

Rissanen, P., The surgical anatomy and pathology of the supraspinosous and interspinosous ligament of the spine with special reference to ligament ruptures, Arch. Orthop. Scand. 46 (1960) 9.

Ritchie, J.H., Fahrni, W.H., Age changes in lumbar intervertebral discs, Canadian J. Surg. 13 (1970) 65.

Ritsema, G.H., Hypoplasia of the articular process in the lumbar vertebral column, Diagnostic Imaging 49 (1980) 89.

Ritz, E., Tschoepe, W., Bommer, J., Andrassy, K., Diagnostik und Therapie der renalen Osteodystrophie, Therapiewoche 27 (1977) 3808.

Rizzi, M., Entwicklung eines verschiebbaren Rueckenprofils fuer Auto- und Ruhesitze, Ergonomics, 12 (1969) 226.

Rizzi, M., Die menschliche Haltung, Klinische und biomech. Betrachtungen, Z. Praeventivmedizin 18 (1973) 341.

Rizzi, M., Untersuchungsmethoden zur Beurteilung der Haltung, Zschr. Praeventivmedizin 18 (1973) 105.

Rizzi, M., Die menschliche Haltung unter Beruecksichtigung der Wirbelsaeule, Die Wirbelsaeule in Forschung und Praxis, Hippokrates Verlag Stuttgart (1979).

Rizzi, M., et al., Einfache Messmethode zur Berechnung der biomechanischen Kraefte der Nackenmuskulatur, Zschr. Unfallmedizin und Berufskrankheiten Nr. 1 (1976) 9.

Rizzi, M., Covelli, B., Biomechanik der Wirbelsaeule unter Beruecksichtigung ihrer Form, Z. Unfallmedizin und Berufskrankh. 1 (1976) 3.

Rizzi, M., Covelli, B., Bivetti, J., Luethi, B., Biomechanisches Verhalten der Wirbelsaeule-Segmente, Arch. orthop. Unfall-Chir. 87 (1977) 111.

Rizzi, M., Gartmann, H., Arbeitsphysiologische Aspekte vertebraler Syundrom und ihrer Prophylaxe durch technische Anpassung der Arbeitsplaetze bei einer Fluggessellschaft, Z. Praeventivmedizin 12 (1967) 191.

Rizzi, M.A., et al., Biomechanical model of the ligamentous spine, Advancements in Bioengineering 17 (1974) 21.

Robson, M.J., Brown, L.J., Sharrard, W.J.W., Cervical spondylolisthesis and other skeletal abnormalities in Rubinstein-Taybi syndrome, Journal of Bone and Joint Surgery 62-B (1980) 297.

Roca, J., Jimeno, F., Die Kraftuebertragung durch den Wirbelbogen und ihre Beziehung mit dem Ursprung der Spondylolyse (photoelastic study), Z. Orthop. 118 (1980) 455.

La Rocca, H., Mac Nab, I., Value of pre-employment radiographic assessment of the lumbar spine, Canadian Medical Association Journal 101 (1969) 49 and Industrial Medicine and Surgery 39 (1970) 253.

Roessler, H., Lumbale Syndrome aus der Sicht des Orthopaeden, Die Wirbelsaeule in Forschung und Praxis, Hippokrates Verlag Stuttgart 83 (1979) 171.

Rohde, H., Griss, P., Vergleichende Ergebnisse der operativen Skoliosebehandlung nach Risser-Hibbs und Harrington, Therapiewoche 29 (1979) 3383.

Roick, H., Albrecht, W.D., Wirbelverschiebungen in der Lumbosakralregion bei jugendlichen Sportlern, Medizin und Sport 13 (1973) 124.

Rompe, G., Zur Haeufigkeitsverteilung roentgenologisch nachweisbarer Strukturunregelmaessigkeiten der Wirbelkoerper-Schlussplatten, Z. Orthop. 100 (1965) 16.

Rompe, G., Die Bedeutung der Scheuermann-Kyphose fuer die Begutachtung, Die Wirbelsaeule in Forschung und Praxis, Hippokrates Verlag Stuttgart 60 (1976) 102.

Rompe, G., Ergebnisse sportmedizinischer Forschung an der Orthopaedischen Universitaetsklinik Heidelberg, Therapiewoche 30 (1980) 3178.

Rompe, G., Steinbrueck, K., Die konstitutionell lockere Wirbelsaeule, Die Wirbelsaeule in Forschung und Praxis, Hippokrates Verlag Stuttgart 87 (1981) 57.

Rompe, G., et al., Beziehungen zwischen Sportpaedagogik und Sporttraumatologie, dargestellt am Beispiel typischer Befunde bei Speerwerfern, Sportarzt und Sportmedizin 22 (1971) 239.

Rompe, G., Dreyer, J., Wirbelsaeulenschaeden bei Speerwerfern, Z. Orthop. Grenzgeb. 110 (1972) 745.

Rompe, G., Krahl, H., Sportschaeden und Sportverletzungen (Wirbelsaeule und Becken), Wirbelschaeden bei Speerwerfern, Ztschr. Orthop. 110 (1972) 745.

Rompe, G., Krahl, H., Spondylolyse durch Leistungssport-Sporttauglichkeit bei Spondylolyse, Orthop. Praxis 11 (1975) 219.

Rompe, G., Rieder, H., Sportmedizin des Haltungs- sund Bewegungsapparates, in: Leistungsmedizin/Sportmedizin, Hrsg.: K.D. Huellemann, Georg Thieme Verlag Stuttgart (1976).

Roofe, P.G., Innervation of anulus fibrosus and posterior longitudinal ligament, fourth and fifth lumbar level, Arch. Neurol. Psychiat. 44 (1940) 100.

Roosen, et al., Dorsale Verklammerungsspondylodese bei posttraumatischer atlanto-axialer Instabilitas, Heft Unfallheilk. 165 (1983) 283.

Roques, C.F., et al., Place de la scintigraphe osseuse dans l'exploration des spondylodiscites infectieuses, Sem. Hop. Paris 53 (1977) 34.

Rosemeyer, B., Optimale Sitzhaltung aus der Sicht des Orthopaeden, Med.-Orthop. Technik 97 (1977) 3.

Rosemeyer, B., Surfen, in Sporttraumatologie, Hrsg.: Pfoerringer et al., perimed Verlag Erlangen (1980/81).

Rosemeyer, B., Windsurfen, in Sporttraumatologie, Hrsg.: Pfoerringer et al., perimed Verlag Erlangen (1980/81).

Rosmanith, J., Zur Frage der Entwicklung der Polyarthritis bei Rundherdpneumokoniose der Stinkohlenbergarbeiter, Arbeitsmedizin, Sozialmedizin, Praeventivmedizin 6 (1971) 296.

Rosomoff, H.L., et al., Axial radiology of the lumbar spine, Clin. Neurosurgery, Proc. 1977, 251 Williams & Wilkins, Baltimore 1978.

Ross, A.H., Swimmer's neck, Journal AOA 53 (1974) 765.

Ross, E., Ergebnisse einer Roentgenreihenuntersuchung der Wirbelsaeule bei 5000 maennlichen Jugendlichen, Fortschr. Roentgenstr. 97 (1962) 734.

Rossi, F., Spondilolisi lombari in atleti, Medicina dello sport 25 (1972) 161.

Rossi, F., Lucarelli, V., Modificazioni strutturali e morfologicamente a livello istemico del segmento lombare delle rachide in atleti pratticanti il sollevamento-pesi, Medicina dello sport 21 (1968) 309.

Rothschuh, K.E., Naturheilbewegung, Reformbewegung, Alternativbewegung, Hippokrates Verlag, Stuttgart (1983).

Rotzler, W., Aspekte der menschlichen Haltung im Spiegel der Kunst, in Rizzi, M.A., "Die menscheliche Haltung und die Wirbelsaeule," Die Wirbelsaeule in Forschung und Praxis, Hippokrates Verlag Stuttgart 85 (1979).

Rousseaux, F., et al., Canal lombaire etroit, Neurochir. 25 (1979) 154.

Rowe, F.A., Psychology of posture, National Health 4 (1922) 60.

Rudi, W., Kurzer Atem, krummer Ruecken, Zeitmagazin, December 1981, 1.

Runge, H., Zippel, H., Untersuchungen zur Entwicklung des Wirbelbogens im Lumbosakralbereich, Beitr. Orthop. und Traumatol. 23 (1976) 19.

Russe, O., Hintere Fusion bei Verrenkung der Halswirbelsaeule, Hefte Unfallheilk. 149 (1980) 95.

Rydevik, B., et al., An experimental study on the structure and function of peripheral nerve tissue in rabbits after local application of chymopapain, Spine 1 (1976) 137.

Rydevik, B., et al., Effect of collagenase on nerve tissue, International Society for the study of the lumbar spine, Annual meeting, Toronto, June (1982).

Saemann, W., Charakteristische Merkmale und Auswirkungen ungeunstiger Arbeitshaltungen, Schriftenreihe Arbeitswiss. und Praxis, Bd. 17 Beuth Cologne (1970).

Saleman, M., et al., Transoral cervical corpectomy with the aid of the microscope, Spine 4 (1979) 209.

Salzer, M., et al., Die totale Wirbelkoerperresektion, Arch. Orthop. Unfall-Chir. 90 (1977) 147.

Sandover, I., Vibration, posture, and low back disorders of professional drivers, Department of Human Science, University of Tech. Loughborough, Rep. Nr. DHS 402 (1981).

Sartor, K., Tumoren der Wirbelsaeule-Computertomographie, Vortrag auf d. 12, Arbeitstagung d. Ges. fuer Wirbelsaeulenforschg. Tuebingen 25/26 (Sept. 1981).

Saunders, E.A., Jacobs, R.R., The multiple operated back, Southern Medical Journal 69 (1976) 868.

Saunders, R.L., Wilson, D.H., The surgery of cervical disk disease, Clinical Orthopaedics and Related Research 146 (1980) 119.

Schaefer, H., Heilen und Heil, oder: von der Selbstbeteiligung des Menschen-Fuenf Thesen zu einer Theorie der Gesundheit-Dtsch. Aerzteblatt H. 47 (1980) 2807.

Schallock, G., Zur Physio-pathologie des bradytrophen Bindegewebes, Sportarzt 27 (1961) 331.

Schanz, A., Wirbelsaeule und Aorta, Z. orthop. Chir. (1930a) 53.

Schanz, A., Wirbelsaeule und Bauch, Ubl. Chir. 57 (1930b) 1598.

Schanz, A., Der Bauch als Hilfstragorgan der Wirbelsaeule, Zur Prophylaxe der Insufficientia vertebrae traumatica, Arch. Chir. 29 (1931) 245.

Schauwecker, C., Selbstihlfegruppen fuer chronisch Kranke, Dtsch. med. Wschr. 107 (1982) 260.

Schede, F., Grundlagen der koerperlichen Erziehung, Enke Stuttgart (1961).

Scheele, K., et al., Vergleichende telemetrische Untersuchungen beim 1000 m-Gehen und -Laufen, Sportarzt und Sportmed. 23 (1972) 94.

Scheele, K., et al., Sportspezifische Verletzungen und Schaeden bei Leichtathleten, Deutsche Ztschr. Sportmedizin 30 (1979) 391.

Scheier, H.J.G., Saner, U., Scheuermann-Erkrankung und Fliegertauglichkeit, Die Wirbelsaeule in Forschung und Praxis, Hippokrates Verlag Stuttgart 68 (1970) 62.

Scheier, H.J.G., Ueberblick ueber die verschiedenen Skolioseformen nach aetiologischen Gesichtspunkten mit prognostischen Hinweisen, Z. Orthop. 113 (1975) 558.

Schenk, R., Funktionelle Anatomie der Wirbelsaeule, Rheumatismus in Forschung und Praxis 11 (1964) 9.

Scherzer, E., Neurologische Folgen der Bandscheibenschaeden an der Lendenwirbelsaeule und ihre arbeitsmedizinischen Folgerungen, Arbeitsmedizin, Sozialmedizin, Arbeitshygiene 7 (1972) 41.

Schilgen, L., Goetze, H., Winkelbestimmungen am Patienten und auf dem Roentgenbild, Z. Orthop. 113 (1975) 414.

Schilling, F., Chronische Polyarthiritis, Handbuch Inn. Med. VI/2 B: Rheumatologie B, Springer Berlin-Heidelberg (1984).

Schilling, F., et al., Veraenderungen der Halswirbelsaeule (Spondylitis cervicalis) bei der chronischen rheumatischen Polyarthritis, Der Radiologe 3 (1963) 483.

Schilling, F., et al., Die Beziehung der Spondylosis hyperostotica zur Konstitution und zu Stoffwechselstoerungen, Med. Klin. 60 (1965) 165.

Schipperges, H., Die Medizin in der Welt von morgen, Econ. Dusseldorf (1976).

Schirmer, M., Untersuchungsbogen bei Lumboischialgie, Dtsch. Aerzteblatt 77 (1980) 755.

Schlegel, K.F., Behandlung und Berufsberatung von Jugendlichen mit Scheuermann-Krankheit, Med. Klin. 59 (1964) 79.

Schlegel, K.F., Angeborene Fehlbildungen und erworbene Deformitaeten, Die Wirbelsaeule in Forschung und Praxis, Hippokrates Verlag Stuttgart 83 (1979) 127.

Schlegel, K.F., Dierks, M., Haltungsforschung im Roentgenbild, Beziehungen zwischen Kopfhaltung und WS-Achse sowie Beckenneigung und Promontoriumwinkel, Z. Orthop. 88 (1958) 451.

Schlenzka, W., Die Besonderheiten der Iliosakralgelenke, Munich med. Wschr. 122 (1980) 1133.

Schliack, H., Zur Segmentdiagnostik der Muskulatur, Nervenarzt 26 (1955) 471 und Dtsch. med. Wschr. 82 (1957) 767.

Schlitt, R., Fallschirmspringen-ein gefaehrlicher Sport? Therapiewochen 26 (1976) 6817.

Schlueter, K., Form und Struktur des normalen und des pathologisch veraenderten Wirbels, Die Wirbelsaeule in Forschung und Praxis, Hippokrates Verlag Stuttgart (1965) 30.

Schmid, J.H.A., Das Iliosakralgelenk in einer Untersuchung mit Roentgenstereophotogrammetrie und einer klinischen Studie, akt. rheumatol. 5 (1980) 163.

Schmidt, C., Bobsport, in Pfoerringer et al., (Hrsg.), Sporttraumatologie, perimed Verlag (1981).

Schmidt, C., Rodelsport, in Pfoerringer et al., (Hrsg.), Sporttraumatologie, perimed Verlag (1981).

Schmidt, C.W., Nachbarschaftsfluorose, Dtsch. Gesundh.-Wesen 31 (1976) 1700.

Schmidt, C.W., Screening auf Nachbarschaftsfluorose mit der Roentgenreihenuntersuchung, Zschr. ges. Hyg. und Grenzgeb. 22 (1976) 815.

Schmidt, H., Orthopaedie im Sport, Sportmedizinische Schriftenreihe 8, Johann Ambrosius Barth, Leipzig (1972).

Schmidt, H., Standardisierte Roentgenauswertung von Wirbelsaeulen-Becken- und Kniegelenksaufnahmen bei Sportlern aus orthopaedisch-sporttraumatologischer Sicht, Medizin und Sport 16 (1974) 14.

Schmidt, H., Sportfaehigkeit bei orthopaedischen Erkrankungen und Veraenderungen im Bereich der Wirbelsaeule, Beitr. Orthop. Traumatol. 22 (1975) 123.

Schmidt, H., Spondylolisthesis und Sport, Medizin und Sport 19 (1979) 73.

Schmidt, K.L., Rehabilitationsprognose der ankylosierenden Spondylitis, Lebensvers. Medizin 32 (1980) 89.

Schmidt, K.L., Physikalische Therapie bei Rueckenschmerzen, Krankenhausarzt 54 (1981) 255.

Schmidt, R.C., Atypische Befunde bei lumbalen Diskographien, Roentgen-Bl. 32 (1979) 203.

Schmidt, R.C., Die lumbale Diskographie, Die Wirbelsaeule in Forschung und Praxis, Hippokrates Stuttgart Bd. 83 (1979) 103.

Schmidt, S., Ein neuer Weg zur Behandlung der schmerzhaften entzuendliehen Osteochondrose? Therapie Gegenw. 96 (1957) 307.

Schmidt, S., Zur Behandlung der Osteochondrose, Aerztl. Praxis IX (1957) 43.

Schmidt, U., Schmidt-Brueggemann, M., Knochenszintigraphie: Indikationen und Ergebnisse, Diagnostik 12 (1979) 23.

Schmidtke, H., Ergonomie 1-Grundlagen menschlicher Arbeit und Leistung, Hanser Munich (1973).

Schmidtke, H., Ergonomie 2-Gestaltung von Arbeitsplatz und Arbeitsumwelt, Hanser Munich (1974).

Schmitt, E., Klinik und Prognose der Scheuermann-Skoliose, Z. Orthop. 113 (1975) 573.

Schmitt, E., Ruhigstellung der Bogengelenke, Die Wirbelsaeule in Forschung und Praxis, Hippokrates Verlag Band 87 (1981).

Schmitt, E., Die Scheuermannsche Erkrankung, Therapiewoche 34 (1984) 6783.

Schmitt, E., Ruckelshausen, D., Zum Bild der Lokkerungssymptomatik und der Hypermobilitaet, Orthop. Praxis 16 (1980) 104.

Schmitt, K., Die krankengymnastische Uebungsbehandlung in der Redressionsorthese bei juveniler Kyphose, Med. Orthop. Techn. 102 (1982) 84.

Schmolinsky, G., Leichtathletik, Sportverlag Berlin DDR (1974).

Schmorl, G., Zur Kenntnis der Ostitis fibrosea, Verh. Dtsch. Patholog. Ges. 21 (1927).

Schmorl, G., Beitraege zur pathologischen Anatomie der Wirbelbandscheiben und ihre Beziehungen zu den Wirbelkoerpern, Acta Orthop. Unfallchir. 29 (1930) 389.

Schmorl, G., Ostitis derformans Paget, Virchows Archiv 283 (1932).

Schmorl, G., Junghanns, H., Die gesunde und die kranke Wirbelsaeule in Roentgenbild und Klinik, 5 Aufl. Thieme, Stuttgart (1968).

Schneider, H., Die Abnutzungserkrankungen der Sehnen und ihre Therapie, Thieme Verlag Stuttgart.

Schneider, H.J., Decker, K., Gedanken zur Gestaltung des Sitzes, Dtsch. med. Wschr. 86 (1961) 1816.

Schneider, P.G., Orthopaedische Probleme des Leistungssportes, Munich med. Wschr. 112 (1970) 452.

Schneider, P.G., Leistungsfaehigkeit und Leistungsgrenze des Muskel-Gelenk-Apparates, Materia med. Nordmark 24 (1972) 140.

Schneider, R.C., Head and neck injuries in football, Williams and Wilkin, Baltimore (1973).

Schneider, U., Will, I., Zum Haltungsverfall der Frau, Heilkunst 71 (1958) 93.

Schneider, W., Einfluss der Scheuermannschen Erkrankung auf den Beruf Jugendlicher, Z. Orthop. 87 (1956) 309.

Schneider, W., et al., Ausbildungskonzept Manuelle Medizin in der Schweiz 1983, Manuelle Medizin 22 (1984) 139.

Schnurrenberger, P.R., Walker, J.F., Martin, R.J., Brucella infections in Illinois veterinarians, Journal of American Veterinary Medicine Association 167 (1975) 1084.

Schoberth, H., Sitzhaltung-Sitzschaeden-Sitzmoebel, Springer, Heidelberg (1962).

Schoberth, H., Verletzungen und Schaeden an der Wirbelsaeule durch den Fussballsport, Kongress Munich 21-25.8. (1972) Mschr. vervielf.

Schoberth, H., Aerzliche Probleme bei der Schaffung einer koerpergerechten Arbeitsitzes im Buero der Zukunft, Arbeitsmedizin, Sozialmedizin, Praeventivmedizin, 14 (1979) 133.

Schoberth, H., Heidensohn, P., Orthopaedische Pathologie und Fussball bei Jugenlichen, Orthop. Praxis 1/XI (1975) 42.

Schoenbauer, H.R., Jugendsport: Belastungsgrenze, Verletzungsrisiko, Orth. Praxis 10 (1974) 445.

Schoenholzer, G., Trainingswirkung auf den Organismus-Uebertraining in Sportmedizin, Hrsg.: Groh, Enke Verlag Stuttgart (1962).

Schoenle, C., et al., Die koerperliche Belastung beim Windsurfen, Mat. Med. Nordm. 33 (1981) 117.

Schoeter, I., Wappenschmidt, J., Die intraspinale Raumforderung im computerassistierten Myelogramm (CAM), Fortschr. Roentgenstr. 133 (1980) 527.

Scholten, R., Ueber die Berechnung der mechanischen Beanspruchung in Knochenstrukturen, Techn. Med. 6 (1976) 85.

Scholz, J.F., Stoephasius, E., Teamarbeit in der Praxis, Jahresb. Dtsch. Vereinigg. fuer Rehab. Behinderter (1973) 251.

Schrader, E., Der Bau der Zwischenwirbelscheiben in seinen Beziehungen zur Beanspruchung, Z. orthop. Chir. 53 (1930) 6.

Schreiber, A., Ungeklaerte Spondylolisthesis-Probleme, Verh. Dtsch. Orthop. Ges. 55 (1968) 154.

Schroeter, G., Die Berufsschaeden des Stuetz- und Bewegungssystems, Heft 31 Arbeitsmedizin J.A. Barth Verlag, Leipzig (1961).

Schroeter, G., Funktionelle Beurteilung der degenerativen Gelenk- und Wirbelsaeulenleiden im Hinblick auf Arbeit und Leistungsfaehigkeit, Schriftenreihe der aerztlichen Fortbildung 24 (1965).

Schroeter, S., et al., Orthesenversorgung der Lendenwirbelsaeule bei chronischen Kreuzschmerzen, Z. Krankengymnastik 33 (1981) 625.

Schroeter, S., Lackner, K., Computertomographische Untersuchung der Lendenwirbelsaeule, Z. Orthop. 118 (1980) 147.

Schubert, J., et al., Die Einschaetzung des Schulsports, Orthopaedische Praxis XIV (1978) 12.

Schubiger, O., Die Computertomographie der Wirbelsaeule, Die Wirbelsaeule in Forschung und Praxis, Hippokrates Verlag Stuttgart 104 (1984).

Schuckmann, W., Skoliose im Wachstumsalter und ihre Belastbarkeit in Schul- und Leistungssport, Beitr. Orthop. 21 (1974) 227.

Schuettmann, W., Die Role der ionisierenden Strahlung als kanzerogener Faktor in der Arbeitsumwelt, Arch. Geschwulstforsch. 43 (1974) 384.

Schuler, P., et al., Lumbale Nucleotomie bei Kindern und Jugendlichen, Z. Orthop. 120 (1982) 735.

Schulitz, K.P., Niethard, F.U., Strain of the interarticular stress distribution, Arch. Orthop. Traumatol. Surg. 96 (1980) 197.

Schulthess, W., Schule und Rueckgratverkruemmung, Z. Schulgesch. Ptl. 15 (1902) 11 und 71.

Schultz, A.B., Andersson, G.B.J., Analysis of loads on the lumbar spine, Spine 6 (1981) 76.

Schultz, A.B., Galante, J.O., A mathematical model for the study of the mechanics of the human vertebral column, Journal of Biomechanics 3 (1970) 405.

Schulze, K.J., Untersuchungen zur Bedeutung der Wirbelrotation fuer die Gesamtdeformitaet der idiopathischen Skoliose, Habilitationsschrift d. Carus Adademie Dresden (1981).

Schulze, K.J., Polster, J., Berufsbedigte Wirbelsaeulenschaeden bei Traktoristen und Landwirten, Beitr. Orthop. und Traumatol. 26 (1979) 356.

Schumacher, G., Rugby, in Sporttraumatologie, Hrsg.: Pfoerringer et al., Perimed Verlag Erlangen (1981/82).

Schwaegerl, W., Belastung nach Bandscheibenoperation, Physiotherapeut (1980) 21.

Schwarz, F., Bewegungstherapie und Schulsonderturnen, Therapiewoche 28 (1978) 7674.

Schwerdtner, H.P., et al., Roentgenologische Verlaufskontrollen der Wirbelsaeule bei Kunstturnern und -turnerinnen nach langjaehrigem Hochleistungstraining, in Sportmedizin, Hrsg.: Kindermann und Hort, Demeter Verlag Graefelfing (1980).

Schwerdtner, H.P., Fohler, N., Roentgenuntersuchungen bei Kunstturnern und Kunstturnerinnen, 22, Kongr. Vereinig. Sueddtsch. Orthop., Baden-Baden 1.5.74.

Schwerdtner, H.P., Schoberth, H., Die Spondylolyse im Hochleistungssport bei Geraeteturnerinnen, Z. Orthop. Grenzgeb. 111 (1973) 934.

Seifert, J., Roentgenologische und nuklearmedizinische Untersuchungsverfahren der Wirbelsaeule (Sammelreferat der Literatur), Die Wirbelsaeule in Forschung und Praxis, Hippokrates Verlag Stuttgart 91 (1976) 10.

Seifert, J., Die zervikale Diskographie, Die Wirbelsaeule in Forschung und Praxis, Hippokrates Verlag Stuttgart 83 (1979) 99.

Seitz, W.A., Anderl, M., Rehabilitation und sozialmedizinischer Dienst. Detsch. Aerztebl. 69 (1972) 2881.

Seliger, V., The influence of sports training on the efficiency of juniors, Intern. Z. angew. Physiol. 26 (1968) 309.

Seliwanow, W.P., et al., Ueber klinisch-roentgenologische, morphologische Veraenderungen und die Behandlung der alkaptonurischen Osteoarthrose, Ort. travt. protez., 7 (1971) 44.

Sell, G., Hastenteufel, Schade, B., et al., Zusammenhaenge zwischen Psyche, Intelligenz und Haltung, Orthop. Praxis 11 (1974) 657.

Sewering, H.J., Teilgebiet Rheumatologie, Dtsch. Aerzteblatt 77 (1980) 1500.

Seyfarth, G., Das sogenannte Ueberlastungssyndrom der oberen Extremitaeten, Zbl. Chir. 82 (1957) 1701.

Seyfarth, H., Degenerative Wirbelsaeulenerkrankungen und Sport, Med. Mschr. 16 (1962) 219.

Seyfarth, H., Sport als Behandlung und Vorbeugung von Wirbelsaeulenschaeden, Schrittenreihe d. Zentralverbandes der Aerzte fuer Naturheilverfahren 8 (1962) 93.

Seyfarth, H., Behandlung und Prophylaxe von Fehlbelastungsfolgen am funktionstuechtigen Gewebe des Haltungs- und Bewegungsapparates, Medizin und Sport 13 (1973) 156.

Seyss, R., Zur Biostatik der Wirbelsaeule, Z. Orthop. 102 (1967) 395.

Seyss, R., Zur Biostatik nach Wirbelkoerperbruechen, Mschr. Unfallhlk. 71 (1968) 23.

Seyss, R., Biostatik bei pathologisch veraendertem Wirbelkoerper, Med. Klin. 64 (1969) 1428.

Seze, S. de., et al., Algie vertebrales et activites sportives, Revue rhumatol. 27 (1960) 277.

Shariaree, H., et al., A family with spondylolisthesis, Journal of Bone and Joint Surgery, Tehran, Iran (1979) 1256.

Shealy, C.N., Facet denervation in the management of back and sciatic pain, Clinical Orthopaedics and Related Research 115 (1976) 157.

Sheikholeslamzaden, S., Aalami-Harandi, B., Fateh, H., Spondylolisthesis of the cervical spine, Journal of Bone and Joint Surgery, 59-B (1977) 95.

Shport, I.U.E., et al., Otsenka trudosposobnosti lits podvergshikhsa laminektomii po povodu gryzhevykh vypadenii poyasnichnykh mezhpozvonkovykh diskov, Klin. Khir. 2 (1978) 10.

Siegfried, J., Eiskunstlauf in Sporttraumatologie, Hrsg.: Pfoerringer et al., perimed Verlag Erlangen (1981/82).

Silberberg, R., Wachstum und Altern des Skeletts, Acta Rheumat. Geigy, Basel, 26 (1971) 12.

Silberberg, R., Response of vertebral cartilage and bone to hormonal imbalances produced by anterior hypophyseal hormones and hypothyroidism, Pathol. Microbiol. 41 (1974) 11.

Silberberg, R., Aufdermaur, A., Adler, J.H., Degeneration of the intervertebral disks and spondylosis in aging sand rats, Archives of Pathology and Laboratory Medicine 103 (1979) 231.

Silberberg, R., Gerritsen, G., Aging changes in intervertebral discs and spondylosis in Chinese hamsters, Diabetes, 25 (1976) 477.

Singer, R.N., Weiss, S.A., Effects of weight reduction on selected anthropometric, physical, and performance measures of wrestlers, Res. Quart. American Association of Health and Physical Education 39 (1968) 361.

Skrgatic, M., Krapac, L., Zergollern, J., Roentgenologische Analyse der Wirbelsaeule bei professionallen Musikern, Medizin und Musik (Medicina i glazba) 101 (1979) 379.

Smagina, N.M., From experience in the prevention of posture disorders in children, Vopr. kurortoi Fiziot. Fiz. Kult. 35 (1970) 343.

Sonoda, T., Studies on the strength for compression tension and torsion of the human vertebral column, J. Kyoto Prof. Med. 71 (1962) 659.

Sozialminister, Hessen, Aktion Jugendarbeitsschutz, Hess. Sozialminister (1974) 1.

Spetzler, R.F., et al., Transoral microsurgical odontoid resection and spinal cord monitoring, Die Wirbelsaeule in Forschung und Praxis, Hippokrates Verlag Stuttgart 93 (1981) 75.

Spranger, J., Mucopolysaccharidosen, Orthopaede 3 (1974) 65.

Staffel, F., Zur Hygiene des Sitzens, Zbl. allg. Gesungh. Ptl. 3 (1884) 403.

Stahl, C., Huth, F., Morphologischer Nachweis synovialer Spaltraeume in der Unco-Vertebral-Region zervikaler Bandscheiben, Z. Orthop. 118 (1980) 721.

Stapleton, J.G., Pre-employment radiographs of the lumbar spine (letter) J. Can. Assoc. Radiol. 29 (1978) 4.

Stasek, V., Lokajicek, M., Palecek, L., et al., Zum Studium des Einflusses der ionisierenden Strahlen auf die wachsende Wirbelsaeule, Strahlenther. 126 (1965) 532.

Stech, E.L., Payne, P.R., Dynamic models of the human body, AMRL-TR-66-157 (1969) AD 701383.

Stedtfeld, G., Traumatische und degenerative Wirbelsaeulenschaeden im Segelflug, Die Wirbelsaeule in Forschung und Praxis, Hippokrates Verlag Stuttgart 68 (1976) 41.

Steinbrueck, A., Paeslack, V., Paraplegie durch Sport unfaelle, Z. Orthop. 116 (1978) 697.

Steinbrueck, K., Hypermobilitaet im Sport, Sportarzt, Sportmed. im Druck.

Steinbrueck, K., Sportmedizinische Probleme bei Gewichthebern, Sportarzt und Sportmedizin, Heft 10 (1977) 289.

Steinbrueck, K., Sportschaeden und Verletzungen der Wirbelsaeule beim Reiten, Z. Orthop. 117 (1979) 591.

Steinbrueck, K., Trampolinspringen und Wirbelsaeule—Belastungen und Risiko, Orthop. Praxis 15 (1979) 740.

Steinbrueck, K., Ringen in: Sporttraumatologie, Hrsg.: Pfoerringer et al., Perimed Verlag Erlangen (1981/82).

Steinbrueck, K., Sportverletzungen der Wirbelsaeule, in: Sportverletzungen und Sportschaeden, Hrsg.: G. Chapchal, Georg Thieme Verlag 1982.

Steinbrueck, K., Sportverletzungen der Wirbelsaeule, in: Sportverietzungen und Sportschaeden, Hrsg.: Chapchal, Thieme Verlag 1983.

Steinbrueck, K., et al., Sporttauglichkeit bei Scheuermann-Kyphose im Breiten- und Leistungssport, Die Wirbelsaeule in Forschung und Praxis, Hippokrates Verlag Stuttgart, Band 89 (1980).

Steinbrueck, K., Krahl, H., Sportschaeden und Sportverletzungen an der Wirbelsaeule, Deutshes Aerzteblatt 80 (1978) 1139.

Steinbrueck, K., Rompe, G., Hochleistungssportplanmaessige Hypermobilitaet, Man. Med. (1980) 62.

Steinbrueck, K., Springorum, H.W., Kontorsionisten und Wettkampfgymnastenerworbene Hypermobilitaet, Z. Orthop. im Druck (1980).

Steinbrueck, K., Tilscher, H., Manuelle Medizin und Sport, Manuelle Medizin 21 (1983) 38.

Steinfeld, J.L., Medical examinations for coal miners, Journal of Occupational Medicine 12 (1970) 462.

Steinhaus, M., Metrische Diagnostik der Skoliosepatienten, Med. Orthop. Techn. 99 (1979) 42.

Steinruecken, H., Chirotherapeutisch beeinflussbare Krankheiten, Hippokrates Verlag, Stuttgart (1980a).

Steinruecken, H., Der pseudoanginoese Herzschmerz im Rahmen des kostovertebralen Syndroms, Klinik und Therapie, Z. Allg. Med. 56 (1980b) 18.

Stender, H.S., Neue Methoden in der Radiologie, Arzt und Krankenhaus 56 (1983) 298.

Steplenski, F., et al., Einfluss horizontaler mechanischer Schwingungen auf die enzymetrische Aktivitaet des Reticulo-Endothelial-Systems der Leber bei Ratten, Inst. Arch. Gewerbepath und Hygiene, 2 (1964) 580.

Stewart, F., Spondylolisthesis without separate neural arch (Pseudospondylolisthesis of Junghanns), Journal of Bone and Joint Surgery 17-A (1935) 640.

Stewart, F.D., The age incidence in Alaskan natives considered from the standpoint of etiology, Journal of Bone and Joint Surgery 35 (1953) 937.

Stilwell, angef. n. Traczuk, (1968).

Stoddard, A., Lehrbuch der osteopathischen Technik, Die Wirbelsaeule in Forschung und Praxis, Hippokrates Verlag Stuttgart 19 (1961).

Stoddard, A., Lehrbuch der osteopathischen Technik an Wirbelsaeule und Becken, 3. Aufl. Hippokrates Stuttgart (1978).

Stoefen, D., Spielt Blei eine Rolle in der Pathogenese der Wirbelsaeulenleiden, Z. Orthop. Grenzgeb. 113 (1975) 59.

Stoehr, M., Iatrogene Nervenlaesionen, New York: Thieme (1980).

Stoelzel, O., Rueckentherapie im Wasser, Z. Krankengymnastik 34 (1982) 535.

Stofft, E., Eine funktionell-anatomische Studie ueber die Strukturen im Bereich der Lendenwirbelsaeule, Anat. Anz. 122 (1968) 48.

Stofft, E., Zur Morphometrie der Gelenkflaechen des oberen Kopfgelenkes, Verh. Anat. Ges. 70 (1976) 575.

Stofft, E., Grosam, K.H., Sport und Wirbelsaeule, Anat. Anz. 137 (1975) 369.

Stofft, E., Ribka, A., Messungen der aktiven Beweglichkeit menschlicher Wirbelsaeulen, Verh. Anat. Ges. 69 (1975) 777.

Strasser, H., Lehrbuch der Muskel- und Gelenkmechanik, Bd. 1-2 Springer Berlin (1908-1913).

Strohal, R., Boxsportverletzungen an der Wirbelsaeule, Medizin und Sport 5 (1965) 177.

Suesse, H.J., Die Haeutigkeit der Zervikalchondrose, Akademie-Verlag Berlin (1957) 10.

Suezawa, Y., Instabiler lumbosakraler Abschnitt, Orthop. Praxis 16 (1980) 368.

Suezawa, Y., et al., Indikation zur operativen Korrektur der schweren Spondylolisthesis und Beeinflussung der lumbalen Fehlhaltung, Z. Orthop. 121 (1983) 555.

Suezawa, Y., Jacob, H.A.C., Zur Aetiologie der Spondylolisthesis, Die Wirbelsaeule in Forschung und Praxis, Hippokrates Verlag Stuttgart.

Suezawa, Y., Jacob, H.A.C., Biomechanische Untersuchungen an der Lendenwirbelsaeule zur Entstehung der Spondylolisthesis, Z. Orthop. 118 (1980) 173.

Suezawa, Y., Jacob, H.A.C., Experimentelle Untersuchung ueber die Biomechanik des lumbosakralen Abschnittes, Wirbelsaeule in Forschung und Praxis 94 (1981).

Sullivan, J.D., Farfan, H.F., The crumpled neural arch, The Othopedic Clinics of North America 6 (1975) 199.

Sund, O., Richtiges Sitzen am Arbeitsplatz, eine arbeitsmedizinische Notwendigkeit, Krankengymnastik 30 (1978) 537.

Sutter, M., Diagnostische Weichteilpalpation des Bewegungsapparates, Manuelle Medizin 21 (1983) 120.

Swiderska, K., Swiderski, G., Zur roentgenografischen Beurteilung der raeumlichen Position der Wirbelsaeule im Lumbosakralabschnitt, Orthopaed. Praxis XIII (1977) 700.

Swiderski, G., Die Klinische Spondylometrie in der Kreuzschmerzdiagnose, Die Wirbelsaeule in Forschung und Praxis, Hippokrates Stuttgart Bd. 83 (1979) 205.

Swiderski, G., et al., Das Spondylogoniometer und seine Anwendung bei der Geschmeidigkeitsmessung der Wirbelsaeule, Orthop. Traumatol. 20 (1973) 593.

Szava, J., Implantate fuer Wirbelkoerperersatz, Die Wirbelsaeule in Forschung un Praxis, Hippokrates Verlag Stuttgart 55 (1972) 134.

Tadie, M., Helias, A., Thebot, J., et al., La phlebographie lombaire sans catheterisme; technique, indications, resultats dans le diagnostic de la hernie discale, Rev. Rhem. 46 (1979) 601.

Taillard, W., Die Spondylolisthese, Die Wirbelsaeule in Forschung und Praxis, Hippokrates Verlag Stuttgart 11 (1959).

Taillard, W., Klassifizierung der Spondylolisthesen, Z. Orthop. 118 (1980) 429.

Taillard, W., Lagier, R., Pseudo-Spondylolisthesis et chondrocalcinose, Rev. Chir. Orthop. 63 (1977) 149.

Tajima, T., et al., Selective lumbosacral radiculography and block, Spine 5 (1980) 68.

Tas, C. van der, Importance of computer-assisted myelography in diseases affecting the vertebral column, Diagnostic Imaging 48 (1979) 71.

Teirich-Leube, H., Grundriss der Bindegewebsmassage, Fischer, Stuttgart 1960.

Tepe, H.J., Haeufigkeit osteobhondrotischer Roentgenbefunde der Halswirbelsaeule bei 400 symptomfreien Erwachsenen, Fortshr. Roentgenstr. (1956) 85.

Terry, C.T., Roberts, V.L., A viscoelastic model of the human spine subjected to +gz accelerations, Journal of Biomechanics 1 (1968) 161.

Teuchmann, K., Untersuchungen ueber den Einfluss der mechanischen Schwingungen auf einige Reaktionen des Nervensystems, Odirony Pracy 13, 79 (1963).

Teysandier, Les atteintes traumatiques du rachis chez le parachutiste (Etude statistique et etiopathogenique a propos de 1033 525 sauts), Revue de Medicine Aeronautique et Spatiale 24 (1967).

Theiss, F., Typische Verletzungen bei Stabhockspringern unter besonderer Beruecksichtigung der Lendenwirbelsaeule, Dtsch. Z. Sportmed. (1980) 161.

Theissen, W., Wittgens, H., Medizinische und aussermedizinische Ursachen der vorzeitigen Pensionierung von Lokfuehrern, Der aerztliche Dienst DB 34 (1973) 33.

Thelen, M., Burman, R., Transfemorale lumbale Venographie, Die Wirbelsaeule in Forschung und Praxis, Hippokrates Verlag Stuttgart 83 (1979) 83.

Theopold, W., Hoevels, O., Hartmann, W., Uhland, R., Beobachtungen ueber das Laengenwachstum in der zweiten Haelfte des 18 Jahrunderts, Dtsch. Aerzteblatt H., 11 (1972) 611.

Thiele, O., Aufrichtung posttraumatischer Kyphosen im thoraco-lumbalen Uebergang mit ventraler osteosynthese, Z. Orthop. 121 (1983) 369.

Thiess, A.M., Versen, P., Arbeitsmedizinische Gedanken zur sorgenannten ''Vinylchloriderkrankung,'' Arbeitsmedizin, Sozialmedizin, Praeventivmedizin 9 (1974) 146.

Thompson, W.A., Keeping the patient with low back pain employable, Industr. Med. Surg. 22 (1953) 18.

Thomsen, W., Orthopaedische Voraussetzung fue die Gestaltung von Sitzen, VDI-Berichte 25 (1957) 35.

Thumb, N., Computergerechte Dokumentation, in Funktionspruefen und Befunddokumentation des Bewegungsapparates, Hrsg.: G. Josenhans, Thieme Stuttgart (1978).

Thurner, J., Amato, V., Das Knochengewebe—Allgemeine Gesichtspunkte seiner Anatomie und Physiologie, Therapiewoche 27 (1977) 19.

Thurner, J., Bodner, E., Funktionsmechanische, deformierend Insertionstendopathien im Bereich der Halswirbelsaeule, Die Wirbelsaeule in Forschung und Praxis, Hippokrates Verlag Stuttgart 26 (1963) 85.

Thurner, J., Caruso, A.M., Insertionstendopathien, Zschr. Orthop. 91 (1959) 209.

Tichauer, E.R., Manual handling and lifting, Journal of Industrial Nursing 13 (1961) 289; (1973).

Tichauer, E.R., Untersuchung der Biomechanik des manuellen Hebens bei simultierten industriellen Arbeitssituationen, J. Vr. safety research USA 3 (1971) 98.

Tichauer, E.R., Miller, M., Nathan, I.M., Lordosimetry: a new technique for the measurement of postural response to materials handling, American Industrial Hygiene Association Journal 34 (1973) 1.

Tichauer, W., Praevention durch Biomechanik, Dtsch. Aerzteblatt 40 (1969) 2736.

Tiisala, R., Kantero, R.L., Tamminen, T., A mixed longitudinal study on skeletal maturation in healthy Finnish children aged 5 to 10 years, Human Biology 43 (1971) 224.

Tillmann, K., Wirbelsaeule, Untersuchungsbogen in Funktionspruefungen und Befunddokumentation des Bewegungsapparates, Hrsg.: G. Josenhans, Thieme Verlag Stuttgart 1978.

Tillmann, K., Dokumentation der Wirbelsaeule im Rahmen der Einstellungsuntersuchung, Die Wirbelsaeule in Forschung und Praxis, Hippokrates Verlag Stuttgart Bd. 92 (1980) 69.

Tilscher, H., Wie schwer darf ein Rucksack sein? Medical Tribune 21.5.82 Nr. 21.

Tilscher, H., Moderne Techniken der manuellen Medizin, Mk. Aertzl. Fortb. 33 (1983) 67.

Tilscher, H., et al., Die topischen Zusammenhaenge zwischen Gesichtsschmerz und subokzipitalen Maximalpunkten, Manuelle Medizin 20 (1982) 127.

Tilscher, H., Bogner, G., Landsiedl, F., Viszerale Erkrankungen als Ursache von Lumbalsyndromen, Z. Rheumatol. 36 (1977) 161.

Tilscher, H., Bogner, G., Das obere Quadrantensyndrom, Orthop. Praxis (1979) 196.

Tilscher, H., Oblak, O., Untersuchungsergebnisse von Leistungsturnerinnen, Journal Sportmed. Austria 3 (1973) 19.

Tilscher, H., Oblak, O., Untersuchungen von chemaligen Jugendleistungssportlern, Orthop. Praxis 10 (1974) 339.

Tilscher, H., Steinbrueck, K., Die Behandlung vertebragener Stoerungen durch die Manuelle Medizin, Orthop. Praxis 15 (1979) 379.

Timmer, G., Wenn Raucher und Trinker krank werden, Frankfurter Allgem. Zeitung 11.10. (1979).

Tischer, H., Eder, M., Die Rehabilitation von Wirbelsaeulengestoerten, Springer Verlag Heidelberg (1983).

Tittel, K., Zur Aetiologie, Morphologie und Prophylaxe der Sportverletzungen und -schaeden am Bewegungsapparat, A. aerztl. Fortbild. 51 (1962) H 1 und 2.

Tittel, K., Zur Anpassungsfaehigkeit einiger Gewebe des Bewegungs-und Halteapparates an Belastungen unterschiedlicher Dauer und Intensitaet, Med. Sport, Berlin 13 (1973) 147.

Tittel, K., Beschreibende und funktionelle Anatomie des Menschen, Stuttgart (1976), 7. Aufl. Fischer Verlag.

Toendury, G., Entwicklungsgeschichte und Fehlbildungen der Wirbelsaeule, Die Wirbelsaeule in Forschung und Praxis, Hippokrates Verlag Stuttgart 7 (1958).

Toendury, G., Gelenke und Baender der Wirbelsaeule, in: Rauber-Kopsch: Lehrbuch und Atlas d. Anatomie des Menschen, Bd. 1-Bewegungsapparat, von G. Toendury, S. 73-104, Georg Thieme Verlag Stuttgart (1968).

Toendury, G., The cervical spine, Huber Bern (1974).

Toendury, G., Angewandte und topographische Anatomie, Thieme Verlag Stuttgart (1981).

Torg, I.S., et al., Unusual fractures caused by football-helmets impact. The physician and sports med. (1976) 73.

Torklus, D. von, Zervikaler Kopfschmerz—Typenbildung I bis III, Orthop. Praxis 15 (1979) 730.

Torklus, D. von, Injektionsbehandlung der Wirbelbogengelenke, Die Wirbelsaeule in Forschung und Praxis, Hippokrates Verlag Stuttgart 87 (1981) 163.

Torklus, D. von, Hamburger Flektionskorsett bei chronischem Lumbalsyndrom und Lumboischialgie, Orthop. Praxis 18 (1982) 239.

Trimming 130, Die neue Richtgeschwindigkeit fuer Ihre Gesundheit, Deutscher Sportbund, Frankfurt/M. (1983).

Trimming 130, Einfaches Handlungskonzept fuer 30- bis 60-jaehrige, Deutsches Aerzteblatt 80 (1983) 13.

Troisier, O., et al., Traitement des lombo-sciatiques par injection intra-discale d'enzymes proteolytiques (nucleolyse), La Nouvelle Presse Medical No. 4 (1980) 227.

Troup, D.G., et al., Measurements of the sagittal mobility of the lumbar spine and hips, Ann. physical. mediraire 9 (1968) 308.

Tscherne, H., et al., Operationsindikationen und chirurgische Technik bei Verletzungen, Tumoren und entzuendlichen Erkrankungen der Wirbelsaeule, 97. Tagung der Deutschen Gesellschaft fuer Chirurgie, 1980 in Munich; in Langenbecks Archiv 352 (1980) 421.

Tscherne, H., Muhr, G., Op Den Winkel, R., Frakturen and Luxationen der HWS, Operative Behandlung, H. Unfallheilk. 149 (1980) 89.

Tsukuda, K., Histologische Studien ueber die Zwischenwirbelscheibe des Menschen, Mitt. med. Akad. Kyoto 25 (1939) 270.

Tuetsch, C., Ulrich, S.P., Wirbelsaeule und Hochleistungsturnen, Schweiz, Rundschau Med. 61 (1973) 1085, Schweiz, Rundschau Med. 63 (1974) 946.

Tuetsch, C.S., Ulrich, P., Wirbelsaeule und Hochleistungsturnen, Sportarzt 9 (1974) 206.

Uffelmann, J., Handbuch der privaten und oeffentlichen Hygiene des Kindes, ECW Vogel Verlag, Leipzig (1881).

Ullman, W., Chirotherapie in der Landpraxis, Man. Med. 18 (1980) 29.

Ulrich, S.P., Rueckenschmerzen bei Jugendlichen, Jugend und Sport 27 (1971) 349.

Ulrich, S.P., Endstadium der vertebralen Dekompensation durch Rudern, Sportarzt und Sportmed. 11 (1972) 284.

Ulrich, S.P., Haeufigkeit von Rueckenschmerzen bei Schuelerinnen, Sportarzt und Sportmed. 26 (1975) 59.

Unterharnscheidt, F., About boxing: review of historical and medical aspects, Texas Reports on Biology and Medicine, 28 (1970) 421.

Urban, J.P.G., Holm, S., Maroudas, A., et al. Nutrition of the intervertebral disc, Clinical Orthopaedics and Related Research 129 (1977) 101.

Urban, J., Maroudas, A., The chemistry of the intervertebral disc in relation to its physiological function and requirements, Clinics in Rheumatic Diseases 6 (1980) 51.

Urist, M.R., et al., The four impressions of the back, from Henri Matisse, Clinical Orthopaedics and Related Research (1972) 117.

Van den Hooff, A., Histological age changes in the anulus fibrosus of the human intervertebral disc, Gerontologia 9 (1964) 136.

Vanderlinden, R.G., Salter, D., Articular facet rhizotomy by percutaneous electrocoagulation, Canadian Journal of Neurology 5 (1978) 349.

Varughese, G., Quartey, R.C., Familial lumbar spinal stenosis with acute disc herniations, Journal of Neurosurgery 51 (1979) 234.

VDI 2057, Beurteilung der Einwirkung mechanischer Schwingungen auf den Menschen, Blatt 1: Grundlagen, Gliederung, Begriffe (Entw. 1975); Blatt 2: Schwingungseinwirkung auf den menschlichen Koerper (Entw. 1979); Blatt 3: Schwingungsbeanspruchung des Menschen (Entw. 1979).

Vernon-Roberts, B., Pirie, C.J., Degenerative changes in the intervertebral discs of the lumbar spine and their sequelae, Rheumatology and Rehabilitation 16 (1977) 13.

Vetter, G., Die Wirbelsaeule als Ausdrucksfeld psychischer Stoerungen, Dtsch. Med. J. 12 (1961) 249.

Vinz, H., Ueber Alternsveraenderungen der festigkeitsmechanischen Eigenschaften des menschlichen Knochengewebes, Orthop. und Traumotol. 22 (1975) 525.

Virchow, H., Die Eigenform der menschlichen Wirbelsaeule, Anat. Anz. 34 (1909) 157.

Virchow, H., Einzelbeitraege bei der sagittalen Biegung der menschlichen Wirbelsaeule, Anat. Anz. 38 (1911) 176.

Virgin, W.J., Anatomical and pathological aspects of the intervertebral disc, Indian Journal of Surgery 20 (1958) 113.

Vogel, J.M., Whittle, M.W., Bone mineral measurement, University of California, School of Medicine, Davis, CA (personal statement) (1975).

Vogelsang, H., Spinale Arteriographie und Phlebographie, Die Wirbelsaeule in Forschung und Praxis, Hippokrates Verlag Stuttgart 83 (1979) 89.

Volek, J., Der Einfluss des Flugdienstes auf die Wirbelsaeule, Voj. zdrav. Listy 32 (1963) 53.

Vortmann, B.J., Kinesiologie der Halswirbelsaeule vor und nach Manipulation, Manuelle Medizin 33 (1984) 53.

Wackenheim, A., Roentgendiagnosis of the craniovertebral region, Springer Berlin 1974.

Wagenhaeuser, F.J., Die Klinik der Haltungssterungen und des M. Scheuermann, Zschr. Praev. Med. 14 (1969) 157.

Wagenhaeuser, F.J., Die Rheumamorbiditaet, Huber Bern (1969).

Wagner, H., Entwicklungsstufen in Sportmedizin, Hrsg.: Groh, Ferdinand Enke Verlag Stuttgart 1962.

Wagner, R., 10 Jahre Jugendarbeitsschutzuntersuchungen, Erfahrungen und Zielsetzung, Fortschr. d. Med. 89 (1971) 129.

Wagner, R., Gesetzlicher Arbeitsschutz—Aktueller Sachstand, Arbeitsmedizin, Sozialmedizin, Praeventivmedizin 10 (1975) 204.

Wagner, R., Untersuchungen nach dem Jugendarbeitsschutzgesetz, Erkenntnisse und Erfahrungen, Deutscher Kongress fuer aerztl. Fortbildung (1976).

Wagner, R., Hasse, H., Die Untersuchungen nach dem Jugendarbeitsschutzgesetz, Chance oder Erschwernis fuer behinderte Jugendliche? Arbeitsmedizin, Sozialmedizin, Praeventivmedizin 9 (1974) 93.

Walker, N., Dambacher, M.A., Rueegsegger, P., Untersuchungen zur Bedeutung der Osteoporose bei der Entstehung der Pseudospondylolisthesis, Z. Orthop. 118 (1980) 451.

Walther, G., Klinische Bedeutung von Tendinosen und Tendoperiostosen der oberen Kostotransversalgelenke, Die Wirbelsaeule in Forschung und Praxis, Hippokrates Verlag Stuttgart 125 (1962) 186.

Wassilev, W., Ultrastruktur des Nucleus pulposus bei bipedalen Maeusen, Comptes rendus de l'Academie bulgare des Sciences 23 (1970) 15611.

Waterloh, E., et al., Die fechtspezifischen Belastungen und ihre Auswirkungen auf Kinder und Jugenliche, Verg: Sportmedizinisches Institut der RWTH Aachen (1978).

Watermann, F., Rehabiliation im Rahmen der gesetzlichen Unfallversicherung unter Beruecksichtigung der sozialen und beruflichen Rueckgliederung, Orthopaede 6 (1977) 92.

Weber, E.H., Anatomisch-physiologische Untersuchung ueber einigen Einrichtungen im Mechanismus der menschlichen Wirbelsaeule, Arch. Anat. Physiol. (1927) 240.

Wegener, C., Weber, U., Schoendorf, T.H., Franz, K., Sekundaere Gefaesserkrankungen bein Spondylolisthesis, Z. Orthop. 118 (1980) 337.

Wehlen, R., Sport-Duden 2 (1976).

Weickert, H., Sind Haltungsschaeden im Kindesalter wirklich ernst zu nehmen? Z. aerztl. Fortb. (Jena) 70 (1976) 899.

Weil, M.P., et al., Rhumatisme et charges sociales, Rev. rhum. 1953, March.

Weintraub, A., Psychosomatische Rueckenbeschwerden, Manuelle Medizin 9 (1971) 125.

Weintraub, A., Die Grenzen der psychosomatischen Kreuzschmerzanalyse, Med. Welt 28 NF (1977) 948.

Weintraub, A., Beitrag zur Diagnostik psychosomatischer Rueckenbeschwerden, Die Wirbelsaeule in Forschung und Praxis, Hippokrates Verlag Stuttgart 82 (1979) 219.

Weiss, J.W., Der Einfluss der Absatzhoehe auf Wirbelsaeule und Becken, Z. Kr. gym. 30 (1978) 100.

Weiss, J.W., Grundlagen der Korsettbehandlung bei der juvenilen Kyphose, Die Wirbelsaeule in Forschung und Praxis 89 (1980) 81.

Weltbrecht, W.U., et al., Langzeitergebnisse verschiedener Operationsmethoden bei lumbalen Bandscheibenvorfaellen, Orthop. Praxis (1980) 8.

Werthemann, Rinetlen, Spondylitis ankylopoetica, Z. Neuro. 142 (1932) 200.

Wertzberger, K.L., Peterson, H.A., Acquired spondylolysis and spondylolisthesis in the young child, Spine 5 (1980) 437.

Wespi, H., Schulaerztliche Beurteilung der Wirbelsaeule, in: Die Funktionsstoerungen der Wirbelsaeule, Huber Verlag Stuttgart (1964).

Wespi, H., Haltungsstoerungen, Scheuermannsche Krankheit und Schularzt, Zschr. Praeventivmed. 14 (1969) 137.

Wespi, H., Beitrag zur Frage der Behandlung der Scheuermannschen Krankheit, Schweiz, Rundschau Med. (Praxis) 65 (1976) 44.

Whincup, M., Back injuries and legal remedies, Occupational Health (London) 23 (1971) 120.

White, A.A., Analysis of the mechanics of the thoracic spine in man; an experimental study of autopsy specimens, Acta Orthop. Scand. Suppl. 127 (1969) 1.

White, A.A., Johnson, R.M., Panjabi, M.M., et al., Biomechanical analysis of clinical stability in the cervical spine, Clinical Orthopaedics and Related Research (1975) 85.

White, A.A., Panjabi, M.M., Clinical biomechanics of the spine, Lippincott, Philadelphia (1976/1978).

Whitman, A., Observations upon an anatomic variation of the lumbo-sacral joint, Ref. Zentr. Org. ges. Chir. 30 (1925) 301.

Wiberg, G., Back pain in relation to the nerve of intervertebral disc, Acta Orthop. Scand. 19 (1949) 211.

Wieg, P., Subjektive Einschaetzung der Laerm- und Schwingungsexpositionen auf Hochseeschiffen, Verk.-Med. 23 (1976) 481.

Wieg, P., Gruener, A., Auswirkungen von Schwingungen auf die Besatzungen von Seeschiffen, Seewirtschaft 9 (1977) 84.

Wieg, P., Gruener, A., Einflussfaktoren auf die subjektive Enschaetzung von Laerm- und Shwingungsexpositionen, Verkehrmedizin 24 (1977) 275.

Wigh, R.E., The thoracolumbar and lumbosacral transitional junctions, Spine 5 (1980) 215.

Wilder, D.G., et al., Objective measurement of L 4-5 instability, Spine 5 (1980) 56.

Wilhelm, W., Orthopaedische Versorgung des Rumpfes durch vorgefertigte Orthesen und masskonfektionierte Mieder, Orthop. Praxis 9 (1980) 759.

Wilkie, R., Beetham, R., Trans-femoral lumbar epidural venography, Spine 5 (1980) 424.

Wilkingson, H.A., Schuman, N., Intradiscal corticosteroids in the treatment of lumbar and cervical disc problems, Spine 5 (1980) 385.

Willert, H.G., Enderle, A., Tumoren der Wirbelbogen gelenke, Die Wirbelsaeule in Forschung und Praxis, Hippokrates Verlag Stuttgart 87 (1981) 115.

Williams, J.G.P., Sportverletzungen, Folia traumatol. Geigy Basel (Switzerland) 1973.

Williams, N., Biological effects of segmental vibration, Journal of Occupational Medicine 17 (1975) 37.

Williams, R.W., Mirolumbar disectomy, A conservative surgical approach to the virgin herniated lumbar disc, Spine 3 (1978) 175.

Willner, S., Moire topography for the diagnosis and documentation of scoliosis, Acta Orthop. Scand. 50 (1979) 295.

Winkler, K.O., Arbeitsmedizinische Befunde, ihre Erfassung und ihre Bedeutung fuer den Arbeitseinsatz, 16. Deutscher Kongress fuer Arbeitsschutz und Arbeitsmedizin, Dusseldorf 14-17 November (1979).

Witt, A.N., Fischer, V., Vibrationsbedingte Wirbelsaeulenschaeden bei Hubschrauberpiloten, Forschung Ber. Wehrmedizin BMVg, FBWM 80-2 (1980).

Woersdoerfer, O., Magerl, F., Funktionelle Anatomie der Wirbelsaeule, Hefte Unfallheilk. 149 (1980) 1.

Wohlenberg, H., Lorbacher, P., Drechsel, U., Schmarsow, R., Die perkutane Wirbelkoerperstanzbiopsie mit der Jamshidi-Biopsienadel, Dtsch. med. Wschr. 103 (1978) 902.

Wolff, H.D., Neurophysiologische Aspekte der Manuellen Medizin, Manuelle Medizin Fischer Heidelberg (1978).

Wolff, H.D., Lumbale Schmerz- und Stoerungszustaende aus chirotherapeutischer Sicht, Die Wirbelsaeule in Forschung und Praxis, Hippokrates Verlag Stuttgart 83 (1979) 175.

Wolff, H.D., Kontraindikationen gezielter Handgrifftherapie an der Wirbelsaeule, Manuelle Medizin 18 (1980) 39.

Wolff, H.D., Manuelle Therapie beim Kopfschmerz, Orth. Klinik Unversitet des Saarlandes, Therapiewoche 30 (1980) 513.

Wolff, H.D., Die Sonderstellung der Kopfgelenke in Gelenkmechanik, Physiologie und Klinik, Orthop. Praxis 19 (1983) 118.

Wolff, J., Das Gesetz der Transformation der Knochen, Hirschwald, Berlin (1892).

Wolter, D., et al., Der Wirbelkoerperersatz und ander operative Massnahmen bei Osteolysen und pathologischen Frakturen der Wirbelsaeule, Hefte Unfallheilk. 165 (1983) 285.

Wood, G.A., Hayes, K.C., A Kinetic Model of Intervertebral Stress During Lifting (Ein biomechanisches Modell der Zwischenwirbelbelastung beim

Gewichtheben, Biomechanik/Wirbelsaeule/ Gewichtheben, British Journal of Sports Medicine, Loughborough 8 (1974) 2/3.

Wotzka, G., Grandjean, E., Burandt, U., et al., Investigations for the development of an auditorium seat, Proc. Symp. "Sitting Posture," Taylor & Francis, London (1969).

Wotzka, G., Grandjean, E., Burandt, U., et al., Untersuchungen zur Entwicklung eines Hoersaalsitzes, Zschr. fuer Praeventivmedizin 14 (1969) 193.

Wrede, A., Haltungsuntersuchungen an Schuelern, Z. Orthop. 114 (1976) 985.

Wright, V., A unifying concept for the spondyloarthropathies, Clinical Orthopaedics and Related Research 143 (1979) 8.

Wuellenweber, R., Lumbale Syndrome aus der Sicht des Neurochirurgen, Die Wirbelsaeule in Forschung und Praxis, Hippokrates Verlag Stuttgart 83 (1979) 189.

Wuensche, O., Scheele, G., Untersuchungen ueber Skelettveraenderungen bei Albinoratten nach Ueberdruckexposition, Deutsche Luft- und Raumfahrt, DLR-FB 71 29 (1971).

Wuensche, O., Scheele, G., Knochenzysten bei Albinoratten nach Dekompression aus Ueberdruck, Arch. orthop. Unfallchir. 77 (1973) 7.

Wuensche, O., Scheele, G., Druckfallkrankheit des Fliegers, Tauchers und Druckluftarbeiters, Sanitaetsdienstliches 1 (1974) 6, Information Dr. A. Wolff Bielefeld.

Wuensche, O., Scheele, G., Roentgen-Reihenuntersuchungen an Druckluftarbeitern zur Feststellung von Skelettveraenderungen als Folge der Ueberdruckexposition, Bundesanstalt fuer Arbeitscchutz und Unfallforschung, Dortmund, Forschungsbericht (1974) 125.

Wuensche, O., Scheele, G., Fruehformen von Skelettveraenderungen nach Ueberdruckexposition im Tierexperiment und Roentgenkontrollen bei Druckluftarbeitern, Zbl. Arbeitsmed. Arbeitsschutz und Prophylaxe 26 (1976) 108.

Wuensche, O., Scheele, G., Spaetschaeden durch Unterdruck-Druckfall, Aerztl. Praxis 28 (1976) 2043.

Wyke, B., Molina, F., Gelenkreflexe der Halswirbelsaeule, 6th International Congress on Physical Medicine Barnosell, Ravella-Barcelona (1972).

Wyke, B.D., The neurological basis of thoracic spinal pain, Rheumatol. Phys. Med. 10 (1967) 356.

Wyke, B.D., Morphological and functional features of the innervation of the costovertebral joints, Folia Morphol. Prague 23 (1975) 296.

Wyndham, C.H., et al., Mechanical efficiency of a champion walker, S.A. Fr. Med. 7 45 (1961) 551.

Wyss, T., Ulrich, S.P., Festigkeitsuntersuchungen und gezielte Extensionsbehandlung der Lendenwirbelsaeule unter Beruecksichtigung des Bandscheiben-Vorfalles, Vierteljahresschr. Naturforsch. Ges. Zurich, Beiheft 3 (1954) 1.

Yamamoto, Isao, et al., Ossification of the posterior longitudinal ligament, Surg. Neurol. 12 (1979) 414.

Yamano, Y., Disc herniation of cervical spine, Arch. Orthop. Traumatol. Surg. 96 (1980) 271.

Yuecel, M., Kontrastdichte und Nebenwirkungsrate bei lumbaler Myelographie, Z. Orthop. 117 (1979) 115.

Yuecel, M., et al., Die Behandlung des floriden dorsalen Morbus Scheuermann mit zwei neuen atmungsaktiven Korsetten und ihre biomechanischen Wirkungsprinzipien, Z. Orthop. 119 (1981) 292.

Zaitseva, M., The influence of working conditions on the development and course of rheumatism, Vop. Reum. 4 (1970) 59.

Zaleske, D.J., et al., Combined biochemical and clinical investigation of chemonucleolysis failures, Clin. Orthop. 126 (1977) 121.

Zapfe, E., Die konservative Behandlung des M. Scheuermann, Die Wirbelsaeule in Forschung und Praxis, Hippokrates Verlag Stuttgart 89 (1980) 59.

Zergollern, J., et al., The painful shoulder syndrome in musicians playing in the orchestra of the Croatian National Theater, Medicina i glazba 101 (1979) 249.

Zettel, H., Ueber Sportschaeden am Stuetz- und Bewegungsapparat, Mschr. Unfallheilk. 63 (1960) 448.

Ziegler, R., Osteoporose: Klinik, Diagnostik, Therapie, Dtsch. Aerzteblatt 81 (1984) 3249.

Zielke, K., Vorteile und Abgrenzung der VDS gegen Dwyer und Harrington, Die Wirbelsaeule in Forschung und Praxis, Hippokrates Verlag Stuttgart 72 (1978) 61.

Zielke, K., Ventrale Derotationsspondylodese, Behandlungsergebnisse bei idiopathischen Lumbalskoliosen, Z. Orthop. 120 (1982) 320.

Zimmermann, K.G., Adophsen, P., Lenz, H., et al., Alkaptonurie und Ochronose, Dtsch. med. Wschr. 97 (1972) 242.

Zimmermann, M., Die physiologischen Grundlagen der Schmerzempfindung und Schmerztherapie, Orthop. Praxis 15 (1979) 12.

Zippel, H., Spondylolisthesis der Halswirbelsaeule, Beitr. Orthop. und Traumatol. 23 (1976) 5.

Zippel, H., Pfeil, E., Wirbelgleiten im Lendenbereich, Geklaerte und ungeklaerte Spondylolisthesisprobleme, Johann Ambrosius Barth, Leipzig (1980).

Zmarzlik, J., Neuregelung des Jugendarbeitsschutzes, Arbeitsschutz 8 (1974) 221.

Zmarzlik, J., Jugendarbeitsschutzgesetz, Modernisiert, Arbeitsschutz, Fachbeilage d. Bundesarbeitsblattes, 5 (1976) 143.

Zorn, E., Laerm- und Vibrationsbelastung an Bord von Schiffen, Schiffsingenieur Journal 20 (1973) 8.

Zsernaviczky, J., Weichel, K., Die funktionellen Schraegaufnahmen der Lendenwirbelsaeule zur Beurteilung der Wirbelbogengelenke, Die Wirbelsaeule in Forschung und Praxis, Hippokrates Verlag Stuttgart 87 (1981) 49.

Zuckschwerdt, L., et al., Wirbelgelenk und Bandscheibe, Hippokrates Verlag, Stuttgart (1955).

Zukschwerdt, L., Mitarb, Wirbelgelenk und Bandscheibe, 2. Aufl. Hippokrates Verlag Stuttgart (1960).

Index

A

Achilles tendon, effects of training on, 5
Acupuncture, 236-237
Adolescents. *See* Children/adolescents
Adults, 209-229. *See also* Aging
    at home, 216
    young, 208-209
        back pain in, 208
        disabling conditions in, 208-209
        posture in, 208
Aging, 225-226
    effects on bones, 36, *36*, 119, *120*
    effects on intervertebral disc, 45-46, 63
        collagen fibers, 43
        fluid content, 39
        metabolism, 39
        mineral content, 42
        stability, 58, *58*
Airplanes, 222-223
Alkaptonuria, 136-137
Angles, 34-35, 144
    articular, 34-35, *35*
    body-isthmus, 34-35, *35*
    isthmus, 34-35, *35*
    lumbosacral, 34, *34*, 144
    promontory, 34, *35*, 144
Ankylosing hyperostosis, 45
Ankylosing spondylitis, 127, *135*, 135-136, 208
    surgery for, *246*
Anterior longitudinal ligament, 20

Aorta, 24, 159
Aquatic sports injuries, 298-306
    due to platform diving, 303-305, *304-305*
    due to rowing and canoeing, 298-301, *299*
    due to sailing, 301
    due to scuba diving, 302-303
    due to surfing, 305
    due to water skiing, 305
    due to wind surfing, 305-306
Archery, 315
Arm-stretching test, 177, *177*, 185
Arteries, 24, *25*
Arteriography, 189
Articular angle, 34-35, *35*
Articular processes, 17-18
Articulations, 26-31. *See also* specific articulations
    arthrosis at, 125-131
        athletic activity for persons with, 327
    effects of training on, 6
    effects of vibration on, 171
    head, 127-128
    of motor unit, 62
    occipital, 29-30, *29-31*
    pseudoarticulations, 129
    sacroiliac, 28, *29*, 127
    sports-related injuries of, 322
    symphysis pubis, 29
    "the 100 articulations of spinal column," 26
    uncovertebral, 30, *31*, 128-129
    vertebral arch, 27-28, *27-28*, 125-127
    vertebrocostal, 30-31, 130-131

Note: Page number in *italics* indicate figures; those followed by "t" indicate tables.

Astronauts, 121, 138-139
Atlantoaxial articulation arthroses, 127-128, *128*
Automobiles, 218-221, *219-221*
Autonomic nervous system, 21-22

B

Baastrup's disease, 95, 115-116, *117*
   cause of, 116
   injection therapy for, 116
   ligament damage in, 116
   sports-related, 284-285, 322
   surgery for, 247-248
Back pain
   chemical changes as cause of, 46
   in children, 199
   diagnostic tests for, 185, *185*
   discogenic, 46
   due to damaged motor segments, 67
   effect on posture, 147
   in late adolescence, 208
   taking history of, 179-180
Badminton, 274, *275*
Ballet, *316*, 316-317
Bang's disease, 131
Basilar impression, 29-30, *30-31*
Basketball, 281
Bechterew's disease, 127, *135*, 135-136, 208
   surgery for, *246*
Bedrest, 223-224
Bending, 152, 211-212
   testing for, 181, *181-183*
Bicycles, 218
   racing of, 263-264, *264*
Biochemistry, 36-48
   of bones, *36*, 36-37
   of intervertebral disc, 37-46. *See also*
      Intervertebral disc
Biomechanics of spinal column, 142-173. *See also*
      specific topics
   definition of, 142
   effect of lack of exercise on, 165-166
   effect of partial body vibrations on, *171*, 171-172
   effect of total body vibrations on, 166-171
   intervertebral disc, 164-165
      models of, 164-165
      stress tolerance values for, 164
   ligaments, 165
   mobility/movement, 148-165
      lifting, carrying, 152-154, *153-154*
      role of blood vessels in, 159-160
      role of muscles in, 154-158, *156-157*
      role of nerves in, 158-159
      standing, sitting, lying, 148-151, *149-151*
      walking, bending, rotating, 151-152
   model of, *172*, 172-173
   posture, 144-148, *146*
   shape, 143-146, *145*
   skeleton, 160-164
      stress tolerance values for, 163-164
      structural analyses and stability studies of, 161-163, 162t-163t
      transformation through stress on, 160-161
Biopsy, vertebral, 185
Block vertebrae, 79-80, 81, *81*
Blood vessels, 24-26, *24-26*, 159-160
   effects of vibration on, 171
Boats, 223
Bobsledding, 306
Body-isthmus angle, 34-35, *35*
Bone spur disease. *See* Spondylosis deformans
Bones. *See also* Vertebral arch; Vertebral body
   disorders of, 119-124. *See also* specific disorders
      hereditary systemic diseases, 123-124
      osteopathies, 122-123
      osteopetrosis, 123
      osteoporosis, 120-122
      pain of, 119
      tumors, 124
   effect of stress on bioarchitecture of, 160-161
      "pressure absorption plates," 160
      reaction to mechanical stresses, 160
      tetracycline marking, 161
   effects of aging on, 36, *36*, 119, *120*
   effects of training on, 4-5
   effects of vibration on, 169-170, 171
   mechanical-biochemical interactions in, 46-47
   metabolism in, *36*, 36-37
   of motor unit, 62
   red vs. yellow marrow in, 36
   stress tolerance values for, 163-164
   structural analyses and stability studies of, 161-163, 162t-163t
   structural types of, 160
Boxing, 276-277, *276-277*
Brucellosis, 131
Buses, 221-222
Butterfly vertebra, 80

C

Cadmium, bone damage due to, 137-138
Canoeing, 298-301, *299*
Caplan's syndrome, 134

Car racing, 263
Carrying, 152-154, 213, *213-215*. *See also* Lifting
Cartilage
    effects of training on, 5-6
    vibration effects on, 170
Case history taking, 179-180
Cervical rib syndrome, 78
Cervico-occipital transition
    syndromes of, 82t, 82-83
    variations of, 78
Cervicodynia, psychosomatic, 179t
Cervicothoracic transition syndromes, 82t, 82-83
Chairs, 200-202, 212, 216, *216*, 228-229, *229*
Chemical substances, 137-138, 224
Chemonucleolysis, 235-236
Children/adolescents
    abdominal homework position for, 207, *207*
    dangers of motorization to, 205-207
    factors adversely affecting spinal columns of, 198
    growth acceleration of, 195
    importance of exercise for, 197-198
    inactivity of, 197
    isometric exercises for, 204, *206*
    lead poisoning in, 197
    postural damage and back pain in, 198-200
    preschool child, 196
    sports and spine of, 328, 328t
    transition to adulthood of, 208-209
        disabling conditions, 208-209
        posture, 208
    treatment for spinal column damage in, 207-208
Chondrodystrophy fetalis, 124
Chondroitin-4-sulfate, 42
Chondroitin-6-sulfate, 42
Chondrosis. *See* Intervertebral chondrosis
Chymopapain injections, 235-236
"Codfish" vertebrae, 47
Cold, 224
Collagen, 43
Collagenase injections, 235
Computed tomography, 189
Conservative treatment, 229-239. *See also* Treatment modalities,conservative
Contact thermography, 186
Contortionists, 317-319, *318-319*
Cribrum, 62
Cross-country skiing, 254-257
Curvatures of spine, 32-34, *33*, 143

D

Dance injuries, *316*, 316-317
Decathlon, 272-273

Dermatome chart, *237*
Desks, 200-202, *201-203*
Diabetes, 44-45, 136
Discography, 189
Discometry, 53, 189
Discus throw, *311*, 311-313
Diving, 303-305, *304-305*
Documentation
    of imaging diagnostics, 191
    of physical exam findings, 187-188, 188t
Dorsalgia, psychosomatic, 179t
Drug therapy, 231

E

Elderly
    spinal column in, 225-226
    sports for, 330-332
Electromyography, 155-157, *156-157*
Endochondral dysostoses, 124
Enzymes, in intervertebral disc, 43
Equestrian sports injuries, 287-289
    due to galloping races, 289
    due to horse jumping and dressage, 289
    due to horseback riding, 287-289, *288-289*
    due to polo, 289
    due to trotting races, 289
Exercise. *See* Physical activity; Sports

F

Fencing, 282-283
Fish vertebrae, 121
Fitness programs, 253-257, 254t
    guidelines for, 254t
    hiking, mountain climbing, cross-country skiing, 254-257
    jogging, 253-254
    for previously damaged spine, 322-328, 323t-325t
        bone damage, 327
        intervertebral disc or articulation damage, 327
        juvenile kyphosis, 323-326, 325t-326t
        scoliosis, 327
        spondylolysis, spondylolisthesis, vertebral dislocations, 327
        surgery, 327-328
    prophylactic examinations for, 329-330
    short, 254, *255*
Flexion, 152, 181, *181-183*, 211-212
Fluorosis, 137
Fractures, surgery for, 244-245, *246-248*

Functional spinal abnormalities, 77-140. *See also* specific disorders
    ankylosing spondylitis, 135-136
    Baastrup's disease, 115-116
    compounded, 81, *81*
    due to anatomical variations, 77-78, *78-79*
    due to arthrosis at spinal articulations, 125-131
    due to chemical substances, 137-138, 224
    due to infections, 131-133
    due to injuries, 139
    due to ionizing radiation, 138
    due to ligament ossification, 119
    due to metabolic disorders, 136-137
    due to muscle disorders, 124-125
    due to narrow vertebral canal and intervertebral canals, 82
    due to rheumatism, 133-134
    due to space flight, 138-139
    due to surgery, 139
    due to tumors, 138
    due to vertebral displacements, 102-104
    due to vertebral slippage, 98-100
    frequency of, 131t
    hypermobility, 118-119
    impairments due to, 83
    instability, 118
    intervertebral chondrosis, 108-110
    intervertebral disc prolapse, 112-115
    intervertebral osteochondrosis, 110-112
    kyphosis, 83-90
        juvenile, 84-89
        senile, 89-90
    lordosis, 94-95
    prognosis of, 139-140
    scoliosis, 90-93
    spinal acroosteoalgia, 116-118
    spondylosis deformans, 105-108
    spondylosis hyperostotica, 108
    stress resistance in, 95-98
    in vertebral arch series, 80-81
    in vertebral body-intervertebral disc series, 79-80, *80*
Furniture
    in schools, 200-202, *201-204,* 205t
    technical improvements in, 228-229, *229*

G

Gentamicin-PMMA balls, 246, *248*
Gliding, 286-287
Golf, 273
Gout, 136

Guentz's sign, 104
Gymnastics, 290-298
    on apparatus, 292-294, *294-295*
    competitive, 294-296, *295-296*
    floor exercises, 291-292, *292-293*
    in school, 198, 202
    trampoline, 296-298, *297*

H

Hammer throw, 311-313, *312*
Handball, 281
Heat, 224
Helicopters, 222-223
Hemispondylus dorsalis, 80
Hiking, 254-257
History taking, 179-180
Hockey, 281-282, 310
Hormones, effects on intervertebral disc, 44-45, 45t
Horseback riding, 287-289, *288-289*
Hurdle running, 267-269, *268*
Hyaline cartilage, 5-6
Hydrotherapy, 235
Hypermobility, 118-119, 178
    causes of, 118
    diagnostic criteria for, 178
    in pregnancy, 118-119
    significance of, 178

I

Ice hockey, 310
Ice skating, 307-310, *309-310*
Immobility, 69
    biomechanical effects of, 165-166
    intervertebral, 72
Immunoglobulins, 43-44
Incarceratio iliosacralis, 73
Infections, 131-133, 132t
Injection therapy, 235-236
Instability. *See* Stability
Interarticularis spondylolysis, 81
Interspinous ligament, 21
Intervertebral chondrosis, 108-110, *110-111*
    biochemistry of, 109
    causes of, 108-109
    diagnosis of, 109
    recognition of, 109
Intervertebral disc
    aging of, 45-46, *58*
    avascularity of, 62
    biochemistry of, 37

chemical changes as cause of pain around, 46
collagenous fibers of, 43
development of
    postnatal, 15, *15-16*
    prenatal, 12
effects of aging on, 39, 63
effects of axial pressure on, 57t, 57-59
effects of traction on, 59, 60t
effects of training on, 6-7
elastic fibers of, 43
enzymes in, 43
fluid content of, 39-41, *40-41*
functional anatomy of, 50-52, *52*
hormonal effects on, 44-45, 45t
immune reactions in, 43-44
impairments of
    areas susceptible to, 105, *105*
    athletic activity for persons with, 327
    intervertebral chondrosis, 108-110
    intervertebral osteochondrosis, 110-112
    protrusion and prolapse, 58, 77, 112-115
    spondylosis deformans, 105-108
    spondylosis hyperostotica, 108
    vertebral body rim detachment, 115
infection of, 132-133, *133*
lymphocytes in, 43
mechanical-biochemical interactions in, 47-48
metabolic pathways in, 37-39, *38*
microstructure of, 44
mineral content of, 41-42
as "mixed articulation," 51
models of, 164-165
morphology of, 18-20, *19-20*
nerve supply of, 15, *23*
nutritional effects on, 44-45, 45t, 109
organic matrix of, 42-43
significance of internal pressure of, 52-53, *52-53*
stability of, 57-58
    rotational, 59-61, 60t, *61*
    shifting, 61-62
stress tolerances of, 57, 57t, 164
tissue of, 18
in vivo pressure measurements in, 53-57, *54-56*
Intervertebral disc prolapse, 112-115
    biomechanical risks of, 113-114
    detachment of portion of vertebral body rim, 115, *116-117*
    functional capacity after surgery for, 115
    posteromedial/posterolateral forms of, 114-115, *116*
    protrusion of back wall leading to, 114, *114*
    Schmorl's nodules in, 113, *113-114*

    surgery for, 241-242, *242-243*
    types of, *112, 115*
Intervertebral foramina (canals)
    morphology of, 17
    narrowness of, 82
    orientations of nerve roots in, 23, *23*
Intervertebral insufficiency, 69-70
    load-bearing capacity in, 74
    terminology of, 69-70
    vs. vertebral insufficiency, 69
Intervertebral motor segment, 32, 49-76, *50*
    anatomy and functions of, 49-50, *50. See also specific structures*
        articulations, 62
        blood vessels, 65
        bones, 62
        intervertebral disc, 50-62
        ligaments, 64
        muscles, 64-65
        nerves, 65-68
        vertebral body-intervertebral disc boundary, 62-64
    chemical changes as cause of pain around, 46
    concept of, 49
    definition of, 49
    external influences on, 68-69
        lack of motion, 69
        sinus vibrations, 68
        stochastic and impacting vibrations, 68-69
    performance-impaired, 69-76
        intervertebral immobility, 72
        intervertebral instability, 70-72, *71-72*
        intervertebral insufficiency, 69-70
        load-bearing capacity in intervertebral insufficiency, 74
        spondylogenic syndromes, 75t, 75-76
        vertebral blockade, 72-74, *73*
Intervertebral osteochondrosis, 110-112, *111-112*
    bone-chip blocking operation for, *240-241*
    mechanism of, 110-111
    radiological diagnosis of, 112
    recognition of, 110
    spinal abnormalities associated with, 111, 112
    surgery for, 112, 242-243
Ionizing radiation, 138
Isometric exercises, 204, *206*
Isthmus angle, 34-35, *35*
Ivory vertebrae, 123, 124

J

Japanese wrestling, 278-279
Javelin throw, *314,* 314-315

Jogging, 253-254
Joints. *See* Articulations
Jump accelerogram, 269, *269*
Jumping, 269-272, *269-272*
    down jump, 270
    high jump, 271-272, *271-272*
    long jump, 270, *270*
    pole vaulting, 272, *273*
    triple jump, *270,* 270-271
Juvenile kyphosis, 84-89. *See also* Kyphosis

K

Kinetosis, 217t, 217-218
"Kissing spines," 116
Klippel-Feil syndrome, 81
Kyphosis, 32-33, *33,* 83-90
    causes of, 79, 83-84
    due to semivertebra, 80
    in gymnasts, 290
    juvenile, 35, 84-89, *145*
        athletic activity for persons with, 323-326, 325t-326t
        cause of, 84, *85*
        development of, 84, *84*
        diagnosis of, 87
        frequency of radiological evidence of, 85, *86*
        of lumbar spine, 85, *86*
        occupational activity and, 96-97
        prevalence of, 84
        range of malformation in, 84
        Schmorl's nodules in, 85, *85*
        stages of, 87
        stress resistance of, 95-97
        surgical correction of, *88*
        of thoracic spine, 86, *87*
    osteoporotic, 121-122
    pathological lordoses and, 94-95
    postural, 198
    senile, 89-90
        development of, 89, *89*
        osteoporosis and, 89, *92*
        progression of, 89, *89-91*
        stress resistance of, 97
        therapy for, 89
    stress resistance of, 95-97
    "student," 83
    surgery for, 243-244, *244-246*
        indications for, 139

L

Lead poisoning, 137, 197
Leisure sports, 251-253
Leukemia, radiation-induced, 138
Lifting, 152-154, *153-154,* 213, *213-215*
    disc pressure measurements during, 53, *55-56*
    effects on internal disc pressure, 52-53, *52-53*
    incorrect posture for, 153, *154*
    internal abdominal pressure during, 153-154
    rotational movements in, 154
    sources of force necessary for, 152
    strain at lumbosacral transition during, 153, *153-154*
    threshold values for, 154, 214t
    weight lifting, 283-286, *284-285*
Ligaments, 165
    Baastrup's disease due to wear of, 115-116
    effects of training on, 5
    functions of, 64
    morphology of, 20-21, *21*
    ossification of, 119
Ligamentum flavum, 20
Lordosis, 32-33, *33, 145,* 145-146
    compensational, 94
    in gymnasts, 291, *291, 294*
    pathomorphological, 94-95
    stress resistance of, 98
Lumbago, due to intervertebral instability, 71
Lumbalization, 78
Lumboischialgia, 71
Lumbosacral angle, 34, *34*
Lumbosacral radioculography, 189
Lumbosacral transition
    high load conditions of, 83
    intervertebral osteochondrosis at, 112
    syndromes of, 82t, 82-83
Luschka joint. *See* Uncovertebral articulation
Luxations, surgery for, 244-245, *246-248*
Lying, 150, *151*
Lymphocytes, in intervertebral disc, 43

M

Malacic osteopathies, 122-123
Maltese fever, 131
Manipulative therapy, *232,* 232-233
Marble vertebrae, 123
Massage, 234
Minitrampoline, 204-205
Mobility. *See also* Immobility
    differences between spinal column section in, 182t
    impairments of, 178
    norms of, 175, *176,* 176t
    rotational, 152, *153*

testing for, 180-185, 181t-182t, *181-185*
Moire photography, 186, *187,* 191
 of corrected juvenile kyphosis, *88*
 of scoliosis, *95*
Motion sickness, 217t, 217-218
Motor unit. *See* Intervertebral motor segment
Motor vehicles, 216-223
 airplanes and helicopters, 222-223
 automobiles, 218-221, *219-221*
 bicycles, 218
 boats, 223
 buses, 221-222
 exercise breaks from, 228
 kinetosis and, 217t, 217-218
 motorcycles, 218
 trains, 222
Motorbike racing, 263
Motorcycles, 205-207, 218
Mountain climbing, 254-257
Movement bath, 235
Mucopolysaccharidoses, 42
Multiplex dysostosis, 42
Muscles, 154-158, *156-157*
 abdominal, effect on intervertebral disc pressure, 155
 analysis of force ratios of, 155
 cervical, 158
 effect of respiratory movements of rib cage on, 154-155
 effect of training on, 4
 effect of vibrations on, 65, 155-157, *157,* 169
 effect on functional capacity of spine, 124-125
 EMG assessment of, 155, *156*
 functions of, 64
 morphology of, 21, *22*
 role in body movements, 154
 tears of, 158
Myelography, 189
Myeloscintigraphy, 189

N

Nerves, 21-23, *23,* 65-68, *66-67,* 158-159
 biochemical influences on, 47
 effects of vibration on, 171
 historical studies of, 65-66
 supplying intervertebral disc, 15
Neural therapy, 236, *237,* 238t, *239*
Notochord
 persistent, 10, *12,* 79
 regressive metamorphosis of, 9-10, *11*
  failures of, 10

Schmorl's nodes and, 11
Nuclear magnetic resonance-computed tomography, 190
Nucleography, 189
Nucleus pulposus
 elasticity of, 18
 fluid absorption capacity of, 52
 functional anatomy of, 51
 internal turgor of, 52, *52*
 pressure exerted by, 52-53, *52-53*
 stability in, 18, *19*
Nutrition, effects on intervertebral disc, 44-45, 45t

O

Occipital articulations, 29-30, *29-31*
Occipital vertebra, 29, *29*
Ochronosis, 45, 136-137
Orthotic devices, 237
Osteochondrosis. *See* Intervertebral osteochondrosis
Osteomyelitis, 132
 surgery for, 246, *248*
Osteomyelroscleroses, 138
Osteopathies, 122-123
Osteopetrosis, 123
Osteoporosis, 47, 120-122
 of astronauts, 121
 blood circulation and, 121
 bony changes in, 160
 causes of, 120-121
 drug-induced, 165-166
 drug therapy for, 231
 effect of inactivity on, 166
 localized, 120
 postmenopausal, 121
 senile, 120, *121,* 225
 therapy for, 121
 vertebral body changes in, 121, *122*

P

Paget's disease, 123, *123*
Parachuting, 286
Pendulum seat, 216, *216*
Pharmacotherapy, 231
Physical activity. *See also* Sports
 for disabled young adults, 208-209
 fitness programs, 253-257, 254t
 lack of, 194-195, 223-224
 leisure, 251-253
 of past years, 194
 of preschool age child, 196

prophylactic, 226-228, *227*
in school, 202-205
exemption from, 204, 207
Physical therapy, 234-235
Physiotherapy, 233-234
Play, 195-196
Pole vaulting, 272, *273*
Polo, 289
Polyvinylchloride, 138
Posterior longitudinal ligament, 20, *21*
Posture, 143-148
the arts and, 147-148, *148*
"bad," 177
damage in children due to, 198-200
effect of pain on, 147
for horseback riding, *288-289*
impairments of, 175-177, *176-177*
internal vs. external, 146-147
"jeans type," 199-200, *200*
kyphosis due to, 198
in late adolescence, 208
lordosis due to, 95
mechanical influences on, 145
"normal," 143
pelvic inclination and, 146
permanent deviations in, 147
problems in women, 215
psyche and, 146-147
psychological factors and, 195
in school, 200-202, *201-203*
school-related effects on, 194
scoliosis due to, 92, 198-199
stress resistance and, 146
types of, 146, *146*
"utilitarian," 145
Pregnancy, spinal hypermobility in, 118-119
Pressure measurements, intradiscal, 53-57, *54-56*
Promontory angle, 34, *35*
Prophylactic measures, 226-229, 238, 330
Pseudoarticulations, arthrotic, 129
Pseudospondylolisthesis, *102*, 102-103
definition of, 102
nomenclature of, 102-103
stress resistance of, 104
symptoms of, 103
treatment of, 103
vertebral displacements in, 102
"Psychobarometer thoracic spinal column," 146
Psychological factors, 146-147
posture and, 195
Psychosomatic back disorders, 179, 179t

Q

Quintathlon, 272-273

R

Racket sports, 273-276, *275*
Radiation, ionizing, 138
Radicular symptoms, 238t
Radioculography, lumbosacral, 189
Radiodiagnostics, 187-189
mandatory, 192
special procedures in, 188-189
Radix arcus vertebrae, 17
Rehabilitation, 249, 330
Retrolisthesis, *103*, 103-104
definition of, 103
stress resistance of, 104
vertebral canal constriction due to, 104
vertebral displacement in, 103-104
Rheumatism, 133-134
degenerative, 134
genuine forms of, 134
nomenclature of, 133-134
silicoarthritis, 134
spinal stress resistance in, 134
spondylodiscitis and, 134
Rib cage, 31
Roentgenograms
cinematographic, 189
functional, 188-189
graduated plan for, 187-188
measuring of, 189
stereophotogrammetry, 190
stereoscopic, 189
Roller skating, 282, *282*
Rotational mobility, 152, *153,* 212
testing for, 181, 182t, *184*
Rotational sliding, 61-62
Rotational stability, 59-61, 60t, *61,* 162, 163t
Rowing, 298-301, *299*
Rugby, 282
Running, 266-269
hurdles, 267-269, *268*
long-distance, 267
medium-distance, 266-267, *267*
obstacle course, 269, *269*
relay racing, 267
sprinting, 266, *266*

S

Sacralization, 18, 78
Sacroiliac articulations
anatomy of, 18, 28, *29*

arthroses of, 127
brucellosis of, 131
Sailing, 301
Salmonellosis, 131-132
Scalenus syndrome, 78
Scheuermann's disease. *See* Kyphosis, juvenile
Schmorl's nodules, 11, 85, *85*, 113, *113-114*
School
   examinations for, 191, 197
   furniture in, 200-202, *201-204*, 205t
   isometric exercises in, 204, *206*
   physical activity in, 202-205
School headache, 199
Sciatica, psychosomatic, 179t
Scintigraphy, 189
Scoliosis, 90-93, *94*
   appearance of, 92, *93*
   athletic activity for persons with, 327
   causes of, 90-93
   degrees of, 91
   due to compounded spinal abnormalities, 81, *81*
   intervertebral disc variations in, 43
   juvenile, 35
   measuring curvature in, 92, *94*
   postural, 198-199
      vs. structural, 92
   prevalence of, 90
   rotational displacement in, 61-62, 104, *104*
   spondylolisthesis and, 101
   stress resistance of, 97-98
   supporting bone spurs in, 91, *92-93*
   surgery for, 243
   torsion vertebra in, 91, *93*
   variations of, 92
Scuba diving, 302-303
Self-help groups, 238, 249
Semivertebrae, 80
Sharpey's fibers, 18
Ships, 223
Shooting, 315
Shot putting, *313*, 313-314
Silicoarthritis, 134
Sinuvertebral nerve, 22, 65
Sitting, 148-150, *149-151*, 212-213, 224
   EMG of lumbar muscles in, 155-156, *156*
   inactivity and, 166
Ski acrobatics, 320
Skiing, 306-307, *308*
   cross-country, 254-257
   water, 305
Sledding, 306

Soccer, 279-280
Sonography, 190
Space flight, 121, 138-139
Spina bifida, 80
Spinal acroosteoalgia, 116-118, *118*
Spinal column
   in adult, 209-225
   biochemistry of, 36-48
      bones, 36-37
      intervertebral disc, 37-46. *See also* Intervertebral disc
   biomechanics of, 142-173. *See also* Biomechanics
   in child/adolescent, 195-209
   constitutionally relaxed, 180
   effect of aging on, 225-226
   effect of cold and heat on, 224
   effect of vibration on, 48, 64-65
      partial body vibration, *171*, 171-172
      total body vibration, 170-171
   in elderly, 225-226
   evolution of, 9, *10-11*
   external influences on, 141-142
   factors affecting functional capacity of, 77-140. *See also* Functional spinal abnormalities
   flexion of, 211-212
   functions of, 141
   in lying position, 150, *151*
   morphology of, 15-36. *See also* specific structures
      articulations, 26-31, *27-31*, 62
      blood vessels, 24-26, *24-26*, 65, 159-160
      bones, 160-164
      curvatures and angles, 32-36, *33-35*
      intervertebral disc, 18-20, *19-20*, 50-62, 164-165
      ligaments, 20-21, *21*, 64, 165
      motor unit, 32, 49-68
      muscles, 21, *22*, 64-65, 154-158
      nerves, 21-23, *23*, 65-68, *66-67*, 158-159
      vertebral body-intervertebral disc junction, 31-32, 62-64
      vertebral bones and sacrum, 17-18, 62
   normal development of, 9-15
      prenatal, 9-12, *11-12*
      stages of, 9
      until conclusion of growth, 12-15, *13-16*
   normal mobility of, 175, *176*, 176t
   role in posture system, 144-145
   rotation of, 152
   self-protection/adaptation of, 140
   shape of, 143-146, *145*
      impairments of, 175-177, *176-177*

in sitting position, 148-150, *149-151,* 212-213, 224
in standing position, 150, *151,* 209-210, *210*
stresses on, 1-7. *See also* Spinal stress injuries
surgery of, 139
tumors of, 124, 138
variations of, 77-78, *78*
when bending, 152
when walking, 151-152, 210-212, *211*
Spinal column examination, 175-192
   diagnostic imaging procedures, 187-191
      arteriography, 189
      cinematographic roentgenograms, 189
      computed tomography, 189
      documentation of, 191
      functional roentgenograms, 188-189
      mandatory, 192
      nuclear magnetic resonance imaging, 190
      roentgenograms, 187-188
      sonography, 190
      specialized procedures, 189
      stereophotogrammetry, 190
      stereoscopic roentgenograms, 189
      thermography, 190, *190*
   documentation of, 185-186, 186t
   general physical exam, 180
      manual, 180
      neurological, 180
   history taking for, 179-180
   principles of, 175-178
      mobility impairments, 178
      normal mobility, 175, *176,* 176t
      shape and postural impairments, 175-176, *177-178*
   purpose of, 143
   in schools, 191
   specific tests, 180-185, 181t-182t, *181-185*
   West German experience with, 191-192
Spinal cord, 22
Spinal stress
   adaptation to, 3-7
      by articulations, 6
      by bones, 4-5
      effect of overstressing, 4
      by hyaline cartilage, 5-6
      by intervertebral disc, 6-7
      by muscular system, 4
      sports training, 4
      stress tolerance, 4
      by tendons and ligaments, 5
   affecting women, 213-216, *215-216*
   of daily living, 193-194
   due to growth acceleration, 195-196
   periods of increased susceptibility to, 194
Spinal stress injuries, 1-7, 139
   chronic mechanical influences and, 2
   factors affecting stress tolerance, 2-3
   questions regarding mechanisms of, 2
   sports-related. *See* Sports injuries
   terminology of, 1-2
   traumatic vs. long-term, 1-2
   vs. "normal" stress, 2
Spinous processes, 17-18
   sports-related separations of, 321-322, *322*
Spondylitis, 131-133
   surgery for, 246
Spondylodiscitis, 132-133, *133*
   rheumatism and, 134
   surgery for, 246
   therapeutic, 133
Spondylogenic syndromes, 75-76
   due to intervertebral instability, 71
   ischemic heart disorders and, 75t
   psychological factors in, 146
   therapy for, 75-76
   vs. muscle tears, 158
Spondylolisthesis
   athletic activity for persons with, 327
   due to spondylolysis, 98-99
   mobility of, 100
   progression of, 100
   scoliosis and, 101
   sports-related, 320-321
   stress resistance of, 101-102
Spondylolysis
   athletic activity for persons with, 327
   bony adaptations in, 5
   causes of, 99-101
   definition of, 98
   forms of, 98, *98-99*
   frequency of, 98-99
   location of, 99
   progression of, 101
   sports-related, 320-321
   stress resistance of, 101-102
   vertebral arch in, 17, 100-101
Spondylosis deformans, 46, 105-108, *106-107,* 169
   development of, 107, *107*
   diagnosis of, 107
   differential diagnosis of, 107
   exogenous causes of, 107
   mechanism of, 105-106, *106*
   mobility in, 107
   pain of, 107

prevalence of, 105, *106*
swallowing problems due to, 247, *248*
Spondylosis hyperostotica, 108, *108-109*, 136
Sports
    for disabled young adults, 208-209
    for fitness, 253-257, 254t
    juvenile spine and, 328, 328t
    for leisure, 251-253
    for older persons, 330-332
    prophylactic examinations for, 329-330
    in school, 202-205
        exemption from, 204, 207
    spinal stress resistance and, 257-259, 258t
    teachers and trainers in, 315
    as therapy, 332
Sports injuries
    in acrobatics, 317-320
        contortionists, 317-319, *318-319*
        on skis, 320
        on trampoline, 319-320
    in air sports, 286-287
        gliding, 286-287
        parachuting, 286
    in aquatic sports, 298-306
        platform diving, 303-305, *304-305*
        rowing and canoeing, 298-301, *299*
        sailing, 301
        scuba diving, 302-303
        surfing, 305
        swimming, 301-302, *301-302*
        water skiing, 305
        wind surfing, 305-306
    of articulations, 322
    Baastrup's disease, 322
    in ballet and dance, *316*, 316-317
    in bicycle racing, 263-264, *264*
    in boxing, 276-277, *276-277*
    in car racing, 263
    cause of, 3
    in equestrian sports, 287-289, *288-289*
    in fencing, 282-283
    in golf, 273
    in gymnastics, 290-298
    in Japanese wrestling, 278-279
    in motorbike racing, 263
    in racket sports, 273-276, *275*
    rehabilitation/reintegration after, 330
    in roller skating, 282, *282*
    secondary damage after, 3
    in shooting and archery, 315
    spinous process separations, 321-322, *322*
    spondylolysis/spondylolisthesis, 320-321

statistics on, 259t-261t, 259-260
    in team sports, 280-282
        basketball, 281
        handball, 281
        hockey, 281-282
        rugby, 282
        soccer, 279-280
        volleyball, 281, *281*
        water polo, 282
    tendopathy/tendinosis, 322
    in throwing sports, 310-315
        discus and hammer throw, *311-312*, 311-313
        javelin throw, *314*, 314-315
        shot put, *313*, 313-314
    in track and field sports, 264-273
        decathlon/quintathlon, 272-273
        jumping, 269-272, *269-272*
        running, 266-269, *266-269*
        walking, *265*, 265-266
    vibrational, 169
    vs. sports damage, 3
    in weight lifting, 283-286, *284-285*
    in winter sports, 306-310
        ice sports, 307-310, *309-310*
        skiing, 306-307, *308*
        sledding and bobsledding, 306
    in wrestling, 277-278, *278*
Sprinting, 266, *266*
Squash, 274, *275*
Stability
    impairments of, 118
    of intervertebral disc, 57-58
        effect of aging on, 58, *58*, 161-162, 162t
        rotational, 56-61, 60t, *61*
        shifting, 61-62
    in nucleus pulposus, 18, *19*
    studies of, 161-163, 162t-163t
    in traction, 162, 163t
Standing, 150, *151*, 209-210, *210*
Statokinesiometer, 180-181
Stereophotogrammetry, 190
Stress resistance
    of bones, 163-164
    factors affecting, 2-3
    of intervertebral disc, 57, 57t, 164
    in kyphosis, 95-97
    limits of, 257-259, 258t
    in lordosis, 98
    posture and, 146
    in pseudospondylolisthesis, 104
    in retrolisthesis, 104

in rheumatism, 104
in scoliosis, 97-98
in spondylolisthesis, 101-102
in spondylolysis, 101-102
of vertebral body, 161-162, 162t
with vertebral displacements, 104
Subluxation, 73
Supraspinous ligament, 21
Surfing, 305
Surgery, 239-249. *See also* Treatment modalities,surgical
athletic activity after, 327-328
Swimming, 234, 252
injuries due to, 301-302, *301-302*
Symphysis pubis
anatomy of, 29
arthroses at, 127

T

Table tennis, 275-276
Tendinosis, sports-related, 322
Tendons, effects of training on, 5
Tendopathy, sports-related, 322
Tennis, 274
Thermography, 190, *190*
contact, 186
Thermotherapy, 235
Thoracolumbar transition
syndromes of, 82t, 82-83
variations of, 78
Track and field sports injuries, 264-273
distribution of, *265*
due to decathlon/quintathlon, 272-273
due to jumping, 269-272, *269-272*
due to running, 266-269, *266-269*
due to walking, 265, 265-266
Traction, 59, 60t, 162, 163t, 233
Training
adaptations to, 3-7
by articulations, 6
by bones, 4-5
by hyaline cartilage, 5-6
by intervertebral disc, 6-7
by muscles, 4
by tendons and ligaments, 5
effect of overstressing, 4
purpose of, 4
Trains, 222
Trampoline acrobatics, 319-320
Trampoline gymnastics, 296-298, *297*
Transitional region syndromes, 82t, 82-83

Transitional vertebrae
variations of, 78, *78-79*
vertebral arch structure in, 15
Transverse processes, bone bridges between, 81
Treatment modalities
conservative, 229-239
acupuncture, 236
avoidance of factors causing pain, 230-231
body's self-healing mechanisms, 230, *230*
diet, 232
drug therapy, 231
injection treatments, 235-236
manual medicine, *232*, 232-233
massage, 234
orthotic devices, 237
physical therapy, 234-235
physiotherapy, 233-234
principles of, 231
prophylactic measures, 226-229, 238, 330
segment and neural therapy, 236, *237*, 238t, *239*
self-help groups, 238
swimming, 234
traction, 233
upside-down hanging, 238
rehabilitation, 249, 330
surgical, 239-249
future tasks for, 248-249
indications for, 239-240, 247-248
for intervertebral disc prolapse, 241-242, *242-243*
for painful disc disorders and arthroses, 242-243
plan for, 240-241
for scoliosis and kyphosis, 243-244, *244-246*
for spinal fractures and luxations, 244-245, *246-248*
for spondylitis and spondylodiscitis, 246, *248*
for tumors and metastases, 246-247
for vertebral slippage and displacement, 243
Tuberculosis, spinal, 131
Tumors, 124; 138
surgery for, 246-247
Tweezer mechanism, 71, *71*
surgery for, 247

U

Uncinate processes, 17
Uncovertebral articulations
anatomy of, 17, 30, *31*
arthroses of, 128-129, *128-130*
development of, 20, *20*

V

Vascular system, 24-26, *24-26*
Vertebral arch
    blood supply of, 24
    development of
        postnatal suture disappearance, 14-15, *15*
        prenatal, 11
    interarticular gaps of, 81, *98*
    malformations of, 15, 80-81
    morphology of, 17-18
    ossification of, 11-12
    in spondylolysis, 100-101
    in transitional vertebra, 15
Vertebral arch articulations
    anatomy of, 27-28, *27-28*
    arthroses of, 125-127, *126,* 225
        surgery for, 242-243
    brucellosis of, 131
    tumors of, 127
Vertebral artery, 24, *25,* 159
Vertebral biopsy, 185
Vertebral blockade, 72-74, *73*
Vertebral body
    abnormalities of, 79-80, *80*
    biomechanics and structure of, 13-14, *14*
    blood supply of, 24, 62-63
    cleft of, 80
    cribrum of, 62
    development of
        prenatal, 11, *12*
        until conclusion of growth, 12-13, *13*
    effects of aging on, 119, *120*
    end plates of, 62
    in juvenile kyphosis, 84-86, *84-86*
    malformations of, 15
    maturation of, 79, *80*
    morphology of, 17
    ossification of, 11-12
    in osteoporosis, 121, *122*
    stress tolerance of, 161-162, 162t
Vertebral body-intervertebral disc junction, 31-32
    anatomy and functions of, 62-64
    effect of vibration on, 64
    histology of, 63
    morphology of, 17
Vertebral canal, narrowness of, 82
Vertebral displacements, 102-104
    athletic activity for persons with, 327
    backward, *103,* 103-104
    forward, *102,* 102-103
    intervertebral osteochondrosis and, 112
    lateral, *93,* 104, *104*
    stress resistance of, 104
    surgery for, 243
Vertebral slippage, 98-100
    due to spondylolysis, 98-101
    measurement of, 100
    progression of, 100
    surgery for, 243
Vertebrocostal articulations, 30-31, 67
    arthroses of, 130-131
        surgery for, 247
    blockade in, 74
Vertical loading, 16, *16*
Vibration
    effects on blood flow, 159
    effects on bones, 169-170
    effects on cartilage, 170
    effects on muscles, 155-157, *157,* 170
    effects on spinal column, 48, 64-65, 142
    intervertebral disc prolapse due to, 114
    lead poisoning and, 197
    partial body, 68, 171-172, 223
        diseases caused by, 171
        effects on spinal column, *171,* 171-172
    sinus, 68
    stochastic and impacting, 68-69
    test for evaluating effects of, 181
    therapeutic, 234-235
    total body, 68, 166-171, 216-223
        airplanes and helicopters and, 222-223
        automobiles and, 218-221, *219-221*
        bicycles and, 218
        boats and, 223
        buses and, 221-222
        directional letters for, 167-168
        effects on body systems, 166-168
        effects on spinal column, 170-171
        frequency range of, 167, *167-168*
        kinetosis and, 217t, 217-218
        motorcycles and, 205-207, 218
        organ self-resonance and, 168
        trains and, 222
        transmission pathways for, 169
    during walking, 210
Vibration sickness, 169-170
Vinylchloride, 138
Volleyball, 281, *281*

W

Walking, 151-152, 210-212, *211*
   injuries due to, 265, 265-266
Water polo, 282
Water skiing, 305
Weight lifting, 283-286, *284-285*
Weightlessness, 121, 138-139
   effect on intervertebral disc fluid, 40, *40-41*
Wind surfing, 305-306
Wrestling, 277-278, *278*
   Japanese, 278-279

About the Author

Herbert Junghanns, the great physician, scientist, teacher, professor, and medical doctor, holder of an honorary medical degree, died in March 1986, thus ending a full, rich life.

Born in 1902, he announced his desire to become a surgeon while still in grade school, worked to improve his manual skills while still a child, and steadily and industriously pursued his goal of self-realization. He experienced and lived through important times in German history: the monarchy as a child; the Weimar Republic as a student and intern; the dictatorship, World War II, and finally the emergence of democracy as a chief surgeon, researcher, and author.

After concluding his studies, he worked with the pathologist Privy Councilor Georg Schmorl in Dresden for more than three years. It was Schmorl who had awakened basic research in the morphology and pathology of the spine from a long sleep. On Christmas Eve, 1930, the famed surgeon Sauerbruch sent a telegram to Junghanns: "Fill position in my clinic on 1st of January." However, Junghanns had already made his decision in favor of the Frankfurt surgeon Schmieden several days earlier. He became Schmieden's assistant (and later head physician and professor) and worked with him until the end of the war. Subsequently, he became medical superintendent of the Protestant Hospital in Oldenburg. In 1962, he was appointed Medical Director of the newly constructed Emergency Hospital of the Professional Cooperative Association in Frankfurt/Main, which soon developed into a model center for emergency surgery. In 1970, Junghanns retired from hospital activity. However, he remained actively involved in research as well as in the politics of his profession until the end.

The stations of his work life also mark his scientific interests and accomplishments. The desire with which his teacher Schmorl researched the spine was regenerated in him. Together with Schmorl, he published his first book on the pathology of the spine in 1932. In it, he described the correlations among the morphology of the spine, clinical practice, and radiology. He developed into a trendsetter in surgical treatment of the spine, and he intensified and improved the active and invasive therapy of spinal injuries. During his entire life, he remained faithful to his goal of researching the axial skeleton. He created the foundations for a common nomenclature for abnormalities of the spine. His publications in spinal and occupational medicine are considered standard textbooks.

Junghanns is credited with a great stylistic talent. In 1955, he started the book series *The Spinal Column in Research and Practice* with the Hippokrates publishing company. His intention was to give every practicing physician and everyone interested in the spine the opportunity to see a comprehensive picture. During the same time period, it was his initiative that caused the establishment of the Society for Spinal Column Research in 1958. Finally, in 1962, the Institute for Spinal Column Research of the Professional Cooperative Association in Frankfurt/Main was opened, and he headed it until 1973.

The world-famous surgeon Schmieden developed the manual talent of his pupil and set the groundwork for Junghanns' later qualifications as a surgeon. In the end, Junghanns had mastered the entire spectrum of surgery. He performed not only spinal surgery but also brain and heart surgery. It was already a given fact that someone could become a surgeon under Schmieden only if he was willing to perform "hard labor" all his life. Junghanns also became a pioneer in the area of emergency surgery. He emphasized the importance of this area at a very early time, and the eventual development of emergency surgery into a separate specialty area proved his foresight to be correct.

Junghanns was eventually elected president of the German Society for Surgery. He remained a permanent member of the chairing body and was also general secretary of this society from 1971 to 1981. Junghanns was an active member, and at various times president of the Society for Emergency Medicine, the Association of North-Western German Surgeons, German Therapy Week, and the International Society for Manipulative Therapy.

Junghanns also always showed involvement in the politics of his profession. He was a defender of interdisciplinary cooperation. In 1961, he founded the Working Union of Scientific Medical Associations. He is considered to be a cofounder of the European Union of the National Surgical Societies and was a member of the European Association of Surgical Specialties in the European Community. It was his concern to achieve an interdisciplinary synchronization of continued education in the fields of surgery.

Junghanns' active groundbreaking involvement in these various areas continued without interruption until his death and was worthy of much admiration. He himself was respected and even adored for his professional as well as his human qualities.